EDITED BY PAUL ARTHUR SCHILPP

Albert Einstein

Philosopher-Scientist

*Volume VII in the Library
of Living Philosophers*

MJF BOOKS
NEW YORK

Published by MJF Books
Fine Communications
322 Eighth Avenue
New York, NY 10001

Albert Einstein: Philosopher-Scientist
LC Control Number 00-135984
ISBN 1-56731-432-5

GENERAL INTRODUCTION*

TO

"THE LIBRARY OF LIVING PHILOSOPHERS"

ACCORDING to the late F. C. S. Schiller, the greatest obstacle to fruitful discussion in philosophy is "the curious etiquette which apparently taboos the asking of questions about a philosopher's meaning while he is alive." The "interminable controversies which fill the histories of philosophy," he goes on to say, "could have been ended at once by asking the living philosophers a few searching questions."

The confident optimism of this last remark undoubtedly goes too far. Living thinkers have often been asked "a few searching questions," but their answers have not stopped "interminable controversies" about their real meaning. It is none the less true that there would be far greater clarity of understanding than is now often the case, if more such searching questions had been directed to great thinkers while they were still alive.

This, at any rate, is the basic thought behind the present undertaking. The volumes of *The Library of Living Philosophers* can in no sense take the place of the major writings of great and original thinkers. Students who would know the philosophies of such men as John Dewey, George Santayana, Alfred North Whitehead, Benedetto Croce, G. E. Moore, Bertrand Russell, Ernst Cassirer, Karl Jaspers, *et al.*, will still need to read the writings of these men. There is no substitute for firsthand contact with the original thought of the philosopher himself. Least of all does this *Library* pretend to be such a substitute. The *Library* in fact will spare neither effort nor expense in offering to the student the best possible guide to the published

* This *General Introduction*, setting forth the underlying conception of this *Library*, is purposely reprinted in each volume (with only very minor changes).

writings of a given thinker. We shall attempt to meet this aim by providing at the end of each volume in our series a complete bibliography of the published work of the philosopher in question. Nor should one overlook the fact that the essays in each volume cannot but finally lead to this same goal. The interpretative and critical discussions of the various phases of a great thinker's work and, most of all, the reply of the thinker himself, are bound to lead the reader to the works of the philosopher himself.

At the same time, there is no denying the fact that different experts find different ideas in the writings of the same philosopher. This is as true of the appreciative interpreter and grateful disciple as it is of the critical opponent. Nor can it be denied that such differences of reading and of interpretation on the part of other experts often leave the neophyte aghast before the whole maze of widely varying and even opposing interpretations. Who is right and whose interpretation shall he accept? When the doctors disagree among themselves, what is the poor student to do? If, finally, in desperation, he decides that all of the interpreters are probably wrong and that the only thing for him to do is to go back to the original writings of the philosopher himself and then make his own decision—uninfluenced (as if this were possible!) by the interpretation of any one else—the result is not that he has actually come to the meaning of the original philosopher himself, but rather that he has set up one more interpretation, which may differ to a greater or lesser degree from the interpretations already existing. It is clear that in this direction lies chaos, just the kind of chaos which Schiller has so graphically and inimitably described.[1]

It is curious that until now no way of escaping this difficulty has been seriously considered. It has not occurred to students of philosophy that one effective way of meeting the problem at least partially is to put these varying interpretations and critiques before the philosopher while he is still alive and to ask him to act at one and the same time as both defendant and judge. If the world's great living philosophers can be induced to coöper-

---

[1] In his essay on "Must Philosophers Disagree?" in the volume by the same title (Macmillan, London, 1934), from which the above quotations were taken.

ate in an enterprise whereby their own work can, at least to some extent, be saved from becoming merely "desiccated lecture-fodder," which on the one hand "provides innocuous sustenance for ruminant professors," and, on the other hand, gives an opportunity to such ruminants and their understudies to "speculate safely, endlessly, and fruitlessly, about what a philosopher must have meant" (Schiller), they will have taken a long step toward making their intentions clearly comprehensible.

With this in mind *The Library of Living Philosophers* expects to publish at more or less regular intervals a volume on each of the greater among the world's living philosophers. In each case it will be the purpose of the editor of *The Library* to bring together in the volume the interpretations and criticisms of a wide range of that particular thinker's scholarly contemporaries, each of whom will be given a free hand to discuss the specific phase of the thinker's work which has been assigned to him. All contributed essays will finally be submitted to the philosopher with whose work and thought they are concerned, for his careful perusal and reply. And, although it would be expecting too much to imagine that the philosopher's reply will be able to stop all differences of interpretation and of critique, this should at least serve the purpose of stopping certain of the grosser and more general kinds of misinterpretations. If no further gain than this were to come from the present and projected volumes of this *Library*, it would seem to be fully justified.

In carrying out this principal purpose of the *Library*, the editor announces that (in so far as humanly possible) each volume will conform to the following pattern:

First, a series of expository and critical articles written by the leading exponents and opponents of the philosopher's thought;

Second, the reply to the critics and commentators by the philosopher himself;

Third, an intellectual autobiography of the thinker whenever this can be secured; in any case an authoritative and authorized biography; and

Fourth, a bibliography of the writings of the philosopher to provide a ready instrument to give access to his writings and thought.

The editor has deemed it desirable to secure the services of an Advisory Board of philosophers to aid him in the selection of the subjects of future volumes. The names of the six prominent American philosophers who have consented to serve appear below. To each of them the editor expresses his deep-felt thanks.

Future volumes in this series will appear in as rapid succession as is feasible in view of the scholarly nature of this *Library*. The next three volumes in this series should be those on Benedetto Croce, Sir Sarvepalli Radhakrishnan, and Karl Jaspers.

The editor is very happy, indeed, to be able to make grateful acknowledgment for the financial assistance this volume has received. The editorial work on the Einstein volume has been largely made possible by a grant received from the Humanities Division of the General Education Board of the Rockefeller Foundation through the mediation and courtesy of the American Council of Learned Societies in Washington, D.C. To both organizations the editor desires to express his sincere gratitude and deep appreciation. However, neither the Rockefeller Foundation nor the A.C.L.S. are in any sense the authors, owners, publishers, or proprietors of this *Library*, and they are therefore not to be understood as approving by virtue of their grants any of the statements made in this volume.

Volumes I to IV (incl.) have, unfortunately, been out of print for some time now, not due to lack of demand for these volumes—there is, in fact, a steady demand for each of them—, but simply because The Library of Living Philosophers, Inc. has lacked the necessary funds to permit reprintings or new editions. It is now hoped, however, that it will be possible to print a second edition of at least the volume on *The Philosophy of John Dewey* within approximately four or five months of the date of publication of the present volume. We had strongly hoped to be able to do this in time for Professor Dewey's ninetieth birthday on October 20th, 1949. Failing in this effort we shall do our best to accomplish this end as soon as possible. It is perhaps hardly necessary to add that the *Library* would gladly welcome gifts and donations which would enable us to reprint the other three volumes. Since November 6th, 1947, moreover, any gifts or donations made to The Library of Living Philosophers, Inc. are deductible by the donors in arriving at their taxable net income in conformity with the Internal Revenue Code of the Treasury Department of the United States of America.

PAUL ARTHUR SCHILPP
FOUNDER AND EDITOR, 1939–1981

TABLE OF CONTENTS

PREFACE

THE contents of this volume speak eloquently enough for the inclusion of *Albert Einstein: Philosopher-Scientist* in this series without any superfluous words from the editor.

Almost all of the matters which need to be mentioned here are of the nature of personal privilege.

There is, first of all, the matter of gratitude for help and co-operation. Foremost here stands Professor Einstein himself. Without his consent and willingness to co-operate, this book could never have appeared. But, how to express the editor's thanks and appreciation to him—in the coldness of mere words —this is something I know not how to do. Perhaps he will understand if I state simply that my obligation and gratitude to him are beyond the possibility of verbal expression.

Among the twenty-five other contributors to this volume there are no less than six Nobel-Prize winners in science; and essays have come from as many as eleven countries (viz., Australia, Belgium, Canada, Denmark, England, France, Germany, Ireland, Scotland, Switzerland, and the U.S.A.); an essay for this volume had also been promised by a leading scientist of the U.S.S.R. (although it has not yet actually reached the editor). The editor is as deeply and sincerely obligated to these important and busy scholars the world around as he is to Professor Einstein.

It proved impossible to bring out this volume at the time originally planned. It had been hoped to lay it on Professor Einstein's birthday-table on March 14th last, on the occasion of his seventieth birthday. No one regrets this delay in publication more than does the editor.

Other regrets are no less poignant. It was a tragedy of no mean importance that Max Planck was already too seriously ill, at the time of the conception of this volume, for him to be able to contribute an essay. Nor has the editor recovered from the sadness caused by Professor Hermann Weyl's inability to carry out his original promise to write for this book.

Three other scholars (from as many countries) finally failed to redeem their pledges given to the editor. In the case of one of these it is at least conceivable that the reason for the failure of his essay to reach us may not have lain with himself. In any case, it is regrettable that the *Library of Living Philosophers* is thus deprived from giving those essays to its interested readers. We can merely assure these readers that no stone was left unturned to secure the essays.

All these regrets are compensated for, however, by our being able to present here Professor Einstein's one and only intellectual autobiography.

Everyone who knows Professor Einstein personally is all too well aware of his extreme shyness and his honest and forthright humility. I do not believe that there would have been one chance in ten thousand that the world would ever have secured an autobiography from the hand of Professor Einstein, if the unique nature of the *Library of Living Philosophers* had not finally convinced him of the worth-while-ness and significance of such an "obituary," as he calls his autobiography.

Einstein's "Autobiographical Notes" in themselves assure, therefore, the unique importance of this volume.

In a kindred category stands Professor Niels Bohr's "Discussion with Einstein,"—an essay, not merely delightfully written but of the utmost and lasting importance in its content. These recollections of conversations with Einstein on the epistemological aspects of physical science would never have come into being, were it not for the peculiar nature of this series.

One could go on in this fashion. How can one adequately praise the care, precision, directness, and beauty of Professor Einstein's "Reply" (or "Remarks," as he calls them) to his commentators and critics!

There are, however, still other persons whose kindness or aid have helped to enhance the value or increase the beauty and correctness of this book. Professor Peter G. Bergmann, of the physics department of Syracuse University, spared neither time nor effort in helping to put Professor von Laue's paper into the same adequate and beautiful form in English as the author himself had used in his original German manuscript. Professor Arnold J. F. Siegert, of the physics department of Northwestern University, carefully checked and corrected— especially the technically scientific aspects of—my own translations of both Einstein essays. Mr. Forrest W. Williams, of Northwestern University, very kindly and ably translated the de Broglie and Bachelard essays.

Mere words of gratitude are also quite inadequate to express the editor's appreciation of the wonderfully careful and exacting work accomplished by the bibliographer of Professor Einstein's published works. Long before the present volume got under way, Miss Margaret C. Shields, at that time Librarian of the Mathematics Library of Princeton University, had been at work gathering the data which have now gone into the Bibliography, which constitutes the important Part IV of the present volume. Her labors have been endless and her efforts almost excruciatingly painstaking. The result speaks for itself. Her exhaustive bibliography of the published work of Einstein will prove to be of inestimable value to scientists and scholars for centuries to come. The abiding knowledge of this fact will be a source of deeper satisfaction to Miss Shields than any words of thanks the editor could offer.

Messrs. Surindar Suri and Kenneth G. Halvorsen saved the editor the arduous and laborious task of providing this volume with its accurate and useful index. A host of other individuals contributed their assistance during various parts of the labor of reading proof and seeing the volume through the press. To all of these the editor says a most sincere and heart-felt, "Thank you."

The order in which the essays appear in Part II was determined, in general, by the order in which Professor Einstein chose to discuss the essays in his replying "Remarks." The only exceptions to this rule are those essays to which Dr. Einstein did not reply or which came in after his "Remarks" had been completed.

In reading and editing the contents of this volume, two possible sub-titles have come to the editor's mind again and again, namely (1) "The Scientific Battle of the Twentieth Century," and (2) "The Future of Physics." Viewed from either point of view, this book has been exciting reading, even to its editor. He may be permitted to express the hope, therefore, that the experience of other readers will be similar.

PAUL ARTHUR SCHILPP

DEPARTMENT OF PHILOSOPHY
NORTHWESTERN UNIVERSITY
EVANSTON, ILLINOIS

October 1, 1949

ACKNOWLEDGMENTS

Grateful Acknowledgment is hereby made to the authors, editors, and publishers of all of Professor Einstein's works as well as of any other books, quotations from which appear in this volume. We are particularly grateful to them for the fact that they have not required us to enumerate these volumes here by author, title, and publisher.

We also wish to express our appreciation to the editors and publishers of the numerous scientific, mathematical, and philosophical journals quoted in these pages, for the privilege of utilizing such source materials therein found relevant to the discussion of Professor Einstein's scientific and philosophical views.

PREFATORY NOTE TO THE THIRD EDITION

It has been said that no man is irreplaceable. Like most generalizations, this one too is not entirely correct. The passing of Albert Einstein, in Princeton, N. J., on April 18, 1955, certainly was an irreplaceable loss to science, to scholarship, to humanitarianism, to the cause of peace, and to the conscience of mankind. For, if the conscience of humanity could ever be said to have been represented by one single living human being, that human being was the great and truly immortal Einstein. To the editor of this LIBRARY Einstein's passing was also a great personal loss. My numerous visits and personal conversations with him constitute an indescribable legacy and indestructible memory of the greatest human being it has ever been my privilege to know personally.

Since the present (third) edition of our *Einstein* volume is the first one to be released since Einstein's even yet untimely passing, the editor felt deeply obliged to say at least that much. But all of us are pleased to know that this volume is, at long last, available again.

After all, this volume contains the only thing even so much as approximating an Autobiography that the great Einstein ever wrote. And this appears both in the great scientist's original German and in English translation, side by side and page by page (for all of 95 pages). This, by itself, is an imperishable document, which is even more significant precisely because it contains much more of Einstein's scientific thought-development than it does mere matters of personal recollection. His "Reply to Criticisms" is equally important and of permanent significance.

This third edition has been (1) corrected for errors, and (2) brought more nearly up-to-date in the Bibliography. We know that it will receive the same enthusiastic reception which greeted the first two editions of this—in a real sense timeless—volume.

The editor wishes to express his appreciation to the new

publishers of THE LIBRARY—The Hegeler Foundation and the Open Court Publishing Company—for undertaking to keep all of the volumes of THE LIBRARY permanently in print; to the Advisory Board of THE LIBRARY, for their help in planning future volumes (the present membership of the Board is listed below); and to the National Endowment for the Humanities, Washington, D. C., for generous grants for the years 1967-1970.

PAUL ARTHUR SCHILPP

DEPARTMENT OF PHILOSOPHY
SOUTHERN ILLINOIS UNIVERSITY
CARBONDALE, ILLINOIS

March 3, 1969

ADVISORY BOARD

ALBERT EINSTEIN
AUTOBIOGRAPHICAL NOTES

AUTOBIOGRAPHISCHES

HIER sitze ich, um mit 67 Jahren so etwas wie den eigenen Nekrolog zu schreiben. Dies tue ich nicht nur, weil mich Dr. Schilpp dazu überredet hat; sondern ich glaube selber dass es gut ist, den Mitstrebenden zu zeigen, wie einem das eigene Streben und Suchen im Rückblick erscheint. Nach einiger Ueberlegung fühlte ich, wie unvollkommen ein solcher Versuch ausfallen muss. Denn wie kurz und beschränkt ein Arbeitsleben ist, wie vorherrschend die Irrwege, so fällt doch die Darstellung des Mitteilungswerten nicht leicht—der jetzige Mensch von 67 ist nicht derselbe wie der von 50, 30 und 20. Jede Erinnerung ist gefärbt durch das jetzige So-Sein, also durch einen trügerischen Blickpunkt. Diese Erwägung könnte wohl abschrecken. Aber man kann doch Manches aus dem Selbst-Erleben schöpfen, was einem andern Bewusstsein nicht zugänglich ist.

Als ziemlich frühreifem jungem Menschen kam mir die Nichtigkeit des Hoffens und Strebens lebhaft zum Bewusstsein, das die meisten Menschen rastlos durchs Leben jagt. Auch sah ich bald die Grausamkeit dieses Treibens, die in jenen Jahren sorgsamer als jetzt durch Hypocrisy und glänzende Worte verdeckt war. Jeder war durch die Existenz seines Magens dazu verurteilt, an diesem Treiben sich zu beteiligen. Der Magen konnte durch solche Teilnahme wohl befriedigt werden, aber nicht der Mensch als denkendes und fühlendes Wesen. Da gab es als ersten Ausweg die Religion, die ja jedem Kinde durch die traditionelle Erziehungs-Maschine eingepflanzt wird. So kam ich—obwohl ein Kind ganz irreligiöser (jüdischer) Eltern—zu einer tiefen Religiosität, die aber im Alter von 12 Jahren bereits ein jähes Ende fand. Durch Lesen populär-

AUTOBIOGRAPHICAL NOTES*

HERE I sit in order to write, at the age of 67, something like my own obituary. I am doing this not merely because Dr. Schilpp has persuaded me to do it; but because I do, in fact, believe that it is a good thing to show those who are striving alongside of us, how one's own striving and searching appears to one in retrospect. After some reflection, I felt how insufficient any such attempt is bound to be. For, however brief and limited one's working life may be, and however predominant may be the ways of error, the exposition of that which is worthy of communication does nonetheless not come easy— today's person of 67 is by no means the same as was the one of 50, of 30, or of 20. Every reminiscence is colored by today's being what it is, and therefore by a deceptive point of view. This consideration could very well deter. Nevertheless much can be lifted out of one's own experience which is not open to another consciousness.

Even when I was a fairly precocious young man the nothingness of the hopes and strivings which chases most men restlessly through life came to my consciousness with considerable vitality. Moreover, I soon discovered the cruelty of that chase, which in those years was much more carefully covered up by hypocrisy and glittering words than is the case today. By the mere existence of his stomach everyone was condemned to participate in that chase. Moreover, it was possible to satisfy the stomach by such participation, but not man in so far as he is a thinking and feeling being. As the first way out there was religion, which is implanted into every child by way of the traditional education-machine. Thus I came—despite the fact that I was the son of entirely irreligious (Jewish) parents—to a deep religiosity, which, however, found an abrupt ending at the age

* Translated from the original German manuscript by Paul Arthur Schilpp.

wissenschaftlicher Bücher kam ich bald zu der Ueberzeugung, dass vieles in den Erzählungen der Bibel nicht wahr sein konnte. Die Folge war eine geradezu fanatische Freigeisterei, verbunden mit dem Eindruck, dass die Jugend vom Staate mit Vorbedacht belogen wird; es war ein niederschmetternder Eindruck. Das Misstrauen gegen jede Art Autorität erwuchs aus diesem Erlebnis, eine skeptische Einstellung gegen die Ueberzeugungen, welche in der jeweiligen sozialen Umwelt lebendig waren—eine Einstellung, die mich nicht wieder verlassen hat, wenn sie auch später durch bessere Einsicht in die kausalen Zusammenhänge ihre ursprüngliche Schärfe verloren haben.

Es ist mir klar, dass das so verlorene religiöse Paradies der Jugend ein erster Versuch war, mich aus den Fesseln des "Nur-Persönlichen" zu befreien, aus einem Dasein, das durch Wünsche, Hoffnungen und primitive Gefühle beherrscht ist. Da gab es draussen diese grosse Welt, die unabhängig von uns Menschen da ist und vor uns steht wie ein grosses, ewiges Rätsel, wenigstens teilweise zugänglich unserem Schauen und Denken. Ihre Betrachtung winkte als eine Befreiung, und ich merkte bald, dass so Mancher, den ich schätzen und bewundern gelernt hatte, in der hingebenden Beschäftigung mit ihr innere Freiheit und Sicherheit gefunden hatte. Das gedankliche Erfassen dieser ausserpersönlichen Welt im Rahmen der uns gebotenen Möglichkeiten, schwebte mir halb bewusst, halb unbewusst als höchstes Ziel vor. Ähnlich eingestellte Menschen der Gegenwart und Vergangenheit sowie die von ihnen erlangten Einsichten waren die unverlierbaren Freunde. Der Weg zu diesem Paradies war nicht so bequem und lockend wie der Weg zum religiösen Paradies; aber er hat sich als zuverlässig erwiesen, und ich habe es nie bedauert, ihn gewählt zu haben.

Was ich da gesagt habe, ist nur in gewissem Sinne wahr, wie eine aus wenigen Strichen bestehende Zeichnung einem komplizierten, mit verwirrenden Einzelheiten ausgestatteten, Objekt nur in beschränktem Sinne gerecht werden kann. Wenn ein Individuum an gutgefügten Gedanken Freude hat, so mag sich diese Seite seines Wesens auf Kosten anderer Seiten stärker ausprägen und so seine Mentalität in steigendem Masse be-

of 12. Through the reading of popular scientific books I soon reached the conviction that much in the stories of the Bible could not be true. The consequence was a positively fanatic [orgy of] freethinking coupled with the impression that youth is intentionally being deceived by the state through lies; it was a crushing impression. Suspicion against every kind of authority grew out of this experience, a skeptical attitude towards the convictions which were alive in any specific social environment —an attitude which has never again left me, even though later on, because of a better insight into the causal connections, it lost some of its original poignancy.

It is quite clear to me that the religious paradise of youth, which was thus lost, was a first attempt to free myself from the chains of the "merely-personal," from an existence which is dominated by wishes, hopes and primitive feelings. Out yonder there was this huge world, which exists independently of us human beings and which stands before us like a great, eternal riddle, at least partially accessible to our inspection and thinking. The contemplation of this world beckoned like a liberation, and I soon noticed that many a man whom I had learned to esteem and to admire had found inner freedom and security in devoted occupation with it. The mental grasp of this extrapersonal world within the frame of the given possibilities swam as highest aim half consciously and half unconsciously before my mind's eye. Similarly motivated men of the present and of the past, as well as the insights which they had achieved, were the friends which could not be lost. The road to this paradise was not as comfortable and alluring as the road to the religious paradise; but it has proved itself as trustworthy, and I have never regretted having chosen it.

What I have here said is true only within a certain sense, just as a drawing consisting of a few strokes can do justice to a complicated object, full of perplexing details, only in a very limited sense. If an individual enjoys well-ordered thoughts, it is quite possible that this side of his nature may grow more pronounced at the cost of other sides and thus may determine his mentality in increasing degree. In this case it is well possi-

stimmen. Es mag dann wohl sein, dass dies Individuum im Rückblick eine einheitliche systematische Entwicklung sieht, während das tatsächliche Erleben in kaleidoskopartiger Einzel-Situation sich abspielt. Die Mannigfaltigkeit der äusseren Situationen und die Enge des momentanen Bewusstsein-Inhaltes bringen ja eine Art Atomisierung des Lebens jedes Menschen mit sich. Bei einem Menschen meiner Art liegt der Wendepunkt der Entwicklung darin, dass das Hauptinteresse sich allmählich weitgehend loslösst vom Momentanen und Nur-Persönlichen und sich dem Streben nach gedanklicher Erfassung der Dinge zuwendet. Von diesem Gesichtspunkt aus betrachtet enthalten die obigen schematischen Bemerkungen so viel Wahres, als sich in solcher Kürze sagen lässt.

Was ist eigentlich "Denken"? Wenn beim Empfangen von Sinnes-Eindrücken Erinnerungsbilder auftauchen, so ist das noch nicht "Denken." Wenn solche Bilder Serien bilden, deren jedes Glied ein anderes wachruft, so ist dies auch noch kein "Denken." Wenn aber ein gewisses Bild in vielen solchen Reihen wiederkehrt, so wird es eben durch seine Wiederkehr zu einem ordnenden Element für solche Reihen, indem es an sich zusammenhangslose Reihen verknüpft. Ein solches Element wird zum Werkzeug, zum Begriff. Ich denke mir, dass der Uebergang vom freien Assoziieren oder "Träumen" zum Denken characterisiert ist durch die mehr oder minder dominierende Rolle, die der "Begriff" dabei spielt. Es ist an sich nicht nötig, dass ein Begriff mit einem sinnlich wahrnehmbaren und reproduzierbaren Zeichen (Wort) verknüpft sei; ist er es aber so wird dadurch Denken mitteilbar.

Mit welchem Recht—so fragt nun der Leser—operiert dieser Mensch so unbekümmert und primitiv mit Ideen auf einem so problematischen Gebiet, ohne den geringsten Versuch zu machen, etwas zu beweisen? Meine Verteidigung: all unser Denken ist von dieser Art eines freien Spiels mit Begriffen; die Berechtigung dieses Spiels liegt in dem Masse der Uebersicht über die Sinnenerlebnisse, die wir mit seiner Hilfe erreichen können. Der Begriff der "Wahrheit" kann auf ein solches Gebilde noch gar nicht angewendet werden; dieser Begriff kann nach meiner Meinung erst dann in Frage kom-

ble that such an individual in retrospect sees a uniformly systematic development, whereas the actual experience takes place in kaleidoscopic particular situations. The manifoldness of the external situations and the narrowness of the momentary content of consciousness bring about a sort of atomizing of the life of every human being. In a man of my type the turning-point of the development lies in the fact that gradually the major interest disengages itself to a far-reaching degree from the momentary and the merely personal and turns towards the striving for a mental grasp of things. Looked at from this point of view the above schematic remarks contain as much truth as can be uttered in such brevity.

What, precisely, is "thinking"? When, at the reception of sense-impressions, memory-pictures emerge, this is not yet "thinking." And when such pictures form series, each member of which calls forth another, this too is not yet "thinking." When, however, a certain picture turns up in many such series, then—precisely through such return—it becomes an ordering element for such series, in that it connects series which in themselves are unconnected. Such an element becomes an instrument, a concept. I think that the transition from free association or "dreaming" to thinking is characterized by the more or less dominating rôle which the "concept" plays in it. It is by no means necessary that a concept must be connected with a sensorily cognizable and reproducible sign (word); but when this is the case thinking becomes by means of that fact communicable.

With what right—the reader will ask—does this man operate so carelessly and primitively with ideas in such a problematic realm without making even the least effort to prove anything? My defense: all our thinking is of this nature of a free play with concepts; the justification for this play lies in the measure of survey over the experience of the senses which we are able to achieve with its aid. The concept of "truth" can not yet be applied to such a structure; to my thinking this concept can come in question only when a far-reaching agreement

men, wenn bereits eine weitgehende Einigung (Convention) über die Elemente und Regeln des Spieles vorliegen.

Es ist mir nicht zweifelhaft, dass unser Denken zum grössten Teil ohne Verwendung von Zeichen (Worte) vor sich geht und dazu noch weitgehend unbewusst. Denn wie sollten wir sonst manchmal dazu kommen, uns über ein Erlebnis ganz spontan zu "wundern"? Dies "sich wundern" scheint dann aufzutreten, wenn ein Erlebnis mit einer in uns hinreichend fixierten Begriffswelt in Konflikt kommt. Wenn solcher Konflikt hart und intensiv erlebt wird dann wirkt er in entscheidender Weise zurück auf unsere Gedankenwelt. Die Entwicklung dieser Gedankenwelt ist in gewissem Sinn eine beständige Flucht aus dem "Wunder."

Ein Wunder solcher Art erlebte ich als Kind von 4 oder 5 Jahren, als mir mein Vater einen Kompass zeigte. Dass diese Nadel in so bestimmter Weise sich benahm passte so gar nicht in die Art des Geschehens hinein, die in der unbewussten Begriffswelt Platz finden konnte (an "Berührung" geknüpftes Wirken). Ich erinnere mich noch jetzt—oder glaube mich zu erinnern—dass dies Erlebnis tiefen und bleibenden Eindruck auf mich gemacht hat. Da musste etwas hinter den Dingen sein, das tief verborgen war. Was der Mensch von klein auf vor sich sieht, darauf reagiert er nicht in solcher Art, er wundert sich nicht über das Fallen der Körper, über Wind und Regen, nicht über den Mond und nicht darüber, dass dieser nicht herunterfällt, nicht über die Verschiedenheit des Belebten und des Nicht-Belebten.

Im Alter von 12 Jahren erlebte ich ein zweites Wunder ganz verschiedener Art: An einem Büchlein über Euklidische Geometrie der Ebene, das ich am Anfang eines Schuljahres in die Hand bekam. Da waren Aussagen wie z.B. das Sich-Schneiden der drei Höhen eines Dreieckes in einem Punkt, die —obwohl an sich keineswegs evident—doch mit solcher Sicherheit bewiesen werden konnten, dass ein Zweifel ausgeschlossen zu sein schien. Diese Klarheit und Sicherheit machte einen unbeschreiblichen Eindruck auf mich. Dass die Axiome unbewiesen hinzunehmen waren beunruhigte mich nicht. Ueberhaupt genügte es mir vollkommen, wenn ich Beweise auf solche Sätze

(*convention*) concerning the elements and rules of the game is already at hand.

For me it is not dubious that our thinking goes on for the most part without use of signs (words) and beyond that to a considerable degree unconsciously. For how, otherwise, should it happen that sometimes we "wonder" quite spontaneously about some experience? This "wondering" seems to occur when an experience comes into conflict with a world of concepts which is already sufficiently fixed in us. Whenever such a conflict is experienced hard and intensively it reacts back upon our thought world in a decisive way. The development of this thought world is in a certain sense a continuous flight from "wonder."

A wonder of such nature I experienced as a child of 4 or 5 years, when my father showed me a compass. That this needle behaved in such a determined way did not at all fit into the nature of events, which could find a place in the unconscious world of concepts (effect connected with direct "touch"). I can still remember—or at least believe I can remember—that this experience made a deep and lasting impression upon me. Something deeply hidden had to be behind things. What man sees before him from infancy causes no reaction of this kind; he is not surprised over the falling of bodies, concerning wind and rain, nor concerning the moon or about the fact that the moon does not fall down, nor concerning the differences between living and non-living matter.

At the age of 12 I experienced a second wonder of a totally different nature: in a little book dealing with Euclidian plane geometry, which came into my hands at the beginning of a schoolyear. Here were assertions, as for example the intersection of the three altitudes of a triangle in one point, which —though by no means evident—could nevertheless be proved with such certainty that any doubt appeared to be out of the question. This lucidity and certainty made an indescribable impression upon me. That the axiom had to be accepted unproved did not disturb me. In any case it was quite sufficient for me if I could peg proofs upon propositions the validity of which did

stützen konnte, deren Gültigkeit mir nicht zweifelhaft erschien. Ich erinnere mich beispielsweise, dass mir der pythagoräische Satz von einem Onkel mitgeteilt wurde, bevor ich das heilige Geometrie-Büchlein in die Hand bekam. Nach harter Mühe gelang es mir, diesen Satz auf Grund der Aehnlichkeit von Dreiecken zu "beweisen"; dabei erschien es mir "evident," dass die Verhältnisse der Seiten eines rechtwinkligen Dreiecks durch einen der spitzen Winkel völlig bestimmt sein müsse. Nur was nicht in ähnlicher Weise "evident" erschien, schien mir überhaupt eines Beweises zu bedürfen. Auch schienen mir die Gegenstände, von denen die Geometrie handelt, nicht von anderer Art zu sein als die Gegenstände der sinnlichen Wahrnehmung, "die man sehen und greifen konnte." Diese primitive Auffassung, welche wohl auch der bekannten Kant'schen Fragestellung betreffend die Möglichkeit "synthetischer Urteile *a priori*" zugrundeliegt, beruht natürlich darauf, dass die Beziehung jener geometrischen Begriffe zu Gegenständen der Erfahrung (fester Stab, Strecke, etc.) unbewusst gegenwärtig war.

Wenn es so schien, dass man durch blosses Denken sichere Erkenntnis über Erfahrungsgegenstände erlangen könne, so beruhte dies "Wunder" auf einem Irrtum. Aber es ist für den, der es zum ersten Mal erlebt, wunderbar genug, dass der Mensch überhaupt imstande ist, einen solchen Grad von Sicherheit und Reinheit im blossen Denken zu erlangen, wie es uns die Griechen erstmalig in der Geometrie gezeigt haben.

Nachdem ich mich nun einmal dazu habe hinreissen lassen, den notdürftig begonnenen Nekrolog zu unterbrechen, scheue ich mich nicht hier in ein paar Sätzen mein erkenntnistheoretisches Credo auszudrücken, obwohl im Vorigen einiges davon beiläufig schon gesagt ist. Dies Credo entwickelte sich erst viel später und langsam und entspricht nicht der Einstellung, die ich in jüngeren Jahren hatte.

Ich sehe auf der einen Seite die Gesamtheit der Sinnen-Erlebnisse, auf der andern Seite die Gesamtheit der Begriffe und Sätze, die in den Büchern niedergelegt sind. Die Beziehungen zwischen den Begriffen und Sätzen unter einander sind logischer Art, und das Geschäft des logischen Denkens ist

not seem to me to be dubious. For example I remember that an uncle told me the Pythagorean theorem before the holy geometry booklet had come into my hands. After much effort I succeeded in "proving" this theorem on the basis of the similarity of triangles; in doing so it seemed to me "evident" that the relations of the sides of the right-angled triangles would have to be completely determined by one of the acute angles. Only something which did not in similar fashion seem to be "evident" appeared to me to be in need of any proof at all. Also, the objects with which geometry deals seemed to be of no different type than the objects of sensory perception, "which can be seen and touched." This primitive idea, which probably also lies at the bottom of the well known Kantian problematic concerning the possibility of "synthetic judgments *a priori,*" rests obviously upon the fact that the relation of geometrical concepts to objects of direct experience (rigid rod, finite interval, etc.) was unconsciously present.

If thus it appeared that it was possible to get certain knowledge of the objects of experience by means of pure thinking, this "wonder" rested upon an error. Nevertheless, for anyone who experiences it for the first time, it is marvellous enough that man is capable at all to reach such a degree of certainty and purity in pure thinking as the Greeks showed us for the first time to be possible in geometry.

Now that I have allowed myself to be carried away sufficiently to interrupt my scantily begun obituary, I shall not hesitate to state here in a few sentences my epistemological credo, although in what precedes something has already incidentally been said about this. This credo actually evolved only much later and very slowly and does not correspond with the point of view I held in younger years.

I see on the one side the totality of sense-experiences, and, on the other, the totality of the concepts and propositions which are laid down in books. The relations between the concepts and propositions among themselves and each other are of a logical nature, and the business of logical thinking is strictly limited

strikte beschränkt auf die Herstellung der Verbindung zwischen
Begriffen und Sätzen untereinander nach festgesetzten Regeln,
mit denen sich die Logik beschäftigt. Die Begriffe und Sätze
erhalten "Sinn" bezw. "Inhalt" nur durch ihre Beziehung zu
Sinnen-Erlebnissen. Die Verbindung der letzteren mit den
ersteren ist rein intuitiv, nicht selbst von logischer Natur. Der
Grad der Sicherheit, mit der diese Beziehung bezw. intuitive
Verknüpfung vorgenommen werden kann, und nichts anderes,
unterscheidet die leere Phantasterei von der wissenschaftlichen
"Wahrheit." Das Begriffssystem ist eine Schöpfung des Menschen samt den syntaktischen Regeln, welche die Struktur der
Begriffssysteme ausmachen. Die Begriffssysteme sind zwar an
sich logisch gänzlich willkürlich, aber gebunden durch das Ziel,
eine möglischst sichere (intuitive) und vollständige Zuordnung
zu der Gesamtheit der Sinnen-Erlebnisse zuzulassen; zweitens
erstreben sie möglichste Sparsamkeit inbezug auf ihre logisch
unabhängigen Elemente (Grundbegriffe und Axiome) d.h.
nicht definierte Begriffe und nicht erschlossene Sätze.

Ein Satz ist richtig, wenn er innerhalb eines logischen Systems nach den accertierten logischen Regeln abgeleitet ist.
Ein System hat Wahrheitsgehalt, entsprechend der Sicherheit
und Vollständigkeit seiner Zuordnungs-Möglichkeit zu der
Erlebnis-Gesamtheit. Ein richtiger Satz erborgt seine "Wahrheit" von dem Wahrheits-Gehalt des Systems, dem er angehört.

Eine Bemerkung zur geschichtlichen Entwicklung. Hume
erkannte klar, dass gewisse Begriffe, z.B. der der Kausalität,
durch logische Methoden nicht aus dem Erfahrungsmaterial
abgeleitet werden können. Kant, von der Unentbehrlichkeit
gewisser Begriffe durchdrungen, hielt sie—so wie sie gewählt
sind—für nötige Prämisse jeglichen Denkens und unter-
schied sie von Begriffen empirischen Ursprungs. Ich bin aber
davon überzeugt, dass diese Unterscheidung irrtümlich ist,
bezw. dem Problem nicht in natürlicher Weise gerecht wird.
Alle Begriffe, auch die erlebnis-nächsten, sind vom logischen
Gesichtspunkte aus freie Setzungen, genau wie der Begriff der
Kausalität, an den sich in erster Linie die Fragestellung an-
geschlossen hat.

to the achievement of the connection between concepts and propositions among each other according to firmly laid down rules, which are the concern of logic. The concepts and propositions get "meaning," viz., "content," only through their connection with sense-experiences. The connection of the latter with the former is purely intuitive, not itself of a logical nature. The degree of certainty with which this relation, viz., intuitive connection, can be undertaken, and nothing else, differentiates empty phantasy from scientific "truth." The system of concepts is a creation of man together with the rules of syntax, which constitute the structure of the conceptual systems. Although the conceptual systems are logically entirely arbitrary, they are bound by the aim to permit the most nearly possible certain (intuitive) and complete co-ordination with the totality of sense-experiences; secondly they aim at greatest possible sparsity of their logically independent elements (basic concepts and axioms), i.e., undefined concepts and underived [postulated] propositions.

A proposition is correct if, within a logical system, it is deduced according to the accepted logical rules. A system has truth-content according to the certainty and completeness of its co-ordination-possibility to the totality of experience. A correct proposition borrows its "truth" from the truth-content of the system to which it belongs.

A remark to the historical development. Hume saw clearly that certain concepts, as for example that of causality, cannot be deduced from the material of experience by logical methods. Kant, thoroughly convinced of the indispensability of certain concepts, took them—just as they are selected—to be the necessary premises of every kind of thinking and differentiated them from concepts of empirical origin. I am convinced, however, that this differentiation is erroneous, i.e., that it does not do justice to the problem in a natural way. All concepts, even those which are closest to experience, are from the point of view of logic freely chosen conventions, just as is the case with the concept of causality, with which this problematic concerned itself in the first instance.

Nun zurück zum Nekrolog. Im Alter von 12-16 machte ich mich mit den Elementen der Mathematik vertraut inklusive der Prinzipien der Differential- und Integral-Rechnung. Dabei hatte ich das Glück auf Bücher zu stossen, die es nicht gar zu genau nahmen mit der logischen Strenge, dafür aber die Hauptgedanken übersichtlich hervortreten liessen. Diese Beschäftigung war im Ganzen wahrhaft fascinierend; es gab darin Höhepunkte, deren Eindruck sich mit dem der elementaren Geometrie sehr wohl messen konnte—der Grundgedanke der analytischen Geometrie, die unendlichen Reihen, der Differential- und Integral-Begriff. Auch hatte ich das Glück, die wesentlichen Ergebnisse und Methoden der gesamten Naturwissenschaft in einer vortrefflichen populären, fast durchweg aufs Qualitative sich beschränkenden Darstellung kennen zu lernen (Bernsteins naturwissenschaftliche Volksbücher, ein Werk von 5 oder 6 Bänden), ein Werk, das ich mit atemloser Spannung las. Auch etwas theoretische Physik hatte ich bereits studiert, als ich mit 17 Jahren auf das Züricher Polytechnikum kam als Student der Mathematik und Physik.

Dort hatte ich vortreffliche Lehrer (z.B. Hurwitz, Minkowski), so dass ich eigentlich eine tiefe mathematische Ausbildung hätte erlangen können. Ich aber arbeitete die meiste Zeit im physikalischen Laboratorium, fasciniert durch die direkte Berührung mit der Erfahrung. Die übrige Zeit benutzte ich hauptsächlich, um die Werke von Kirchhoff, Helmholtz, Hertz, etc. zuhause zu studieren. Dass ich die Mathematik bis zu einem gewissen Grade vernachlässigte, hatte nicht nur den Grund, dass das naturwissenschaftliche Interesse stärker war als das mathematische, sondern das folgende eigentümliche Erlebnis. Ich sah, dass die Mathematik in viele Spezialgebiete gespalten war, deren jedes diese kurze uns vergönnte Lebenszeit wegnehmen konnte. So sah ich mich in der Lage von Buridans Esel, der sich nicht für ein besonderes Bündel Heu entschliessen konnte. Dies lag offenbar daran, dass meine Intuition auf mathematischem Gebiete nicht stark genug war, um das Fundamental-Wichtige, Grundlegende sicher von dem Rest der mehr oder weniger entbehrlichen Gelehrsamkeit zu unterscheiden. Ausserdem war aber auch das Interesse für die Natur-Erkennt-

And now back to the obituary. At the age of 12-16 I familiarized myself with the elements of mathematics together with the principles of differential and integral calculus. In doing so I had the good fortune of hitting on books which were not too particular in their logical rigour, but which made up for this by permitting the main thoughts to stand out clearly and synoptically. This occupation was, on the whole, truly fascinating; climaxes were reached whose impression could easily compete with that of elementary geometry—the basic idea of analytical geometry, the infinite series, the concepts of differential and integral. I also had the good fortune of getting to know the essential results and methods of the entire field of the natural sciences in an excellent popular exposition, which limited itself almost throughout to qualitative aspects (Bernstein's *People's Books on Natural Science*, a work of 5 or 6 volumes), a work which I read with breathless attention. I had also already studied some theoretical physics when, at the age of 17, I entered the Polytechnic Institute of Zürich as a student of mathematics and physics.

There I had excellent teachers (for example, Hurwitz, Minkowski), so that I really could have gotten a sound mathematical education. However, I worked most of the time in the physical laboratory, fascinated by the direct contact with experience. The balance of the time I used in the main in order to study at home the works of Kirchhoff, Helmholtz, Hertz, etc. The fact that I neglected mathematics to a certain extent had its cause not merely in my stronger interest in the natural sciences than in mathematics but also in the following strange experience. I saw that mathematics was split up into numerous specialities, each of which could easily absorb the short lifetime granted to us. Consequently I saw myself in the position of Buridan's ass which was unable to decide upon any specific bundle of hay. This was obviously due to the fact that my intuition was not strong enough in the field of mathematics in order to differentiate clearly the fundamentally important, that which is really basic, from the rest of the more or less dispensable erudition. Beyond this, however, my interest in the knowledge of nature was also unqualifiedly stronger; and it was not clear

nis unbedingt stärker; und es wurde mir als Student nicht klar, dass der Zugang zu den tieferen prinzipiellen Erkenntnissen in der Physik an die feinsten mathematischen Methoden gebunden war. Dies dämmerte mir erst allmählich nach Jahren selbständiger wissenschaftlicher Arbeit. Freilich war auch die Physik in Spezialgebiete geteilt, deren jedes ein kurzes Arbeitsleben verschlingen konnte, ohne dass der Hunger nach tieferer Erkenntnis befriedigt würde. Die Masse des erfahrungsmässig Gegebenen und ungenügend Verbundenen war auch hier überwältigend. Aber bald lernte ich es hier, dasjenige herauszuspüren, was in die Tiefe führen konnte, von allem Andern aber abzusehen, von dem Vielen, das den Geist ausfüllt und von dem Wesentlichen ablenkt. Der Haken dabei war freilich, dass man für die Examina all diesen Wust in sich hineinstopfen musste, ob man nun wollte oder nicht. Dieser Zwang wirkte so abschreckend, dass mir nach überstandenem Endexamen jedes Nachdenken über wissenschaftliche Probleme für ein ganzes Jahr verleidet war. Dabei muss ich sagen, dass wir in der Schweiz unter solchem den wahren wissenschaftlichen Trieb erstickenden Zwang weniger zu leiden hatten, als es an vielen andern Orten der Fall ist. Es gab im Ganzen nur zwei Examina; im übrigen konnte man so ziemlich tun und lassen, was man wollte. Besonders war dies so, wenn man wie ich einen Freund hatte, der die Vorlesungen regelmässig besuchte und den Inhalt gewissenhaft ausarbeitete. Dies gab Freiheit in der Wahl der Beschäftigung bis auf wenige Monate vor dem Examen, eine Freiheit die ich weitgehend genossen habe und das mit ihr verbundene schlechte Gewissen als das weitaus kleinere Uebel gerne in den Kauf nahm. Es ist eigentlich wie ein Wunder, dass der moderne Lehrbetrieb die heilige Neugier des Forschens noch nicht ganz erdrosselt hat; denn dies delikate Pflänzchen bedarf neben Anregung hauptsächlich der Freiheit; ohne diese geht es unweigerlich zugrunde. Es ist ein grosser Irrtum zu glauben dass Freude am Schauen und Suchen durch Zwang und Pflichtgefühl gefördert werden könne. Ich denke, dass man selbst einem gesunden Raubtier seine Fressgier wegnehmen könnte, wenn es gelänge, es mit Hilfe der Peitsche fortgesetzt zum Fressen zu zwingen, wenn es keinen Hunger

to me as a student that the approach to a more profound knowledge of the basic principles of physics is tied up with the most intricate mathematical methods. This dawned upon me only gradually after years of independent scientific work. True enough, physics also was divided into separate fields, each of which was capable of devouring a short lifetime of work without having satisfied the hunger for deeper knowledge. The mass of insufficiently connected experimental data was overwhelming here also. In this field, however, I soon learned to scent out that which was able to lead to fundamentals and to turn aside from everything else, from the multitude of things which clutter up the mind and divert it from the essential. The hitch in this was, of course, the fact that one had to cram all this stuff into one's mind for the examinations, whether one liked it or not. This coercion had such a deterring effect [upon me] that, after I had passed the final examination, I found the consideration of any scientific problems distasteful to me for an entire year. In justice I must add, moreover, that in Switzerland we had to suffer far less under such coercion, which smothers every truly scientific impulse, than is the case in many another locality. There were altogether only two examinations; aside from these, one could just about do as one pleased. This was especially the case if one had a friend, as did I, who attended the lectures regularly and who worked over their content conscientiously. This gave one freedom in the choice of pursuits until a few months before the examination, a freedom which I enjoyed to a great extent and have gladly taken into the bargain the bad conscience connected with it as by far the lesser evil. It is, in fact, nothing short of a miracle that the modern methods of instruction have not yet entirely strangled the holy curiosity of inquiry; for this delicate little plant, aside from stimulation, stands mainly in need of freedom; without this it goes to wreck and ruin without fail. It is a very grave mistake to think that the enjoyment of seeing and searching can be promoted by means of coercion and a sense of duty. To the contrary, I believe that it would be possible to rob even a healthy beast of prey of its voraciousness, if it were possible, with the aid of a whip, to force the beast to devour continuously,

hat, besonders wenn man die unter solchem Zwang verabreichten Speisen entsprechend auswählte. – – –

Nun zur Physik, wie sie sich damals präsentierte. Bei aller Fruchtbarkeit im Einzelnen herrschte in prinzipiellen Dingen dogmatische Starrheit: Am Anfang (wenn es einen solchen gab), schuf Gott Newtons Bewegungsgesetze samt den notwendigen Massen und Kräften. Dies ist alles; das Weitere ergibt die Ausbildung geeigneter mathematischer Methoden durch Deduktion. Was das 19. Jahrhundert fussend auf diese Basis geleistet hat, insbesondere durch die Anwendung der partiellen Differenzialgleichungen, musste die Bewunderung jedes empfänglichen Menschen erwecken. Newton war wohl der erste, der die Leistungsfähigkeit der partiellen Differentialgleichung in seiner Theorie der Schall-Fortpflanzung offenbarte. Euler hatte schon das Fundament der Hydrodynamik geschaffen. Aber der feinere Ausbau der Mechanik diskreter Massen, als Basis der gesamten Physik, war das Werk des 19. Jahrhunderts. Was aber auf den Studenten den grössten Eindruck machte, war weniger der technische Aufbau der Mechanik und die Lösung komplizierter Probleme, sondern die Leistungen der Mechanik auf Gebieten, die dem Anscheine nach nichts mit Mechanik zu tun hatten: die mechanische Lichttheorie, die das Licht als Wellenbewegung eines quasi-starren elastischen Aethers auffasste, vor allem aber die kinetische Gastheorie:—Die Unabhängigkeit der spezifischen Wärme einatomiger Gase vom Atomgewicht, die Ableitung der Gasgleichung und deren Beziehung zur spezifischen Wärme, die kinetische Theorie der Dissoziation der Gase, vor allem aber der quantitative Zusammenhang von Viskosität, Wärmeleitung und Diffusion der Gase, welche auch die absolute Grösse des Atoms lieferte. Diese Ergebnisse stützten gleichzeitig die Mechanik als Grundlage der Physik und der Atomhypothese. welch letztere ja in der Chemie schon fest verankert war. In der Chemie spielten aber nur die Verhältnisse der Atommassen eine Rolle, nicht deren absolute Grössen, sodass die Atomtheorie mehr als veranschaulichendes Gleichnis denn als Erkenntnis über den faktischen Bau der Materie betrachtet werden konnte. Abgesehen davon war es auch von

even when not hungry, especially if the food, handed out under such coercion, were to be selected accordingly. – – –

Now to the field of physics as it presented itself at that time. In spite of all the fruitfulness in particulars, dogmatic rigidity prevailed in matters of principles: In the beginning (if there was such a thing) God created Newton's laws of motion together with the necessary masses and forces. This is all; everything beyond this follows from the development of appropriate mathematical methods by means of deduction. What the nineteenth century achieved on the strength of this basis, especially through the application of the partial differential equations, was bound to arouse the admiration of every receptive person. Newton was probably first to reveal, in his theory of sound-transmission, the efficacy of partial differential equations. Euler had already created the foundation of hydrodynamics. But the more precise development of the mechanics of discrete masses, as the basis of all physics, was the achievement of the 19th century. What made the greatest impression upon the student, however, was less the technical construction of mechanics or the solution of complicated problems than the achievements of mechanics in areas which apparently had nothing to do with mechanics: the mechanical theory of light, which conceived of light as the wave-motion of a quasi-rigid elastic ether, and above all the kinetic theory of gases:—the independence of the specific heat of monatomic gases of the atomic weight, the derivation of the equation of state of a gas and its relation to the specific heat, the kinetic theory of the dissociation of gases, and above all the quantitative connection of viscosity, heat-conduction and diffusion of gases, which also furnished the absolute magnitude of the atom. These results supported at the same time mechanics as the foundation of physics and of the atomic hypothesis, which latter was already firmly anchored in chemistry. However, in chemistry only the ratios of the atomic masses played any rôle, not their absolute magnitudes, so that atomic theory could be viewed more as a visualizing symbol than as knowledge concerning the factual construction of matter. Apart from this it was also of profound

tiefem Interesse, dass die statistische Theorie der klassischen
Mechanik imstande war, die Grundgesetze der Thermodynamik zu deduzieren, was dem Wesen nach schon von Boltzmann geleistet wurde.

Wir dürfen uns daher nicht wundern, dass sozusagen alle
Physiker des letzten Jahrhunderts in der klassischen Mechanik
eine feste und endgültige Grundlage der ganzen Physik, ja
der ganzen Naturwissenschaft sahen, und dass sie nicht müde
wurden zu versuchen, auch die indessen langsam sich durch-
setzende Maxwell'sche Theorie des Elektromagnetismus auf
die Mechanik zu gründen. Auch Maxwell und H. Hertz, die
im Rückblick mit Recht als diejenigen erscheinen, die das Vertrauen auf die Mechanik als die endgültige Basis alles physikalischen Denkens erschüttert haben, haben in ihrem bewussten
Denken durchaus an der Mechanik als gesicherter Basis der
Physik festgehalten. Ernst Mach war es, der in seiner Geschichte der Mechanik an diesem dogmatischen Glauben rüt-
telte; dies Buch hat gerade in dieser Beziehung einen tiefen
Einfluss auf mich als Student ausgeübt. Ich sehe Machs wahre
Grösse in der unbestechlichen Skepsis und Unabhängigkeit; in
meinen jungen Jahren hat mich aber auch Machs erkenntnis-
theoretische Einstellung sehr beeindruckt, die mir heute als im
Wesentlichen unhaltbar erscheint. Er hat nämlich die dem
Wesen nach konstruktive und spekulative Natur alles Denkens
und im Besonderen des wissenschaftlichen Denkens nicht richtig ins Licht gestellt und infolge davon die Theorie gerade an
solchen Stellen verurteilt, an welchen der konstruktiv-speku-
lative Charakter unverhüllbar zutage tritt, z.B. in der kinetischen Atomtheorie.

Bevor ich nun eingehe auf eine Kritik der Mechanik als
Grundlage der Physik, muss erst etwas Allgemeines über die
Gesichtspunkte gesagt werden, nach denen physikalische Theorien überhaupt kritisiert werden können. Der erste Gesichtspunkt liegt auf der Hand: die Theorie darf Erfahrungstatsachen nicht widersprechen. So einleuchtend diese Forderung
auch zunächst erscheint, so subtil gestaltet sich ihre Anwendung.
Man kann nämlich häufig, vielleicht sogar immer, an einer
allgemeinen theoretischen Grundlage festhalten, indem man

interest that the statistical theory of classical mechanics was able to deduce the basic laws of thermodynamics, something which was in essence already accomplished by Boltzmann.

We must not be surprised, therefore, that, so to speak, all physicists of the last century saw in classical mechanics a firm and final foundation for all physics, yes, indeed, for all natural science, and that they never grew tired in their attempts to base Maxwell's theory of electro-magnetism, which, in the meantime, was slowly beginning to win out, upon mechanics as well. Even Maxwell and H. Hertz, who in retrospect appear as those who demolished the faith in mechanics as the final basis of all physical thinking, in their conscious thinking adhered throughout to mechanics as the secured basis of physics. It was Ernst Mach who, in his *History of Mechanics,* shook this dogmatic faith; this book exercised a profound influence upon me in this regard while I was a student. I see Mach's greatness in his incorruptible skepticism and independence; in my younger years, however, Mach's epistemological position also influenced me very greatly, a position which today appears to me to be essentially untenable. For he did not place in the correct light the essentially constructive and speculative nature of thought and more especially of scientific thought; in consequence of which he condemned theory on precisely those points where its constructive-speculative character unconcealably comes to light, as for example in the kinetic atomic theory.

Before I enter upon a critique of mechanics as the foundation of physics, something of a broadly general nature will first have to be said concerning the points of view according to which it is possible to criticize physical theories at all. The first point of view is obvious: the theory must not contradict empirical facts. However evident this demand may in the first place appear, its application turns out to be quite delicate. For it is often, perhaps even always, possible to adhere to a general theoretical foundation by securing the adaptation of the theory

durch künstliche zusätzliche Annahmen ihre Anpassung an die Tatsachen möglich macht. Jedenfalls aber hat es dieser erste Gesichtspunkt mit der Bewährung der theoretischen Grundlage an einem vorliegenden Erfahrungsmaterial zu tun.

Der zweite Gesichtspunkt hat es nicht zu schaffen mit der Beziehung zu dem Beobachtungsmaterial sondern mit den Prämissen der Theorie selbst, mit dem, was man kurz aber undeutlich als "Natürlichkeit" oder "logische Einfachheit" der Prämissen (der Grundbegriffe und zugrunde gelegten Beziehungen zwischen diesen) bezeichnen kann. Dieser Gesichtspunkt, dessen exakte Formulierung auf grosse Schwierigkeiten stösst, hat von jeher bei der Wahl und Wertung der Theorien eine wichtige Rolle gespielt. Es handelt sich dabei nicht einfach um eine Art Abzählung der logisch unabhängigen Prämissen (wenn eine solche überhaupt eindeutig möglich wäre) sondern um eine Art gegenseitiger Abwägung inkommensurabler Qualitäten. Ferner ist von Theorien mit gleich "einfacher" Grundlage diejenige als die Ueberlegene zu betrachten, welche die an sich möglichen Qualitäten von Systemen am stärksten einschränkt (d.h. die bestimmtesten Aussagen enthält). Von dem "Bereich" der Theorien brauche ich hier nichts zu sagen, da wir uns auf solche Theorien beschränken, deren Gegenstand die *Gesamtheit* der physikalischen Erscheinungen ist. Der zweite Gesichtspunkt kann kurz als der die "innere Vollkommenheit" der Theorie betreffende bezeichnet werden, während der erste Gesichtspunkt sich auf die "äussere Bewährung" bezieht. Zur "inneren Vollkommenheit" einer Theorie rechne ich auch folgendes: Wir schätzen eine Theorie höher, wenn sie nicht eine vom logischen Standpunkt willkürliche Wahl unter an sich gleichwertigen und analog gebauten Theorien ist.

Die mangelhafte Schärfe der in den letzten beiden Absätzen enthaltenen Aussagen will ich nicht mit dem Mangel an genügendem zur Verfügung stehendem Druck-Raum zu entschuldigen suchen, sondern bekenne hiermit, dass ich nicht ohne Weiteres, vielleicht überhaupt nicht fähig wäre, diese Andeutungen durch scharfe Definitionen zu ersetzen. Ich glaube aber, dass eine schärfere Formulierung möglich wäre. Jedenfalls zeigt es sich, dass zwischen den "Auguren" meist Uebereinstim-

to the facts by means of artificial additional assumptions. In any case, however, this first point of view is concerned with the confirmation of the theoretical foundation by the available empirical facts.

The second point of view is not concerned with the relation to the material of observation but with the premises of the theory itself, with what may briefly but vaguely be characterized as the "naturalness" or "logical simplicity" of the premises (of the basic concepts and of the relations between these which are taken as a basis). This point of view, an exact formulation of which meets with great difficulties, has played an important rôle in the selection and evaluation of theories since time immemorial. The problem here is not simply one of a kind of enumeration of the logically independent premises (if anything like this were at all unequivocally possible), but that of a kind of reciprocal weighing of incommensurable qualities. Furthermore, among theories of equally "simple" foundation that one is to be taken as superior which most sharply delimits the qualities of systems in the abstract (i.e., contains the most definite claims). Of the "realm" of theories I need not speak here, inasmuch as we are confining ourselves to such theories whose object is the *totality* of all physical appearances. The second point of view may briefly be characterized as concerning itself with the "inner perfection" of the theory, whereas the first point of view refers to the "external confirmation." The following I reckon as also belonging to the "inner perfection" of a theory: We prize a theory more highly if, from the logical standpoint, it is not the result of an arbitrary choice among theories which, among themselves, are of equal value and analogously constructed.

The meager precision of the assertions contained in the last two paragraphs I shall not attempt to excuse by lack of sufficient printing space at my disposal, but confess herewith that I am not, without more ado [immediately], and perhaps not at all, capable to replace these hints by more precise definitions. I believe, however, that a sharper formulation would be possible. In any case it turns out that among the "augurs" there usually is agreement in judging the "inner perfection" of the

mung besteht bezüglich der Beurteilung der "inneren Vollkommenheit" der Theorien und erst recht über den Grad der
"äusseren Bewährung."

Nun zur Kritik der Mechanik als Basis der Physik.

Vom ersten Gesichtspunkte (Bewährung an den Tatsachen)
musste die Einverleibung der Wellenoptik ins mechanische
Weltbild ernste Bedenken erwecken. War das Licht als Wellenbewegung in einem elastischen Körper aufzufassen (Aether) so
musste es ein alles durchdringendes Medium sein, wegen der
Transversalität der Lichtwellen in der Hauptsache ähnlich
einem festen Körper, aber inkompressibel, so dass longitudinale
Wellen nicht existierten. Dieser Aether musste neben der sonstigen Materie ein Gespensterdasein führen, indem er den Bewegungen der "ponderabeln" Körper keinerlei Widerstand zu
leisten schien. Um die Brechungs-Indices durchsichtiger Körper
sowie die Prozesse der Emission und Absorption der Strahlung
zu erklären, hätte man verwickelte Wechselwirkungen zwischen
beiden Arten von Materie annehmen müssen, was nicht einmal
ernstlich versucht, geschweige geleistet wurde.

Ferner nötigten die elekromagnetischen Kräfte zur Einführung elektrischer Massen, die zwar keine merkliche Trägheit
besassen, aber Wechselwirkungen auf einander ausübten, und
zwar, im Gegensatz zur Gravitations-Kraft, solche von polarer
Art.

Was die Physiker nach langem Zaudern langsam dazu
brachte, den Glauben an die Möglichkeit zu verlassen, dass die
gesamte Physik auf Newtons Mechanik gegründet werden
könne, war die Faraday-Maxwell'sche Elektrodynamik. Diese
Theorie und ihre Bestätigung durch die Hertz'schen Versuche
zeigten nämlich, dass es elektromagnetische Vorgänge gibt, die
ihrem Wesen nach losgelöst sind von jeglicher ponderabeln
Materie—die aus elektromagnetischen "Feldern" im leeren
Raume bestehenden Wellen. Wollte man die Mechanik als
Grundlage der Physik aufrecht halten, so mussten die Maxwell'schen Gleichungen mechanisch interpretiert werden. Dies
wurde eifrigst aber erfolglos versucht, während sich die Gleichungen in steigendem Masse als fruchtbar erwiesen. Man
gewöhnte sich daran, mit diesen Feldern als selbständigen

theories and even more so concerning the "degree" of "external confirmation."

And now to the critique of mechanics as the basis of physics.

From the first point of view (confirmation by experiment) the incorporation of wave-optics into the mechanical picture of the world was bound to arouse serious misgivings. If light was to be interpreted as undulatory motion in an elastic body (ether), this had to be a medium which permeates everything; because of the transversality of the lightwaves in the main similar to a solid body, yet incompressible, so that longitudinal waves did not exist. This ether had to lead a ghostly existence alongside the rest of matter, inasmuch as it seemed to offer no resistance whatever to the motion of "ponderable" bodies. In order to explain the refraction-indices of transparent bodies as well as the processes of emission and absorption of radiation, one would have had to assume complicated reciprocal actions between the two types of matter, something which was not even seriously tried, let alone achieved.

Furthermore, the electromagnetic forces necessitated the introduction of electric masses, which, although they had no noticeable inertia, yet interacted with each other, and whose interaction was, moreover, in contrast to the force of gravitation, of a polar type.

The factor which finally succeeded, after long hesitation, to bring the physicists slowly around to give up the faith in the possibility that all of physics could be founded upon Newton's mechanics, was the electrodynamics of Faraday and Maxwell. For this theory and its confirmation by Hertz's experiments showed that there are electromagnetic phenomena which by their very nature are detached from every ponderable matter—namely the waves in empty space which consist of electromagnetic "fields." If mechanics was to be maintained as the foundation of physics, Maxwell's equations had to be interpreted mechanically. This was zealously but fruitlessly attempted, while the equations were proving themselves fruitful in mounting degree. One got used to operating with these fields as independent substances without finding it necessary

Wesenheiten zu operieren, ohne dass man sich über ihre mechanische Natur auszuweisen brauchte; so verliess man halb unvermerkt die Mechanik als Basis der Physik, weil deren Anpassung an die Tatsachen sich schliesslich als hoffnungslos darstellte. Seitdem gibt es zweierlei Begriffselemente, einerseits materielle Punkte mit Fernkräften zwischen ihnen, andererseits das kontinuierliche Feld. Es ist ein Zwischenzustand der Physik ohne einheitliche Basis für das Ganze, der—obwohl unbefriedigend—doch weit davon entfernt ist überwunden zu sein. – – –

Nun einiges zur Kritik der Mechanik als Grundlage der Physik vom zweiten, dem inneren Gesichtspunkte aus. Solche Kritik hat bei dem heutigen Stande der Wissenschaft, d.h. nach dem Verlassen des mechanischen Fundamentes, nur noch methodisches Interesse. Sie ist aber recht geeignet eine Art des Argumentierens zu zeigen, die in der Zukunft bei der Auswahl der Theorien eine umso grössere Rolle spielen muss, je weiter sich die Grundbegriffe und Axiome von dem direkt Wahrnehmbaren entfernen, sodass das Konfrontieren der Implikationen der Theorie mit den Tatsachen immer schwieriger und langwieriger wird. Da ist in erster Linie das Mach'sche Argument zu erwähnen, das übrigens von Newton schon ganz deutlich erkannt worden war (Eimer Versuch). Alle "starren" Koordinationssysteme sind vom Standpunkt der rein geometrischen Beschreibung unter einander logisch gleichwertig. Die Gleichungen der Mechanik (z.B. schon das Trägheits-Gesetz) beanspruchen Gültigkeit nur gegenüber einer besonderen Klasse solcher Systeme, nämlich gegenüber den "Inertialsystemen." Das Koordinationssystem als körperliches Objekt ist hierbei ohne Bedeutung. Man muss also für die Notwendigkeit dieser besonderen Wahl etwas suchen, was ausserhalb der Gegenstände (Massen, Abstände) liegt, von denen die Theorie handelt. Newton führte als ursächlich bestimmend deshalb ganz explicite den "absoluten Raum" ein als allgegenwärtigen aktiven Teilnehmer bei allen mechanischen Vorgängen; unter "absolut" versteht er offenbar unbeeinflusst von den Massen und ihren Bewegungen. Was den Tatbestand besonders hässlich erscheinen lässt, ist die Tatsache, dass es unendlich viele,

to give one's self an account of their mechanical nature; thus mechanics as the basis of physics was being abandoned, almost unnoticeably, because its adaptability to the facts presented itself finally as hopeless. Since then there exist two types of conceptual elements, on the one hand, material points with forces at a distance between them, and, on the other hand, the continuous field. It presents an intermediate state in physics without a uniform basis for the entirety, which—although unsatisfactory—is far from having been superseded. – – –

Now for a few remarks to the critique of mechanics as the foundation of physics from the second, the "interior," point of view. In today's state of science, i.e., after the departure from the mechanical foundation, such critique has only an interest in method left. But such a critique is well suited to show the type of argumentation which, in the choice of theories in the future will have to play an all the greater rôle the more the basic concepts and axioms distance themselves from what is directly observable, so that the confrontation of the implications of theory by the facts becomes constantly more difficult and more drawn out. First in line to be mentioned is Mach's argument, which, however, had already been clearly recognized by Newton (bucket experiment). From the standpoint of purely geometrical description all "rigid" co-ordinate systems are among themselves logically equivalent. The equations of mechanics (for example this is already true of the law of inertia) claim validity only when referred to a specific class of such systems, i.e., the "inertial systems." In this the co-ordinate system as bodily object is without any significance. It is necessary, therefore, in order to justify the necessity of the specific choice, to look for something which lies outside of the objects (masses, distances) with which the theory is concerned. For this reason "absolute space" as originally determinative was quite explicitly introduced by Newton as the omnipresent active participant in all mechanical events; by "absolute" he obviously means uninfluenced by the masses and by their motion. What makes this state of affairs appear particularly offensive is the fact that there are supposed to be infinitely many inertial systems, relative to each

gegen einander gleichförmig und rotationsfrei bewegte Inertialsysteme geben soll, die gegenüber allen andern starren Systemen ausgezeichnet sein sollen.

Mach vermutet, dass in einer wirklich vernünftigen Theorie
die Trägheit, genau wie bei Newton die übrigen Kräfte, auf
Wechselwirkung der Massen beruhen müsse, eine Auffassung
die ich lange für im Prinzip die richtige hielt. Sie setzt aber
implicite voraus, dass die basische Theorie eine solche vom
allgemeinen Typus der Newton'schen Mechanik sein solle:
Massen und Wirkungen zwischen diesen als ursprüngliche
Begriffe. In eine konsequente Feldtheorie passt ein solcher
Lösungsversuch nicht hinein, wie man unmittelbar einsieht.

Wie stichhaltig die Mach'sche Kritik aber an sich ist, kann
man besonders deutlich aus folgender Analogie ersehen. Wir
denken uns Leute, die eine Mechanik aufstellen, nur ein kleines
Stück der Erdoberfläche kennen und auch keine Sterne wahrnehmen können. Sie werden geneigt sein, der vertikalen Dimension des Raumes besondere physikalische Eigenschaften
zuzuschreiben (Richtung der Fallbeschleunigung) und auf
Grund einer solchen begrifflichen Basis es begründen, dass der
Erdboden überwiegend horizontal ist. Sie mögen sich nicht
durch das Argument beeinflussen lassen, dass bezüglich der
geometrischen Eigenschaften der Raum isotrop ist, und dass es
daher unbefriedigend sei, physikalische Grundgesetze aufzu-
stellen, gemäss welchen es eine Vorzugsrichtung geben soll;
sie werden wohl geneigt sein (analog zu Newton) zu erklären,
die Vertikale sei absolut, das zeige eben die Erfahrung und
man müsse sich damit abfinden. Die Bevorzugung der Vertikalen gegen alle anderen Raum-Richtungen ist genau analog
der Bevorzugung der Inertialsysteme gegen andere starre
Koordinationssysteme.

Nun zu anderen Argumenten die sich ebenfalls auf die innere Einfachheit bezw. Natürlichkeit der Mechanik beziehen.
Wenn man die Begriffe Raum (inklusive Geometrie) und
Zeit ohne kritischen Zweifel hinnimmt, so besteht an sich kein
Grund, die Zugrundelegung von Fernkräften zu beanstanden,
wenn ein solcher Begriff auch nicht zu denjenigen Ideen passt,
die man sich auf Grund der rohen Erfahrung des Alltags bildet.

other in uniform translation, which are supposed to be distinguished among all other rigid systems.

Mach conjectures that in a truly rational theory inertia would have to depend upon the interaction of the masses, precisely as was true for Newton's other forces, a conception which for a long time I considered as in principle the correct one. It presupposes implicitly, however, that the basic theory should be of the general type of Newton's mechanics: masses and their interaction as the original concepts. The attempt at such a solution does not fit into a consistent field theory, as will be immediately recognized.

How sound, however, Mach's critique is in essence can be seen particularly clearly from the following analogy. Let us imagine people construct a mechanics, who know only a very small part of the earth's surface and who also can not see any stars. They will be inclined to ascribe special physical attributes to the vertical dimension of space (direction of the acceleration of falling bodies) and, on the ground of such a conceptual basis, will offer reasons that the earth is in most places horizontal. They might not permit themselves to be influenced by the argument that as concerns the geometrical properties space is isotrope and that it is therefore supposed to be unsatisfactory to postulate basic physical laws, according to which there is supposed to be a preferential direction; they will probably be inclined (analogously to Newton) to assert the absoluteness of the vertical, as proved by experience as something with which one simply would have to come to terms. The preference given to the vertical over all other spatial directions is precisely analogous to the preference given to inertial systems over other rigid co-ordination systems.

Now to [a consideration of] other arguments which also concern themselves with the inner simplicity, i.e., naturalness, of mechanics. If one puts up with the concepts of space (including geometry) and time without critical doubts, then there exists no reason to object to the idea of action-at-a-distance, even though such a concept is unsuited to the ideas which one forms on the basis of the raw experience of daily life. However, there

Dagegen gibt es eine andere Ueberlegung, welche die Mechanik als Basis der Physik aufgefasst als primitiv erscheinen lässt. Es gibt im Wesentlichen zwei Gesetze

1) das Bewegungsgesetz
2) den Ausdruck für die Kraft bezw. die potentielle Energie.

Das Bewegungsgesetz ist präzis, aber leer, solange der Ausdruck für die Kräfte nicht gegeben ist. Für die Setzung der letzteren besteht aber ein weiter Spielraum für Willkür, besonders wenn man die an sich nicht natürliche Forderung fallen lässt, dass die Kräfte von den Koordinaten allein (und z.B. nicht von deren Differentialquotienten nach der Zeit) abhängen. Im Rahmen der Theorie ist es an sich ganz willkürlich, dass die von einem Punkte ausgehenden Gravitations- (und elektrischen) Kraftwirkungen durch die Potentialfunktion ($1/r$) beherrscht werden. Zusätzliche Bemerkung: es ist schon lange bekannt, dass diese Funktion die zentralsymmetrische Lösung der einfachsten (drehungs-invarianten) Differentialgleichung $\Delta\varphi = 0$ ist; es wäre also naheliegend gewesen, dies als ein Anzeichen dafür zu betrachten, dass man diese Funktion als durch ein Raumgesetz bestimmt anzusehen hätte, wodurch die Willkür in der Wahl des Kraftgesetzes beseitigt worden wäre. Dies ist eigentlich die erste Erkenntnis, welche eine Abkehr von der Theorie der Fernkräfte nahelegt, welche Entwicklung —durch Faraday, Maxwell und Hertz angebahnt—unter dem äusseren Druck von Erfahrungstatsachen erst später einsetzt.

Ich möchte auch als eine innere Unsymmetrie der Theorie erwähnen, dass die im Bewegungsgesetz auftretende träge Masse auch im Kraftgesetz der Gravitation, nicht aber im Ausdruck der übrigen Kraftgesetze auftritt. Endlich möchte ich darauf hinweisen, dass die Spaltung der Energie in zwei wesensverschiedene Teile, kinetische und potentielle Energie, als unnatürlich empfunden werden muss; dies hat H. Hertz als so störend empfunden, dass er in seinem letzten Werk versuchte, die Mechanik von dem Begriff der potentiellen Energie (d.h. der Kraft) zu befreien. - - -

Genug davon. Newton verzeih' mir; du fandst den einzigen Weg der zu deiner Zeit für einen Menschen von höchster

is another consideration which causes mechanics, taken as the basis of physics, to appear as primitive. Essentially there exist two laws

1) the law of motion
2) the expression for force or potential energy.

The law of motion is precise, although empty, as long as the expression for the forces is not given. In postulating the latter, however, there exists great latitude for arbitrary [choice], especially if one omits the demand, which is not very natural in any case, that the forces depend only on the co-ordinates (and, for example, not on their differential quotients with respect to time). Within the framework of theory alone it is entirely arbitrary that the forces of gravitation (and electricity), which come from one point are governed by the potential function $(1/r)$. Additional remark: it has long been known that this function is the central-symmetrical solution of the simplest (rotation-invariant) differential equation $\Delta\varphi = 0$; it would therefore have been a suggestive idea to regard this as a sign that this function is to be regarded as determined by a law of space, a procedure by which the arbitrariness in the choice of the law of energy would have been removed. This is really the first insight which suggests a turning away from the theory of distant forces, a development which—prepared by Faraday, Maxwell and Hertz—really begins only later on under the external pressure of experimental data.

I would also like to mention, as one internal asymmetry of this theory, that the inert mass occuring in the law of motion also appears in the expression for the gravitational force, but not in the expression for the other forces. Finally I would like to point to the fact that the division of energy into two essentially different parts, kinetic and potential energy, must be felt as unnatural; H. Hertz felt this as so disturbing that, in his very last work, he attempted to free mechanics from the concept of potential energy (i.e., from the concept of force). — — —

Enough of this. Newton, forgive me; you found the only way which, in your age, was just about possible for a man of highest thought- and creative power. The concepts, which you

Denk- und Gestaltungskraft eben noch möglich war. Die Begriffe, die du schufst, sind auch jetzt noch führend in unserem physikalischen Denken, obwohl wir nun wissen, dass sie durch andere, der Sphäre der unmittelbaren Erfahrung ferner stehende ersetzt werden müssen, wenn wir ein tieferes Begreifen der Zusammenhänge anstreben.

"Soll dies ein Nekrolog sein?" mag der erstaunte Leser fragen. Im wesentlichen ja, möchte ich antworten. Denn das Wesentliche im Dasein eines Menschen von meiner Art liegt in dem *was* er denkt und *wie* er denkt, nicht in dem, was er tut oder erleidet. Also kann der Nekrolog sich in der Hauptsache auf Mitteilung von Gedanken beschränken, die in meinem Streben eine erhebliche Rolle spielten. Eine Theorie ist desto eindrucksvoller, je grösser die Einfachheit ihrer Prämissen ist, je verschiedenartigere Dinge sie verknüpft, und je weiter ihr Anwendungsbereich ist. Deshalb der tiefe Eindruck, den die klassische Thermodynamik auf mich machte. Es ist die einzige physikalische Theorie allgemeinen Inhaltes, von der ich überzeugt bin, dass sie im Rahmen der Anwendbarkeit ihrer Grundbegriffe niemals umgestossen werden wird (zur besonderen Beachtung der grundsätzlichen Skeptiker).

Der faszinierendste Gegenstand zur Zeit meines Studiums war die Maxwell'sche Theorie. Was sie als revolutionär erscheinen liess, war der Übergang von den Fernwirkungskräften zu Feldern als Fundamentalgrössen. Die Einordnung der Optik in die Theorie des Elektromagnetismus mit ihrer Beziehung der Lichtgeschwindigkeit zum elektrischen und magnetischen absoluten Masssystem sowie die Beziehung des Brechungsexponenten zur Dielektrizitätskonstante, die qualitative zwischen Reflexionsfähigkeit und metallischer Leitfähigkeit des Körpers—es war wie eine Offenbarung. Abgesehen vom Übergang zur Feldtheorie, d.h. des Ausdrucks der elementaren Gesetze durch Differentialgleichungen, hatte Maxwell nur einen einzigen hypothetischen Schritt nötig—die Einführung des elektrischen Verschiebungsstromes im Vacuum und in den Dielektrica und seiner magnetischen Wirkung, eine Neuerung, die durch die formalen Eigenschaften der Differentialgleichungen beinahe vorgeschrieben war. In diesem Zusammenhang

created, are even today still guiding our thinking in physics, although we now know that they will have to be replaced by others farther removed from the sphere of immediate experience, if we aim at a profounder understanding of relationships.

"Is this supposed to be an obituary?" the astonished reader will likely ask. I would like to reply: essentially yes. For the essential in the being of a man of my type lies precisely in *what* he thinks and *how* he thinks, not in what he does or suffers. Consequently, the obituary can limit itself in the main to the communicating of thoughts which have played a considerable rôle in my endeavors.—A theory is the more impressive the greater the simplicity of its premises is, the more different kinds of things it relates, and the more extended is its area of applicability. Therefore the deep impression which classical thermodynamics made upon me. It is the only physical theory of universal content concerning which I am convinced that, within the framework of the applicability of its basic concepts, it will never be overthrown (for the special attention of those who are skeptics on principle).

The most fascinating subject at the time that I was a student was Maxwell's theory. What made this theory appear revolutionary was the transition from forces at a distance to fields as fundamental variables. The incorporation of optics into the theory of electromagnetism, with its relation of the speed of light to the electric and magnetic absolute system of units as well as the relation of the refraction coëfficient to the dielectric constant, the qualitative relation between the reflection coëfficient and the metallic conductivity of the body—it was like a revelation. Aside from the transition to field-theory, i.e., the expression of the elementary laws through differential equations, Maxwell needed only one single hypothetical step —the introduction of the electrical displacement current in the vacuum and in the dielectrica and its magnetic effect, an innovation which was almost prescribed by the formal properties of the differential equations. In this connection I cannot sup-

kann ich die Bemerkung nicht unterdrücken, dass das Paar
Faraday-Maxwell so merkwürdige innere Aehnlichkeit hat
mit dem Paar Galileo-Newton—der erste jedes Paares die
Zusammenhänge intuitiv erfassend, der zweite sie exakt formu-
lierend und quantitativ anwendend.

Was die Einsicht in das Wesen der elektromagnetischen
Theorie zu jener Zeit erschwerte, war folgender eigentüm-
licher Umstand. Elektrische bezw. magnetische "Feldstärken"
und "Verschiebungen" wurden als gleich elementare Grössen
behandelt, der leere Raum als Spezialfall eines dielektrischen
Körpers. Die *Materie* erschien als Träger des Feldes, nicht der
Raum. Dadurch war impliziert, dass der Träger des Feldes
einen Geschwindigkeitszustand besitze, und dies sollte natürlich auch vom "Vacuum" gelten (Aether). Hertz' Elektrodynamik bewegter Körper ist ganz auf diese grundsätzliche
Einstellung gegründet.

Es war das grosse Verdienst von H. A. Lorentz, dass er hier
in überzeugender Weise Wandel schuf. Im Prinzip gibt es
nach ihm ein Feld nur im leeren Raume. Die atomistisch
gedachte Materie ist einziger Sitz der elektrischen Ladungen;
zwischen den materiellen Teilchen ist leerer Raum, der Sitz
des elektromagnetischen Feldes, das erzeugt ist durch die Lage
und Geschwindigkeit der auf den materiellen Teilchen sitzenden
punktartigen Ladungen. Dielektrizität, Leitungsfähigkeit, etc.
sind ausschliesslich durch die Art der mechanischen Bindung
der Teilchen bedingt, aus welchen die Körper bestehen. Die
Teilchen-Ladungen erzeugen das Feld, das andererseits Kräfte
auf die Ladungen der Teilchen ausübt, die Bewegungen des
letzteren gemäss Newtons Bewegungsgesetz bestimmend. Ver-
gleicht man dies mit Newtons System, so besteht die Aende-
rung darin: Die Fernkräfte werden ersetzt durch das Feld,
welches auch die Strahlung mitbeschreibt. Die Gravitation
wird meist ihrer relativen Kleinheit wegen unberücksichtigt
gelassen; ihre Berücksichtigung war aber stets möglich durch
Bereicherung der Feldstruktur, bezw. Erweiterung des Maxwell'schen Feldgesetzes. Der Physiker der gegenwärtigen Generation betrachtet den von Lorentz errungenen Standpunkt als
den einzig möglichen; damals aber war es ein überraschender

press the remark that the pair Faraday-Maxwell has a most remarkable inner similarity with the pair Galileo-Newton—the former of each pair grasping the relations intuitively, and the second one formulating those relations exactly and applying them quantitatively.

What rendered the insight into the essence of electromagnetic theory so much more difficult at that time was the following peculiar situation. Electric or magnetic "field intensities" and "displacements" were treated as equally elementary variables, empty space as a special instance of a dielectric body. *Matter* appeared as the bearer of the field, not *space*. By this it was implied that the carrier of the field could have velocity, and this was naturally to apply to the "vacuum" (ether) also. Hertz's electrodynamics of moving bodies rests entirely upon this fundamental attitude.

It was the great merit of H. A. Lorentz that he brought about a change here in a convincing fashion. In principle a field exists, according to him, only in empty space. Matter—considered as atoms—is the only seat of electric charges; between the material particles there is empty space, the seat of the electromagnetic field, which is created by the position and velocity of the point charges which are located on the material particles. Dielectricity, conductivity, etc., are determined exclusively by the type of mechanical tie connecting the particles, of which the bodies consist. The particle-charges create the field, which, on the other hand, exerts forces upon the charges of the particles, thus determining the motion of the latter according to Newton's law of motion. If one compares this with Newton's system, the change consists in this: action at a distance is replaced by the field, which thus also describes the radiation. Gravitation is usually not taken into account because of its relative smallness; its consideration, however, was always possible by means of the enrichment of the structure of the field, i.e., expansion of Maxwell's law of the field. The physicist of the present generation regards the point of view achieved by Lorentz as the only possible one; at that time, however, it was a surprising and

und kühner Schritt, ohne den die spätere Entwicklung nicht möglich gewesen wäre.

Betrachtet man diese Phase der Entwicklung der Theorie kritisch, so fällt der Dualismus auf, der darin liegt, dass materieller Punkt im Newton'schen Sinne und das Feld als Kontinuum als elementare Begriffe neben einander verwendet werden. Kinetische Energie und Feld-Energie erscheinen als prinzipiell verschiedene Dinge. Dies erscheint umso unbefriedigender, als gemäss der Maxwell'schen Theorie das Magnetfeld einer bewegten elektrischen Ladung Trägheit repräsentierte. Warum also nicht die *ganze* Trägheit? Dann gäbe es nur noch Feldenergie, und das Teilchen wäre nur ein Gebiet besonders grosser Dichte der Feldenergie. Dann durfte man hoffen, den Begriff des Massenpunktes samt den Bewegungsgleichungen des Teilchens aus den Feldgleichungen abzuleiten —der störende Dualismus wäre beseitigt.

H. A. Lorentz wusste dies sehr wohl. Die Maxwell'schen Gleichungen aber erlaubten nicht, das Gleichgewicht der der ein Teilchen konstituierenden Elektrizität abzuleiten. Nur andere, *nicht lineare* Gleichungen des Feldes konnten solches vielleicht leisten. Es gab aber keine Methode, derartige Feldgleichungen herauszufinden, ohne in abenteuerliche Willkür auszuarten. Jedenfalls durfte man glauben, auf dem von Faraday und Maxwell so erfolgreich begonnenen Wege nach und nach eine neue, sichere Grundlage für die gesamte Physik zu finden. – – –

Die durch die Einführung des Feldes begonnene Revolution war demnach keineswegs beendet. Da ereignete es sich, dass um die Jahrhundertwende unabhängig hiervon eine zweite fundamentale Krise einsetzte, deren Ernst durch Max Plancks Untersuchungen über die Wärmestrahlung (1900) plötzlich ins Bewusstsein trat. Die Geschichte dieses Geschehens ist umso merkwürdiger, weil sie wenigstens in ihrer ersten Phase nicht von irgend welchen überraschenden Entdeckungen experimenteller Art beeinflusst wurde.

Kirchhoff hatte auf thermodynamischer Grundlage geschlossen, dass die Energiedichte und spektrale Zusammensetzung der Strahlung in einem von undurchlässigen Wänden von der

audacious step, without which the later development would not have been possible.

If one views this phase of the development of theory critically, one is struck by the dualism which lies in the fact that the material point in Newton's sense and the field as continuum are used as elementary concepts side by side. Kinetic energy and field-energy appear as essentially different things. This appears all the more unsatisfactory inasmuch as, according to Maxwell's theory, the magnetic field of a moving electric charge represents inertia. Why not then *total* inertia? Then only field-energy would be left, and the particle would be merely an area of special density of field-energy. In that case one could hope to deduce the concept of the mass-point together with the equations of the motion of the particles from the field equations—the disturbing dualism would have been removed.

H. A. Lorentz knew this very well. However, Maxwell's equations did not permit the derivations of the equilibrium of the electricity which constitutes a particle. Only other, non-linear field equations could possibly accomplish such a thing. But no method existed by which this kind of field equations could be discovered without deteriorating into adventurous arbitrariness. In any case one could believe that it would be possible by and by to find a new and secure foundation for all of physics upon the path which had been so successfully begun by Faraday and Maxwell. ---

Accordingly, the revolution begun by the introduction of the field was by no means finished. Then it happened that, around the turn of the century, independently of what we have just been discussing, a second fundamental crisis set in, the seriousness of which was suddenly recognized due to Max Planck's investigations into heat radiation (1900). The history of this event is all the more remarkable because, at least in its first phase, it was not in any way influenced by any surprising discoveries of an experimental nature.

On thermodynamic grounds Kirchhoff had concluded that the energy density and the spectral composition of radiation in a *Hohlraum*, surrounded by impenetrable walls of the tempera-

Temperatur T umschlossenen Hohlraum unabhängig sei von der Natur der Wände. Das heisst die nonchromatische Strahlungsdichte ϱ ist eine universelle Funktion der Frequenz ν und der absoluten Temperatur T. Damit entstand das interessante Problem der Bestimmung dieser Funktion $\varrho(\nu,T)$. Was konnte auf theoretischem Wege über diese Funktion ermittelt werden? Nach Maxwells Theorie musste die Strahlung auf die Wände einen durch die totale Energiedichte bestimmten Druck ausüben. Hieraus folgerte Boltzmann auf rein thermodynamischem Wege, dass die gesamte Energiedichte der Strahlung ($\int\varrho d\nu$) proportional T^4 sei. Er fand so eine theoretische Begründung einer bereits vorher von Stefan empirisch gefundenen Gesetzmässigkeit, bezw. er verknüpfte sie mit dem Fundament der Maxwell'schen Theorie. Hierauf fand W. Wien durch eine geistvolle thermodynamische Überlegung, die ebenfalls von der Maxwell'schen Theorie Gebrauch machte, dass die universelle Funktion ρ der beiden Variabeln ν und T von der Form sein musse

$$\rho \approx \nu^3 f\left(\frac{\nu}{T}\right),$$

wobei $f(\nu/T)$ eine universelle Funktion der einzigen Variable ν/T bedeutet. Es war klar, dass die theoretische Bestimmung dieser universellen Funktion f von fundamentaler Bedeutung war—dies war eben die Aufgabe, vor welcher Planck stand. Sorgfältige Messungen hatten zu einer recht genauen empirischen Bestimmung der Funktion f geführt. Es gelang ihm zunächst, gestützt auf diese empirischen Messungen, eine Darstellung zu finden, welche die Messungen recht gut wiedergab:

$$\rho = \frac{8\pi h \nu^3}{c^3} \cdot \frac{1}{exp(h\nu/kT) - 1}$$

wobei h und k zwei universelle Konstante sind, deren erste zur Quanten-Theorie führte. Diese Formel sieht wegen des Nenners etwas sonderbar aus. War sie auf theoretischem Wege begründbar? Planck fand tatsächlich eine Begründung, deren Unvollkommenheiten zunächst verborgen blieben, welch letz-

ture T, would be independent of the nature of the walls. That is to say, the nonchromatic density of radiation ϱ is a universal function of the frequency ν and of the absolute temperature T. Thus arose the interesting problem of determining this function $\varrho(\nu,T)$. What could theoretically be ascertained about this function? According to Maxwell's theory the radiation had to exert a pressure on the walls, determined by the total energy density. From this Boltzmann concluded by means of pure thermodynamics, that the entire energy density of the radiation ($\int \varrho d\nu$) is proportional to T^4. In this way he found a theoretical justification of a law which had previously been discovered empirically by Stefan, i.e., in this way he connected this empirical law with the basis of Maxwell's theory. Thereafter, by way of an ingenious thermodynamic consideration, which also made use of Maxwell's theory, W. Wien found that the universal function ϱ of the two variables ν and T would have to be of the form

$$\rho \approx \nu^3 f\left(\frac{\nu}{T}\right),$$

whereby $f(\nu/T)$ is a universal function of one variable ν/T only. It was clear that the theoretical determination of this universal function f was of fundamental importance—this was precisely the task which confronted Planck. Careful measurements had led to a very precise empirical determination of the function f. Relying on those empirical measurements, he succeeded in the first place in finding a statement which rendered the measurements very well indeed:

$$\rho = \frac{8\pi h\nu^3}{c^3} \frac{1}{exp(h\nu/kT) - 1}$$

whereby h and k are two universal constants, the first of which led to quantum theory. Because of the denominator this formula looks a bit queer. Was it possible to derive it theoretically? Planck actually did find a derivation, the imperfections of which remained at first hidden, which latter fact was most for-

terer Umstand ein wahres Glück war für die Entwicklung der Physik. War diese Formel richtig, so erlaubte sie mit Hilfe der Maxwell'schen Theorie die Berechnung der mittleren Energie E eines in dem Strahlungsfelde befindlichen quasi-monochromatischen Oszillators:

$$E = \frac{h\nu}{exp(h\nu/kT) - 1}$$

Planck zug es vor zu versuchen, diese letztere Grösse theoretisch zu berechnen. Bei diesem Bestreben half zunächst die Thermodynamik nicht mehr, und ebensowenig die Maxwell'sche Theorie. Was nun an dieser Formel ungemein ermutigend war, war folgender Umstand. Sie lieferte für hohe Werte der Temperatur (bei festem ν) den Ausdruck

$$E = kT.$$

Es ist dies derselbe Ausdruck, den die kinetische Gastheorie für die mittlere Energie eines in einer Dimension elastisch schwingungsfähigen Massenpunktes liefert. Diese liefert nämlich

$$E = (R/N)T,$$

wobei R die Konstante der Gasgleichung und N die Anzahl der Moleküle im Grammmolekül bedeutet, welche Konstante die absolute Grösse des Atoms ausdrückt. Die Gleichsetzung beider Ausdrücke liefert

$$N = R/k.$$

Die eine Konstante der Planck'schen Formel liefert also exakt die wahre Grösse des Atoms. Der Zahlenwert stimmte befriedigend überein mit den allerdings wenig genauen Bestimmungen von N mit Hilfe der kinetischen Gastheorie.

Dies war ein grosser Erfolg, den Planck klar erkannte. Die Sache hat aber eine bedenkliche Kehrseite, die Planck zunächst glücklicher Weise übersah. Die Ueberlegung verlangt nämlich, das die Beziehung $E = kT$ auch für kleine Temperaturen gelten müsse. Dann aber wäre es aus mit der Planck'schen Formel und mit der Konstante h. Die richtige Konsequenz aus der bestehenden Theorie wäre also gewesen: Die mittlere

tunate for the development of physics. If this formula was correct, it permitted, with the aid of Maxwell's theory, the calculation of the average energy E of a quasi-monochromatic oscillator within the field of radiation:

$$E = \frac{h\nu}{exp(h\nu/kT) - 1}$$

Planck preferred to attempt calculating this latter magnitude theoretically. In this effort, thermodynamics, for the time being, proved no longer helpful, and neither did Maxwell's theory. The following circumstance was unusually encouraging in this formula. For high temperatures (with a fixed ν) it yielded the expression

$$E = kT.$$

This is the same expression as the kinetic theory of gases yields for the average energy of a mass-point which is capable of oscillating elastically in one dimension. For in kinetic gas theory one gets

$$E = (R/N)T,$$

whereby R means the constant of the equation of state of a gas and N the number of molecules per mol, from which constant one can compute the absolute size of the atom. Putting these two expressions equal to each other one gets

$$N = R/k.$$

The one constant of Planck's formula consequently furnishes exactly the correct size of the atom. The numerical value agreed satisfactorily with the determinations of N by means of kinetic gas theory, even though these latter were not very accurate.

This was a great success, which Planck clearly recognized. But the matter has a serious drawback, which Planck fortunately overlooked at first. For the same considerations demand in fact that the relation $E = kT$ would also have to be valid for low temperatures. In that case, however, it would be all over with Planck's formula and with the constant h. From the existing theory, therefore, the correct conclusion would have

kinetische Energie des Oszillators wird entweder durch die Gastheorie falsch geliefert, was eine Widerlegung der Mechanik bedeuten würde; oder die mittlere Energie des Oszillators ergibt sich unrichtig aus der Maxwell'schen Theorie, was eine Widerlegung der letzteren bedeuten würde. Am Wahrscheinlichsten ist es unter diesen Verhältnissen, dass beide Theorien nur in der Grenze richtig, im Uebrigen aber falsch sind; so verhält es sich auch in der Tat, wie wir im Folgenden sehen werden. Hätte Planck so geschlossen, so hätte er vielleicht seine grosse Entdeckung nicht gemacht, weil seiner Ueberlegung das Fundament entzogen worden wäre.

Nun zurück zu Planck's Ueberlegung. Boltzmann hatte auf Grund der kinetischen Gastheorie gefunden, dass die Entropie abgesehen von einem konstanten Faktor gleich dem Logarithmus der "Wahrscheinlichkeit" des ins Auge gefassten Zustandes sei. Er hat damit das Wesen der im Sinne der Thermodynamik "nicht umkehrbaren" Vorgänge erkannt. Vom molekular-mechanischen Gesichtspunkte aus gesehen sind dagegen alle Vorgänge umkehrbar. Nennt man einen molekulartheoretisch definierten Zustand einen mikroskopisch beschriebenen oder kurz Mikrozustand, einen im Sinne der Thermodynamik beschriebenen Zustand einen Makrozustand, so gehören zu einem makroskopischen Zustand ungeheuer viele (Z) Zustände. Z ist dann das Mass für die Wahrscheinlichkeit eines ins Auge gefassten Makrozustandes. Diese Idee erscheint auch darum von überragender Bedeutung, dass ihre Anwendbarkeit nicht auf die mikroskopische Beschreibung auf der Grundlage der Mechanik beschränkt ist. Dies erkannte Planck und wendete das Boltzmann'sche Prinzip auf ein System an, das aus sehr vielen Resonatoren von derselben Frequenz ν besteht. Der makroskopische Zustand ist gegeben durch die Gesamtenergie der Schwingung aller Resonatoren, ein Mikrozustand durch Angabe der (momentanen) Energie jedes einzelnen Resonators. Um nun die Zahl der zu einem Makrozustand gehörigen Mikrozustände durch eine endliche Zahl ausdrücken zu können, teilte er die Gesamtenergie in eine grosse aber endliche Zahl von gleichen Energie-Elementen ε und fragte: auf wieviele Arten können diese Energie-Elemente unter die Resonatoren

been: the average kinetic energy of the oscillator is either given incorrectly by the theory of gases, which would imply a refutation of [statistical] mechanics; or else the average energy of the oscillator follows incorrectly from Maxwell's theory, which would imply a refutation of the latter. Under such circumstances it is most probable that both theories are correct only at the limits, but are otherwise false; this is indeed the situation, as we shall see in what follows. If Planck had drawn this conclusion, he probably would not have made his great discovery, because the foundation would have been withdrawn from his deductive reasoning.

Now back to Planck's reasoning. On the basis of the kinetic theory of gases Boltzmann had discovered that, aside from a constant factor, entropy is equivalent to the logarithm of the "probability" of the state under consideration. Through this insight he recognized the nature of courses of events which, in the sense of thermodynamics, are "irreversible." Seen from the molecular-mechanical point of view, however, all courses of events are reversible. If one calls a molecular-theoretically defined state a microscopically described one, or, more briefly, micro-state, and a state described in terms of thermodynamics a macro-state, then an immensely large number (Z) of states belong to a macroscopic condition. Z then is a measure of the probabality of a chosen macro-state. This idea appears to be of outstanding importance also because of the fact that its usefulness is not limited to microscopic description on the basis of mechanics. Planck recognized this and applied the Boltzmann principle to a system which consists of very many resonators of the same frequency ν. The macroscopic situation is given through the total energy of the oscillation of all resonators, a micro-condition through determination of the (instantaneous) energy of each individual resonator. In order then to be able to express the number of the micro-states belonging to a macro-state by means of a finite number, he [Planck] divided the total energy into a large but finite number of identical energy-elements ε and asked: in how many ways can these energy-elements be divided among the resonators. The logarithm of

verteilt werden. Der Logarithmus dieser Zahl liefert dann die Entropie und damit (auf thermodynamischem Wege) die Temperatur des Systems. Planck erhielt nun seine Strahlungsformel, wenn er seine Energieelemente ε von der Grösse $\varepsilon = h\nu$ wählte. Das Entscheidende dabei ist, dass das Ergebnis daran gebunden ist, dass man für ε einen bestimmten endlichen Wert nimmt, also nicht zum Limes $\varepsilon = 0$ übergeht. Diese Form der Ueberlegung lässt nicht ohne Weiteres erkennen, dass dieselbe mit der mechanischen und elektrodynamischen Basis im Widerspruch steht, auf welcher die Ableitung im Uebrigen beruht. In Wirklichkeit setzt die Ableitung aber implicite voraus, dass die Energie nur in "Quanten" von der Grösse $h\nu$ von dem einzelnen Resonator absorbiert und emittiert werden kann, dass also sowohl die Energie eines schwingungsfähigen mechanischen Gebildes als auch die Energie der Strahlung nur in solchen Quanten umgesetzt werden kann—im Gegensatz mit den Gesetzen der Mechanik und Elektrodynamik. Hierbei war der Widerspruch mit der Dynamik fundamental, während der Widerspruch mit der Elektrodynamik weniger fundamental sein konnte. Der Ausdruck für die Dichte der Strahlungsenergie ist nämlich zwar *vereinbar* mit den Maxwell'schen Gleichungen, aber keine notwendige Folge dieser Gleichungen. Dass dieser Ausdruck wichtige Mittelwerte liefert, zeigt sich ja dadurch, dass die auf ihm beruhenden Gesetze von Stefan-Boltzmann und Wien mit der Erfahrung im Einklang sind.

All dies war mir schon kurze Zeit nach dem Erscheinen von Plancks grundlegender Arbeit klar, sodass ich, ohne einen Ersatz für die klassische Mechanik zu haben, doch sehen konnte, zu was für Konsequenzen dies Gesetz der Temperaturstrahlung für den licht-elektrischen Effekt und andere verwandte Phänomene der Verwandlung von Strahlungsenergie sowie für die spezifische Wärme (insbesondere) fester Körper führt. All meine Versuche, das theoretische Fundament der Physik diesen Erkenntnissen anzupassen, scheiterten aber völlig. Es war wie wenn einem der Boden unter den Füssen weggezogen worden wäre, ohne dass sich irgendwo fester Grund zeigte, auf dem man hätte bauen können. Dass diese schwankende und widerspruchsvolle Grundlage hinreichte um einen

this number, then, furnishes the entropy and thus (via thermodynamics) the temperature of the system. Planck got his radiation-formula if he chose his energy-elements ε of the magnitude $\varepsilon = h\nu$. The decisive element in doing this lies in the fact that the result depends on taking for ε a definite finite value, i.e., that one does not go to the limit $\varepsilon = 0$. This form of reasoning does not make obvious the fact that it contradicts the mechanical and electrodynamic basis, upon which the derivation otherwise depends. Actually, however, the derivation presupposes implicitly that energy can be absorbed and emitted by the individual resonator only in "quanta" of magnitude $h\nu$, i.e., that the energy of a mechanical structure capable of oscillations as well as the energy of radiation can be transferred only in such quanta—in contradiction to the laws of mechanics and electrodynamics. The contradiction with dynamics was here fundamental; whereas the contradiction with electrodynamics could be less fundamental. For the expression for the density of radiation-energy, although it is *compatible* with Maxwell's equations, is not a necessary consequence of these equations. That this expression furnishes important average-values is shown by the fact that the Stefan-Boltzmann law and Wien's law, which are based on it, are in agreement with experience.

All of this was quite clear to me shortly after the appearance of Planck's fundamental work; so that, without having a substitute for classical mechanics, I could nevertheless see to what kind of consequences this law of temperature-radiation leads for the photo-electric effect and for other related phenomena of the transformation of radiation-energy, as well as for the specific heat of (especially) solid bodies. All my attempts, however, to adapt the theoretical foundation of physics to this [new type of] knowledge failed completely. It was as if the ground had been pulled out from under one, with no firm foundation to be seen anywhere, upon which one could have built. That this insecure and contradictory foundation was sufficient to en-

Mann mit dem einzigartigen Instinkt und Feingefühl Bohrs
in den Stand zu setzen, die hauptsächlichen Gesetze der
Spektrallinien und der Elektronenhüllen der Atome nebst
deren Bedeutung für die Chemie aufzufinden, erschien mir
wie ein Wunder—und erscheint mir auch heute noch als ein
Wunder. Dies ist höchste Musikalität auf dem Gebiete des
Gedankens.

Mein eingenes Interesse in jenen Jahren war weniger auf
die Einzel-Folgerungen aus dem Planck'schen Ergebnis ge-
richtet, so wichtig diese auch sein mochten. Meine Hauptfrage
war: Was für allgemeine Folgerungen können aus der Strahlungsformel betreffend die Struktur der Strahlung und überhaupt betreffend das elektromagnetische Fundament der Physik
gezogen werden? Bevor ich hierauf eingehe, muss ich einige
Untersuchungen kurz erwähnen, die sich auf die Brown'sche
Bewegung und verwandte Gegenstände (Schwankungs-Phä-
nomene) beziehen und sich in der Hauptsache auf die klas-
sich Molekularmechanik gründen. Nicht vertraut mit den
früher erschienen und den Gegenstand tatsächlich erschöpfenden Untersuchungen von Boltzmann und Gibbs, entwickelte ich die statistische Mechanik und die auf sie gegründete molekular-kinetische Theorie der Thermodynamik.
Mein Hauptziel dabei war es, Tatsachen zu finden, welche die
Existenz von Atomen von bestimmter endlicher Grösse
möglichst sicher stellten. Dabei entdeckte ich, dass es nach der
atomistischen Theorie eine der Beobachtung zugängliche Bewegung suspendierter mikroskopischer Teilchen geben müsse,
ohne zu wissen, dass Beobachtungen über die "Brown'sche Bewegung" schon lange bekannt waren. Die einfachste Ableitung
beruhte auf folgender Erwägung. Wenn die molekular-kinetische Theorie im Prinzip richtig ist, muss eine Suspension
von sichtbaren Teilchen ebenso einen die Gasgesetze erfül-
lenden osmotischen Druck besitzen wie eine Lösung von
Molekülen. Dieser osmotische Druck hängt ab von der wahren
Grösse der Moleküle, d.h. von der Zahl der Moleküle in
einem Gramm-Aequivalent. Ist die Suspension von ungleich-
mässiger Dichte, so gibt die damit vorhandene räumliche
Variabilität dieses osmotischen Druckes Anlass zu einer aus-

able a man of Bohr's unique instinct and tact to discover the major laws of the spectral lines and of the electron-shells of the atoms together with their significance for chemistry appeared to me like a miracle—and appears to me as a miracle even today. This is the highest form of musicality in the sphere of thought.

My own interest in those years was less concerned with the detailed consequences of Planck's results, however important these might be. My major question was: What general conclusions can be drawn from the radiation-formula concerning the structure of radiation and even more generally concerning the electro-magnetic foundation of physics? Before I take this up, I must briefly mention a number of investigations which relate to the Brownian motion and related objects (fluctuation-phenomena) and which in essence rest upon classical molecular mechanics. Not acquainted with the earlier investigations of Boltzmann and Gibbs, which had appeared earlier and actually exhausted the subject, I developed the statistical mechanics and the molecular-kinetic theory of thermodynamics which was based on the former. My major aim in this was to find facts which would guarantee as much as possible the existence of atoms of definite finite size. In the midst of this I discovered that, according to atomistic theory, there would have to be a movement of suspended microscopic particles open to observation, without knowing that observations concerning the Brownian motion were already long familiar. The simplest derivation rested upon the following consideration. If the molecular-kinetic theory is essentially correct, a suspension of visible particles must possess the same kind of osmotic pressure fulfilling the laws of gases as a solution of molecules. This osmotic pressure depends upon the actual magnitude of the molecules, i.e., upon the number of molecules in a gram-equivalent. If the density of the suspension is inhomogeneous, the osmotic pressure is inhomogeneous, too, and gives rise to a

gleichenden Diffusionsbewegung, welche aus der bekannten Beweglichkeit der Teilchen berechenbar ist. Dieser Diffusionsvorgang kann aber andererseits auch aufgefasst werden als das Ergebnis der zunächst ihrem Betrage nach unbekannten regellosen Verlagerung der suspendierten Teilchen unter der Wirkung der thermischen Agitation. Durch Gleichsetzung der durch beide Ueberlegungen erlangten Beträge für den Diffusionsfluss erhält man quantitativ das statistiche Gesetz für jene Verlagerungen, d.h. das Gesetz der Brown'schen Bewegung. Die Uebereinstimmung dieser Betrachtung mit der Erfahrung zusammen mit der Planck'schen Bestimmung der wahren Molekülgrösse aus dem Strahlungsgesetz (für hohe Temperaturen) überzeugte die damals zahlreichen Skeptiker (Ostwald, Mach) von der Realität der Atome. Die Abneigung dieser Forscher gegen die Atomtheorie ist ohne Zweifel auf ihre positivistische philosophische Einstellung zurückzuführen. Es ist dies ein interessantes Beispiel dafür, dass selbst Forscher von kühnem Geist und von feinem Instinkt durch philosophische Vorurteile für die Interpretation von Tatsachen gehemmt werden können. Das Vorurteil—welches seither keineswegs ausgestorben ist—liegt in dem Glauben, dass die Tatsachen allein ohne freie begriffliche Konstruktion wissenschaftliche Erkenntnis liefern könnten und sollten. Solche Täuschung ist nur dadurch möglich, dass man sich der freien Wahl von solchen Begriffen nicht leicht bewusst werden kann, die durch Bewährung und langen Gebrauch unmittelbar mit dem empirischen Material verknüpft zu sein scheinen.

Der Erfolg der Theorie der Brown'schen Bewegung zeigte wieder deutlich, dass die klassische Mechanik stets dann zuverlässige Resultate lieferte, wenn sie auf Bewegungen angewandt wurde, bei welchen die höheren zeitlichen Ableitungen der Geschwindigkeit vernachlässigbar klein sind. Auf diese Erkenntnis lässt sich eine verhältnismässig direkte Methode gründen, um aus der Planck'schen Formel etwas zu erfahren über die Konstitution der Strahlung. Man darf nämlich schliessen, dass in einem Strahlungsraume ein (senkrecht zu seiner Ebene) frei bewegter, quasi monochromatisch reflektierender Spiegel eine Art Brown'sche Bewegung ausführen muss, deren

compensating diffusion, which can be calculated from the well known mobility of the particles. This diffusion can, on the other hand, also be considered as the result of the random displacement—unknown in magnitude originally—of the suspended particles due to thermal agitation. By comparing the amounts obtained for the diffusion current from both types of reasoning one reaches quantitatively the statistical law for those displacements, i.e., the law of the Brownian motion. The agreement of these considerations with experience together with Planck's determination of the true molecular size from the law of radiation (for high temperatures) convinced the sceptics, who were quite numerous at that time (Ostwald, Mach) of the reality of atoms. The antipathy of these scholars towards atomic theory can indubitably be traced back to their positivistic philosophical attitude. This is an interesting example of the fact that even scholars of audacious spirit and fine instinct can be obstructed in the interpretation of facts by philosophical prejudices. The prejudice—which has by no means died out in the meantime—consists in the faith that facts by themselves can and should yield scientific knowledge without free conceptual construction. Such a misconception is possible only because one does not easily become aware of the free choice of such concepts, which, through verification and long usage, appear to be immediately connected with the empirical material.

The success of the theory of the Brownian motion showed again conclusively that classical mechanics always offered trustworthy results whenever it was applied to motions in which the higher time derivatives of velocity are negligibly small. Upon this recognition a relatively direct method can be based which permits us to learn something concerning the constitution of radiation from Planck's formula. One may conclude in fact that, in a space filled with radiation, a (vertically to its plane) freely moving, quasi monochromatically reflecting mirror would have to go through a kind of Brownian movement, the average

mittlere kinetische Energie gleich $\frac{1}{2}(R/N)T$ ist (R = Konstante der Gasgleichung für ein Gramm-Molekül, N gleich Zahl der Moleküle in einem Gramm-Molekül, T = absolute Temperatur). Wäre die Strahlung keinen lokalen Schwankungen unterworfen, so würde der Spiegel allmählich zur Ruhe kommen, weil er auf seiner Vorderseite infolge seiner Bewegung mehr Strahlung reflektiert als auf seiner Rückseite. Er muss aber gewisse aus der Maxwell'schen Theorie berechenbare unregelmässige Schwankungen des auf ihn wirkenden Druckes dadurch erfahren, dass die die Strahlung konstituierenden Wellenbündel miteinander interferieren. Diese Rechnung zeigt nun, dass diese Druckschwankungen (insbesondere bei geringen Strahlungsdichten) keineswegs hinreichen, um dem Spiegel die mittlere kinetische Energie $\frac{1}{2}(R/N)T$ zu erteilen. Um dies Resultat zu erhalten, muss man vielmehr annehmen, dass es eine zweite aus der Maxwell'schen Theorie nicht folgende Art Druckschwankungen gibt, welche der Annahme entspricht, dass die Strahlungsenergie aus unteilbaren punktartig lokalisierten Quanten von der Energie $h\nu$ (und dem Impuls $h\nu/c$, (c = Lichtgeschwindigkeit)) besteht, die ungeteilt reflektiert werden. Diese Betrachtung zeigte in einer drastischen und direkten Weise, dass den Planck'schen Quanten eine Art unmittelbare Realität zugeschrieben werden muss, dass also die Strahlung in energetischer Beziehung eine Art Molekularstruktur besitzen muss, was natürlich mit der Maxwell'schen Theorie im Widerspruch ist. Auch Ueberlegungen über die Strahlung, die unmittelbar auf Boltzmanns Entropie-Wahrscheinlichkeits-Relation gegründet sind (Wahrscheinlichkeit = statistische zeitliche Häufigkeit gesetzt) führten zu demselben Resultat. Diese Doppelnatur von Strahlung (und materiellen Korpuskeln) ist eine Haupteigenschaft der Realität, welche die Quanten-Mechanik in einer geistreichen und verblüffend erfolgreichen Weise gedeutet hat. Diese Deutung welche von fast allen zeitgenössischen Physikern als im wesentlichen endgültig angesehen wird, erscheint mir als ein nur temporärer Ausweg; einige Bemerkungen darüber folgen später. – – –

Ueberlegungen solcher Art machten es mir schon kurz nach

kinetic energy of which equals $\frac{1}{2}(R/N)T$ (R = constant of the gas-equation for one gram-molecule, N equals the number of the molecules per mol, T = absolute temperature). If radiation were not subject to local fluctuations, the mirror would gradually come to rest, because, due to its motion, it reflects more radiation on its front than on its reverse side. However, the mirror must experience certain random fluctuations of the pressure exerted upon it due to the fact that the wave-packets, constituting the radiation, interfere with one another. These can be computed from Maxwell's theory. This calculation, then, shows that these pressure variations (especially in the case of small radiation-densities) are by no means sufficient to impart to the mirror the average kinetic energy $\frac{1}{2}(R/N)T$. In order to get this result one has to assume rather that there exists a second type of pressure variations, which can not be derived from Maxwell's theory, which corresponds to the assumption that radiation energy consists of indivisible point-like localized quanta of the energy $h\nu$ (and of momentum ($h\nu/c$), (c = velocity of light)), which are reflected undivided. This way of looking at the problem showed in a drastic and direct way that a type of immediate reality has to be ascribed to Planck's quanta, that radiation must, therefore, possess a kind of molecular structure in energy, which of course contradicts Maxwell's theory. Considerations concerning radiation which are based directly on Boltzmann's entropy-probability-relation (probability taken equal to statistical temporal frequency) also lead to the same result. This double nature of radiation (and of material corpuscles) is a major property of reality, which has been interpreted by quantum-mechanics in an ingenious and amazingly successful fashion. This interpretation, which is looked upon as essentially final by almost all contemporary physicists, appears to me as only a temporary way out; a few remarks to this [point] will follow later. – – –

Reflections of this type made it clear to me as long ago as

1900, d.h. kurz nach Plancks bahnbrechender Arbeit klar, dass weder die Mechanik noch die Electrodynamik (ausser in Grenzfällen) exakte Gültigkeit beanspruchen können. Nach und nach verzweifelte ich an der Möglichkeit die wahren Gesetze durch auf bekannte Tatsachen sich stützende konstruktive Bemühungen herauszufinden. Je länger und verzweifelter ich mich bemühte, desto mehr kam ich zu der Ueberzeugung, dass nur die Auffindung eines allgemeinen formalen Prinzipes uns zu gesicherten Ergebnissen führen könnte. Als Vorbild sah ich die Thermodynamik vor mir. Das allgemeine Prinzip war dort in dem Satze gegeben: die Naturgesetze sind so beschaffen, dass es unmöglich ist, ein *perpetuum mobile* (erster und zweiter Art) zu konstruieren. Wie aber ein solches allgemeines Prinzip finden? Ein solches Prinzip ergab sich nach zehn Jahren Nachdenkens aus einem Paradoxon, auf das ich schon mit 16 Jahren gestossen bin: Wenn ich einem Lichtstrahl nacheile mit der Geschwindigkeit c (Lichtgeschwindigkeit im Vacuum), so sollte ich einen solchen Lichtstrahl als ruhendes, räumlich oszillatorisches elektromagnetisches Feld wahrnehmen. So etwas scheint es aber nicht zu geben, weder auf Grund der Erfahrung noch gemäss den Maxwell'schen Gleichungen. Intuitiv klar schien es mir von vornherein, dass von einem solchen Beobachter aus beurteilt alles sich nach denselben Gesetzen abspielen müsse wie für einen relativ zu Erde ruhenden Beobachter. Denn wie sollte der erste Beobachter wissen bezw. konstatieren können, dass er sich im Zustand rascher gleichförmiger Bewegung befindet?

Man sieht, dass in diesem Paradoxon der Keim zur speziellen Relativitätstheorie schon enthalten ist. Heute weiss natürlich jeder, dass alle Versuche, dies Paradoxon befriedigend aufzuklären, zum Scheitern verurteilt waren, solange das Axiom des absoluten Charakters der Zeit, bezw. der Gleichzeitigkeit, unerkannt im Unbewussten verankert war. Dies Axiom und seine Willkür klar erkennen bedeutet eigentlich schon die Lösung des Problems. Das kritische Denken, dessen es zur Auffindung dieses zentralen Punktes bedurfte, wurde bei mir entscheidend gefördert insbesondere durch die Lektüre von David Humes und Ernst Machs philosophischen Schriften.

shortly after 1900, i.e., shortly after Planck's trailblazing work, that neither mechanics nor electrodynamics could (except in limiting cases) claim exact validity. By and by I despaired of the possibility of discovering the true laws by means of constructive efforts based on known facts. The longer and the more despairingly I tried, the more I came to the conviction that only the discovery of a universal formal principle could lead us to assured results. The example I saw before me was thermodynamics. The general principle was there given in the theorem: the laws of nature are such that it is impossible to construct a *perpetuum mobile* (of the first and second kind). How, then, could such a universal principle be found? After ten years of reflection such a principle resulted from a paradox upon which I had already hit at the age of sixteen: If I pursue a beam of light with the velocity *c* (velocity of light in a vacuum), I should observe such a beam of light as a spatially oscillatory electromagnetic field at rest. However, there seems to be no such thing, whether on the basis of experience or according to Maxwell's equations. From the very beginning it appeared to me intuitively clear that, judged from the standpoint of such an observer, everything would have to happen according to the same laws as for an observer who, relative to the earth, was at rest. For how, otherwise, should the first observer know, i.e., be able to determine, that he is in a state of fast uniform motion?

One sees that in this paradox the germ of the special relativity theory is already contained. Today everyone knows, of course, that all attempts to clarify this paradox satisfactorily were condemned to failure as long as the axiom of the absolute character of time, viz., of simultaneity, unrecognizedly was anchored in the unconscious. Clearly to recognize this axiom and its arbitrary character really implies already the solution of the problem. The type of critical reasoning which was required for the discovery of this central point was decisively furthered, in my case, especially by the reading of David Hume's and Ernst Mach's philosophical writings.

Man hatte sich darüber klar zu werden, was die räumlichen Koordinaten und der Zeitwert eines Ereignisses in der Physik bedeuteten. Die physikalische Deutung der räumlichen Koordinaten setzten einen starren Bezugskörper voraus, der noch dazu von mehr oder minder bestimmtem Bewegungszustande (Inertialsystem) sein musste. Bei gegebenem Inertialsystem bedeuteten die Koordinaten Ergebnisse von bestimmten Messungen mit starren (ruhenden) Stäben. (Dass die Voraussetzung der prinzipiellen Existenz starrer Stäbe eine durch approximative Erfahrung nahe gelegte aber im Prinzip willkürliche Voraussetzung ist, dessen soll man sich stets bewusst sein.) Bei solcher Interpretation der räumlichen Koordinaten wird die Frage der Gültigkeit der Euklidischen Geometrie zum physikalischen Problem.

Sucht man nun die Zeit eines Ereignisses analog zu deuten, so braucht man ein Mittel zur Messung der Zeitdifferenz (in sich determinierter periodischer Prozess realisiert durch ein System von hinreichend geringer räumlicher Abmessung). Eine relativ zum Inertialsystem ruhend angeordnete Uhr definiert eine (Orts-Zeit). Die Ortszeiten aller räumlichen Punkte zusammen genommen sind die "Zeit," die zu dem gewählten Inertialsystem gehört, wenn man noch ein Mittel gegeben hat, diese Uhren gegeneinander zu "richten." Man sieht, dass es *a priori* gar nicht nötig ist, dass die in solcher Weise definierten "Zeiten" verschiedener Inertialsysteme miteinander übereinstimmen. Man würde dies längst gemerkt haben, wenn nicht für die praktische Erfahrung des Alltags (wegen des hohen Wertes von c) das Licht nicht als Mittel für die Konstatierung absoluter Gleichzeitigkeit erschiene.

Die Voraussetzung von der (prinzipiellen) Existenz (idealer bezw. vollkommener) Massstäbe und Uhren ist nicht unabhängig voneinander, denn ein Lichtsignal, welches zwischen den Enden eines starren Stabes hin und her reflektiert wird, stellt eine ideale Uhr dar, vorausgesetzt, dass die Voraussetzung von der Konstanz der Vacuum-Lichtgeschwindigkeit nicht zu Widersprüchen führt.

Das obige Paradoxon lässt sich nun so formulieren. Nach den in der klassischen Physik verwendeten Verknüpfungsregeln

One had to understand clearly what the spatial co-ordinates and the temporal duration of events meant in physics. The physical interpretation of the spatial co-ordinates presupposed a fixed body of reference, which, moreover, had to be in a more or less definite state of motion (inertial system). In a given inertial system the co-ordinates meant the results of certain measurements with rigid (stationary) rods. (One should always be conscious of the fact that the presupposition of the existence in principle of rigid rods is a presupposition suggested by approximate experience, but which is, in principle, arbitrary.) With such an interpretation of the spatial co-ordinates the question of the validity of Euclidean geometry becomes a problem of physics.

If, then, one tries to interpret the time of an event analogously, one needs a means for the measurement of the difference in time (in itself determined periodic process realized by a system of sufficiently small spatial extension). A clock at rest relative to the system of inertia defines a local time. The local times of all space points taken together are the "time," which belongs to the selected system of inertia, if a means is given to "set" these clocks relative to each other. One sees that *a priori* it is not at all necessary that the "times" thus defined in different inertial systems agree with one another. One would have noticed this long ago, if, for the practical experience of everyday life light did not appear (because of the high value of c), as the means for the statement of absolute simultaneity.

The presupposition of the existence (in principle) of (ideal, viz., perfect) measuring rods and clocks is not independent of each other; since a lightsignal, which is reflected back and forth between the ends of a rigid rod, constitutes an ideal clock, provided that the postulate of the constancy of the light-velocity in vacuum does not lead to contradictions.

The above paradox may then be formulated as follows. According to the rules of connection, used in classical physics, of the spatial co-ordinates and of the time of events in the transi-

von räumlichen Koordinaten und Zeit von Ereignissen beim
Uebergang von einem Inertialsystem zu einem andern sind die
beiden Annahmen

1) Konstanz der Lichtgeschwindigkeit
2) Unabhängigkeit der Gesetze (also speziell auch des Gesetzes von der Konstanz der Lichtgeschwindigkeit) von
der Wahl des Inertialsystems (spezielles Relativitätsprinzip)

miteinander unvereinbar (trotzdem beide einzeln durch die
Erfahrung gestützt sind).

Die der speziellen Rel. Th. zugrunde liegende Erkenntnis
ist: Die Annahmen 1) und 2) sind miteinander vereinbar, wenn
für die Umrechnung von Koordinaten und Zeiten der Ereignisse neuartige Beziehungen ("Lorentz-Transformation")
zugrunde gelegt werden. Bei der gegebenen physikalischen Interpretation von Koordinaten und Zeit bedeutet dies nicht etwa
nur einen konventionellen Schritt sondern involviert bestimmte
Hypothesen über das tatsächliche Verhalten bewegter Massstäbe und Uhren, die durch Experiment bestätigt bezw. wider-
legt werden können.

Das allgemeine Prinzip der speziellen Relativitätstheorie
ist in dem Postulat enthalten: Die Gesetze der Physik sind invariant mit Bezug auf Lorentz-Transformationen (für den
Uebergang von einem Inertialsystem zu einem beliebigen andern Inertialsystem). Dies ist ein einschränkendes Prinzip für
die Naturgesetze, vergleichbar mit dem der Thermodynamik
zugrunde liegenden einschränkenden Prinzip von der Nichtexistenz des *perpetuum mobile*.

Zunächst eine Bemerkung über die Beziehung der Theorie
zum "vierdimensionalen Raum." Es ist ein verbreiteter Irrtum,
dass die spezielle Rel. Th. gewissermassen die Vierdimensionalität des physikalischen Kontinuums entdeckt bezw. neu eingeführt hätte. Dies ist natürlich nicht der Fall. Auch der klassischen Mechanik liegt das vierdimensionale Kontinuum von
Raum und Zeit zugrunde. Nur haben im vierdimensionalen
Kontinuum der klassischen Physik die "Schnitte" konstanten
Zeitwertes eine absolute, d.h. von der Wahl des Bezugssystems
unabhängige, Realität. Das vierdimensionale Kontinuum zer-

tion from one inertial system to another the two assumptions of

(1) the constancy of the light velocity

(2) the independence of the laws (thus specially also of the law of the constancy of the light velocity) of the choice of the inertial system (principle of special relativity)

are mutually incompatible (despite the fact that both taken separately are based on experience).

The insight which is fundamental for the special theory of relativity is this: The assumptions (1) and (2) are compatible if relations of a new type ("Lorentz-transformation") are postulated for the conversion of co-ordinates and the times of events. With the given physical interpretation of co-ordinates and time, this is by no means merely a conventional step, but implies certain hypotheses concerning the actual behavior of moving measuring-rods and clocks, which can be experimentally validated or disproved.

The universal principle of the special theory of relativity is contained in the postulate: The laws of physics are invariant with respect to the Lorentz-transformations (for the transition from one inertial system to any other arbitrarily chosen system of inertia). This is a restricting principle for natural laws, comparable to the restricting principle of the non-existence of the *perpetuum mobile* which underlies thermodynamics.

First a remark concerning the relation of the theory to "four-dimensional space." It is a wide-spread error that the special theory of relativity is supposed to have, to a certain extent, first discovered, or at any rate, newly introduced, the four-dimensionality of the physical continuum. This, of course, is not the case. Classical mechanics, too, is based on the four-dimensional continuum of space and time. But in the four-dimensional continuum of classical physics the subspaces with constant time value have an absolute reality, independent of the choice of the reference system. Because of this [fact], the four-dimensional continuum falls naturally into a three-

fällt dadurch natürlich in ein dreidimensionales und ein ein-
dimensionales (Zeit), sodass die vierdimensionale Betrach-
tungsweise sich nicht als *notwendig* aufdrängt. Die spezielle
Relativitätstheorie dagegen schafft eine formale Abhängigkeit
zwischen der Art und Weise, wie die räumlichen Koordinaten
einerseits und die Zeitkoordinate andrerseits in die Naturgesetze
eingehen müssen.

Minkowskis wichtiger Beitrag zu der Theorie liegt in Folgendem: Vor Minkowskis Untersuchung hatte man an einem
Gesetze eine Lorentz-Transformation auszuführen, um seine
Invarianz bezüglich solcher Transformationen zu prüfen; ihm
dagegen gelang es, einen solchen Formalismus einzuführen,
dass die mathematische Form des Gesetzes selbst dessen Invarianz bezüglich Lorentz-Transformationen verbürgt. Er leistete durch Schaffung eines vierdimensionalen Tensorkalküls
für den vierdimensionalen Raum dasselbe, was die gewöhnliche Vektorkalkül für die drei räumlichen Dimensionen leistet.
Er zeigte auch, dass die Lorentz-Transformation (abgesehen
von einem durch den besonderen Charakter der Zeit bedingten
abweichenden Vorzeichen) nichts anderes ist als eine Drehung
des Koordinatensystems im vierdimensionalen Raume.

Zunächst eine kritische Bemerkung zur Theorie, wie sie
oben charakterisiert ist. Es fällt auf, dass die Theorie (ausser
dem vierdimensionalen Raum) zweierlei physikalische Dinge
einführt, nämlich 1) Massstäbe und Uhren, 2) alle sonstigen
Dinge, z.B. das elektromagnetische Feld, den materiellen
Punkt, etc. Dies ist in gewissem Sinne inkonsequent; Massstäbe
und Uhren müssten eigentlich als Lösungen der Grundgleichungen (Gegenstände bestehend aus bewegten atomistischen Gebilden) dargestellt werden, nicht als gewissermassen theoretisch
selbstständige Wesen. Das Vorgehen rechtfertigt sich aber
dadurch, dass von Anfang an klar war, dass die Postulate der
Theorie nicht stark genug sind, um aus ihr genügend vollständige Gleichungen für das physikalische Geschehen genügend frei von Willkür zu deduzieren, um auf eine solche
Grundlage eine Theorie der Massstäbe und Uhren zu gründen.
Wollte man nicht auf eine physikalische Deutung der Koordinaten überhaupt verzichten (was an sich möglich wäre), so

dimensional and a one-dimensional (time), so that the four-dimensional point of view does not force itself upon one as *necessary*. The special theory of relativity, on the other hand, creates a formal dependence between the way in which the spatial co-ordinates, on the one hand, and the temporal co-ordinates, on the other, have to enter into the natural laws.

Minkowski's important contribution to the theory lies in the following: Before Minkowski's investigation it was necessary to carry out a Lorentz-transformation on a law in order to test its invariance under such transformations; he, on the other hand, succeeded in introducing a formalism such that the mathematical form of the law itself guarantees its invariance under Lorentz-transformations. By creating a four-dimensional tensor-calculus he achieved the same thing for the four-dimensional space which the ordinary vector-calculus achieves for the three spatial dimensions. He also showed that the Lorentz-transformation (apart from a different algebraic sign due to the special character of time) is nothing but a rotation of the co-ordinate system in the four-dimensional space.

First, a remark concerning the theory as it is characterized above. One is struck [by the fact] that the theory (except for the four-dimensional space) introduces two kinds of physical things, i.e., (1) measuring rods and clocks, (2) all other things, e.g., the electro-magnetic field, the material point, etc. This, in a certain sense, is inconsistent; strictly speaking measuring rods and clocks would have to be represented as solutions of the basic equations (objects consisting of moving atomic configurations), not, as it were, as theoretically self-sufficient entities. However, the procedure justifies itself because it was clear from the very beginning that the postulates of the theory are not strong enough to deduce from them sufficiently complete equations for physical events sufficiently free from arbitrariness, in order to base upon such a foundation a theory of measuring rods and clocks. If one did not wish to forego a physical interpretation of the co-ordinates in general (something which, in itself, would be possible), it was better to permit such inconsistency—

war es besser, solche Inkonsequenz zuzulassen—allerdings mit der Verpflichtung, sie in einem späteren Stadium der Theorie zu eliminieren. Man darf aber die erwähnte Sünde nicht so weit legitimieren, dass man sich etwa vorstellt, dass Abstände physikalische Wesen besonderer Art seien, wesensverschieden von sonstigen physikalischen Grössen ("Physik auf Geometrie zurückführen," etc.). Wir fragen nun nach den Erkenntnissen von definitivem Charakter, den die Physik der speziellen Relativitätstheorie verdankt.

1) Es gibt keine Gleichzeitigkeit distanter Ereignisse; es gibt also auch keine unvermittelte Fernwirkung im Sinne der Newton'schen Mechanik. Die Einführung von Fernwirkungen, die sich mit Lichtgeschwindigkeit ausbreiten, bleibt zwar nach dieser Theorie denkbar, erscheint aber unnatürlich; in einer derartigen Theorie könnte es nämlich keinen vernünftigen Ausdruck für das Energieprinzip geben. Es erscheint deshalb unvermeidlich, dass die physikalische Realität durch kontinuierliche Raumfunktionen zu beschreiben ist. Der materielle Punkt dürfte deshalb als Grundbegriff der Theorie nicht mehr in Betracht kommen.

2) Die Sätze der Erhaltung des Impulses und der Erhaltung der Energie werden zu einem einzigen Satz verschmolzen. Die träge Masse eines abgeschlossenen Systems ist mit seiner Energie identisch, sodass die Masse als selbstständiger Begriff eliminiert ist.

Bemerkung. Die Lichtgeschwindigkeit c ist eine der Grössen, welche in physikalischen Gleichungen als "universelle Konstante" auftritt. Wenn man aber als Zeiteinheit statt der Sekunde die Zeit einführt, in welcher das Licht 1 cm zurücklegt, so tritt c in den Gleichungen nicht mehr auf. Man kann in diesem Sinne sagen, dass die Konstante c nur eine *scheinbare* universelle Konstante ist.

Es ist offenkundig und allgemein angenommen, dass man auch noch zwei andere universelle Konstante dadurch aus der Physik eliminieren könnte, dass man an Stelle des Gramms und Centimeters passend gewählte "natürliche" Einheiten einführt (z.B. Masse und Radius des Elektrons).

Denkt man sich dies ausgeführt, so würden in den Grund-

with the obligation, however, of eliminating it at a later stage of the theory. But one must not legalize the mentioned sin so far as to imagine that intervals are physical entities of a special type, intrinsically different from other physical variables ("reducing physics to geometry," etc.).

We now shall inquire into the insights of definite nature which physics owes to the special theory of relativity.

(1) There is no such thing as simultaneity of distant events; consequently there is also no such thing as immediate action at a distance in the sense of Newtonian mechanics. Although the introduction of actions at a distance, which propogate with the speed of light, remains thinkable, according to this theory, it appears unnatural; for in such a theory there could be no such thing as a reasonable statement of the principle of conservation of energy. It therefore appears unavoidable that physical reality must be described in terms of continuous functions in space. The material point, therefore, can hardly be conceived any more as the basic concept of the theory.

(2) The principles of the conservation of momentum and of the conservation of energy are fused into one single principle. The inert mass of a closed system is identical with its energy, thus eliminating mass as an independent concept.

Remark. The speed of light c is one of the quantities which occurs as "universal constant" in physical equations. If, however, one introduces as unit of time instead of the second the time in which light travels 1 cm, c no longer occurs in the equations. In this sense one could say that the constant c is only an *apparently* universal constant.

It is obvious and generally accepted that one could eliminate two more universal constants from physics by introducing, instead of the gram and the centimeter, properly chosen "natural" units (for example, mass and radius of the electron).

If one considers this done, then only "dimension-less" con-

Gleichungen der Physik nur mehr "dimensionslose" Konstante auftreten können. Bezüglich dieser möchte ich einen Satz aussprechen, der vorläufig auf nichts anderes gegründet werden kann als auf ein Vertrauen in die Einfachheit, bezw. Verständlichkeit, der Natur: derartige *willkürliche* Konstante gibt es nicht; d.h. die Natur ist so beschaffen, dass man für sie logisch derart stark determinierte Gesetze aufstellen kann, dass in diesen Gesetzen nur rational völlig bestimmte Konstante auftreten (also nicht Konstante, deren Zahlwerte verändert werden könnten, ohne die Theorie zu zerstören). – – –

Die spezielle Relativitätstheorie verdankt ihre Entstehung den Maxwell'schen Gleichungen des elektromagnetischen Feldes. Umgekehrt werden die letzteren erst durch die spezielle Relativitätstheorie in befriedigender Weise formal begriffen. Es sind die einfachsten Lorentz-invarianten Feldgleichungen, die für einen aus einem Vektorfeld abgeleiteten schief symmetrischen Tensor aufgestellt werden können. Dies wäre an sich befriedigend, wenn wir nicht aus den Quanten-Erscheinungen wüssten, dass die Maxwell'sche Theorie den energetischen Eigenschaften der Strahlung nicht gerecht wird. Wie aber die Maxwell'sche Theorie in natürlicher Weise modifiziert werden könnte, dafür liefert auch die spezielle Relativitätstheorie keinen hinreichenden Anhaltspunkt. Auch auf die Mach'sche Frage: "wie kommt es, dass die Inertialsysteme gegenüber anderen Koordinationssystemen physikalisch ausgezeichnet sind?" liefert diese Theorie keine Antwort.

Dass die spezielle Relativitätstheorie nur der erste Schritt einer notwendigen Entwicklung sei, wurde mir erst bei der Bemühung völlig klar die Gravitation im Rahmen dieser Theorie darzustellen. In der feldartig interpretierten klassischen Mechanik erscheint das Potential der Gravitation als ein *skalares* Feld (die einfachste theoretische Möglichkeit eines Feldes mit einer einzigen Komponente). Eine solche Skalar-Theorie des Gravitationsfeldes kann zunächst leicht invariant gemacht werden inbezug auf die Gruppe der Lorentz-Transformationen. Folgendes Programm erscheint also natürlich: Das physikalische Gesamtfeld besteht aus einem Skalarfeld (Gravitation) und einem Vektorfeld (elektromagnetisches

stants could occur in the basic equations of physics. Concerning such I would like to state a theorem which at present can not be based upon anything more than upon a faith in the simplicity, i.e., intelligibility, of nature: there are no *arbitrary* constants of this kind; that is to say, nature is so constituted that it is possible logically to lay down such strongly determined laws that within these laws only rationally completely determined constants occur (not constants, therefore, whose numerical value could be changed without destroying the theory). – – –

The special theory of relativity owes its origin to Maxwell's equations of the electromagnetic field. Inversely the latter can be grasped formally in satisfactory fashion only by way of the special theory of relativity. Maxwell's equations are the simplest Lorentz-invariant field equations which can be postulated for an anti-symmetric tensor derived from a vector field. This in itself would be satisfactory, if we did not know from quantum phenomena that Maxwell's theory does not do justice to the energetic properties of radiation. But how Maxwell's theory would have to be modified in a natural fashion, for this even the special theory of relativity offers no adequate foothold. Also to Mach's question: "how does it come about that inertial systems are physically distinguished above all other co-ordinate systems?" this theory offers no answer.

That the special theory of relativity is only the first step of a necessary development became completely clear to me only in my efforts to represent gravitation in the framework of this theory. In classical mechanics, interpreted in terms of the field, the potential of gravitation appears as a *scalar* field (the simplest theoretical possibility of a field with a single component). Such a scalar theory of the gravitational field can easily be made invariant under the group of Lorentz-transformations. The following program appears natural, therefore: The total physical field consists of a scalar field (gravitation) and a vector field (electromagnetic field); later insights may eventually

Feld); spätere Erkenntnisse mögen eventuell die Einführung noch komplizierterer Feldarten nötig machen, aber darum brauchte man sich zunächst nicht zu kümmern.

Die Möglichkeit der Realisierung dieses Programms war aber von vornherein zweifelhaft, weil die Theorie folgende Dinge vereinigen musste.

1) Aus allgemeinen Ueberlegungen der speziellen Relativitätstheorie war klar, dass die *träge* Masse eines physikalischen Systems mit der Gesamtenergie (also z.B. mit der kinetischen Energie) wachse.

2) Aus sehr präzisen Versuchen (insbesondere aus den Eötvös'schen Drehwage-Versuchen) war mit sehr grosser Präzision empirisch bekannt, dass die *schwere* Masse eines Körpers seiner *trägen* Masse genau gleich sei.

Aus 1) und 2) folgte, dass die *Schwere* eines Systems in genau bekannter Weise von seiner Gesamtenergie abhänge. Wenn die Theorie dies nicht oder nicht in natürlicher Weise leistete, so war sie zu verwerfen. Die Bedingung lässt sich am natürlichsten so aussprechen: die Fall-Beschleunigung eines Systems in einem gegebenen Schwerefelde ist von der Natur des fallenden Systems (speziell also auch von seinem Energie-Inhalte) unabhängig.

Es zeigte sich nun, dass im Rahmen des skizzierten Programmes diesem elementaren Sachverhalte überhaupt nicht oder jedenfalls nicht in natürlicher Weise Genüge geleistet werden konnte. Dies gab mir die Ueberzeugung, dass im Rahmen der speziellen Relativitätstheorie kein Platz sei für eine befriedigende Theorie der Gravitation.

Nun fiel mir ein: Die Tatsache der Gleichheit der trägen und schweren Masse, bezw. die Tatsache der Unabhängigkeit der Fallbeschleunigung von der Natur der fallenden Substanz, lässt sich so ausdrücken: In einem Gravitationsfelde (geringer räumlicher Ausdehnung) verhalten sich die Dinge so wie in einem gravitationsfreien Raume, wenn man in diesem statt eines "Inertialsystems" ein gegen ein solches beschleunigtes Bezugssystem einführt.

Wenn man also das Verhalten der Körper inbezug auf das

make necessary the introduction of still more complicated types of fields; but to begin with one did not need to bother about this.

The possibility of the realization of this program was, however, dubious from the very first, because the theory had to combine the following things:

(1) From the general considerations of special relativity theory it was clear that the *inert* mass of a physical system increases with the total energy (therefore, e.g., with the kinetic energy).

(2) From very accurate experiments (specially from the torsion balance experiments of Eötvös) it was empirically known with very high accuracy that the gravitational mass of a body is exactly equal to its *inert* mass.

It followed from (1) and (2) that the *weight* of a system depends in a precisely known manner on its total energy. If the theory did not accomplish this or could not do it naturally, it was to be rejected. The condition is most naturally expressed as follows: the acceleration of a system falling freely in a given gravitational field is independent of the nature of the falling system (specially therefore also of its energy content).

It then appeared that, in the framework of the program sketched, this elementary state of affairs could not at all or at any rate not in any natural fashion, be represented in a satisfactory way. This convinced me that, within the frame of the special theory of relativity, there is no room for a satisfactory theory of gravitation.

Now it came to me: The fact of the equality of inert and heavy mass, i.e., the fact of the independence of the gravitational acceleration of the nature of the falling substance, may be expressed as follows: In a gravitational field (of small spatial extension) things behave as they do in a space free of gravitation, if one introduces in it, in place of an "inertial system," a reference system which is accelerated relative to an inertial system.

If then one conceives of the behavior of a body, in reference

letztere Bezugssystem als durch ein "wirkliches" (nicht nur scheinbares) Gravitationsfeld bedingt auffasst, so kann man dieses Bezugssystem mit dem gleichen Rechte als ein "Inertialsystem" betrachten wie das ursprüngliche Bezugssystem.

Wenn man also beliebig ausgedehnte, nicht von vornherein durch räumliche Grenzbedingungen eingeschränkte, Gravitationsfelder als möglich betrachtet, so wird der Begriff des Inertialsystems völlig leer. Der Begriff "Beschleunigung gegenüber dem Raume" verliert dann jede Bedeutung und damit auch das Trägheitsprinzip samt dem Mach'schen Paradoxon.

So führt die Tatsache der Gleichheit der trägen und schweren Masse ganz natürlich zu den Auffassungen, dass die Grund-Forderung der speziellen Relativitätstheorie (Invarianz der Gesetze bezüglich Lorentz-Transformationen) zu eng sei, d.h. dass man eine Invarianz der Gesetze auch bezüglich *nicht linearer* Transformationen der Koordinaten im vierdimensionalen Kontinuum zu postulieren habe.

Dies trug sich 1908 zu. Warum brauchte es weiterer 7 Jahre für die Aufstellung der allgemeinen Rel. Theorie? Der hauptsächliche Grund liegt darin, dass man sich nicht so leicht von der Auffassung befreit, dass den Koordinaten eine unmittelbare metrische Bedeutung zukommen müsse. Die Wandlung vollzog sich ungefähr in folgender Weise.

Wir gehen aus von einem leeren, feldfreien Raume, wie er —auf ein Inertialsystem bezogen—im Sinne der speziellen Relativitätstheorie als der einfachste aller denkbaren physikalischen Tatbestände auftritt. Denken wir uns nun ein Nicht-Inertialsystem dadurch eingeführt, dass das neue System gegen das Inertialsystem (in dreidimensionaler Beschreibungsart) in einer Richtung (geeignet definiert) gleichförmig beschleunigt ist, so besteht inbezug auf dieses System ein statisches paralleles Schwerefeld. Das Bezugssystem kann dabei als starr gewählt werden, in den dreidimensionalen metrischen Beziehungen von euklidischem Charakter. Aber jene Zeit, in welcher das Feld statisch erscheint, wird *nicht* durch *gleich beschaffene* ruhende Uhren gemessen. Aus diesem speziellen Beispiel erkennt man schon, dass die unmittelbare metrische Bedeutung der Koordinaten verloren geht, wenn man überhaupt nichtlineare

to the latter reference system, as caused by a "real" (not merely apparent) gravitational field, it is possible to regard this reference system as an "inertial system" with as much justification as the original reference system.

So, if one regards as possible, gravitational fields of arbitrary extension which are not initially restricted by spatial limitations, the concept of the "inertial system" becomes completely empty. The concept, "acceleration relative to space," then loses every meaning and with it the principle of inertia together with the entire paradox of Mach.

The fact of the equality of inert and heavy mass thus leads quite naturally to the recognition that the basic demand of the special theory of relativity (invariance of the laws under Lorentz-transformations) is too narrow, i.e., that an invariance of the laws must be postulated also relative to *non-linear* transformations of the co-ordinates in the four-dimensional continuum.

This happened in 1908. Why were another seven years required for the construction of the general theory of relativity? The main reason lies in the fact that it is not so easy to free oneself from the idea that co-ordinates must have an immediate metrical meaning. The transformation took place in approximately the following fashion.

We start with an empty, field-free space, as it occurs—related to an inertial system—in the sense of the special theory of relativity, as the simplest of all imaginable physical situations. If we now think of a non-inertial system introduced by assuming that the new system is uniformly accelerated against the inertial system (in a three-dimensional description) in one direction (conveniently defined), then there exists with reference to this system a static parallel gravitational field. The reference system may thereby be chosen as rigid, of Euclidian type, in three-dimensional metric relations. But the time, in which the field appears as static, is *not* measured by *equally constituted* stationary clocks. From this special example one can already recognize that the immediate metric significance of the co-ordinates is lost if one admits non-linear transforma-

Transformationen der Koordinaten zulässt. Letzteres *muss* man aber, wenn man der Gleichheit von schwerer und träger Masse durch das Fundament der Theorie gerecht werden will, und wenn man das Mach'sche Paradoxon bezüglich der Inertialsysteme überwinden will.

Wenn man nun aber darauf verzichten muss, den Koordinaten eine unmittelbare metrische Bedeutung zu geben (Koordinatendifferenzen = messbare Längen bezw. Zeiten), so wird man nicht umhin können, alle durch kontinuierliche Transformationen der Koordinaten erzeugbare Koordinatensysteme als gleichwertig zu behandeln.

Die allgemeine Relativitätstheorie geht demgemäss von dem Grundsatz aus: Die Naturgesetze sind durch Gleichungen auszudrücken, die kovariant sind bezüglich der Gruppe der kontinuierlichen Koordinaten-Transformationen. Diese Gruppe tritt also hier an die Stelle der Gruppe der Lorentz-Transformationen der speziellen Relativitätstheorie, welch letztere Gruppe eine Untergruppe der ersteren bildet.

Diese Forderung für sich alleine genügt natürlich nicht als Ausgangspunkt für eine Ableitung der Grundgleichungen der Physik. Zunächst kann man sogar bestreiten, dass die Forderung allein eine wirkliche Beschränkung für die physikalischen Gesetze enthalte; denn es wird stets möglich sein, ein zunächst nur für gewisse Koordinatensysteme postuliertes Gesetz so umzuformulieren, dass die neue Formulierung der Form nach allgemein kovariant wird. Ausserdem ist es von vornherein klar, dass sich unendlich viele Feldgesetze formulieren lassen, die diese Kovarianz-Eigenschaft haben. Die eminente heuristische Bedeutung des allgemeinen Relativitätsprinzips liegt aber darin, dass es uns zu der Aufsuchung jener Gleichungssysteme führt, welche *in allgemein kovarianter* Formulierung *möglichst einfach* sind; unter diesen haben wir die Feldgesetze des physikalischen Raumes zu suchen. Felder, die durch solche Transformationen ineinander übergeführt werden können, beschreiben denselben realen Sachverhalt.

Die Hauptfrage für den auf diesem Gebiete Suchenden ist diese: Von welcher mathematischen Art sind die Grössen (Funktionen der Koordinaten), welche die physikalischen

tions of co-ordinates at all. To do the latter is, however, *obligatory* if one wants to do justice to the equality of gravitational and inert mass by means of the basis of the theory, and if one wants to overcome Mach's paradox as concerns the inertial systems.

If, then, one must give up the attempt to give the co-ordinates an immediate metric meaning (differences of co-ordinates = measurable lengths, viz., times), one will not be able to avoid treating as equivalent all co-ordinate systems, which can be created by the continuous transformations of the co-ordinates.

The general theory of relativity, accordingly, proceeds from the following principle: Natural laws are to be expressed by equations which are covariant under the group of continuous co-ordinate transformations. This group replaces the group of the Lorentz-transformations of the special theory of relativity, which forms a sub-group of the former.

This demand by itself is of course not sufficient to serve as point of departure for the derivation of the basic concepts of physics. In the first instance one may even contest [the idea] that the demand by itself contains a real restriction for the physical laws; for it will always be possible thus to reformulate a law, postulated at first only for certain co-ordinate systems, such that the new formulation becomes formally universally covariant. Beyond this it is clear from the beginning that an infinitely large number of field-laws can be formulated which have this property of covariance. The eminent heuristic significance of the general principles of relativity lies in the fact that it leads us to the search for those systems of equations which are *in their general covariant* formulation the *simplest ones possible;* among these we shall have to look for the field equations of physical space. Fields which can be transformed into each other by such transformations describe the same real situation.

The major question for anyone doing research in this field is this: Of which mathematical type are the variables (functions of the co-ordinates) which permit the expression of the physical

Eigenschaften des Raumes auszudrücken gestatten ("Struktur")? Dann erst: welchen Gleichungen genügen jene Grössen? Wir können heute diese Fragen noch keineswegs mit Sicherheit beantworten. Der bei der ersten Formulierung der allgemeinen Rel. Theorie eingeschlagene Weg lässt sich so kennzeichnen. Wenn wir auch nicht wissen, durch was für Feldvariable (Struktur) der physikalische Raum zu charakterisieren ist, so kennen wir doch mit Sicherheit einen speziellen Fall: den des "feldfreien" Raumes in der speziellen Relativitätstheorie. Ein solcher Raum ist dadurch charakterisiert, dass für ein passend gewähltes Koordinatensystem der zu zwei benachbarten Punkten gehörige Ausdruck

$$ds^2 = dx_1{}^2 + dx_2{}^2 + dx_3{}^2 - dx_4{}^2 \tag{1}$$

eine messbare Grösse darstellt (Abstandsquadrat), also eine reale physikalische Bedeutung hat. Auf ein beliebiges System bezogen drückt sich diese Grösse so aus

$$ds^2 = g_{ik}dx_idx_k \tag{2}$$

wobei die Indices von 1 bis 4 laufen. Die g_{ik} bilden einen symmetrischen Tensor. Wenn, nach Ausführung einer Transformation am Felde (1), die ersten Ableitungen der g_{ik} nach den Koordinaten nicht verschwinden, so besteht, mit Bezug auf dies Koordinatensystem, ein Gravitationsfeld im Sinne der obigen Ueberlegung, und zwar ein Gravitationsfeld ganz spezieller Art. Dies besondere Feld lässt sich dank der Riemann'schen Untersuchung n-dimensionaler metrischer Räume invariant charakterisieren:

1) Der aus den Koeffizienten der Metric (2) gebildete Riemann'sche Krümmungstensor R_{iklm} verschwindet.

2) Die Bahn eines Massenpunktes ist inbezug auf das Inertialsystem (inbezug auf welches (1) gilt) eine gerade Linie, also eine Extremale (Geodete). Letzteres ist aber bereits eine auf (2) sich stützende Charakterisierung des Bewegungsgesetzes.

Das *allgemeine* Gesetz des physikalischen Raumes muss nun eine Verallgemeinerung des soeben charakterisierten Gesetzes sein. Ich nahm nun an, dass es zwei Stufen der Verallgemeinerung gibt:

properties of space ("structure")? Only after that: Which equations are satisfied by those variables?

The answer to these questions is today by no means certain. The path chosen by the first formulation of the general theory of relativity can be characterized as follows. Even though we do not know by what type field-variables (structure) physical space is to be characterized, we do know with certainty a special case: that of the "field-free" space in the special theory of relativity. Such a space is characterized by the fact that for a properly chosen co-ordinate system the expression

$$ds^2 = dx_1^2 + dx_2^2 + dx_3^2 - dx_4^2 \tag{1}$$

belonging to two neighboring points, represents a measurable quantity (square of distance), and thus has a real physical meaning. Referred to an arbitrary system this quantity is expressed as follows:

$$ds^2 = g_{ik}dx_idx_k \tag{2}$$

whereby the indices run from 1 to 4. The g_{ik} form a (real) symmetrical tensor. If, after carrying out a transformation on field (1), the first derivatives of the g_{ik} with respect to the coordinates do not vanish, there exists a gravitational field with reference to this system of co-ordinates in the sense of the above consideration, a gravitational field, moreover, of a very special type. Thanks to Riemann's investigation of n-dimensional metrical spaces this special field can be invariantly characterized:

(1) Riemann's curvature-tensor R_{iklm}, formed from the coefficients of the metric (2) vanishes.

(2) The orbit of a mass-point in reference to the inertial system (relative to which (1) is valid) is a straight line, therefore an extremal (geodetic). The latter, however, is already a characterization of the law of motion based on (2).

The *universal* law of physical space must now be a generalization of the law just characterized. I now assume that there are two steps of generalization:

a) reines Gravitationsfeld
b) allgemeines Feld (in welchem auch Grössen auftreten, die irgendwie dem elektromagnetischen Felde entsprechen).

Der Fall a) war dadurch charakterisiert, dass das Feld zwar immer noch durch eine Riemann-Metrik (2) bezw. durch einen symmetrischen Tensor darstellbar ist, wobei es aber (ausser im Infinitesimalen) keine Darstellung in der Form (1) gibt. Dies bedeutet, dass im Falle a) der Riemann-Tensor *nicht* verschwindet. Es ist aber klar, dass in diesem Falle ein Feldgesetz gelten muss, das eine Verallgemeinerung (Abschwächung) dieses Gesetzes ist. Soll auch dies Gesetz von der zweiten Differentiationsordnung und in den zweiten Ableitungen linear sein, so kam nur die durch einmalige Kontraktion zu gewinnende Gleichung

$$0 = R_{kl} = g^{im} R_{iklm}$$

als Feldgleichung im Falle a) in Betracht. Es erscheint ferner natürlich anzunehmen, dass auch im Falle a) die geodätische Linie immer noch das Bewegungsgesetz des materiellen Punktes darstelle.

Es erschien mir damals aussichtslos, den Versuch zu wagen, das Gesamtfeld b) darzustellen und für dieses Feldgesetze zu ermitteln. Ich zog es deshalb vor, einen vorläufigen formalen Rahmen für eine Darstellung der ganzen physikalischen Realität hinzustellen; dies war nötig, um wenigstens vorläufig die Brauchbarkeit des Grundgedankens der allgemeinen Relativität untersuchen zu können. Dies geschah so.

In der Newton'schen Theorie kann man als Feldgesetz der Gravitation

$$\Delta \varphi = 0$$

schreiben ($\varphi =$ Gravitationspotential) an solchen Orten, wo die Dichte ϱ der Materie verschwindet. Allgemein wäre zu setzen (Poissonsche Gleichung)

$$\Delta \varphi = 4\pi k \varrho \cdot (\varrho = \text{Massen-Dichte}).$$

Im Falle der relativistischen Theorie des Gravitationsfeldes tritt R_{ik} an die Stelle von $\Delta \varphi$. Auf die rechte Seite haben wir

(a) pure gravitational field
(b) general field (in which quantities corresponding some-
     how to the electromagnetic field occur, too).

The instance (a) was characterized by the fact that the field can
still be represented by a Riemann-metric (2), i.e., by a symmetric tensor, whereby, however, there is no representation in
the form (1) (except in infinitesimal regions). This means that
in the case (a) the Riemann-tensor does not vanish. It is clear,
however, that in this case a field-law must be valid, which is a
generalization (loosening) of this law. If this law also is to be
of the second order of differentiation and linear in the second
derivations, then only the equation, to be obtained by a single
contraction

$$0 = R_{kl} = g^{im}R_{iklm}$$

came under consideration as field-equation in the case of (a).
It appears natural, moreover, to assume that also in the case of
(a) the geodetic line is still to be taken as representing the law
of motion of the material point.

It seemed hopeless to me at that time to venture the attempt
of representing the total field (b) and to ascertain field-laws
for it. I preferred, therefore, to set up a preliminary formal
frame for the representation of the entire physical reality; this
was necessary in order to be able to investigate, at least pre-
liminarily, the usefulness of the basic idea of general relativity.
This was done as follows.

In Newton's theory one can write the field-law of gravitation thus:

$$\Delta\varphi = 0$$

(φ = gravitation-potential) at points, where the density of
matter, ϱ, vanishes. In general one may write (Poisson equation)

$$\Delta\varphi = 4\pi k\varrho \cdot (\varrho = \text{mass-density}).$$

In the case of the relativistic theory of the gravitational field
R_{ik} takes the place of $\Delta\varphi$. On the right side we shall then have

dann an die Stelle von ϱ ebenfalls einen Tensor zu setzen. Da wir aus der speziellen Rel. Th. wissen, dass die (träge) Masse gleich ist der Energie, so wird auf die rechte Seite der Tensor der Energie-Dichte zu setzen sein—genauer der gesamten Energiedichte, soweit sie nicht dem reinen Gravitationsfelde angehört. Man gelangt so zu den Feldgleichungen

$$R_{ik} - \tfrac{1}{2} g_{ik} R = -k T_{ik}.$$

Das zweite Glied der linken Seite ist aus formalen Gründen zugefügt; die linke Seite ist nämlich so geschrieben, dass ihre Divergenz im Sinne des absoluten Differentialkalküls identisch verschwindet. Die rechte Seite ist eine formale Zusammenfassung aller Dinge, deren Erfassung im Sinne einer Feldtheorie noch problematisch ist. Natürlich war ich keinen Augenblick darüber im Zweifel, dass diese Fassung nur ein Notbehelf war, um dem allgemeinen Relativitätsprinzip einen vorläufigen geschlossenen Ausdruck zu geben. Es war ja nicht wesentlich *mehr* als eine Theorie des Gravitationsfeldes, das einigermassen künstlich von einem Gesamtfelde noch unbekannter Struktur isoliert wurde.

Wenn irgend etwas—abgesehen von der Forderung der Invarianz der Gleichungen bezüglich der Gruppe der kontinuierlichen Koordinaten-Transformationen—in der skizzierten Theorie möglicherweise endgültige Bedeutung beanspruchen kann, so ist es die Theorie des Grenzfalles des reinen Gravitationsfeldes und dessen Beziehung zu der metrischen Struktur des Raumes. Deshalb soll im unmittelbar Folgenden nur von den Gleichungen des reinen Gravitationsfeldes die Rede sein.

Das Eigenartige an diesen Gleichungen ist einerseits ihr komplizierter Bau, besonders ihr nichtlinearer Charakter inbezug auf die Feldvariabeln und deren Ableitungen, andererseits, die fast zwingende Notwendigkeit, mit welcher die Transformationsgruppe dies komplizierte Feldgesetz bestimmt. Wenn man bei der speziellen Relativitätstheorie, d.h. bei der Invarianz bezüglich der Lorentz-Gruppe, stehen geblieben wäre, so würde auch im Rahmen dieser engeren Gruppe das Feldgesetz $R_{ik} = 0$ invariant sein. Aber vom Standpunkte der engeren Gruppe bestünde zunächst keinerlei Anlass dafür, dass

to place a tensor also in place of ϱ. Since we know from the special theory of relativity that the (inert) mass equals energy, we shall have to put on the right side the tensor of energy-density—more precisely the entire energy-density, insofar as it does not belong to the pure gravitational field. In this way one gets the field-equations

$$R_{ik} - \tfrac{1}{2} g_{ik} R = -k T_{ik}.$$

The second member on the left side is added because of formal reasons; for the left side is written in such a way that its divergence disappears identically in the sense of the absolute differential calculus. The right side is a formal condensation of all things whose comprehension in the sense of a field-theory is still problematic. Not for a moment, of course, did I doubt that this formulation was merely a makeshift in order to give the general principle of relativity a preliminary closed expression. For it was essentially not anything *more* than a theory of the gravitational field, which was somewhat artificially isolated from a total field of as yet unknown structure.

If anything in the theory as sketched—apart from the demand of the invariance of the equations under the group of the continuous co-ordinate-transformations—can possibly make the claim to final significance, then it is the theory of the limiting case of the pure gravitational field and its relation to the metric structure of space. For this reason, in what immediately follows we shall speak only of the equations of the pure gravitational field.

The peculiarity of these equations lies, on the one hand, in their complicated construction, especially their non-linear character as regards the field-variables and their derivatives, and, on the other hand, in the almost compelling necessity with which the transformation-group determines this complicated field-law. If one had stopped with the special theory of relativity, i.e., with the invariance under the Lorentz-group, then the field-law $R_{ik} = 0$ would remain invariant also within the frame of this narrower group. But, from the point of view of the nar-

die Gravitation durch eine so komplizierte Struktur dargestellt werden müsse, wie sie der symmetrische Tensor g_{ik} darstellt. Würde man aber doch hinreichende Gründe dafür finden, so gäbe es eine unübersehbare Zahl von Feldgesetzen aus Grössen g_{ik}, die alle kovariant sind bezüglich Lorentz-Transformationen (nicht aber gegenüber der allgemeinen Gruppe). Selbst aber wenn man von all den denkbaren Lorentz-invarianten Gesetzen zufällig gerade das zu der weiteren Gruppe gehörige Gesetz erraten hätte, so wäre man immer noch nicht auf der durch das allgemeine Relativitätsprinzip erlangten Stufe der Erkenntnis. Denn vom Standpunkt der Lorentz-Gruppe wären zwei Lösungen fälschlich als physikalisch voneinander verschieden zu betrachten, wenn sie durch eine nichtlineare Koordinaten-Transformation ineinander transformierbar sind, d.h. vom Standpunkt der weiteren Gruppe nur verschiedene Darstellungen desselben Feldes sind.

Noch eine allgemeine Bemerkung über Struktur und Gruppe. Es ist klar, dass man im Allgemeinen eine Theorie als umso vollkommener beurteilen wird, eine je einfachere "Struktur" sie zugrundelegt und je weiter die Gruppe ist, bezüglich welcher die Feldgleichungen invariant sind. Man sieht nun, dass diese beiden Forderungen einander im Wege sind. Gemäss der speziellen Relativitätstheorie (Lorentz-Gruppe) kann man z.B. für die denkbar einfachste Struktur (skalares Feld) ein kovariantes Gesetz aufstellen, während es in der allgemeinen Relativitätstheorie (weitere Gruppe der kontinuierlichen Koordinaten-Transformationen) erst für die kompliziertere Struktur des symmetrischen Tensors ein invariantes Feldgesetz gibt. Wir haben *physikalische* Gründe dafür angegeben, dass Invarianz gegenüber der weiteren Gruppe in der Physik gefordert werden muss;[1] vom rein mathematischen Gesichtspunkte aus sehe ich keinen Zwang, die einfachere Struktur der Weite der Gruppe zum Opfer zu bringen.

Die Gruppe der allgemeinen Relativität bringt es zum ersten

[1] Bei der engeren Gruppe zu bleiben und gleichzeitig die kompliziertere Struktur der allgemeinen Rel. Theorie zugrunde zu legen, bedeutet eine naive Inkonsequenz. Sünde bleibt Sünde, auch wenn sie von sonst respektabeln Männern begangen wird.

rower group there would at first exist no reason for representing gravitation by so complicated a structure as is represented by the symmetric tensor g_{ik}. If, nonetheless, one would find sufficient reasons for it, there would then arise an immense number of field-laws out of quantities g_{ik}, all of which are covariant under Lorentz-transformations (not, however, under the general group). However, even if, of all the conceivable Lorentz-invariant laws, one had accidentally guessed precisely the law which belongs to the wider group, one would still not yet be on the plane of insight achieved by the general principle of relativity. For, from the standpoint of the Lorentz-group two solutions would incorrectly have to be viewed as physically different from each other, if they can be transformed into each other by a non-linear transformation of co-ordinates, i.e., if they are, from the point of view of the wider field, only different representations of the same field.

One more general remark concerning field-structure and the group. It is clear that in general one will judge a theory to be the more nearly perfect the simpler a "structure" it postulates and the broader the group is concerning which the field-equations are invariant. One sees now that these two demands get in each other's way. For example: according to the special theory of relativity (Lorentz-Group) one can set up a covariant law for simplest structure imaginable (a scalar field), whereas in the general theory of relativity (wider group of the continuous transformations of co-ordinates) there is an invariant field-law only for the more complicated structure of the symmetric tensor. We have already given *physical* reasons for the fact that in physics invariance under the wider group has to be demanded:[1] from a purely mathematical standpoint I can see no necessity for sacrificing the simpler structure to the generality of the group.

The group of the general relativity is the first one which

[1] To remain with the narrower group and at the same time to base the relativity theory of gravitation upon the more complicated (tensor-) structure implies a naïve inconsequence. Sin remains sin, even if it is committed by otherwise ever so respectable men.

Male mit sich, dass das einfachste invariante Gesetz nicht linear und homogen in den Feldvariabeln und ihren Differentialquotienten ist. Dies ist aus folgendem Grunde von fundamentaler Wichtigkeit. Ist das Feldgesetz linear (und homogen), so ist die Summe zweier Lösungen wieder eine Lösung; so ist es z.B. bei den Maxwell'schen Feldgleichungen des leeren Raumes. In einer solchen Theorie kann aus dem Feldgesetz allein nicht auf eine Wechselwirkung von Gebilden geschlossen werden, die isoliert durch Lösungen des Systems dargestellt werden können. Daher bedurfte es in den bisherigen Theorien neben den Feldgesetzen besonderer Gesetze für die Bewegung der materiellen Gebilde unter dem Einfluss der Felder. In der relativistischen Gravitationstheorie wurde nun zwar ursprünglich neben dem Feldgesetz das Bewegungsgesetz (Geodätische Linie) unabhängig postuliert. Es hat sich aber nachträglich herausgestellt, dass das Bewegungsgesetz nicht unabhängig angenommen werden muss (und darf), sondern dass es in dem Gesetz des Gravitationsfeldes implicite enthalten ist.

Das Wesen dieser an sich komplizierten Sachlage kann man sich wie folgt veranschaulichen. Ein einziger ruhender materieller Punkt wird durch ein Gravitationsfeld repräsentiert, das überall endlich und regulär ist ausser an dem Orte, an dem der materielle Punkt sitzt; dort hat das Feld eine Singularität. Berechnet man aber durch Integration der Feldgleichungen das Feld, welches zu zwei ruhenden materiellen Punkten gehört, so hat dieses ausser den Singularitäten am Orte der materiellen Punkte noch eine aus singulären Punkten bestehende Linie, welche die beiden Punkte verbindet. Man kann aber eine Bewegung der materiellen Punkte in solcher Weise vorgeben, dass das durch sie bestimmte Gravitationsfeld ausserhalb der materiellen Punkte nirgends singulär wird. Es sind dies gerade jene Bewegungen, die in erster Näherung durch die Newton'schen Gesetze beschrieben werden. Man kann also sagen: Die Massen bewegen sich so, dass die Feldgleichung im Raume ausserhalb der Massen nirgends Singularitäten des Feldes bedingt. Diese Eigenschaft der Gravitationsgleichungen hängt unmittelbar zusammen mit ihrer Nicht-Linearität, und diese

demands that the simplest invariant law be no longer linear or homogeneous in the field-variables and in their differential quotients. This is of fundamental importance for the following reason. If the field-law is linear (and homogeneous), then the sum of two solutions is again a solution; as, for example: in Maxwell's field-equations for the vacuum. In such a theory it is impossible to deduce from the field equations alone an interaction between bodies, which can be described separately by means of solutions of the system. For this reason all theories up to now required, in addition to the field equations, special equations for the motion of material bodies under the influence of the fields. In the relativistic theory of gravitation, it is true, the law of motion (geodetic line) was originally postulated independently in addition to the field-law equations. Afterwards, however, it became apparent that the law of motion need not (and must not) be assumed independently, but that it is already implicitly contained within the law of the gravitational field.

The essence of this genuinely complicated situation can be visualized as follows: A single material point at rest will be represented by a gravitational field which is everywhere finite and regular, except at the position where the material point is located: there the field has a singularity. If, however, one computes by means of the integration of the field-equations the field which belongs to two material points at rest, then this field has, in addition to the singularities at the positions of the material points, a line consisting of singular points, which connects the two points. However, it is possible to stipulate a motion of the material points in such a way that the gravitational field which is determined by them does not become singular anywhere at all except at the material points. These are precisely those motions which are described in first approximation by Newton's laws. One may say, therefore: The masses move in such fashion that the solution of the field-equation is nowhere singular except in the mass points. This attribute of the gravitational equations is intimately connected with their non-linearity,

ihrerseits wird durch die weitere Transformationsgruppe bedingt.

Nun könnte man allerdings den Einwand machen: Wenn am Orte der materiellen Punkte Singularitäten zugelassen werden, was für eine Berechtigung besteht dann, das Auftreten von Singularitäten im übrigen Raume zu verbieten? Dieser Einwand wäre dann berechtigt, wenn die Gleichungen der Gravitation als Gleichungen des Gesamtfeldes anzusehen wären. So aber wird man sagen müssen, dass das Feld eines materiellen Teilchens desto weniger als *reines Gravitationsfeld* wird betrachtet werden dürfen, je näher man dem eigentlichen Ort des Teilchens kommt. Würde man die Feldgleichung des Gesamtfeldes haben, so müsste man verlangen, dass die Teilchen selbst als *überall* singularitätsfreie Lösungen der vollständigen Feldgleichungen sich darstellen lassen. Dann erst wäre die allgemeine Relativitätstheorie eine *vollständige* Theorie.

Bevor ich auf die Frage der Vollendung der allgemeinen Relativitätstheorie eingehe, muss ich Stellung nehmen zu der erfolgreichsten physikalischen Theorie unserer Zeit, der statistischen Quantentheorie, die vor etwa 25 Jahren eine konsistente logische Form angenommen hat (Schrödinger, Heisenberg, Dirac, Born). Es ist die einzige gegenwärtige Theorie, welche die Erfahrungen über den Quanten-Charakter der mikromechanischen Vorgänge einheitlich zu begreifen gestattet. Diese Theorie auf der einen Seite und die Relativitätstheorie auf der andern Seite werden beide in gewissem Sinne für richtig gehalten, obwohl ihre Verschmelzung allen bisherigen Bemühungen widerstanden hat. Damit hängt es wohl zusammen, dass unter den theoretischen Physikern der Gegenwart durchaus verschiedene Meinungen darüber bestehen, wie das theoretische Fundament der künftigen Physik aussehen wird. Ist es eine Feldtheorie; ist es eine im Wessentlichen statistische Theorie? Ich will hier kurz sagen, wie ich darüber denke.

Die Physik ist eine Bemühung das Seiende als etwas begrifflich zu erfassen, was unabhängig vom Wahrgenommen-Werden gedacht wird. In diesem Sinne spricht man vom "Physikalisch-Realen." In der Vor-Quantenphysik war kein Zweifel, wie dies zu verstehen sei. In Newtons Theorie war das Reale

and this is a consequence of the wider group of transformations.

Now it would of course be possible to object: If singularities are permitted at the positions of the material points, what justification is there for forbidding the occurrence of singularities in the rest of space? This objection would be justified if the equations of gravitation were to be considered as equations of the total field. [Since this is not the case], however, one will have to say that the field of a material particle may the less be viewed as a *pure gravitational field* the closer one comes to the position of the particle. If one had the field-equation of the total field, one would be compelled to demand that the particles themselves would *everywhere* be describable as singularity-free solutions of the completed field-equations. Only then would the general theory of relativity be a *complete* theory.

Before I enter upon the question of the completion of the general theory of relativity, I must take a stand with reference to the most successful physical theory of our period, viz., the statistical quantum theory which, about twenty-five years ago, took on a consistent logical form (Schrödinger, Heisenberg, Dirac, Born). This is the only theory at present which permits a unitary grasp of experiences concerning the quantum character of micro-mechanical events. This theory, on the one hand, and the theory of relativity on the other, are both considered correct in a certain sense, although their combination has resisted all efforts up to now. This is probably the reason why among contemporary theoretical physicists there exist entirely differing opinions concerning the question as to how the theoretical foundation of the physics of the future will appear. Will it be a field theory; will it be in essence a statistical theory? I shall briefly indicate my own thoughts on this point.

Physics is an attempt conceptually to grasp reality as it is thought independently of its being observed. In this sense one speaks of "physical reality." In pre-quantum physics there was no doubt as to how this was to be understood. In Newton's theory reality was determined by a material point in space and

durch materielle Punkte in Raum und Zeit, in der Maxwell'schen Theorie durch ein Feld in Raum und Zeit dargestellt. In der Quantenmechanik ist es weniger durchsichtig.
Wenn man fragt: Stellt eine ψ-Funktion der Quantentheorie
einen realen Sachverhalt in demselben Sinne dar wie ein ma-
terielles Punktsystem oder ein elektromagnetisches Feld, so
zögert man mit der simpeln Antwort "ja" oder "nein";
warum? Was die ψ-Funktion (zu einer bestimmten Zeit) aus-
sagt, das ist: Welches ist die Wahrscheinlichkeit dafür, eine
bestimmte physikalische Grösse q (oder p) in einem bestimmten
gegebenen Intervall vorzufinden, wenn ich sie zur Zeit t messe?
Die Wahrscheinlichkeit ist hierbei als eine empirisch feststell-
bare, also gewiss "reale" Grösse anzusehen, die ich feststellen
kann, wenn ich dieselbe ψ-Funktion sehr oft erzeuge und je-
desmal eine q-Messung vornehme. Wie steht es nun aber mit
dem einzelnen gemessenen Wert von q? Hatte das betreffende
individuelle System diesen q-Wert schon vor der Messung? Auf
diese Frage gibt es im Rahmen der Theorie keine bestimmte
Antwort, weil ja die Messung ein Prozess ist, der einen endlichen äusseren Eingriff in das System bedeutet; es wäre daher
denkbar, dass das System einen bestimmten Zahlwert für q
(bezw. p) den gemessenen Zahlwert erst durch die Messung
selbst erhält. Für die weitere Diskussion denke ich mir zwei
Physiker A und B, die bezüglich des durch die ψ-Funktion
beschriebenen realen Zustandes eine verschiedene Auffassung
vertreten.

A. Das einzelne System hat (vor der Messung) einen bestimmten Wert von q (bezw. p) für alle Variabeln des
Systems, und zwar *den* Wert, der bei einer Messung dieser
Variabeln festgestellt wird. Ausgehend von dieser Auffassung wird er erklären: Die ψ-Funktion ist keine erschöpfende Darstellung des realen Zustandes des Systems, sondern eine unvollständige Darstellung; sie drückt nur dasjenige aus, was wir auf Grund früherer Messungen über
das System wissen.

B. Das einzelne System hat (vor der Messung) keinen bestimmten Wert von q (bezw. p). Der Messwert kommt
unter Mitwirkung der ihm vermöge der ψ-Funktion eigen-

time; in Maxwell's theory, by the field in space and time. In quantum mechanics it is not so easily seen. If one asks: does a ψ-function of the quantum theory represent a real factual situation in the same sense in which this is the case of a material system of points or of an electromagnetic field, one hesitates to reply with a simple "yes" or "no"; why? What the ψ-function (at a definite time) asserts, is this: What is the probability for finding a definite physical magnitude q (or p) in a definitely given interval, if I measure it at time t? The probability is here to be viewed as an empirically determinable, and therefore certainly as a "real" quantity which I may determine if I create the same ψ-function very often and perform a q-measurement each time. But what about the single measured value of q? Did the respective individual system have this q-value even before the measurement? To this question there is no definite answer within the framework of the [existing] theory, since the measurement is a process which implies a finite disturbance of the system from the outside; it would therefore be thinkable that the system obtains a definite numerical value for q (or p), i.e., the measured numerical value, only through the measurement itself. For the further discussion I shall assume two physicists, A and B, who represent a different conception with reference to the real situation as described by the ψ-function.

A. The individual system (before the measurement) has a definite value of q (i.e., p) for all variables of the system, and more specifically, *that* value which is determined by a measurement of this variable. Proceeding from this conception, he will state: The ψ-function is no exhaustive description of the real situation of the system but an incomplete description; it expresses only what we know on the basis of former measurements concerning the system.

B. The individual system (before the measurement) has no definite value of q (i.e., p). The value of the measurement only arises in cooperation with the unique probability which is given to it in view of the ψ-function only through the

tümlichen Wahrscheinlichkeit erst durch den Akt der Messung zustande. Ausgehend von dieser Auffassung wird (oder wenigstens darf) er erklären: Die ψ-Funktion ist eine erschöpfende Darstellung des realen Zustandes des Systems.

Nun präsentieren wir diesen beiden Physikern folgenden Fall. Es liege ein System vor das zu der Zeit t unserer Betrachtung aus zwei Teilsystemen S_1 und S_2 bestehe, die zu dieser Zeit räumlich getrennt und (im Sinne der klassischen Physik) ohne erhebliche Wechselwirkung sind. Das Gesamtsystem sei durch eine bekannte ψ-Funktion $ψ_{12}$ im Sinne der Quantenmechanik vollständig beschrieben. Alle Quantentheoretiker stimmen nun im Folgenden überein. Wenn ich eine vollständige Messung an S_1 mache, so erhalte ich aus den Messresultaten und aus $ψ_{12}$ eine völlig bestimmte ψ-Funktion $ψ_2$ des Systems S_2. Der Charakter von $ψ_2$ hängt dann davon ab, was *für eine Art* Messung ich an S_1 vornehme. Nun scheint es mir, dass man von dem realen Sachverhalt des Teilsystems S_2 sprechen kann. Von diesem realen Sachverhalt wissen wir vor der Messung an S_1 von vornherein noch weniger als bei einem durch die ψ-Funktion beschriebenen System. Aber an *einer* Annahme sollten wir nach meiner Ansicht unbedingt festhalten: Der reale Sachverhalt (Zustand) des Systems S_2 ist unabhängig davon, was mit dem von ihm räumlich getrennten System S_1 vorgenommen wird. Je nach der Art der Messung, welche ich an S_1 vornehme, bekomme ich aber ein andersartiges $ψ_2$ für das zweite Teilsystem. ($ψ_2$, $ψ_2^1$ . . .). Nun muss aber der Realzustand von S_2 unabhängig davon sein, was an S_1 geschieht. Für denselben Realzustand von S_2 können also (je nach Wahl der Messung an S_1) verschiedenartige ψ-Funktionen gefunden werden. (Diesem Schlusse kann man nur dadurch ausweichen, dass man entweder annimmt, dass die Messung an S_1 den Realzustand von S_2 (telepathisch) verändert, oder aber dass man Dingen, die räumlich voneinander getrennt sind, unabhängige Realzustände überhaupt abspricht. Beides scheint mir ganz inacceptabel.)

Wenn nun die Physiker A und B diese Ueberlegung als stichhaltig annehmen, so wird B seinen Standpunkt aufgeben

act of measurement itself. Proceeding from this conception, he will (or, at least, he may) state: the ψ-function is an exhaustive description of the real situation of the system.

We now present to these two physicists the following instance: There is to be a system which at the time t of our observation consists of two partial systems S_1 and S_2, which at this time are spatially separated and (in the sense of the classical physics) are without significant reciprocity. The total system is to be completely described through a known ψ-function ψ_{12} in the sense of quantum mechanics. All quantum theoreticians now agree upon the following: If I make a complete measurement of S_1, I get from the results of the measurement and from ψ_{12} an entirely definite ψ-function ψ_2 of the system S_2. The character of ψ_2 then depends upon *what kind* of measurement I undertake on S_1.

Now it appears to me that one may speak of the real factual situation of the partial system S_2. Of this real factual situation, we know to begin with, before the measurement of S_1, even less than we know of a system described by the ψ-function. But on one supposition we should, in my opinion, absolutely hold fast: the real factual situation of the system S_2 is independent of what is done with the system S_1, which is spatially separated from the former. According to the type of measurement which I make of S_1, I get, however, a very different ψ_2 for the second partial system (Ψ_2, Ψ_2^1,...). Now, however, the real situation of S_2 must be independent of what happens to S_1. For the same real situation of S_2 it is possible therefore to find, according to one's choice, different types of ψ-function. (One can escape from this conclusion only by either assuming that the measurement of S_1 ((telepathically)) changes the real situation of S_2 or by denying independent real situations as such to things which are spatially separated from each other. Both alternatives appear to me entirely unacceptable.)

If now the physicists, A and B, accept this consideration as valid, then B will have to give up his position that the Ψ-func-

müssen, dass die ψ-Funktion eine vollständige Beschreibung eines realen Sachverhaltes sei. Denn es wäre in diesem Falle unmöglich, dass demselben Sachverhalt (von S_2) zwei verschiedenartige ψ-Funktionen zugeordnet werden könnten. Der statistische Charakter der gegenwärtigen Theorie würde dann eine notwendige Folge der Unvollständigkeit der Beschreibung der Systeme in der Quantenmechanik sein, und es bestände kein Grund mehr für die Annahme, dass eine zukünftige Basis der Physik auf Statistik gegründet sein müsse. – – –

Meine Meinung ist die, dass die gegenwärtige Quantentheorie bei gewissen festgelegten Grundbegriffen, die im Wesentlichen der klassischen Mechanik entnommen sind, eine optimale Formulierung der Zusammenhänge darstellt. Ich glaube aber, dass diese Theorie keinen brauchbaren Ausgangspunkt für die künftige Entwicklung bietet. Dies ist der Punkt, in welchem meine Erwartung von derjenigen der meisten zeitgenössischen Physiker abweicht. Sie sind davon überzeugt, dass den wesentlichen Zügen der Quantenphänomene (scheinbar sprunghafte und zeitlich nicht determinierte Aenderungen des Zustandes eines Systems, gleichzeitig korpuskuläre und undulatorische Qualitäten der elementaren energetischen Gebilde) nicht Rechnung getragen werden kann durch eine Theorie, die den Realzustand der Dinge durch kontinuierliche Funktionen des Raumes beschreibt, für welche Differentialgleichungen gelten. Sie denken auch, dass man auf solchem Wege die atomistische Struktur der Materie und Strahlung nicht wird verstehen können. Sie erwarten, dass Systeme von Differentialgleichungen, wie sie für eine solche Theorie in Betracht kämen, überhaupt keine Lösungen haben, die überall im vierdimensionalen Raume regulär (singularitätsfrei) sind. Vor allem aber glauben sie, dass der anscheinend sprunghafte Charakter der Elementarvorgänge nur durch eine im Wesen statistische Theorie dargestellt werden kann, in welcher den sprunghaften Aenderungen der Systeme durch *kontinuierliche* Aenderungen von Wahrscheinlichkeiten der möglichen Zustände Rechnung getragen wird.

All diese Bemerkungen erscheinen mir recht eindrucksvoll. Die Frage, auf die es ankommt, scheint mir aber die zu sein:

tion constitutes a complete description of a real factual situation. For in this case it would be impossible that two different types of ψ-functions could be co-ordinated with the identical factual situation of S_2.

The statistical character of the present theory would then have to be a necessary consequence of the incompleteness of the description of the systems in quantum mechanics, and there would no longer exist any ground for the supposition that a future basis of physics must be based upon statistics. $---$

It is my opinion that the contemporary quantum theory by means of certain definitely laid down ·basic concepts, which on the whole have been taken over from classical mechanics, constitutes an optimum formulation of the connections. I believe, however, that this theory offers no useful point of departure for future development. This is the point at which my expectation departs most widely from that of contemporary physicists. They are convinced that it is impossible to account for the essential aspects of quantum phenomena (apparently discontinuous and temporally not determined changes of the situation of a system, and at the same time corpuscular and undulatory qualities of the elementary bodies of energy) by means of a theory which describes the real state of things [objects] by continuous functions of space for which differential equations are valid. They are also of the opinion that in this way one can not understand the atomic structure of matter and of radiation. They rather expect that systems of differential equations, which could come under consideration for such a theory, in any case would have no solutions which would be regular (free from singularity) everywhere in four-dimensional space. Above everything else, however, they believe that the apparently discontinuous character of elementary events can be described only by means of an essentially statistical theory, in which the discontinuous changes of the systems are taken into account by way of the continuous changes of the probabilities of the possible states.

All of these remarks seem to me to be quite impressive. However, the question which is really determinative appears to me

Was kann bei der heutigen Situation der Theorie mit einiger
Aussicht auf Erfolg versucht werden? Da sind es die Erfahrungen in der Gravitationstheorie, die für meine Erwartungen richtung-gebend sind. Diese Gleichungen haben nach
meiner Ansicht mehr Aussicht, etwas *Genaues* auszusagen als
alle andern Gleichungen der Physik. Man ziehe etwa die Maxwell'schen Gleichungen des leeren Raumes zum Vergleich
heran. Diese sind Formulierungen, die den Erfahrungen an
unendlich schwachen elektromagnetischen Feldern entsprechen.
Dieser empirische Ursprung bedingt schon ihre lineare Form;
dass aber die wahren Gesetze nicht linear sein können, wurde
schon früher betont. Solche Gesetze erfüllen das Superpositions-
Prinzip für ihre Lösungen, enthalten also keine Aussagen über
die Wechselwirkungen von Elementargebilden. Die wahren
Gesetze können nicht linear sein und aus solchen auch nicht
gewonnen werden. Noch etwas anderes habe ich aus der Gravitationstheorie gelernt: Eine noch so umfangreiche Sammlung
empirischer Fakten kann nicht zur Aufstellung so verwickelter
Gleichungen führen. Eine Theorie kann an der Erfahrung
geprüft werden, aber es gibt keinen Weg von der Erfahrung
zur Aufstellung einer Theorie. Gleichungen von solcher Kom-
pliziertheit wie die Gleichungen des Gravitationsfeldes können
nur dadurch gefunden werden, dass eine logisch einfache mathematische Bedingung gefunden wird, welche die Gleichungen
völlig oder nahezu determiniert. Hat man aber jene hinreichend starken formalen Bedingungen, so braucht man nur
wenig Tatsachen-Wissen für die Aufstellung der Theorie;
bei den Gravitationsgleichungen ist es die Vierdimensionalität
und der symmetrische Tensor als Ausdruck für die Raum-
struktur, welche zusammen mit der Invarianz bezüglich der
kontinuierlichen Transformationsgruppe die Gleichungen prak-
tisch vollkommen determinieren.

Unsere Aufgabe ist es, die Feldgleichungen für das totale
Feld zu finden. Die gesuchte Struktur muss eine Verallgemeinerung des symmetrischen Tensors sein. Die Gruppe darf
nicht enger sein als die der kontinuierlichen Koordinaten-
Transformationen. Wenn man nun eine reichere Struktur einführt, so wird die Gruppe die Gleichungen nicht mehr so stark

to be as follows: What can be attempted with some hope of success in view of the present situation of physical theory? At this point it is the experiences with the theory of gravitation which determine my expectations. These equations give, from my point of view, more warrant for the expectation to assert something *precise* than all other equations of physics. One may, for example, call on Maxwell's equations of empty space by way of comparison. These are formulations which coincide with the experiences of infinitely weak electro-magnetic fields. This empirical origin already determines their linear form; it has, however, already been emphasized above that the true laws can not be linear. Such linear laws fulfill the super-position-principle for their solutions, but contain no assertions concerning the interaction of elementary bodies. The true laws can not be linear nor can they be derived from such. I have learned something else from the theory of gravitation: No ever so inclusive collection of empirical facts can ever lead to the setting up of such complicated equations. A theory can be tested by experience, but there is no way from experience to the setting up of a theory. Equations of such complexity as are the equations of the gravitational field can be found only through the discovery of a logically simple mathematical condition which determines the equations completely or [at least] almost completely. Once one has those sufficiently strong formal conditions, one requires only little knowledge of facts for the setting up of a theory; in the case of the equations of gravitation it is the four-dimensionality and the symmetric tensor as expression for the structure of space which, together with the invariance concerning the continuous transformation-group, determine the equations almost completely.

Our problem is that of finding the field equations for the total field. The desired structure must be a generalization of the symmetric tensor. The group must not be any narrower than that of the continuous transformations of co-ordinates. If one introduces a richer structure, then the group will no longer determine the equations as strongly as in the case of the sym-

determinieren wie im Falle des symmetrischen Tensors als Struktur. Deshalb wäre es am schönsten, wenn es gelänge, die Gruppe abermals zu erweitern in Analogie zu dem Schritte, der von der speziellen Relativität zur allgemeinen Relativität geführt hat. Im Besonderen habe ich versucht, die Gruppe der komplexen Koordinaten-Transformationen heranzuziehen. Alle derartigen Bemühungen waren erfolglos. Eine offene oder verdeckte Erhöhung der Dimensionszahl des Raumes habe ich ebenfalls aufgegeben, eine Bemühung, die von Kaluza begründet wurde und in ihrer projektiven Variante noch heute ihre Anhänger hat. Wir beschränken uns auf den vierdimensionalen Raum und die Gruppe der kontinuierlichen reellen Koordinaten-Transformationen. Nach vielen Jahren vergeblichen Suchens halte ich die im Folgenden skizzierte Lösung für die logischerweise am meisten befriedigende.

Anstelle des symmetrischen g_{ik} ($g_{ik} = g_{ki}$) wird der nichtsymmetrische Tensor g_{ik} eingeführt. Diese Grösse setzt sich aus einem symmetrischen Teil s_{ik} und einem reellen oder gänzlich imaginären antisymmetrischen a_{ik} so zusammen:

$$g_{ik} = s_{ik} + a_{ik}.$$

Vom Standpunkte der Gruppe aus betrachtet ist diese Zusammenfügung von s und a willkürlich, weil die Tensoren s und a einzeln Tensor-Charakter haben. Es zeigt sich aber, dass diese g_{ik} (als Ganzes betrachtet) im Aufbau der neuen Theorie eine analoge Rolle spielen wie die symmetrischen g_{ik} in der Theorie des reinen Gravitationsfeldes.

Diese Verallgemeinerung der Raum-Struktur scheint auch vom Standpunkt unseres physikalischen Wissens natürlich, weil wir wissen, dass das elektromagnetische Feld mit einem schief symmetrischen Tensor zu tun hat.

Es ist ferner für die Gravitationstheorie wesentlich, dass aus den symmetrischen g_{ik} die skalare Dichte $\sqrt{|g_{ik}|}$ gebildet werden kann sowie der kontravariante Tensor g^{ik} gemäss der Definition

$$g_{ik}g^{il} = \delta_k{}^l \quad (\delta_k{}^l = \text{Kronecker-Tensor}).$$

Diese Bildungen lassen sich genau entsprechend für die nichtsymmetrischen g_{ik} definieren, ebenso Tensor-Dichten.

metrical tensor as structure. Therefore it would be most beautiful, if one were to succeed in expanding the group once more, analogous to the step which led from special relativity to general relativity. More specifically I have attempted to draw upon the group of the complex transformations of the co-ordinates. All such endeavors were unsuccessful. I also gave up an open or concealed raising of the number of dimensions of space, an endeavor which was originally undertaken by Kaluza and which, with its projective variant, even today has its adherents. We shall limit ourselves to the four-dimensional space and to the group of the continuous real transformations of co-ordinates. After many years of fruitless searching I consider the solution sketched in what follows as the logically most satisfactory.

In place of the symmetrical g_{ik} ($g_{ik} = g_{ki}$), the non-symmetrical tensor g_{ik} is introduced. This magnitude is constituted by a symmetric part s_{ik} and by a real or purely imaginary anti-symmetric a_{ik}, thus:

$$g_{ik} = s_{ik} + a_{ik}.$$

Viewed from the standpoint of the group the combination of s and a is arbitrary, because the tensors s and a individually have tensor-character. It turns out, however, that these g_{ik} (viewed as a whole) play a quite analogous rôle in the construction of the new theory as the symmetric g_{ik} in the theory of the pure gravitational field.

This generalization of the space structure seems natural also from the standpoint of our physical knowledge, because we know that the electro-magnetic field has to do with an anti-symmetric tensor.

For the theory of gravitation it is furthermore essential that from the symmetric g_{ik} it is possible to form the scalar density $\sqrt{|g_{ik}|}$ as well as the contravariant tensor g^{ik} according to the definition

$$g_{ik}g^{il} = \delta_k{}^l \ (\ \delta_k{}^l = \text{Kronecker-Tensor}).$$

These concepts can be defined in precisely corresponding manner for the non-symmetric g_{ik}, also for tensor-densities.

In der Gravitationstheorie ist es ferner wesentlich, dass sich zu einem gegebenen symmetrischen g_{ik}-Feld ein Feld Γ^l_{ik} definieren lässt, das in den unteren Indices symmetrisch ist und geometrisch betrachtet die Parallel-Verschiebung eines Vektors beherrscht. Analog lässt sich zu den nicht-symmetrischen g_{ik} ein nicht-symmetrisches Γ^l_{ik} definieren, gemäss der Formel

$$g_{ik,l} - g_{sk}\Gamma^s_{il} - g_{is}\Gamma^s_{lk} = 0, \ldots \tag{A}$$

welche mit der betreffenden Beziehung der symmetrischen g übereinstimmt, nur dass hier natürlich auf die Stellung der unteren Indices in den g und Γ geachtet werden muss.

Wie in der reellen Theorie kann aus den Γ eine Krümmung R^i_{klm} gebildet werden und aus dieser eine kontrahierte Krümmung R_{kl}. Endlich kann man unter Verwendung eines Variationsprinzips mit (A) zusammen kompatible Feldgleichungen finden:

$$\mathfrak{g}^{ik} = \tfrac{1}{2}(g^{ik} - g^{ki})\sqrt{-|g_{ik}|}) \tag{B$_1$}$$

$$\Gamma_{is}{}^s = 0(\Gamma_{is}{}^s = \tfrac{1}{2}(\Gamma_{is}{}^s - \Gamma_{si}{}^s)) \tag{B$_2$}$$

$$R_{\underline{ik}} = 0 \tag{C$_1$}$$

$$R_{\underline{kl},m} + R_{\underline{lm},k} + R_{\underline{mk},l} = 0 \tag{C$_2$}$$

Hierbei ist jede der beiden Gleichungen (B_1), (B_2) eine Folge der andern, wenn (A) erfüllt ist. R_{kl} bedeutet den symmetrischen, $R_{\underline{kl}}$ den antisymmetrischen $\overline{\text{T}}$eil von R_{kl}.

Im Falle des Verschwindens des antisymmetrischen Teils von g_{ik} reduzieren sich diese Formeln auf (A) und (C_1)— Fall des reinen Gravitationsfeldes.

Ich glaube, dass diese Gleichungen die natürlichste Verallgemeinerung der Gravitationsgleichungen darstellen.[2] Die Prüfung ihrer physikalischen Brauchbarkeit ist eine überaus schwierige Aufgabe, weil es mit Annäherungen nicht getan

---

[2] Die hier vorgeschlagene Theorie hat nach meiner Ansicht ziemliche Wahrscheinlichkeit der Bewährung, wenn sich der Weg einer erschöpfenden Darstellung der physischen Realität auf der Grundlage des Kontinuums überhaupt als gangbar erweisen wird.

In the theory of gravitation it is further essential that for a given symmetrical g_{ik}-field a field F^l_{ik} can be defined, which is symmetric in the lower indices and which, considered geometrically, governs the parallel displacement of a vector. Analogously for the non-symmetric g_{ik} a non-symmetric Γ^l_{ik} can be defined, according to the formula

$$g_{ik,l} - g_{sk}\Gamma^s_{il} - g_{is}\Gamma^s = 0, \dots \qquad (A)$$

which coincides with the respective relation of the symmetrical g, only that it is, of course, necessary to pay attention here to the position of the lower indices in the g and Γ.

Just as in the theory of a symmetrical g_{ik}, it is possible to form a curvature R^i_{klm} out of the Γ and a contracted curvature R_{kl}. Finally, with the use of a variation principle, together with (A), it is possible to find compatible field-equations:

$$\mathfrak{g}^{ik} = \tfrac{1}{2}(g^{ik} - g^{ki})\sqrt{-|g_{ik}|)} \qquad (B_1)$$

$$\Gamma_{is}^s = 0(\Gamma_{is}^s = \tfrac{1}{2}(\Gamma_{is}^s - \Gamma_{si}^s)) \qquad (B_2)$$

$$R_{ik} = 0 \qquad (C_1)$$

$$R_{kl,m} + R_{lm,k} + R_{mk,l} = 0 \qquad (C_2)$$

Each of the two equations (B_1), (B_2) is a consequence of the other, if (A) is satisfied. R_{kl} means the symmetric, R_{kl} the anti-symmetric part of R_{kl}.

If the anti-symmetric part of g_{ik} vanishes, these formulas reduce to (A) and (C_1)—the case of the pure gravitational field.

I believe that these equations constitute the most natural generalization of the equations of gravitation.[2] The proof of their physical usefulness is a tremendously difficult task, inasmuch as mere approximations will not suffice. The question is:

[2] The theory here proposed, according to my view, represents a fair probability of being found valid, if the way to an exhaustive description of physical reality on the basis of the continuum turns out to be possible at all.

ist. Die Frage ist: Was für im ganzen Raume singularitätsfreie Lösungen dieser Gleichungen gibt es? − − −

Diese Darlegung hat ihren Zweck erfüllt, wenn sie dem Leser zeigen, wie die Bemühungen eines Lebens miteinander zusammenhängen und warum sie zu Erwartungen bestimmter Art geführt haben.

A. Einstein.

INSTITUTE FOR ADVANCED STUDY
PRINCETON, NEW JERSEY

AUTOBIOGRAPHICAL NOTES

What are the everywhere regular solutions of these equations? − − −

This exposition has fulfilled its purpose if it shows the reader how the efforts of a life hang together and why they have led to expectations of a definite form.

A. Einstein.

INSTITUTE FOR ADVANCED STUDY
PRINCETON, NEW JERSEY

Ich hatte sehr tüchtige Lehrer (z. B. Hurwitz, Minkowski), so dass ich eigentlich eine hohe mathematische Ausbildung hätte erlangen können. Ich aber arbeitete die meiste Zeit im physikalischen Laboratorium, fasziniert durch die direkte Berührung mit der Erfahrung. Die übrige Zeit benützte ich zum Hauptteile dazu, um die Werke von Kirchhoff, Helmholtz, Hertz etc. zu Hause zu studieren. Denn ich die Mathematik bis zu einem gewissen Grade vernachlässigte, hatte nicht nur darin den Grund, dass das naturwissenschaftliche Interesse stärker war als das mathematische, sondern das folgende eigentümliche Erlebnis. Ich sah, dass die Mathematik in viele Spezialgebiete gespalten war, deren jedes diese kurze uns vergönnte Lebenszeit wegnehmen konnte. Ich sah mich in der Lage von Buridans Esel, der sich nicht für ein besonderes Bündel Heu entschliessen konnte. Dies lag offenbar daran, dass meine Intuition auf mathematischem Gebiete nicht stark genug war, um das Fundamental-Wichtige, Grundlegende

FACSIMILE OF PART OF A PAGE FROM ALBERT EINSTEIN'S AUTOBIOGRAPHY WRITTEN ESPECIALLY FOR THIS VOLUME (see p. 14 *supra*)

THE EDITOR WITH ALBERT EINSTEIN IN THE LATTER'S STUDY
IN PRINCETON, NEW JERSEY, DECEMBER 28, 1947

I

Arnold Sommerfeld

TO ALBERT EINSTEIN'S SEVENTIETH BIRTHDAY

TO ALBERT EINSTEIN'S SEVENTIETH BIRTHDAY*

I AM TOLD that Adolf Harnack once said, in the conference-room of the University of Berlin: "People complain that our generation has no philosophers. Quite unjustly: it is merely that today's philosophers sit in another department, their names are Planck and Einstein." And it is indeed true that with the great work of Einstein of 1905 the mutual distrust, which existed during the last century between philosophy and physics, has disappeared. Einstein at this point touches upon the old epistemological basic questions of space and time, and, proceeding from the most general results of physics, gives them a new content. Be it noted that that essay does not bear the widely misunderstood and not very fortunate name of "theory of relativity," but the much more harmless yet at the same time more significant title, "On the Electrodynamics of Moving Bodies." It is the relation between material motion and the universal speed of light which has led Einstein to the new analysis of space and time, that is to say, to their indissoluble connection. Not the *relativizing* of the perceptions of length and duration are the chief point for him, but the *independence of natural laws*, particularly those of electrodynamics and optics, *of the standpoint of the observer*. The essay has, of course, absolutely nothing whatsoever to do with ethical relativism, with the "Beyond Good and Evil." This invariance of natural laws exists in that group of motions (the uniform translations),

* From the original German essay, "Zum Siebzigsten Geburtstag Albert Einsteins," which appeared in *Deutsche Beiträge* (Eine Zweimonatsschrift, Vol. III, No. 2, Nymphenburger Verlagshandlung, München, 1949), translated (with the permission of author and publisher) specifically for this volume by Paul Arthur Schilpp.

to which Einstein, after the prior work of the great Dutchman
H. A. Lorentz, has given the name of "Lorentz-transformations," although their true nature was first really grasped only
by Einstein himself. Since that time the so-called "special
theory of relativity," which is based upon these [Lorentz
transformations], forms the unshakable foundation of physics
and astronomy.

Immediately after 1905 Einstein attacked the problem of
Newtonian gravitation. How is this [latter] to be reconciled
with the postulate of invariance? We know fictitious forces,
which come into being as the result of the non-uniform motion
of material bodies, for example the centrifugal force of rotation. One of the factors which appears here is the common mechanical mass, which we call "inert mass" because of its connection with the law of inertia. The same magnitude occurs
also in the law of gravitation as "heavy mass." The equality of
heavy and inert mass had already been emphasized by Newton,
tested by Bessel, and confirmed with extreme precision by Ro-
land Eötvös. This made Einstein wonder. For him there could
be no doubt that the equality of the masses pointed to an
equality of causes; that is to say, that gravitation also would
have to be a kind of inertia effect. With this the problem of
space and time assumed a new empirical aspect. The structure
of space and time had to be determined by the spatially-
temporally distributed masses (stated more generally, energies). Einstein wrestled with the program of this structural
theory of the space-time continuum in the years 1905-1915.
We shall let him speak for himself. In reply to several
letters of mine he answered on November 28, 1915, as follows:

During the last month I experienced one of the most exciting and most
exacting times of my life, true enough, also one of the most successful.
[Letter-] Writing was out of the question.

For I realized that all of my field equations of gravitation up till now
were entirely without support. Instead of that the following points of
departure turned up. . . .

After all confidence in the former theory has thus disappeared, I saw
clearly that a satisfactory solution could be found only by means of a

connection with the universal theory of covariants of Riemann. . . . The final result is as follows: . . .

Now the marvellous thing which I experienced was the fact that not only did Newton's theory result as first approximation but also the perihelion motion of Mercury (43" per century) as second approximation. For the deflection of light by the sun twice the former amount resulted.

Naturally I reacted somewhat incredulously. To this he remarked, on a postcard dated February 8th[, 1916]:

Of the general theory of relativity you will be convinced, once you have studied it. Therefore I am not going to defend it with a single word.

We may elaborate on Einstein's letter by saying: The marvellous thing which we experienced was that now the paths of the planets could be calculated as "shortest lines" in the structurally modified space, analogous to the straight lines in Euclidean space. The space-time continuum has become "non-Euclidean" in Riemann's most generalized sense, it has received a "curvature" which is impressed upon it by local energies.

The experimental verification was not to be long delayed. In the year 1918 a British solar eclipse expedition to the tropics had photographed the surroundings of the eclipsed sun and compared the positions of the fixed stars nearest to the sun with their normal positions. They showed deviations from these latter to the extent of the effect predicted by Einstein. The light-rays of these stars in passing close by the edge of the sun, go through an area of modified spatial structure and thereby are deflected, just as the rays of the sun are deflected in the inhomogeneous atmosphere of the earth and no longer follow a straight line. The great, now already deceased, British astronomer, Sir Arthur Eddington, became an inspired apostle of Einstein's doctrine and has worked it out in its manifold consequences.

From then on this doctrine entered into the publicity of home and foreign countries. When a representative of the *Kölnische Zeitung* asked me for further information about it in the year 1920, I told him that this was no matter for the general public, which lacked every prerequisite for the mathematical understanding of this theory. Nevertheless there began, in Berlin's newspapers, the "relativity-rumpus" with a passionate pro and con Einstein. Einstein suffered greatly under this. He was not made to be a newspaper-celebrity; every form of vanity was foreign to him. He has always retained something of the "boy of nature" and of the "Bohemian." Even his golden humor, which often took the form of very drastic statements, was not able to help him surmount the discomforts and obligations of a famous celebrity.

At this point a few biographical notes may be inserted. Born in a small Swabian Jewish community, Einstein attended the Humanistische Gynmasium in Munich, where his father was temporarily a businessman. After graduation he first went with his family to Italy and then studied at the Federal Institute of Technology in Zürich. Strangely enough no personal contacts resulted between his teacher of mathematics, Hermann Minkowski, and Einstein. When, later on, Minkowski built up the special theory of relativity into his "world-geometry," Einstein said on one occasion: "Since the mathematicians have invaded the theory of relativity, I do not understand it myself any more." But soon thereafter, at the time of the conception of the general theory of relativity, he readily acknowledged the indispensability of the four-dimensional scheme of Minkowski. At the time when Einstein discovered his special theory of relativity, in 1905, he was working in the Federal Patent-Office in Bern. From there he was called to the University of Zürich as associate professor. Thereafter he was, in passing, active as full professor of theoretical physics in Prague and returned then to an identical position in the Federal Institute of Technology in Zürich. Nernst succeeded in getting him to accept a research professorship in Berlin. The lecture cycles, to which his Zürich position obligated him, were not to Einstein's taste. He never had any orderly lecture-manuscripts. By the time a certain lecture came around again, he had lost his former notes. In Berlin he could freely choose to give university-lectures, but he had no obligation whatsoever to do so. We owe the completion of his general theory of relativity to his leisure while in Berlin. When, at the beginning of the first world-war, I visited him in Berlin and we read a war-report concerning the use of gas-bombs on the part of the enemies, Einstein remarked: "This is supposed to say that they stunk first, but we know better how to do it." This latter he knew from his friend, Fritz Haber. Politically he was, of course, definitely left of center, and possibly expected something good from the Russian revolution. During the "relativity-rumpus," which occasionally sank to the level of anti-Semitic mass-meetings, he had considered leaving Berlin. The decision came at the Nauheim Congress of Natural Scientists, in 1920: thanks to the efforts of Planck, he decided "to remain faithful to his friends in Berlin." I visited him for the last time in 1930 in Kaputh near Potsdam, where he pursued the sport of sailing. This was the only sport which he enjoyed; he had no use for physical exertion. Concerning the joy of intellectual work he once remarked: "Whoever knows it, does not go tearing after it." This means to say: His results did not fall into his lap, but had to be achieved by way of hard work and laborious mathematical investigations.

The battle over the theory of relativity had also slightly reached over into America, where youth was warned by a Boston Cardinal to beware of Einstein the atheist. Thereupon Rabbi Herbert S. Goldstein of New York cabled Einstein: "Do you believe in God?" Einstein cabled back: "I believe in Spinoza's God, who reveals himself in the harmony of all being, not in a God who concerns himself with the fate and actions of men." It would have been impossible for Einstein to give the rabbi a more pointed reply or one which came closer to his own innermost convictions. Many a time, when a new theory appeared to him arbitrary or forced, he remarked: "God doesn't do anything like that." I have often felt and occasionally also stated that Einstein stands in particularly intimate relation to the God of Spinoza.

Then came the shameful year 1933. Einstein was driven out of Berlin and robbed of his possessions.

A number of countries vied for his immigration. He chose America, where he found a worthy field of activity as a member of the Institute for Advanced Studies in Princeton. After Hahn's discovery of uranium fission he was the first to call President Roosevelt's attention to the possible military consequences of this discovery. The interpretation of this discovery, after all, was based directly upon Einstein's law of the equivalence of mass and energy. He did not participate in the technical development of the atom-bomb; I presume that he belonged to that group of American physicists who advised against the aggressive use of the new weapon. As an active pacifist, Einstein is an exponent of the organization "One World or None."*

Last year the newspapers carried the announcement that Einstein would make a lecture-tour in the interests of this organization. When I asked him not to forget Munich on this occasion, he replied: "Now I am an old duck and am no longer travelling, after I have come to know men sufficiently from all angles. The newspaper report was of course false, as usual."

We must once more return to the year 1905. Besides the special theory of relativity Einstein published in this year a still far more revolutionary work: the discovery of light-quanta. The old question, whether light is undulatory or corpuscular, was being raised again. The photo-electric effect and the phenomena of fluorescence can be understood only from the latter point of view. This was Einstein's first step on the road of the quantum theory indicated by Planck, which was later followed by further important steps, for example his theory of specific heat, and the theory of the fluctuation-phenomena of the black body radiation. Today we know that light unites both characteristics, that, according to the type of experiment, it shows us either its undulatory or its corpuscular aspect. The logical dissonance which seems to lie in this dualism, we consider as a direct consequence of the existence of the quantum of action discovered by Planck.

Out of the year 1905 comes also Einstein's brief note on Brownian motion. It has nothing to do with quantum theory or with the atomism of action, but rests entirely upon the atomism

---

* EDITOR'S NOTE: There is no such organization. However, the Federation of American Scientists, of which Professor Einstein is honorary president, late in 1945 published a volume by this title, *One World or None*. This Federation of American Scientists, therefore, is undoubtedly the organization to which Geheimrat Sommerfeld refers here. It must be added, moreover, that this Federation is by no means pacifist. *Ed.*

of matter and upon the general principles of statistical thermodynamics. The old fighter against atomistics, Wilhelm Ostwald, told me once that he had been converted to atomistics by the complete explanation of the Brownian motion.

Boltzmann's idea to reduce thermodynamics to statistics and entropy to the enumeration of probabilities, Einstein brought to manifold application as the "Boltzmann principle." He also has improved the explanation of the blueness of the sky by his statistical calculation of the small scale fluctuations in the density of air. Einstein is therefore also a scientist of first rank in the field of atomic theory.

In spite of all this, in the old question "continuum versus discontinuity," he has taken his position most decisively on the side of the continuum. Everything of the nature of quanta—to which, in the final analysis, the material atoms and the elementary particles belong also—he would like to derive from a continuum-physics by means of methods which relate to his general theory of relativity and expand this theory. His unceasing efforts, since he resides in America, have been directed towards this end. Until now, however, they have led to no tangible success. Even his most recent note, written for the *Review of Modern Physics* on the occasion of Robert Millikan's 80th birthday, still contains a mathematical attack in this direction, which, in his opinion, has hope of success. By far the most of today's physicists consider Einstein's aim as unachievable and, consequently, aim to get along with the dualism: wave-corpuscle, which he himself first clearly uncovered. However, in view of the total work of Einstein we want to remind ourselves of the beautiful couplet, which Schiller dedicated to Columbus:

> With the genius nature remains in eternal union:
> What the one promises, the other certainly redeems.

ARNOLD SOMMERFELD

UNIVERSITÄT MÜNCHEN
GERMANY

2

Louis de Broglie

A GENERAL SURVEY OF THE SCIENTIFIC WORK
OF ALBERT EINSTEIN

A GENERAL SURVEY OF THE SCIENTIFIC WORK
OF ALBERT EINSTEIN*

FOR ANY educated man, whether or not a professional scientist, the name of Albert Einstein calls to mind the intellectual effort and genius which overturned the most traditional notions of physics and culminated in the establishment of the relativity of the notions of space and time, the inertia of energy, and an interpretation of gravitational forces which is in some sort purely geometrical. Therein lies a magnificent achievement comparable to the greatest that may be found in the history of the sciences; comparable, for example, to the achievements of Newton. This alone would have sufficed to assure its author imperishable fame. But, great as it was, this achievement must not cause us to forget that Albert Einstein also rendered decisive contributions to other important advances in contemporary physics. Even if we were to overlook his no less remarkable work on the Brownian movement, statistical thermodynamics, and equilibrium fluctuations, we could not fail to take note of the tremendous import of his research upon a developing quantum theory and, in particular, his conception of "light quanta" which, reintroducing the corpuscular notion into optics, was to send physicists in search of some kind of synthesis of Fresnel's wave theory of light and the old corpuscular theory. The latter, after having been held by such men as Newton, was, as we know, destined for oblivion. Thus, Einstein became the source of an entire movement of ideas which, as wave mechanics and quantum mechanics, was to cast so disturbing a light upon atomic phenomena twenty years later.

* Translated from the French manuscript by Forrest W. Williams.

Before attempting to describe briefly the principal ideas which Einstein introduced into the scientific thought of our time, I would like to isolate some of the essential traits of his work.

Albert Einstein wrote, especially during his youth, numerous papers, almost all of them brief. He wrote only a few comparatively comprehensive expositions, and even these were quite succinct. Generally, he left to the care of others the task of presenting in complete works the theories whose foundations were laid by his powerful mind. Nevertheless, if most of his articles were short, there was not one among them that did not contain marvelous new ideas destined to revolutionize science, or acute and profound remarks penetrating to the most obscure recesses of the problem under consideration and opening in a few words almost unlimited perspectives. The work of Einstein is above all a "work of quality" in which elaboration and detailed development are not to be found. His articles might be compared to blazing rockets which in the dark of the night suddenly cast a brief but powerful illumination over an immense unknown region.

In every inquiry which he undertook Einstein always was able—and this is the mark of his genius—to master all the questions which faced him and to envisage them in some novel aspect which had escaped his precursors. Thus, he saw in the transformation formulas of Lorentz, not a pure and simple mathematical artifice, as did those before him, but the very expression of the bond which exists physically between space and time. Again, he saw in the laws of the photoelectric effect, unforeseen and inexplicable by classical notions, the necessity for returning in some fashion to a corpuscular conception of light. Example after example could be cited: each would prove to us the originality and genius of a mind which can perceive in a single glance, through the complex maze of difficult questions, the new and simple idea which enabled him to elicit their true significance and suddenly to bring clarity and light where darkness had reigned.

It is not to the discredit of great inventors to say that a discovery always comes "in the fulness of time," having been, in a sense, prepared by a number of previous investigations. The fruit was ripe, but no one as yet had been able to see it and pluck it.

When, in 1905, Albert Einstein with marvelous insight enunciated the principle of relativity and perceived its meaning and consequences, physicists had known for two decades that the old theories were beset with difficulties whose origin they were not able to comprehend. These older theories, in fact, admitted the existence of an ether, that is to say, a subtle medium filling all space, which served, so to speak, to materialize the classical conception of absolute space. This medium, support of all electrical and luminous phenomena, remained quite mysterious. A half-century of research had not enabled the successors of Fresnel to specify its physical properties in any plausible fashion. In the quite abstract theories of the electromagnetic field developed principally by Maxwell, Hertz, and Lorentz, the ether functioned as little more than a medium of reference; and, even in this modest rôle, it caused some discomfiture, for the assumption of its existence led to prediction of phenomena which, in fact, did not transpire. These phenomena would be extremely minute under any realizable conditions, and for a long time the impossibility of making them evident could be attributed to the lack of sufficiently precise instruments of measurement. But the great progress effected in the field of precision measurement by the technique of interferometric measures enabled physicists such as Michelson to assert, in respect to the earth's motion relative to the ether, the absence of any of the effects upon optic phenomena which had been predicted by the theories hitherto advanced. Stimulated by this discrepancy between observation and theoretical prediction, theorists examined the problem from all sides, subjecting the electromagnetic theory to all manner of critical study and reconstruction. H. A. Lorentz, the great specialist in this field who had gained the distinction of establishing a solid foundation for the electron theory and of deducing from his conclusions certain predictions thoroughly authenticated by the facts, notably the Zeeman effect, perceived an important fact. Examining the manner in which the Max-

well equations are transformed when one passes from one
frame of reference to a second in a motion rectilinear and
uniform relative to the first, he showed that these equations
remain invariant when one utilizes certain variables, x', y', z',
and t', bound to the initial variables by linear relations constituting what has since come to be known as the "Lorentz
transformation." But, according to the ideas then prevailing in
regard to the absolute character of space and time, the variables
x', y', z', and t', of the Lorentz transformation could not coincide with the true co-ordinates of space-time in the new frame
of reference. Consequently, Lorentz considered them to be
merely kinds of fictitious variables facilitating certain calculations. Nevertheless, he came very close to the correct solution
of the problem by defining a "local time" with the aid of the
variable, t', whereas Fitzgerald, interpreting in his own fashion
the Lorentz formulas, attributed the "failure" [*l'échec*] of the
Michelson experiments to a flattening or longitudinal contraction suffered by every moving solid. The Lorentz transformation, local time, and the Fitzgerald contraction appeared to be
artifices permitting one to account for certain aspects of the
electromagnetic field without disclosing their profound significance.

Then came Albert Einstein.

With great vigor he attacked this formidable problem, which
had already been the object of so much study, by resolutely
adopting a new point of view. For him, the Lorentz transformation formulas were not simple mathematical relations
defining a change of variables, convenient for studying the
equations of electromagnetism; rather, they were the expression of the relations which *physically* exist between the spatial
and temporal co-ordinates of two Galilean observers. A daring
hypothesis indeed, before which the perspicacious mind of
Lorentz recoiled! It carried in its wake, in fact, an abandonment of the ideas, traditional since Newton, regarding the
absolute nature of space and time, and established between
these two elements of the schema [*cadre*], in which all our
perceptions are ordered, an unforeseen relation entirely contrary to the immediate data of our intuitions. It was the high

distinction of Albert Einstein to succeed in showing, by means of an extremely minute and subtle analysis of the manner in which the physicist is led by his measuring operations to constitute his own schema of space and time, that the co-ordinates of space and time of different Galilean observers are really interlocked by the Lorentz formulas. Revealing that the absence of signals which travel at infinite speed results in the impossibility of verifying the simultaneity of two events occurring at points distant from each other, he analyzed the manner in which observers related to the same Galilean system nevertheless are able, through synchronization of clocks by exchanges of signals, to define a simultaneity within their system of reference; however, this simultaneity would be valid only for them, and events which would seem to them to be thus simultaneous would not be so for observers in motion relative to them. Central to this reasoning is the fact that no signal can travel with a speed greater than that of light in a void.

It is not our intention to explain here in detail how the ideas of Einstein led to the development of a precise and subtle mathematical theory, the special theory of relativity, which reveals the manner in which space and time co-ordinates are transformed by a change of Galilean reference systems in rectilinear and uniform motion with respect to each other. We must be confined to enumerating later some of the chief consequences of this theory. But we must underscore the magnificent effort, having few precedents in the history of the sciences, by which Einstein succeeded in isolating the fundamental new conceptions which removed at a stroke all the obstacles which lay in the path of the electrodynamics of moving bodies.

The new ideas regarding space and time were represented by introducing space-time or the world of Minkowski. This four-dimensional continuum preserves the *a priori* character which accrued separately, according to thinkers before Einstein, to absolute space and absolute time. Distances and elements of volume have, in fact, an invariant value, that is to say, have the same value for all Galilean observers notwithstanding the diversity of space co-ordinates and time co-ordinates which they employ. Space and time cease to possess an absolute nature, but the space-time which reunites them preserves this character. In space-time, each observer carves out in his own fashion his space and his time, and the Lorentz transformation formulas show us how the different portions are inter-related.

In space-time, everything which for each of us constitutes the past, the present, and the future is given in block, and the entire collection of events, successive for us, which form the existence of a material particle is represented by a line, the world-line of the particle. Moreover, this new conception defers to the principle of causality and in no way prejudices the determinism of phenomena. Each observer, as his time passes, discovers, so to speak, new slices of space-time which appear to him as successive aspects of the material world, though in reality the ensemble of events constituting space-time exist prior to his knowledge of them. Although overturning a large number of the notions held by classical physics, the special theory of relativity may in one sense be considered as the crown or culmination of that physics, for it maintains the possibility of each observer localizing and describing all the phenomena in the schema of space and time, as well as maintaining the rigorous determinism of those phenomena, from which it follows that the aggregate of past, present, and future phenomena are in some sense given *a priori*. Quantum physics, which issued from the study of atomic phenomena, led to quite different conceptions on these points, which were far from those of classical physics. We will not pursue this question, which would lead us too far astray, but will only say that, in any case, for all macroscopic phenomena investigated by classical physics, phenomena in which an enormous number of quantum processes intervene, the conceptions of the theory of relativity retain their validity throughout by virtue of the most exact statistical approximations.

As soon as Albert Einstein had laid the foundation of the special theory of relativity, innumerable consequences of great interest flowed from these unusual ideas. Some of the chief consequences were the Lorentz-Fitzgerald contraction, the apparent retardation of moving clocks, the variation of mass with velocity among high-speed particles, new formulas containing second-order terms [*termes supplémentaires*] for aberration and the Doppler effect, and new formulas for the compounding of velocities, yielding as a simple consequence of relative kinematics the celebrated formula of Fresnel, verified by Fizeau, specifying the light-wave-trains [*l'entrainement des ondes lumineuses*] of refracting bodies in motion. And these are not merely theoretical notions: one can not insist sufficiently upon the fact that the special theory of relativity today rests upon innumerable experimental verifications, for we can regularly obtain particles of velocities approaching that of light in vacuum, particles in regard to which it is necessary to take account of corrections introduced by the special theory of relativity. To cite only two examples among many, let us recall that the variation of mass with velocity deduced by Einstein from relativistic dynamics, after having been firmly established by the experiments of Guye and Lavanchy, is verified daily by observation of the motion of the high-speed particles of which nuclear physics currently makes such extensive use; let us also recall that some of the beautiful experiments of Mr. Ives have made possible verification of the relativistic formulas of the Doppler effect, and thus, indirect verification of the existence of the retardation of clocks of which they are a consequence.

If the special theory of relativity was thus directly verified by experiment in a number of ways, it also indirectly demonstrated its full worth by serving as a point of departure for new and fruitful theories. It performed this function in regard to the theory of photons (quanta of light), and the Compton effect, obtaining experimental verifications from the study of the photoelectric effect and the diffraction of electrons in the presence of high-velocity particles for which the variation of mass to velocity is detectable. Consideration of the Bohr atomic theory in the light of relativity dynamics enabled Sommerfeld to derive for the first time a theory of the fine structure of spectral rays which, at the time, constituted considerable progress. The author of the present article cannot forget the rôle of relativity considerations in the reasoning which led him to the basic ideas of wave mechanics. Finally, the electron theory of Dirac made possible a relativistic theory of "spin" and dis-closed a slender, well-concealed link between relativistic ideas and the spin notion.

Today, even a summary analysis of the special theory of relativity requires mention of the inertia of energy. In relativity dynamics, the expression of the energy of a material particle reveals that in each Galilean system of reference the energy is equal to the product of the square of the velocity of light and the mass which the material particle under consideration pos-sesses by virtue of its movement in the given system of refer-ence. From this proposition Albert Einstein concluded by means of a momentous generalization that every mass necessarily corresponds to an energy equal to the product of the mass and the square of the velocity of light, and he showed by ingenious examples how this idea could be verified in particular cases. An enormous simplification of prevailing conceptions resulted from this single idea, since the two principles of conservation of mass and conservation of energy, hitherto considered to be absolutely distinct, became in a sense amalgamated. Since radiation transmits energy, it followed that a radiating body loses mass and that an absorbing body gains mass. These new ideas were, moreover, entirely in accord with the existence of a momentum of radiation which had been indicated by the work of Henri Poincaré and Max Abraham.

One of the most important consequences of this principle of inertial energy was that the least fragment of matter con-tains, in virtue of its mass, an enormous quantity of energy. Henceforth, matter was regarded as an immense reservoir of energy congealed, so to speak, in the form of mass, and nothing prevented one from imagining that some day man would suc-ceed in liberating and using a portion of this hidden treasure. We know how, exactly forty years after the preliminary work of Einstein on relativity, this prediction received a dazzling, and sufficiently terrifying, verification.

The principle of the inertia of energy also explains why the exothermal formation of an atomic nucleus from its con-stituents yields a lesser mass than the sum of the masses of the constituents. Thus originated the explanation, as Paul

Langevin once observed, of the "mass-defects" of nuclei. Inertial energy thus enters significantly into energy-balances relative to nuclear reactions. The principle established by Einstein today plays a fundamental rôle in nuclear physics and chemistry and has found a wide range of application in this realm. It is one of the most magnificent conquests which we owe to the creator of the theory of relativity.

The special theory of relativity is a marvelous advance, but in itself, incomplete. For it deals only with the description of phenomena in Galilean systems of reference, that is to say, in systems of reference which are in rectilinear and uniform motion relative to the aggregate of fixed stars. Thus, on the one hand, it treats only of changes of variables corresponding to rectilinear and uniform relative motions, and on the other hand, it grants a kind of primacy to reference-systems in respect to the ensemble of fixed stars. It seemed necessary to break free of these restrictions in constructing a more general theory which would extend the principle of relativity to cases of any kind of accelerated motion and relate the apparently absolute character of velocities to the existence of the ensemble of stellar masses. Albert Einstein, keenly aware from the outset of his investigations of the necessity for such a generalization, arrived step by step at the solution sought. In this investigation he was guided by the ideas of certain precursors such as Mach, and by his extensive knowledge of tensor- and absolute differential-calculus, of which the special theory of relativity had already made some use; but, once again, it was the genius and originality of his mind which enabled him to attain the goal, which was definitively reached in 1916.

No attempt can be made here to analyze the general theory of relativity, which requires for its exposition extensive reference to difficult mathematical theories. Let us only say that it rests essentially upon the notion that all the laws of physics can be expressed by "covariant" equations, that is to say, equations which have the same mathematical form regardless of the system of reference selected or the space-time variables used. If this notion is applied to a reference system in rotation, it is evident that the centrifugal forces [*forces centrifuges et centrifuges composés*] which are involved in the motion of a moving body in respect to this system may be considered as resulting from the metrical form of the space-time element and the variables used by the observer in rotation.

The new flash of Einstein's genius during this investigation was to perceive the possibility of deriving a geometrical interpretation of gravitational forces analogous to that of centrifugal forces. The centrifugal forces are proportional to the mass of the body, and this seems only natural. But, what is far more extraordinary, the same may be said of gravitational forces inasmuch as the gravitational force experienced by a body is likewise always proportional to its mass. This proportionality of "inertial mass" and "gravitational mass" was verified in precise experiments conducted by Eötvös and seems to hold rigorously. It follows that the trajectory of a material particle in a field of gravitation is independent of its mass. This analogy between centrifugal and gravitational forces suggests that they be similarly interpreted as resulting from the expression of the metrical form of space-time with the aid of the variables employed by the observer embedded in the gravitational field. Pursuing this line of thought, Einstein showed the "equivalence" of inertial force and gravitational force, and illustrated it by the famous example of a free-falling elevator: an observer inside an elevator could say that he maintains contact with the floor by his weight, but he could as well say that he has no weight at all and that the elevator is propelled upward by a velocity of motion equal to *g*.

However, the analogy between centrifugal and gravitational forces is not complete. One can, in fact, eliminate centrifugal forces by placing oneself in a Galilean system of co-ordinates; in which case one calls upon the formulas of special relativity. Yet one cannot, by any apposite choice of the system of reference, eliminate the gravitational forces. Einstein discovered the geometrical interpretation of this fact.

In the absence of gravitational force, space-time is Euclidean.[1] One can select Cartesian reference systems in which there are no centrifugal forces: these forces appear only if one adopts

[1] Or, more precisely, pseudo-Euclidean.

curvilinear co-ordinates, which amounts to placing oneself in an accelerated reference system, for example, in a rotating system. On the other hand, space-time is not Euclidean in the presence of a gravitational field; hence, as for a curved surface, it is impossible to adopt Cartesian co-ordinates. Gravitation is thus reduced to an effect of the curvature of space-time dependent upon the existence of masses scattered through the universe. It follows that the structure of the universe, and in particular its curvature in a geometrical sense, depends upon the masses contained in the universe. Relying upon the Riemannian theory of curved space, the general theory of relativity develops, by means of tensor-calculus, an interpretation of gravitational phenomena whose elegance and beauty is incontestable. This will remain one of the finest monuments of mathematical physics of the twentieth century.

Verifications of the general theory of relativity are few in number and still rather inaccurate. The rotation of the perihelion of Mercury, whose exact value had not been predictable by classical celestial mechanics, appears to conform to the predictions of the relativistic theory of gravitation. But since there subsists a residual effect after one has taken into account the perturbations due to other bodies of the solar system, and precise calculations are long and difficult and have not been verified often, this verification of relativity theory calls for further examination and debate. The deviation of light rays passing through a strong field of gravitation, predicted by Einstein's theory, was sought by studying the light rays of a distant star as they passed near the edge of the sun during a total solar eclipse. The results were encouraging, but further measurements would be desirable. As for the red-shift of rays emitted by a source located in a strong gravitational field, this has been the subject of much debate. It seems that this phenomenon has been observed at the surface of the sun, but the very minute displacements detected could perhaps be due to other causes (pressure, magnetic fields, etc. . . . .). A more significant displacement was foreseen in regard to the "white dwarfs," very small stars of extremely high density whose surfaces have a very intense gravitational field. A very great displacement of rays has actually been observed in the spectrum of the Companion of Sirius, and this appears to be one of the best experimental verifications of the relativity theory of gravitation.

The assimilation of space-time to a four-dimensional curved surface leads necessarily to the question of whether the universe is infinite, or partially—or totally—bent back upon itself like a cylinder or a sphere. One arrives, in pursuing this question, at cosmological theories, naturally of a rather conjectural character, concerning the structure of the whole universe. Einstein himself led the way by introducing into the theory of gravitation a cosmological constant related to the dimensions of a universe considered as finite, and by developing the hypothesis of a cylindrical universe; whereas the Dutch astronomer, de Sitter, studied the hypothesis of a spherical universe. These bold theories led to predictions for which the actual state of astronomy permitted no verification, and they would have remained somewhat sterile if Abbé Lemaître had not succeeded, by slightly modifying them, in extracting an explanation of that most curious phenomenon, the recession of distant nebulae, and of the linear law of Hubble. Lemaître conceived the universe, not as a static sphere in the style of de Sitter, but as a sphere whose dimensions increase (the expanding universe), and demonstrated that the hypothesis may logically be introduced into the framework of the general theory of relativity. No one can say at present with any certainty whether the explanation thus derived of the apparent recession of nebulae is appropriate, but it seems that no other valid explanation has yet been proposed. Without wishing to pass upon questions which only a study of the limits of the sky by the most powerful instruments of contemporary astronomy might succeed in resolving, we might note the extent to which Einstein's theory was fecund with new conceptions of all kinds and how, beginning in pure physics, it came to exercise a stimulating influence upon the highest of astronomical research.

The general theory of relativity advances a geometrical interpretation of the notion of "force." It succeeds satisfactorily in regard to gravitational forces. Its goal, therefore, would be entirely achieved if it were to succeed also in interpreting electromagnetic forces; for it certainly seems that all forces existing in nature are either gravitational or electromagnetic in character. But electromagnetic forces are proportional to the charge, and not to the mass, of the body upon which they act. It follows that the trajectory of a charged particle in an electromagnetic field depends upon the relation between its charge and its mass and varies according to the nature of the particle. Therein lies a fundamental difference between gravitational and electromagnetic fields which does not allow an extension to the latter of the geometrical interpretation which succeeded in respect to the former. Innumerable attempts have been made in the past thirty years to complete the general theory of relativity on this point and transform it into a "unified theory" capable of interpreting at once the existence of gravitational forces and electromagnetic forces. The theories of Weyl, Eddington, Kaluza, etc., are well known, but none appears to have had complete success. Naturally, Einstein also applied himself to the solution of this problem, and for twenty years or more has published, sometimes as sole author, sometimes in collaboration, a number of papers on new forms of unified theories. Einstein's efforts in this direction, ever characterized by the salient originality of his thought, will not be examined here. Despite their indisputable interest, they have not, to the best of our knowledge, attained any decisive success, and form, rather, landmarks placed on a road as yet uncleared. Moreover, the nature of the electromagnetic field is so intimately bound to the existence of quantum phenomena that any non-quantum unified theory is necessarily incomplete. These are problems of redoubtable complexity whose solution is still "in the lap of the gods."

The work of Albert Einstein on fluctuations, on the Brownian movement, on statistical thermodynamics, doubtless possesses less general significance than his trail-blazing research on the theory of relativity. However, the former alone would suffice to make the reputation of a great physicist. Accomplished during the years 1905-1912 and paralleling in its development the remarkable theoretical studies of Mr. Smoluchovski on the same subject, it was most timely, for during this period direct or indirect proofs of the reality of molecules were being sought on all sides. A great number of first-rate experimenters, including Jean Perrin and Mr. The. Svedberg, were supplying the decisive proofs desired for the existence of molecules, by their observations of the equilibrium of emulsions, the Brownian movement, fluctuations of density, critical opalescence, etc. All of these studies were guided and clarified by Einstein's calculations. And the conceptions or methods which Einstein, with his customary acuity, had introduced in the course of his theoretical studies, brought new light to certain aspects of the statistical interpretation of thermodynamics.

If, for the sake of brevity, I must pass rapidly over this portion, however important, of the work of Albert Einstein, I must in contrast dwell at greater length upon the capital contribution which he made to the development of quantum theory. It should not be forgotten that it was particularly for his photoelectric research that Einstein received the Nobel prize for physics in 1921.

At the time that Einstein was undertaking his first investigations, Planck was introducing into physics the startling hypothesis regarding quanta and revealing that they enabled one to find the experimental laws of the spectral distribution of the radiation of thermal equilibrium, of which the classical theories had been unable to give any account. Planck had assumed, in disturbing contradiction to the most inveterate conceptions of the old physics, that the electron oscillators within matter which are responsible for the emission and absorption of radiation could emit radiant energy only as finite quantities, by quanta, whose value was proportional to the frequency emitted. Thus, he was led to introduce as the factor of proportionality the famous Planck constant whose importance on the atomic scale has never ceased to be reconfirmed to an increasing degree. Planck thus obtained as well the correct law of blackbody radiation and, comparing his formula with experimental results, ascertained the value of the constant, h. Moreover, the introduction of the quantum hypothesis proved necessary to obtain a correct representation of the properties of blackbody radiation. The work of Lord Rayleigh, Jeans, Planck himself, and somewhat later that of Henri Poincaré, proved that the old conceptions must lead to inexact laws and that the introduction of the element of discontinuity represented by the quantum of action was inevitable.

In his first works on this subject, Planck held that radiation was emitted *and absorbed* in quanta: this was the first version of the quantum theory. But, if radiation is always absorbed in quanta, it seemed necessary to admit that radiant energy arrived in quanta, that is to say, that electromagnetic waves, instead of being homogeneous (as had always been supposed), must consist of local concentrations of energy, packets of energy. Such a constitution of electromagnetic waves and, in particular, of light waves seemed, however, difficult to reconcile with the known properties of radiation, notably the phenomena of interference and diffraction so precisely described by the theory of homogeneous waves advanced by Fresnel and Maxwell. Since one could, strictly speaking, grant that the emission of radiation is accomplished in quanta without therefore postulating a corpuscular structure of radiation, the prudent mind of Planck, accustomed to the methods of classical physics, preferred to revise his theory of black-body radiation by the hypothesis that emission, but not absorption, proceeds in quantum fashion: this was the second, somewhat hybrid, version of the quantum theory.

The young Einstein reflected deeply upon this difficult subject and, in 1905, at the age of twenty-six, when he was laying the foundations of the theory of relativity, he proposed to adopt quite frankly the more radical point of view by granting the hypothesis of a corpuscular structure of radiation; and derived therefrom an interpretation of the mysterious laws of the photoelectric effect. Thus, with the vigor of an exceptional mind, Einstein, in the same year, founded *one* of the two great theories (relativity and quantum) which today reign supreme over the whole of contemporary physics, and made a capital contribution to the progress of the *other*.

The photoelectric effect, discovered by Hertz in 1887, obeys laws which long seemed incomprehensible. A metal subjected to an irradiation ejects electrons if the frequency of incident radiation lies above a certain threshold: the kinetic energy of the ejected electrons increasing in linear fashion as a function of the difference between the excitatory frequency and the threshold frequency. Thus the elementary phenomenon of the ejection of an electron by the metal depends uniquely upon the frequency of incident radiation and in no way upon its amplitude, only the number of these elementary phenomena increasing with the intensity of the excitatory radiation. The classical theories of the constitution of light could not predict anything of the sort and the laws of the photoelectric effect remained inexplicable. Einstein, abandoning the prudent attitude of Planck, perceived in these laws the proof that the radiation possesses a corpuscular structure, the energy in a wave of frequency v being concentrated in a corpuscle of energy content equal to hv. He derived with admirable simplicity an interpretation of photoelectric laws. If an electron, in order to be ejected from matter, must spend an amount of energy ω equal to hv_0, it could not, after having absorbed a quantum equal to hv, be ejected unless v is greater than v_0; hence the existence of a threshold frequency. If v is greater than v_0, the electron will be ejected with a kinetic energy equal to $h(v - v_0)$; hence the linear growth of this energy as a function of $v - v_0$. This theory of such great simplicity has since been verified by Millikan for ordinary light, by Maurice de Broglie for X-rays, and by Jean Thibaud and Ellis for γ-rays. Their experiments furnished a new means of measuring the value of the constant, h. Thus did precise experiments directly require a return in some fashion to a corpuscular conception of light, already maintained by Newton and other thinkers before the success of the wave theory, as a consequence of the fine work of Fresnel, almost led to its abandonment by all physicists. In order to signify its quantum origin, Einstein called this new corpuscular theory of light "the theory of light-quanta" (*Licht-Quanta*). Today, we call it the "photon theory."

During the succeeding years, Einstein did not cease to reflect upon this new conception of light. Assisted by arguments drawn from the theory of relativity, studies of the equilibrium between radiation and matter, and research into the fluctuations of energy in black-body radiation, he showed that photons must not only have an energy equal to hv, but a momentum equal to hv/c. This conclusion was later verified by the discovery and study of the Compton effect. To be sure, Einstein's conceptions immediately encountered strong opposition. Masters of science such as Lorentz and Planck were not slow to point out that a purely corpuscular theory of light could not account for the phenomena of diffraction and coherence of wave-trains, for which the wave theory offered a ready interpretation. Einstein did not deny these difficulties, yet insisted upon the need for introducing into light waves an element of discontinuity, supporting his contentions by some penetrating observations. He inclined toward a "mixed theory" which would admit the existence of packets of radiant energy, but would link their movement and their localization to the propagation of a homogeneous wave of the Maxwell-Fresnel type. Later, the author of the present article was to attempt, at the outset of the development of wave mechanics, to develop an analogous idea for interpreting the general relation between the corpuscles and their associated waves. These attempts were unsuccessful, and it was necessary to find a very different interpretation connected with the indeterminacy relations of Heisenberg: we shall speak of this later. But it is certain that the ideas of Einstein on the constitution of light played a decisive rôle in the evolution of quantum theory and the growth of wave mechanics.

Pursuing his study of the applications of Planck's hypothesis, Albert Einstein demonstrated that it furnished a new theory of specific heats and removed the difficulties which had beset this domain. The Einsteinian formula for specific heats, though based upon hypotheses which were too simple to be truly applicable to real cases, clearly revealed the rôle of the quantum of action in these phenomena and served as a model for the more detailed research subsequently undertaken by Lindeman, Debye, Born, and Karman. . . .

However, the theory of quanta was elsewhere making enormous progress. In 1913 Bohr published his quantum theory of the atom, the immense repercussion of which upon the whole field of physics is well known. In 1916 Sommerfeld perfected Bohr's theory by introducing the corrections of relativity and accounted, at least in part, for the fine structures observed in spectra. Einstein followed all these investigations with great interest. In a paper he formulated the method of quantization employed by Sommerfeld and, when Bohr enunciated his "correspondence principle," Einstein published a celebrated work in which, studying the thermodynamic equilibrium between blackbody radiation and a gas, he revealed the connection between Planck's formula and Bohr's law of frequencies. In accord with the correspondence principle, he gave expression to the probability of quantum transitions which may be undergone by an atom in a field of incident radiation. Thus, once again, he made a capital contribution to the development of quantum theory.

When the author of the present article expounded in his Doctoral thesis in 1924 the ideas which remained at the foundation of wave mechanics, Einstein learned of them through Paul Langevin. Realizing their interest, he published in January of 1925 in the *Proceedings* of the Berlin Academy a note in which, drawing upon these new ideas and upon a then-recent work by the Indian physicist Bose, he formulated the statistics applicable to a group of particles indistinguishable one from another. This statistics, which is applicable to photons, α-particles, and more generally to any complex particle containing an even number of elementary corpuscles, today goes by the name of the "Bose-Einstein statistics." As we now know, electrons, protons, neutrons, and complex particles composed of an odd number of elementary corpuscles fall under the Pauli principle of exclusion, and groups of them obey a different statistics, that of Fermi-Dirac. By calling attention to the new ideas of wave mechanics, Einstein's paper certainly contributed greatly toward hastening this development.

Between 1924 and 1928 the new quantum theories, wave mechanics and quantum mechanics, rapidly gained great momentum, largely due to the work of Heisenberg, Born, Schrödinger, and Dirac. In 1927 Heisenberg made public his indeterminacy relations. His work, together with Bohr's penetrating analyses, led to a physical interpretation of the new mechanics in which the notion of probability plays a primordial rôle and which, abandoning the ideas dearest to classical physics, ceases to attribute simultaneously a position and a velocity to particles on the atomic scale and refuses to impose a rigorous determinism upon the succession of their observable manifestations. Einstein, along with certain physicists of his generation or of preceding generations (Langevin, Planck), never granted, it seems, the new ideas of Bohr and Heisenberg. At the Solvay Conference of October, 1927, he was already raising serious objections. A few years later, in a paper written with Podolsky and Rosen, he expounded the difficulties which the actual interpretation of quantum mechanics appeared to him to raise. To Einstein's objections various physicists, and notably Mr. Bohr, composed acute replies, and it rather seems today that the physicists of the younger generation are almost unanimously in favor of granting the Bohr-Heisenberg interpretation, which seems to be the only one compatible with the totality of the known facts. Nevertheless, Einstein's objections, which bear the imprint of his profound mind, were surely useful because they forced the champions of the new conceptions to clarify subtle points. Even if one considers it possible to circumvent them, it is useful to have studied and reflected upon them at length.

The first half of the twentieth century was marked by an extraordinary impetus to physics which will remain one of the most brilliant chapters in the history of science. In these few years, human science raised two monuments which will stand in future centuries: the theory of relativity and the quantum theory. The first emerged wholly from the creative brain of Albert Einstein. The second, whose first stones were laid by Planck, owes to the mind of Einstein some of its most noteworthy advances.

One could not contemplate a work at once so profound and so powerfully original, accomplished in a few years, without astonishment and admiration. The name of Albert Einstein will be forever joined to two of the most magnificent achievements in which the human mind may take pride.

LOUIS DE BROGLIE

INSTITUT DE FRANCE
ACADÉMIE DES SCIENCES

3

Ilse Rosenthal-Schneider

PRESUPPOSITIONS AND ANTICIPATIONS IN EINSTEIN'S PHYSICS

3

PRESUPPOSITIONS AND ANTICIPATIONS IN EINSTEIN'S PHYSICS

THE PRESUPPOSITIONS in Einstein's physics which I am discussing here are not the well known and often explicitly stated fundamental hypotheses of the theory of relativity; nor are the "anticipations" those consequences of the theory which provided the possibilities of testing the relativity theory's theoretical results and of verifying them. My remarks are concerned with some fundamental ideas which, I think, are determining principles of Einstein's work, and with his anticipations as to the possibilities of future developments in theoretical physics. The evidence will be drawn from his own methods in his scientific work and from his epistemological statements in publications as well as in personal discussions and correspondence.

Einstein's views on the comprehensibility of the world of our sense-experiences will be contrasted with Planck's, and some other problems, as for instance the significance of the constants of nature, will be touched upon.

Einstein's contention that "the axiomatic basis of theoretical physics cannot be an inference from experience," but is a "free invention" of the human mind, has been reasserted by him again and again.[1] This contention represents the starting point

---

[1] "On the Methods of Theoretical Physics," Herbert Spencer Lecture (Oxford, 1933, Clarendon Press). (Afterwards referred to as M.T.P.)

"Physik und Realität," *J. Franklin Inst.*, v. 221 (1933), n. 3. (Afterwards referred to as P.R.)

"Russell's Theory of Knowledge," *The Library of Living Philosophers*, v. 5 (1944). (Afterwards referred to as R.T.K.)

Translations from the German of all quotations except those from R.T.K. are mine.

of a much debated problem. The most debatable point is "the gulf—logically unbridgeable—which separates the world of sensory experiences from the world of concepts and propositions."[2] Taking the existence of sense-experiences as "given" and "knowable," Einstein states, that the concept of the "real external world" of our everyday thinking rests exclusively on sense-impressions, and that physics . . . deals with sense-experiences and with "comprehending" connections between them. The notions of bodily objects are formed by assigning concepts to repeatedly occurring complexes of sense-impressions "arbitrarily" selected from the multitude of sensory experiences. Logically viewed the concepts of bodily objects are "free creations of the human (or animal) mind,"[3] but they owe their meaning and their "justification" exclusively to the totality of sense-impressions to which they are co-ordinated and with which they are directly and intuitively connected. We attribute to the concept of the object real existence, i.e., a meaning which is largely independent of the sense-impressions to which the concept was assigned. We are justified in setting up "real objects" only because, by means of these concepts and their mutual relations (also set up by us), we are in a position to find our way in the "labyrinth of sense-impressions." Just like these "primary" concepts of everyday thinking, the "secondary" concepts and the basic laws connecting them, which form the foundation of scientific theory, are "free inventions."

To the question whether any principle can be established in accordance with which a co-ordinating selection is performed (or, as Eddington would have said, must be performed), Einstein's answer would be a definite "no." He emphasizes that concepts do not originate from experience by way of abstraction, a conception which he regards as "fateful." In order to illustrate that concepts are not abstracted from, but logically independent of sense-experiences, he refers to the series of integers as an invention of the human mind, and he states that "there is no way in which this concept could be made to grow, as it

[2] R.T.K., 287.
[3] P.R., 314.

were, directly out of sense-experiences."[4] This illustration, seen from a different angle, represents the same complications as the still unsolved—and perhaps insoluble—μέθεξις-problem which, ever since it impeded the unity of Plato's philosophy and eluded attempts at its solution by Aristotle's theory of substance, has constituted a stumbling-block for metaphysicians and epistemologists.

For Einstein the concepts are to the sense-experiences "not like the soup to the beef, but more like the cloakroom number to the coat."[5] However, I think, we should not forget that there are *complexes* of sense-experiences: to the coat there belongs a hat and gloves, etc.; we have to select them as a complex, and they, as a complex, must be suitable to be designated by the *one* cloakroom number.

It may be argued that the arbitrary selection of complexes of sense-experiences represents a sort of interference with the given totality of sense-impressions. We should be conscious that such interference, implied in the formation of primary concepts, is of still greater significance when secondary concepts and the laws of their interrelations, basic to physical theory, are concerned.

Eddington's presentation of the scientist's interference with the things he studies refers not only to this selection (representing interference at the "early" stage, where concepts are co-ordinated to sense-experiences) but also to interference at "later" stages. "It makes no difference whether we create or whether we select the conditions we study,"[6] may be an overstatement, but it is by no means a commonplace. The truth it contains had rarely been admitted by scientists. Poincaré, one of the few who did admit it, drew attention to interference by selection; the problem, however, came to the fore with the growth of quantum ideas—especially those of complementarity. The interference to which the scientist is compelled by the intrinsic nature of objects represents a type of "physical"

[4] R.T.K., 287.

[5] P.R., 317.

[6] A. Eddington, *The Philosophy of Physical Science* (Cambridge, 1939, University Press), 110.

interference which has far reaching philosophical implications, some of which will be touched upon in connection with Einstein's anticipations.

Eddington, in his "selective subjectivism," or "structuralism," sees the "Procrustean method" not only in the physical violence but also in the interference through selection brought about by our "sensory and intellectual equipment,"[7] the framework into which the observationally acquired knowledge is fitted. Eddington's framework is by no means identical with Kant's, to which it may be compared; but the basic idea of looking for a frame of thought originated from similar considerations, i.e., to find the conditions of the possibility of experience. In Kant's epistemology, too, we find some Procrustean methods; they form an integral part of his transcendental deduction. Our understanding "imposes laws on nature,"[8] but —to prevent misunderstanding—only universal principles (like the principles of causality and of substantiality), not laws concerning special facts which can only be ascertained by "experience," or, we may say, by the special sciences. Eddington, however, goes much further than Kant; he regards also special laws, and even the constants of nature, as deducible from epistemological considerations only, so that we can have *a priori* knowledge of them. This point is of interest when compared with Einstein's anticipations concerning the universal constants.

A few more lines on Kant's epistemology may help in elucidating Einstein's views on the comprehensibility of the external world, in contradistinction to Planck's, whose philosophical attitude is largely based on that of Kant—though of a Kant slightly distorted by Helmholtz. Kant did not stop at subjectivism, as Eddington did, but tried to find a "bridge," as I may call it, from the human mind to the phenomena of the external world which we perceive and judge. This bridge is to be found in his critical or transcendental idealism. The laws of nature are, for Kant, the laws of the experience of nature.

[7] *Ibid.*, 16.
[8] I. Kant, *Critik der reinen Vernunft*, 2. Aufl. (Riga, 1787), J. F. Hartknoch, 163.

He saw the harmony between laws of thinking and nature in the principle of the synthetic unity of thinking. Our intellectual equipment (to use Eddington's term, though I am fully conscious of its being completely un-Kantian) contains the forms of intuition, space and time,—which Einstein once jokingly compared to the emperor's new clothes in Andersen's story—as well as the principles of pure understanding. Both are elements of "knowledge restricted to objects of experience, though not wholly borrowed from experience."[9] These elements are *a priori;* but Kant's *a priori* is not a temporal—previous to experience—it is a logical *a priori:* independent of experience. For him, just as for Locke, there are only acquired, no innate, ideas.

Einstein writes: "That the totality of our sense-experiences is such that they can be arranged in an order by means of thinking . . . is a fact which strikes us with amazement, but which we shall never be able to comprehend."[10] There is no *a priori* framework, and apparently nothing—even *a posteriori* —that can be established about the co-ordination of concepts to sense-experiences or amongst each other. His statements that they are "somehow" (*irgendwie*)[11] connected, or "that enough propositions of the conceptual system be firmly enough connected with sensory experiences"[12] appear to be, perhaps deliberately, somewhat vague formulations. But he thinks it necessary that rules are fixed for building up a "system," like rules of a game, the fixation of which rules, though arbitrary, makes the game possible. He also stresses that this fixation of rules will never be a final one but will be valid only for a particular field of application, and that "there are no final categories in the sense of Kant." Any set of rules for the game is permissible as long as it leads to the desired result.

The question is whether the game can be played at all unless certain fundamental rules of thinking, or at least a scheme for their fixation, are established to which all players of all games

[9] *Ibid.,* 166.
[10] P.R., 315.
[11] P.R., 315.
[12] R.T.K., 289.

have to conform. Einstein agrees with Kant that "in thinking we use, with a certain 'right,' concepts to which there is no access from the materials of sensory experience, if the situation is viewed from the logical point of view."[13] This "right," just as Poincaré's *"conventions justifiées"*[14] (conventions justified on the grounds of intuition), seems to be very similar to Kant's *a priori* correctly interpreted as "logical independence of experience," though Einstein stresses that neither its certainty nor its inherent necessity can be upheld.

At this juncture we are in a position to compare Einstein's with Planck's views on the comprehensibility of the external world—certainly the most essential presupposition of science. Planck's standpoint may briefly be sketched as follows: We believe in the real external world, but we have no possibility of investigating it. The symbols we use in physics are constituents of the world picture and to a certain extent arbitrary; there are no observables in the world picture. Observables belong to the world of sense-experiences, and behind this, there is the real world which we can perceive only by means of the world of our sense-experiences. It is this real world which Planck presupposes as the "absolute," and it is this absolute which he tried to establish in physics: in the absolute value of the energy and of the entropy, or even in the space-time metric.

Whoever discussed such problems with Planck will have felt the powerful impact of his basic philosophical ideas on his scientific work. His attitude towards the problem of the comprehensibility of the external world is revealed in the beginning of his autobiography:

The fact which led me to my science and filled me with enthusiasm for it, from my youth onwards, and which is by no means self-evident, is that our laws of thinking coincide with the lawfulness in the course of impressions which we receive from the external world, so that man is enabled to obtain enlightenment on this lawfulness by means of pure thinking. In this it is of essential significance that the external world represents something independent of ourselves, something absolute that we are

[13] R.T.K., 287.
[14] H. Poincaré, *Dernières Pensées* (Paris, Flamarion), 94.

facing, and the search for the laws that hold for this absolute seem to me the most satisfying task for the life's work of a scientist.[15]

Unlike Einstein, Planck does not see an "unbridgeable gulf" separating the world of sense-experiences from the world of concepts. For him there *is* a bridge, i.e., the Kantian solution. When Planck says that our laws of thinking coincide with[16] the lawfulness in the course of sense-impressions, it is obvious that he thinks of Kant's forms of intuition and concepts of pure understanding as bridging the gulf, and therewith guaranteeing the comprehensibility of the external world. The reality of the external world is presupposed as absolute and independent of ourselves.

This is very different from the views of Einstein, who in all his writings starts his fundamental considerations not with the "reality of the external world," whose existence is a problem he does not discuss, but with our sense-experiences. Nevertheless, Einstein's statement: "All knowledge about reality begins with experience and terminates in it," is exactly in agreement with Planck's philosophy (and with Kant's), viz., with the idea of a logically formed coherent physical theory based on experience, which theory has to stand the test of verification when its results are confronted by the facts of experience.

Very important in Einstein's presuppositions is the notion of simplicity, imposed as a condition on the formation of a basis, and, on the deduction from this basis, of a logical theory of physics. This simplicity is to be understood as including the reduction in number of the logically independent basic elements, i.e., concepts and fundamental hypotheses, and is generally agreed upon as a goal of all scientific theory. The logically simpler is not always the mathematically simpler. The essential point is that for a physical theory a type of mathematics be chosen which allows of the description of a coherent theory consistent as a whole. It sometimes appears as if Einstein were identifying a purely logical with a purely mathematical derivation. I do not think that he does so in the sense Leibniz did— or did at least in theory. Leibniz's theory of pure logic as *ars*

[15] M. Planck, *Wissenschaftliche Selbstbiographie* (Leipzig, 1948, J. A. Barth).
[16] Or: are identical with (*stimmen überein*).

demonstrandi et ars inveniendi, being capable of embracing the whole of mathematics and providing the means for mathematical progress by logical analytical methods only, excludes all synthetic, all intuitional aspects, and was not practised by himself, as can easily be shown, e.g., in his "synthetic" approach to the problem which led him to his invention of the differential calculus.

In contrast to this, Einstein's achievements seem to have been attained by means of exactly those methods which he described as the appropriate methods of theoretical physics: the physical world is represented as a four-dimensional continuum, a Riemannian metric is adopted, and, in looking for the "simplest" laws which such a metric can satisfy, he arrives at his relativistic theory of gravitation of empty space. Adopting in this space a vector field, or the antisymmetrical tensor field derived from it, and looking again for the "simplest" laws which such a field can satisfy he arrives at the Maxwell equations for free space. He also states that in the paucity of the mathematically existent field types, and of the relations between them, lies the hope of comprehending "reality in its depth."[17]

Simplicity and comprehensiveness are actualized in the theory of relativity in a most impressive way: the general theory includes the special theory for the special limiting case of $g_{\mu\nu}$ = const. The form of the laws of nature must be covariant with respect to arbitrary transformations, and the tensor analysis makes such a formulation possible. The immense heuristic value embodied in this postulate of general covariance is obvious; it restricts the possible laws of nature to those that satisfy the covariance condition.[18]

[17] M.T.P., 14.

[18] Theoretically, it is possible to express all laws of nature in covariant form (cf. E. Kretschmann, *Ann. Phys.*, v. 53, 1917, n. 16, and A. Einstein, *Ann. Phys.*, v. 55, 1918, n. 4). Therefore covariance in itself provides no sufficient criterion for the admissibility of an equation as expression of a law of nature. Combined, however, with the conditions of simplicity and, of course, of compatibility with experience, the principle of covariance has its great heuristic value, as Einstein's derivation of the gravitation law demonstrated clearly enough. In case there were two theoretical systems "possible," i.e., both compatible with experience, the selec-

Also, the unity built on the paucity of independent assumptions is reached in relativity theory as never before. After having discarded the inconsistent concept of a stationary ether, and after having replaced Lorentz's *ad hoc* invented hypothesis of contraction by the relativistic interpretation, Einstein was, as shown above, guided throughout by the ideal of mathematical simplicity and of an epistemologically satisfying unification. He felt, for instance, not satisfied with having to introduce into the equations the cosmological constant λ, which seemed to disturb the logical coherence and homogeneity of the system. That is why he welcomed every suggestion[19] which promised a way out of the dilemma, as, e.g., Friedmann's assumption of a spherical space with a radius varying with time, avoiding the unsatisfactory λ.

The fundamental assumptions of physical theory and the consequences of such theory to be tested by experiment are separated by a gap widening progressively with the unification of the logical structure. This drifting away from phenomenological physics, this loss of closeness to experience for the sake of greater comprehensiveness and unity, can be seen in the whole development of modern physics. In general relativity, for instance, the four co-ordinates by themselves had no longer any direct physical meaning, they were only mathematical symbols, and the theory obtained its physical foundation by the introduction of the invariant infinitesimal distance $ds^2 = \sum_{\mu,\nu=1}^{4} g_{\mu\nu} dx_\mu dx_\nu$ The remoteness from experience, however, of the theory, which in its unity and comprehensiveness has surpassed the fondest

tion would have to be guided by the covariance principle, in preferring the system which is simpler (from the viewpoint of the absolute differential calculus). "Someone should just try to formulate the Newtonian mechanics of gravitation in the form of absolutely covariant equations (four-dimensional), and he will certainly be convinced, that the principle (of covariance) excludes this theory practically, even if not theoretically!" (Einstein, *loc. cit.*) From the epistemological point of view, the covariant form is natural for a law of nature, because it expresses its independence of any frame of reference, and excludes all laws that appear simple only when a special co-ordinate system is used. In contrast to P. W. Bridgman (*The Nature of Physical Theory*, 81), I feel that the principle of covariance is very important.

[19] *Berl. Preuss. Akad. Wiss., Berlin,* 16.4.1931; and *The Meaning of Relativity,* 3 ed. (London, 1946, Methuen & Co.), 106-107.

expectations of physicists, has not impeded its verifiability.

Planck, too, like Einstein, pointed to the remarkable, and at first sight paradoxical, fact that the physical world picture is becoming more and more perfect, in spite of its continuously growing distance from the world of senses. But Planck insisted that the only reasonable interpretation of this fact was that: "The increasing distance of the physical world picture from the world of senses means nothing but a progressive approach to the real world." He added that there was no possibility of proving this opinion by logic, since not even the existence of the real world could be logically proved.[20] The difference in Einstein's and Planck's attitudes is obvious, although as physicists they are in complete agreement, so that a logically unified theory, and its significance to the world of senses, have the same meaning for both of them.

The axiomatic basis of such a theory, i.e., the fundamental concepts and the relations between them, should be as narrow as possible, freely selected, but with a view to parsimony. The freedom, however,

is not much of a freedom, it is not like the freedom of a fiction writer, but rather like that of a person who has to solve a cleverly-designed word-puzzle. He may suggest any word as a solution, but there is probably only *o n e* which really solves the puzzle in all its parts. That nature . . . has the character of such a well designed puzzle is a faith which is, however, to a certain extent encouraged by the successes of science up to date.[21]

If we were to assume Planck's viewpoint, we should say: a condition of finding a solution at all is that the person who tries to solve the puzzle uses the same laws of thinking in accordance with which the puzzle was designed.

Einstein's analogy suggests that he sees the final aim of physics in an approach to the unique solution, that of a unified and most comprehensive theory, and one which, we know, should be of the greatest possible logical simplicity. Einstein feels that "experience will guide us aright" and that "there is a correct path and, moreover, that it is in our power to find

[20] M. Planck, *Wege zur physikalischen Erkenntnis*, 2. Aufl. (Leipzig, 1934, S. Hirzel), 184.
[21] P.R., 318.

it;" he also speaks of feeling sure that "in nature is actualized the ideal of mathematical simplicity," and that "pure mathematical construction enables us to discover the concepts and the laws connecting them which give us the key to the understanding of the phenomena of nature." He stresses that an agreement with experience remains "the sole criterion of the serviceability of a mathematical construction for physics," a view generally agreed upon; and—perhaps not so unanimously agreed upon—that "the truly creative principle resides in mathematics," so that he can say: "In a certain sense, therefore, I hold it to be true that pure thought is competent to comprehend the real, as the ancients dreamed."[22] These words are almost identical with Planck's;[23] but, whereas "pure thinking" for Planck includes the Kantian solution and its *a priori* with its necessity and universality, the same words have a different meaning for Einstein. The "pure thought" to which he refers is to be understood as "mathematical thinking;" and the understanding of the phenomena of nature, viz., comprehending the real, refers to nature in which the ideal of mathematical simplicity is actualized. However, Einstein emphasizes that mathematical concepts contain "nothing of the certainty, of the inherent necessity, which Kant had attributed to them."[24]

Einstein's ideas of a complete and unified theory have led to an exciting controversy on the significance of the physical world picture provided by quantum mechanics, a controversy which, I am sure, will be discussed by other contributors to this volume. I shall, therefore, only briefly mention a few points in so far as they reveal Einstein's anticipations concerning the future development of physics.

His criterion for the reality of a physical quantity is "the possibility of predicting it with certainty without disturbing the system."[25] In quantum mechanics, there is no possibility of such prediction of complementary quantities. Quite apart from this "incompleteness" and from the statistical character

[22] M.T.P., 13.
[23] Cf. fn. 15 above.
[24] R.T.K., 285.
[25] A. Einstein, B. Podolsky, N. Rosen, *Phys. Rev.* (v. 47, 1935), 777.

of the laws, quite apart from the influence of the measuring process on the measured system, Einstein feels that quantum mechanics is *not* likely to furnish the *basis* of a complete theory for the whole of physics,—though it may be deducible from this basis—, because of the fact that the ψ-function does not describe the happenings in a single system, but relates to an ensemble of systems only. He also stresses the point that the relative independence of spatially distant things should be maintained, if possible, in all its consequences (without admitting action-at-a-distance), as it is carried out most consistently in the field theory, otherwise "the existence of (quasi-)closed systems, and therewith the setting up of laws to be tested empirically in the usual sense, would be made impossible."[26]

In contrast to Bohr, who claims that quantum theory—seen from the viewpoint of complementarity—appears as "a completely rational description of physical phenomena," and thinks that "a radical revision of our attitude as regards physical reality"[27] is needed, Einstein regards this description as incomplete, and anticipates that a comprehensive unified field theory may finally include a satisfactory explanation of quantum phenomena. His aim is a theory which represents "events themselves and not merely the probability of their occurrence,"[28] and he expressed[29] the opinion that there may be a chance of solving the quantum puzzle without having to renounce the representation of "reality."

The existence of empirically observed and calculated constants of nature, and the numerical agreement between the results of observations and calculations of such constants,—even if arrived at by widely diverging methods—, provides a strong support for the belief in the lawfulness of nature, and therewith for the hope of its comprehensibility. The endeavour to form the basis and the methods of physical theories in conformity with the law of parsimony may lead us to expect the same tendency with respect to the universal constants of na-

[26] "Quantenmechanik und Wirklichkeit," *Dialectica*, v. 2 (1948), n. 3/4, 322.
[27] N. Bohr, *Phys. Rev.*, v. 48 (1935), 702; also: *Dialectica, loc. cit.*, 313.
[28] M.T.P., 15.
[29] In a letter to the author, March 1944.

ture; attempts to follow up this line of thought have actually been made. Very important problems are linked up with the nature and the significance of these constants.

Planck, in accordance with his ideas of reality, regarded the universal constants, e.g., the gravitational constant, the velocity of light, the masses and charges of protons and electrons, as "the most tangible signs of a real world," which also keep their significance as "foundation stones," (together with the conservation laws of energy and impulse, the second principle of thermodynamics, and the principle of relativity) in the new world picture into which the new universal constant, his elementary quantum of action, entered as "a mysterious messenger from the real world."[30] Planck's opinion concerning the possibility of finding connections between the universal constants was: "it is without doubt an attractive idea to link them up as closely as possible, by reducing them to a single one. I myself, however, doubt that this endeavour will be successful. But I may be mistaken."[31]

The idea of deducing the constants of nature in a purely epistemological way had been expressed by Eddington in his earlier writings and was mathematically treated in his *Fundamental Theory*.[32] I do not feel competent to judge whether his efforts to carry out his certainly fascinating, though somewhat fantastic, plans were successful.

Einstein's anticipations as to the constants of nature and the rôle they may play in the structure of a unified theory are very different indeed. In reply to some questions, he expressed his views. I should like to emphasize, however, that the communications I am here permitted [by Einstein] to use should by no means be taken as categorical statements, but only as conjectures based merely on intuition.

Einstein begins with the elimination of conventional units; in order to arrive at dimensionless constants he proceeds in the following way: Let there be a *complete* theory of physics in whose fundamental equations the "universal" constants

[30] Cf. fn. 20 above, 187.
[31] Letter from Planck to the author, dated: 30.3.1947.
[32] Cambridge, 1946, University Press.

c_1 .... c_n appear. The quantities shall somehow be reduced to gr.cm.sec. The choice of these three units is evidently completely a matter of convention. Each of the c_1 ... (which Einstein, in another letter, called "apparent" constants) has a dimension in these units. We now will choose conditions so that c_1, c_2, c_3 have such dimensions that it is not possible to build from these c_1, c_2, c_3 a dimensionless product $c_1{}^\alpha$, $c_2{}^\beta$, $c_3{}^\gamma$. Then we can multiply c_4, c_5, etc., in such a way, by factors built from powers of c_1, c_2, c_3, that these new symbols c_4^*, c_5^*, c_6^* are pure numbers. These are the genuine (*eigentlichen*) universal constants of the theoretical system, which have nothing to do with conventional units.

Einstein now expects that these constants c_4^*, etc. must be rational (*rationelle*) numbers whose values are established by the logical foundation of the whole theory. As rational (*rationell*) he regards such numbers

which appear in some sense with necessity in the logical evolution of mathematics as unique individual formations, as e.g.,

$$e = 1 + 1 + \tfrac{1}{2!} + \tfrac{1}{3!} + \cdots$$

It is the same with π, which indeed is closely connected with e. In contrast to such rational numbers are the remaining numbers which are not derived from 1 by means of a clear construction.

There follow more remarks about such rational numbers, as far as they are "simple," resp. "natural" formations. Einstein characterizes these remarks as not fundamental; they may, however, be taken as further proof of his desire for simplicity in physical theory.

He expressed his anticipations concerning the true universal constants c_4^* ... , also in the following way: "In a reasonable theory, there are no (dimensionless) numbers whose values are only empirically determinable." He stressed again, however, that he, naturally, has no proof for this, but that he could not imagine a unified and reasonable theory explicitly to contain a number which the mood of the creator could just as well have chosen differently, whereby a world of a qualitatively different lawfulness would have resulted.[33] Or, in other words: a theory which in its fundamental equations would explicitly contain a non-rational constant would have to be built up from logically independent bits and pieces. But Einstein is confident that "this world is not such as to make such an 'ugly' construction necessary for its theoretical comprehension. Of course, up to now there is no consistent theoretical foundation for the whole of physics, and still less a foundation satisfying such a radical postulation." Einstein's main concern is not merely that of overcoming the mathematical difficulties in finding the field equations for such a comprehensive theory, but—true to his whole scientific attitude—it is his desire to arrive at verifiable consequences.

From all that has been stated it may be gathered that Einstein regards the significance of the constants of nature as fundamental; and I think I have understood him correctly when I assume that a really complete unified field theory would have to provide the possibility of finding these constants mathematically. In such a generalized general theory of relativity a definite solution of the field equations would have to give information about all details of the atomic arrangement in a space lattice; and again, a solution would have to correspond to the frequency in an H-atom. In that way it should be possible to derive, for instance, the velocity of light mathematically from the field equations.

Presuppositions and anticipations in science are not—in the first instance, certainly—open to experimental or logical proof. The faith, the endeavour, and the expectations, as they manifest themselves in the basis, the methods, and the aim of physical science, are grounded in a personal philosophy which transcends the sphere of science itself. The deep satisfaction found in scientific work, akin to the delight derived from

[33] Einstein letter to the author, dated: 13.10.1945. The last sentence refers probably to Kant's remarks that God could have chosen a different law of gravitation, with, e.g., inverse proportionality to the third power, and that from such a law a space of different properties and dimensions would have resulted. Details about this first hint at a connection between physics and geometry, cf. Ilse Schneider, *Das Raum-Zeit-Problem bei Kant und Einstein* (Berlin, 1921, J. Springer), 69.

genuine art, is one of the fundamental human emotions which is highly intensified by personal contact with the creative mind.

I feel extremely grateful, therefore, for having been privileged not only to attend Einstein's regular lectures, but also to have had the opportunity very frequently of discussing scientific problems with him. He was at all times ready to listen patiently to questions and to answer them in detail. I shall never forget the animating hours when, together, we were reading a book full of objections to his theory, or the humorous remarks with which he had adorned the book. I am conscious that, like so many others, I shall never be able to express my gratitude in an adequate way; but I hope that my small contribution to this volume will show my great indebtedness to him.

ILSE ROSENTHAL-SCHNEIDER

THE UNIVERSITY OF SYDNEY
SYDNEY, AUSTRALIA

4

Wolfgang Pauli

EINSTEIN'S CONTRIBUTIONS TO QUANTUM THEORY

4

EINSTEIN'S CONTRIBUTIONS TO QUANTUM THEORY

IF NEW features of the phenomena of nature are discovered that are incompatible with the system of theories assumed at that time, the question arises, which of the known principles used in the description of nature are general enough to comprehend the new situation and which have to be modified or abandoned. The attitude of different physicists on a problem of this kind, which makes strong demands on the intuition and tact of a scientist, depends to some extent on the personal temperament of the investigator. In the case of Planck's discovery in 1900 of the quantum of action during the course of his famous investigations of the law of the black-body radiation, it was clear that Boltzmann's principle connecting entropy and probability, and the law of the conservation of energy and momentum were two pillars sufficiently strong to stand unshaken by the development resulting from the new discovery. It was indeed the faithfulness to these principles which enabled Planck to introduce the new constant h, the quantum of action, into his statistical theory of the thermodynamic equilibrium of radiation.

The earlier work of Planck, however, had treated only with a certain discretion the question whether the new "quantum-hypothesis" implied the necessity of changing the laws of microscopic phenomena themselves independent of statistical applications, or whether one had to use only an improvement of the statistical method to enumerate equally probable states. In any case, the tendency towards a compromise between the older ideas of physics, now called the "classical" ones, and the quantum theory was always favored by Planck, both in his earlier and later work on the subject, although such a possibility had diminished considerably the significance of his own discovery.

This was the background of Einstein's first paper* on quantum theory [1], which was preceded by his papers on the fundamentals of statistical mechanics[1] and accompanied, in the same year 1905, by his other fundamental papers on the theory of the Brownian movement[2] and the theory of relativity.[3] In this and subsequent papers [2, 3, 4b], Einstein clarified and strengthened the thermodynamical arguments underlying Planck's theory so much that he was able to draw definite conclusions on the microscopic phenomena themselves. He gave to Boltzmann's equation between entropy S and "probability" W

$$S = k \log W + \text{constant} \tag{1}$$

a definite physical meaning by defining W for a given state, as the relative duration in which this state (which may deviate more or less from the state of thermodynamical equilibrium) is realized in a closed system with a given value of its energy (time-ensemble). Hence, Boltzmann's relation is not only a definition of W, but also gives a connection between quantities which are in principle observable. For instance, one obtains for the mean value of the square of the energy-fluctuation ε of a small partial volume of a closed system, as a consequence of (1), the expression

$$\overline{\varepsilon^2} = k \left[- \left(\frac{\partial^2 S}{\partial E^2} \right)_{T,V} \right]^{-1} = k T^2 \left(\frac{\partial E}{\partial T} \right)_V \tag{2}$$

where T is the temperature and E the average energy (we disregard here the complication of the formula due to density fluctuations, because it is absent in the case of radiation). This relation must hold independent of the theoretical model of

---

* EDITOR'S NOTE: All numerals appearing in brackets [ ] in this paper refer to Einstein's papers, dealing with the quantum theory, appearing under equivalent numbers at the close of this paper. *Ed.*

[1] Ann. Phys. (4) *9*, 417 (1902); *11*, 170 (1903); *14*, 354 (1904).

[2] Ann. Phys. (4) *17*, 549 (1905).

[3] Ann. Phys. (4) *17*, 891 (1905).

the system. If the energy of a system as a function of the temperature is empirically known, the model has to be in accordance with the fluctuation computed with help of equation (2) and inversely, the assumption of such a theoretical model prescribes the choice of states supposed to be equally probable in Boltzmann's relation (1). For the mean square of the energy fluctuation of the part of the radiation within the frequency interval $(v, v + dv)$, in the small partial volume V of a hole filled with radiation in thermodynamical equilibrium, Planck's radiation formula gives, according to (2), the expression, first derived by Einstein [4b]

$$\overline{\epsilon^2} = h\nu E + \frac{c^3}{8\pi\nu^2 d\nu} \frac{E^2}{V} \tag{3}$$

if E is the mean energy of the radiation in V of the frequency interval in question. Whereas the second term can easily be interpreted with help of the classical wave theory as due to the interferences between the partial waves,[4] the first term is in obvious contradiction to classical electrodynamics. It can, however, be interpreted by analogy to the fluctuations of the number of molecules in ideal gases with the help of the picture that the energy of radiation stays concentrated in limited regions of space in energy amounts $h\nu$, which behave like independent particles, called "light-quanta" or "photons."

As one was reluctant to apply statistical methods to the radiation itself, Einstein also considered the Brownian motion of a mirror which perfectly reflects radiation in the frequency interval $(v, v + dv)$, but transmits for all other frequencies, [4b]. If Pv is the frictional force corresponding to the velocity v of the mirror normal to its surface, Einstein's general theory of the Brownian movement gives, for the irregular change of the momentum of the mirror in the normal direction during the time interval τ, the statistical relation.

$$\overline{\Delta^2} = 2Pm\overline{v^2}\tau = 2PkT\tau \tag{4}$$

[4] For a quantitative computation, see H. A. Lorentz "Théories statistiques en thermodynamiques," Leipzig 1916, Appendix No. IX.

since $m\overline{v^2} = kT$ (m is the mass of the mirror). One first computes P according to the usual wave theory as given by

$$P = \frac{3}{2c}\left(\rho - \frac{1}{3}\nu\frac{\partial\rho}{\partial\nu}\right)d\nu\cdot f \qquad (5)$$

where $\rho d\nu$ is the radiative energy in the unit of volume of the frequency interval, $(\nu, \nu + d\nu)$ considered, and f the surface of the mirror. Inserting (5) into (4), and using Planck's formula, one obtains

$$\frac{\overline{\Delta^2}}{\tau} = \frac{1}{c}\left[h\nu\rho + \frac{c^3}{8\pi\nu^2}\rho^2\right]d\nu\cdot f \qquad (6)$$

This formula is very closely connected with (3), since using $E = \rho d\nu V$ one has

$$\frac{\overline{\Delta^2}}{\tau} = \frac{1}{c}f\frac{\overline{\epsilon^2}}{V} \qquad (6a)$$

Just as in (3), it is only the last term in (6) which can be explained by the classical wave theory, whereas the first term can be interpreted with the picture of corpuscular light-quanta of the energy $h\nu$ and the momentum $h\nu/c$ in the direction of their propagation.

We have to add two remarks. 1°) If one starts with the simplified law of Wien for the black-body radiation, which holds for $h\nu \gg kT$, only the first term in (3) is obtained. 2°) In his first paper [1], Einstein computed for the region of validity of Wien's law, with help of a direct application of equation (1), the probability of the rare state in which the entire radiation energy is contained in a certain partial volume (instead of considering the mean square of the energy fluctuation). Also in this case he could interpret the results with the help of the above mentioned picture of corpuscular "light-quanta."

In this way Einstein was led to his famous "light-quantum hypothesis," which he immediately applied to the photoelectric effect and to Stockes' law for fluorescence [1], later also to the generation of secondary cathode rays by X-rays [5] and to the prediction of the high frequency limit in the *Bremsstrah-*

lung [9]. All this is so well known today that it is hardly necessary to go into a detailed discussion of these consequences. We are only briefly recalling that, by this earlier work of Einstein, it became clear that the existence of the quantum of action implies a radical change in the laws governing microphenomena. In the case of radiation, this change is expressed in the contrast between the use of the particle picture and the wave picture for different phenomena.

The consequences of Planck's theory, that material harmonic oscillators with the *eigen*frequency v can only have discrete energy values, given by integral multiples of *h*v [2], was also successfully applied by Einstein to the theory of the specific heat of solids [3]. Methodically it has to be pointed out that on this occasion Einstein for the first time applied the simpler method of the canonical ensemble to the derivation of the free energy and the mean energy of such oscillators as a function of the temperature, whereas in the earlier papers of Planck the entropy as a function of the energy was calculated with aid of Boltzmann's method in which the microcanonic ensemble is used. Regarding the physical content of the theory, it was obvious that the assumption of only a single value of the frequency of the oscillators in the solid body could not be correct. In connection with Madelung[5] and Sutherland's[6] discovery of a relation between the assumed value of this frequency and the elastic properties of the solid, this problem was discussed in several subsequent papers of Einstein [7, 8, 9], among which Einstein's report at the Solvay Congress in 1911 is most interesting, since it was given after the establishment of the empirical formula of Nernst and Lindemann for the thermal energy of solids and just before the problem was solved theoretically by Born and Karman[7] and independently, by Debye.[8] It may be considered as rather strange today that these later theories were not found much earlier, all the more since the method of *eigen*vibrations was applied to the black-body radiation from the standpoint of the classical theory much

[5] J. Madelung, Phys. ZS. *11*, 898 (1910).

[6] W. Sutherland, Phil. Mag. (6) *20*, 657 (1910).

[7] M. Born and Th. van Karman, Phys. ZS. *13*, 297 (1912).

[8] P. Debye, Ann. Phys. (4) *39*, 789 (1912).

earlier by Rayleigh and Jeans. One has to bear in mind, however, that until then no general rule for determining the discrete energy values of states had been found and also that physicists wre rather hesitant to apply quantum laws to objects so widely extended in space as a proper vibration.

Einstein's report on the constitution of radiation at the physics meeting in Salzburg [5] in 1909, where he appeared before a larger audience for the first time, can be considered as one of the landmarks in the development of theoretical physics. It deals with both special relativity and quantum theory and contains the important conclusion that the elementary process must be directed (needle radiation) not only for absorption, but also for emission of radiation, although this postulate was in open conflict with the classical idea of emission in a spherical wave, which is indispensable for the understanding of the coherence properties of radiation, as they appear in interference experiments. Einstein's postulate of a directed emission process has been further supported by strong thermodynamical arguments in his subsequent work. In papers published with L. Hopf [6] (which later also caused an interesting discussion with von Laue [12] on the degree of disorder in the "black" radiation) he could extend the earlier work on the fluctuations of momentum of a mirror under the influence of a radiation field to the corresponding momentum fluctuations of a harmonic oscillator. In this way, it was possible, at least for this particular system which played such an important rôle in Planck's original theory, to compute the translatory motion in equilibrium with the surrounding radiation, besides their oscillating motion which had been treated much earlier by Planck. The result was disappointing for those who still had the vain hope of deriving Planck's radiation formula by merely changing the statistical assumption rather than by a fundamental break with the classical ideas regarding the elementary microphenomena themselves: The classical computation of the fluctuation of momentum of an harmonic oscillator in its interaction with a radiation field is only compatible with the wellknown value $3/2 \ kT$ for its kinetic energy in thermodynamic equilibrium, if the radiation field fulfills the classical law of

Rayleigh-Jeans instead of the law of Planck. If inversely the latter law is assumed, the fluctuation of momentum of the oscillators must be due to irregularities in the radiation field, which have to be much larger than the classical ones for a small density of the radiation energy.

With Bohr's successful application of quantum theory to the explanation of the line spectra of the elements with help of his well-known two "fundamental postulates of quantum theory" (1913), a rapid development started, in the course of which the quantum theory was liberated from the restriction to such particular systems as Planck's oscillators.

Therefore the problem arose of deriving Planck's radiation formula using general assumptions holding for all atomic systems in accordance with Bohr's postulates. This problem was solved by Einstein in 1917 in a famous paper [13] which can be considered as the peak of one stage of Einstein's achievements in quantum theory (see also [10] and [11]) and as the ripe fruit of his earlier work on the Brownian movement. With the help of general statistical laws for the spantaneous and induced emission processes and for the absorption processes which are the inverse of the former, he could derive Planck's formula under the assumption of the validity of two general relations between the three co-efficients which determine the frequency of these processes and which, if one of these co-efficients is given, permits the computation of the other two. As these results of Einstein are today contained in all textbooks of quantum theory, it is hardly necessary to discuss here the details of this theory and its later generalization to more complicated radiation processes [15]. Besides this derivation of Planck's formula, the same paper discusses also the exchange of momentum between the atomic system and the radiation in a definite and very general way, using again equation (4) of the theory of the Brownian movement, which connects the mean square of the exchange of momentum in a certain time interval and the friction force Pv. The latter can be computed, using the general assumption indicated by both experience and classical electrodynamics that the absorption or emission of light induced from pencils with different directions are independent of each other.[9] The condition (4) is then fulfilled in Planck's radiation field, only if the spontaneous emission is assumed to be directed in such a way that for every elementary process of radiation an amount $h\nu/c$ of momentum is emitted in a random direction and that the atomic system suffers a corresponding recoil in the opposite direction. The latter consequence was later confirmed experimentally by Frisch.[10]

Insufficient attention has been paid, according to the author's opinion, to Einstein's own critical judgement of the fundamental rôle ascribed to "chance" in this description of the radiation processes by statistical laws. We are therefore quoting the following passage from the end of his paper of 1917:

Die Schwäche der Theorie liegt einerseits darin, dass sie uns dem Anschluss an die Undulationstheorie nicht näher bringt, andererseits darin, dass sie Zeit und Richtung der Elementarprozesse dem „Zufall" überlässt; trotzdem hege ich das volle Vertrauen in die Zuverlässigkeit des eingeschlagenen Weges.[11]

The contrast between the interference properties of radiation, for the description of which the superposition principle of the wave theory is indispensable, and the properties of exchange of energy and momentum between radiation and matter, which can only be described with the help of the corpuscular picture, was undiminished and seemed at first to be irreconcilable. As is well known, de Broglie later quantitatively formulated the idea that a similar contrast will appear again with matter. Einstein was very much in favour of this new idea; the author remembers that, in a discussion at the physics meeting in Innsbruck in the autumn of 1924, Einstein proposed to search for interference and diffraction phenomena with molecular beams.[12]

---

[9] Compare to this point the discussion between Einstein and Jordan [16].

[10] R. Frisch, ZS. f. Phys. *86*, 42 (1933).

[11] "The weakness of the theory lies, on the one hand, in the fact that it does not bring us any closer to a merger with the undulatory theory, and, on the other hand, in the fact that it leaves the time and direction of elementary processes to 'chance'; in spite of this I harbor full confidence in the trustworthiness of the path entered upon." (Tr. by the editor.)

[12] Compare in this connection also the earlier discussion by Einstein and Ehrenfest [14] of questions regarding molecular beams.

At the same time, in a paper of S.N. Bose, a derivation of Planck's formula was given, in which only the corpuscular picture, but no wave mechanical concept was used. This inspired Einstein to give an analogous application to the theory of the so-called degeneration of ideal gases [17], now known to describe the thermodynamical properties of a system of particles with symmetrical wave functions (Einstein-Bose statistics). It is interesting that later an attempt was made to apply this theory to liquid helium. The fundamental difference between the statistical properties of like and unlike particles, which is also discussed in the cited papers of Einstein, is connected, according to wave mechanics, with the circumstance that due to Heisenberg's principle of indeterminacy, which belongs to the foundation of the new theory, the possibility of distinguishing between different like particles, with help of the continuity of their motion in space and time, is getting lost. Shortly after Einstein's paper appeared, the thermodynamical consequence of the other alternative of particles with antisymmetric wave functions, which applies to electrons, was discussed in literature ("Fermi-Dirac statistics").

The formulation of quantum mechanics which soon followed the publication of de Broglie's paper was not only decisive, for the first time since Planck's discovery, in establishing again a self-consistent theoretical description of such phenomena in which the quantum of action plays an essential rôle, but it made also possible the achievement of a deeper insight into the general epistemological situation of atomic physics in connection with the point of view termed by Bohr "complementarity."[13] The writer belongs to those physicists who believe that the new epistemological situation underlying quantum mechanics is satisfactory, both from the standpoint of physics and from the broader standpoint of the conditions of human knowledge in general. He regrets that Einstein seems to have a different opinion on this situation; and this all the more, because the new aspect of the description of nature, in contrast to the ideas underlying classical physics, seems to open up hopes for a fu-

[13] An account of Einstein's position during this development is given in the subsequent article of N. Bohr.

ture development of different branches of science towards a greater unity.

Inside physics in the proper sense we are well aware that the present form of quantum mechanics is far from anything final, but, on the contrary, leaves problems open which Einstein considered long ago. In his previously cited paper of 1909 [4b], he stresses the importance of Jeans' remark that the elementary electric charge e, with the help of the velocity of light c, determines the constant e^2/c of the same dimension as the quantum of action h (thus aiming at the now well known fine structure constant $2\pi e^2/hc$). He recalled "that the elementary quantum of electricity e is a stranger in Maxwell-Lorentz' electrodynamics" and expressed the hope that "the same modification of the theory which will contain the elementary quantum e as a consequence, will also have as a consequence the quantum theory of radiation." The reverse certainly turned out to be not true, since the new quantum theory of radiation and matter does not have the value of the elementary electric charge as a consequence, which is still a stranger in quantum mechanics, too.

The theoretical determination of the fine structure constant is certainly the most important of the unsolved problems of modern physics. We believe that any regression to the ideas of classical physics (as, for instance, to the use of the classical field concept) cannot bring us nearer to this goal. To reach it, we shall, presumably, have to pay with further revolutionary changes of the fundamental concepts of physics with a still farther digression from the concepts of the classical theories.

WOLFGANG PAULI

Zürich, Switzerland

List of Einstein's Papers on Quantum Theory Referred to:

1. *Ann. Phys.*, Lpz. (4) *17*, 132 (1905): "Über einen die Erzeugung und Verwandlung des Lichtes betreffenden heuristischen Gesichtspunkt."

2. *Ann. Phys.*, Lpz. (4) *20*, 199 (1906): "Zur Theorie der Lichterzeugung und Lichtabsorption."

3. *Ann. Phys.*, Lpz. (4) 22, 180 and 800 (1907): "Die Planck'sche Theorie der Strahlung und die Theorie der spezifischen Wärme."

4. Discussion with W. Ritz: a) W. Ritz, *Phys. ZS.* 9, 903, (1908) and 10, 224, (1908); b) A. Einstein, *Phys. ZS.* 10, 185, (1909) "Zum gegenwärtigen Stand des Strahlungsproblems." c) W. Ritz and A. Einstein, *Phys. ZS.* 10, 323, (1909) "Zur Aufklärung."

5. *Phys. ZS.* 10, 817, (1909): "Über die Entwicklung unserer Anschauungen über das Wesen und die Konstitution der Strahlung." (Report given at the physics meeting in Salzburg, September 1909).

6. a) A. Einstein and L. Hopf, *Ann. Phys.*, Lpz. 33, 1096, (1910) "Über einen Satz der Wahrscheinlichkeitsrechnung und seine Anwendung in der Quantentheorie" (compare also below, reference 12).
   b) A. Einstein and L. Hopf, *Ann. Phys.*, Lpz. 33, 1105, (1910): "Statistische Untersuchung der Bewegung eines Resonators in einem Strahlungsfeld."

7. *Ann. Phys.*, Lpz. 34, 170 and 590, (1911): "Eine Beziehung zwischen dem elastischen Verhalten und der spezifischen Wärme bei festen Körpern mit einatomigem Molekül."

8. *Ann. Phys.*, Lpz. 35, 679, (1911): "Elementare Betrachtungen über die thermische Molekularbewegung in festen Körpern."

9. *Rapport et discussions de la Réunion Solvay*, 1911: "La théorie du Rayonnement et les Quanta," Paris, 1912. Report by Einstein: "L'état actuel du problème des chaleurs spécifiques."

10. *Ann. Phys.*, Lpz. 37, 832, (1912) and 38, 881 (1912): "Thermodynamische Begründung des photochemischen Aequivalentgesetzes."

11. A. Einstein and O. Stern, *Ann Phys.*, Lpz. 40, 551, (1913): "Einige Argumente für die Annahme einer molekularen Agitation beim absoluten Nullpunkt."

12. Discussion Einstein and v. Laue: a) M. v. Laue, *Ann. Phys.*, Lpz. 47, 853, (1915); b) A. Einstein, *Ann. Phys.*, Lpz. 47, 879, (1915); c) M. v. Laue, *Ann. Phys.*, Lpz. 48, 668, (1915).

13. *Phys. ZS.* 18, 121, (1917) (compare also *Verhandlungen der deutschen physikalischen Gesellschaft*, No. 13/14, 1916): "Zur Quantentheorie der Strahlung."

14. A. Einstein and P. Ehrenfest, *Z. Phys.* 11, 326, (1922): "Quan-

tentheoretische Bemerkungen zum Experiment von Stern und Gerlach."

15. A. Einstein and P. Ehrenfest, Z. *Phys. 19*, 301, (1923): "Zur Quantentheorie des Strahlungsgleichgewichtes." (See also: W. Pauli, Z. *Phys. 18*, 272, 1923).

16. Discussion Jordan-Einstein: a) P. Jordan, Z. *Phys. 30*, 297, (1924). b) A. Einstein, Z. *Phys. 31*, 784, (1925).

17. *Berl. Ber.* (1924), p. 261 and (1925), p. 3 and 18: "Zur Quantumtheorie des einatomigen idealen Gases." (See also: S. N. Bose, Z. *Phys. 26*, 178, 1924 and *27*, 384, 1924).

5

Max Born

EINSTEIN'S STATISTICAL THEORIES

EINSTEIN'S STATISTICAL THEORIES

ONE of the most remarkable volumes in the whole of scientific literature seems to me Vol. 17 (4th series) of *Annalen der Physik*, 1905. It contains three papers by Einstein, each dealing with a different subject, and each to-day acknowledged to be a masterpiece, the source of a new branch of physics. These three subjects, in order of pages, are: theory of photons, Brownian motion, and relativity.

Relativity is the last one, and this shows that Einstein's mind at that time was not completely absorbed by his ideas on space and time, simultaneity and electro-dynamics. In my opinion he would be one of the greatest theoretical physicists of all times even if he had not written a single line on relativity—an assumption for which I have to apologise, as it is rather absurd. For Einstein's conception of the physical world cannot be divided into watertight compartments, and it is impossible to imagine that he should have by-passed one of the fundamental problems of the time.

Here I propose to discuss Einstein's contributions to statistical methods in physics. His publications on this subject can be divided into two groups: an early set of papers deals with classical statistical mechanics, whereas the rest is connected with quantum theory. Both groups are intimately connected with Einstein's philosophy of science. He has seen more clearly than anyone before him the statistical background of the laws of physics, and he was a pioneer in the struggle for conquering the wilderness of quantum phenomena. Yet later, when out of his own work a synthesis of statistical and quantum principles emerged which seemed to be acceptable to almost all physicists, he kept himself aloof and sceptical. Many of us regard this as a tragedy—for him, as he gropes his way in loneliness, and for us who miss our leader and standard-bearer. I shall not try to suggest a resolution of this discord. We have to accept the fact that even in physics fundamental convictions are prior to reasoning, as in all other human activities. It is my task to give an account of Einstein's work and to discuss it from my own philosophical standpoint.

Einstein's first paper of 1902, "Kinetische Theorie des Wärmegleichgewichtes und des zweiten Hauptsatzes der Thermodynamik"[1] is a remarkable example of the fact that when the time is ripe important ideas are developed almost simultaneously by different men at distant places. Einstein says in his introduction that nobody has yet succeeded in deriving the conditions of thermal equilibrium and of the second law of thermodynamics from probability considerations, although Maxwell and Boltzmann came near to it. Willard Gibbs is not mentioned. In fact, Einstein's paper is a re-discovery of all essential features of statistical mechanics and obviously written in total ignorance of the fact that the whole matter had been thoroughly treated by Gibbs a year before (1901). The similarity is quite amazing. Like Gibbs, Einstein investigates the statistical behaviour of a virtual assembly of equal mechanical systems of a very general type. A state of the single system is described by a set of generalised co-ordinates and velocities, which can be represented as a point in a $2n$-dimensional "phase-space;" the energy is given as function of these variables. The only consequence of the dynamical laws used is the theorem of Liouville according to which any domain in the $2n$-dimensional phase-space of all co-ordinates and momenta preserves its volume in time. This law makes it possible to define regions of equal weight and to apply the laws of probability. In fact, Einstein's method is essentially identical with Gibb's theory of canonical assemblies. In a second paper, of the following year, entitled "Eine Theorie der Grundlagen der Thermodynamik,"[2] Einstein builds the theory on another basis not used by Gibbs, namely on the consideration of a single system in course of time (later called "Zeit-Gesammtheit," time

---

[1] *Annalen der Physik* (4), *9*, p. 477, (1902).
[2] *Annalen der Physik* (4), *11*, p. 170, (1903).

assembly), and proves that this is equivalent to a certain virtual assembly of many systems, Gibb's micro-canonical assembly. Finally, he shows that the canonical and micro-canonical distribution lead to the same physical consequences.

Einstein's approach to the subject seems to me slightly less abstract than that of Gibbs. This is also confirmed by the fact that Gibbs made no striking application of his new method, while Einstein at once proceeded to apply his theorems to a case of utmost importance, namely to systems of a size suited for demonstrating the reality of molecules and the correctness of the kinetic theory of matter.

This was the theory of Brownian movement. Einstein's papers on this subject are now easily accessible in a little volume edited and supplied with notes by R. Fürth, and translated into English by A. D. Cowper.[3] In the first paper (1905) he sets out to show "that, according to the molecular-kinetic theory of heat, bodies of microscopically visible size suspended in a liquid will perform movements of such magnitude that they can be easily observed in a microscope, on account of the molecular motion of heat," and he adds that these movements are possibly identical with the "Brownian motion" though his information about the latter is too vague to form a definite judgment.

The fundamental step taken by Einstein was the idea of raising the kinetic theory of matter from a possible, plausible, useful hypothesis to a matter of observation, by pointing out cases where the molecular motion and its statistical character can be made visible. It was the first example of a phenomenon of thermal fluctuations, and his method is the classical paradigma for the treatment of all of them. He regards the movement of the suspended particles as a process of diffusion under the action of osmotic pressure and other forces, among which friction due to the viscosity of the liquid is the most important one. The logical clue to the understanding of the phenomenon consists in the statement that the actual velocity of the suspended particle, produced by the impacts of the molecules of the liquid on it, is unobservable; the visible effect in a finite interval of

[3] *Investigations on the Theory of the Brownian Movement;* Methuen & Co., London, (1926).

time τ consists of irregular displacements, the probability of which satisfies a differential equation of the same type as the equation of diffusion. The diffusion coefficient is nothing but the mean square of the displacement divided by 2τ. In this way Einstein obtained his celebrated law expressing the mean square displacement for τ in terms of measurable quantities (temperature, radius of the particle, viscosity of the liquid) and of the number of molecules in a gramme-molecule (Avogadro's number N). By its simplicity and clarity this paper is a classic of our science.

In the second paper (1906) Einstein refers to the work of Siedentopf (Jena) and Gouy (Lyons) who convinced themselves by observations that the Brownian motion was in fact caused by the thermal agitation of the molecules of the liquid, and from this moment on he takes it for granted that the "irregular motion of suspended particles" predicted by him is identical with the Brownian motion. This and the following publications are devoted to the working out of details (e.g., rotatory Brownian motion) and presenting the theory in other forms; but they contain nothing essentially new.

I think that these investigations of Einstein have done more than any other work to convince physicists of the reality of atoms and molecules, of the kinetic theory of heat, and of the fundamental part of probability in the natural laws. Reading these papers one is inclined to believe that at that time the statistical aspect of physics was preponderant in Einstein's mind; yet at the same time he worked on relativity where rigorous causality reigns. His conviction seems always to have been, and still is to-day, that the ultimate laws of nature are causal and deterministic, that probability is used to cover our ignorance if we have to do with numerous particles, and that only the vastness of this ignorance pushes statistics into the fore-front.

Most physicists do not share this view to-day, and the reason for this is the development of quantum theory. Einstein's contribution to this development is great. His first paper of 1905, mentioned already, is usually quoted for the interpretation of the photo-electric effect and similar phenomena (Stokes law of photo-luminescence, photo-ionisation) in terms of light-quanta (light-darts, photons). As a matter of fact, the main argument of Einstein is again of a statistical nature, and the phenomena just mentioned are used in the end for confirmation. This statistical reasoning is very characteristic of Einstein, and produces the impression that for him the laws of probability are central and by far more important than any other law. He starts with the fundamental difference between an ideal gas and a cavity filled with radiation: the gas consists of a finite number of particles, while radiation is described by a set of functions in space, hence by an infinite number of variables. This is the root of the difficulty of explaining the law of black body radiation; the monochromatic density of radiation turns out to be proportional to the absolute temperature (later known as the law of Rayleigh-Jeans) with a factor independent of frequency, and therefore the total density becomes infinite. In order to avoid this, Planck (1900) had introduced the hypothesis that radiation consists of quanta of finite size. Einstein, however, does not use Planck's radiation law, but the simpler law of Wien, which is the limiting case for low radiation density, expecting rightly that here the corpuscular character of the radiation will be more evident. He shows how one can obtain the entropy S of black body radiation from a given radiation law (monochromatic density as function of frequency) and applies then Boltzmann's fundamental relation between entropy S and thermodynamic probability W

$$S = k \log W$$

where k is the gas constant per molecule, for determining W. This formula was certainly meant by Boltzmann to express the physical quantity S in terms of the combinatory quantity W, obtained by counting all possible configurations of the atomistic elements of the statistical ensemble. Einstein inverts this process: he starts from the known function S in order to obtain an expression for the probability which can be used as a clue to the interpretation of the statistical elements. (The same trick has been applied by him later in his work on fluctuations;[4] although this is of considerable practical importance,

[4] *Annalen der Physik* (4), *19*, p. 373, (1906).

I shall only mention it, since it introduces no new fundamental concept apart from that "inversion.")

Substituting the entropy derived from Wien's law into Boltzmann's formula, Einstein obtains for the probability of finding the total energy E by chance compressed in a fraction αV of the total volume V

$$W = \alpha^{E/\mathrm{hv}}$$

that means, the radiation behaves as if it consisted of independent quanta of energy of size and number $\mathrm{n} = E/\mathrm{hv}$. It is obvious from the text of the paper that this result had an overwhelming power of conviction for Einstein, and that it led him to search for confirmation of a more direct kind. This he found in the physical phenomena mentioned above (e.g., photoelectric effect) whose common feature is the exchange of energy between an electron and light. The impression produced on the experimentalists by these discoveries was very great. For the facts were known to many, but not correlated. At that time Einstein's gift for intuiting such correlations was almost uncanny. It was based on a thorough knowledge of experimental facts combined with a profound understanding of the present state of theory, which enabled him to see at once where something strange was happening. His work at that period was essentially empirical in method, though directed to building up a consistent theory—in contrast to his later work when he was more and more led by philosophical and mathematical ideas.

A second example of the application of this method is the work on specific heat.[5] It started again with a theoretical consideration of that type which provided the strongest evidence in Einstein's mind, namely on statistics. He remarks that Planck's radiation formula can be understood by giving up the continuous distribution of statistical weight in the phase-space which is a consequence of Liouville's theorem of dynamics; instead, for vibrating systems of the kind used as absorbers and emitters in the theory of radiation most states have a vanishing statistical weight and only a selected number (whose energies are multiples of a quantum) have finite weights.

[5] "Die Planck'sche Theorie der Strahlung und die Theorie der specifischen Wärme," *Annalen der Physik* (4), 22, p. 180, (1907).

Now if this is so, the quantum is not a feature of radiation but of general physical statistics, and should therefore appear in other phenomena where vibrators are involved. This argument was obviously the moving force in Einstein's mind, and it became fertile by his knowledge of facts and his unfailing judgment of their bearing on the problem. I wonder whether he knew that there were solid elements for which the specific heat per mole was lower than its normal value 5.94 calories, given by the law of Dulong-Petit, or whether he first had the theory and then scanned the tables to find examples. The law of Dulong-Petit is a direct consequence of the law of equipartition of classical statistical mechanics, which states that each co-ordinate or momentum contributing a quadratic term to the energy should carry the same average energy, namely $\frac{1}{2} RT$ per mole where R is the gas constant; as R is a little less than 2 calories per degree and an oscillator has 3 co-ordinates and 3 momenta, the energy of one mole of a solid element per degree of temperature should be $6 \times \frac{1}{2}RT$, or 5.94 calories. If there are substances for which the experimental value is essentially lower, as it actually is for carbon (diamond), boron, silicon, one has a contradiction between facts and classical theory. Another such contradiction is provided by some substances with poly-atomic molecules. Drude had proved by optical experiments that the atoms in these molecules were performing oscillations about each other; hence the number of vibrating units per molecule should be higher than 6 and therefore the specific heat higher than the Dulong-Petit value—but that is not always the case. Moreover Einstein could not help wondering about the contribution of the electrons to the specific heat. At that time vibrating electrons in the atom were assumed for explaining the ultra-violet absorption; they did apparently not contribute to the specific heat, in contradiction to the equipartition law.

All these difficulties were at once swept away by Einstein's suggestion that the atomic oscillators do not follow the equipartition law, but the same law which leads to Planck's radiation formula. Then the mean energy would not be proportional to the absolute temperature but decrease more quickly with falling temperature in a way which still depends on the frequencies of the oscillators. High frequency oscillators like the electrons would at ordinary temperature contribute nothing to the specific heat, atoms only if they were not too light and not too strongly bound. Einstein confirmed that these conditions were satisfied for the cases of poly-atomic molecules for which Drude had estimated the frequencies, and he showed that the measurements of the specific heat of diamond agreed fairly well with his calculation.

But this is not the place to enter into a discussion of the physical details of Einstein's discovery. The consequences with regard to the principles of scientific knowledge were far reaching. It was now proved that the quantum effects were not a specific property of radiation but a general feature of physical systems. The old rule *"natura non facit saltus"* was disproved: there are fundamental discontinuities, quanta of energy, not only in radiation but in ordinary matter.

In Einstein's model of a molecule or a solid these quanta are still closely connected with the motion of single vibrating particles. But soon it became clear that a considerable generalisation was necessary. The atoms in molecules and crystals are not independent but coupled by strong forces. Therefore the motion of an individual particle is not that of a single harmonic oscillator, but the superposition of many harmonic vibrations. The carrier of a simple harmonic motion is nothing material at all; it is the abstract "normal mode," well known from ordinary mechanics. For crystals in particular each normal mode is a standing wave. The introduction of this idea opened the way to a quantitative theory of thermodynamics of molecules and crystals and demonstrated the abstract character of the new quantum physics which began to emerge from this work. It became clear that the laws of micro-physics differed fundamentally from those of matter in bulk. Nobody has done more to elucidate this than Einstein. I cannot report all his contributions, but shall confine myself to two outstanding investigations which paved the way for the new micro-mechanics which physics at large has accepted to-day—while Einstein himself stands aloof, critical, sceptical, and hoping that this episode may pass by and physics return to classical principles.

The first of these two investigations has again to do with the law of radiation and statistics.[6] There are two ways of tackling problems of statistical equilibrium. The first is a direct one, which one may call the combinatory method: After having established the weights of elementary cases one calculates the number of combinations of these elements which correspond to an observable state; this number is the statistical probability W, from which all physical properties can be obtained (e.g. the entropy by Boltzmann's formula). The second method consists in determining the rates of all competing elementary processes, which lead to the equilibrium in question. This is, of course, much more difficult; for it demands not only the counting of equally probable cases but a real knowledge of the mechanism involved. But, on the other hand, it carries much further, providing not only the conditions of equilibrium but also of the time-rate of processes starting from non-equilibrium configurations. A classical example of this second method is Boltzmann's and Maxwell's formulation of the kinetic theory of gases; here the elementary mechanism is given by binary encounters of molecules, the rate of which is proportional to the number-density of both partners. From the "collision equation" the distribution function of the molecules can be determined not only in statistical equilibrium, but also for the case of motion in bulk, flow of heat, diffusion etc. Another example is the law of mass-action in chemistry, established by Guldberg and Waage; here again the elementary mechanism is provided by multiple collisions of groups of molecules which combine, split, or exchange atoms at a rate proportional to the number-density of the partners. A special case of these elementary processes is the monatomic reaction, where the molecules of one type spontaneously explode with a rate proportional to their number-density. This case has a tremendous importance in nuclear physics: it is the law of radio-active decay. Whereas in the few examples of ordinary chemistry, where monatomic reaction has been observed, a dependence of reaction velocity on the physical conditions (e.g. temperature) could be assumed or even observed, this was not the case for radio-activity:

[6] "Zur Quantentheorie der Strahlung," *Phys. Z. 18*, p. 121, (1917).

The decay constant seemed to be an invariable property of the nucleus, unchangeable by any external influences. Each individual nucleus explodes at an unpredictable moment; yet if a great number of nuclei are observed, the average rate of disintegration is proportional to the total number present. It looks as if the law of causality is put out of action for these processes.

Now what Einstein did was to show that Planck's law of radiation can just be reduced to processes of a similar type, of a more or less non-causal character. Consider two stationary states of an atom, say the lowest state 1 and an excited state 2. Einstein assumes that if an atom is found to be in the state 2 it has a certain probability of returning to the ground state 1, emitting a photon of a frequency which, according to the quantum law, corresponds to the energy difference between the two states; i.e. in a big assembly of such atoms the number of atoms in state 2 returning to the ground state 1 per unit time is proportional to their initial number—exactly as for radio-active disintegration. The radiation, on the other hand, produces a certain probability for the reverse process $1 \rightarrow 2$ which represents absorption of a photon of frequency ν_{12} and is proportional to the radiation density for the frequency.

Now these two processes alone balancing one another would not lead to Planck's formula; Einstein is compelled to introduce a third one, namely an influence of the radiation on the emission process $2 \rightarrow 1$, "induced emission," which again has a probability proportional to the radiation density for ν_{12}.

This extremely simple argument together with the most elementary principle of Boltzmann's statistics leads at once to Planck's formula without any specification of the magnitude of the transition probabilities. Einstein has connected it with a consideration of the transfer of momentum between atom and radiation, showing that the mechanism proposed by him is not consistent with the classical idea of spherical waves but only with a dart-like behaviour of the quanta. Here we are not concerned with this side of Einstein's work, but with its bearing on his attitude to the fundamental question of causal and statistical laws in physics. From this point of view this paper is of particular interest. For it meant a decisive step in the direction of non-causal, indeterministic reasoning. Of course, I am sure that Einstein himself was—and is still—convinced that there are structural properties in the excited atom which determine the exact moment of emission, and that probability is called in only because of our incomplete knowledge of the pre-history of the atom. Yet the fact remains that he has initiated the spreading of indeterministic statistical reasoning from its original source, radio-activity, into other domains of physics.

Still another feature of Einstein's work must be mentioned which was also of considerable assistance to the formulation of indeterministic physics in quantum mechanics. It is the fact that it follows from the validity of Planck's law of radiation that the probabilities of absorption ($1 \rightarrow 2$) and induced emission ($2 \rightarrow 1$) are equal. This was the first indication that interaction of atomic systems always involves two states in a symmetrical way. In classical mechanics an external agent like radiation acts on one definite state, and the result of the action can be calculated from the properties of this state and the external agent. In quantum mechanics each process is a transition between two states which enter symmetrically into the laws of interaction with an external agent. This symmetrical property was one of the deciding clues which led to the formulation of matrix mechanics, the earliest form of modern quantum mechanics. The first indication of this symmetry was provided by Einstein's discovery of the equality of up- and down-ward transition probabilities.

The last of Einstein's investigations which I wish to discuss in this report is his work on the quantum theory of monatomic ideal gases.[7] In this case the original idea was not his but came from an Indian physicist, S. N. Bose; his paper appeared in a translation by Einstein[8] himself who added a remark that he regarded this work as an important progress. The essential point in Bose's procedure is that he treats photons like particles of a gas with the method of statistical mechanics but with the difference that these particles are not distinguishable. He does not distribute individual particles over a set of states, but counts

[7] *Berl. Ber.* 1924, p. 261, 1925, p. 318.
[8] S. N. Bose, *Zeitschrift für Physik*, 26, 178, (1924).

the number of states which contain a given number of particles. This combinatory process together with the physical conditions (given number of states and total energy) leads at once to Planck's radiation law. Einstein added to this idea the suggestion that the same process ought to be applied to material atoms in order to obtain the quantum theory of a monatomic gas. The deviation from the ordinary gas laws derived from this theory is called "gas degeneracy." Einstein's papers appeared just a year before the discovery of quantum mechanics; one of them contains moreover (p. 9 of the second paper) a reference to de Broglie's celebrated thesis, and the remark that a scalar wave field can be associated with a gas. These papers of de Broglie and Einstein stimulated Schroedinger to develop his wave mechanics, as he himself confessed at the end of his famous paper.[9] It was the same remark of Einstein's which a year or two later formed the link between de Broglie's theory and the experimental discovery of electron diffraction; for, when Davisson sent me his results on the strange maxima found in the reflexion of electrons by crystals, I remembered Einstein's hint and directed Elsasser to investigate whether those maxima could be interpreted as interference fringes of de Broglie waves. Einstein is therefore clearly involved in the foundation of wave mechanics, and no alibi can disprove it.

I cannot see how the Bose-Einstein counting of equally probable cases can be justified without the conceptions of quantum mechanics. There a state of equal particles is described not by noting their individual positions and momenta, but by a symmetric wave function containing the co-ordinates as arguments; this represents clearly only one state and has to be counted once. A group of equal particles, even if they are perfectly alike, can still be distributed between two boxes in many ways—you may not be able to distinguish them individually but that does not affect their being individuals. Although arguments of this kind are more metaphysical than physical, the use of a symmetric wave function as representation of a state seems to me preferable. This way of thinking has morover led to the other case of

[9] "Quantisierung als Eigenwertproblem," *Annalen der Physik* (4), 70, p. 361, (1926); s. p. 373.

gas degeneracy, discovered by Fermi and Dirac, where the wave function is skew, and to a host of physical consequences confirmed by experiment.

The Bose-Einstein statistics was, to my knowledge, Einstein's last decisive positive contribution to physical statistics. His following work in this line, though of great importance by stimulating thought and discussion, was essentially critical. He refused to acknowledge the claim of quantum mechanics to have reconciled the particle and wave aspects of radiation. This claim is based on a complete re-orientation of physical principles: causal laws are replaced by statistical ones, determinism by indeterminism. I have tried to show that Einstein himself has paved the way for this attitude. Yet some principle of his philosophy forbids him to follow it to the end. What is this principle?

Einstein's philosophy is not a system which you can read in a book; you have to take the trouble to abstract it from his papers on physics and from a few more general articles and pamphlets. I have found no definite statement of his about the question "What is Probability?"; nor has he taken part in the discussions going on about von Mises' definition and other such endeavours. I suppose he would have dismissed them as metaphysical speculation, or even joked about them. From the beginning he has used probability as a tool for dealing with nature just like any scientific device. He has certainly very strong convictions about the value of these tools. His attitude toward philosophy and epistemology is well described in his obituary article on Ernst Mach:[10]

Nobody who devotes himself to science from other reasons than superficial ones, like ambition, money making, or the pleasure of brain-sport, can neglect the questions, what are the aims of science, how far are its general results true, what is essential and what based on accidental features of the development?

Later in the same article he formulates *his empirical creed* in these words:

Concepts which have been proved to be useful in ordering things easily acquire such an authority over us that we forget their human origin and accept them as invariable. Then they become "necessities of thought," "given *a priori*," etc. The path of scientific progress is then, by such errors, barred for a long time. It is therefore no useless game if we are practising to analyse current notions and to point out on what conditions their justification and usefulness depends, how they have grown especially from the data of experience. In this way their exaggerated authority is broken. They are removed, if they cannot properly legitimate themselves; corrected, if their correspondence to the given things was too negligently established; replaced by others, if a new system can be developed that we prefer for good reasons.

That is the core of the young Einstein, thirty years ago. I am sure the principles of probability were then for him of the same kind as all other concepts used for describing nature, so impressively formulated in the lines above. The Einstein of to-day is changed. I translate here a passage of a letter from him which I received about four years ago (7th November, 1944): "In our scientific expectation we have grown antipodes. You believe in God playing dice and I in perfect laws in the world of things existing as real objects, which I try to grasp in a wildly speculative way." These speculations distinguish indeed his present work from his earlier writing. But if any man has the right to speculate it is he whose fundamental results stand like rock. What he is aiming at is a general field-theory which preserves the rigid causality of classical physics and restricts probability to masking our ignorance of the initial conditions or, if you prefer, of the pre-history, of all details of the system considered. This is not the place to argue about the possibility of achieving this. Yet I wish to make one remark, using Einstein's own picturesque language: If God has made the world a perfect mechanism, he has at least conceded so much to our imperfect intellect that, in order to predict little parts of it, we need not solve innumerable differential equations but can use dice with fair success. That this is so I have learned, with many of my contemporaries, from Einstein himself. I think, this situation has not changed much by the introduction of quantum statistics; it is still we mortals who are playing dice for our little purposes of prognosis—God's actions are as mysterious in classical Brownian motion as in radio-activity and quantum radiation, or in life at large.

Einstein's dislike of modern physics has not only been expressed in general terms, which can be answered in a similarly general and vague way, but also in very substantial papers in which he has formulated objections against definite statements of wave mechanics. The best known paper of this kind is one published in collaboration with Podolsky and Rosen.[11] That it goes very deep into the logical foundations of quantum mechanics is apparent from the reactions it has evoked. Niels Bohr has answered in detail; Schroedinger has published his own sceptical views on the interpretation of quantum mechanics; Reichenbach deals with this problem in the last chapter of his excellent book, *Philosophic Foundations of Quantum Mechanics,* and shows that a complete treatment of the difficulties pointed out by Einstein, Podolsky, and Rosen needs an overhaul of logic itself. He introduces a three-valued logic, in which apart from the truth-values "true" and "false," there is an intermediate one, called "indeterminate," or, in other words, he rejects the old principle of *"tertium non datur,"* as has been proposed long before, from purely mathematical reasons, by Brouwer and other mathematicians. I am not a logician, and in such disputes always trust that expert who last talked to me. My attitude to statistics in quantum mechanics is hardly affected by formal logics, and I venture to say that the same holds for Einstein. That his opinion in this matter differs from mine is regrettable, but it is no object of logical dispute between us. It is based on different experience in our work and life. But in spite of this, he remains my beloved master.

MAX BORN

DEPARTMENT OF MATHEMATICAL PHYSICS
UNIVERSITY OF EDINBURGH
EDINBURGH, SCOTLAND

[11] A. Einstein, B. Podolsky, N. Rosen: "Can Quantum Mechanical Description of Physical Reality be Considered Complete?" *Phys. Rev.* 47, p. 777, (1935).

6

Walter Heitler

THE DEPARTURE FROM CLASSICAL THOUGHT IN MODERN PHYSICS

6

THE DEPARTURE FROM CLASSICAL THOUGHT IN MODERN PHYSICS

THE beginning of the twentieth century is the milestone of a marked change in the direction of scientific thought as far as the science of the inanimate world, i.e., physics, is concerned. What is now termed classical physics is an unbroken line of continuous development lasting roughly 300 years, which began in earnest with Galileo, Newton and others and culminated in the completion of analytical dynamics, Maxwell's theory of the electromagnetic field and the inclusion of optics as a consequence of the latter by Hertz. If we also include Boltzmann's statistical interpretation of the second law of thermodynamics, the list of what constitutes the major parts of classical physics will be fairly complete.

The logical structure of all these theories is roughly as follows: The happenings in the outside world (always confined to dead nature) follow a strictly causal development, governed by strict laws in space and time. The space and time in which these events occur is the absolute space-time of Newton and identical with what we are used to in daily life. The term "outside world" presupposes a sharp distinction between an "objective" outside reality, of which we have knowledge ultimately through sense perception, but which is completely independent of us, and "us," the onlookers, and ultimately those who think about the results of our observations. The term "causal development" is meant in the following, rather narrow, sense: Given at any time the complete[1] knowledge of the state of a physical object (which may be a mechanical system, an

---

[1] What "complete knowledge" means is defined in each part of physics, as the knowledge of a well defined set of initial conditions.

electromagnetic field, etc.), the future development of the object (or for that matter, its previous development until it has reached the state in question) follows then with mathematical certainty from the laws of nature, and is exactly predictable.

It was Einstein who, in 1905, made the first inroad into this logical structure. The greatness and courage of this step can only be measured by the fact that it was a departure from a 300 years old, and exceedingly successful, tradition. The change which our concepts of space and time have since undergone, through his special and general theories of relativity, are well known and adequately dealt with in other parts of this book. In this essay I want to deal with the second great departure from the classical program, namely quantum theory. It was also Einstein who has taken here some of the most decisive steps and who has paved the way short till the completion of quantum mechanics.

As far as the theory of relativity is concerned, that part of the classical structure which is concerned with the causal development of events (in the above sense) and with the relation of object and observer remained intact, or very nearly so. It is true that in the theory of relativity, the simultaneity of two events depends on the state of motion of the "observer," but it is equally true that nothing is changed in the happenings of the outside world if no observer is there at all, or if he is replaced by some lifeless mechanism, and the events follow in the same causal chain as in classical physics.

It is in the microscopical world and in quantum mechanics, which describes it, that a change in these concepts has come about.

In 1900 Planck discovered, through his analysis of the radiation emitted by a hot black body, that light of a given frequency v could not be emitted in any arbitrary intensity, but that the emitted energy must be an integral multiple of a certain smallest unit hv where h is a universal constant—Planck's constant—whose value is fixed once and for always. Consequently, when light is emitted by matter, this does not happen evenly or continuously, but must happen in jumps, a whole quantum hv being emitted at a time. No doubt this picture contains traces of an atomic structure of light and is quite at variance with the classical picture according to which all changes in the world occur continuously. However, Planck still supposed that light, once it is emitted, followed the laws of the Maxwell-Hertz theory. The discontinuity of the emission and absorption act were attributed to the material body rather than to the structure of light.

Planck's ideas were carried further, and to the extreme, by Einstein in 1905, when he gave us an understanding of the photoelectric phenomena. Here, Einstein, almost going back to the old ideas of Newton which had long been discarded, supposed an atomistic structure of light. The logical consequence of Planck's idea is evidently that light, of a given frequency ν, cannot itself exist with an arbitrary intensity. Quite independently of the way in which it is emitted or absorbed by material bodies, it consists of quanta (hardly anything else but another word for light-atoms) each containing an energy $h\nu$ and having quite a number of other characteristics (for instance momentum) of material corpuscles. Naturally, this hypothesis was now in flat contradiction to the Maxwell-Hertz theory of light, which was thought to be well established at the time and supported by innumerable facts. Moreover, it was felt that the picture of a discontinuous emission or absorption process, connected with a discontinuous change in the number of light-quanta, is rather difficult to reconcile with the general frame work of the classical theory. It is true, discontinuous happenings, or jumps, need not necessarily contradict what we have described above as the general structure of classical physics: It may be that the jumps are "caused" by some outside influence, and knowing the cause can be predicted exactly as regards the time and other characteristics of their occurrence. Many physicists hoped it would turn out to be so. Yet, the more sensitive of the physicists felt the very profound changes in the classical picture required by the introduction of jumps, and no one was more sensitive to this necessity than Einstein.

In fact it became quite clear that the jumps were not predictable as to the exact time of their occurence nor that they were caused by an outside influence taking place at the time when they did occur, when Niels Bohr, in 1913, developed the quantum theory of the hydrogen atom. The essence of Planck's hypothesis found its more precise formulation in Bohr's statement: An atom can only exist in a discrete series of stationary states with various energies E_n, say, n = 0, 1, 2. . . . A change from the state E_n, say, to another E_m ($E_m < E_n$) takes place discontinuously with emission of one light-quantum whose frequency is determined by the change of energy $E_n — E_m = h\nu$. There exists a lowest state, the normal state of the atom, with energy E_o. This state is stable and the atom is incapable of emitting light. It followed further from the very fact that the black-body radiation had to be accounted for by these emission processes (Einstein 1917) that the jumps occurred *spontaneously*, and were not caused by any outside influence which happened to occur at the very time when the jump took place. Moreover, it was assumed from the start that the time which the atom spent in the higher state —supposing it had been brought to the higher state at a time $t = O$—was not a fixed interval of time which for all the atoms in the same excited state was the same, but that the life times of individual atoms followed the distribution law of *chance*. Only the average life time, taken for a large number of like atoms in the same excited state, was determined and a characteristic quantity for the atom and the excited state in question. It was here for the first time that statistical and probability considerations entered into the laws governing individual physical objects. Before, statistics was by definition to be applied only to an assembly of a large number of objects, in whose individual behaviour one was not interested, but who individually followed the strictly causal laws of classical physics. If one might have entertained any doubts as to whether the life time of an excited atom was not perhaps a fixed interval of time, which alone would have conformed with the classical idea of exact predictability (I am not aware that anyone thought that this might be the case), such doubts must have been dispelled by innumerable physical facts, such as the decay of radioactive bodies where the statistical nature of the jumps was proved by experiments.

As far as the nature of light was concerned, the situation was one—so it seemed—of flat contradictions. On the one hand the wave nature of light was used, and with complete success, to describe the phenomena of diffraction and countless other phenomena. On the other hand the light quanta of Planck and Einstein, equally indispensable to describe the phenomena of light emission and absorption and an ever increasing number of similar facts, had all or nearly all the characteristics of material particles. The two natures of light seemed quite irreconcilable.

The dynamics of material particles, atoms and electrons, was brought into an equally confusing state by the introduction of Planck's and Bohr's quantum ideas. Not only was it impossible to understand that in the lowest state of an atom an electron, i.e., a negatively charged particle, could forever rotate about a positively charged nucleus in an orbit of finite dimensions without radiating light and ultimately falling into the nucleus, but also the very nature of the quantum jumps seemed to escape any detailed description on the lines of classical dynamics or otherwise.

The next step which Einstein took was one that was likely to aggravate the situation by carrying the contradictions yet a step further, but in a way—as it turned out later—which contained many of the elements for the final clarification.

In 1924 Bose published a paper in which he treated light quanta like a gas of material particles rather than considering them as energy quanta of the electromagnetic waves as which Planck had conceived them. In order not to be at variance with Planck's formula for the black-body radiation, Bose was forced to apply a statistical treatment which was somewhat different from that usually applied to a gas of material particles. Attracted by the similarity of light quanta and a gas of material particles, Einstein turned round (1924/25) and applied Bose's statistical methods to a gas of atoms. That differences in the gas laws arose then was not surprising. Particular attention was paid by Einstein to the density fluctuations of such a gas. The energy fluctuations of the electromagnetic radiation was previously known to consist of two parts of which one was attributed

to the interference of the waves; the other part was due to
the existence of the quanta and would not be there if the classical (i.e., not quantum-) theory of light had been used. On
the other hand, the density fluctuations of a gas, treated according to the older statistical methods were quite analogous to
the second part (thus stressing the similarity of light quanta
and material particles), the first part being absent. Now when
Einstein applied the new statistical methods to a gas of atoms,
the first contribution to the fluctuations also appeared which in
the case of radiation was due to the interference of waves.
Upon this Einstein remarked:

One can interpret it (i.e., this part of the fluctuations) *in an analogous
way by attributing to a gas some kind of radiation in a suitable way,
and by calculating its interference-fluctuations. I go into further details
because I believe that this is more than an analogy.*

*Mr. E. de Broglie has shown, in a very remarkable thesis, how one
can attribute a wave field to a material particle, or to a system of particles.
To a material particle of mass* m *first a frequency is attributed.... Relative to a system in which the particle moves with a velocity* v *a wave
exists. Frequency and phase velocity are given by ... whilst* v *is at the
same time—as Mr. de Broglie has shown—the group velocity of this
wave.*

A formula is given which expresses the phase velocity of the
wave by the velocity of the particle v. If v is small compared
with the velocity of light, the formula boils down to one for
the *wave length* λ of the wave "accompanying" the particle,
namely $\lambda = h/mv$. ($m =$ mass of particle). Here Planck's
constant h appears again. It always appears as a connecting link
between concepts relating to a particle (v, energy E) and concepts relating to a wave (λ, v).

In 1905 Einstein had put forward and stressed the "opposite nature" of light—its particle nature. Twenty years later,
his considerations led him to draw attention to de Broglie's
work, and put forward the "opposite nature" of what was always thought to be corpuscles—their wave nature. In this way
he created the same paradoxical situation, that existed for
light, also for material particles, putting the two on—so to
speak—the same level.

Here Einstein's contribution to the development of quantum mechanics ends. He had given it two major impulses. Their strength can be measured by the fact that two or three years after the publication of the last mentioned work the problem was clarified and the structure of quantum mechanics was complete in its major outline. In particular the contrasting of the wave and particle natures of all physical objects has proved to be very fruitful, and it will be seen that it is just this contrast which leads most easily to an understanding of the typical features of quantum mechanics.

Following de Broglie and Einstein, Schrödinger developed the wave picture of an electron into a consistent mathematical theory, in which each electron was described by a wave field. At the same time and independently, a different more abstract line was pursued by Heisenberg, Born, and Jordan, and it soon turned out that both lines were in reality partly identical and partly supplemented each other. In particular the existence of a discrete set of energy levels of an atom appeared as a mathematical consequence of this theory. In 1927 Davisson and Germer verified the wave nature of the electron by proving experimentally that a beam of electrons showed much the same diffraction phenomena as a beam of light. Finally, and this gave the final solution of the apparent contradictions in the two pictures, Born (1926) gave his statistical interpretation of the wave field.

At first sight, Schrödinger's wave equation had much in common with other classical field theories. The wave field attributed to an electron develops in space and time in the same causal manner as an electromagnetic field, and the wave equation allows one to predict its future values at any point (in space) if the field is known at the present. Yet there were some marked differences, from the very beginning. In the first place, it turned out that the wave function was, in some cases, not real but necessarily complex. In the second place, when the problem of several (say n) electrons was considered, it turned out that the wave function was necessarily in a $3n$-dimensional space. These are not features which are shared by the electromagnetic field (or gravitational field) and make it unlikely that the wave field of an electron could be a measurable physical object (as the other known fields are). The statistical interpretation by Born has finally decided against this idea.

What is now the logical structure of the new quantum mechanics, how are the double rôles of all physical objects as particles and waves to be reconciled, and how does the new theory differ from the classical ideas of space, time, and causality? The simplest way to explain this is to consider an example. In the following we shall give preference to the case of of the electron for the following reason: Although historically quantum theory originated from the idea of light quanta, the electron case is now the one better understood. In fact light quanta belong to the realm of relativistic quantum mechanics (they move always with the velocity of light) and the latter presents us still with very deep unsolved problems. However, as far as the following considerations go, not much would be changed if we substitute a beam of light for a beam of electrons and a light quantum for an electron.

Let us consider a beam of electrons and an experiment by which its wave nature is put into evidence. For this purpose we let the beam pass through a slit. On a screen behind the slit we observe the intensity of the electron beam arriving there. We make sure that the beam is monochromatic and that all electrons have the same wave length, or, by the wave length-velocity relation, the same velocity. We find then a characteristic diffraction pattern, maxima and minima of intensity in alternation, as would be the case if a monochromatic beam of light or X-rays had passed. The intensity distribution on the screen is exactly predictable from the wave equation, as would be the case for a classical field. So far the wave picture is successful and all the theoretical predictions were found to be true. In particular the relation between wave length and velocity could be verified.

On the other hand it is clear that the beam of electrons consists of a large number of individual particles. The atomistic structure of electricity had long ago been established beyond doubt, and we know in fact exactly how many electrons there are in a beam of given intensity. The contrast between the two pictures we have formed of the electron is brought to a head, if we now ask: What will happen, if we use a beam of very weak intensity so that we can observe individual electrons one by one passing through the slit and arriving on the screen? If the wave picture were still correct in the more classical sense, we could at once predict that the diffraction pattern on the screen would be left intact and would appear with exactly the same distribution of maxima and minima, only with very much smaller overall intensity. All maxima and minima would have decreased in intensity in the same proportion. The absurdity of this proposition is clear. The diffraction pattern on the screen has an extension in space of several centimeters and this would mean that an individual electron would in fact have this extension! This is not indeed what has been found.[2] What is observed is this: Each individual electron arrives on the screen on one point, but each on a different point. When a sufficiently large number of electrons has passed (say a few dozens) it becomes more and more clear that the points at which the particles arrive are not distributed at random on the screen but lie *preferably* in the regions where in the former experiment with an intense beam the *maxima* of the diffraction pattern were found. Very few electrons arrive in the minima regions. This evidently means: The intensity distribution of the diffraction pattern is the *probability distribution* for the arrival (i.e., the position) of each individual electron. Now the diffraction pattern is nothing but the square of the amplitude of the wave function derived from the wave picture. We are therefore led to interpret the wave function not as the amplitude of some physical field analogous to the electromagnetic field, but as the *probability* (amplitude) *for finding the electron,* pictured as a particle, *at a given position.* This is Born's statistical interpretation.

From the very use of the world "probability" it is inferred that the *orbit of the electron* is *no longer precisely predictable.*

[2] The above experiment with individual particles has in fact been performed, although in a somewhat different way. The above description is, of course, an idealization, which, however, differs from the actual experiment in no essential point.

What can be predicted is only the probability of finding the electron at some point. This will amount to a certainty in general only if we have an assembly of a very *large number* of particles. Here then a drastic departure is made from the classical idea of strict determinism. The behaviour of atomistic particles no longer conforms with that idea. The departure is forced upon us by the necessity of reconciling the otherwise contradictory pictures of an electron behaving sometimes like a particle and sometimes like a wave. Through the statistical interpretation a first step is taken in reconciling the two "natures," but we must examine the situation more thoroughly. When the electron passes through the slit its wave function has a large extension in space and this means the probability distribution of its position extends also over a large area. We say then that the position of the electron is "not sharp." We then observe its position on the screen and find it, say, at some point x. Supposing now we can make the screen exceedingly thin so that the electron can pass through the screen. And supposing we place a second screen immediately behind the first one and observe the position of the electron again on the second screen. Where would we expect to find the particle? If the probability distribution for the position of the electron is the same as before we have no reason whatsoever to expect that we should find it at the same point (rather at the projection of x on the second screen). It would be just as probable to find it elsewhere at x', a few centimetres away, where, according to the probability distribution, the probability is just as great as in x. This again is absurd. It would mean that having observed the particle at a point x, we still know nothing about its position, and we could find it just as well at x', a moment afterwards. This cannot be so. On the second screen, the electron will, of course, appear at precisely the same position as on the first screen, i.e., on the projection of x. But then it follows that through the appearance of the electron on the first screen, the probability distribution for the position must have changed and *contracted into one of certainty*, i.e., into a distribution which is zero everywhere except in x where it is one. The wave function of the electron has, therefore, suddenly changed. This sudden change of the probability distribution must have been effected by the *observation* on the first screen. It is indeed the outcome of an observation which changes a situation of "probability" into one of certainty. By this observation the *position* of the electron has suddenly become *sharp or certain*. It is here, for the first time in physics, that a measurement or observation has a decisive influence on the course of events and cannot be separated, as was the case in classical physics, from the physical picture. We come back to this point below.

There is now one further question to be answered before we can obtain a logically consistent picture. When the electron is observed on the screen, its position has become certain. Why can we then not work from the start with electrons with sharp positions and observe their positions before they pass the slit and thus return to a situation in which their orbits would be predictable? The answer is this: In order that the diffraction experiment works we had to use a monochromatic beam, which, as we have seen, means that all electrons have the same velocity, and hence wave length. Now a wave track with a given wave length has necessarily a long extension in space and therefore leads to a great uncertainty of the position of the electron. On the other hand, if the position is sharp, the wave function is such that it is different from zero only in a very small region of space. There is no trace of what we usually call a wave. As is well known, from Fourier analysis, such a "wave packet," as it is called, can be built up by a superposition of many monochromatic waves with many very different wave lengths. It follows then that we cannot assign a given wave length or, by the relation $\lambda = h/mv$, a given velocity, to such an electron. In other words: *the velocity is not sharp.* (Quantum mechanics allows us then to calculate a probability distribution for the various values of the velocity.) We see therefore that we have the *choice of either having the position* OR *the velocity sharp, but* WE CANNOT HAVE BOTH. (This is essentially Heisenberg's uncertainty principle.) Whereas in classical physics it is taken for granted that a body has a clearly defined position in space, as well as an equally clearly defined velocity, this is not the case in quantum mechanics. Only one of the two quantities can have a sharp value, whereas the other is very uncertain. There are, of course, also intermediate cases, where both position and velocity are to some extent sharp,—say within a certain range of values,—and to some extent unsharp.

It is important to note that it is not possible to determine position and velocity of a particle at the same time, thus refuting the uncertainty principle by measurements. The measuring instrument exerts a non-negligible influence on the object to be measured, and since the instrument is also subjected to the quantum mechanical uncertainty relation, this influence is to some extent uncertain. Following this up in detail one finds that a measurement of the position changes the velocity of the object in an uncertain way (and vice versa), whereas it does not change the position of the object. A measure for the uncertainties with which we have to reckon is Planck's constant. In fact the uncertainty relation is $\Delta x \, \Delta v = h/m$ where Δx is the uncertainty of position, Δv that of velocity. Which of the two quantities, x or v, has a sharp value is determined solely by an observation. When beginning our diffraction experiment we had to make sure that the electrons had a sharp velocity (monochromatic beam). This meant: We have made an observation of their velocity somehow beforehand. In this way we have forced them into a state of sharp velocity, sacrificing any definite knowledge of their position. Afterwards we observe the position on the screen. From what was said above, it is clear that henceforth our *previous knowledge of the velocity is destroyed,* the electron has no longer a sharp velocity. Any further diffraction experiment would not show a clear diffraction pattern.

It is clear now why the orbit of the electron is not exactly predictable. For this purpose we would have to know, according to classical physics, the initial position *and* velocity. But the knowledge of both is contradictory to the uncertainty relation. With only half the knowledge sharp, the orbit is naturally not determined.

In the sudden change of the probability distribution (or the wave function) caused by an observation we have the prototype of a quantum jump. Supposing we have an atom which we know to be in an excited state at the time $t = 0$. If we solve the wave equation for this case we find the following result: The wave function changes *gradually* and in course of time from that of the excited state into that of the ground state, owing to the very possibility of light emission. It allows us to predict a probability to find the atom either in the excited or in the ground state, at any later time. If we later make an observation of the state of the atom, we may find it, with a certain probability, in the ground state (and in that case we *always* find that also a light quantum has been emitted) and we say then for short: The atom has jumped down. The probability for the atom to be in the ground state changes steadily. We enforce a sudden change into certainty, by making the observation.

We have stated above that the wave function of an electron develops in space and time much in the same way as a classical field does, i.e., its future course is predictable when it is given at a time, say, $t = 0$. But its very nature and its physical interpretation (as a probability distribution) makes it clear that it is not itself the physical object we investigate (in contrast to the electromagnetic field of the classical theory, which *is* a physical object which we may consider, observe, and measure), although it is inseparable from the object under consideration (the electron, for instance). Its predictable course of development—causal development in the narrow sense of the introduction—continues so long as and until an observation is made. Then the chain of causal development is interrupted, the wave function changes suddenly, giving the quantity observed a sharp value. From here onwards a new, steady, causal development begins allowing us to predict probabilities for future observations, until the next observation is made, and so on. It appears that we are dealing with different aspects of the object: One is the world of observations in space and time, in which the objects under consideration have measurable positions, velocities, etc. Only one of these quantities has a sharply defined value at a time. The future values of these quantities are not precisely or entirely predictable. The other aspect from which we can consider the object is the one of the wave function. It escapes our immediate observation by apparatus or (ultimately) sense perception entirely. It can be grasped by us only through our thinking, our spirit, not through our senses. It is in this world where the development is causal (in the sense used above). It casts its projection into the world of happenings in space and time, allowing us to predict probabilities for the results of any observations we choose to make (in some cases also their exact results). It is futile to argue which of the two aspects is the "real" one. Both are.[3] For both are but two *different projections of one and the same reality*, both are inseparable from each other, and both together only give the complete description of the object we consider.

The relationship that exists between position and velocity and between the causal development of the wave functions and the observations, namely that of mutual exclusiveness, which is so characteristic for quantum mechanics, is called by Bohr "complementarity."

The word "observation" used above requires perhaps still a more precise explanation. One may ask if it is sufficient to carry out a measurement by a self-registering apparatus or whether the presence of an observer is required. The above example of a position measurement by two screens may elucidate the situation. Supposing the first screen is a kind of thin photographic plate which retains an image of the point where the electron has passed through. Supposing we develop this plate only some time after the observation on the second screen has been made. It is then evidently impossible to predict with certainty the result of this observation. We shall, in fact, only be able to predict the probability distribution for the results of the observation on the second screen, and this is the same as that found before on the first screen. When we develop the first screen, it can, however, be said with certainty that the image will appear at the same point where it has been found on the second screen. The self-registering first screen does not itself make future observations certain, unless the result is acknowledged by a *conscious being*. We see, therefore, that here the *observer* appears, as a *necessary* part of the whole structure, and in his full capacity as a conscious being. The separation of the world into an "objective out-

---

[3] What we call "real" requires a clear statement.

side reality," and "us," the self-conscious onlookers, can no longer be maintained. Object and subject have become inseparable from each other. Their separation is an idealization which holds—approximately—where classical physics holds. The approximation is an exceedingly good one—as we shall presently see—in the macroscopical world, when we deal with bodies of our daily life.

It has often been argued whether the indeterminacy of quantum mechanics, with its profound consequences, may not be the result of an insufficient description, and whether it might not be possible that there is an underlying mechanism which has not been found yet, but which, when it is found, would allow us to return to the perfect determinism of classical physics. I believe it has been proved that quantum mechanics, when put on an axiomatic basis, is *logically complete* and permits therefore no such underlying mechanism. The following remark may also help to explain that this can hardly be expected. Classical mechanics (for instance the laws of motion of a heavy body) is certainly complete, in the sense that no unknown mechanism or so is omitted. Now classical mechanics is contained in quantum mechanics as a *special case*. If we consider the behaviour of particles with heavier and heavier masses according to quantum mechanics, it turns out that, owing to the small value of Planck's constant, all probability distributions contract into almost certainty. It is then possible to assign to both position and velocity almost sharp values and the behaviour of such bodies is one of near determinism. This amounts to practically complete determinism when the masses are as big as say those of a dust particle.

This being so, it is hardly conceivable that there could be any incompleteness in quantum mechanics, as the latter contains a complete theory as a special case. The lack of complete determinism does, of course, not mean that quantum mechanics is any less rich in precise predictions than classical physics. The complete mastering of the atomic world which it has given us should suffice to refute any such suggestions.

We summarize: What has been achieved in quantum mechanics is a new category of thinking, which, as far as I am aware, has not been thought of either by scientists or philosophers before. Apparently contradictory pictures of the structure of an object have been reconciled by this new mode of thinking. The happenings in the world of our sense perceptions supported by physical instruments are no longer strictly deterministic in the old sense. Instead, the full reality contains features which escape our senses (or their supporting instruments) and can only be grasped by our thought. No sharp line can be drawn between an outside world and the self-conscious observer who plays a vital rôle in the whole structure, and cannot be separated from it.

The departure from the classical idealization cannot fail to have, in course of time, its profound influences on other domains of human thought. It seems to be in the nature of the human spirit to give way to easy generalizations. When classical physics had its triumphs in the past, in particular in the nineteenth century, its logical structure was, consciously or unconsciously, taken over to almost all parts of human thought. Some have taken it for granted that a living organism is nothing more than a complicated mechanical and chemical system that is entirely subjected to the laws of classical physics and therefore itself deterministic in the same sense. Functions of the mind can, in such a picture, only be regarded as by-products of a deterministic mechanism, and must therefore be precisely predictable themselves. Clearly such views would destroy entirely the concepts of free will and ethical behaviour, and indeed, of "life" itself. And perhaps they have gone some way to destroy both. In the decline of ethical standards which the history of the past fifteen years has exhibited, it is not difficult to trace the influence of mechanistic and deterministic concepts which have unconsciously, but deeply, crept into human minds. That this would be the consequence of the nineteenth century scientific thought, with its subsequent visible destruction, was predicted by Dostojevski eighty years ago.

Of course, there is nothing, even in classical physics, which warrants such generalizations. What is true for a stone, a steam engine, or a water wave, need not hold for a tree and even less so for a mouse. The generalization is not much more logical than the argument: The sky is blue; clouds are in the sky; therefore clouds are blue.

Physics has now taken the first step towards a different attitude. The new way of thinking opens up prospects also for an entirely different approach to problems which are outside the domain of physics. We mention, as an example, briefly some considerations of Niels Bohr concerning the borderline between lifeless matter and a living organism. We may enquire whether in the latter the same laws of physics are valid or not which hold for dead matter. If the answer would be in the affirmative (and even if the laws of physics are those of quantum mechanics) then a living organism would differ in no essential point from inanimate matter and no room would be left for the very concept of life. Now it is known that some of the most important life functions have their material seat in very small units of living matter which are indeed of almost molecular size. In order to answer our question we would therefore have to go into a detailed investigation of the atomic and molecular structure of the organism and then to ask whether the probability and other predictions of quantum mechanics are true or not. These observations must be made with physical instruments (X-rays, etc.) and cannot fail to have a profound influence on the object under consideration, i.e., the living organism. It may be now— and this is what Bohr assumes—that these detailed investigations with instruments would *destroy the life of the organism* and be therefore *incompatible with the very existence of life.* After having made our measurements we would be dealing with the dead body of the organism. It would therefore be impossible to verify or refute the validity of physics in the organism, as long as the latter is alive. In short, Bohr assumes that a similar relation of complementarity exists between life-matter and life-less matter as exists in quantum mechanics between the position and velocity of a particle. The very fact that an organism is living may be incompatible with too detailed a knowledge of its atomic and molecular structure, just as the knowledge of the position of a particle is incompatible with the knowledge of its momentum.

All this may or may not be so. But what is clear is that the new situation, with which we are confronted in quantum mechanics, has *created room* for an approach to the problem of life, (and other domains of human thought) which is no longer chained to the deterministic views of classical physics.

Finally, we return once more to the problems of physics. Quantum mechanics, for which Einstein has done so much to pave the way, is as yet essentially a non-relativistic theory, i.e., it applies to particles which move slowly and for which all gravitational effects can be neglected. It is as yet not reconciled with the great work of Einstein's, the theory of relativity. The two great theories, relativity and quantum mechanics, both creations of the twentieth century, and both departing profoundly from the classical picture, stand as yet apart from each other. A great deal of work has been done to bring about their unification,—and no doubt a certain amount of insight has been gained—, but the final solution is still in abeyance. We are concerned with the behaviour of fast moving atomistic particles, with the structure of the fundamental particles themselves, electrons, protons, the newly discovered mesons, etc., their creation and annihilation; with an understanding of the elementary unit of the electric charge, and with the understanding of such important dimensionless numbers as the universal constant hc/e^2 ($e =$ elementary charge, $h =$ Planck's constant, $c =$ velocity of light), which has the curious value 137. This is the domain of quantum-electrodynamics.

We are as yet far away from a solution of these problems. But when the solution is found, may we expect that it will bring us nearer to the classical ideal again? This can certainly not be the case. The non-quantum-mechanics theory of relativity, and the non-relativistic quantum mechanics must both be contained as specializations of the more general quantum electrodynamics. A generalization can hardly mean a return to the views of a still more special theory, classical physics. Instead we must be prepared for a further departure from the classical ideas. Further limitations will be imposed on the applicability of our present concepts. Perhaps some change will have to be made in our ideas of the continuity of space and time (atomistic structure of space?) or some other change in well established concepts, of which we have as yet not been able to think.

WALTER HEITLER

DUBLIN INSTITUTE FOR ADVANCED STUDIES
DUBLIN, IRELAND

7

Niels Bohr

DISCUSSION WITH EINSTEIN ON
EPISTEMOLOGICAL PROBLEMS
IN ATOMIC PHYSICS

7

DISCUSSION WITH EINSTEIN ON EPISTEMOLOGICAL PROBLEMS IN ATOMIC PHYSICS

WHEN invited by the Editor of the series, "Living Philosophers," to write an article for this volume in which contemporary scientists are honouring the epoch-making contributions of Albert Einstein to the progress of natural philosophy and are acknowledging the indebtedness of our whole generation for the guidance his genius has given us, I thought much of the best way of explaining how much I owe to him for inspiration. In this connection, the many occasions through the years on which I had the privilege to discuss with Einstein epistemological problems raised by the modern development of atomic physics have come back vividly to my mind and I have felt that I could hardly attempt anything better than to give an account of these discussions which, even if no complete concord has so far been obtained, have been of greatest value and stimulus to me. I hope also that the account may convey to wider circles an impression of how essential the open-minded exchange of ideas has been for the progress in a field where new experience has time after time demanded a reconsideration of our views.

———

From the very beginning the main point under debate has been the attitude to take to the departure from customary principles of natural philosophy characteristic of the novel development of physics which was initiated in the first year of this century by Planck's discovery of the universal quantum of action. This discovery, which revealed a feature of atomicity in the laws of nature going far beyond the old doctrine of the limited divisibility of matter, has indeed taught us that the classical theories of physics are idealizations which can be unambiguously applied only in the limit where all actions involved are large compared with the quantum. The question at issue has been whether the renunciation of a causal mode of description of atomic processes involved in the endeavours to cope with the situation should be regarded as a temporary departure from ideals to be ultimately revived or whether we are faced with an irrevocable step towards obtaining the proper harmony between analysis and synthesis of physical phenomena. To describe the background of our discussions and to bring out as clearly as possible the arguments for the contrasting viewpoints, I have felt it necessary to go to a certain length in recalling some main features of the development to which Einstein himself has contributed so decisively.

As is well known, it was the intimate relation, elucidated primarily by Boltzmann, between the laws of thermodynamics and the statistical regularities exhibited by mechanical systems with many degrees of freedom, which guided Planck in his ingenious treatment of the problem of thermal radiation, leading him to his fundamental discovery. While, in his work, Planck was principally concerned with considerations of essentially statistical character and with great caution refrained from definite conclusions as to the extent to which the existence of the quantum implied a departure from the foundations of mechanics and electrodynamics, Einstein's great original contribution to quantum theory (1905) was just the recognition of how physical phenomena like the photo-effect may depend directly on individual quantum effects.[1] In these very same years when, in developing his theory of relativity, Einstein laid a new foundation for physical science, he explored with a most daring spirit the novel features of atomicity which pointed beyond the whole framework of classical physics.

With unfailing intuition Einstein thus was led step by step to the conclusion that any radiation process involves the emission or absorption of individual light quanta or "photons" with energy and momentum

$$E = h\nu \quad \text{and} \quad P = h\sigma \tag{1}$$

[1] A. Einstein, *Ann. d. Phys.*, *17*, 132, (1905).

respectively, where h is Planck's constant, while ν and σ are the number of vibrations per unit time and the number of waves per unit length, respectively. Notwithstanding its fertility, the idea of the photon implied a quite unforeseen dilemma, since any simple corpuscular picture of radiation would obviously be irreconcilable with interference effects, which present so essential an aspect of radiative phenomena, and which can be described only in terms of a wave picture. The acuteness of the dilemma is stressed by the fact that the interference effects offer our only means of defining the concepts of frequency and wavelength entering into the very expressions for the energy and momentum of the photon.

In this situation, there could be no question of attempting a causal analysis of radiative phenomena, but only, by a combined use of the contrasting pictures, to estimate probabilities for the occurrence of the individual radiation processes. However, it is most important to realize that the recourse to probability laws under such circumstances is essentially different in aim from the familiar application of statistical considerations as practical means of accounting for the properties of mechanical systems of great structural complexity. In fact, in quantum physics we are presented not with intricacies of this kind, but with the inability of the classical frame of concepts to comprise the peculiar feature of indivisibility, or "individuality," characterizing the elementary processes.

The failure of the theories of classical physics in accounting for atomic phenomena was further accentuated by the progress of our knowledge of the structure of atoms. Above all, Rutherford's discovery of the atomic nucleus (1911) revealed at once the inadequacy of classical mechanical and electromagnetic concepts to explain the inherent stability of the atom. Here again the quantum theory offered a clue for the elucidation of the situation and especially it was found possible to account for the atomic stability, as well as for the empirical laws governing the spectra of the elements, by assuming that any reaction of the atom resulting in a change of its energy involved a complete transition between two so-called stationary quantum states and that, in particular, the spectra were emitted by a step-like process in which each transition is accompanied by the emission of a monochromatic light quantum of an energy just equal to that of an Einstein photon.

These ideas, which were soon confirmed by the experiments of Franck and Hertz (1914) on the excitation of spectra by impact of electrons on atoms, involved a further renunciation of the causal mode of description, since evidently the interpretation of the spectral laws implies that an atom in an excited state in general will have the possibility of transitions with photon emission to one or another of its lower energy states. In fact, the very idea of stationary states is incompatible with any directive for the choice between such transitions and leaves room only for the notion of the relative probabilities of the individual transition processes. The only guide in estimating such probabilities was the so-called correspondence principle which originated in the search for the closest possible connection between the statistical account of atomic processes and the consequences to be expected from classical theory, which should be valid in the limit where the actions involved in all stages of the analysis of the phenomena are large compared with the universal quantum.

At that time, no general self-consistent quantum theory was yet in sight, but the prevailing attitude may perhaps be illustrated by the following passage from a lecture by the writer from 1913:[2]

I hope that I have expressed myself sufficiently clearly so that you may appreciate the extent to which these considerations conflict with the admirably consistent scheme of conceptions which has been rightly termed the classical theory of electrodynamics. On the other hand, I have tried to convey to you the impression that—just by emphasizing so strongly this conflict—it may also be possible in course of time to establish a certain coherence in the new ideas.

Important progress in the development of quantum theory was made by Einstein himself in his famous article on radiative equilibrium in 1917,[3] where he showed that Planck's law for thermal radiation could be simply deduced from assumptions

---

[2] N. Bohr, *Fysisk Tidsskrift*, *12*, 97, (1914). (English version in *The Theory of Spectra and Atomic Constitution*, Cambridge, University Press, 1922).

[3] A. Einstein, *Phys. Zs.*, *18*, 121, (1917).

conforming with the basic ideas of the quantum theory of atomic constitution. To this purpose, Einstein formulated general statistical rules regarding the occurrence of radiative transitions between stationary states, assuming not only that, when the atom is exposed to a radiation field, absorption as well as emission processes will occur with a probability per unit time proportional to the intensity of the irradiation, but that even in the absence of external disturbances spontaneous emission processes will take place with a rate corresponding to a certain *a priori* probability. Regarding the latter point, Einstein emphasized the fundamental character of the statistical description in a most suggestive way by drawing attention to the analogy between the assumptions regarding the occurrence of the spontaneous radiative transitions and the well-known laws governing transformations of radioactive substances.

In connection with a thorough examination of the exigencies of thermodynamics as regards radiation problems, Einstein stressed the dilemma still further by pointing out that the argumentation implied that any radiation process was "unidirected" in the sense that not only is a momentum corresponding to a photon with the direction of propagation transferred to an atom in the absorption process, but that also the emitting atom will receive an equivalent impulse in the opposite direction, although there can on the wave picture be no question of a preference for a single direction in an emission process. Einstein's own attitude to such startling conclusions is expressed in a passage at the end of the article (*loc. cit.*, p. 127 f.), which may be translated as follows:

These features of the elementary processes would seem to make the development of a proper quantum treatment of radiation almost unavoidable. The weakness of the theory lies in the fact that, on the one hand, no closer connection with the wave concepts is obtainable and that, on the other hand, it leaves to chance (*Zufall*) the time and the direction of the elementary processes; nevertheless, I have full confidence in the reliability of the way entered upon.

When I had the great experience of meeting Einstein for the first time during a visit to Berlin in 1920, these fundamental questions formed the theme of our conversations. The discussions, to which I have often reverted in my thoughts, added to all my admiration for Einstein a deep impression of his detached attitude. Certainly, his favoured use of such picturesque phrases as "ghost waves (*Gespensterfelder*) guiding the photons" implied no tendency to mysticism, but illuminated rather a profound humour behind his piercing remarks. Yet, a certain difference in attitude and outlook remained, since, with his mastery for co-ordinating apparently contrasting experience without abandoning continuity and causality, Einstein was perhaps more reluctant to renounce such ideals than someone for whom renunciation in this respect appeared to be the only way open to proceed with the immediate task of co-ordinating the multifarious evidence regarding atomic phenomena, which accumulated from day to day in the exploration of this new field of knowledge.

In the following years, during which the atomic problems attracted the attention of rapidly increasing circles of physicists, the apparent contradictions inherent in quantum theory were felt ever more acutely. Illustrative of this situation is the discussion raised by the discovery of the Stern-Gerlach effect in 1922. On the one hand, this effect gave striking support to the idea of stationary states and in particular to the quantum theory of the Zeeman effect developed by Sommerfeld; on the other hand, as exposed so clearly by Einstein and Ehrenfest,[4] it presented with unsurmountable difficulties any attempt at forming a picture of the behaviour of atoms in a magnetic field. Similar paradoxes were raised by the discovery by Compton (1924) of the change in wave-length accompanying the scattering of X-rays by electrons. This phenomenon afforded, as is well known, a most direct proof of the adequacy of Einstein's view regarding the transfer of energy and momentum in radiative processes; at the same time, it was equally clear that no simple picture of a corpuscular collision could offer an exhaustive description of the phenomenon. Under the impact of such difficulties, doubts

[4] A. Einstein and P. Ehrenfest, *Zs. f. Phys.*, *11*, 31, (1922).

were for a time entertained even regarding the conservation of energy and momentum in the individual radiation processes;[5] a view, however, which very soon had to be abandoned in face of more refined experiments bringing out the correlation between the deflection of the photon and the corresponding electron recoil.

The way to the clarification of the situation was, indeed, first to be paved by the development of a more comprehensive quantum theory. A first step towards this goal was the recognition by de Broglie in 1925 that the wave-corpuscle duality was not confined to the properties of radiation, but was equally unavoidable in accounting for the behaviour of material particles. This idea, which was soon convincingly confirmed by experiments on electron interference phenomena, was at once greeted by Einstein, who had already envisaged the deep-going analogy between the properties of thermal radiation and of gases in the so-called degenerate state.[6] The new line was pursued with the greatest success by Schrödinger (1926) who, in particular, showed how the stationary states of atomic systems could be represented by the proper solutions of a wave-equation to the establishment of which he was led by the formal analogy, originally traced by Hamilton, between mechanical and optical problems. Still, the paradoxical aspects of quantum theory were in no way ameliorated, but even emphasized, by the apparent contradiction between the exigencies of the general superposition principle of the wave description and the feature of individuality of the elementary atomic processes.

At the same time, Heisenberg (1925) had laid the foundation of a rational quantum mechanics, which was rapidly developed through important contributions by Born and Jordan as well as by Dirac. In this theory, a formalism is introduced, in which the kinematical and dynamical variables of classical mechanics are replaced by symbols subjected to a non-commutative algebra. Notwithstanding the renunciation of orbital pictures, Hamilton's canonical equations of mechanics are kept unaltered and

[5] N. Bohr, H. A. Kramers and J. C. Slater, *Phil. Mag.*, 47, 785, (1924).
[6] A. Einstein, *Berl. Ber.*, (1924), 261, and (1925), 3 and 18.

Planck's constant enters only in the rules of commutation

$$qp - pq = \sqrt{-1} \, \frac{h}{2\pi} \qquad (2)$$

holding for any set of conjugate variables q and p. Through a representation of the symbols by matrices with elements referring to transitions between stationary states, a quantitative formulation of the correspondence principle became for the first time possible. It may here be recalled that an important preliminary step towards this goal was reached through the establishment, especially by contributions of Kramers, of a quantum theory of dispersion making basic use of Einstein's general rules for the probability of the occurrence of absorption and emission processes.

This formalism of quantum mechanics was soon proved by Schrödinger to give results identical with those obtainable by the mathematically often more convenient methods of wave theory, and in the following years general methods were gradually established for an essentially statistical description of atomic processes combining the features of individuality and the requirements of the superposition principle, equally characteristic of quantum theory. Among the many advances in this period, it may especially be mentioned that the formalism proved capable of incorporating the exclusion principle which governs the states of systems with several electrons, and which already before the advent of quantum mechanics had been derived by Pauli from an analysis of atomic spectra. The quantitative comprehension of a vast amount of empirical evidence could leave no doubt as to the fertility and adequacy of the quantum-mechanical formalism, but its abstract character gave rise to a widespread feeling of uneasiness. An elucidation of the situation should, indeed, demand a thorough examination of the very observational problem in atomic physics.

This phase of the development was, as is well known, initiated in 1927 by Heisenberg,[1] who pointed out that the knowledge obtainable of the state of an atomic system will always involve a peculiar "indeterminacy." Thus, any measurement of the position of an electron by means of some device,

[1] W. Heisenberg. *Zs. f. Phys.*, *43*, 172, (1927).

like a microscope, making use of high frequency radiation, will, according to the fundamental relations (1), be connected with a momentum exchange between the electron and the measuring agency, which is the greater the more accurate a position measurement is attempted. In comparing such considerations with the exigencies of the quantum-mechanical formalism, Heisenberg called attention to the fact that the commutation rule (2) imposes a reciprocal limitation on the fixation of two conjugate variables, q and p, expressed by the relation

$$\Delta q \cdot \Delta p \approx h, \qquad (3)$$

where Δq and Δp are suitably defined latitudes in the determination of these variables. In pointing to the intimate connection between the statistical description in quantum mechanics and the actual possibilities of measurement, this so-called indeterminacy relation is, as Heisenberg showed, most important for the elucidation of the paradoxes involved in the attempts of analyzing quantum effects with reference to customary physical pictures.

The new progress in atomic physics was commented upon from various sides at the International Physical Congress held in September 1927, at Como in commemoration of Volta. In a lecture on that occasion,[8] I advocated a point of view conveniently termed "complementarity," suited to embrace the characteristic features of individuality of quantum phenomena, and at the same time to clarify the peculiar aspects of the observational problem in this field of experience. For this purpose, it is decisive to recognize that, *however far the phenomena transcend the scope of classical physical explanation, the account of all evidence must be expressed in classical terms.* The argument is simply that by the word "experiment" we refer to a situation where we can tell others what we have done and what we have learned and that, therefore, the account of the experimental arrangement and of the results of the observations must be expressed in unambiguous language with suitable application of the terminology of classical physics.

This crucial point, which was to become a main theme of the

[8] Atti del Congresso Internazionale dei Fisici, Como, Settembre 1927 (reprinted in *Nature*, *121*, 78 and 580, 1928).

discussions reported in the following, implies the *impossibility of any sharp separation between the behaviour of atomic objects and the interaction with the measuring instruments which serve to define the conditions under which the phenomena appear.* In fact, the individuality of the typical quantum effects finds its proper expression in the circumstance that any attempt of subdividing the phenomena will demand a change in the experimental arrangement introducing new possibilities of interaction between objects and measuring instruments which in principle cannot be controlled. Consequently, evidence obtained under different experimental conditions cannot be comprehended within a single picture, but must be regarded as *complementary* in the sense that only the totality of the phenomena exhausts the possible information about the objects.

Under these circumstances an essential element of ambiguity is involved in ascribing conventional physical attributes to atomic objects, as is at once evident in the dilemma regarding the corpuscular and wave properties of electrons and photons, where we have to do with contrasting pictures, each referring to an essential aspect of empirical evidence. An illustrative example, of how the apparent paradoxes are removed by an examination of the experimental conditions under which the complementary phenomena appear, is also given by the Compton effect, the consistent description of which at first had presented us with such acute difficulties. Thus, any arrangement suited to study the exchange of energy and momentum between the electron and the photon must involve a latitude in the space-time description of the interaction sufficient for the definition of wave-number and frequency which enter into the relation (1). Conversely, any attempt of locating the collision between the photon and the electron more accurately would, on account of the unavoidable interaction with the fixed scales and clocks defining the space-time reference frame, exclude all closer account as regards the balance of momentum and energy.

As stressed in the lecture, an adequate tool for a complementary way of description is offered precisely by the quantum-mechanical formalism which represents a purely symbolic scheme permitting only predictions, on lines of the correspondence principle, as to results obtainable under conditions specified by means of classical concepts. It must here be remembered that even in the indeterminacy relation (3) we are dealing with an implication of the formalism which defies unambiguous expression in words suited to describe classical physical pictures. Thus, a sentence like "we cannot know both the momentum and the position of an atomic object" raises at once questions as to the physical reality of two such attributes of the object, which can be answered only by referring to the conditions for the unambiguous use of space-time concepts, on the one hand, and dynamical conservation laws, on the other hand. While the combination of these concepts into a single picture of a causal chain of events is the essence of classical mechanics, room for regularities beyond the grasp of such a description is just afforded by the circumstance that the study of the complementary phenomena demands mutually exclusive experimental arrangements.

The necessity, in atomic physics, of a renewed examination of the foundation for the unambiguous use of elementary physical ideas recalls in some way the situation that led Einstein to his original revision on the basis of all application of space-time concepts which, by its emphasis on the primordial importance of the observational problem, has lent such unity to our world picture. Notwithstanding all novelty of approach, causal description is upheld in relativity theory within any given frame of reference, but in quantum theory the uncontrollable interaction between the objects and the measuring instruments forces us to a renunciation even in such respect. This recognition, however, in no way points to any limitation of the scope of the quantum-mechanical description, and the trend of the whole argumentation presented in the Como lecture was to show that the viewpoint of complementarity may be regarded as a rational generalization of the very ideal of causality.

––––––

At the general discussion in Como, we all missed the presence of Einstein, but soon after, in October 1927, I had the opportunity to meet him in Brussels at the Fifth Physical Conference of the Solvay Institute, which was devoted to the theme "Electrons and Photons." At the Solvay meetings, Einstein had from their beginning been a most prominent figure, and several

of us came to the conference with great anticipations to learn
his reaction to the latest stage of the development which, to our
view, went far in clarifying the problems which he had himself
from the outset elicited so ingeniously. During the discussions,
where the whole subject was reviewed by contributions from
many sides and where also the arguments mentioned in the
preceding pages were again presented, Einstein expressed, however, a deep concern over the extent to which causal account in
space and time was abandoned in quantum mechanics.

To illustrate his attitude, Einstein referred at one of the ses-
sions[9] to the simple example, illustrated by Fig. 1, of a particle
(electron or photon) penetrating through a hole or a narrow
slit in a diaphragm placed at some distance before a photographic plate. On account of the diffraction of the wave con-

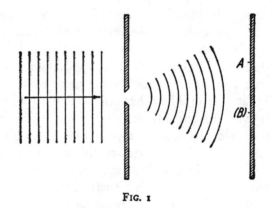

FIG. 1

nected with the motion of the particle and indicated in the figure
by the thin lines, it is under such conditions not possible to
predict with certainty at what point the electron will arrive at
the photographic plate, but only to calculate the probability
that, in an experiment, the electron will be found within any
given region of the plate. The apparent difficulty, in this description, which Einstein felt so acutely, is the fact that, if in the
experiment the electron is recorded at one point A of the plate,

[9] Institut International de Physique Solvay, *Rapport et discussions* du 5ᵉ Conseil, Paris 1928, 253 ff.

then it is out of the question of ever observing an effect of this electron at another point (B), although the laws of ordinary wave propagation offer no room for a correlation between two such events.

Einstein's attitude gave rise to ardent discussions within a small circle, in which Ehrenfest, who through the years had been a close friend of us both, took part in a most active and helpful way. Surely, we all recognized that, in the above example, the situation presents no analogue to the application of statistics in dealing with complicated mechanical systems, but rather recalled the background for Einstein's own early conclusions about the unidirection of individual radiation effects which contrasts so strongly with a simple wave picture (cf. p. 205). The discussions, however, centered on the question of whether the quantum-mechanical description exhausted the possibilities of accounting for observable phenomena or, as Einstein maintained, the analysis could be carried further and, especially, of whether a fuller description of the phenomena could be obtained by bringing into consideration the detailed balance of energy and momentum in individual processes.

To explain the trend of Einstein's arguments, it may be illustrative here to consider some simple features of the momentum and energy balance in connection with the location of a particle in space and time. For this purpose, we shall examine the simple case of a particle penetrating through a hole in a diaphragm without or with a shutter to open and close the hole, as indicated in Figs. 2a and 2b, respectively. The equidistant parallel lines to the left in the figures indicate the train of plane waves corresponding to the state of motion of a particle which, before reaching the diaphragm, has a momentum P related to the wave-number σ by the second of equations (1). In accordance with the diffraction of the waves when passing through the hole, the state of motion of the particle to the right of the diaphragm is represented by a spherical wave train with a suitably defined angular aperture ϑ and, in case of Fig. 2b, also with a limited radial extension. Consequently, the description of this state involves a certain latitude Δp in the momentum component of the particle parallel to the diaphragm and, in the case of a diaphragm with a shutter, an additional latitude ΔE of the kinetic energy.

Since a measure for the latitude Δq in location of the particle in the plane of the diaphragm is given by the radius a of the hole, and since $\vartheta \approx (1/\sigma a)$, we get, using (1), just $\Delta p \approx \vartheta P \approx (h/\Delta q)$, in accordance with the indeterminacy relation (3). This result could, of course, also be obtained directly by noticing that, due to the limited extension of the wave-field at the place of the slit, the component of the wave-number parallel to the plane of the diaphragm will involve a latitude $\Delta \sigma \approx (1/a) \approx (1/\Delta q)$. Similarly, the spread of the frequencies

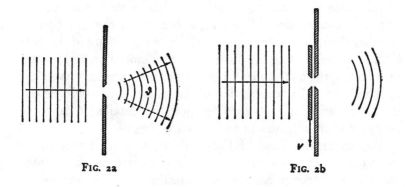

FIG. 2a   FIG. 2b

of the harmonic components in the limited wave-train in Fig. 2b is evidently $\Delta v \approx (1/\Delta t)$, where Δt is the time interval during which the shutter leaves the hole open and, thus, represents the latitude in time of the passage of the particle through the diaphragm. From (1), we therefore get

$$\Delta E \cdot \Delta t \approx h, \qquad (4)$$

again in accordance with the relation (3) for the two conjugated variables E and t.

From the point of view of the laws of conservation, the origin of such latitudes entering into the description of the state of the particle after passing through the hole may be traced to the possibilities of momentum and energy exchange with the diaphragm or the shutter. In the reference system considered in Figs. 2a and 2b, the velocity of the diaphragm may be disregarded and only a change of momentum Δp between the particle and the diaphragm needs to be taken into consideration. The shutter, however, which leaves the hole opened during the time Δt, moves with a considerable velocity $v \approx (a/\Delta t)$, and a momentum transfer Δp involves therefore an energy exchange with the particle, amounting to $v\Delta p \approx (1/\Delta t) \Delta q \Delta p \approx (h/\Delta t)$, being just of the same order of magnitude as the latitude ΔE given by (4) and, thus, allowing for momentum and energy balance.

The problem raised by Einstein was now to what extent a control of the momentum and energy transfer, involved in a location of the particle in space and time, can be used for a further specification of the state of the particle after passing through the hole. Here, it must be taken into consideration that the position and the motion of the diaphragm and the shutter have so far been assumed to be accurately co-ordinated with the space-time reference frame. This assumption implies, in the description of the state of these bodies, an essential latitude as to their momentum and energy which need not, of course, noticeably affect the velocities, if the diaphragm and the shutter are sufficiently heavy. However, as soon as we want to know the momentum and energy of these parts of the measuring arrangement with an accuracy sufficient to control the momentum and energy exchange with the particle under investigation, we shall, in accordance with the general indeterminacy relations, lose the possibility of their accurate location in space and time. We have, therefore, to examine how far this circumstance will affect the intended use of the whole arrangement and, as we shall see, this crucial point clearly brings out the complementary character of the phenomena.

Returning for a moment to the case of the simple arrangement indicated in Fig. 1, it has so far not been specified to what use it is intended. In fact, it is only on the assumption that the diaphragm and the plate have well-defined positions in space that it is impossible, within the frame of the quantum-mechanical formalism, to make more detailed predictions as to the point of the photographic plate where the particle will be recorded. If, however, we admit a sufficiently large latitude in the knowledge of the position of the diaphragm it should, in principle, be possible to control the momentum transfer to the diaphragm and, thus, to make more detailed predictions as to the direction of the electron path from the hole to the recording point. As regards the quantum-mechanical description, we have to deal here with a two-body system consisting of the diaphragm as well as of the particle, and it is just with an explicit application of conservation laws to such a system that we are concerned in the Compton effect where, for instance, the observation of the recoil of the electron by means of a cloud chamber allows us to predict in what direction the scattered photon will eventually be observed.

The importance of considerations of this kind was, in the course of the discussions, most interestingly illuminated by the examination of an arrangement where between the diaphragm with the slit and the photographic plate is inserted another

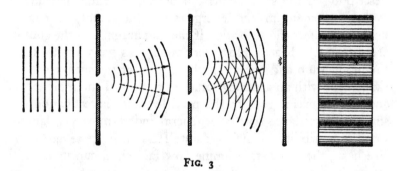

FIG. 3

diaphragm with two parallel slits, as is shown in Fig. 3. If a parallel beam of electrons (or photons) falls from the left on the first diaphragm, we shall, under usual conditions, observe on the plate an interference pattern indicated by the shading of the photographic plate shown in front view to the right of the figure. With intense beams, this pattern is built up by the accumulation of a large number of individual processes, each giving rise to a small spot on the photographic plate, and the distribution of these spots follows a simple law derivable from the wave analysis. The same distribution should also be found in the statistical account of many experiments performed with beams so faint that in a single exposure only one electron (or photon) will arrive at the photographic plate at some spot shown in the figure as a small star. Since, now, as indicated by the broken arrows, the momentum transferred to the first diaphragm ought to be different if the electron was assumed to pass through the upper or the lower slit in the second diaphragm, Einstein suggested that a control of the momentum transfer would permit a closer analysis of the phenomenon and, in particular, to decide through which of the two slits the electron had passed before arriving at the plate.

A closer examination showed, however, that the suggested control of the momentum transfer would involve a latitude in the knowledge of the position of the diaphragm which would exclude the appearance of the interference phenomena in question. In fact, if ω is the small angle between the conjectured paths of a particle passing through the upper or the lower slit, the difference of momentum transfer in these two cases will, according to (1), be equal to $h\sigma\omega$ and any control of the momentum of the diaphragm with an accuracy sufficient to measure this difference will, due to the indeterminacy relation, involve a minimum latitude of the position of the diaphragm, comparable with $1/\sigma\omega$. If, as in the figure, the diaphragm with the two slits is placed in the middle between the first diaphragm and the photographic plate, it will be seen that the number of fringes per unit length will be just equal to $\sigma\omega$ and, since an uncertainty in the position of the first diaphragm of the amount of $1/\sigma\omega$ will cause an equal uncertainty in the positions of the fringes, it follows that no interference effect can appear. The same result is easily shown to hold for any other placing of the second diaphragm between the first diaphragm and the plate, and would also be obtained if, instead of the first diaphragm, another of these three bodies were used for the control, for the purpose suggested, of the momentum transfer.

This point is of great logical consequence, since it is only the circumstance that we are presented with a choice of *either* tracing the path of a particle *or* observing interference effects, which allows us to escape from the paradoxical necessity of concluding that the behaviour of an electron or a photon should depend on the presence of a slit in the diaphragm through which it could be proved not to pass. We have here to do with a typical example of how the complementary phenomena appear under mutually exclusive experimental arrangements (cf. p. 210) and are just faced with the impossibility, in the analysis of quantum effects, of drawing any sharp separation between an independent behaviour of atomic objects and their interaction with the measuring instruments which serve to define the conditions under which the phenomena occur.

Our talks about the attitude to be taken in face of a novel situation as regards analysis and synthesis of experience touched naturally on many aspects of philosophical thinking, but, in spite of all divergencies of approach and opinion, a most humorous spirit animated the discussions. On his side, Einstein mockingly asked us whether we could really believe that the providential authorities took recourse to dice-playing (". . . *ob der liebe Gott würfelt*"), to which I replied by pointing at the great caution, already called for by ancient thinkers, in ascribing attributes to Providence in every-day language. I remember also how at the peak of the discussion Ehrenfest, in his affectionate manner of teasing his friends, jokingly hinted at the apparent similarity between Einstein's attitude and that of the opponents of relativity theory; but instantly Ehrenfest added that he would not be able to find relief in his own mind before concord with Einstein was reached.

———

Einstein's concern and criticism provided a most valuable incentive for us all to reexamine the various aspects of the situation as regards the description of atomic phenomena. To me it was a welcome stimulus to clarify still further the rôle played by the measuring instruments and, in order to bring into strong relief the mutually exclusive character of the experimental conditions under which the complementary phenomena appear, I tried in those days to sketch various apparatus in a pseudo-realistic style of which the following figures are examples. Thus, for the study of an interference phenomenon of the type indicated in Fig. 3, it suggests itself to use an experimental arrangement like that shown in Fig. 4, where the solid parts of the apparatus, serving as diaphragms and plate-holder, are

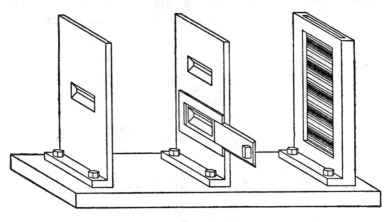

firmly bolted to a common support. In such an arrangement, where the knowledge of the relative positions of the diaphragms and the photographic plate is secured by a rigid connection, it is obviously impossible to control the momentum exchanged between the particle and the separate parts of the apparatus. The only way in which, in such an arrangement, we could insure that the particle passed through one of the slits in the second diaphragm is to cover the other slit by a lid, as indicated in the figure; but if the slit is covered, there is of course no question of any interference phenomenon, and on the plate we shall simply observe a continuous distribution as in the case of the single fixed diaphragm in Fig. 1.

In the study of phenomena in the account of which we are dealing with detailed momentum balance, certain parts of the whole device must naturally be given the freedom to move independently of others. Such an apparatus is sketched in Fig. 5, where a diaphragm with a slit is suspended by weak springs from a solid yoke bolted to the support on which also other immobile parts of the arrangement are to be fastened. The scale on the diaphragm together with the pointer on the bearings of

the yoke refer to such study of the motion of the diaphragm, as
may be required for an estimate of the momentum transferred
to it, permitting one to draw conclusions as to the deflection
suffered by the particle in passing through the slit. Since, however, any reading of the scale, in whatever way performed, will

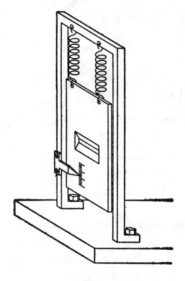

FIG. 5

involve an uncontrollable change in the momentum of the
diaphragm, there will always be, in conformity with the indeterminacy principle, a reciprocal relationship between our
knowledge of the position of the slit and the accuracy of the
momentum control.

In the same semi-serious style, Fig. 6 represents a part of an
arrangement suited for the study of phenomena which, in contrast to those just discussed, involve time co-ordination explicitly. It consists of a shutter rigidly connected with a robust
clock resting on the support which carries a diaphragm and on
which further parts of similar character, regulated by the same
clock-work or by other clocks standardized relatively to it, are
also to be fixed. The special aim of the figure is to underline
that a clock is a piece of machinery, the working of which can
completely be accounted for by ordinary mechanics and will be

affected neither by reading of the position of its hands nor by the interaction between its accessories and an atomic particle. In securing the opening of the hole at a definite moment, an apparatus of this type might, for instance, be used for an accurate measurement of the time an electron or a photon takes to come from the diaphragm to some other place, but evidently, it would leave no possibility of controlling the energy transfer to

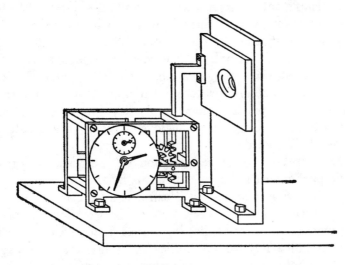

FIG. 6

the shutter with the aim of drawing conclusions as to the energy of the particle which has passed through the diaphragm. If we are interested in such conclusions we must, of course, use an arrangement where the shutter devices can no longer serve as accurate clocks, but where the knowledge of the moment when the hole in the diaphragm is open involves a latitude connected with the accuracy of the energy measurement by the general relation (4).

The contemplation of such more or less practical arrangements and their more or less fictitious use proved most instructive in directing attention to essential features of the problems. The main point here is the distinction between the *objects* under investigation and the *measuring instruments* which serve to define, in classical terms, the conditions under which the phenomena appear. Incidentally, we may remark that, for the illustration of the preceding considerations, it is not relevant that experiments involving an accurate control of the momentum or energy transfer from atomic particles to heavy bodies like diaphragms and shutters would be very difficult to perform, if practicable at all. It is only decisive that, in contrast to the proper measuring instruments, these bodies together with the particles would in such a case constitute the system to which the quantum-mechanical formalism has to be applied. As regards the specification of the conditions for any well-defined application of the formalism, it is moreover essential that the *whole experimental arrangement* be taken into account. In fact, the introduction of any further piece of apparatus, like a mirror, in the way of a particle might imply new interference effects essentially influencing the predictions as regards the results to be eventually recorded.

The extent to which renunciation of the visualization of atomic phenomena is imposed upon us by the impossibility of their subdivision is strikingly illustrated by the following example to which Einstein very early called attention and often has reverted. If a semi-reflecting mirror is placed in the way of a photon, leaving two possibilities for its direction of propagation, the photon may either be recorded on one, and only one, of two photographic plates situated at great distances in the two directions in question, or else we may, by replacing the plates by mirrors, observe effects exhibiting an interference between the two reflected wave-trains. In any attempt of a pictorial representation of the behaviour of the photon we would, thus, meet with the difficulty: to be obliged to say, on the one hand, that the photon always chooses *one* of the two ways and, on the other hand, that it behaves as if it had passed *both* ways.

It is just arguments of this kind which recall the impossibility of subdividing quantum phenomena and reveal the ambiguity in ascribing customary physical attributes to atomic objects. In particular, it must be realized that—besides in the account of the placing and timing of the instruments forming the experimental arrangement—all unambiguous use of space-time concepts in the description of atomic phenomena is confined to the recording of observations which refer to marks on a photographic plate or to similar practically irreversible amplification effects like the building of a water drop around an ion in a cloud-chamber. Although, of course, the existence of the quantum of action is ultimately responsible for the properties of the materials of which the measuring instruments are built and on which the functioning of the recording devices depends, this circumstance is not relevant for the problems of the adequacy and completeness of the quantum-mechanical description in its aspects here discussed.

These problems were instructively commented upon from different sides at the Solvay meeting,[10] in the same session where Einstein raised his general objections. On that occasion an interesting discussion arose also about how to speak of the appearance of phenomena for which only predictions of statistical character can be made. The question was whether, as to the occurrence of individual effects, we should adopt a terminology proposed by Dirac, that we were concerned with a choice on the part of "nature" or, as suggested by Heisenberg, we should say that we have to do with a choice on the part of the "observer" constructing the measuring instruments and reading their recording. Any such terminology would, however, appear dubious since, on the one hand, it is hardly reasonable to endow nature with volition in the ordinary sense, while, on the other hand, it is certainly not possible for the observer to influence the events which may appear under the conditions he has arranged. To my mind, there is no other alternative than to admit that, in this field of experience, we are dealing with individual phenomena and that our possibilities of handling the measuring instruments allow us only to make a choice between the different complementary types of phenomena we want to study.

The epistemological problems touched upon here were more explicitly dealt with in my contribution to the issue of *Naturwissenschaften* in celebration of Planck's 70th birthday in 1929. In this article, a comparison was also made between the lesson derived from the discovery of the universal quantum of action

[10] *Ibid.,* 248ff.

and the development which has followed the discovery of the finite velocity of light and which, through Einstein's pioneer work, has so greatly clarified basic principles of natural philosophy. In relativity theory, the emphasis on the dependence of all phenomena on the reference frame opened quite new ways of tracing general physical laws of unparalleled scope. In quantum theory, it was argued, the logical comprehension of hitherto unsuspected fundamental regularities governing atomic phenomena has demanded the recognition that no sharp separation can be made between an independent behaviour of the objects and their interaction with the measuring instruments which define the reference frame.

In this respect, quantum theory presents us with a novel situation in physical science, but attention was called to the very close analogy with the situation as regards analysis and synthesis of experience, which we meet in many other fields of human knowledge and interest. As is well known, many of the difficulties in psychology originate in the different placing of the separation lines between object and subject in the analysis of various aspects of psychical experience. Actually, words like "thoughts" and "sentiments," equally indispensable to illustrate the variety and scope of conscious life, are used in a similar complementary way as are space-time co-ordination and dynamical conservation laws in atomic physics. A precise formulation of such analogies involves, of course, intricacies of terminology, and the writer's position is perhaps best indicated in a passage in the article, hinting at the mutually exclusive relationship which will always exist between the practical use of any word and attempts at its strict definition. The principal aim, however, of these considerations, which were not least inspired by the hope of influencing Einstein's attitude, was to point to perspectives of bringing general epistemological problems into relief by means of a lesson derived from the study of new, but fundamentally simple physical experience.

———

At the next meeting with Einstein at the Solvay Conference in 1930, our discussions took quite a dramatic turn. As an objection to the view that a control of the interchange of momentum and energy between the objects and the measuring instruments was excluded if these instruments should serve their purpose of defining the space-time frame of the phenomena, Einstein brought forward the argument that such control should be possible when the exigencies of relativity theory were taken into consideration. In particular, the general relationship between energy and mass, expressed in Einstein's famous formula

$$E = mc^2 \qquad (5)$$

should allow, by means of simple weighing, to measure the total energy of any system and, thus, in principle to control the energy transferred to it when it interacts with an atomic object.

As an arrangement suited for such purpose, Einstein proposed the device indicated in Fig. 7, consisting of a box with

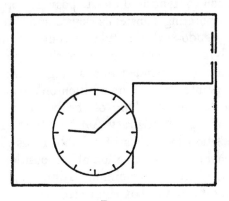

FIG. 7

a hole in its side, which could be opened or closed by a shutter moved by means of a clock-work within the box. If, in the beginning, the box contained a certain amount of radiation and the clock was set to open the shutter for a very short interval at a chosen time, it could be achieved that a single photon was released through the hole at a moment known with as great accuracy as desired. Moreover, it would apparently also be possible, by weighing the whole box before and after this event, to measure the energy of the photon with any accuracy wanted, in definite contradiction to the reciprocal indeterminacy of time and energy quantities in quantum mechanics.

This argument amounted to a serious challenge and gave rise to a thorough examination of the whole problem. At the outcome of the discussion, to which Einstein himself contributed effectively, it became clear, however, that this argument could not be upheld. In fact, in the consideration of the problem, it was found necessary to look closer into the consequences of the identification of inertial and gravitational mass implied in the application of relation (5). Especially, it was essential to take into account the relationship between the rate of a clock and its position in a gravitational field—well known from the red-shift of the lines in the sun's spectrum—following from Einstein's principle of equivalence between gravity effects and the phenomena observed in accelerated reference frames.

Our discussion concentrated on the possible application of an apparatus incorporating Einstein's device and drawn in Fig. 8 in the same pseudo-realistic style as some of the preceding figures. The box, of which a section is shown in order to exhibit its interior, is suspended in a spring-balance and is furnished with a pointer to read its position on a scale fixed to the balance support. The weighing of the box may thus be performed with any given accuracy Δm by adjusting the balance to its zero position by means of suitable loads. The essential point is now that any determination of this position with a given accuracy Δq will involve a minimum latitude Δp in the control of the momentum of the box connected with Δq by the relation (3). This latitude must obviously again be smaller than the total impulse which, during the whole interval T of the balancing procedure, can be given by the gravitational field to a body with a mass Δm, or

$$\Delta p \approx \frac{h}{\Delta q} < T \cdot g \cdot \Delta m, \qquad (6)$$

where g is the gravity constant. The greater the accuracy of the reading q of the pointer, the longer must, consequently, be the balancing interval T, if a given accuracy Δm of the weighing of the box with its content shall be obtained.

Now, according to general relativity theory, a clock, when displaced in the direction of the gravitational force by an amount of Δq, will change its rate in such a way that its reading

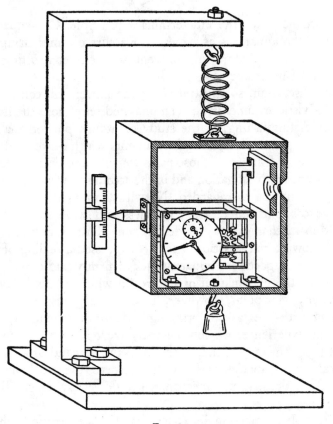

Fig. 8

in the course of a time interval T will differ by an amount ΔT given by the relation

$$\frac{\Delta T}{T} = \frac{1}{c^2} g\Delta q. \qquad (7)$$

By comparing (6) and (7) we see, therefore, that after the weighing procedure there will in our knowledge of the adjustment of the clock be a latitude

$$\Delta T > \frac{h}{c^2 \Delta m}.$$

Together with the formula (5), this relation again leads to

$$\Delta T \cdot \Delta E > h,$$

in accordance with the indeterminacy principle. Consequently, a use of the apparatus as a means of accurately measuring the energy of the photon will prevent us from controlling the moment of its escape.

The discussion, so illustrative of the power and consistency of relativistic arguments, thus emphasized once more the necessity of distinguishing, in the study of atomic phenomena, between the proper measuring instruments which serve to define the reference frame and those parts which are to be regarded as objects under investigation and in the account of which quantum effects cannot be disregarded. Notwithstanding the most suggestive confirmation of the soundness and wide scope of the quantum-mechanical way of description, Einstein nevertheless, in a following conversation with me, expressed a feeling of disquietude as regards the apparent lack of firmly laid down principles for the explanation of nature, in which all could agree. From my viewpoint, however, I could only answer that, in dealing with the task of bringing order into an entirely new field of experience, we could hardly trust in any accustomed principles, however broad, apart from the demand of avoiding logical inconsistencies and, in this respect, the mathematical formalism of quantum mechanics should surely meet all requirements.

The Solvay meeting in 1930 was the last occasion where, in common discussions with Einstein, we could benefit from the stimulating and mediating influence of Ehrenfest, but shortly before his deeply deplored death in 1933 he told me that Einstein was far from satisfied and with his usual acuteness had discerned new aspects of the situation which strengthened his critical attitude. In fact, by further examining the possibilities for the application of a balance arrangement, Einstein had perceived alternative procedures which, even if they did not allow the use he originally intended, might seem to enhance the paradoxes beyond the possibilities of logical solution. Thus, Einstein had pointed out that, after a preliminary weighing of the box with the clock and the subsequent escape of the photon, one was still left with the choice of either repeating the weighing or opening the box and comparing the reading of the clock with the standard time scale. Consequently, we are at this stage still free to choose whether we want to draw conclusions either about the energy of the photon or about the moment when it left the box. Without in any way interfering with the photon between its escape and its later interaction with other suitable measuring instruments, we are, thus, able to make accurate predictions pertaining *either* to the moment of its arrival *or* to the amount of energy liberated by its absorption. Since, however, according to the quantum-mechanical formalism, the specification of the state of an isolated particle cannot involve both a well-defined connection with the time scale and an accurate fixation of the energy, it might thus appear as if this formalism did not offer the means of an adequate description.

Once more Einstein's searching spirit had elicited a peculiar aspect of the situation in quantum theory, which in a most striking manner illustrated how far we have here transcended customary explanation of natural phenomena. Still, I could not agree with the trend of his remarks as reported by Ehrenfest. In my opinion, there could be no other way to deem a logically consistent mathematical formalism as inadequate than by demonstrating the departure of its consequences from experience or by proving that its predictions did not exhaust the possibilities of observation, and Einstein's argumentation could be directed to neither of these ends. In fact, we must realize that in the problem in question we are not dealing with a *single* specified experimental arrangement, but are referring to *two* different, mutually exclusive arrangements. In the one, the balance together with another piece of apparatus like a spectrometer is used for the study of the energy transfer by a photon; in the other, a shutter regulated by a standardized clock together with another apparatus of similar kind, accurately timed relatively to the clock, is used for the study of the time of propagation of a photon over a given distance. In both these cases, as also assumed by Einstein, the observable effects are expected to be in complete conformity with the predictions of the theory.

The problem again emphasizes the necessity of considering the *whole* experimental arrangement, the specification of which is imperative for any well-defined application of the quantum-mechanical formalism. Incidentally, it may be added that paradoxes of the kind contemplated by Einstein are encountered also in such simple arrangements as sketched in Fig. 5. In fact, after a preliminary measurement of the momentum of the diaphragm, we are in principle offered the choice, when an electron or photon has passed through the slit, either to repeat the momentum measurement or to control the position of the diaphragm and, thus, to make predictions pertaining to alternative subsequent observations. It may also be added that it obviously can make no difference as regards observable effects obtainable by a definite experimental arrangement, whether our plans of constructing or handling the instruments are fixed beforehand or whether we prefer to postpone the completion of our planning until a later moment when the particle is already on its way from one instrument to another.

In the quantum-mechanical description our freedom of constructing and handling the experimental arrangement finds its proper expression in the possibility of choosing the classically defined parameters entering in any proper application of the formalism. Indeed, in all such respects quantum mechanics exhibits a correspondence with the state of affairs familiar from classical physics, which is as close as possible when considering the individuality inherent in the quantum phenomena. Just in helping to bring out this point so clearly, Einstein's concern had therefore again been a most welcome incitement to explore the essential aspects of the situation.

The next Solvay meeting in 1933 was devoted to the problems of the structure and properties of atomic nuclei, in which field such great advances were made just in that period due to the experimental discoveries as well as to new fruitful applications of quantum mechanics. It need in this connection hardly be recalled that just the evidence obtained by the study of artificial nuclear transformations gave a most direct test of Einstein's fundamental law regarding the equivalence of mass and energy, which was to prove an evermore important guide for researches in nuclear physics. It may also be mentioned how Einstein's intuitive recognition of the intimate relationship between the law of radioactive transformations and the probability rules governing individual radiation effects (cf. p. 205) was confirmed by the quantum-mechanical explanation of spontaneous nuclear disintegrations. In fact, we are here dealing with a typical example of the statistical mode of description, and the complementary relationship between energy-momentum conservation and time-space co-ordination is most strikingly exhibited in the well-known paradox of particle penetration through potential barriers.

Einstein himself did not attend this meeting, which took place at a time darkened by the tragic developments in the political world which were to influence his fate so deeply and add so greatly to his burdens in the service of humanity. A few months earlier, on a visit to Princeton where Einstein was then guest of the newly founded Institute for Advanced Study to which he soon after became permanently attached, I had, however, opportunity to talk with him again about the epistemological aspects of atomic physics, but the difference between our ways of approach and expression still presented obstacles to mutual understanding. While, so far, relatively few persons had taken part in the discussions reported in this article, Einstein's critical attitude towards the views on quantum theory adhered to by many physicists was soon after brought to public attention through a paper[11] with the title "Can Quantum-Mechanical Description of Physical Reality Be Considered Complete?," published in 1935 by Einstein, Podolsky and Rosen.

The argumentation in this paper is based on a criterion which the authors express in the following sentence: "If, without in any way disturbing a system, we can predict with certainty (i.e., with probability equal to unity) the value of a physical quantity, then there exists an element of physical reality correspond-

---

[11] A. Einstein, B. Podolsky and N. Rosen, *Phys. Rev.*, 47, 777, (1935).

ing to this physical quantity." By an elegant exposition of the consequences of the quantum-mechanical formalism as regards the representation of a state of a system, consisting of two parts which have been in interaction for a limited time interval, it is next shown that different quantities, the fixation of which cannot be combined in the representation of one of the partial systems, can nevertheless be predicted by measurements pertaining to the other partial system. According to their criterion, the authors therefore conclude that quantum mechanics does not "provide a complete description of the physical reality," and they express their belief that it should be possible to develop a more adequate account of the phenomena.

Due to the lucidity and apparently incontestable character of the argument, the paper of Einstein, Podolsky and Rosen created a stir among physicists and has played a large rôle in general philosophical discussion. Certainly the issue is of a very subtle character and suited to emphasize how far, in quantum theory, we are beyond the reach of pictorial visualization. It will be seen, however, that we are here dealing with problems of just the same kind as those raised by Einstein in previous discussions, and, in an article which appeared a few months later,[12] I tried to show that from the point of view of complementarity the apparent inconsistencies were completely removed. The trend of the argumentation was in substance the same as that exposed in the foregoing pages, but the aim of recalling the way in which the situation was discussed at that time may be an apology for citing certain passages from my article.

Thus, after referring to the conclusions derived by Einstein, Podolsky and Rosen on the basis of their criterion, I wrote:

Such an argumentation, however, would hardly seem suited to affect the soundness of quantum-mechanical description, which is based on a coherent mathematical formalism covering automatically any procedure of measurement like that indicated. The apparent contradiction in fact discloses only an essential inadequacy of the customary viewpoint of natural philosophy for a rational account of physical phenomena of the type with which we are concerned in quantum mechanics. Indeed the *finite interaction between object and measuring agencies* conditioned

[12] N. Bohr, *Phys. Rev.*, *48*, 696, (1935).

by the very existence of the quantum of action entails—because of the impossibility of controlling the reaction of the object on the measuring instruments, if these are to serve their purpose—the necessity of a final renunciation of the classical ideal of causality and a radical revision of our attitude towards the problem of physical reality. In fact, as we shall see, a criterion of reality like that proposed by the named authors contains—however cautious its formulation may appear—an essential ambiguity when it is applied to the actual problems with which we are here concerned.

As regards the special problem treated by Einstein, Podolsky and Rosen, it was next shown that the consequences of the formalism as regards the representation of the state of a system consisting of two interacting atomic objects correspond to the simple arguments mentioned in the preceding in connection with the discussion of the experimental arrangements suited for the study of complementary phenomena. In fact, although any pair q and p, of conjugate space and momentum variables obeys the rule of non-commutative multiplication expressed by (2), and can thus only be fixed with reciprocal latitudes given by (3), the difference $q_1 - q_2$ between two space-co-ordinates referring to the constituents of the system will commute with the sum $p_1 + p_2$ of the corresponding momentum components, as follows directly from the commutability of q_1 with p_2 and q_2 with p_1. Both $q_1 - q_2$ and $p_1 + p_2$ can, therefore, be accurately fixed in a state of the complex system and, consequently, we can predict the values of either q_1 or p_1 if either q_2 or p_2, respectively, are determined by direct measurements. If, for the two parts of the system, we take a particle and a diaphragm, like that sketched in Fig. 5, we see that the possibilities of specifying the state of the particle by measurements on the diaphragm just correspond to the situation described on p. 220 and further discussed on p. 230, where it was mentioned that, after the particle has passed through the diaphragm, we have in principle the choice of measuring either the position of the diaphragm or its momentum and, in each case, to make predictions as to subsequent observations pertaining to the particle. As repeatedly stressed, the principal point is here that such measurements demand mutually exclusive experimental arrangements.

The argumentation of the article was summarized in the following passage:

From our point of view we now see that the wording of the above-mentioned criterion of physical reality proposed by Einstein, Podolsky, and Rosen contains an ambiguity as regards the meaning of the expression 'without in any way disturbing a system.' Of course there is in a case like that just considered no question of a mechanical disturbance of the system under investigation during the last critical stage of the measuring procedure. But even at this stage there is essentially the question of *an influence on the very conditions which define the possible types of predictions regarding the future behaviour of the system.* Since these conditions constitute an inherent element of the description of any phenomenon to which the term "physical reality" can be properly attached, we see that the argumentation of the mentioned authors does not justify their conclusion that quantum-mechanical description is essentially incomplete. On the contrary, this description, as appears from the preceding discussion, may be characterized as a rational utilization of all possibilities of unambiguous interpretation of measurements, compatible with the finite and uncontrollable interaction between the objects and the measuring instruments in the field of quantum theory. In fact, it is only the mutual exclusion of any two experimental procedures, permitting the unambiguous definition of complementary physical quantities, which provides room for new physical laws, the coexistence of which might at first sight appear irreconcilable with the basic principles of science. It is just this entirely new situation as regards the description of physical phenomena that the notion of *complementarity* aims at characterizing.

Rereading these passages, I am deeply aware of the inefficiency of expression which must have made it very difficult to appreciate the trend of the argumentation aiming to bring out the essential ambiguity involved in a reference to physical attributes of objects when dealing with phenomena where no sharp distinction can be made between the behaviour of the objects themselves and their interaction with the measuring instruments. I hope, however, that the present account of the discussions with Einstein in the foregoing years, which contributed so greatly to make us familiar with the situation in quantum physics, may give a clearer impression of the necessity of a radical revision of basic principles for physical explanation in order to restore logical order in this field of experience.

Einstein's own views at that time are presented in an article "Physics and Reality," published in 1936 in the *Journal of the Franklin Institute*.[13]." Starting from a most illuminating exposition of the gradual development of the fundamental principles in the theories of classical physics and their relation to the problem of physical reality, Einstein here argues that the quantum-mechanical description is to be considered merely as a means of accounting for the average behaviour of a large number of atomic systems and his attitude to the belief that it should offer an exhaustive description of the individual phenomena is expressed in the following words: "To believe this is logically possible without contradiction; but it is so very contrary to my scientific instinct that I cannot forego the search for a more complete conception."

Even if such an attitude might seem well-balanced in itself, it nevertheless implies a rejection of the whole argumentation exposed in the preceding, aiming to show that, in quantum mechanics, we are not dealing with an arbitrary renunciation of a more detailed analysis of atomic phenomena, but with a recognition that such an analysis is *in principle* excluded. The peculiar individuality of the quantum effects presents us, as regards the comprehension of well-defined evidence, with a novel situation unforeseen in classical physics and irreconcilable with conventional ideas suited for our orientation and adjustment to ordinary experience. It is in this respect that quantum theory has called for a renewed revision of the foundation for the unambiguous use of elementary concepts, as a further step in the development which, since the advent of relativity theory, has been so characteristic of modern science.

In the following years, the more philosophical aspects of the situation in atomic physics aroused the interest of ever larger circles and were, in particular, discussed at the Second International Congress for the Unity of Science in Copenhagen in July 1936. In a lecture on this occasion,[14] I tried especially to

[13] A. Einstein, *Journ. Frankl. Inst.*, 221, 349, (1936).
[14] N. Bohr, *Erkenntnis*, 6, 293, (1937), and *Philosophy of Science*, 4, 289, (1937).

stress the analogy in epistemological respects between the limitation imposed on the causal description in atomic physics and situations met with in other fields of knowledge. A principal purpose of such parallels was to call attention to the necessity in many domains of general human interest to face problems of a similar kind as those which had arisen in quantum theory and thereby to give a more familiar background for the apparently extravagant way of expression which physicists have developed to cope with their acute difficulties.

Besides the complementary features conspicuous in psychology and already touched upon (cf. p. 224), examples of such relationships can also be traced in biology, especially as regards the comparison between mechanistic and vitalistic viewpoints. Just with respect to the observational problem, this last question had previously been the subject of an address to the International Congress on Light Therapy held in Copenhagen in 1932,[15] where it was incidentally pointed out that even the psycho-physical parallelism as envisaged by Leibniz and Spinoza has obtained a wider scope through the development of atomic physics, which forces us to an attitude towards the problem of explanation recalling ancient wisdom, that when searching for harmony in life one must never forget that in the drama of existence we are ourselves both actors and spectators.

Utterances of this kind would naturally in many minds evoke the impression of an underlying mysticism foreign to the spirit of science; at the above mentioned Congress in 1936 I therefore tried to clear up such misunderstandings and to explain that the only question was an endeavour to clarify the conditions, in each field of knowledge, for the analysis and synthesis of experience.[14] Yet, I am afraid that I had in this respect only little success in convincing my listeners, for whom the dissent among the physicists themselves was naturally a cause of scepticism as to the necessity of going so far in renouncing customary demands as regards the explanation of natural phenomena. Not least through a new discussion with Einstein in Princeton in 1937, where we did not get beyond a humourous contest con-

---

[15] II° Congrès international de la Lumière, Copenhague 1932 (reprinted in *Nature*, *131*, 421 and 457, 1933).

cerning which side Spinoza would have taken if he had lived to see the development of our days, I was strongly reminded of the importance of utmost caution in all questions of terminology and dialectics.

These aspects of the situation were especially discussed at a meeting in Warsaw in 1938, arranged by the International Institute of Intellectual Co-operation of the League of Nations.[16] The preceding years had seen great progress in quantum physics due to a number of fundamental discoveries regarding the constitution and properties of atomic nuclei as well as due to important developments of the mathematical formalism taking the requirements of relativity theory into account. In the last respect, Dirac's ingenious quantum theory of the electron offered a most striking illustration of the power and fertility of the general quantum-mechanical way of description. In the phenomena of creation and annihilation of electron pairs we have in fact to do with new fundamental features of atomicity, which are intimately connected with the non-classical aspects of quantum statistics expressed in the exclusion principle, and which have demanded a still more far-reaching renunciation of explanation in terms of a pictorial representation.

Meanwhile, the discussion of the epistemological problems in atomic physics attracted as much attention as ever and, in commenting on Einstein's views as regards the incompleteness of the quantum-mechanical mode of description, I entered more directly on questions of terminology. In this connection I warned especially against phrases, often found in the physical literature, such as "disturbing of phenomena by observation" or "creating physical attributes to atomic objects by measurements." Such phrases, which may serve to remind of the apparent paradoxes in quantum theory, are at the same time apt to cause confusion, since words like "phenomena" and "observations," just as "attributes" and "measurements," are used in a way hardly compatible with common language and practical definition.

As a more appropriate way of expression I advocated the ap-

[16] *New Theories in Physics* (Paris 1938), 11.

plication of the word *phenomenon* exclusively to refer to the observations obtained under specified circumstances, including an account of the whole experimental arrangement. In such terminology, the observational problem is free of any special intricacy since, in actual experiments, all observations are expressed by unambiguous statements referring, for instance, to the registration of the point at which an electron arrives at a photographic plate. Moreover, speaking in such a way is just suited to emphasize that the appropriate physical interpretation of the symbolic quantum-mechanical formalism amounts only to predictions, of determinate or statistical character, pertaining to individual phenomena appearing under conditions defined by classical physical concepts.

Notwithstanding all differences between the physical problems which have given rise to the development of relativity theory and quantum theory, respectively, a comparison of purely logical aspects of relativistic and complementary argumentation reveals striking similarities as regards the renunciation of the absolute significance of conventional physical attributes of objects. Also, the neglect of the atomic constitution of the measuring instruments themselves, in the account of actual experience, is equally characteristic of the applications of relativity and quantum theory. Thus, the smallness of the quantum of action compared with the actions involved in usual experience, including the arranging and handling of physical apparatus, is as essential in atomic physics as is the enormous number of atoms composing the world in the general theory of relativity which, as often pointed out, demands that dimensions of apparatus for measuring angles can be made small compared with the radius of curvature of space.

In the Warsaw lecture, I commented upon the use of not directly visualizable symbolism in relativity and quantum theory in the following way:

Even the formalisms, which in both theories within their scope offer adequate means of comprehending all conceivable experience, exhibit deepgoing analogies. In fact, the astounding simplicity of the generalization of classical physical theories, which are obtained by the use of multidimensional geometry and non-commutative algebra, respectively, rests in both cases essentially on the introduction of the conventional symbol $\sqrt{-1}$. The abstract character of the formalisms concerned is indeed, on closer examination, as typical of relativity theory as it is of quantum mechanics, and it is in this respect purely a matter of tradition if the former theory is considered as a completion of classical physics rather than as a first fundamental step in the thoroughgoing revision of our conceptual means of comparing observations, which the modern development of physics has forced upon us.

It is, of course, true that in atomic physics we are confronted with a number of unsolved fundamental problems, especially as regards the intimate relationship between the elementary unit of electric charge and the universal quantum of action; but these problems are no more connected with the epistemological points here discussed than is the adequacy of relativistic argumentation with the issue of thus far unsolved problems of cosmology. Both in relativity and in quantum theory we are concerned with new aspects of scientific analysis and synthesis and, in this connection, it is interesting to note that, even in the great epoch of critical philosophy in the former century, there was only question to what extent *a priori* arguments could be given for the adequacy of space-time co-ordination and causal connection of experience, but never question of rational generalizations or inherent limitations of such categories of human thinking.

Although in more recent years I have had several occasions of meeting Einstein, the continued discussions, from which I always have received new impulses, have so far not led to a common view about the epistemological problems in atomic physics, and our opposing views are perhaps most clearly stated in a recent issue of *Dialectica*,[17] bringing a general discussion of these problems. Realizing, however, the many obstacles for mutual understanding as regards a matter where approach and background must influence everyone's attitude, I have welcomed this opportunity of a broader exposition of the development by which, to my mind, a veritable crisis in physical science has been overcome. The lesson we have hereby received would seem to have brought us a decisive step further in the never-

[17] N. Bohr, *Dialectica*, 1, 312 (1948).

ending struggle for harmony between content and form, and taught us once again that no content can be grasped without a formal frame and that any form, however useful it has hitherto proved, may be found to be too narrow to comprehend new experience.

Surely, in a situation like this, where it has been difficult to reach mutual understanding not only between philosophers and physicists but even between physicists of different schools, the difficulties have their root not seldom in the preference for a certain use of language suggesting itself from the different lines of approach. In the Institute in Copenhagen, where through those years a number of young physicists from various countries came together for discussions, we used, when in trouble, often to comfort ourselves with jokes, among them the old saying of the two kinds of truth. To the one kind belong statements so simple and clear that the opposite assertion obviously could not be defended. The other kind, the so-called "deep truths," are statements in which the opposite also contains deep truth. Now, the development in a new field will usually pass through stages in which chaos becomes gradually replaced by order; but it is not least in the intermediate stage where deep truth prevails that the work is really exciting and inspires the imagination to search for a firmer hold. For such endeavours of seeking the proper balance between seriousness and humour, Einstein's own personality stands as a great example and, when expressing my belief that through a singularly fruitful co-operation of a whole generation of physicists we are nearing the goal where logical order to a large extent allows us to avoid deep truth, I hope that it will be taken in his spirit and may serve as an apology for several utterances in the preceding pages.

The discussions with Einstein which have formed the theme of this article have extended over many years which have witnessed great progress in the field of atomic physics. Whether our actual meetings have been of short or long duration, they have always left a deep and lasting impression on my mind, and when writing this report I have, so-to-say, been arguing with Einstein all the time even when entering on topics apparently far removed from the special problems under debate at our meetings. As regards the account of the conversations I am, of course, aware that I am relying only on my own memory, just as I am prepared for the possibility that many features of the development of quantum theory, in which Einstein has played so large a part, may appear to himself in a different light. I trust, however, that I have not failed in conveying a proper impression of how much it has meant to me to be able to benefit from the inspiration which we all derive from every contact with Einstein.

NIELS BOHR

UNIVERSITETETS INSTITUT
FOR TEORETISK FYSIK
COPENHAGEN, DENMARK

8

Henry Margenau

EINSTEIN'S CONCEPTION OF REALITY

EINSTEIN'S CONCEPTION OF REALITY

1. Introduction

AN ARTICLE which concerns itself with the philosophical views of a living scientist requires justification beyond the desire to honor his work; for such honor would be bestowed more properly by the pursuit and publication of significant research along lines marked out by the scientist himself. This consideration weighs heavily in relation to Einstein, a man who is particularly sensitive to writings about his person.

It is one thing to write a scientific exposition of the theory of relativity, but quite another to leave the realm of factual statement and to enter the wider domain of discourse in which words have a variety of meanings, where what is known is difficult to set apart from what is surmised and where, after all, Einstein's interest has never centered. This paper is not an attempt to *interpret* his views on reality, nor to embody them into a system for the reader's acceptance or rejection. If that were to be done, the originator of these views should be the author of their interpretation.

It is equally far from my intentions to present a criticism of ideas, physical or metaphysical, which inhere in the theory of relativity. The literature attempting this is already wide, too wide for the good of either physics or philosophy. A knowledge of the physical and mathematical structure of relativity theory will here be assumed, and its fundamental validity will never be drawn into question as far as present evidence goes. In fact this theory is now so well corroborated by experience and by assimilation into the whole of modern physics that its denial is almost unthinkable. The physicist is impressed not solely by its far flung empirical verifications, but above all by the intrinsic beauty of its conception which predisposes the discriminating mind for acceptance even if there were no experimental evidence for the theory at all.

The purpose of the subsequent remarks is simply this: To distill from Einstein's work those elements of method, to draw from his miscellaneous writings those basic conceptions, which combine into a picture of what, to him, must be reality. That philosophers and physicists are interested in this picture, the background of the most creative effort of our time, goes without saying. That it be accurate can be insured, theoretically, by the opportunity available to its hero to point out its defects. The paper is written, therefore, in full expectation of being disavowed or corrected where it is in error. This valuable possibility of later correction has, I understand, inspired the publication of the present and of similar volumes.

Scientists, among them Einstein, have warned philosophers to give attention to their deeds rather than their words. Failure to heed this advice has produced a rather deplorable lack of understanding between philosophy and physics today. Every discoverer of a new physical principle makes an important contribution to philosophy, even though he may not discuss it in philosophic terms. The metaphysical wealth reposing largely untapped in modern physical theory is enormous and challenging to the investigator; it is available for everyone who will acquire the tools needed to explore it. The methodological content of relativity theory, both special and general, has not been exhausted and will here be made the primary source of information. Its author's own remarks on reality, illuminating indeed despite their relative paucity, will be used as corroborating evidence.

It is possible to construe a contradiction between the methodological implications of the theory of relativity and its founder's interpretative comments. Misconceptions have arisen as a result of this, and since they involve an erroneous identification of reality they should at once be exposed. One of the famous consequences of the special theory is the need for non-Newtonian time. According to Newton, time was a unique process of flow, independent of the circumstances of the observer. This empirical uniqueness was epitomized in Kant's system by a rationalization which attached transcendental necessity to the uniqueness of time, thus lifting it above empirical examination. Relativity shattered this isolation and again made time a matter for experimental inquiry. Indeed it went much farther than that, farther than Newton or anyone had ever gone; it wholly renounced rational preconceptions and made the meaning of time dependent upon one very specific physical process: the propagation of light. There was insistence on a definition of time which could be operationally circumscribed in great detail, a definition that stood the test of pragmatism. If the results of this innovation contradicted the alleged dictates of reason, common reasoning had to be modified: empirical facts forced inquiry into unaccustomed channels. It is hard to ignore the undercurrent of empiricism, and one might be tempted to impute the success of the relativity theory to a philosophic attitude which banishes rational, or mental, elements from the description of nature and replaces them by the solid facts of sensible experience. This is often done.

And yet, in his writings, Einstein frequently states that his position differs from Newton's inasmuch as he takes issue with the thought that time and space are concepts derived from experience. He claims that the distance between theoretical construction and verifiable conclusion in modern physics grows larger as theories take on simpler forms; indeed he regards fundamental principles as "free inventions of the human intellect."[1] Superficial examination senses here a contradiction which only closer analysis can remove. Einstein's position cannot be labelled by any one of the current names of philosophic attitudes; it contains features of rationalism and extreme empiricism, but not in logical isolation.

2. Ontological Beliefs

There is every indication that, to Einstein, reality means *physical* reality. While everywhere considerable respect is

[1] "On the Method of Theoretical Physics," by Albert Einstein (The Clarendon Press, Oxford, 1933; "The Herbert Spencer Lecture delivered at Oxford, 10 June 1933"); reprinted in *The World As I See It*, Covici Friede (1934), 33.

shown for those phases of experience which have not as yet been penetrated by scientific method, one feels, in reading his utterances, that all existence is essentially fathomable by means of the peculiar interplay of experience and analysis which characterizes physics. A certain pathos for the unknown, though often displayed, always intimates the ultimately knowable character of existence, knowable in scientific terms.

Little can be found which is at all relevant to the traditional questions of ontology: whether the real world contains traces of the human observer in a Kantian sense; whether it contains merely sensory qualities or the idealizations called laws of nature as well; whether logical concepts are to be regarded as part of it. In fact, one does not find a definition of reality. For my own part, I do not regard this as a lack, for it is increasingly evident that the best of modern physics avoids the term and operates entirely within the realm of epistemology, or methodology; leaving it for the spectator to construe the meaning of reality in any way he wishes. To some extent this seems to be true for the discoverer of relativity. Nevertheless there is a good deal of consistency in his usage of the word.

It is perfectly clear that Einstein, in common with practically all scientists, assumes the existence of an external world, an objective world, i.e., one that is largely independent of the human observer. To quote:

The belief in an external world independent of the perceiving subject is the basis of all natural science. Since, however, sense perception only gives information of this external world or of 'physical reality' indirectly, we can only grasp the latter by speculative means. It follows from this that our notions of physical reality can never be final. We must always be ready to change these notions—that is to say, the axiomatic structure of physics —in order to do justice to perceived facts in the most logically perfect way.[2]

On the one hand one has here an identification of physical reality with the external world, on the other an insistence upon the difference between an essence of reality and what it appears

[2] "Clerk Maxwell's Influence on the Evolution of the Idea of Physical Reality," from Einstein, A., *The World As I See It*, 60.

to be. Indeed there is implied a three-fold distinction between an *external world*, the observer's *perception of that external world*, and our *notions* of it; for as we have seen before, the axiomatic structure of physics is not abstracted from sensory experience.

To some of the interesting questions which arise at this point answers seem to be lacking. Having been reared in the Kantian tradition Einstein conceivably espouses a *Ding an sich* which is intrinsically unknowable. More likely, however, he would hold any characterization of reality in terms other than those provided by science as irrelevant and regard the question as to the metaphysical attributes of reality as unimportant. Under those conditions, what is meant by the assertion that there *is* an external world independent of the perceiving subject becomes problematical. Like most scientists, Einstein leaves unanswered the basic metaphysical problem underlying all science, the meaning of externality.

There may be perceived a curious trace of rationalism in the passage last quoted. Sense perception, we are told, gives information about physical reality in a manner called indirect. This innocent word, of course, hides a multitude of epistemological problems upon which the scientist does not care to express himself. But the hint that, because of the indirect nature of sensuous knowledge, recourse is to be taken to speculation, is intensely interesting and reminds us again of that thoroughgoing conviction which separates Einstein, Planck and others who have had much to do with the creation of modern physics, from the more popular schools of current positivism and empiricism. However, to state this conviction very precisely is difficult, as the following quotation shows.

Behind the tireless efforts of the investigator there lurks a stronger, more mysterious drive: it is existence and reality that one wishes to comprehend. But one shrinks from the use of such words, for one soon gets into difficulties when one has to explain what is really meant by 'reality' and by 'comprehend' in such a general statement.[8]

[8] Address at Columbia University from, *The World As I See It*, 137f.

3. RELATION OF THEORY TO REALITY

While the exact manner in which theory represents physical reality is difficult to construe, it is quite clear from Einstein's work and writings that he was an opponent of the view according to which theory *copies* reality. On this point he takes sharp issue with Newton, and implicitly with the whole of British empiricism. The central recognition of the theory of relativity is that geometry, regarded by Newton as a set of descriptive propositions flowing from and summarizing physical experience, is a construct of the intellect. Only when this discovery is accepted can the mind feel free to tamper with the time-honored notions of space and time, to survey the range of possibilities available for defining them, and to select that formulation which agrees with observation. Conformation with experience must be achieved, not in the initial stages of theoretical analysis but in its final consequences. "The structure of the system is the work of reason; the empirical contents and their mutual relations must find their representation in the conclusions of the theory."[4]

Just how the contact with reality is to be made is obvious in the physical content of relativity theory, and is also a matter on which Einstein has expressed himself unambiguously. There is something ineffable about the real, something occasionally described as mysterious and awe-inspiring; the property alluded to is no doubt its ultimacy, its spontaneity, its failure to present itself as the perfect and articulate consequence of rational thought. On the other hand mathematics, and especially geometry, have exactly those attributes of internal order, the elements of predictability, which reality seems to lack. How do these incongruous counterparts of our experience get together? "As far as the laws of mathematics refer to reality, they are not certain; and as far as they are certain, they do not refer to reality."[5]

The point is that the two do not of themselves get together,

---

[4] "On the Method of Theoretical Physics" (1933); in *The World As I See It*, 33.

[5] "Geometry and Experience." An expanded form of an address to the Prussian Academy of Sciences, Berlin, Jan. 27, 1921, quoted from Einstein's *Sidelights of Relativity* (London, 1922).

but have to be brought together forcibly by means of a special postulate. Euclidean geometry is a hypothetical discipline based upon axioms which in themselves claim no relevance to reality. Other axioms generate different geometries. Reality, on the other hand, does not present the investigator with axioms. A physical theory, i.e., an intelligible picture of reality, results when one geometry is postulationally said to correspond to observation. Contact with reality has then been made. Mystic experience of the real is like a vast but formless reservoir of life-giving substance; mathematics alone is a gallery of robots. Select one of them and connect him with the real. If you have chosen the right one, you may witness the spectacle of man-made life; blood will course through the previously empty veins of the artifact and a functioning organism has been created. No one can tell in advance which robot will cause this success to be achieved; the scientist of genius makes the proper selection.

I should like to think that this crude pictorization will not do violence to Einstein's view. It emphasizes a point to which I have attached very great importance, namely that the central elements of any methodology of physics are these: the sensory facts of experience, the constructs generated to explain them, and the rules of correspondence which make possible the fruitful and valid intercommunication between the former two areas. All through "Geometry and Experience" one finds evidence for the need of such rules of correspondence.

In a number of places Einstein expresses his indebtedness to Mach, and it is easy to trace his concern over observability directly to this philosopher. Both reject theoretical concepts which by their nature do not lend themselves to verification. To get around the notion of unobservable absolute space, Mach tries to save the laws of mechanics by substituting for an acceleration with respect to absolute space an acceleration relative to the inertial system moving with the center of mass of all masses in the universe. This same attitude led Einstein to the rejection of the ether and, indeed, of Mach's proposal, for the latter annuls itself when thought through completely. To measure acceleration with reference to a universal inertial frame, and even to define that frame, requires the concept of action at a distance and this, in turn, presupposes universal simultaneity which is operationally absurd. By this chain of logical reduction does the suggestion of Mach finally destroy itself. This example is nearly symbolic, for it happens that in many other instances the delicacy and the consistency of Einstein's physical reasoning controverts the original Machian stand, and the thoughtful observer sees throughout his work a progressive denial of the attitude that regards theories as inessential, labor saving adornments of reality which, though important for a time, are shed like dry leaves as the organism of science develops, to use Mach's phraseology.

4. THE CONCEPT OF OBJECTIVITY

What makes the theory of relativity extraordinarily important for philosophy is its incisive answer to the problem of objectivity. It is agreed that the formalization which goes as the accepted view of reality must have the quality of being objective, or independent of the observer; it must have as few anthropomorphic traits as possible. One might mean thereby that reality must appear the same to all, appear, that is, in sensory perception. But this can certainly never be assured in view of the intrinsic subjectivity of all our sensory knowledge. Nor is there any use in wondering how reality could be constructed apart from sensory specification, for this would lead to an endless variety of reals. What the world would appear to be if our eyes were sensitive not to the range of optical frequencies but to X-rays, or even how a three-dimensional map of all electric and magnetic fields at any instant might be drawn, are philosophically not very significant questions. Relativity teaches that the meaning of objectivity can not be captured wholly in the external realm of science.

In Newton's physics space and time were objective because they manifested themselves unmistakably in everyone's experience. But this idea of objectivity was completely shattered when several different spaces and times suddenly clamored for acceptance. It then became necessary to distinguish between the subjective time and space of every observer, and several kinds of formalized or public spaces and times. The latter had certain ideal properties such as being finite, or being isotropic, or constancy of metric, which the subjective counterparts did not possess. However, these ideal properties did not constitute them as objective.

Does objectivity, then, arise from agreement between experience and the predictions of theory? Is *any valid* theory objective? The answer to these questions is doubtless affirmative, but does not give a clue to the problem under consideration, for a theory, to be valid, must *also* be objective; correct prediction of events is not enough. It is thus seen that the criterion of objectivity lies somehow within the very structure of theory itself, that it must reside within some formal property of the ideal scheme which pretends to correspond to reality. And that is where the theory of relativity places it.

Objectivity becomes equivalent to *invariance* of physical laws, not physical phenomena or observations. A falling object may describe a parabola to an observer on a moving train, a straight line to an observer on the ground. These differences in appearance do not matter so long as the law of nature in its general form, i.e., in the form of a differential equation, is the same for both observers. Einstein's concept of objectivity takes every pretense to uniformity out of the sphere of perception and puts it in the basic form of theoretical statements. He rejected Newtonian mechanics because of its failure to satisfy this principle; he discarded the ether for that reason. Having produced the special theory of relativity, the conviction with regard to the ultimate significance of the axiom of invariance kept alive in Einstein, through the stunning series of successes encountered by the special theory, an acute realization of its limits. For the special theory had recognized invariance only with respect to inertial systems and had therefore not pushed objectivity far enough. From this defect the general theory took its origin.

The amazing results of Einstein's interpretation of objectivity have silenced almost completely all philosophical inquiry into its logical status. On the face of it, it seems satisfactory to impose the demands of invariability upon the most basic tenets of theory, even though this creates variability in the sphere of immediate experience. From the mathematical point of view, however, this procedure fails to be impartial, for it favors differential equations over ordinary equations. The laws of physics, which are to remain invariant, are always differential equations. Their solutions, i.e., ordinary equations, contain constants which vary from one observer to the next. Now what distinguishes differential equations logically from ordinary ones is that they are less committal, and that requirements placed on them have less drastic effects than similar requirements on their solutions. One may put the meaning of objectivity, then, perhaps in this form: It amounts to invariance of that group of theoretical statements which are least specific.

The idea of invariance is the nucleus of the theory of relativity. To the layman, and sometimes to the philosopher, this theory represents quite the contrary, a set of laws which allow for variability from one observer to another. This one-sided conception is linguistically implied by the word relativity which does not characterize the theory as centrally as it should. The true state of affairs can be seen when attention is directed to the aforementioned postulate of objectivity, which requires that the basic laws (the differential equations of highest order used in the description of reality) shall be invariant with respect to certain transformations. From this the variability, or relativity, of detailed observation may be shown to follow as a logical consequence. To give a simple example: the basic laws of electrodynamics involve the speed of light, c. If these laws are to be invariant, c must be constant. But the constancy of c in different inertial systems requires that moving objects contract, that moving clocks be retarded, that there can be no universal simultaneity, and so forth. To achieve *objectivity* of basic description, the theory must confer *relativity* upon the domain of immediate observations. In philosophic discussions, too much emphasis has been placed upon the incidental consequence, doubtless because the spectacular tests of the theory involve this consequence.

5. SIMPLICITY AS A CRITERION OF REALITY

Coupled with the hypothesis that our conception of reality must be objective one finds, throughout Einstein's work, the implicit belief that the best description of the world is the simplest. "Our experience . . . justifies us in believing that nature is the realisation of the simplest conceivable mathematical ideas."[6] The criterion of simplicity is frequently used by methodologists of science to distinguish acceptable from unacceptable theories. But it does not often attain complete clarity of statement.

Logically, it is extremely difficult to state the conditions under which a set of axioms may be regarded as simple or even as simpler than another, and this situation is likely to remain until theoretical physics has been penetrated completely by the methods of symbolic logic. Only when the number of independent fundamental axioms involved in a theory can be counted will simplicity become a quantitative concept.

Meanwhile, however, the scientist proceeds to use it intuitively, as a sort of topological measure upon which he relies when two competing theories, equally well verified, present themselves for acceptance. This happened, for example, in the days of Copernicus. The issue of simplicity was raised and it favored the heliocentric theory, although it would have been quite possible to patch up the Ptolemean system by adding deferents and epicycles *ad libitum*. It seems historically correct to say that Copernicus adopted his theory not because he held it to be true but because it was simpler. Similar instances have occurred in the later history of science.

Einstein's use of the principle of simplicity is not merely discriminating, it is constructive. In proposing new theories he employs it as a guide. This is made possible by limiting its meaning to some extent, by restricting it to the form of mathematical equations. For here it is not difficult to agree, for example, that a linear equation is simpler than one of higher order, that a constant is the simplest function, that a four-vector is a simpler construct than a tensor of the second rank, etc. Also,

---

[6] "On the Method of Theoretical Physics" (1933); in *The World As I See It*, 36.

in the mathematical field the hypothesis of simplicity combines beautifully with the postulate or invariance treated in the preceding section. To quote again, "In the limited nature of the mathematically existent simple fields and the simple equations possible between them, lies the theorist's hope of grasping the real in all its depth."[7]

We see this method at work, first of all, in the special theory with its choice of linear transformation equations;[8] in the explanation of the photoelectric effect where the simplest of all possible mathematical formulations worked so well; in the theory of radiation where mathematical simplicity and necessity led to the introduction of the coefficient of spontaneous emission for which the physical need was at the time not clear; in the formulation of Einstein's cosmological equation of the general theory of relativity; and finally in his discovery that the quantities used by Dirac in his successful theory of the electron were actually the simplest field quantities (spinors) suitable for that purpose.

It may well be that Einstein has carried his reliance on simplicity too far, for it has led him to criticize the recent advances in quantum theory on the basis of that criterion. But we shall defer discussion of this matter to a later section.

Although it is nowhere stated, the idea of simplicity seems to present itself to the man who used it so skillfully as one facet of a larger background of conviction, namely that our conception of reality while changing as time goes on, nevertheless converges toward some goal. The goal may never be reached, but it functions as a limit. And unless I am greatly in error, Einstein regards that goal as simple, and hence a simple theory as the best vehicle on which to approach it.

Considerations of mathematical simplicity play an important rôle in modern theories of cosmology. One of the chief arguments for supposing the universe to be bounded in space was the reminder that the boundary condition for a finite closed surface is very much simpler than the corresponding condition

---

[7] *Ibid.*, 38.

[8] This is not a good example, for there are reasons other than simplicity why linear equations must here be chosen; but we thought it worth mentioning.

at infinity, needed for a quasi-Euclidean universe. The story of the "cosmological constant" also throws an interesting side light on this issue. The simplest law of gravitation, which related the second order, divergence-free tensor $R_{\mu\nu}' - \frac{1}{2}g_{\mu\nu} R$ directly to the matter-energy tensor $T_{\mu\nu}$, was regretfully found to be in error because it failed to account for the finite mean density of matter in the universe. Proceeding under the restraint of the simplicity conviction, Einstein introduced into his law the minimum complication by adding the term ΛG_{ik}, Λ being the cosmological constant. This amounted to a most unwelcome sacrifice. In reading the Appendix for the Second Edition of *The Meaning of Relativity* (1945) one senses the relief which the author of this augmented law of gravitation experienced at the work of Friedmann, who showed that the cosmological constant is, after all, not needed. Yet there looms a final dilemma, as yet unresolved. Friedmann's equations imply an age of the universe of a mere billion years, whereas all other evidence demands a greater span.

6. The Form of Physical Theories

Pre-quantum physics was marred by a peculiar dualism of conception, the irreconcilability of particles with fields, or, in more fundamental terms, the contrast between the discrete and the continuous. The particle notion received its confirmation at the hands of Newton and culminated in the brilliant speculations of Helmholtz. But the very idea of a particle becomes logically unsound unless it is stabilized by an absolute space or an ether to provide an invariable reference for its instantaneous position. The situation is well described by Einstein whom we quote at length.

—Before Clerk Maxwell people conceived of physical reality—in so far as it is supposed to represent events in nature—as material points, whose changes consist exclusively of motions, which are subject to *ordinary* [partial] differential equations. After Maxwell they conceived physical reality as represented by continuous fields, not mechanically explicable, which are subject to partial differential equations. This change in the conception of reality is the most profound and fruitful one that has come to physics since Newton; but it has at the same time to be admitted that the programme has by no means been completely carried out yet. The successful systems of physics which have been evolved since rather represent compromises between these two schemes, which for that very reason bear a provisional, logically incomplete character, although they may have achieved great advances in certain particulars.

The first of these that calls for mention is Lorentz's theory of electrons, in which the field and the electrical corpuscles appear side by side as elements of equal value for the comprehension of reality. Next come the special and general theories of relativity, which, though based entirely on ideas connected with the field-theory, have so far been unable to avoid the independent introduction of material points and *ordinary* [total] differential equations.[9]

The author's preference is here very clearly stated. Reality is to be regarded as a continuous manifold. This view has inspired Einstein's recent researches, his quest for a unified field-theory on the model of general relativity which would include the laws of the electromagnetic as well as those of the gravitational fields. Simplicity would demand the absence of singularities in such a manifold, but if singularities appeared, and these could be correlated with electrical or material particles, that too would be a major achievement. But the successes of this research have thus far been limited, partly because it has been a lonely road and most physicists are preoccupied with the problems of quantum theory, which promise a better immediate yield.

Nevertheless, the need for unification, perhaps after the fashion of a continuum theory, is greater than would appear from philosophic considerations, or from predilections with regard to the representation of reality. For it must not be overlooked that one faces here also a problem of factual consistency. If the theory of relativity is correct, even only in its special form, the meaning of independent particles is an absurdity because their states cannot be specified in principle. There are further difficulties. Indications are that particles may not be re-

---

[9] From "Clark Maxwell's Influence on the Evolution of the Idea of Physical Reality," in Einstein's *The World As I See It*, pp. 65f. The only printed translation available uses the words "partial" and "total" differential equations in a manner confusing to me. I have taken the liberty, therefore, of replacing these words in accordance with presumed meanings (but I have been careful to *italicize* my own replacements and to print the original translations in brackets). *H.M.*

garded as points but as structures of finite size. Hence their states cannot be presumed to be given by a finite set of variables, and this condition threatens the validity of all causal description in an embarrassing way. It is clear, therefore, that physical description must either avail itself of the simplifying facilities offered by fields which satisfy partial differential equations and thereby insure sufficient regularity for causal analysis, or else it must entirely abandon the four-dimensional manifold and follow new lines such as those indicated by quantum mechanics. Einstein's view on these possibilities, which we shall now examine, throws further interesting light on his conception of reality.

7. CLASSICAL AND QUANTUM-MECHANICAL DESCRIPTION

As an introduction we first remind the reader of the essential differences between what is called *classical* and *quantum mechanical* description of reality. In Newtonian mechanics one conceives of matter as an aggregate of mass points, and the state of each mass point is specified by means of 6 numbers, three coordinates and three momenta. When the state is known at any instant, all future and all past states can be calculated from the laws of motion. Probabilities are introduced into this scheme only by ignorance of the states of all the particles, an ignorance occasioned only by difficulties of measurement, not of conception. According to the classical view, a particle *has* position and velocity in a simple possessive sense, just as a visible object has size, or color; and to say that quantities like position and velocity of a particle are *real* is an obvious statement which seems to require no further scrutiny.

The theory of relativity has greatly sharpened the outlines of this picture and has given it a degree of evidence and naturalness which is almost irresistible. For by showing that time may be regarded as a fourth co-ordinate, and by representing the changing universe as a system of world lines, it made the representation both more symmetrical and esthetically more appealing, and the sense in which particles *have* position, time, velocity has become even more obvious. But to this most perfect picture, as well as to its Newtonian predecessor, one may object on the grounds that it takes no account of the finite size of particles and their internal structure, and that if it tried to do so it would become hopelessly non-causal.

Quantum mechanics changes all this by introducing a different concept of state. To be sure, it still uses particle language, but requires us no longer to commit ourselves to stating precisely where the particle is, or what is its velocity. It operates in fact with state functions, ψ (x,y,z), which have definite values for *all* positions of the physical system (e.g., particle). They are the best we have in the way of representing reality, but they do not in general permit a prediction of future and past positions, velocities etc. of the system. If we continue to use the word state in the classical sense of the term, these functions do not define a state at all.

Nevertheless they are immensely useful. For by simple and well-known mathematical procedures they allow the calculation of the *mean values* of all the measurements which can possibly be performed on the system. Or, if desired, the *probability* that a certain measurement shall yield a given value can be computed by similar rules. Many writers on quantum mechanics follow classical language to the extent of saying: Quantum mechanics allows the calculation of the probability that a certain *quantity*, such as momentum, shall be found to have a certain value upon measurement. To the physicist and his practical concerns this statement is acceptable as a working rule. To the philosopher, however, it carries a falsification which is most unfortunate because it looks so innocent. In fact, quantum mechanics never refers to *quantities* of systems; it gives no hint whatever that the system possesses quantities in the older sense. All it does is to say, in probability terms, what may be found when a measurement is made. All further implications arise from an injudicious use of classical language in a field foreign to such lingo. We shall see that Einstein's appreciation of quantum mechanics is troubled by this misfortune.

Knowledge of the state function represents the maximum knowledge attainable with regard to a physical system, and the quantum mechanical theory dealing with this optimum representation is called the theory of *pure cases* or *pure states*.

Almost all of useful modern atomic theory belongs to it; on the classical level it corresponds to ordinary dynamics. But classical physics includes also statistical mechanics, where states are known with a lesser measure of certainty. In quantum mechanics, too, there arises the possibility that knowledge exhausts itself in specifying merely the probabilities, w_i, that a system shall have given state functions ψ_i. As far as observation, or measurement is concerned, we are then dealing with a superposition of two kinds of probabilities; for even if we knew for certain that the system was in the state ψ_i, the results of measurements could still be calculated with probability only, and the uncertainty expressed by the w_i would further diffuse this knowledge. A state Φ, corresponding to this imperfect knowledge, and written $\Phi = \sum_v w_i \psi_i$, is called a mixture. The theory of mixtures has been developed by Von Neumann; its main fields of application are quantum-thermodynamics and the theory of measurement. Since Einstein is much interested in the latter it was necessary to mention it here. We shall briefly return to it.

To summarize these introductory considerations: Quantum mechanics does not define its states in terms of the classical variables of state. It uses functions which, however they may be related to reality, do not imply the *existence* of the old variables of state. These functions are connected with experience (observation, measurement) in a perfectly satisfactory way inasmuch as they allow prediction of probabilities of events, not of quantities or properties of systems. Less certain knowledge is represented in quantum mechanics by the idea of a mixture, which is subject to special treatment and must be distinguished from a pure case.

8. Quantum Theory and Reality

In contemplation of the changes induced by quantum theory in the description of physical states, Einstein, Rosen and Podolski published a paper with the significant title "Can Quantum-Mechanical Description of Physical Reality be Considered Complete?"[10] Aside from giving a negative answer to this ques-

[10] *Physical Review*, vol. 47, 777 (1935).

tion, the article contains a more or less systematic exposition of what the authors mean by reality, limited, to be sure, to the purposes at hand and confirming some of the points already made in this article. Here we read at length:

> Any serious consideration of a physical theory must take into account the distinction between the objective reality, which is independent of any theory, and the physical concepts with which the theory operates. These concepts are intended to correspond with the objective reality, and by means of these concepts we picture this reality to ourselves. . . .
>
> Whatever the meaning assigned to the term *complete*, the following requirement for a complete theory seems to be a necessary one: *every element of the physical reality must have a counterpart in the physical theory.* We shall call this the condition of completeness. The second question is thus easily answered, as soon as we are able to decide what are the elements of the physical reality.
>
> The elements of the physical reality cannot be determined by *a priori* philosophical considerations, but must be found by an appeal to results of experiments and measurements. A comprehensive definition of reality, is, however, unnecessary for our purpose. We shall be satisfied with the following criterion, which we regard as reasonable. *If, without in any way disturbing a system, we can predict with certainty (i.e., with probability equal to unity) the value of a physical quantity, then there exists an element of physical reality corresponding to this physical quantity.* It seems to us that this criterion, while far from exhausting all possible ways of recognizing a physical reality, at least provides us with one such way, whenever the conditions set down in it occur. Regarded not as a necessary, but merely as a sufficient, condition of reality, this criterion is in agreement with classical as well as quantum-mechanical ideas of reality.

Attention is called to the two italicised statements. The first sets up a correspondence between the elements of physical reality and physical theory. Unfortunately, one finds nowhere a concise exposition of the meaning of physical reality apart from physical theory; indeed it is my conviction that reality cannot be defined except by reference to successful physical theory. If this is true, Einstein's proposition becomes tautological, as I suspect it to be. On the other hand there is the possibility of a more favorable interpretation by construing physical reality, as used in that particular sentence, to mean sensory experience alone, or perhaps the sum total of all possible experience, past, present and future. The disadvantage of this position is its divergence from the usual attitude with regard to reality. For the latter term customarily implies more permanence and uniformity than bare sense experience can convey.

As to the second italicised statement in the quotation above, we find it somewhat too specific for general use, and heavily weighted in favor of the classical definition of state. Reality is conferred upon physical quantities by their predictability. But what if physical quantities were ghostlike things to which no primary interest attaches, as indeed they are in quantum mechanics? What if physical theory seized upon the elements of experience directly, addressed itself at once to outcomes of observations without the interpolation of ideal quantities like position and momentum? To this question we shall return at the end of this article. For the present let it be said that, if the second italicised statement is accepted, the argument of Einstein, Podolski and Rosen does precisely what it sets out to do; it proves that quantum mechanical description of reality is not complete when the discussion is limited to pure cases, and this limitation is made in the paper, even if it is not explicitly stated. Nor is this an insignificant contribution, for the independent-quantity view of reality implicit in the quotation, here criticised as an incongruous relic from earlier days, was actually widely held by physicists and is still in vogue today.

We now examine briefly the logical content of the paper in question and present the detailed conclusions. This need not detain us long, for the steps are simple, clearly stated and the results are definite. Confusion which has subsequently arisen stems largely from the discussions which this paper has stimulated, discussions which did not always confine themselves to the issues clearly marked in that paper. The main content may be summarized in the following example.[11]

Let two physical systems be isolated from each other from the beginning of time to the present. Now, for a finite period, they interact, only to be isolated again forever after. According

---

[11] The following review is greatly condensed and will probably be somewhat incomprehensible to the reader who has not previously studied reference 10.

to the laws of quantum mechanics it is possible to represent the state function of the two isolated systems after interaction in two equivalent ways by means of biorthogonal expansions. One expansion correlates the probabilities for the outcomes of an observation of type A_1 on system 1 with those for observation of type A_2 on system 2, the other correlates the probabilities for outcomes of observation B_1 on system 1 with those for observation B_2 on system 2. In Einstein's language, A_1, A_2, B_1, B_2 are *quantities*, as they would be in classical physics. If now a measurement of type A_2 is made after isolation upon system 2, and the value measured is A_2, certain inferences can be drawn with regard to the state of system 1. The usual inference is this.

After the measurement, we know exactly what the state of system 2 must be. It is in fact such that further repetition of the measurement would yield the same value. In other words, the measurement has converted the original state function into an *Eigenstate*[12] for that kind of measurement. But associated with this eigenstate of system 2 there is also an eigenstate of system 1 corresponding to the value a_1, the existence of which may thus be concluded as a result of a measurement performed on system 2. This will in general correspond to some other "observable" than that measured on 1.

This inference leads to trouble. For suppose we had chosen to observe, after isolation, the outcome of another type of measurement, say of type B_2, on system 2, and let the measured value be b_2. This would then be correlated with certainty of measuring b_1 on system 1. If now b_1 were different from a_1 we should face the curious fact of a measurement on system 2 influencing the state of system 1, the systems being not at the time interacting. The situation is indeed worse than this, for it can be shown by definite examples that the results a_1 and b_1 not only may be different, they may even be *incompatible* (belong to non-commuting operators). They are of a kind which experience can never provide simultaneously. The following conclusion, within the framework of Einstein's query, is thus inescapable.

In accordance with his criterion, we must in one case regard

[12] For terminology, see any book on quantum mechanics.

a_1 as an element of reality, in the other case b_1. But both belong to the same reality, for system 1 has not been disturbed in the act of measurement. Hence, by slight further elaboration, Einstein, Podolski and Rosen finally remark: "We are thus forced to conclude that the quantum-mechanical description of physical reality given by wave functions (i.e., state functions) is not complete."

To judge the seriousness of this indictment, certain presuppositions of the argument must be examined. We note that the authors operate throughout with simple state functions and hence pure cases, and that they accept the axiom according to which a measurement converts a state into an eigenstate of the measured observable. In my opinion, as stated elsewhere,[13] this view cannot be maintained in spite of its reasonableness and its close alignment with classical physics. Empirically, the effect of a measurement upon the state of a system is extremely complicated, sometimes slight, sometimes—as in the case of absorption of photons—destructive to the identity of the physical system. It is difficult to make a simple theory about the dynamical fate of a system during measurement. Now quantum mechanics may be said to be that discipline which successfully overcomes this difficulty by recasting its entire method of physical description, by taking care of the uncertainties of empirical cognition in its very foundation. If we apply it correctly we must not ask: what happens to a system during measurement; but content ourselves with the information given to us in that measurement. Furthermore, a state function does not fix the outcome of a single observation; why should a single observation determine a state function? It thus appears that Einstein's analysis focuses attention upon an inadvertency frequently exhibited in the discussion of the foundations of quantum mechanics, and one which it was important to expose.

The fate of a system during measurement cannot be satisfactorily described by the formalism employed in the work under discussion. Its analysis requires the use of mixtures. It

[13] "Critical Points of Modern Physical Theory;" *Journal of Philosophy of Science*, vol. 4, 337 (1937).

has indeed been shown by various authors, first by Von Neumann, that the effect of a measurement is to convert a pure case into a mixture. When this is recognized, the logical difficulties disappear.

To round out the picture, let it be emphasized once more that a reformulation of the criterion of reality which regards classical quantities as parts of reality is greatly needed. Quantum theory denies the attachment of quantities to physical systems in a possessive manner. To say that an electron *has* momentum when it is not in an eigenstate of the momentum operator is meaningless, and in that state its momentum is not a significant component of reality. The possibility of "measuring its momentum" is of course always at hand; but properly speaking this is no more than an act of creating experience of a certain kind; this experience *is* a component of reality, as is the fact that, when the measurement is repeated, its result may be different from the first. Such positive experiences are honored by the quantum mechanical way of describing reality, yet the possibility of assigning persistent properties like position, momentum, is not. What Einstein has always correctly stressed is that classical continuity of properties is contradicted by quantum physics.

He has further objections to the new discipline. In reference 1 we read:

> Unfortunately, it [quantum mechanics] compels us to use a continuum the number of whose dimensions is not that ascribed to space by physics hitherto (4) but rises indefinitely with the number of particles constituting the system under consideration. I can not but confess that I attach only a transitory importance to this interpretation. I still believe in the possibility of a model of reality—that is to say, of a theory which represents things themselves and not merely the probability of their occurrence.

Here one might wonder what would become of models with preassigned properties if experience itself threw doubts upon their existence. Would not a model of an electron force us to a commitment as to whether it is a particle or a wave? This question, however, is unanswerable in the face of recent developments.

Einstein regards the Heisenberg uncertainty principle as true and important, but he prefers another kind of description.

. . . to account for the atomic character of electricity, the field equations need only lead to the following conclusions: A portion of space (three-dimensional) at whose boundaries electrical density disappears everywhere, always contains a total electrical charge whose size is represented by a whole number. In a continuum-theory atomic characteristics would be satisfactorily expressed by integral laws without localization of the formation entity which constitutes the atomic structure.

Not until the atomic structure has been successfully represented in such a manner would I consider the quantum-riddle solved.[14]

In conclusion, one is moved to this reflection. It is everywhere apparent that Einstein, with a keen intuitive sense for what is physically real, has come to recognize an impasse in the time-honored description of the universe. The independent particle concept must be abandoned because of the failure of space or ether to be absolute in the Newtonian sense. Furthermore, the assumption of a three-dimensional infinity of point particles, needed to account for structures of finite size, threatens the simplicity and indeed the feasibility of causal analysis. There are other indications of this kind.

One can at present see two paths leading out of the dilemma. One is to retain the epistemology of classical physics, to describe reality in terms of systems defined by stable properties having significance at all times. This is possible only by means of field theories, in which every point of a four-dimensional continuum becomes the permanent bearer of qualities, such as a metric, or an electromagnetic potential. To make the program practicable the field quantities must be subjected to partial differential equations which allow a large region of the continuum to be controlled by the properties of an infinitesimal portion of it, thus establishing a basis for causality. This is the path favored by Einstein.

The other road passes through less familiar terrain. To travel it, one must leave much of classical physics behind; one must redefine the notion of physical state and accept the more rhapsodic form of reality which it entails. This requires the

14 "On the Method of Theoretical Physics" (1933); in *The World As I See It*, 40.

abandonment of the attempt to map experience upon a four-dimensional continuum, but leads into a branch of mathematics which has peculiar attractions of its own and is not unmanageable. Present successes in the exploration of the atom definitely recommend this road, which is quantum mechanics. But there are difficulties, already very vexing in the quantum theory of electromagnetic fields, which are beginning to dampen the enthusiasm of its travellers.

Perhaps the two roads will meet beyond our present horizon.

HENRY MARGENAU

SLOANE PHYSICS LABORATORY
YALE UNIVERSITY

9

Philipp Frank

EINSTEIN, MACH, AND LOGICAL POSITIVISM

EINSTEIN, MACH, AND LOGICAL POSITIVISM

ROUGHLY speaking, we may distinguish, according to Max Planck, two conflicting conceptions in the philosophy of science: the metaphysical and the positivistic conception. Each of these regards Einstein as its chief advocate and most distinguished witness. If there were a legal case to be decided, it would be possible to produce satisfactory evidence on behalf of either position by quoting Einstein. We do not, however, intend here to stretch the meaning of words like "positivism" and "metaphysics" as is done—a necessary evil—in legal disputes; we intend, rather, to describe Einstein's position in the philosophy of science and to use some arbitrary but precise meanings of "positivism" and "metaphysics" as points of reference for this description. As a matter of fact, Einstein has always felt the need for describing his position with respect to this frame of reference.

If we mean by "positivism" the philosophy of science which was advocated by Ernst Mach, we may describe it by quoting Einstein's essay of 1916, published as an obituary on Mach in the *Physikalische Zeitschrift*, as follows:

Science is nothing else but the comparing and ordering of our observations according to methods and angles which we learn practically by trial and error. . . . As results of this ordering abstract concepts and the rules of their connection appear. . . . Concepts have meaning only if we can point to objects to which they refer and to the rules by which they are assigned to these objects. . . .

He [Mach] conceived every science as the task of bringing order into the elementary single observations which he described as 'sensations.' This denotation was probably responsible for the fact that this sober and cautious thinker was called a philosophical idealist or solipsist by people who had not studied his work thoroughly.[1]

[1] *Physikalische Zeitschrift*, XVII (1916), 101ff.

We note here that Einstein obviously does not share a very common misinterpretation of Mach's philosophy. The "idealistic" (mis-)interpretation of Mach's philosophy, which Einstein rightly repudiates, has, as a matter of fact, become of historic importance by virtue of the fact that Lenin took it as the point of departure in this book on *Materialism and Empirio-Criticism*, in which he made a spirited attack on Mach's "idealism." As a result of this pronouncement by the highest Soviet political authority, Mach's philosophy of science has become a target of attack in every textbook and in every classroom in the Soviet Union where philosophy is being taught. Because of the close connection, which obviously exists between Einstein's theory of relativity and Mach's philosophy, Lenin feared that Einstein's theories might become a Trojan horse for the infiltration of idealistic currents of thought among Russian scientists and among educated classes in general. This suspicion accounts for the bittersweet reception which Einstein's theories frequently met in the first years of the Soviet regime in Russia.

In 1916 Einstein himself asserted:

I can say with certainty that the study of Mach and Hume has been directly and indirectly a great help in my work. . . . Mach recognized the weak spots of classical mechanics and was not very far from requiring a general theory of relativity half a century ago [this was written in 1916]. . . . It is not improbable that Mach would have discovered the theory of relativity, if, at the time when his mind was still young and susceptible, the problem of the constancy of the speed of light had been discussed among physicists. . . . Mach's considerations about Newton's bucket experiment show how close to his way of thinking was the search for relativity in a general sense (relativity of acceleration).[2]

It is easy to see which lines of Mach's thought have been particularly helpful to Einstein. The definition of simultaneity in the special theory of relativity is based on Mach's requirement, that every statement in physics has to state relations between observable quantities. The same requirement appeared when Einstein started the theory of gravitation by asking what conditions are responsible for the flattening of a rotating liquid sphere.

[2] *Ibid.*, 103.

In this case Mach decided that the cause of flattening does not have to be the rotation in empty space, but the rotations with respect to some material and therefore observable bodies.

There is no doubt that in both cases Mach's requirement, the "positivistic" requirement, was of great heuristic value to Einstein. When Einstein actually developed his general theory, however, he found that it was an oversimplification to require that every statement of physics must be directly translatable into relations between observable quantities. Actually, in Einstein's general theory of relativity, the general statements of physics are relations between symbols (general co-ordinates, gravitational potentials, etc.) from which conclusions can be drawn, which latter are translatable into statements about observable quantities.

The original "positivistic requirement," as advocated by Mach and his immediate followers, had to be replaced by a more general requirement, which allows for any symbols or words in the formulation of the principles, provided that statements about observable quantities can logically be derived from them. In the original "positivistic conception of science," as advocated by Mach, the concepts of which the principles consisted were very near to direct observation and, therefore, very near to possible physical experiments. The road from these experiments to the principles was short and easy to understand.

In his Herbert Spencer Lecture, delivered in London in 1933, Einstein says:

The natural philosophers of those days [18th and 19th centuries] were . . . most of them possessed with the idea that the fundamental concepts and postulates of physics were not in the logical sense free inventions of the human mind but could be deduced from experience by 'abstraction' —that is to say by logical means. A clear recognition of the erroneousness of this notion really only came with the general theory of relativity, . . . the fictitious character of the fundamental principles is perfectly evident from the fact that we can point to two essentially different principles, both of which correspond with experience to a large extent. . . .

These bases are Newton's and Einstein's principles of gravitation. "This proves," Einstein continues, "that every attempt at a logical deduction of the basic concepts and postulates of mechanics from elementary experiences is doomed to failure."[3]

This logical derivation of laws from experience by "abstraction" was certainly not regarded as possible by Mach. But it was a typical belief of nineteenth century physicists as represented, for instance, in J. Tyndall's famous *Fragments of Science*. It is, however, probable that Mach did not believe that there was a wide gap between the concepts which were used in the description of our physical experiments and the concepts used in the formulation of general laws. Einstein, however, emphasized

... the distance in thought between the fundamental concepts and laws on one side and, on the other, the conclusions which have to be brought into relation with our experience grows larger and larger, the simpler the logical structure becomes—that is to say, the smaller the number of logically independent conceptual elements which are found necessary to support the structure.[4]

Einstein's conception of modern science departs from Mach's "positivistic requirement" in the following point: According to Mach and his immediate followers, the fundamental laws of physics should be formulated so that they would contain only concepts which could be defined by direct observations or at least by a short chain of thoughts connected with direct observations. Einstein, however, recognized that this requirement is an oversimplification. In twentieth-century physics the general principles have been formulated by using words or symbols which are connected with observational concepts by long chains of mathematical and logical argument. Einstein, of course, holds in addition that there must be some consequences of these general principles which can be formulated in terms of observational concepts and which can, therefore, be checked by direct observation. This requirement is "positivistic" in the sense that the "truth" of general principles is ultimately based on a check by direct physical experiment and observation. Einstein does not believe—as Mach's contemporaries did—that the basic principles can be checked directly or by means of a short chain of

[3] "On the Methods of Theoretical Physics," in *The World As I See It*, 35f.
[4] *Ibid.*, 34.

conclusions. It had now become clear that the road between principles and observation was a long and arduous one. In the same Herbert Spencer Lecture already quoted, Einstein says that "it is the grand object of all theory to make these irreducible elements as simple and as few in number as possible, without having to renounce the adequate representation of any empirical content whatever."[5]

Einstein requires, accordingly, that two criteria have to be met by a set of basic principles: logical consistency and simplicity, on the one hand, and agreement with the observed facts, on the other—briefly speaking, a logical and an empirical criterion. It is irrelevant by means of what concepts or symbols the principles are formulated. They become, from the purely logical viewpoint, free creations of the human mind. But they also have to meet the empirical criterion; they have to obey the restriction of the free imagination which is necessary to represent the data of experience.

The growing understanding of the general theory of relativity and similar theories accounted for a new development within the views held by Mach's "positivistic" followers. A modification and generalization of Mach's "positivistic requirement" occurred among the scientists who worked in the logic of science after 1920. They tried to adjust their formulations to the methods which had been used successfully in general relativity. Under the name of "logical empiricism" a new school of thought appeared, which can be regarded as an attempt to develop Mach's philosophy of science according to the new developments in theoretical physics. The basic principles of physics were no longer to contain only concepts like "red," "warm," "one spot touching a second spot," etc., which were called "elementary terms" or "observational terms." Instead, the principles themselves were regarded as products of the free human imagination and could contain any "abstract terms" or symbols. But these principles cannot be proved or validated by an appeal to the imagination, to intuition, or even to logical simplicity or beauty. The principles are regarded as "true" only if by logical conclusions statements about observations can be

[5] *Ibid.*, 33f.

derived which can be confirmed by actual experience.

As an example of this line of thought, I quote from Rudolf Carnap's *Foundations of Logic and Mathematics,* which was published in the *Encyclopedia of Unified Science* in 1939:

> Would it be possible to formulate all laws of physics in elementary terms, admitting more abstract terms only as abbreviations? If so, we would have that ideal of a science in sensationalistic form which Goethe in his polemic against Newton, as well as some positivists, seems to have had in mind. But it turns out—this is an empirical fact, not a logical necessity—that it is not possible to arrive in this way at a powerful and efficacious system of laws. To be sure, historically, science started with laws formulated in terms of a low level of abstractness. But for any law of this kind, one nearly always later found some exceptions and thus had to confine it to a narrower realm of validity. Hence we understand that they [the physicists] are inclined to choose the *second method.* This method begins at the top of the system, . . . It consists in taking a few abstract terms as primitive science and a few fundamental laws of great generality as axioms. . . . If, . . . abstract terms are taken as primitive—according to the second method, the one used in scientific physics—then the semantical rules [which connect the abstract terms with observational terms] have no direct relations to the primitive [abstract] terms of the system but refer to terms introduced by long chains of definitions. The calculus is first constructed floating in the air, so to speak; the construction begins at the top and then adds lower and lower levels. Finally, by the semantical rules, the lowest level is anchored at the solid ground of the observable facts. The laws . . . are not directly interpreted, but only the singular sentences.[6]

This conception of logical empiricism seems to be fairly in accordance with the way Einstein anchored his theory of gravitation in the solid grounds of observable facts by deriving phenomena like the redshift of spectral lines, etc. Whether this generalized conception of the relation between theory and facts is a "positivistic conception" is certainly a question of terminology. Some authors in the United States have given to this conception the name "logical positivism," whereas Charles W. Morris recommends the name "logical empiricism," which I have used in this paper. It is simply a matter of a practical

[6] R. Carnap, *Foundations of Logic and Mathematics,* 64f.

scheme in one's history of thought, whether one includes this conception in his chapter on "positivism" or whether one starts a new chapter.

One thing is certain: the classical authors of "positivism," Ernst Mach and even Auguste Comte, understood very well that to say that the laws of science can be expressed in terms of observational concepts is an oversimplification. They hinted quite pointedly at the necessity of a more general conception; but they did not elaborate this hint at length, because at that time theories of the type of Einstein's theory of gravitation did not exist. But, from the strictly logical viewpoint, it is certain that even Newton's mechanics can not be formulated correctly unless we make use of the Einsteinian type of theory, which Carnap calls "starting from the top" or, in other words, unless we start from relations between symbols and draw conclusions which later can then be interpreted in terms of observable facts.

In 1894 Ernst Mach gave a lecture on the topic, "The Principle of Comparison in Physics" (published in his *Popular Scientific Lectures*), in which he distinguishes between "direct description" and "indirect description." The latter type does not describe facts in observational terms but by comparison with a mathematical scheme. Mach uses the example of the wave theory of light, which describes the optical phenomena by starting from a purely symbolic system of axioms which allows a much more practical description of the observed optical phenomena than a "direct" description in terms of optical sensations.

Auguste Comte, the founder of "positivism," was far from assuming that a physical theory should be expressed in observational terms only. He stresses the point, in fact, that no observation is possible without a theory or, at least, no description of observations is possible without previous acceptance of a conceptual scheme. In 1829 Comte wrote in his *Positive Philosophy:*

If, on the one hand, every positive theory has to be based on observations, it is, on the other hand, also true that our mind needs a theory in order to make observations. If in contemplating the phenomena we did not link them immediately with some principles, it would not only be impossible to combine the isolated observation and draw any useful conclusions, we would not even be able to remember them, and, for the most part, the facts would not be noticed by our eyes.[7]

Comte was so profoundly convinced of the necessity of having to start from a theory that he regarded man at the beginning of scientific research as being entangled in a vicious circle. He continues:

Hence, squeezed between the necessity of observing in order to form real theories, and the no less urgent necessity of producing some theories in order to make coherent observations, the human mind had not been able to break this circle if not a natural way out had been opened by the spontaneous growth of theological conceptions.[8]

From these quotations it seems to become clear that even the "classical positivism" of Comte or Mach did not hold the opinion that the laws of nature could be simply "derived" from experience. These men knew very well that there must be a theoretical starting-point, a system of principles constructed by the human imagination in order to compare its consequences with observations. This feeling was so strong that Comte accepted even the theological principles as a starting-point to "get science going."

The principal feature which modern logical empiricism has in common with classical positivism is the requirement that, whatever the basic symbols and the laws of their connection may look like, there must be logical conclusions from these principles which can be confronted with direct experience. A set of principles from which no consequences of this type could be derived were called "meaningless" or "metaphysical" by the logical empiricists, thus giving to the time-honored word "metaphysics" a slightly derogatory meaning.

In order to understand Einstein's attitude towards this conception, we may quote his remarks in the volume on *The Philosophy of Bertrand Russell* in the present series:

In order that thinking might not degenerate into "metaphysics," or into empty talk, it is only necessary that enough propositions of the con-

[7] Comte, A., *Cours de philosophie positive*, Premiére leçon.
[8] *Ibid.*

ceptual system be firmly enough connected with sensory experience and that the conceptual system, in view of its task of ordering and surveying sense-experience, should show as much unity and parsimony as possible. Beyond that, however, the "system" is (as regards logic) a free play with symbols according to (logical) arbitrarily given rules of the game. . . . The concepts which arise in our thought and in our linguistic expressions are all—when viewed logically—the free creations of thought which can not inductively be gained from sense-experiences.[9]

Einstein speaks here almost completely in the line of the logical empiricists; which is not surprising, inasmuch as logical empiricism is, to a considerable extent, a formulation of the very way in which Einstein envisaged the logical structure of his later theories, e.g., the theory of gravitation. Occasionally even Einstein himself uses the term "metaphysics" in exactly the same sense in which it has been used by the logical empiricists. He speaks of "metaphysics or empty talk," meaning by it any set of principles from which no conclusion—i.e., no statement about possible sense-experience—can be derived. Einstein shares the opinion of logical empiricism that the principles of science, e.g., the theories of physics, contain tools which are invented by human ingenuity in order to enable us to survey our sense-experiences in as simple a way as possible. He says, e.g., about the integer numbers: ". . . the series of integers is obviously an invention of the human mind, a self-created tool which simplifies the ordering of certain sensory experiences."[10]

In this context it is instructive to learn how Einstein himself describes the psychology of his creative work. The great French mathematician, Jacques Hadamard, in 1945 published a work on *The Psychology of Invention in the Mathematical Field*, in which he put some questions to prominent scientists concerning their respective way of procedure in mathematical science. Among these was Einstein, who described his work in a letter to Hadamard. Einstein, in this letter, stresses particularly the

[9] Albert Einstein, in "Remarks on Bertrand Russell's Theory of Knowledge" in Paul A. Schilpp's *The Philosophy of Bertrand Russell* (1944), 289 and, the last part of the quotation: 287.

[10] Einstein, A., in *ibid.*, 287.

way in which he finds the symbolic structure which is at the top of every theory:

The words or the language, as they are written or spoken, do not seem to play any role in my mechanism of thought. The psychical entities which seem to serve as elements in thought are certain signs and more or less clear images which can be "voluntarily" reproduced and combined.

There is, of course, a certain connection between those elements and relevant logical concepts. It is also clear that the desire to arrive finally at logically connected concepts is the emotional basis of this rather vague play with the above mentioned elements. But taken from the psychological viewpoint, this combinatory play seems to be the essential feature in productive thought.[11]

According to the conception of logical empiricism the relations between symbols which form the "top" of any scientific theory cannot be produced by any logical method. Their origin can only be explained psychologically. This production is the real nucleus of what one may call "creative thinking." This conception is fairly well confirmed by Einstein's statements. According to his own experience, the "combinatory play with symbols is the essential feature of productive thought."

These relations between symbols are, according to logical empiricism, the first part of any scientific theory. But there is a second part, which connects these symbols with the words of our everyday language: the "semantical rules" or, as P. W. Bridgman puts it, the "operational definitions."

Einstein continues the description of the procedure involved in developing new theories: "Conventional words or other signs have to be sought for laboriously only in a secondary stage, when the mentioned associative play is sufficiently established and can be reproduced at will. . . ." Then starts what Einstein calls "the connection with logical construction in words or other signs which can be communicated to others."[12] This means exactly that "semantical rules" have to be added to the symbolic expressions.

[11] Einstein, A., in Jacques Hadamard's *An Essay on the Psychology of Invention in the Mathematical Field* (Princeton, 1945), Appendix II, 142.
[12] *Ibid.*, 143, 142.

Although Einstein seems to be in considerable agreement with the logical empiricists on a great many points, he speaks occasionally of the "fateful 'fear of metaphysics' . . . which has come to be a malady of contemporary empiricistic philosophizing."[13] It is obvious that in this statement, by which "metaphysics" is being encouraged, he does *not* mean the same type of "metaphysics" which he discouraged in the statement, quoted above, where he uses the phrase, "metaphysics and empty talk." If we read this statement in *The Philosophy of Bertrand Russell* carefully, we see clearly that he disagreed with the belief "that all those concepts and propositions which cannot be deduced from the sensory raw material are, on account of their 'metaphysical' character, to be removed from thinking."[14] Einstein calls here "metaphysical" every concept that cannot be deduced from sensory raw material. But this kind of "metaphysical" concepts have certainly not been rejected by the logical empiricists. The admission of these concepts is exactly the point which distinguishes twentieth century logical empiricism from nineteenth century "positivism" of men like Mach. One could, therefore, give good reasons for not regarding logical empiricism as a kind of "positivism." It has often been called "logical positivism" because it rejected principles, from which, according to their structure, no observable facts could be deduced. But in this rejection there was again agreement with Einstein who called such systems "metaphysics and empty talk" exactly as they have been called by the logical empiricists and, for that matter, already by Hume, Mach, and Comte.

There is even the question, whether Mach, if pinned down, would not have agreed that the general conceptions of science are not "derived" from sensory experience, but constructed by the human imagination to derive observable facts logically from these concepts. This becomes probable if we consider Einstein's personal talk with Mach which occurred in 1913. From this conversation[15] it seems plausible that Mach could be pinned

[13] Einstein, in *The Philosophy of Bertrand Russell* (Schilpp, ed.), 289.
[14] *Ibid.*, 287-9.
[15] Frank, Philipp, *Einstein, His Life and Times* (New York, 1947), 104f.

down to admit the usefulness of these constructed concepts in science, although his emphasis and predilection belonged to the direct deduction from sensory material.

Concerning this question the difference between Einstein's approach and that of logical empiricism is only a verbal one. Whereas Einstein would, apparently, not use the term "positivism" for his twentieth century group, they in turn would not use the term "metaphysical" for concepts which are constructed by the human imagination in the process of deriving our sense-perceptions.

The extent of this agreement can best be judged, perhaps, by some of Einstein's statements from his Princeton Lecture of 1921, which do not deal with philosophy but with a presentation of the theory of relativity to physicists. In this lecture occur the following remarks:

> The object of all science, whether natural science or psychology, is to coördinate our experiences and to bring them into a logical system. . . . The only justification for our concepts is that they serve to represent the complex of our experiences; beyond this they have no legitimacy. I am convinced that the philosophers have had a harmful effect upon the progress of scientific thinking in removing certain fundamental concepts from the domain of empiricism, where they are under control, to the intangible heights of the *a priori*. For even if it should appear that the universe of ideas cannot be deduced from experience by logical means, but is, in a sense, a creation of the human mind, without which no science is possible, nevertheless the universe of ideas is just as little independent of the nature of our experiences as clothes are of the form of the human body. This is particularly true of our conceptions of time and space, which physicists have been obliged by the facts to bring down from the Olympus of the *a priori* in order to adjust them and put them in a serviceable condition.[16]

Briefly, I do not see in the question of the origin of the fundamental concepts of science any essential divergence between Einstein and twentieth century logical empiricism. But from the belief that the basic conceptions of science are creations of the human imagination—a belief which is common to both Einstein and the logical empiricists—one could easily draw the conclusion

[16] Einstein, A., *The Meaning of Relativity* (Princeton, 1923), 2f.

that we shall never reach the definitive basic principles of science. One could even be inclined to believe that such a "correct basis" does not at all exist. Conclusions of this kind have been widely drawn by Henri Poincaré, the godfather of logical empiricism, and by a great many of his followers. Einstein, however, in his Herbert Spencer Lecture of 1933, says:

> If it is true that this axiomatic basis of theoretical physics cannot be extracted from experience but must be freely invented, can we ever hope to find the right way? Nay more, has this right way any existence outside our illusions? . . . I answer without hesitation that there is, in my opinion, a right way, and that we are capable of finding it. . . . I am convinced that we can discover by means of purely mathematical constructions the concepts and the laws connecting them with each other, which furnish the key to the understanding of natural phenomena.[17]

By extolling the great heuristic value of mathematics Einstein does not want to suggest that a statement of physics could be proved to be true by this purely logical argument. For he continues: "Experience remains, of course, the sole criterion of the physical utility of a mathematical construction. But the creative principle resides in mathematics."[18] This means that the criterion of truth in physics is experience, but that the method by which the principles are found, or, in other words, produced, is mathematics. Einstein is so convinced of the creative power of mathematics that he says: "In a certain sense . . . I hold it to be true that pure thought can grasp reality, as the ancients dreamed."[19]

This statement could be interpreted as meaning that Einstein agrees with the Platonic belief that a statement of physics could be proved by mathematics. According to Einstein, however, this is true only "in a certain sense." This "certain sense" means "in the sense of heuristic method," but not "in the sense of a criterion of truth."

Nobody would deny the fact that this heuristic method, looking for mathematical simplicity and beauty, has led to successful theories, which have turned out to be "true" in the empiri-

[17] Einstein, A., in *The World As I See It*, 36.
[18] *Ibid.*, 36f.
[19] *Ibid.*, 37.

cal sense. Everybody, notwithstanding his special philosophic creed, who has had any glimpse of theoretical physics, will agree that this fact is a property of our world. It is itself an empirical fact. It is even—as some people like to express themselves— a "hard fact." The emotional reaction to this "hard fact" can, of course, be of various kinds. Einstein calls this fact the basis of cosmic religion. It is a "mystical experience." As "hard facts" cannot be "explained" but only derived from principles which are themselves "inexplicable hard facts," we can say that the most mystical experience is the experience of hard facts. In his paper "On Physical Reality" (1936) Einstein said: "The most incomprehensible thing about the world is that it is comprehensible."[20]

There are, however, scientists whose personal reaction to this fact is different. As an example we may quote P. W. Bridgman. In his *Logic of Modern Physics* (1927), Bridgman writes:

With regard to the general question of simple laws, there are at least two attitudes; one is that there are probably simple general laws still undiscovered, the other is that nature has a predilection for simple laws. I do not see how there can be any quarrel with the first of these attitudes. Let us examine the second. We have in the first place to notice that "simple" means simple to us, when stated in terms of our concepts. This is in itself sufficient to raise a presumption against this general attitude. It is evident that our thinking must follow those lines imposed by the nature of our thinking mechanism: does it seem likely that all nature accepts these same limitations? If this were the case, our conceptions ought to stand in certain simple and definite relations to nature. Now if our discussion has brought out any one thing, it is that our concepts are not well defined things, but they are hazy and do not fit nature exactly, and many of them fit even approximately only within restricted range. . . . Considering, then, the nature of our conceptual material, it seems to me that the overwhelming presumption is against the laws of nature having any predisposition to simplicity as formulated in terms of our concepts (which is of course all that simplicity means), and the wonder is that there are apparently so many simple laws. There is this observation to be made about all the simple laws of nature that have hitherto been formulated; they apply only over a certain range.

[20] Einstein, A., "On Physical Reality," in *Franklin Institute, Journal*, vol. 221 (1936), 349ff.

. . . It does not seem so very surprising that over a limited domain, in which the most important phenomena are a restricted type, the conduct of nature should follow comparatively simple rules.[21]

Although this interpretation of the simplicity of nature sounds very different from Einstein's, the difference lies not in the assertion of facts or of logical relations but in the emphasis. Einstein stresses the marvelous simplicity and beauty of such symbolic structures as Maxwell's equations of the electro-magnetic field or the field equations of the general theory of relativity. This beauty produces, according to Einstein, the feeling of admiration and even of "awe;" whereas Bridgman, in the passage quoted, is simply "wondering" about the exist-ence of so many simple laws. These attitudes do not imply dif-ferent assertions about the physical world or about the logical system by which this world is scientifically described. The dif-ference is totally within the domain of personal reaction. In his address to the Conference on Science, Philosophy and Religion (1940), Einstein states clearly that the belief in the existence of this regularity in nature belongs to religion.

To this [sphere of religion] there also belongs the faith in the possi-bility that the regulations valid for the world of existence are rational, that is comprehensible to reason. I cannot conceive of a genuine scientist without that profound faith. The situation may be expressed by an image: science without religion is lame, religion without science is blind.[22]

Although this personal reaction, which, with Einstein, we may call "cosmic religion," is not implied logically by the facts and principles of physics, it may well be that the kind of re-action which is produced in the mind of the physicists is of rele-vance for his creative power in science. This is obviously Ein-stein's opinion. He stresses that this "knowledge, this feeling, is at the center of true religiousness. In this sense, and in this sense only, I belong to the ranks of devoutly religious men."

We see from these words that for Einstein this belief in the

[21] Bridgman, P. W., *The Logic of Modern Physics*, (New York, 1927); 2nd ed., (1946), 201, 203.

[22] *Science, Philosophy and Religion*, A Symposium (New York, Harper, 1941), 211.

"possibility of mathematical physics," if we put it perfunctorily, is almost identical with religion. But, on the other hand, Einstein has never agreed with some contemporary philosophical interpretations of physics, according to which relativity and quantum theory are interpreted as having been a decisive step in the reconciliation between science and religion. He has never agreed with men like Jeans or Eddington, who regarded the Heisenberg principle of indeterminacy in quantum theory as an argument for the freedom of the will and for the moral responsibility of man in contrast to the "iron causality of classical physics." Einstein's cosmic religion has been the belief in the possibility of a symbolic system of great beauty and conceptual simplicity from which the observed facts can be logically derived. Whatever his system may look like and whatever symbols may be used does not matter. Newtonian physics bolsters up cosmic religion in this sense just as well as twentieth century physics does.

Eventually the truly interested student of science should follow Einstein's advice, when he says: "If you want to find out anything from the theoretical physicists about the methods they use, . . . don't listen to their words, fix your attention on their deeds."

PHILIPP FRANK

RESEARCH LABORATORY OF PHYSICS
HARVARD UNIVERSITY

10

Hans Reichenbach

THE PHILOSOPHICAL SIGNIFICANCE OF THE THEORY OF RELATIVITY

THE PHILOSOPHICAL SIGNIFICANCE OF THE THEORY OF RELATIVITY

I

THE philosophical significance of the theory of relativity has been the subject of contradictory opinions. Whereas many writers have emphasized the philosophical implications of the theory and have even tried to interpret it as a sort of philosophical system, others have denied the existence of such implications and have voiced the opinion that Einstein's theory is merely a physical matter, of interest only to the mathematical physicist. These critics believe that philosophical views are constructed by other means than the methods of the scientist and are independent of the results of physics.

Now it is true that what has been called the philosophy of relativity represents, to a great extent, the fruit of misunderstandings of the theory rather than of its physical content. Philosophers who regard it as an ultimate wisdom that everything is relative are mistaken when they believe that Einstein's theory supplies evidence for such a sweeping generalization; and their error is even deeper when they transfer such a relativity to the field of ethics, when they claim that Einstein's theory implies a relativism of men's duties and rights. The theory of relativity is restricted to the cognitive field. That moral conceptions vary with the social class and the structure of civilization is a fact which is not derivable from Einstein's theory; the parallelism between the relativity of ethics and that of space and time is nothing more than a superficial analogy, which blurs the essential logical differences between the fields of volition and cognition. It appears understandable that those who were trained in the precision of mathematico-physical

methods wish to divorce physics from such blossoms of philosophizing.

Yet it would be another mistake to believe that Einstein's
theory is not a philosophical theory. This discovery of a physicist
has radical consequences for the theory of knowledge. It com-
pels us to revise certain traditional conceptions that have played
an important part in the history of philosophy, and it offers
solutions for certain questions which are as old as the history
of philosophy and which could not be answered earlier. Plato's
attempt to solve the problems of geometry by a theory of ideas,
Kant's attempt to account for the nature of space and time by a
"reine Anschauung" and by a transcendental philosophy, these
represent answers to the very questions to which Einstein's
theory has given a different answer at a later time. If Plato's
and Kant's doctrines are philosophical theories, then Einstein's
theory of relativity is a philosophical and not a merely physical
matter. And the questions referred to are not of a secondary
nature but of primary import for philosophy; that much is evident from the central position they occupy in the systems of
Plato and Kant. These systems are untenable if Einstein's answer is put in the place of the answers given to the same questions by their authors; their foundations are shaken when space
and time are not the revelations of an insight into a world of
ideas, or of a vision grown from pure reason, which a philosophical apriorism claimed to have established. The analysis of
knowledge has always been the basic issue of philosophy; and
if knowledge in so fundamental a domain as that of space and
time is subject to revision, the implications of such criticism will
involve the whole of philosophy.

To advocate the philosophical significance of Einstein's
theory, however, does not mean to make Einstein a philosopher;
or, at least, it does not mean that Einstein is a philosopher of
primary intent. Einstein's primary objectives were all in the
realm of physics. But he saw that certain physical problems
could not be solved unless the solutions were preceded by a
logical analysis of the fundamentals of space and time, and he
saw that this analysis, in turn, presupposed a philosophic read-
justment of certain familiar conceptions of knowledge. The

physicist who wanted to understand the Michelson experiment had to commit himself to a philosophy for which the meaning of a statement is reducible to its verifiability, that is, he had to adopt the verifiability theory of meaning if he wanted to escape a maze of ambiguous questions and gratuitous complications. It is this positivist, or let me rather say, empiricist commitment which determines the philosophical position of Einstein. It was not necessary for him to elaborate on it to any great extent; he merely had to join a trend of development characterized, within the generation of physicists before him, by such names as Kirchhoff, Hertz, Mach, and to carry through to its ultimate consequences a philosophical evolution documented at earlier stages in such principles as Occam's razor and Leibnitz' identity of indiscernibles.

Einstein has referred to this conception of meaning in various remarks, though he has never felt it necessary to enter into a discussion of its grounds or into an analysis of its philosophical position. The exposition and substantiation of a philosophical theory is nowhere to be found in his writings. In fact, Einstein's philosophy is not so much a philosophical system as a philosophical attitude; apart from occasional remarks, he left it to others to say what philosophy his equations entail and thus remained a philosopher by implication, so to speak. That is both his strength and his weakness; his strength, because it made his physics so conclusive; his weakness, because it left his theory open to misunderstandings and erroneous interpretations.

It seems to be a general law that the making of a new physics precedes a new philosophy of physics. Philosophic analysis is more easily achieved when it is applied to concrete purposes, when it is done within the pursuit of research aimed at an interpretation of observational data. The philosophic results of the procedure are often recognized at a later stage; they are the fruit of reflection about the methods employed in the solution of the concrete problem. But those who make the new physics usually do not have the leisure, or do not regard it as their objective, to expound and elaborate the philosophy implicit in their constructions. Occasionally, in popular presentations, a physicist attempts to explain the logical background of his theories; thus many a physicist has been misled into believing that philosophy of physics is the same as a popularization of physics. Einstein himself does not belong to this group of writers who do not realize that what they achieve is as much a popularization of philosophy as it is one of physics, and that the philosophy of physics is as technical and intricate as is physics itself. Nevertheless, Einstein is not a philosopher in the technical sense either. It appears to be practically impossible that the man who is looking for new physical laws should also concentrate on the analysis of his method; he will perform this second task only when such analysis is indispensable for the finding of physical results. The division of labor between the physicist and the philosopher seems to be an inescapable consequence of the organization of the human mind.

It is not only a limitation of human capacities which calls for a division of labor between the physicist and the philosopher. The discovery of general relations that lend themselves to empirical verification requires a mentality different from that of the philosopher, whose methods are analytic and critical rather than predictive. The physicist who is looking for new discoveries must not be too critical; in the initial stages he is dependent on guessing, and he will find his way only if he is carried along by a certain faith which serves as a directive for his guesses. When I, on a certain occasion, asked Professor Einstein how he found his theory of relativity, he answered that he found it because he was so strongly convinced of the harmony of the universe. No doubt his theory supplies a most successful demonstration of the usefulness of such a conviction. But a creed is not a philosophy; it carries this name only in the popular interpretation of the term. The philosopher of science is not much interested in the thought processes which lead to scientific discoveries; he looks for a logical analysis of the completed theory, including the relationships establishing its validity. That is, he is not interested in the context of discovery, but in the context of justification. But the critical attitude may make a man incapable of discovery; and, as long as he is successful, the creative physicist may very well prefer his creed to the logic of the analytic philosopher.

The philosopher has no objections to a physicist's beliefs, so long as they are not advanced in the form of a philosophy. He knows that a personal faith is justified as an instrument of finding a physical theory, that it is but a primitive form of guessing, which is eventually replaced by the elaborate theory, and that it is ultimately subject to the same empirical tests as the theory. The philosophy of physics, on the other hand, is not a product of creed but of analysis. It incorporates the physicist's beliefs into the psychology of discovery; it endeavors to clarify the meanings of physical theories, independently of the interpretation by their authors, and is concerned with logical relationships alone.

Seen from this viewpoint it appears amazing to what extent the logical analysis of relativity coincides with the original interpretation by its author, as far as it can be constructed from the scanty remarks in Einstein's publications. In contradistinction to some developments in quantum theory, the logical schema of the theory of relativity corresponds surprisingly with the program which controlled its discovery. His philosophic clarity distinguishes Einstein from many a physicist whose work became the source of a philosophy different from the interpretation given by the author. In the following pages I shall attempt to outline the philosophical results of Einstein's theory, hoping to find a friendly comment by the man who was the first to see all these relations, even though he did not always formulate them explicitly. And the gratitude of the philosopher goes to this great physicist whose work includes more implicit philosophy than is contained in many a philosophical system.

II

The logical basis of the theory of relativity is the discovery that many statements, which were regarded as capable of demonstrable truth or falsity, are mere definitions.

This formulation sounds like the statement of an insignificant technical discovery and does not reveal the far-reaching implications which make up the philosophical significance of the theory. Nonetheless it is a complete formulation of the *logical* part of the theory.

Consider, for instance, the problem of geometry. That the unit of measurement is a matter of definition is a familiar fact; everybody knows that it does not make any difference whether we measure distances in feet or meters or light-years. However, that the comparison of distances is also a matter of definition is known only to the expert of relativity. This result can also be formulated as the definitional character of congruence. That a certain distance is congruent to another distance situated at a different place can never be proved to be true; it can only be maintained in the sense of a definition. More precisely speaking, it can be maintained as true only after a definition of congruence is given; it therefore depends on an original comparison of distances which is a matter of definition. A comparison of distances by means of the transport of solid bodies is but one definition of congruence. Another definition would result if we regarded a rod, once it had been transported to another location, as twice as long, thrice transported as three times as long, and so on. A further illustration refers to time: that the simultaneity of events occurring at distant places is a matter of definition was not known before Einstein based his special theory of relativity on this logical discovery.

The definitions employed for the construction of space and time are of a particular kind: they are co-ordinative definitions. That is, they are given by the co-ordination of a physical object, or process, to some fundamental concept. For instance, the concept "equal length" is defined by reference to a physical object, a solid rod, whose transport lays down equal distances. The concept "simultaneous" is defined by the use of light-rays which move over equal distances. The definitions of the theory of relativity are all of this type; they are co-ordinative definitions.

In the expositions of the theory of relativity the use of different definitions is often illustrated by a reference to different observers. This kind of presentation has led to the erroneous conception that the relativity of space-time measurements is connected with the subjectivity of the observer, that the privacy of the world of sense perception is the origin of the relativity maintained by Einstein. Such Protagorean interpretation of Einstein's relativity is utterly mistaken. The definitional character of simultaneity, for instance, has nothing to do with the perspective variations resulting for observers located in different frames of reference. That we co-ordinate different definitions of simultaneity to different observers merely serves as a simplification of the presentation of logical relationships. We could as well interchange the co-ordination and let the observer located in the "moving" system employ the time definition of the observer located in the system "at rest," and vice versa; or we could even let both employ the same time definition, for instance that of the system "at rest." Such variations would lead to different transformations; for instance, the last mentioned definition would lead, not to the Lorentz transformation, but to the classical transformation from a system at rest to a moving system. It is convenient to identify one definitional system with one observer; to speak of different observers is merely a mode of speech expressing the plurality of definitional systems. In a logical exposition of the theory of relativity the observer can be completely eliminated.

Definitions are arbitrary; and it is a consequence of the definitional character of fundamental concepts that with the change of the definitions various descriptional systems arise. But these systems are equivalent to each other, and it is possible to go from each system to another one by a suitable transformation. Thus the definitional character of fundamental concepts leads to a plurality of equivalent descriptions. A familiar illustration is given by the various descriptions of motion resulting when the system regarded as being at rest is varied. Another illustration is presented by the various geometries resulting, for the same physical space, through changes in the definition of congruence. All these descriptions represent different languages saying the same thing; equivalent descriptions, therefore, express the same physical content. The theory of equivalent descriptions is also applicable to other fields of physics; but the domain of space and time has become the model case of this theory.

The word "relativity" should be interpreted as meaning "relative to a certain definitional system." That relativity implies plurality follows because the variation of definitions leads to the plurality of equivalent descriptions. But we see that the plurality implied is not a plurality of different views, or of systems of contradictory content; it is merely a plurality of equivalent languages and thus of forms of expression which do not contradict each other but have the same content. Relativity does not mean an abandonment of truth; it only means that truth can be formulated in various ways.

I should like to make this point quite clear. The two statements "the room is 21 feet long" and "the room is 7 yards long" are quivalent descriptions; they state the same fact. That the simple truth they express can be formulated in these two ways does not eliminate the concept of truth; it merely illustrates the fact that the number characterizing a length is relative to the unit of measurement. All relativities of Einstein's theory are of this type. For instance, the Lorentz transformation connects different descriptions of space-time relations which are equivalent in the same sense as the statements about a length of 21 feet and a length of 7 yards.

Some confusion has arisen from considerations referring to the property of simplicity. One descriptional system can be simpler than another; but that fact does not make it "truer" than the other. The decimal system is simpler than the yard-foot-inch system; but an architect's plan drawn in feet and inches is as true a description of a house as a plan drawn in the decimal system. A simplicity of this kind, for which I have used the name of *descriptive simplicity*, is not a criterion of truth. Only within the frame of inductive considerations can simplicity be a criterion of truth; for instance, the simplest curve between observational data plotted in a diagram is regarded as "truer," i.e., more probable, than other connecting curves. This *inductive simplicity*, however, refers to non-equivalent descriptions and does not play a part in the theory of relativity, in which only equivalent descriptions are compared. The simplicity of descriptions used in Einstein's theory is therefore always a descriptive simplicity. For instance, the fact that non-Euclidean geometry often supplies a simpler description of physical space than does Euclidean geometry does not make the non-Euclidean description "truer."

Another confusion must be ascribed to the theory of conventionalism, which goes back to Poincaré. According to this theory, geometry is a matter of convention, and no empirical meaning can be assigned to a statement about the geometry of physical space. Now it is true that physical space can be described by both a Euclidean and a non-Euclidean geometry; but it is an erroneous interpretation of this relativity of geometry to call a statement about the geometrical structure of physical space meaningless. The choice of a geometry is arbitrary only so long as no definition of congruence is specified. Once this definition is set up, it becomes an empirical question *which* geometry holds for a physical space. For instance, it is an empirical fact that, when we use solid bodies for the definition of congruence, our physical space is practically Euclidean within terrestrial dimensions. If, in a different part of the universe, the same definition of congruence were to lead to a non-Euclidean geometry, that part of universal space would have a geometrical structure different from that of our world. It is true that a Euclidean geometry could also be introduced for that part of the universe; but then the definition of congruence would no longer be given by solid bodies.[1] The combination of a statement about a geometry with a statement of the co-ordinative definition of congruence employed is subject to empirical test and thus expresses a property of the physical world. The conventionalist overlooks the fact that only the incomplete statement of a geometry, in which a reference to the definition of congruence is omitted, is arbitrary; if the statement is made complete by the addition of a reference to the definition of congruence, it becomes empirically verifiable and thus has physical content.

Instead of speaking of conventionalism, therefore, we should speak of the relativity of geometry. Geometry is relative in precisely the same sense as other relative concepts. We might call it a convention to say that Chicago is to the left of New York; but we should not forget that this conventional statement can be made objectively true as soon as the point of refer-

---

[1] Poincaré believed that the definition of a solid body could not be given without reference to a geometry. That this conception is mistaken, is shown in the present author's *Philosophie der Raum-Zeit-Lehre* (Berlin, 1928) §5.

ence is included in the statement. It is not a convention but a physical fact that Chicago is to the left of New York, seen, for instance, from Washington, D.C. The relativity of simple concepts, such as left and right, is well known. That the fundamental concepts of space and time are of the same type is the essence of the theory of relativity.

The relativity of geometry is a consequence of the fact that different geometries can be represented on one another by a one-to-one correspondence. For certain geometrical systems, however, the representation will not be continuous throughout, and there will result singularities in individual points or lines. For instance, a sphere cannot be projected on a plane without a singularity in at least one point; in the usual projections, the North Pole of the sphere corresponds to the infinity of the plane. This peculiarity involves certain limitations for the relativity of geometry. Assume that in one geometrical description, say, by a spherical space, we have a normal causality for all physical occurrences; then a transformation to certain other geometries, including the Euclidean geometry, leads to violations of the principle of causality, to *causal anomalies*. A light signal going from a point A by way of the North Pole to a point B in a finite time will be so represented within a Euclidean interpretation of this space, that it moves from A in one direction towards infinity and returns from the other side towards B, thus passing through an infinite distance in a finite time. Still more complicated causal anomalies result for other transformations.[2] If the principle of normal causality, i.e., a continuous spreading from cause to effect in a finite time, or *action by contact*, is set up as a necessary prerequisite of the description of nature, certain worlds cannot be interpreted by certain geometries. It may well happen that the geometry thus excluded is the Euclidean one; if Einstein's hypothesis of a closed universe is correct, a

---

[2] Cf. the author's *Philosophie der Raum-Zeit-Lehre* (Berlin, 1928), §12. It has turned out that within the plurality of descriptions applicable to quantum mechanics the problem of causal anomalies plays an even more important part, since we have there a case where no description exists which avoids causal anomalies. (Cf. also the author's *Philosophic Foundations of Quantum Mechanics*, Berkeley, 1944), §§5-7, §26.

Euclidean description of the universe would be excluded for all adherents of a normal causality.

It is this fact which I regard as the strongest refutation of the Kantian conception of space. The relativity of geometry has been used by Neo-Kantians as a back door through which the apriorism of Euclidean geometry was introduced into Einstein's theory: if it is always possible to select a Euclidean geometry for the description of the universe, then the Kantian insists that it be this description which should be used, because Euclidean geometry, for a Kantian, is the only one that can be visualized. We see that this rule may lead to violations of the principle of causality; and since causality, for a Kantian, is as much an *a priori* principle as Euclidean geometry, his rule may compel the Kantian to jump from the frying pan into the fire. There is no defense of Kantianism, if the statement of the geometry of the physical world is worded in a complete form, including all its physical implications; because in this form the statement is empirically verifiable and depends for its truth on the nature of the physical world.[3]

It should be clear from this analysis that the plurality of equivalent description does not rule out the possibility of true empirical statements. The empirical content of statements about space and time is only stated in a more complicated way.

III

Though we now possess, in Einstein's theory, a complete statement of the relativity of space and time, we should not forget that this is the result of a long historical development. I mentioned above Occam's razor and Leibnitz' identity of indiscernibles in connection with the verifiability theory of meaning. It is a matter of fact that Leibnitz applied his principle successfully to the problem of motion and that he arrived at a relativity of motion on logical grounds. The famous correspondence between Leibnitz and Clarke,—the latter a contemporary defender of Newton's absolutism,—presents us with the same type of discussion which is familiar from the modern discussions

---

[3] This refutation of Kantianism was presented in the author's *Relativitätstheorie und Erkenntnis A priori* (Berlin, 1920).

of relativity and reads as though Leibnitz had taken his arguments from expositions of Einstein's theory. Leibnitz even went so far as to recognize the relationship between causal order and time order.[4] This conception of relativity was carried on at a later time by Ernst Mach, who contributed to the discussion the important idea that a relativity of rotational motion requires an extension of relativism to the concept of inertial force. Einstein has always acknowledged Mach as a forerunner of his theory.

Another line of development, which likewise found its completion through Einstein's theory, is presented by the history of geometry. The discovery of non-Euclidean geometries by Gauss, Bolyai, and Lobachewski was associated with the idea that physical geometry might be non-Euclidean; and it is known that Gauss tried to test the Euclidean character of terrestrial geometry by triangular measurements from mountain tops. But the man to whom we owe the philosophical clarification of the problem of geometry is Helmholtz. He saw that physical geometry is dependent on the definition of congruence by means of the solid body and thus arrived at a clear statement of the nature of physical geometry, superior in logical insight to Poincaré's conventionalism developed several decades later. It was Helmholtz, too, who clarified the problem of a visual presentation of non-Euclidean geometry by the discovery that visualization is a fruit of experiences with solid bodies and light-rays. We find in Helmholtz' writings the famous statement that imagining something visually means depicting the series of sense perceptions which one would have if one lived in such a world. That Helmholtz did not succeed in dissuading contemporary philosophers from a Kantian apriorism of space and time is not his fault. His philosophical views were known only among a small group of experts. When, with Einstein's theory, the public interest turned toward these problems, philosophers began to give in and to depart from Kant's apriorism. Let us hope that this development will continue and eventually include even those philosophers who in our day still defend an apriorist philosophy against the attacks of the mathematical physicist.

[4] For an analysis of Leibnitz' views see the author's "Die Bewegungslehre bei Newton, Leibnitz und Huyghens," *Kantstudien* [vol. 29, 1924], 416.

Although there exists a historical evolution of the concepts of space and motion, this line of development finds no analogue in the concept of time. The first to speak of a relativity of the measure of time, i.e., of what is called the uniform flow of time, was Mach. However, Einstein's idea of a relativity of simultaneity has no forerunners. It appears that this discovery could not be made before the perfection of experimental methods of physics. Einstein's relativity of simultaneity is closely associated with the assumption that light is the fastest signal, an idea which could not be conceived before the negative outcome of such experiments as that by Michelson.

It was the combination of the relativity of time and of motion which made Einstein's theory so successful and led to results far beyond the reach of earlier theories. The discovery of the special theory of relativity, which none of Einstein's forerunners had thought of, thus became the key to a general theory of space and time, which included all the ideas of Leibnitz, Gauss, Riemann, Helmholtz, and Mach, and which added to them certain fundamental discoveries which could not have been anticipated at an earlier stage. In particular, I refer to Einstein's conception according to which the geometry of physical space is a function of the distribution of masses, an idea entirely new in the history of geometry.

This short account shows that the evolution of philosophical ideas is guided by the evolution of physical theories. The philosophy of space and time is not the work of the ivory tower philosopher. It was constructed by men who attempted to combine observational data with mathematical analysis. The great synthesis of the various lines of development, which we owe to Einstein, bears witness to the fact that philosophy of science has taken over a function which philosophical systems could not perform.

IV

The question of what is space and time has fascinated the authors of philosophical systems over and again. Plato answered it by inventing a world of "higher" reality, the world of ideas, which includes space and time among its ideal objects and reveals their relations to the mathematician who is able to per-

form the necessary act of vision. For Spinoza space was an attribute of God. Kant, on the other hand, denied the reality of
space and time and regarded these two conceptual systems as
forms of visualization, i.e., as constructions of the human mind,
by means of which the human observer combines his perceptions
so as to collect them into an orderly system.

The answer we can give to the question on the basis of Einstein's theory is very different from the answers of these philosophers. The theory of relativity shows that space and time
are neither ideal objects nor forms of order necessary for the
human mind. They constitute a relational system expressing
certain general features of physical objects and thus are descriptive of the physical world. Let us make this fact quite clear.

It is true that, like all concepts, space and time are inventions
of the human mind. But not all inventions of the human mind
are fit to describe the physical world. By the latter phrase we
mean that the concepts refer to certain physical objects and differentiate them from others. For instance, the concept "cen-
taur" is empty, whereas the concept "bear" refers to certain
physical objects and distinguishes them from others. The concept "thing," on the other hand, though not empty, is so general that it does not differentiate between objects. Our examples
concern one-place predicates, but the same distinction applies to
two-place predicates. The relation "telepathy" is empty,
whereas the relation "father" is not. When we say that non-
empty one-place predicates like "bear" describe real objects, we
must also say that non-empty many-place predicates like
"father" describe real relations.

It is in this sense that the theory of relativity maintains the
reality of space and time. These conceptual systems describe
relations holding between physical objects, namely, solid bodies,
light-rays, and watches. In addition, these relations formulate
physical laws of great generality, determining some fundamental features of the physical world. Space and time have as much
reality as, say, the relation "father" or the Newtonian forces of
attraction.

The following consideration may serve as a further explanation why geometry is descriptive of physical reality. As long as

only one geometry, the Euclidean geometry, was known, the fact that this geometry could be used for a description of the physical world represented a problem for the philosopher; and Kant's philosophy must be understood as an attempt to explain why a structural system derived from the human mind can account for observational relations. With the discovery of a plurality of geometries the situation changed completely. The human mind was shown to be capable of inventing all kinds of geometrical systems, and the question, which of the systems is suitable for the description of physical reality, was turned into an empirical question, i.e., its answer was ultimately left to empirical data. Concerning the empirical nature of this answer we refer the reader to our considerations in Section II; it is the combined statement of geometry and co-ordinative definitions which is empirical. But, if the statement about the geometry of the physical world is empirical, geometry describes a property of the physical world in the same sense, say, as temperature or weight describe properties of physical objects. When we speak of the reality of physical space we mean this very fact.

As mentioned above, the objects whose general relationship is expressed in the spatio-temporal order are solid bodies, light-rays, and natural watches, i.e., closed periodic systems, like revolving atoms or revolving planets. The important part which light-rays play in the theory of relativity derives from the fact that light is the fastest signal, i.e., represents the fastest form of a causal chain. The concept of causal chain can be shown to be the basic concept in terms of which the structure of space and time is built up. The spatio-temporal order thus must be regarded as the expression of the causal order of the physical world. The close connection between space and time on the one hand and causality on the other hand is perhaps the most prominent feature of Einstein's theory, although this feature has not always been recognized in its significance. Time order, the order of *earlier* and *later*, is reducible to causal order; the cause is always earlier than the effect, a relation which cannot be reversed. That Einstein's theory admits of a reversal of time order for certain events, a result known from the relativity of simultaneity, is merely a consequence of this fundamental fact.

Since the speed of causal transmission is limited, there exist events of such a kind that neither of them can be the cause or the effect of the other. For events of this kind a time order is not defined, and either of them can be called earlier or later than the other.

Ultimately even spatial order is reducible to causal order; a space point B is called closer to A than a space point C, if a direct light-signal, i.e., a fastest causal chain, from A to C passes by B. For a construction of geometry in terms of light-rays and mass-points, i.e., a light-geometry, I refer to another publication.[5]

The connection between time order and causal order leads to the question of the direction of time. I should like to add some remarks about this problem which has often been discussed, but which has not always been stated clearly enough. The relation between cause and effect is an asymmetrical relation; if P is the cause of Q, then Q is not the cause of P. This fundamental fact is essential for temporal order, because it makes time a serial relation. By a serial relation we understand a relation that orders its elements in a linear arrangement; such a relation is always asymmetrical and transitive, like the relation "smaller than." The time of Einstein's theory has these properties; that is necessary, because otherwise it could not be used for the construction of a serial order.

But what we call the direction of time must be distinguished from the asymmetrical character of the concepts "earlier" and "later." A relation can be asymmetrical and transitive without distinguishing one direction from the opposite one. For instance, the points of a straight line are ordered by a serial relation which we may express by the words "before" and "after." If A is before B, then B is not before A, and if A is before B and B is before C, then A is before C. But which direction of the line we should call "before" and which one "after" is not indicated by the nature of the line; this definition can only be set up by an arbitrary choice, for instance, by pointing into one direction and calling it the direction of "before." In other words, the relations "before" and "after" are structurally indistinguish-

[5] H. Reichenbach, *Philosophie der Raum-Zeit-Lehre* (Berlin, 1928), §27.

able and therefore interchangeable; whether we say that point *A* is before point *B* or after point *B* is a matter of arbitrary definition. It is different with the relation "smaller than" among real numbers. This relation is also a serial relation and thus asymmetrical and transitive; but in addition, it is structurally different from its converse, the relation "larger than," a fact expressible through the difference of positive and negative numbers. The square of a positive number is a positive number, and the square of a negative number is also a positive number. This peculiarity enables us to define the relation "smaller than:" a number which cannot be the square of another number is smaller than a number which is the square of another number. The series of real numbers possesses therefore a direction: the direction "smaller than" is not interchangeable with the direction "larger than;" these relations are therefore not only asymmetrical but also *unidirectional*.

The problem of the time relation is whether it is unidirectional. The relation "earlier than" which we use in everyday life is structurally different from the relation "later than." For instance, we may make up our mind to go to the theatre tomorrow; but it would be nonsensical to make up our mind to go to the theatre yesterday. The physicist formulates this distinction as the *irreversibility of time:* time flows in one direction, and the flow of time cannot be reversed. We see that, in the language of the theory of relations, the question of the irreversibility of time is expressed, not by the question of whether time is an asymmetrical relation, but by the question of whether it is a unidirectional relation.

For the theory of relativity, time is certainly an asymmetrical relation, since otherwise the time relation would not establish a serial order; but it is not unidirectional. In other words, the irreversibility of time does not find an expression in the theory of relativity. We must not conclude that that is the ultimate word which the physicist has to say about time. All we can say is that, as far as the theory of relativity is concerned, we need not make a qualitative distinction between the two directions of time, between the "earlier" and "later." A physical theory may very well abstract from certain properties of the physical world; that does not mean that these properties do not exist. The irreversibility of time has so far been dealt with only in thermodynamics, where it is conceived as being merely of a statistical nature, not applicable to elementary processes. This answer is none too satisfactory; particularly in view of the fact that it has led to certain paradoxes. Quantum physics so far, however, has no better answer. I would like to say that I regard this problem as at present unsolved and do not agree with those who believe that there is no genuine problem of the direction of time.

It is an amazing fact that the mathematico-physical treatment of the concept of time formulated in Einstein's theory has led to a clarification which philosophical analysis could not achieve. For the philosopher such concepts as time order and simultaneity were primitive notions inaccessible to further analysis. But the claim that a concept is exempt from analysis often merely springs from an inability to understand its meaning. With his reduction of the time concept to that of causality and his generalization of time order toward a relativity of simultaneity, Einstein has not only changed our conceptions of time; he has also clarified the meaning of the classical time concept which preceded his discoveries. In other words, we know better today what absolute time means than anyone of the adherents of the classical time conceptions. Absolute simultaneity would hold in a world in which there exists no upper limit for the speed of signals, i.e., for causal transmission. A world of this type is as well imaginable as Einstein's world. It is an empirical question to which type our world belongs. Experiment has decided in favor of Einstein's conception. As in the case of geometry, the human mind is capable of constructing various forms of a temporal schema; the question which of these schemes fits the physical world, i.e., is true, can only be answered by reference to observational data. What the human mind contributes to the problem of time is not one definite time order, but a plurality of possible time orders, and the selection of one time order as the real one is left to empirical observation. Time is the order of causal chains; that is the outstanding result of Einstein's discoveries. The only philosopher who anticipated this result was Leibnitz; though, of course, in his day it was impossible to conceive of a relativity of simultaneity. And Leibnitz was a mathematician as well as a philosopher. It appears that the solution of the problem of time and space is reserved to philosophers who, like Leibnitz, are mathematicians, or to mathematicians who, like Einstein, are philosophers.

V

From the time of Kant, the history of philosophy shows a growing rift between philosophical systems and the philosophy of science. The system of Kant was constructed with the intention of proving that knowledge is the resultant of two components, a mental and an observational one; the mental component was assumed to be given by the laws of pure reason and conceived as a synthetic element different from the merely analytic operations of logic. The concept of a *synthetic a priori* formulates the Kantian position: there is a *synthetic a priori* part of knowledge, i.e., there are non-empty statements which are absolutely necessary. Among these principles of knowledge Kant includes the laws of Euclidean geometry, of absolute time, of causality and of the conservation of mass. His followers in the 19th century took over this conception, adding many variations.

The development of science, on the other hand, has led away from Kantian metaphysics. The principles which Kant regarded as *synthetic a priori* were recognized as being of a questionable truth; principles contradictory to them were developed and employed for the construction of knowledge. These new principles were not advanced with a claim to absolute truth but in the form of attempts to find a description of nature fitting the observational material. Among the plurality of possible systems, the one corresponding to physical reality could be singled out only by observation and experiment. In other words, the synthetic principles of knowledge which Kant had regarded as *a priori* were recognized as *a posteriori*, as verifiable through experience only and as valid in the restricted sense of empirical hypotheses.

It is this process of a dissolution of the *synthetic a priori* into which we must incorporate the theory of relativity, when we desire to judge it from the viewpoint of the history of philosophy. A line which began with the invention of non-Euclidean geometries 20 years after Kant's death runs uninterruptedly right up and into Einstein's theory of space and time. The laws of geometry, for 2000 years regarded as laws of reason, were recognized as empirical laws, which fit the world of our environment to a high degree of precision; but they must be abandoned for astronomic dimensions. The apparent self-evidence of these laws, which made them seem to be inescapable presuppositions of all knowledge, turned out to be the product of habit; through their suitability to all experiences of everyday life these laws had acquired a degree of reliability which erroneously was taken for absolute certainty. Helmholtz was the first to advocate the idea that human beings, living in a non-Euclidean world, would develop an ability of visualization which would make them regard the laws of non-Euclidean geometry as necessary and self-evident, in the same fashion as the laws of Euclidean geometry appear self-evident to us. Transferring this idea to Einstein's conception of time, we would say that human beings, in whose daily experiences the effects of the speed of light would be noticeably different from those of an infinite velocity, would become accustomed to the relativity of simultaneity and regard the rules of the Lorentz-transformation as necessary and self-evident, just as we regard the classical rules of motion and simultaneity self-evident. For instance, if a telephone connection with the planet Mars were established, and we would have to wait a quarter of an hour for the answer to our questions, the relativity of simultaneity would become as trivial a matter as the time difference between the standard times of different time zones is today. What philosophers had regarded as laws of reason turned out to be a conditioning through the physical laws of our environment; we have ground to assume that in a different environment a corresponding conditioning would lead to another adaptation of the mind.

The process of the dissolution of the *synthetic a priori* is one of the significant features of the philosophy of our time. We should not commit the mistake of considering it a breakdown of human abilities, if conceptions which we regarded as absolutely true are shown to be of limited validity and have to be abandoned in certain fields of knowledge. On the contrary, the fact that we are able to overcome these conceptions and to replace them by better ones reveals unexpected abilities of the human mind, a versatility vastly superior to the dogmatism of a pure reason which dictates its laws to the scientist.

Kant believed himself to possess a proof for his assertion that his *synthetic a priori* principles were necessary truths: According to him these principles were necessary conditions of knowledge. He overlooked the fact that such a proof can demonstrate the truth of the principles only if it is taken for granted that knowledge within the frame of these principles will always be possible. What has happened, then, in Einstein's theory is a proof that knowledge within the framework of Kantian principles is not possible. For a Kantian, such a result could only signify a breakdown of science. It is a fortunate fact that the scientist was not a Kantian and, instead of abandoning his attempts of constructing knowledge, looked for ways of changing the so-called *a priori* principles. Through his ability of dealing with space-time relations essentially different from the traditional frame of knowledge, Einstein has shown the way to a philosophy superior to the philosophy of the *synthetic a priori*.

It is the philosophy of empiricism, therefore, into which Einstein's relativity belongs. It is true, Einstein's empiricism is not the one of Bacon and Mill, who believed that all laws of nature can be found by simple inductive generalizations. Einstein's empiricism is that of modern theoretical physics, the empiricism of mathematical construction, which is so devised that it connects observational data by deductive operations and enables us to predict new observational data. Mathematical physics will always remain empiricist as long as it leaves the ultimate criterion of truth to sense perception. The enormous amount of deductive method in such a physics can be accounted for in terms of analytic operations alone. In addition to deductive operations there is, of course, an inductive element included in the physics of mathematical hypotheses; but even the principle of induction, by far the most difficult obstacle to a radical empiricism, can be shown today to be justifiable without a belief in a *synthetic a priori.* The method of modern science can be completely accounted for in terms of an empiricism which recognizes only sense perception and the analytic principles of logic as sources of knowledge. In spite of the enormous mathematical apparatus, Einstein's theory of space and time is the triumph of such a radical empiricism in a field which had always been regarded as a reservation for the discoveries of pure reason.

The process of the dissolution of the *synthetic a priori* is going on. To the abandonment of absolute space and time quantum physics has added that of causality; furthermore, it has abandoned the classical concept of material substance and has shown that the constituents of matter, the atomic particles, do not possess the unambiguous nature of the solid bodies of the macroscopic world. If we understand by metaphysics the belief in principles that are non-analytic, yet derive their validity from reason alone, modern science is anti-metaphysical. It has refused to recognize the authority of the philosopher who claims to know the truth from intuition, from insight into a world of ideas or into the nature of reason or the principles of being, or from whatever super-empirical source. There is no separate entrance to truth for philosophers. The path of the philosopher is indicated by that of the scientist: all the philosopher can do is to analyze the results of science, to construe their meanings and stake out their validity. Theory of knowledge is analysis of science.

I said above that Einstein is a philosopher by implication. That means that making the philosophic implications of Einstein's theory explicit is the task of the philosopher. Let us not forget that it is implications of an enormous reach which are derivable from the theory of relativity, and let us realize that it must be an eminently philosophical physics that lends itself to such implications. It does not happen very often that physical systems of such philosophical significance are presented to us; Einstein's predecessor was Newton. It is the privilege of our generation that we have among us a physicist whose work occupies the same rank as that of the man who determined the philosophy of space and time for two centuries. If physicists present us with implicational philosophies of such excellence, it is a pleasure to be a philosopher. The lasting fame of the philosophy of modern physics will justly go to the man who made the physics rather than to those who have been at work deriving the implications of his work and who are pointing out its position in the history of philosophy. There are many who have contributed to the philosophy of Einstein's theory, but there is only one Einstein.

HANS REICHENBACH

DEPARTMENT OF PHILOSOPHY
UNIVERSITY OF CALIFORNIA AT LOS ANGELES

II

H. P. Robertson

GEOMETRY AS A BRANCH OF PHYSICS

GEOMETRY AS A BRANCH OF PHYSICS

IS SPACE REALLY CURVED? That is a question which, in one form or another, is raised again and again by philosophers, scientists, T. C. Mits and readers of the weekly comic supplements. A question which has been brought into the limelight above all by the genial work of Albert Einstein, and kept there by the unceasing efforts of astronomers to wrest the answer from a curiously reluctant Nature.

But what is the meaning of the question? What, indeed, is the meaning of each word in it? Properly to formulate and adequately to answer the question would require a critical excursus through philosophy and mathematics into physics and astronomy, which is beyond the scope of the present modest attempt. Here we shall be content to examine the rôles of deduction and observation in the problem of physical space, to exhibit certain high points in the history of the problem, and in the end to illustrate the viewpoint adopted by presenting a relatively simple caricature of Einstein's general theory of relativity. It is hoped that this, certainly incomplete and possibly naïve, description will present the essentials of the problem from a neutral mathematico-physical viewpoint in a form suitable for incorporation into any otherwise tenable philosophical position. Here, for example, we shall not touch directly upon the important problem of form versus substance—but if one wishes to interpret the geometrical substratum here considered as a formal backdrop against which the contingent relations of nature are exhibited, one should be able to do so without distorting the scientific content.

First, then, we consider geometry as a deductive science, a branch of mathematics in which a body of theories is built up by logical processes from a postulated set of axioms (not "self-evident truths"). In logical position geometry differs not in kind from any other mathematical discipline—say the theory of numbers or the calculus of variations. As mathematics, it is not the science of measurement, despite the implications of its name—even though it did, in keeping with the name, originate in the codification of rules for land surveying. The principal criterion of its validity as a mathematical discipline is whether the axioms as written down are self-consistent, and the sole criterion of the truth of a theorem involving its concepts is whether the theorem can be deduced from the axioms. This truth is clearly relative to the axioms; the theorem that the sum of the three interior angles of a triangle is equal to two right angles, true in Euclidean geometry, is false in any of the geometries obtained on replacing the parallel postulate by one of its contraries. In the present sense it suffices for us that geometry is a body of theorems, involving among others the concepts of point, angle and a unique numerical relation called distance between pairs of points, deduced from a set of self-consistent axioms.

What, then, distinguishes Euclidean geometry as a mathematical system from those logically consistent systems, involving the same category of concepts, which result from the denial of one or more of its traditional axioms? This distinction cannot consist in its "truth" in the sense of observed fact in physical science; its truth, or applicability, or still better appropriateness, in this latter sense is dependent upon observation, and not upon deduction alone. The characteristics of Euclidean geometry, as mathematics, are therefore to be sought in its internal properties, and not in its relation to the empirical.

First, Euclidean geometry is a *congruence geometry*, or equivalently the space comprising its elements is *homogeneous and isotropic;* the intrinsic relations between points and other elements of a configuration are unaffected by the position or orientation of the configuration. As an example, in Euclidean geometry all intrinsic properties of a triangle—its angles, area, etc.,—are uniquely determined by the lengths of its three sides; two triangles whose three sides are respectively equal are "congruent;" either can by a "motion" of the space into itself be brought into complete coincidence with the other, whatever its original position and orientation may be. These motions of Euclidean space are the familiar translations and rotations, use of which is made in proving many of the theorems of Euclid. That the existence of these motions (the axiom of "free mobility") is a desideratum, if not indeed a necessity, for a geometry applicable to physical space, has been forcibly argued on *a priori* grounds by von Helmholtz, Whitehead, Russell and others; for only in a homogeneous and isotropic space can the traditional concept of a rigid body be maintained.[1]

But the Euclidean geometry is only one of several congruence geometries; there are in addition the "hyperbolic" geometry of Bolyai and Lobachewsky, and the "spherical" and "elliptic" geometries of Riemann and Klein. Each of these geometries is characterized by a real number K, which for the Euclidean geometry is zero, for the hyperbolic negative, and for the spherical and elliptic geometries positive. In the case of 2-dimensional congruence spaces, which *may* (but need not) be conceived as surfaces embedded in a 3-dimensional Euclidean space, the constant K may be interpreted as the *curvature* of the surface into the third dimension—whence it derives its name. This name and this representation are for our purposes at least psychologically unfortunate, for we propose ultimately to deal exclusively with properties intrinsic to the space under consideration—properties which in the later physical applications can be measured within the space itself—and are not dependent upon some extrinsic construction, such as its relation to an hypothesized higher dimensional embedding space. We must accordingly seek some determination of K—which we nevertheless continue to call curvature—in terms of such inner properties.

[1] Technically this requirement, as expressed by the axiom of free mobility, is that there exist a motion of the 3-dimensional space into itself which takes an arbitrary configuration, consisting of a point, a direction through the point, and a plane of directions containing the given direction, into a standard such configuration. For an excellent presentation of this standpoint see B. A. W. Russell's *The Foundations of Geometry* (Cambridge, 1897), or Russell and A. N. Whitehead's article "Geometry VI: Non-Euclidean Geometry" 11th Ed. *Encyclopædia Brittanica.*

In order to break into such an intrinsic characterization of curvature, we first relapse into a rather naïve consideration of measurements which may be made on the surface of the earth, conceived as a sphere of radius R. This surface is an example of a 2-dimensional congruence space of positive curvature $K = 1/R^2$ on agreeing that the abstract geometrical concept "distance" r between any two of its points (not the extremities of a diameter) shall correspond to the lesser of the two distances *measured on the surface* between them along the unique great circle which joins the two points.[2] Consider now a "small circle" of radius r (measured on the surface!) about a point P of the surface; its perimeter L and area A (again measured on the surface!) are clearly less than the corresponding measures $2\pi r$ and πr^2 of the perimeter and area of a circle of radius r in the Euclidean plane. An elementary calculation shows that for sufficiently small r (i.e., small compared with R) these quantities on the sphere are given approximately by:

$$L = 2\pi r \left(1 - Kr^2/6 + \dots\right),$$

(1)

$$A = \pi r^2 \left(1 - Kr^2/12 + \dots\right).$$

Thus, the ratio of the area of a small circle of radius 400 miles on the surface of the earth to that of a circle of radius 40 miles is found to be only 99.92, instead of 100.00 as in the plane.

Another consequence of possible interest for astronomical applications is that in spherical geometry the sum σ of the three angles of a triangle (whose sides are arcs of great circles) is *greater* than 2 right angles; it can in fact be shown that this "spherical excess" is given by

(2) $\sigma - \pi = K\delta,$

where δ is the area of the spherical triangle and the angles are measured in radians (in which $180° = \pi$). Further, each full

---

[2] The motions of the surface of the earth into itself, which enable us to transform a point and a direction through it into any other point and direction, as demanded by the axiom of free mobility, are here those generated by the 3-parameter family of rotations of the earth about its center (not merely the 1-parameter family of diurnal rotations about its "axis."!).

line (great circle) is of finite length $2\pi R$, and any two full lines meet in two points—there are no parallels!

In the above paragraph we have, with forewarning, slipped into a non-intrinsic quasi-physical standpoint in order to present the formulae (1) and (2) in a more or less intuitive way. But the essential point is that these formulae are in fact independent of this mode of presentation; they are relations between the mathematical concepts distance, angle, perimeter and area which follow as logical consequences from the axioms of this particular kind of non-Euclidean geometry. And since they involve the space-constant K, this "curvature" may in principle at least be determined *by measurements made on the surface*, without recourse to its embedment in a higher dimensional space.

Further, these formulae may be shown to be valid for a circle or triangle in the hyperbolic plane, a 2-dimensional congruence space for which $K < 0$. Accordingly here the perimeter and area of a circle are *greater*, and the sum of the three angles of a triangle *less*, than the corresponding quantities in the Euclidean plane. It may also be shown that each full line is of infinite length, that through a given point outside a given line an infinity of full lines may be drawn which do not meet the given line (the two lines bounding the family are said to be "parallel" to the given line), and that two full lines which meet do so in but one point.

The value of the intrinsic approach is especially apparent in considering 3-dimensional congruence spaces, where our physical intuition is of little use in conceiving them as "curved" in some higher-dimensional space. The intrinsic geometry of such a space of curvature K provides formulae for the surface area S and the volume V of a "small sphere" of radius r, whose leading terms are

$$S = 4\pi r^2 \left(1 - Kr^2/3 + \ldots\right),$$
(3)
$$V = 4/3\pi r^3 \left(1 - Kr^2/5 + \ldots\right).$$

It is to be noted that in all these congruence geometries, except the Euclidean, there is at hand a natural unit of length $R =$

$1/|K|^{1/2}$; this length we shall, without prejudice, call the "radius of curvature" of the space.

So much for the congruence geometries. If we give up the axiom of free mobility we may still deal with the geometry of spaces which have only limited or no motions into themselves.[3] Every smooth surface in 3-dimensional Euclidean space has such a 2-dimensional geometry; a surface of revolution has a 1-parameter family of motions into itself (rotations about its axis of symmetry), but not enough to satisfy the axiom of free mobility. Each such surface has at a point $P(x, y)$ of it an intrinsic "total curvature" $K(x, y)$, which will in general vary from point to point; knowledge of the curvature at all points essentially determines all intrinsic properties of the surface.[4] The determination of $K(x, y)$ by measurements on the surface is again made possible by the fact that the perimeter L and area A of a closed curve, every point of which is at a given (sufficiently small) distance r from $P(x, y)$, are given by the formulae (1), where K is no longer necessarily constant from point to point. Any such variety for which $K = 0$ throughout is a ("developable") surface which may, on ignoring its macroscopic properties, be rolled out without tearing or stretching onto the Euclidean plane.

From this we may go on to the contemplation of 3- or higher dimensional ("Riemannian") spaces, whose intrinsic properties vary from point to point. But these properties are no longer describable in terms of a single quantity, for the "curvature" now acquires at each point a directional character which requires in 3-space 6 components (and in 4-space 20) for its specification. We content ourselves here to call attention to a single combination of the 6, which we call the "mean curvature" of the space at the point $P(x, y, z)$, and which we again denote by K— or more fully by $K(x, y, z)$; it is in a sense the mean of the curvatures of various surfaces passing through P, and reduces

[3] We are here confining ourselves to metric (Riemannian) geometries, in which there exists a differential element ds of distance, whose square is a homogeneous quadratic form in the co-ordinate differentials.

[4] That is, the "differential," as opposed to the "macroscopic," properties. Thus the Euclidean plane and a cylinder have the same differential, but not the same macroscopic, structure.

to the previously contemplated space-constant K when the space in question is a congruence space.[5] This concept is useful in physical applications, for the surface area S and the volume V of a sphere of radius r about the point $P(x, y, z)$ as center are again given by formulae (3), where now K is to be interpreted as the mean curvature $K(x, y, z)$ of the space at the point P. In four and higher dimensions similar concepts may be introduced and similar formulae developed, but for them we have no need here.

We have now to turn our attention to the world of physical objects about us, and to indicate how an ordered description of it is to be obtained in accordance with accepted, preferably philosophically neutral, scientific method. These objects, which exist for us in virtue of some pre-scientific concretion of our sense-data, are positioned in an extended manifold which we call physical space. The mind of the individual, retracing at an immensely accelerated pace the path taken by the race, bestirs itself to an analysis of the interplay between object and extension. There develops a notion of the permanence of the object and of the ordering and the change in time—another form of extension, through which object and subject appear to be racing together—of its extensive relationships. The study of the ordering of actual and potential relationships, the physical problem of space and time, leads to the consideration of geometry and kinematics as a branch of physical science. To certain aspects of this problem we now turn our attention.

We consider first that proposed solution of the problem of space which is based upon the postulate that space is an *a priori* form of the understanding. Its geometry must then be a congruence geometry, independent of the physical content of space;

---

[5] The quantities here referred to are the six independent components of the Riemann-Christoffel tensor in 3 dimensions, and the "mean curvature" here introduced (not to be confused with the mean curvature of a surface, which is an extrinsic property depending on the embedment) is $K = - R'/6$, where R' is the contracted Ricci tensor. I am indebted to Professor Herbert Busemann, of the University of Southern California, for a remark which suggested the usefulness for my later purposes of this approach. A complete exposition of the fundamental concepts involved is to be found in L. P. Eisenhart's *Riemannian Geometry* (Princeton 1926).

and since for Kant, the propounder of this view, there existed but one geometry, space must be Euclidean—and the problem of physical space is solved on the epistemological, pre-physical, level.

But the discovery of other congruence geometries, characterized by a numerical parameter K, perforce modifies this view, and restores at least in some measure the objective aspect of physical space; the *a posteriori* ground for this space-constant K is then to be sought in the contingent. The means for its intrinsic determination is implicit in the formulae presented above; we have merely (!) to measure the volume V of a sphere of radius r or the sum σ of the angles of a triangle of measured area δ, and from the results to compute the value of K. On this modified Kantian view, which has been expounded at length by Russell,[6] it is inconceivable that K might vary from point to point—for according to this view the very possibility of measurement depends on the constancy of space-structure, as guaranteed by the axiom of free mobility. It is of interest to mention in passing, in view of recent cosmological findings, the possibility raised by A. Calinon (in 1889!) that the space-constant K might vary with time.[7] But this possibility is rightly ignored by Russell, for the same arguments which would on this *a priori* theory require the constancy of K in space would equally require its constancy in time.

In the foregoing sketch we have dodged the real hook in the problem of measurement. As physicists we should state clearly those aspects of the physical world which are to correspond to elements of the mathematical system which we propose to employ in the description ("realisation" of the abstract system). Ideally this program should prescribe fully the operations by

[6] In the works already referred to in footnote 1 above.

[7] "Les espaces géometriques," *Revue Philosophique*, vol. 27, pp. 588-595 (1889). The possibilities at which Calinon arrives are, to quote in free translation:

"1. Our space is and remains rigorously Euclidean;

"2. Our space realizes a geometrical space which differs very little from the Euclidean, but which always remains the same;

"3. Our space realizes successively in time different geometrical spaces; otherwise said, our spatial parameter varies with the time, whether it departs more or less away from the Euclidean parameter or whether it oscillates about a definite parameter very near to the Euclidean value."

which numerical values are to be assigned to the physical counterparts of the abstract elements. How is one to achieve this in the case in hand of determining the numerical value of the space-constant K?

Although K. F. Gauss, one of the spiritual fathers of non-Euclidean geometry, at one time proposed a possible test of the flatness of space by measuring the interior angles of a terrestrial triangle, it remained for his Göttingen successor K. Schwarzschild to formulate the procedure and to attempt to evaluate K on the basis of astronomical data available at the turn of the century.[8] Schwarzschild's pioneer attempt is so inspiring in its conception and so beautiful in its expression that I cannot refrain from giving here a few short extracts from his work. After presenting the possibility that physical space may, in accordance with the neo-Kantian position outlined above, be non-Euclidean, Schwarzschild states (in free translation):

One finds oneself here, if one but will, in a geometrical fairyland, but the beauty of this fairy tale is that one does not know but what it may be true. We accordingly bespeak the question here of how far we must push back the frontiers of this fairyland; of how small we must choose the curvature of space, how great its radius of curvature.

In furtherance of this program Schwarzschild proposes:

A triangle determined by three points will be defined as the paths of light-rays from one point to another, the lengths of its sides a, b, c, by the times it takes light to traverse these paths, and the angles α, β, γ will be measured with the usual astronomical instruments.

Applying Schwarzschild's prescription to observations on a given star, we consider the triangle ABC defined by the position A of the star and by two positions B, C of the earth—say six months apart—at which the angular positions of the star are measured. The base BC $= a$ is known, by measurements within the solar system consistent with the prescription, and the interior angles β, γ which the light-rays from the star make with the base-line are also known by measurement. From these the *parallax* $p = \pi - (\beta + \gamma)$ may be computed; in Euclidean

[8] "Über das zulässige Krümmungsmaass des Raumes," *Vierteljahrsschrift der astronomischen Gesellschaft*, vol. 35, pp. 337-347 (1900). The *annual parallax*, as used in practice, is one-half that defined below.

space this parallax is simply the inferred angle α subtended at the star by the diameter of the earth's orbit. In the other congruence geometries the parallax is seen, with the aid of formula (2) above, to be equal to

$$(2') \qquad p = \pi - (\beta + \gamma) = \alpha - K\delta,$$

where α is the (unknown) angle at the star A, and δ is the (unknown) area of the triangle ABC. Now in spite of our incomplete knowledge of the elements on the far right, certain valid conclusions may be drawn from this result. First, if space is hyperbolic ($K < 0$), for distant stars (for which $\alpha \sim 0$), the parallax p will remain positive; hence if stars are observed whose parallax is zero to within the errors of observation, this estimated error will give an upper limit to the absolute value $-K$ of the curvature. Second, if space is spherical ($K > 0$), for a sufficiently distant star (more distant than one-quarter the circumference of a Euclidean sphere of radius $R = 1/K^{\frac{1}{2}}$, as may immediately be seen by examining a globe) the sum $\beta + \gamma$ will exceed two right angles; hence the parallax p of such a star should be negative, and if no stars are in fact observed with negative parallax, the estimated error of observation will give an upper limit to the curvature K. Also, in this latter case the light sent out by the star must return to it after traversing the full line of length $2\pi R$, (πR in elliptic space), and hence we should, but for absorption and scattering, be able to observe the returning light as an anti-star in a direction opposite to that of the star itself!

On the basis of the evidence then available, Schwarzschild concluded that if space is hyperbolic its radius of curvature $R = 1/(-K)^{\frac{1}{2}}$ cannot be less than 64 light-years (i.e., the distance light travels in 64 years), and that if the space is elliptic its radius of curvature $R = 1/K^{\frac{1}{2}}$ is at least 1600 light-years. Hardly imposing figures for us today, who believe on other astronomical grounds that objects as distant as 500 million light-years have been sighted in the Mt. Wilson telescope, and who are expecting to find objects at twice that distance with the new Mt. Palomar mirror! But the value for us of the work of Schwarzschild lies in its sound operational approach to the problem of physical geometry—in refreshing contrast to the pontifical pronouncement of H. Poincaré, who after reviewing the subject stated:[9]

> If therefore negative parallaxes were found, or if it were demonstrated that all parallaxes are superior to a certain limit, two courses would be open to us; we might either renounce Euclidean geometry, or else modify laws of optics and suppose that light does not travel rigorously in a straight line.
>
> It is needless to add that all the world would regard the latter solution as the more advantageous.
>
> The Euclidean geometry has, therefore, nothing to fear from fresh experiments. [!]

So far we have tied ourselves into the neo-Kantian doctrine that space must be homogeneous and isotropic, in which case our proposed operational approach is limited in application to the determination of the numerical value of the space-constant K. But the possible scope of the operational method is surely broader than this; what if we do apply it to triangles and circles and spheres in various positions and at various times and find that the K so determined is in fact dependent on position in space and time? Are we, following Poincaré, to attribute these findings to the influence of an external force postulated for the purpose? Or are we to take our findings at face value, and accept the geometry to which we are led as a natural geometry for physical science?

The answer to this methodological question will depend largely on the *universality* of the geometry thus found—whether the geometry found in one situation or field of physical discourse may consistently be extended to others—and in the end partly on the predilection of the individual or of his colleagues or of his times. Thus Einstein's special theory of relativity, which offers a physical kinematics embracing measurements in space and time, has gone through several stages of acceptance and use, until at present it is a universal and indispensable tool of modern physics. Thus Einstein's general theory of relativity, which offers an extended kinematics which includes in its geometrical structure the universal force of gravitation,

[9] *Science and Hypothesis*, p. 81; transl. by G. B. Halsted (Science Press 1929).

was long considered by some contemporaries to be a *tour de force*, at best amusing but in practice useless. And now, in extending this theory to the outer bounds of the observed universe, the kind of geometry suggested by the present marginal data seems to many so repugnant that they would follow Poincaré in postulating some *ad hoc* force, be it a double standard of time or a secular change in the velocity of light or Planck's constant, rather than accept it.

But enough of this general and historical approach to the problem of physical geometry! While we should like to complete this discussion with a detailed operational analysis of the solution given by the general theory of relativity, such an undertaking would require far more than the modest mathematical background which we have here presupposed. Further, the field of operations of the general theory is so unearthly and its *experimenta crucis* so delicate that an adequate discussion would take us far out from the familiar objects and concepts of the workaday world, and obscure the salient points we wish to make in a welter of unfamiliar and esoteric astronomical and mathematical concepts. What is needed is a homely experiment which could be carried out in the basement with parts from an old sewing machine and an Ingersoll watch, with an old file of *Popular Mechanics* standing by for reference! This I am, alas, afraid we have not achieved, but I do believe that the following example of a simple theory of measurement in a heat-conducting medium is adequate to expose the principles involved with a modicum of mathematical background. The very fact that it will lead to a rather bad and unacceptable physical theory will in itself be instructive, for its very failure will emphasize the requirement of universality of application—a requirement most satisfactorily met by the general theory of relativity.

The background of our illustration is an ordinary laboratory, equipped with Bunsen burners, clamps, rulers, micrometers and the usual miscellaneous impedimenta there met—at the turn of the century, no electronics required! In it the practical Euclidean geometry reigns (hitherto!) unquestioned, for even though measurements are there to be carried out with quite reasonable standards of accuracy, there is no need for sophisticated qualms concerning the effect of gravitational or magnetic or other general extended force-fields on its metrical structure. Now that we feel at home in these familiar, and disarming, surroundings, consider the following experiment:

Let a thin, flat metal plate be heated in any way—just so that the temperature T is not uniform over the plate. During the process clamp or otherwise constrain the plate to keep it from buckling, so that it can reasonably be said to remain flat by ordinary standards. Now proceed to make simple geometrical measurements on the plate with a short metal rule, which has a certain coefficient of expansion c, taking care that the rule is allowed to come into thermal equilibrium with the plate at each setting before making the measurement. The question now is, what is the geometry of the plate *as revealed by the results of these measurements?*

It is evident that, unless the coefficient of expansion c of the rule is zero, the geometry will not turn out to be Euclidean, for the rule will expand more in the hotter regions of the plate than in the cooler, distorting the (Euclidean) measurements which would be obtained by a rule whose length did not change according to the usual laboratory standards. Thus the perimeter L of a circle centered at a point at which a burner is applied will surely turn out to be greater than π times its measured diameter $2r$, for the rule will expand in measuring through the hotter interior of the circle and hence give a smaller reading than if the temperature were uniform. On referring to the first of formulae (1) above it is seen that the plate would seem to have a negative curvature K at the center of the circle—the kind of structure exhibited by an ordinary twisted surface in the neighborhood of a "saddle-point." In general the curvature will vary from point to point in a systematic way; a more detailed mathematical analysis of the situation shows that, on removing heat sources and neglecting radiation losses from the faces of the plate, K is everywhere negative and that the "radius of curvature" $R = 1/(-K)^{1/2}$ at any point P is inversely proportional to the rate s at which heat flows past P. (R is in fact equal to k/cs, where k is the coefficient of heat conduction *of the plate* and c is as before the coefficient of expansion *of the rule.*) The hyperbolic geometry is accordingly realized when the heat flow is constant throughout the plate, as when the long sides of an elongated rectangle are kept at different fixed temperatures.[10]

And now comes the question, what is the true geometry of the plate? The flat Euclidean geometry we had uncritically agreed upon at the beginning of the experiment, or the un-Euclidean geometry revealed by measurement? It is obvious that the question is improperly worded; the geometry is determinate only when we prescribe the method of measurement, i.e., when we set up a correspondence between the physical aspects (here readings on a definite rule obtained in a prescribed way) and the elements (here distances, in the abstract sense) of the mathematical system. Thus our original common-sense requirement that the plate not buckle, or that it be measured with an invar rule (for which $c \sim 0$), leads to Euclidean geometry, while the use of a rule with a sensible coefficient of expansion leads to a locally hyperbolic type of Riemannian geometry, which is in general not a congruence geometry.

There is no doubt that anyone examining this situation will prefer Poincaré's common-sense solution of the problem of the physical geometry of the plate—i.e., to attribute to it Euclidean geometry, and to consider the measured deviations from this geometry as due to the action of a force (thermal stresses in the rule). Most compulsive to this solution is the fact that this disturbing force lacks the requirement of universality; on employing a brass rule in place of one of steel we would find that the local curvature is trebled—and an ideal rule ($c = 0$) would, as we have noted, lead to the Euclidean geometry.

In what respect, then, does the general theory of relativity differ in principle from this geometrical theory of the hot plate? The answer is: *in its universality;* the force of gravitation which it comprehends in the geometrical structure acts equally on all

---

[10] This case, in which the geometry is that of the Poincaré half-plane, has been discussed in detail by E. W. Barankin "Heat Flow and Non-Euclidean Geometry," *American Mathematical Monthly*, vol. 49, pp. 4-14 (1942). For those who are numerically-minded it may be noted that for a steel plate ($k = 0.1$ cal/cm deg) 1 cm thick, with a heat flow of 1 cal/cm^2 sec, the natural unit of length R of the geometry, as measured by a steel rule ($c = 10^{-5}$/deg), is 10^4 cm $\sim$ 328 feet!

matter. There is here a close analogy between the gravitational mass M of the field-producing body (Sun) and the inertial mass m of the test-particle (Earth) on the one hand, and the heat conduction k of the field (plate) and the coefficient of expansion c of the test-body (rule) on the other. *The success of the general relativity theory of gravitation as a physical geometry of space-time is attributable to the fact that the gravitational and inertial masses of any body are observed to be rigorously proportional for all matter.* Whereas in our geometrical theory of the thermal field the ratio of heat conductivity to coefficient of expansion varies from substance to substance, resulting in a change of the geometry of the field on changing the test-body.

From our present point of view the great triumph of the theory of relativity lies in its absorbing the universal force of gravitation into the geometrical structure; its success in accounting for minute discrepancies in the Newtonian description of the motions of test-bodies in the solar field, although gratifying, is nevertheless of far less moment to the philosophy of physical science.[11] Einstein's achievements would be substantially as great even though it were not for these minute observational tests.

[11] Even here an amusing and instructive analogy exists between our caricature and the relativity theory. On extending our notions to a 3-dimensional heat-conducting medium (without worrying too much about how our measurements are actually to be carried out!), and on adopting the standard field equation for heat conduction, the "mean curvature" introduced above is found at any point to be $-(cs/k)^2$, which is of second order in the characteristic parameter c/k. (The case in which the temperature is proportional to $a^2 - r^2$, which requires a continuous distribution of heat sources, has been discussed in some detail by Poincaré, *Loc. cit.* pp. 76-78, in his discussion of non-Euclidean geometry.) The field equation may now itself be given a geometrical formulation, at least to first approximation, by replacing it by the requirement that the mean curvature of the space *vanish* at any point at which no heat is being supplied to the medium—in complete analogy with the procedure in the general theory of relativity by which the classical field equations are replaced by the requirement that the Ricci contracted curvature tensor vanish. Here, as there, will now appear certain deviations, whose magnitude here depends upon the ratio c/k, between the standard and the modified theories. One curious consequence of this treatment is that on solving the modified field equation for a spherically-symmetric source (or better, sink) of heat, one finds precisely the same spatial structure as in the Schwarzschild solution for the gravitational field of a spherically-symmetric gravitational mass—the correspondence being such that the geometrical effect of a sink which removes 1 calorie per second from the medium is equivalent to the gravitational effect of a mass of 10^{22} gm, e.g., of a chunk of rock 200 miles in diameter!

Our final illustration of physical geometry consists in a brief reference to the cosmological problem of the geometry of the observed universe as a whole—a problem considered in greater detail elsewhere in this volume. *If* matter in the universe can, taken on a sufficiently large scale (spatial gobs millions of light-years across), be considered as uniformly distributed, and if (as implied by the general theory of relativity) its geometrical structure is conditioned by matter, then to this approximation our 3-dimensional astronomical space must be homogeneous and isotropic, with a spatially-constant K which may however depend upon time. Granting this hypothesis, how do we go about measuring K, using of course only procedures which can be operationally specified, and to which congruence geometry are we thereby led? The way to the answer is suggested by the second of the formulae (3), for if the nebulae are by-and-large uniformly distributed, then the number N within a sphere of radius r must be proportional to the volume V of this sphere. We have then only to examine the dependence of this number N, as observed in a sufficiently powerful telescope, on the distance r to determine the deviation from the Euclidean value. But how is r operationally to be defined?

If all the nebulae were of the same intrinsic brightness, then their apparent brightness as observed from the Earth should be an indication of their distance from us; we must therefore examine the exact relation to be expected between apparent brightness and the abstract distance r. Now it is the practice of astronomers to assume that brightness falls off inversely with the square of the "distance" of the object—as it would do in Euclidean space, if there were no absorption, scattering, and the like. We must therefore examine the relation between this astronomer's "distance" d, as inferred from apparent brightness, and the distance r which appears as an element of the geometry. It is clear that *all* the light which is radiated at a given moment from the nebula will, after it has traveled a distance r, lie on the surface of a sphere whose area S is given by the first of the formulae (3). And since the practical procedure involved in determining d is equivalent to assuming that all this light lies on the surface of a Euclidean sphere of radius d, it follows immediately that the relationship between the "distance" d used in practice and the distance r dealt with in the geometry is given by the equation

$$4\pi d^2 = S = 4\pi r^2 (1 - Kr^2/3 + \ldots);$$

whence, to our approximation

(4)
$$d = r(1 - Kr^2/6 + \ldots), \text{ or}$$

$$r = d(1 + Kd^2/6 + \ldots).$$

But the astronomical data give the number N of nebulae counted out to a given inferred "distance" d, and in order to determine the curvature from them we must express N, or equivalently V, to which it is assumed proportional, in terms of d. One easily finds from the second of the formulae (3) and the formula (4) just derived that, again to the approximation here adopted,

(5) $$V = 4/3 \, \pi \, d^3 \, (1 + 3/10 \, Kd^2 + \ldots).$$

And now on plotting N against inferred "distance" d and comparing this empirical plot with the formula (5), it should be possible operationally to determine the "curvature" K.[12]

The search for the curvature K indicates that, after making all known corrections, the number N seems to increase faster with d than the third power, which would be expected in Euclidean space, hence K is *positive*. The space implied thereby is therefore bounded, of finite total volume, and of a present "radius of curvature" $R = 1/K^{1/2}$ which is found to be of the order of 500 million light-years. Other observations, on the "red-shift" of light from these distant objects, enable us to

[12] This is, of course, an outrageously over-simplified account of the assumptions and procedures involved. All nebulae are *not* of the same intrinsic brightness, and the modifications required by this and other assumptions tacitly made lead one a merry astronomical chase through the telescope, the Earth's atmosphere, the Milky Way and the Magellanic Clouds to Andromeda and our other near extragalactic neighbors, and beyond. The story of this search has been delightfully told by E. P. Hubble in his *The Realm of the Nebulae* (Yale 1936) and in his *Observational Approach to Cosmology* (Oxford 1937), the source of the data mentioned below.

conclude with perhaps more assurance that this radius is increasing in time at a rate which, if kept up, would double the present radius in something less than 2000 million years.

With this we have finished our brief account of Geometry as a branch of Physics, a subject to which no one has contributed more than Albert Einstein, who by his theories of relativity has brought into being physical geometries which have supplanted the tradition-steeped *a priori* geometry and kinematics of Euclid and Newton.

H. P. ROBERTSON

DEPARTMENT OF PHYSICS
CALIFORNIA INSTITUTE OF TECHNOLOGY

12

P. W. Bridgman

EINSTEIN'S THEORIES AND THE OPERATIONAL POINT OF VIEW

EINSTEIN'S THEORIES AND THE OPERATIONAL POINT OF VIEW

THIS exposition will endeavor to show that Einstein did not carry over into his general relativity theory the lessons and insights which he himself has taught us in his special theory.

Let us examine what Einstein did in his special theory. In the first place, he recognized that the meaning of a term is to be sought in the operations employed in making application of the term. If the term is one which is applicable to concrete physical situations, as "length" or "simultaneity," then the meaning is to be sought in the operations by which the length of concrete physical objects is determined, or in the operations by which one determines whether two concrete physical events are simultaneous or not. This is well brought out by the following quotation from Einstein himself in connection with a discussion of the simultaneity of two lightning strokes:

The concept does not exist for the physicist until he has the possibility of discovering whether or not it is fulfilled in an actual case. We thus require a definition of simultaneity such that this definition supplies us with the means by which, in the present case, he can decide by experiment whether both lightning strokes occurred simultaneously. As long as this requirement is not satisfied, I allow myself to be deceived as a physicist (and of course the same applies if I am not a physicist) when I imagine that I am able to attach a meaning to the statement of simultaneity.[1]

It is to be questioned whether this criterion of meaning by itself is very revolutionary. It is easy to imagine that even Sir Isaac Newton would have assented to it if he had been asked.

[1] From *Relativity*, 26, translated by Lawson, Henry Holt and Co. (1920).

But before Einstein people had not considered the matter to any great extent, and probably only seldom if ever consciously formulated or applied the criterion. Einstein's revolutionary contribution consisted in his self-conscious use of it in new situations and in the way in which he applied it. What Einstein did was to make a more detailed analysis of the physical operations used in the measurement of length and time than had ever been made before. In doing this he uncovered necessary details which are always involved in any measurement of length, but which had formerly been ignored simply because of their universality, and because no one had had the imagination to formulate them or to see that they might be significant. For example, Einstein's analysis brought to light that in measuring the length of moving objects manipulations with clocks as well as with meter sticks are involved. Before the analysis it had never occurred to anyone that the operations for measuring a moving object were not the same as those for measuring an object at rest, with the result that an "absolute" significance had been attributed to the concept of length. When Einstein's analysis also suggested that there are several conceivable procedures for measuring the length of a moving object, no one of which has any logical or even physical inevitability, the way was prepared for the recognition that the length of a moving object might not be the same as its length at rest, and that the precise way in which the length varies with the motion will be a function of the definition of the length of the moving object. Everyone now knows that the contraction of length of a moving object is embedded in this special theory of relativity, and that experimentally the contraction is found to exist, but that it is too small to be detectible under ordinary conditions and becomes important only at high velocities approaching the velocity of light.

The new vision given to physicists by Einstein through his special theory of relativity is the vision that the conventional operations of physics may involve details of which we are not ordinarily aware because of their apparent irrelevance or universality or minuteness, that when we extend our experience into new fields, as by going to very high velocities, we may expect new types of phenomena which from the point of view of the old may be paradoxical, and that the paradox may perhaps be resolved when we consider details in our operations which we had disregarded when dealing with ordinary phenomena. Einstein has conditioned us to regard it as a matter of the highest importance, when pushing into new ground, to acquire as vivid a consciousness as possible of all the details of our present operations and of the tacit assumptions back of them, and to anticipate that some of the factors which we have hitherto been able to disregard may prove to be the key to the new situation. Or, put negatively, we have come to see that it is not safe, when we penetrate into new ground, to disregard the effect of factors which could be disregarded in a narrower range of experience.

However, even when we have analyzed the operations which we now employ in as great detail as we are capable of, we can have no assurance that the particular details which our analysis may uncover will be pertinent to the particular new situation that confronts us. It would be difficult to set any limit to the details which more and more penetrating analysis can disclose. At least we must always anticipate the possibility of continually uncovering finer and finer details (or, from another point of view, presuppositions of increasingly great generality) as we push our analysis further. Whether the particular new details that our analysis discloses are pertinent in the new situation can be determined only by the test of effectiveness in application. Einstein's analysis of the operations of measuring length and time was by no means an exhaustive or unique analysis, any more than any analysis can be exhaustive or unique. Einstein's genius consisted, even more than in seeing that the measuring operations involve certain details that had hitherto been neglected as irrelevant, in picking out those particular details which in actual application proved to be the key to the new physical situations when we penetrate into the realm of hitherto unexperienced high velocities.

Now let us turn to the general theory and inquire what are the tacit assumptions in the operations required to give the general theory its meaning. Consider in the first place that part of the general theory embodied in the mathematical equations, such as the equation of light propagation,

$$ds^2 (\equiv \sum g_{mn}dx_m dx_n) = 0,$$

or the equation of motion of a particle,

$$\frac{d^2 x^\mu}{ds^2} + \Gamma^\mu_{\alpha\beta} \frac{dx^\alpha}{ds} \times \frac{dx^\beta}{ds} = 0.$$

Formally, the equations contain only co-ordinates and functions of the co-ordinates which can for the present be treated as given. But the co-ordinates are co-ordinates of something, and what it is that they are the co-ordinates of, or how we are to determine the co-ordinates in any concrete case, cannot be specified by the mathematical machinery of the equations alone, but must be known in other ways. What are the operations which one has to employ in applying the equations to any concrete physical situation? Evidently we must be able to determine the co-ordinates which correspond to the phenomenon under observation (such as propagation of a light-signal or motion of a mass particle) and this involves identifying the point at which the phenomenon occurs to the extent at least of being able to tag it with the co-ordinates. But how shall a point be identified? "Empty" space is amorphous and its "points" have no identity. Identifiability demands some physical substratum. That is, the framework in which the co-ordinates are determined must be a physical framework, and the specification of the framework involves a specification of at least some of its physical properties. In particular, if we use a framework which allows the conventional separation into space and time co-ordinates, then one specification of the framework is that the spatial co-ordinates shall be determined by "rigid" members, and the time co-ordinates by "clocks." Logically, we should be able to ascribe an independent meaning to "rigid" and to "clock," but as far as I know this has not been accomplished. In particular, the specification of what is meant by "clock" has given much difficulty, and at present "clock" seems to be circularly defined by implication as a physical apparatus so constructed that it functions in the way in which the theory of relativity says that a "clock" functions.

It would appear then that the complete operational specification of the framework still offers certain difficulties. Passing over the difficulties, what is the operational situation with regard to the phenomenon whose co-ordinates are to be determined in the framework? In the first place, the equations may refer to different kinds of events. What kind of event it is has to be specified by means not contained in the equations, and by means which are not usually made the subject of analysis. Consider, for example, the equation of light-propagation. The equation states that if the co-ordinates of a light-signal are determined physically, the equation will be satisfied when the co-ordinates are substituted into it. The implication is that the light-signal has identifiability and individuality, and that it can be followed observationally as it is propagated. Or whatever other equation we have to deal with or whatever other phenomenon, it would seem that as a very minimum a certain amount of individuality or identifiability in the phenomenon is demanded. This would seem to involve a certain amount of discreteness. But how much discreteness? Physical happenings never are mathematically sharp, but are always surrounded by an instrumental haze. How much haze is permissible is a question that seems not to have been discussed; it is quite conceivably a question that might become important when we enter fields remote from ordinary experience.

In general comment, Einstein seems to have concentrated his analytical attack almost exclusively on the co-ordinate system used in specifying physical events, and to have neglected the events themselves. In fact, the events are conventionally treated as primitive or unanalyzed and unanalyzable elements. Of course no theory can avoid ultimately its unanalyzed elements. The question can only be whether the analysis has been carried as far as the physical situation demands.

As far as the mathematical aspects of the general theory go, perhaps most essential feature is the use of generalized co-ordinates. The arguments by which the equations are derived assert as a fundamental thesis that the frame of reference used in describing a phenomenon is a matter of indifference, and the possibility is contemplated of passing back and forth from one co-ordinate system to another, an enterprise for which the use of generalized co-ordinates is especially well adapted. This thesis is usually understood to have a physical content in addition to its purely formal content. From the purely formal point of view the content of the thesis is: given a certain physical phenomenon which is described in terms of a certain co-ordinate system, then it may equally well be described in terms of another co-ordinate system. This is to be done merely by translating the co-ordinates as measured in the first system into the corresponding co-ordinates in the second system, and this translation is to be made by applying certain purely formal procedures for correlating any set of co-ordinates in the first system with others in the second system. The operations for passing from the first to the second co-ordinate system are here purely paper and pencil operations, and are sterile with respect to any physical implications. From the point of view of the physicist they are trivial. Physical content is injected into the situation, however, by the supplementary thesis that the co-ordinates obtained by the paper and pencil operations are the co-ordinates that would have been obtained if the observer had originally measured the phenomenon in the second co-ordinate system, or, alternately, that they are the co-ordinates which would have been obtained by a second observer, observing the same phenomenon in the second co-ordinate frame. At any rate, the possibility is assumed of observing the same phenomenon or event[2] from two different frames of reference.

What does it mean to say that the same event has been observed in two frames of reference? The question hardly arises under ordinary conditions, when the two frames do not differ much from each other, and is, as far as I am aware, not raised by Einstein. That is, as we have already remarked, in Einstein's argument the event itself, which is the subject of the co-ordinate measurement, is not recognized as in need of analysis, but is treated as a primitive element. This may be entirely legitimate

---

[2] I use *event* in the usual sense, and not in the technical sense of an aggregate of three space and one time co-ordinates.

for present needs as long as we are concerned with only a single frame of reference, but it seems to me that the event, when regarded as something that can be equally viewed from two frames of reference, can by no means be treated as primitive or unanalyzable. If the two frames are allowed to vary without restriction, as they are in the general theory, the question of what it means to say that the same event has been observed in two frames of reference becomes far from academic. If, for example, the event whose co-ordinates are being determined is for the first observer the arrival of a train of radiation which he perceives as a flash of light in his eye or which he may register on a photographic plate, the second observer, moving with high relative velocity, may not be able to detect ocularly at all, but he perceives it as a sensation of warmth in his finger or registers it instrumentally on a bolometer. Unsophisticated procedure would not at first incline one to recognize these two experiences of the two observers, involving different sense organs or different instruments, as pertaining to the same phenomenon or event. The attribute of sameness can perhaps be recognized in the two experiences if the two observers are allowed to communicate with each other. If the first observer can say to the second observer, "Something just happened to me," and if the second can also make the same remark to the first, and if what happens to each observer is sufficiently discrete so that it does not overlap with other happenings, then we probably would be willing to say that both had observed the "same" event. But the "sameness" which can thereby be ascribed to the two experiences is obviously a sophisticated thing, involving considerations by no means simple, among which the ascription of a "sufficient" amount of discreteness to the signal would seem to be a very minimum.

Even more complexity is involved in the apparently necessary assumption that the two observers are able to communicate meanings to each other. This assumption appears, for example, when we talk about similarly constructed apparatus in the two systems, as two similar clocks. What are the operations by which observers in two different frames of reference communicate meanings with each other, and decide that their clocks are similar? A certain similarity in the observers themselves is necessary, but how much similarity? Even the inhabitants of this planet with different cultural backgrounds do not find it always easy to communicate. If the difference between the two frames is not excessive, it is possible to think of one of the observers as myself and the other as a vicarious edition of myself, who can step back and forth from one frame of reference to the other. But how shall we discover what are the relevant operational details which are involved in the possibility of thinking about two observers in this way? He would be rash indeed who would try to conceptualize what it means to communicate meanings with another observer moving with 99 per cent of the velocity of light, or living in the gravitational field occurring at the center of a giant star, or in a part of the stellar universe not yet explored by the solar system in its secular wanderings. Under such conditions we would do well to replace the "similar observers" and their biological connotations, with "physical observing apparatus." But what can we mean under these conditions by "similarity of two photographic plates," for example, which will not already assume a knowledge of the physical properties which it is the purpose of the analysis to deduce? We cannot, for example, adopt the easy answer of saying that we will manufacture the photographic plates both in the one frame of reference, and then transfer one of them bodily to the second frame, because this would assume that the process of transfer had introduced no essential changes in the properties of the plate, and we have no operational criterion for this.

In other words, when in our analysis of the physical operations involved in observing systems at high velocities or in intense gravitational fields, or in remote parts of the stellar universe, we neglect as irrelevant an analysis of the operations by which observations are transferred between different frames of reference, we are in effect saying that our understanding of the mechanism of transfer is so good that we are justified in anticipating that none of the details ordinarily neglected are pertinent. It seems to me that this point of view assumes an understanding of the details of the processes of communication be-

tween different observing systems to which no human being
is as yet entitled.

There is another method of assigning a meaning to the
"sameness" of the event which is the subject of observation in
two frames of reference. If I could assume in the background
a third observer, observing both the phenomenon itself and
the two observers observing the phenomenon, then obviously
a meaning could be assigned to the sameness of a phenomenon
observed by the two observers whenever the third observer reports that the two observers are observing the same thing. It
does indeed seem that such a conceptual observer in the background is implied in the argument of Einstein, for we have
already seen that a meaning is assigned to the event in its own
right apart from the frame of reference which yields the co-
ordinates. This in itself amounts to the assumption of a certain
amount of pre-Einsteinian "absoluteness" in the event. Operationally this "absoluteness" means merely that we are getting
along without analyzing the details of what is involved when
we say we can treat a thing in its own right independent of the
frame of reference. In addition to the objection that the third
observer in the background involves a preferred system of reference, there is the fundamental objection that even the third
ghostly observer does not eliminate the necessity of assuming
that two observers may observe the same event.

To what extent is it true that two observers may observe the
same event? The assumption that this is possible is almost universal in modern science. It is often stated that science is by its
very nature public, not private. This means, among other
things, that the same phenomenon may be observed by different
observers, and that when so observed their reports will be found
to agree. What about the operational details? The complete
situations are never exactly the same for the two observers for
the reason, among others, that two observers never observe with
the same beam of light. In neglecting the fact that the light-
beams are different by which different observers observe, we
are saying that this is irrelevant. Ordinary experience justifies
us amply, but what assurance have we that we will continue

to be justified when we push into new territory? Recognition of the discrete structure of light, a recognition which we owe in large part to Einstein's analysis of the photo-electric effect, would prepare us to anticipate failure at least when we push into the domain of the very small.

The question of the meaning of "sameness" in an event observed by different observers does not force itself prominently on the attention as general relativity theory is ordinarily expounded. The events tend to be replaced by "pointer readings," that is by the aggregate of the four numbers which are the co-ordinates of the event in the particular frame of reference. In fact, "event" has sometimes come to be used in the technical sense of the aggregate of these four numbers. The tendency is to fix the attention exclusively on the co-ordinates and the equations connecting them. But any such treatment can at best be only partial. It cannot offer even an adequate description of a physical situation, to say nothing of being able to establish correlations. For it obviously is impossible to reproduce the original physical situation, given only the co-ordinates (pointer readings) into which it is analyzed. We must know in addition what it is that the co-ordinates are of. Are they co-ordinates of an electron, or a proton, or larger mass particle, or are they co-ordinates determined by the arrival of a photon?

In attempting to assess the importance of these considerations I think we have to keep distinctly in view whether the proposed application is to large or small scale phenomena. So far, the success of the general theory has been confined to large scale phenomena; attempts to extend the application to the small phenomena of the quantum domain have not been fruitful, in spite of the most serious efforts of physicists of the highest ability. From the large scale point of view and in the range of ordinary experience it certainly must be conceded by everyone that the assumption of the public nature of science and the possibility of observation of the same event by two observers from two frames of reference is a very close approximation. But even here we have seen that a certain amount of discreteness has to be presupposed. The term "object" or event implies a certain amount of differentiation from the matrix in which it is embedded, and therefore a boundary of the object or event. Even in the realm of ordinary experience instruments now in our possession are capable of showing that the boundaries of objects or events are not absolutely sharp, but there is always a haziness of outline. If this haziness were to become too great we would lose the identifiability of the object and the "sameness" of the event. If now we enter new realms of experience and attempt to foresee what would be found by observers moving with very high relative velocities, or in very intense gravitational fields, we must, by our general maxim, be prepared to find that the outlines of objects or events have become so blurred that we can no longer uniquely correlate readings made in one frame of reference with those made in anotner, and hence can no longer describe the events experienced in one frame of reference, as the "same" as those experienced in the other.

So much by way of general methodology. We may, however, play a hunch that these considerations are not as a matter of fact very important when it comes to large scale phenomena, and that we may neglect them. This is essentially what Einstein did in assuming the possibility of the observation of large scale events by two observers. The theory developed on this basis has been successful in embracing at least three types of large scale phenomena which could not be included in former theories. We must not conclude, however, that the success of the theory has been in *consequence* of the assumption of the possibility of two observers, that is, the assumption of the possibility of the description of the phenomenon in covariant form in generalized co-ordinates. The assumption of covariance is itself sterile in physical consequences, as was pointed out by Kretschmann[3] and admitted by Einstein. The physical content entered into the theory in other ways during the detailed working out, chiefly through the demand for mathematical simplicity. This meant that the equations in generalized co-ordinates were taken as linear, of the second order, and that they reduce to the already familiar equations under proper limiting conditions. Among other things this sort of mathematical formulation in-

[3] E. Kretschmann, *Annalen der Physik*, vol. 53, 575 (1917); A. Einstein, *Annalen der Physik*, vol. 55, 241 (1918).

volved the validity of the physical principle of superposition which states that two "causes" acting simultaneously produce the sum of their separate effects. I have discussed this matter more in detail in other places, especially in the chapter on "Relativity" in my book *The Nature of Physical Theory*, where most of the considerations presented here are also given.

The situation is entirely different, however, when we come to small scale events. We might perhaps make a fairly plausible argument for the thesis that the description of small scale situations can be adequately broken down into terms of pointer readings only. For although it is true that a specification of the pointer readings alone, without a specification of what the pointer readings are of, does not constitute adequate description for the reason that we cannot reproduce the primitive situation when given the pointer readings; nevertheless in the microscopic domain there are only a few distinct sorts of things to which pointer readings could refer, contrasted with the infinite variety of possible events on the large scale. Hence, if in addition to the pointer readings themselves we are told to what sort of elementary event the pointer readings refer, such as the motion of an electron or a proton or a photon, we believe, in our present state of physical knowledge, that we would be able uniquely to reproduce the primitive situation. It is probably considerations of this sort that are back of the contention of Eddington and others that the only important features in a physical situation are the pointer readings. This is also essentially the position of Einstein himself when he states that the *intersections* of the co-ordinate meshes are the only things with physical significance. But this thesis necessarily draws us into the microscopic domain, and in the microscopic domain we encounter phenomena diametrically contradictory to the spirit of the relativistic approach. The emission or reception of a photon cannot be observed by two observers or recorded in two frames of reference. The elementary processes or "objects" do not have individuality or identifiability, nor can they be repeated. The concept of "sameness" does not apply in the microscopic domain of quantum phenomena. It is natural to think that the failure of general relativity theory in the realm of the small is no accident, but is due to a fundamental contradiction between the presuppositions and attitude of mind of the general theory and the actual construction of nature.

Two general aspects of the general theory of relativity may be recognized. Firstly, there is the mathematical edifice of the system of equations and the rules by which the symbols of the equations are to be correlated with the results of physical operations; and secondly, there is the attitude of mind, or what I may call the philosophy, that leads to the arguments used in deriving the equations and to the expectation that the equations so derived will have physical validity. These two aspects are not uniquely connected; from a given mathematical edifice one cannot uniquely deduce the philosophy that led to the erection of the edifice, and even less can one infer from the success of the mathematics in reproducing certain aspects of experience that therefore the philosophy back of it was true. In this paper we are concerned with the philosophy of Einstein rather than with the equations which he deduced by the philosophy.

Although it is not possible to deduce uniquely from the equations what Einstein's philosophy is, we know pretty definitely what it is like from his writings. It seems to me that the things Einstein does and the way he talks about his theory are like the acts and words of a man who would say that there is a "reality" back of all our multifarious experience. Although explicit use of the world "reality" does not figure prominently, if at all, in Einstein's exposition, nevertheless without some such notion in the background it is difficult to understand such things as his continued insistence on the indifference of the language (co-ordinate system) in which a phenomenon is described. Again and again in Einstein's exposition appears his feeling for the importance of getting away from any special frame of reference, and his conviction that it *must* be possible to do this and that by so doing one may hope to arrive at something pretty fundamental. Something much akin to this is involved in the common thesis that science is by its very nature public, or universal, although such a thesis is much weaker than the thesis of an underlying reality. One may, if one chooses, make the public nature of science a matter of definition, but even so, one need not refrain from inquiring what the processes are by which the publicity is arrived at.

If one analyzes what one does when engaging in any scientific activity I think it will be recognized that the raw material of science is in the beginning private or individual before it becomes public or universal. The public "real" object, with its permanence and individuality, to which we correlate our private sensations, involves a tremendous amount of complex intermediate detail, as anyone might realize who has witnessed the struggles of an infant during its early months to acquire the concept of object. The concept of object thus arrived at is itself complex, and passes, one may guess, through a stage of private object before the concept of public object emerges. "Object" is palpably a construction, and as far as we know or can give meaning, is a construction only of the human nervous system. The apparent fact that different human beings can so universally agree and arrive at the concept of public object may excite our wonder, but it is not more wonderful than the fact that the human nervous system has the biological stability to reproduce itself over billions of examples and eons of time. The common sense notion of "object" with its reality and individuality apart from any frame of reference, is a concept of stark simplicity, from which all consciousness of the complexity of the processes by which it was engendered and maintained has been ruthlessly discarded. In other words, the common sense concept of object is a pre-Einsteinian concept, a carry-over from the days when we were not sophisticated enough to realize the complexities concealed in apparently simple situations, nor practiced enough in analysis to be able to bring these complexities into evidence.

If one examines the range of practical conditions within which the concept of "object" is known to be valid, it will appear that the range is exceedingly narrow. It occurs as far as we know only in connection with human nervous systems, which occur only in comparatively narrow temperature ranges, on the surface of a particular planet, in an approximately constant gravitational field of low intensity, in organisms that never have relative velocities of more than an infinitesimal fraction of the velocity of light, and which have not existed for an interval of time long enough for the planet on which they live to have moved through more than an infinitesimal fraction of the sidereal universe. Yet we are apparently so convinced of the necessity for the universal validity of this so complicated concept, checked under such a narrow range of conditions, as to use the assumption of its validity as a tool to determine the behavior under unknown conditions of such comparatively simple things as a light-ray in a gravitational field. Surely the plausible method of attack is to start with things which we feel we understand well and from them try to deduce the probable behavior of things we understand less. But who would maintain that we understand better the processes by which we arrive at the concept of an underlying reality than we understand the behavior of light in a gravitational field? This, however, is precisely what we have done in assuming to know that the terribly complex processes back of our mentation will not be modified in novel conditions, although at the same time we anticipate an effect of the gravitational field on light-beams. Surely the reason we have acted in this way has been lack of consideration. Once our eyes have been opened it seems to me that the tactics of our attack lose their plausibility.

Perhaps the most sweeping characterization of Einstein's attitude of mind with regard to the general theory is that he believes it possible to get away from the special point of view of the individual observer and sublimate it into something universal, "public," and "real." I on the other hand would take the position that a detailed analysis of everything that we do in physics discloses the universal impossibility of getting away from the individual starting-point. It is a matter of simple observation that the private comes before the public. For each one of us the very meaning of "public" is to be found in certain aspects of his "private." Not only is the starting-point in any scientific activity always private, but after it has emerged into the domain of the public, the story is not completed until we can return to the private from which we came. For the final test of scientific description or theory is that it enables us to reconstruct or to anticipate the immediate (private) situation. The concepts back of the first and second laws of thermodynamics, perhaps the most sweeping generalizations we have in physics, get their meaning from the possibility of recovering the starting-point. For neither energy nor entropy can be defined without reference to a standard state of the system to which we can always return by suitable manipulation.

In much the same way the fundamental measuring operations, without which even description of a physical system would not be possible, have to be defined by reference to some standard set of conditions. Consider, for example, the operation for determining "interval," which is perhaps the most characteristic concept of relativity theory. For the purposes of illustration consider this in the simplest case, when we determine the geometrical distance between two points at rest with respect to us. This is determined by the simple operation of laying a meter stick between the two points and taking the difference of the readings of the two points on the stick. If for some reason it is not convenient to make the observation by direct laying on of the meter stick, but if we know the Cartesian co-ordinates of the two points, then it is possible to calculate by a simple rule the results that we would have obtained with the meter stick. Or, if the physical situation becomes more complicated, and the two points are in motion with respect to our frame of reference, the operations for determining the length become more complicated, being now compounded of operations with meter sticks and clocks in a specified manner combined with computation in a specified manner according to mathematical formulas. The object of all the complicated procedure is to be able to get a numerical result which is the same as the result obtained in an original frame of reference in which the points are at rest. That is, "interval" is an invariant, and the meaning of invariance is merely that it is always possible when measurements are made in strange and complicated systems of reference to return, by suitable calculation, to the results which would have been obtained with the original uniquely simple operation of reading the distance on a resting meter stick. All the complicated processes receive their meaning and significance from the fact that there is in the background a single definite procedure to which we can return, and from which *we do not want* permanently to get away. If one asks "why" it is that the interval is so fundamental for description, I think there is no answer. It is a brute fact that every individual observer finds that the interval as determined by him with meter sticks stationary with respect to him is especially adapted to the description of nature. The fact that nature itself provides this unique method of description would seem to rob the contention that all frames of reference are equally significant of some of its intuitive appeal.

Not only does nature provide us with a unique operation for measuring interval, but it also provides us with a unique frame of reference, namely a frame fixed with respect to the stellar universe, as was pointed out by Mach. Einstein, however, rejects this frame as having significance, because the ascription of significance to it would not be consistent with the "field" point of view. According to the field point of view local happenings are to be significantly correlated, not with distant happenings, but with happenings or conditions in the immediate vicinity, the aggregate of which constitute the "field." The advantage and necessity of the field point of view is usually considered to be that it avoids the difficulties of the old action-at-a-distance point of view. These difficulties are, I believe, generally recognized not to be of a strictly logical character, but to be connected with the difficulty of imagining any "mechanism" by which action at a distance occurs. I believe, however, that an analysis of the operations that are used in specifying what the field is will show that the conceptual dilemma has by no means been successfully met, but has merely been smothered in a mass of neglected operational detail. For the field at a point (considering the electrostatic field for simplicity) is determined by placing a charge at the point, measuring the force on the charge, and then proceeding to the limit by letting the charge become vanishingly small and calculating the limit of ratio of force to charge. The result is conceptualized as something characteristic of the point alone, from which any effect which the test charge may have exerted has disappeared with the vanishing of the charge. But this is plainly an improper conceptualization of this limiting process, because force as well as charge vanishes, and the indispensable rôle of the charge by no means disappears. I know of no means that has been proposed for giving operational meaning to the statement that a condition exists at a point of space independent of the presence at the point of something else, nor have I been able to think of any method by which such a meaning might be given. What one has done when he has shown how to obtain the force on a given distribution of charges in terms of the field, is at bottom nothing more than to find the force on a complicated distribution in terms of the forces on a simpler set of standard charges. It does not seem surprising that this should be feasible, nor would one anticipate that any very fundamental conclusions could be drawn about whatever mechanism there may be which determines the forces on the standard charges. The same considerations apply to dynamic as well as static conditions. One visualizes a "propagation" of a modification in the "field," but operationally one observes only the way in which a force which at one moment acts on a test-body acts a moment later on another test-body. One has in no wise exorcised the mystery of the successive appearance of a force at successive test-bodies by the invention of the field.

It seems to me that the broadest and least restrictive base that can be imagined for the attack on the problem of understanding nature is correlation between the parts. For the broadest attack, we must set up no thesis as to what sort of correlations we will accept as significant, but any universally observed correlation must be given potential significance. Nature presents us with a unique frame of reference; the meaning of "unique" implies a correlation with our measuring operations. Furthermore, this unique frame has a correlation with ordinary mechanical phenomena (Foucault pendulum). When Einstein refuses to accept this frame as having significance, but on the contrary sets up the thesis that it is not possible in the nature of things that there should be a unique frame, I think he is being influenced by the special and, to my mind, erroneous considerations back of the field concept in a way opposed to the spirit of his own general approach.

It has already been intimated that unique frames of reference or preferred starting-points have some of the attributes of the "absolute." It might appear therefore that to recognize their existence is a throw-back to the Newtonian point of view. I think any misgivings on this score will vanish, however, when it is appreciated that operationally the preferred starting-point is different for each individual observer. That this is true is a matter of simple observation, whether or not we like it. There is here nothing of the old Newtonian absolute, metaphysically existing in its own right, the same for all observers. One can see that a complete working out of the implications of each observer having his own unique frame of reference is a matter of the very widest philosophical import, but it is not necessary for present purposes to go into it further here.

In Einstein's argument another type of consideration plays an important part. A distinction is made between the general "laws" of nature and phenomena which are special, local, and adventitious. The velocity of light or the gravitational constant are taken as manifestations of general laws, while the acceleration of gravity at the surface of the earth would be an example of the second sort of thing. The distinction is made fundamental, because it is the general laws that are required to be capable of covariant formulation. I believe, however, that analysis will show that there is no way by which the concept of "general law" can be made operationally sharp. If, when we have telescopes a million times more powerful than any at present, we find that there is reason to think that the gravitational constant varies in different parts of space, and that its value in any particular region cannot be correlated with anything observable, any more than the actual size of the earth can at present be correlated with anything observable, I think we would not maintain that the gravitational constant is connected with some universal law. The point is that the meaning of the concept of general law becomes operationally hazy as we extend our measurements of our thinking toward domains as yet unexplored. It would seem that a sound scientific methodology would not allow us to use as a tool for stupendous extrapolations any concepts which have the slightest recognizable amount of haziness. Such an extrapolation should not be made until we have at least some basis for estimating the order of magnitude of the haze and its probable effect on such an extrapolation. It is difficult for me to imagine a way of doing this that would not involve some prior knowledge of the region into which we are trying to penetrate.

In summary, the obvious structure of experience is based on the individual and particular. Our fundamental operations of description and measurement do not get away from it. We find it present in the structure of the universe in a unique frame of reference when we go to the very large; and when we go to the very small we find it in the impossibility of public knowledge or observation in the quantum domain. The indictment that this article would bring against Einstein is therefore the following: That in his conviction of the possibility of getting away from any special co-ordinate system, in his conviction of the fruitfulness of so doing, and in his treatment of the event as something primitive and unanalyzed, he has carried into general relativity theory precisely that uncritical, pre-Einsteinian point of view which he has so convincingly shown us, in his special theory, conceals the possibility of disaster.

P. W. Bridgman

Research Laboratory of Physics
Harvard University

13

Victor F. Lenzen

EINSTEIN'S THEORY OF KNOWLEDGE

EINSTEIN'S THEORY OF KNOWLEDGE

I

THEORY of knowledge, or epistemology, is the philosophical discipline that deals with the aims, methods, and achievements of cognition. Subject matter for epistemological analysis is exemplified by the perceptions and opinions of daily life, by the procedures and laws of natural science, by the axioms and deductions of mathematics. Theoretical physics, which is a mathematical scheme for the ordering of certain refined concepts of daily life, provides a fruitful object for epistemological analysis. The science combines the functions of experience and reason in the constitution of knowledge. The impulse to construct a physical theory originates in perception as a mode of experience, but a theory is constructed rationally out of mathematical concepts. In the present essay I shall expound the theory of knowledge which Einstein has formulated in the light of his constructive work in theoretical physics.[1]

Creative advance in exact science historically has provided

---

[1] In preparing this essay Einstein's theoretical works have been consulted, and in addition the following contributions which are of especial philosophical significance:

1) "Ernst Mach." *Physikalische Zeitschrift*, Vol. 17, 101-104 (1916).
2) "Address in honor of Planck." Quoted by A. Moszkowski, *Einstein*, 67-69 (1921).
3) "Time, Space, and Gravitation." Reprinted from the *London Times*. *Science*, 8-10, January 2 (1920).
4) *Aether und Relativitätstheorie* (1920).
5) *Geometrie und Erfahrung* (1921).
6) *Vier Vorlesungen über Relativitätstheorie* (1922).
7) "Newton's Mechanik und ihr Einfluss auf die Gestaltung der theoretischen Physik." *Die Naturwissenschaften*, Vol. 15, 273-276 (1927).
8) "Maxwell's Influence on the Development of the Conception of Physical Reality." *Essays on James Clerk Maxwell* (1931).

(Continued on next page)

material for new points of view in theory of knowledge. In antiquity the mathematical discoveries of the Pythagoreans gave rise to rationally constructed deductive systems for numbers and geometrical figures. Plato explained the possibility of mathematical knowledge by the theory of ideas, or forms, which were exact, eternal objects of rational insight. In the modern era the creation of classical mechanics and its application by Newton to construct a system of the world provided mathematical knowledge of motion. Kant explained the possibility of a mathematical science of nature by the doctrine that space and time are *a priori* forms of sensibility, and substance and causality are *a priori* categories of the understanding. Since the dawn of the twentieth century new bases for theoretical physics have been created by the theory of relativity and quantum theory. One may expect that new conceptions in theory of knowledge will be required in order to comprehend these new achievements in physical theory. The epistemological analysis of theoretical physics should provide the pathway to a comprehensive theory of knowledge.

Theory of knowledge does not, however, await the completion of a new theoretical physics. There may be invariable principles, so that epistemological analysis is an element in the criticism of prevailing concepts and in the creation of new physical theories. This creative function of epistemology has been acknowledged by Einstein to have been an essential constituent in his own creative work. In an essay on the work of Ernst Mach,

9) "Prologue by Albert Einstein." Max Planck, *Where Is Science Going?* Translated by James Murphy (1932).
10) *The Origins of the General Theory of Relativity* (1933).
11) *On the Method of Theoretical Physics* (1933).
12) A. Einstein, B. Podolsky and N. Rosen, "Can Quantum-Mechanical Description of Physical Reality be Considered Complete?" *Physical Review*, Vol. 47, 777-780 (1935).
13) "Physik und Realität." *Journal of the Franklin Institute*, 313-347 (1936).
14) "Remarks on Bertrand Russell's Theory of Knowledge." *The Philosophy of Bertrand Russell.* Edited by Paul Arthur Schilpp (1944).
The following biographical works also have been consulted:
1) Alexander Moszkowski, *Einstein* (1921).
2) Anton Reiser, *Albert Einstein* (1930).
3) H. Gordon Garbedian, *Albert Einstein* (1939).
4) Marianoff and Wayne, *Einstein* (1944).

Einstein describes the subject matter of *Erkenntnistheorie* as the aims and nature of science, the extent to which its results are true, the discrimination between what is essential and that which rests on accidents of development. He asserts that the truth about these problems must be mastered again and again in conformity to the needs of an era, for reflective insight which is not continually recreated in general becomes lost. Concepts that have proved useful in the constitution of an order of things readily win such an authority over us that we forget their earthly origin and take them to be changeless data. Such concepts then become stamped as necessities of thought, as given *a priori*, so that the path of scientific progress often becomes impassable for a long period. Einstein declared that it is no idle play, therefore, if we engage in analysis of concepts that have been long current and show on what their justification and usefulness depends. The all too great authority of customary concepts is thereby broken: they are set aside, if they can not be justified adequately, corrected if their correlation with given experience was too careless, or replaced by other concepts if it is possible to set up a preferable new system. Einstein has stated that the critical discussions of Hume and Mach influenced him directly and indirectly in the reconstruction of the concepts of space and time for the creation of the theory of relativity. Despite the protests of those philosophers who had placed these concepts in a treasure chest of the absolute, of the *a priori*, critical analysis replaced them by more sharply defined concepts in order to further the development of physical science.

Einstein also has expounded general conclusions concerning the nature of knowledge as exemplified by theoretical physics. His views constitute a contribution to the development of theory of knowledge as a philosophical discipline. As preparation for a preliminary statement of his doctrine I recall the distinction between sensory experience and conceptual description. Empirical knowledge originates in sense-impressions, but its goal is understanding through concepts. The media of scientific knowledge are concepts of properties of things and processes which constitute natural phenomena. A basic problem of theory of knowledge is the relation of concepts to sensory experience; in this question one may distinguish between the rôle of experience in the origin of concepts and the function of concepts in ordering experience. According to empiricism concepts are abstracted from experience. An observer perceives several white things, for example, and abstracts from these particulars the common quality whiteness. The concept of the property whiteness, a universal, thus is explained as derived from experiences that exemplify the universal. The doctrine of empiricism as applied to natural science is that concepts and natural laws are abstracted from experience. It can be claimed that Newton viewed the principles by which he described gravitational phenomena as derived from experience. Einstein has declared that Newton's *"hypotheses non fingo"* can be interpreted only in the sense that Newton held that the concepts of mass, acceleration, and force, and the laws connecting them, were directly borrowed from experience.[2] Although Einstein acknowledges the stimulus which he owes to the empiricists Hume and Mach, he rejects an empirical account of the origin of concepts.

According to Einstein, the concepts which arise in thought and in our linguistic expressions logically are free creations of thought which can not be derived inductively from sensory experiences. Like Plato, Einstein stresses the gap between data of sense and concepts of thought. He contends that there is a gulf, logically unbridgeable, which separates the world of sensory experiences from the realm of concepts and conceptual relations which constitute propositions. The constructive nature of concepts is not easily noticed, Einstein asserts, because we have the habit of combining certain concepts and conceptual relations definitely with certain sensory experiences. In contrast to John Stuart Mill, who held that propositions of mathematics are inductions from experience, Einstein offers the series of integers as obviously an invention of the human mind, a self-created tool which simplifies the ordering of sensory experiences.[3] He asserts that there is no way in which the concept could be made to grow, as it were, directly out of sensory experiences. The concept of number belongs to pre-scientific thought, but its constructive character is still easily recognizable.

In support of Einstein's doctrine of concepts, one can cite

---

[2] *Method of Theoretical Physics,* 10.

[3] "Remarks on Bertrand Russell's Theory of Knowledge," 286. (cf. 14 in fn. 1).

examples of constructive concepts in physical theory. Although Newton thought of mechanics as derived from experience, its universe of discourse contains conceptual objects, particles and rigid bodies, which are not exactly exemplified in experience. Observation of the results of an experiment involves assignment of physical quantities to a perceptible body. This operation requires a constructive act which may be exemplified by the measurement of distance between two points; in this operation each of the points is brought into coincidence simultaneously with corresponding points on a standard body that is idealized as rigid. Even if a crude concept of distance were held to be abstracted from perceptions of coincidence, the exact concept requires the constructive act of idealization of points and rigid bodies. As Einstein has emphasized, the hypothesis of atomism is based on constructive-speculative concepts. Atoms are conceptual objects, the properties of which are not perceptible but are assigned hypothetically.

Although Einstein recognizes the spontaneity of thought, he agrees with Kant that all thought acquires material content only through its relationship to sensory experiences. Pure logical thinking can give us no knowledge of the world of experience; all knowledge about reality begins with experience and terminates in it. The function of concepts is to order and survey experience, so that a conceptual system is tested by its success in establishing order in the manifold of sense-experiences. Thus reason builds the structure in a system of knowledge. Einstein declares that our experience up to date justifies us in feeling sure that in Nature is actualized the ideal of mathematical simplicity. Accordingly he asserts, "In a certain sense, therefore, I hold it to be true that pure thought is competent to comprehend the real, as the ancients dreamed."[4]

Einstein holds that the truly creative principle in theoretical physics is mathematical construction. It enables us to discover the concepts and laws connecting them which give us the key to the understanding of natural phenomena. Experience may guide us in our choice of mathematical concepts; experience also remains the sole criterion of the serviceability of a mathematical construction for physics; but it cannot possibly be the

[4] *Method of Theoretical Physics*, 12.

source from which a theory is derived. The aim of theory is to reduce the concepts for a field of knowledge to as simple and as few irreducible basic elements as possible. Einstein has further stated, "The basic concepts and laws which are not logically further reducible constitute the indispensable and not rationally deducible part of the theory."[5] The reference to a non-rational element may be explained by a passage from an address in honor of Planck.[6] On this occasion Einstein stated that the development of physics has shown that among all conceivable constructions at a given time, one has proved itself unconditionally superior to all others; that the world of perceptions practically determines the theoretical system, although no logical path leads from perceptions to the principles of the theory, only intuition which rests upon an intimacy with experience. It is appropriate to apply to Einstein his own characterization of Planck: The longing for the vision of the pre-established harmony which was recognized by Leibniz is the source of the inexhaustible patience with which Einstein has been able to devote himself to the general problems of theoretical physics.

II

Einstein has recognized that science is a refinement of the thinking of daily life. Accordingly, he initiates his critical reflections concerning theoretical physics with an analysis of concepts which serve to interpret common experience. The physicist in ordinary activities as well as in science is cognizant of an environment constituted by things that are extended in space and variable in time. Subject matter for physical science is the pattern of basic processes in the spatio-temporal environment. Physical knowledge is expressed by organized sets of propositions which express conceptual relations exemplified in physical processes. The basic concept is that of bodily object by which we interpret the data of perception; a manifold of bodily objects comprises the external world which stands in cognitive relations to observers. As a foundation for the present essay we need to understand the concept of bodily object as set forth,

[5] *Ibid.*, 9.
[6] Moszkowski, *Einstein*, 69.

for example, in Einstein's monograph "Physik und Realität."

Natural science during the modern era generally has presupposed dualism in theory of knowledge. Data of perception have been acknowledged to be relative to percipient events; objects have been conceived as independent of perception. In dualism a physical object is held to be an independent reality which manifests itself by initiating a chain of processes that act on a sensory mechanism. The resulting perception is interpreted as mediate cognition of an independent object. Einstein has remarked that this dualist conception is an application of physical ways of thinking to the problem of cognition. Dualism was criticized by Berkeley and Hume, but for physical scientists the significant alternative was set forth by Ernst Mach. In his theory the object of perception is a complex of elements, which Mach called sensations but viewed as neutral with respect to the distinction between mental and material. In essays on the philosophy of physics Planck has argued repeatedly against the positivism of Mach, contending that a realist conception of the physical world is necessary for the progress of physical science. Einstein in an essay on Maxwell appears to have accepted the realist doctrine, for he says, "The belief in an external world independent of the percipient subject is the foundation of all science. But since sense-perceptions inform us only indirectly of this external world, of Physical Reality, it is only by speculation that it can become comprehensible to us."[7] In his essay on the method of theoretical physics he expresses the conviction that pure mathematical construction is the method of discovering the concepts and laws for the comprehension of nature. He declares, "Our experience up to date justifies us in feeling sure that in Nature is actualized the ideal of mathematical simplicity."[8] Perhaps it is permissible to conjecture that according to Einstein the relational structure of an independent reality can be cognized by virtue of a pre-established harmony between thought and reality.

The realist language occasionally used by Einstein is exemplified in a discussion of quantum mechanics in collaboration

[7] "Maxwell's Influence," 66.
[8] Op. cit., 12.

with B. Podolsky and N. Rosen. It is asserted that any consideration of a physical theory must take into account the distinction between objective reality, which is independent of any theory, and the physical concepts with which the theory operates. These concepts are intended to correspond with the objective reality, and by means of the concepts we picture this reality to ourselves. The following requirement for a complete theory is held to be necessary: every element of the physical reality must have a counterpart in the physical theory. The criterion of reality is: "If, without in any way disturbing a system, we can predict with certainty the value of a physical quantity, then there exists an element of physical reality corresponding to the physical quantity."[9] This criterion is regarded not as necessary but merely as sufficient, and accords with classical as well as quantum mechanical ideas of reality. In my judgment the presupposition of this criterion is that physical reality is conceived to have only those characters that are manifested in observable results of experiments. In so far as physical reality is independent in the sense of a realistic theory of knowledge, its only character which is relevant to physical theory is form as exhibited in the pattern of observable objects.

The realist language of Einstein is further neutralized by his recognition that the significance of concepts depends on sense-impressions. In his systematic discussion in "Physik und Realität" Einstein starts with sensory experiences as would a positivist. He begins his analysis with the observation that upon the stage of our experience there appear in colorful succession sense-impressions, recollections thereof, representations, and feelings. The distinction between sense-impressions, or sensations, and representations is problematic, but Einstein proceeds on the assumption that sense-impressions as such are given and cognizable. The concept of "real external world" of daily life is based upon sense-impressions. Physical science deals with sense-impressions and aims to comprehend the connections between them.

The first step in positing a "real external world" is the construction of the concept of bodily object, respectively, bodily objects of different kinds. Certain recurring complexes of sensation are arbitrarily selected by thought out of the fulness of sensations and to them is assigned the concept of bodily object. Einstein holds that, logically considered, the concept of bodily object is not identical with the totality of those sensations, but is a free creation of the human (or animal) spirit. However, the concept of bodily object owes its significance and justification to the totality of sensations to which it is assigned. In positing a "real external world" we attribute "real existence" to the bodily object, and thereby endow the concept with an independent existence. With the help of such concepts and relations which are thought of between them, we are able to find our way in the maze of sensations. The real objects, although free posits of thought, seem more fixed and changeless than individual sense-impressions, whose character in contrast to illusion or hallucination is never completely certified. The world of sense-impressions is comprehensible in the following sense: One fashions general concepts and relations between them, imposes relations between concepts and sense-impressions, and thereby establishes an order between sense-impressions. Einstein declares that it is one of the great discoveries of Immanuel Kant that the positing of a real external world would be meaningless without such comprehensibility. In virtue of the connections between complexes of sense-impressions and concepts, the purely conceptual propositions of science become general assertions about complexes of sense-impressions. The method of forming concepts and connections between them, and the mode of assigning concepts to sense-impressions, is decided only by success in establishing an order of sense-impressions. The rules of correlation can never be definitive, but can claim validity only for a specified region of applicability. Einstein declares that there are no definitive categories in the sense of Kant. He asserts that we must always be ready to alter our conceptions of physical reality, in order to take account of perceptions with the greatest possible logical completeness. The connections between complexes of sense impressions and the elementary concepts of daily life are not comprehensible conceptually and can only be grasped intuitively. Einstein declares that the comprehensibility of the world is the eternally incomprehensible.

Einstein's concept of bodily object may be compared with a theory of Bertrand Russell, according to which a physical object is a collection of sense-data. In his discussion of Russell's theory of knowledge Einstein rejects the conception of a thing as a bundle of qualities which are taken from sensory raw material. He attributes the origin of such a concept of thing to a fear of metaphysics created by Hume. Einstein declares, however, that he can see no "metaphysical danger" in taking the thing (the object in the sense of physics) as an independent concept into the system together with the proper spatio-temporal structure.[10]

In my judgment the minimal significance of the concept of bodily object expresses a matrix to which thought refers sense-impressions. This conception of bodily object as a matrix for the arrangement of sense-impressions can be fashioned so that a decision between idealism and realism is not required for science. Einstein recognizes that the function of the bodily object is to order sense-impressions. Since he rejects the view that the object is only a complex of sensations, his view need not be idealism. He holds that the concept of bodily object is independent, but since the object is not characterized explicitly as the cause of sensations, one extreme of dualism can be avoided. Indeed, since the propositions of physical science are about complexes of sense-impressions, the independent concept of bodily object need not refer to a reality beyond experience. In language occasionally used by Einstein, however, the term bodily object seems to signify an element of an independent reality, whose structure is grasped through the conceptual scheme which orders the manifold of sense-impressions.

III

Einstein's exposition of scientific method starts with the concept of bodily object and then introduces concepts which are fashioned for daily life and refined by science. In the passage from ordinary experience to theories of physics Einstein recog-

[10] "Remarks on Bertrand Russell's Theory of Knowledge," 290.

nizes strata, or levels of knowledge. A primary level has the closest relation to sense-impressions; the primary concepts formed on this level are connected intuitively and directly with typical complexes of sense-impressions. Concepts on deeper levels are significant for experience only to the extent that they can be brought into relation with primary concepts through propositions. Among propositions are definitions of concepts as well as propositions logically deducible from them. Natural laws are propositions which are not deducible from definitions, but which assert relations between primary concepts and thereby between sense-impressions. Einstein states that the distinction between definitions and natural laws depends to a considerable extent on the chosen mode of representation. He remarks that the distinction needs to be carried out actually only if one seeks to investigate to what extent a conceptual system is meaningful from the physical point of view.

On the primary level of natural knowledge the concepts of space and time play a fundamental role. The laboratory of experimental physics has a place in space during an epoch of time. Qualitative concepts of these frames of events are used in daily life; in physical science the definitions of these concepts are progressively reformed and sharpened for the investigation of processes in space and time under controlled conditions. The primary concept for the theory of space and time is that of bodily object. According to Einstein the characteristic property assigned to a bodily object is existence independent of subjective time and of sensory perception. We ascribe independence to the object, although we observe changes in qualities and position during time. The term "independence" suggests a realist conception of objects, but in my judgment the term may be applied to a construct of thought which serves to establish order among sense-impressions. The following discussion does not require a decision concerning the ontological status of bodily objects.

Einstein explains the concepts of objective space and objective time in terms of the properties of a specific kind of bodily object, the practically rigid body.[11] Practically rigid bodies are exemplified by solid bodies of common experience. Solid bodies

---

[11] "Physik u. Realität."

can undergo changes of position which can be reversed by arbitrary motions of an observer's body and are thereby distinguished from changes of state. In a pair of solid bodies each can change its position without change in position of the pair. One thereby attains the concept of relative position and thus the concept of relative position of each body. A special case of relative position is contact of two bodies at a point. Experience shows that if two adjacent bodies are in contact at two points, this contact can be continued during changes of position, and after separation can be restored. By this concept of coincidence of points one describes the properties of a solid body which are expressed by the term "practically rigid body." Two points on a practically rigid body determine a stretch. The stretches on two bodies are called equal to each other if the points of one coincide with the corresponding points of the other. It is postulated that if two stretches determined by points on practically rigid bodies have been found equal, they are always and everywhere equal. This postulate is the basis of equality of stretches at a distance.

A specific body K_0 can be continued by a second body which is in contact with it at three or more points. The quasi-rigid continuation of a body is unlimited. The collection of conceivable quasi-rigid continuations of a body K_0 is the infinite space determined by this body as frame of reference. The concept of space conceptually transforms the manifold of positional relations of bodily objects into the manifold of positions of bodily objects in space. Every proposition about position thereby becomes one about contact. That a point of a bodily object is to be found at the spatial point P signifies that the given point of the object is in contact, or coincides with, the point P on the suitably conceived continuation of the body of reference K_0. In pre-scientific thought the earth's crust plays the rôle of the body of reference K_0 and its continuation. The term geometry for the mathematical theory of the properties of space indicates that for the Greek creators of the science the concept of space was relative to the earthly body of reference. Einstein describes space in general as the totality of possibilities of relative position of practically rigid bodies.

In geometry as a branch of mathematics the practically rigid body is transformed into an ideal rigid body. The axioms of geometry implicitly define the properties of points, lines, planes, and rigid bodies. Euclidean geometry, for example, consists of the totality of propositions for the relative positions of rigid bodies which are independent of time. Its formal simplicity is characterized by the properties of homogeneity, isotropy and existence of similar figures in space. The central significance of Euclidean geometry from the physical point of view lies in the fact that its validity is independent of the qualitative nature of bodies. The description of position by co-ordinates, as in the geometry of Descartes, has been a powerful tool in the quantitative development of the subject. Einstein points out that the content of Euclidean geometry can be based axiomatically on the propositions:

1) Two points on a rigid body determine a stretch.

2) To any point of space one can assign a triplet of co-ordinate numbers so that to a stretch one can assign a positive number, the square of which is the sum of squares of the co-ordinate differences. The positive number is called the length of the stretch, or the distance of the points, and is independent of position of the given body as well as all other bodies.

Einstein declares that the formulation of geometry in terms of co-ordinates clearly exhibits the connection between conceptual constructions and sense-impressions, upon which rests the significance of geometry for physics. The propositions of Euclidean geometry indeed are embodied in an approximate manner in configurations of solid bodies of common experience. In particular, Euclidean geometry is approximately exemplified in apparatus for measuring quantities such as distance, time, and in general the quantities of classical physics. The axiomatic construction of Euclidean geometry has an empirical foundation, and Einstein declares that forgetfulness of this fact was responsible for the fatal error that Euclidean geometry is a necessity of thought which is prior to all experience.

The concept of objective time is introduced through the intermediary of space. Just as the rigid body is a basis for space, so is the clock for time. Einstein introduces time by two independent posits:

1) Objective local time is based on the correlation of the temporal course of experience with the indications of a "clock," i.e., a periodically running isolated system.

2) Objective extended time is based upon synchronization of distant clocks by signals.

The postulate for stretches in space also applies to time. The propagation of light in empty space correlates to every interval of local time a stretch, the corresponding light path. If two immediately adjacent, ideal clocks run at the same rate at any time and at any place, they will run at the same rate whenever and wherever they are compared at the same place.[12] An empirical basis for this postulate is provided by the agreement of the frequencies of light emitted by individual atoms of the same chemical element.

The distinction between time and local time was vague prior to the creation of the special theory of relativity. Simultaneity of sight and simultaneity of occurrence were not distinguished, because the time required for the propagation of light was neglected in science as well as in daily life. The presupposition of classical mechanics that space and time are independent of bodies obscured the unsharpness of the concept of time from the empirical point of view, but it did facilitate the development of mechanics. Einstein has remarked that the hypostatization of concepts may serve a useful purpose in science; there is danger, however, that the origin of concepts in experience may be forgotten and concepts considered changeless. The Kantian doctrine of the fixity of concepts is not a constituent of Einstein's theory of knowledge.

The concepts of space, time, and bodily object are basic concepts in the cognitions of daily life. Physical science in its initial stage of development employs as media of cognition primary concepts which are intuitively correlated with the perceptions of common experience. An example is the concept of water as primary substance in the cosmological theory of Thales. Einstein

[12] *Geometrie u. Erfahrung*, 9.

declares that the scientific mind is not satisfied with such a primary stage of cognition, on account of lack of logical unity among concepts and their relations. Accordingly, a secondary system is invented with fewer concepts and relations, and from it the primary concepts and relations of the first stratum are logically derived. The greater logical unity of the secondary system is achieved at the sacrifice of immediate correlation between its concepts and complexes of sense-impressions. The first and second stages of physical science may be exemplified respectively by descriptions of the perceptible properties of matter and the kinetic-molecular theory of matter. In the kinetic-molecular theory a material like the water of Thales is reduced to an assembly of molecules whose different modes of arrangement furnish the basis of solid, liquid, and gaseous states. Further striving for logical unity leads to the creation of an even more impoverished tertiary system from which the concepts and relations of the secondary system can be derived. The process goes on until one arrives at a system with the greatest conceivable unity and poverty of concepts, and which is consistent with the structure introduced into the manifold of sense-impressions by primary concepts. The strata are not sharply separated. In the present unfinished state of theoretical physics the strata represent stages of partial success. The science as a whole consists of parts in different stages of development, and contains apparently inconsistent constituents. If a definitive, unified system should be created, the intermediate stages would disappear.

Consideration of the construction of a system of theoretical physics raises the question as to how we shall choose concepts and principles so that we may hope for confirmation of their consequences by experience. Einstein offers two guides for construction, one empirical, one rational. The aim of theory is to achieve the most complete conceptual comprehension of sense-impressions. Hence the most favorable results are to be expected from hypotheses which are suggested by experience. Such hypotheses establish what Einstein has called theories of principle.[18] He gives as examples the hypothesis of the non-exist-

---

[18] "Time, Space, and Gravitation."

ence of a *perpetuum mobile* as a foundation for thermodynamics, and Galileo's law of inertia as a constituent of classical mechanics. The fundamental hypotheses of the special theory of relativity are similar in nature. The special theory rests upon:

1) The principle of relativity of uniform motion, a proposition which has been confirmed negatively by the failure to detect the effects of the earth's motion with respect to an ether.

2) The principle of the constancy of the velocity of light, a principle which serves to represent the Maxwell-Lorentz theory of electromagnetic phenomena in moving bodies.

The union of the two principles requires that the velocity of light be the same in all inertial frames of reference. The principles of the theory of relativity determine time and space to be relative to the frame of reference. The four-dimensional space-time of Minkowski then provides the approximate frame for events.

The construction of physical theory is also guided by ideals of reason. Reason demands the greatest possible simplicity in a physical theory. Simplicity is understood to consist in a minimum number of fundamental concepts and relations together with a maximum of abstractness. The creative function of such logical ideals was especially exemplified by the creation of the general theory of relativity. The general theory was constructed to conform to a general principle of relativity, according to which the equations which express physical laws are covariant under all transformations of co-ordinates. The creative function of mathematical ideals has been succinctly expressed by Einstein:

The physical world is represented as a four-dimensional continuum. If in this I adopt a Riemannian metric, and look for the simplest laws which such a metric can satisfy, I arrive at the relativistic gravitation theory of empty space. If I adopt in this space a vector-field, or the anti-symmetrical tensor-field derived from it, and if I look for the simplest laws which such a field can satisfy, I arrive at the Maxwell equations for free space.[14]

[14] *Method of Theoretical Physics*, 13.

The use of rational criteria for the construction of physical theories confirms Einstein's doctrine that concepts are free creations of the mind. The fundamental axioms, he declares, can be chosen freely. To be sure, the freedom is controlled to the extent that consequences of the axioms must be confirmed by experience. The freedom is not that of a novelist, but of the person who solves a cross-word puzzle. Any word can be proposed as a solution, but there is only one that fits the puzzle in all parts. In view of Einstein's distinction between theories of principle, which are suggested by experience, and constructive theories, it might be thought that the creative nature of concepts does not hold for theories of principle. But theories of principle, such as thermodynamics, are formulated in terms of sharply defined concepts of properties that are never exactly exemplified in experience. Again, the synthesis of principles for the special theory of relativity created the concepts of relative space and time and thus provided the basis for space-time. Hence it is justifiable to agree with Einstein that physical concepts in a logical sense are free creations of the human mind.

Einstein states that during the classical period scientists believed that the basic concepts and laws of physics were derivable from experience by abstraction. The great successes of the Newtonian theory of gravitation prevented recognition of the constructive nature of its principles. According to Einstein, it is the general theory of relativity which showed in a convincing manner the incorrectness of the view that concepts are derived from experience. This theory revealed that by using principles quite differently conceived from those of Newton it was possible to comprehend the entire range of the data of experience in a manner even more complete and satisfactory than on Newton's principles. The constructive character of the principles is made obvious by the fact that it is possible to exhibit two essentially different bases, each of which yields consequences in agreement with experience to a large extent. This indicates, Einstein declares, that an attempt to derive logically the concepts and laws of mechanics from the ultimate data of experience is doomed to failure. There is no inductive method that can lead to the fundamental concepts or principles. The truly creative principle of theoretical physics is mathematical construction.

IV

The aim of theoretical physics is the unified conceptual representation of physical reality. This end has been accomplished in large part by the construction of models for physical processes. The pattern of common experience has provided models, such as particles and waves, with which to picture physical reality. Solid bodies perceived in daily life suggest the concept of a bodily object that is relatively small in extent; ripples on water suggest the concept of a wave by which a continuous field is propagated through space. I have already discussed Einstein's conception of theories of principle, and shall now examine his doctrine of constructive theories in physics.

A relatively small solid body provides the empirical basis for the precisely defined concept of the material point as a bodily object concentrated in a point. Classical mechanics is a theory of motion of material points, the positions of which can be described in terms of co-ordinates relative to a space K_o. The law of inertia states that the acceleration of a material point vanishes if it is sufficiently far removed from all other points. The law of motion is that force equals mass times acceleration. As Einstein has remarked, the laws of mechanics constitute a general schema. The laws acquire content through laws of force which express interactions between material points in accordance with the law of action and reaction. Newton's law of gravitation is a law of force which made possible application of classical mechanics to planetary motions. The laws of motion in classical mechanics hold only with respect to bodies of reference K_o with a specific type of motion, and hence such spaces of reference are endowed with a physical property which is foreign to the geometrical concept of space. Einstein has declared that it is a defect of classical mechanics that laws of force can not be won through formal-logical considerations; the choice of such laws is to a great extent arbitrary *a priori*. Newton's law of gravitation is marked out from other conceivable laws of force through its success in prediction. By constrast, Einstein's law of gravitation was found by seeking the simplest covariant law for space-time with a Riemannian metric. Einstein's criticism of Newton's law of gravitation recalls to the student of Plato that philosopher's criticism of the employment of hypotheses in mathematics without rational comprehension obtained by dialectic. The formal-logical considerations which Einstein employed in creating the general theory of relativity accord with the Platonic conception of "episteme."

Einstein declares that classical mechanics leads necessarily to the atomic constitution of matter, a result which demonstrates that the theory of atomism does not arise inductively out of experience. The atomistic point of view, however, is limited by phenomenological physics, which operates with concepts intuitively correlated with experience. Thus the configuration of a rigidly connected system of material points can be described in terms of a number of generalized co-ordinates. Again, a deformable system of material points can be treated approximately as a continuous distribution of matter. Such a fiction, which avoids the explicit introduction of material points, is made the basis of theories of elasticity and hydrodynamics. The program of phenomenological physics also called for the description of heat, electricity, and light in terms of variables in addition to the mechanical ones. The functional dependence of these variables on one another and on the time was to be found empirically. During the latter half of the nineteenth century many scientists, in particular Ernst Mach, envisaged the goal of physical science as the representation of processes through concepts inductively derived from sensory experience. On Einstein's view the consistent application of Newtonian mechanics carried theoretical physics beyond the phenomenological standpoint. The kinetic-molecular theory of gases correlated phenomena which seemed to be independent. Statistical mechanics furnished a mechanical interpretation of the concepts and laws of thermodynamics. This reduction of the phenomenological stratum to an atomistic one required assignment of real structure to material points which thereby became atoms or molecules. Einstein declares that the speculative-constructive character of these particles was obvious; no one could hope to perceive an atom directly. The kinetic-molecular theory of matter was opposed by an empiricism which was represented by Ernst Mach. Mach viewed atoms as auxiliary fictions which were to be discarded after the complete correlation of sensations was achieved. A creative exponent of atomism was Boltzmann, who in his statistical mechanical theory of thermodynamics expressed entropy as proportional to the probability of the state of an assembly of particles. Planck applied Boltzmann's methods to heat radiation, and in the first year of the twentieth century invented the concept of quantum of energy from which he derived a law for black body radiation that agreed with experimental results.

Einstein contributed significantly to the theory of atomism. An early work was a statistical mechanical theory of thermodynamics. He applied statistical methods to the Brownian movement, the irregular thermal motion of colloidal particles suspended in a liquid. Of special significance was his application of Boltzmann's theory of entropy as probability to radiation in order to introduce the concept of discrete quanta of radiant energy. He further extended Planck's theory of the quantized oscillator to atomic motions in a solid and derived the result that the specific heat of a monatomic solid is a function of the temperature. The quantum theory received great impetus when Bohr introduced stationary states determined by quantum conditions into the nuclear model of the atom. The stationary states of atomic hydrogen, for example, were represented as motions of a single electron in quantized orbits about a positive nucleus. In conformity with Einstein's quantum theory of radiation, Bohr also postulated that atoms jump from one stationary state to another with the emission or absorption of a quantum of radiant energy. Einstein then constructed a theory for the emission and absorption of radiation in equilibrium with an assembly of atoms characterized by stationary states and obtained Planck's law of radiation. Later, Bose applied a new kind of statistics to photons in order to derive Planck's law; Einstein then extended the Bose statistics to an ideal gas. One may summarize Einstein's contributions to constructive theories based on atomism: initially he founded his statistical investigations upon classical mechanics and in the course of development applied and extended the concepts of quantum theory to obtain new statistical theories.

The mechanical theory of atomism was applied in Newton's corpuscular theory to explain the phenomena of light. Later, particles that carry electric charges were conceived for the explanation of electric and magnetic phenomena. Wave motion in material media then suggested more suitable models for optical and electromagnetic phenomena. The interference and diffraction of light required explanation in terms of waves. Electric and magnetic forces, which were initially conceived to act at a distance like gravitation, were interpreted to be manifestations of a continuous field which transmits actions by contact. The theory of partial differential equations, which had been developed for the continuous functions of phenomenological mechanics, provided mathematical methods for the theory of the field.

A wave theory of light initially represented the physical basis of visual sensations as wave motion in a mechanical ether. Faraday invented, and Maxwell developed, the concept of field as a region in which electric and magnetic forces are continuous functions of position. According to Einstein, the theory of electromagnetic field constituted a further step in the direction of constructive speculation. For the existence of the field is manifested only if electrically charged bodies are brought into it. Electric charges are regions of non-vanishing divergence of electric force. Maxwell's differential equations correlate the spatial and temporal rates of change of electric and magnetic forces. Light consists of undulatory processes in the electromagnetic field. Maxwell sought to construct mechanical models for the field, but gradually the field acquired a fundamental rôle. Under the influence of Heinrich Hertz the equations of electromagnetism came to be interpreted as representations of fundamental realities. Thus the strictly mechanical view of nature was gradually abandoned. H. A. Lorentz applied the theory of electromagnetism to material media with the aid of the concept of electron. He considered the ether to be the seat of electromagnetic fields within material bodies as well as in empty space. Electrons, that is elementary particles which carry electric charges, enabled Lorentz to account for electromagnetic phenomena in moving bodies. Einstein has remarked that Lorentz took from the ether all its mechanical properties except immobility.[15] The electron theory was a synthesis of the Newtonian mechanics of material points and Maxwell's theory of the electromagnetic field. This dualism of theoretical foundations inspired attempts to explain the electron in terms of the field.

The special theory of relativity was based on the Maxwell-Lorentz theory of the electromagnetic field. According to the special theory, physical phenomena can be described with equal correctness in a multiplicity of inertial frames of reference. If the seat of electromagnetic processes is called an ether, it must be deprived of a definite state of motion. Einstein thus considers that the special theory of relativity completed the work of establishing the electromagnetic field as a fundamental reality. He has said, "This change in the conception of Reality is the most profound and the most fruitful that physics has experienced since the time of Newton; but it must be confessed that the complete realization of the program contained in this idea has so far by no means been attained."[16]

The conception of field as physical reality was further developed by Einstein in the general theory of relativity. According to this theory, the metrical properties of the space-time continuum are dependent upon matter. The formulation of this field theory, however, required the concept of material particle. Einstein has sought to resolve the dualism between field and particle. He declares that in the foundations of a consistent field theory the concept of particle must not occur alongside that of field. The whole theory must be based on partial differential equations and solutions thereof which are free from singularities. Concerning the problem of quanta, Einstein looks for a solution by which the foundations of field physics are united with the facts of quanta. This basis is the only one which

[15] *Aether u. Relativitätstheorie*, 7.
[16] "Maxwell's Influence," 71.

in the light of the present status of mathematical methods fits the postulate of general relativity.[17]

V

As a final topic in this essay on Einstein's theory of knowledge I consider his evaluation of the achievements of theoretical physics in attaining knowledge of reality. For this discussion we need to distinguish between empirical science and pure mathematics.

The universe of discourse for empirical science is the properties of things and processes known through sensory experience. For example, the relation between the lengths of perceptible rods that constitute a triangle is matter of fact for geometry as a branch of experimental physics. The concept of measurement of theoretical physics presupposes that an immediate repetition of a measurement will yield the same result. In actual practice, however, measurements are carried out with instruments made of practically rigid bodies, and results are only approximately reproducible. Thus the properties of bodily objects as found by perception lack complete consistency. A proposition which expresses a relation between sharply defined concepts admits only approximate confirmation by experience. In contrast, the propositions of mathematics have been credited with certainty. Although empiricists like John Stuart Mill have held mathematics to be empirical, there is wide acceptance to-day of the doctrine that mathematics is abstract. Einstein accepts the standpoint of Axiomatics, according to which the formal-logical content of mathematics is neatly separated from the factual or intuitive content. The formal-logical content is the object of pure mathematics, the factual content is a concrete interpretation of applied mathematics.

The axioms of mathematics exemplify Einstein's view that concepts are free creations of the human mind. The construction of a mathematical system occurs when propositions, more precisely propositional functions, are postulated to hold exactly for a set of objects. The objects of the system are realized in

[17] "Physik u. Realität," 344.

thought by postulates for conceptual relations between the objects. In so far as he acknowledges mathematical objects to be constructions, the theory of Einstein reminds one of Kant who held that objects of mathematics were constructed in pure intuition. In Kant, however, the creative activity of mind was limited by *a priori* forms of intuition. Mathematical thought was liberated by the invention of non-Euclidean geometries, and hence it is fitting that Einstein should endow thought with greater freedom for creation than Kant. Einstein is allied to Kant in that he recognizes spontaneity of thinking. In view of his emphasis on the distinction between thought and sense, Einstein's doctrine has elements in common with the Platonic conception of mathematical objects as exact forms that transcend sense. Einstein has said, "In so far as the propositions of mathematics refer to reality they are not certain and in so far as they are certain they do not refer to reality."[18] The certainty of mathematical axioms, more adequately, the precision with which they hold, is founded on the function of creating their objects.

Theoretical physics, when adequately developed for a field of physical processes, can be reduced to a set of principles which express functional relations between variables. The theory based on the principles further includes theorems which are derived by transformation from the principles. The certainty of the theory resides in the mathematical transformations of the deductive system.

Systems of physical theory were based initially on propositions which were refinements of generalizations from experience. For example, propositions which expressed positional relations of practically rigid bodies were taken as precise for Euclidean geometry. The transition from generalizations of empirical science to the principles of a deductive system is also exemplified by the creation of classical mechanics for material points. A principle of stationary action serves as a fundamental principle in this field. The mathematical physicist further may set up principles for any conceivable set of objects and unfold the logical implications of the principles. However, physical theories are constructed for the comprehension of experience,

[18] *Geometrie u. Erfahrung*, 3.

and therefore are subject to confirmation or disconfirmation, if only approximately, by experience. The mathematical physicist enjoys freedom to create whatsoever forms he wishes, but if he presumes to represent physical reality, he is subject to the control of experience.

Confirmation of an applied theory by perception is only approximate. The variables in a physical theory are interpreted by results of measurement which are never completely consistent. One reason for the inconsistency of measurements is that the establishment of conditions under which controlled experimentation is carried out requires a method of successive approximation. A standard measuring rod, for example, exemplifies unit distance only under conditions which are specified in terms of quantities that are themselves defined in terms of distance. The concept of distance, as defined to a given approximation, must be used in order to specify conditions under which it is precise to a higher approximation. As Einstein has emphasized, laws of classical physics are limiting cases of laws based on the theory of relativity or the quantum theory. Experimental apparatus is constructed in terms of approximate classical laws. Einstein has stated that Newtonian mechanics would continue to be a basis for physics. Bohr has taught that the interpretation of experiments requires the concepts of classical physics. If there should be created the unified theory for the physical world, which Einstein believes embodies the ideal of mathematical simplicity, this theory could only be confirmed by successive approximation.

Einstein's conception of physical theory is expressed in his criticism of quantum mechanics. This theory has given a relatively adequate account of the extra-nuclear structure of atoms in terms of concepts adapted from the classical mechanics of particles. The interpretation of quantum mechanics as given by Bohr limits the applicability of classical concepts to the elements of physical reality. Heisenberg's principle of indeterminacy expresses the limit of precision to which co-ordinates of position and momentum can be assigned simultaneously to a particle.

The interpretation of the formalism of quantum mechanics is based on the doctrine that in any investigation a line must be drawn between the object of observation and the measuring apparatus of the observer. The apparatus must be presupposed in an operation of measurement, and it falls outside the field of quantum mechanics during a given investigation.[19] If the behaviour of apparatus is considered in order to find the result of a measurement, classical physics is employed. The determination of position is with respect to a space-frame of reference, for example, a screen which is attached to a massive table rigidly attached to the earth. The employment of the screen for the definition of position is illustrated by the passage of an electron through a hole in the screen. During its passage through the hole the electron interacts with the screen and exchanges an uncontrollable quantity of momentum with the screen. The momentum acquired by the screen is absorbed by the frame of reference, presupposed in the experiment, and can not be used to calculate by the conservation law the change in momentum of the electron during the observation. After position is determined, the result is immediately reproducible, and therefore the value of the quantity has physical reality in conformity to the criterion of reality as formulated by Einstein, Podolsky, and Rosen. The result of a measurement of momentum is unpredictable, and therefore this quantity is without reality. The momentum of an electron could be found from its original momentum, and the change resulting from passage through a mobile screen, the momentum of which is determined before and after the passage. But a screen mobile with respect to the space-frame would lose its function for definition of position. Preparation of conditions under which position is defined excludes conditions under which momentum is defined, and vice versa. The experimental arrangements for the determination of conjugate quantities are mutually exclusive, and hence the state of a system is not describable in terms of simultaneous values of classically defined conjugate quantities. The state is represented by a wavefunction which satisfies Schrödinger's equation, whose characteristic values are the possible results of measurement and whose characteristic functions determine the probabilities of obtaining specific results. According to Bohr, the uncontrollable

[19] N. Bohr, *Physical Review*, Vol. 48, 696 (1935).

disturbance of the object by the instrument of observation is responsible for the use of statistical concepts for the description of atomic systems. The finite reaction of the measuring instruments on an object renders it impossible to take into account the momentum exchanged with separate parts of the apparatus and thus prevents us from drawing conclusions regarding the "course" of such processes, for example, to determine through which one of two slits in a diaphragm a particle passes on its way to a photographic plate. Bohr has declared that the essential property of atomic phenomena is the character of individuality which is completely foreign to classical physics. The limitation imposed upon the description of atomic processes is expressed by Dirac who says that the only object of theoretical physics is to calculate results that can be compared with experiment, and that it is quite unnecessary that any satisfying description of the whole course of the phenomena should be given.[20]

Einstein holds that quantum mechanics is limited to a statistical point of view.[21] On his view the wave-function does not describe the state of a single system; it refers rather to an ensemble of systems in the sense of statistical mechanics. If, except for certain special cases, the wave-function furnishes only statistical propositions for measurable quantities, the reason lies not only in the fact that the operation of measuring introduces unknown elements, but that the wave-function does not describe the state of a single system. What happens to a single system remains unclarified by this mode of consideration. Einstein declares that it is contrary to his scientific instinct to refrain from seeking a detailed mode of representation. He demands a theory that will represent the "course" of events, not merely probabilities of results of observation. Quantum mechanics expresses an element of truth, but it can not serve as starting point for a more adequate theory. Quantum mechanics must be derived as a limiting case of some future theory, just as electrostatics is deducible from electrodynamics, and thermodynamics from classical mechanics. Einstein has declared that he continues to believe in the possibility of constructing a model of reality.

[20] P. A. M. Dirac, *Quantum Mechanics,* 7 (1930).
[21] "Physik u. Realität," 341.

The preceding remark may serve to introduce a concluding summary of Einstein's theory of knowledge.

The postulates of a mathematical system implicitly define the conceptual relations of a set of objects which are thereby realized in thought. Theorems are derivable from the postulates by logical deductions which may be viewed as certain. Cognition of reality, however, originates in sensory experience, is tested by sensory experience, and shares the uncertainty of such experience. Cognition of physical reality occurs through the media of concepts which express properties of objects in a spatio-temporal environment. Theoretical physics represents reality by models, such as particles and continuous fields. A model of reality serves to order sense-impressions; the theory based upon it is confirmed by approximate agreement of logical consequences with sense-impressions. The concepts of theoretical physics need to be correlated with sense-impressions, but in the last analysis concepts are created by the spontaneity of thinking. Experience may suggest theories which operate with concepts which are intuitively related to experience, but for deeply lying objects the search for principles is guided by ideas of mathematical simplicity and generality. Methodical, intimate consideration of a problematic situation is the foundation of an intuition which gives insight into the order of reality. That the model of reality represents an order independent of experience is justified by the belief, founded on past successes, that nature embodies an ideal of mathematical simplicity. The pursuit of truth under the guidance of mathematical ideals is founded on the faith that a preestablished harmony between thought and reality will win for the human mind, after patient effort, an intuition of the depths of Reality.

VICTOR F. LENZEN

DEPARTMENT OF PHYSICS
UNIVERSITY OF CALIFORNIA
BERKELEY, CAL.

14

F. S. C. Northrop

EINSTEIN'S CONCEPTION OF SCIENCE

EINSTEIN'S CONCEPTION OF SCIENCE

ALBERT EINSTEIN is as remarkable for his conception of scientific method as he is for his achievements by means of that method. It might be supposed that these two talents would always go together. An examination, however, of statements upon scientific method by truly distinguished scientists indicates that this is far from being the case. Nor is the reason difficult to understand. The scientist who is making new discoveries must have his attention continuously upon the subject matter of his science. His methods are present, but he must have them so incorporated in his habits that he operates according to them without having to give any conscious attention to them. He is like the truly natural athlete, who performs spontaneously, but who often cannot teach others how he does it. Albert Einstein, however, is an exception to this frequently illustrated rule. He has given as much attention consciously and technically to the method of science as he has given to the theoretical foundations of physics to which he has applied scientific method.

Moreover, his analysis of scientific method has taken him beyond empirical logic into epistemology. In fact, his technical epoch-making contributions to theoretical physics owe their discovery and success in considerable part to the more careful attention which he has given, as compared with his predecessors, to the epistemological relation of the scientist as knower to the subject matter of physics as known. It happens, therefore, that to understand Albert Einstein's conception of scientific method is to have a very complete and precisely analyzed epistemological philosophy—an epistemological philosophy, moreover, which, while influenced by positivism on the one hand and ancient Greek and Kantian formal thinking on the other, departs nonetheless rather radically from both and steers a course of its own, checked at every point by actual methodological practices of scientists. The result is an epistemology which has fitted itself to an expert understanding and analysis of scientific method rather than an epistemology, such as Kantianism or positivism, which has come to science with certain epistemological premises and prescriptions and tried to fit scientific procedure to these prescriptions.

In this connection, Albert Einstein himself gives us very important advice. At the very beginning of a paper "On the Method of Theoretical Physics" he writes, "If you want to find out anything from the theoretical physicists about the methods they use, I advise you to stick closely to one principle: don't listen to their words, fix your attention on their deeds."[1] Obviously this is excellent advice, and, as we shall see, Einstein has followed it, illustrating all his statements about scientific method and epistemology by specific illustrations from technical scientific theories and the technical scientific methods which they entail in their formulation, discovery and verification.

Nonetheless, his words as thus stated might easily mislead one who has not read everything which Albert Einstein has written on scientific method. One might suppose that, when he talks about fixing one's attention on the deeds of physicists, he means by "deeds" the denotatively given operations and experiments performed in a laboratory; in other words, one might suppose that he means something identical with P. W. Bridgman's operationalism.

Actually, however, Albert Einstein's meaning is almost the reverse of this, as the very next sentence in the aforementioned paper clearly indicates: "To him who is a discoverer in this field, the products of his imagination appear so necessary and natural that he regards them, and would like to have them regarded by others, not as creations of thought but as given realities."

What Einstein means here is that the full meaning of verified mathematical physics is only given in part empirically in sense awareness or in denotatively given operations or experiments,

---

[1] P. 30 in a volume of his collected papers, entitled *The World As I See It* (Covici Friede, Publishers, New York, 1934).

and hence involves also meanings which only the imagination can envisage and which only deductively formulated, systematic, mathematical constructions, intellectually conceived rather than merely sensuously immediate, can clearly designate. But because these deductively formulated constructions, as the scientist becomes more at home with them, so capture his imagination as to appear both "necessary and natural," and also because their deductive consequences become empirically confirmed, the tendency of the scientist is to think that they are merely denotative, empirically "given realities," rather than empirically unobservable, purely imaginatively or intellectually known, theoretically designated factors, related in very complicated ways to the purely empirically given.

This counsel by Albert Einstein is something which philosophers especially need to take seriously. If one approaches epistemology by itself, simple answers to epistemological questions often seem very satisfactory. It is obviously much more simple to affirm that all meanings in science come down to purely empirically given, positivistically immediate, denotative particulars than to hold that the source of scientific meanings is much more complicated than this. Consequently, if some philosopher, especially one with a position in a physics department, holds this simple-minded theory and asserts that this is the scientific epistemology, he can fool most philosophers, even those who are experts in epistemology. There is only one cure for this, and this cure is an examination of the technical theories of the physical sciences, their technical concepts, the specific scientific methods used actually by the scientist who introduced the concepts, and the attendant specification of the epistemological relations joining the meanings of the concepts as specified by the deductively formulated theory to meanings denotatively exhibited in empirical experience. Albert Einstein has the competence to construct such an epistemology, and he happens to have directed his attention seriously and technically to this end.

It is valuable also that Albert Einstein is a theoretical rather than an experimental physicist. The experimental physicist's business is to perform denotatively given operations. This tends to cause him to have his attention upon, and consequently to emphasize, the purely empirical, positivistically immediate side of scientific theory. It tends also to cause him to want to reduce all other meanings in science to such purely empirical, positivistically immediate operational meanings. The theoretical physicist, on the other hand, tends to approach science from the standpoint of its basic theoretical problems, as these problems are defined either by the points of difference between major theories in different parts of the science or by points of difference between the deductions from a single systematic scientific theory and propositions incompatible with these deductions, which are nonetheless called for by the experimental evidence. Thus the experimental physicist who writes on the methodology, epistemology and theory of physics tends naturally to reduce imaginatively constructed, systematically and deductively formulated scientific meanings to positivistically immediate, purely denotatively given meanings. The theoretical physicist, on the other hand, tends to see that the problems of physics are only theoretically formulatable, since facts cannot contradict each other; only the theoretically prescribed conceptualizations of the facts can contradict one another.

Albert Einstein has seen that in scientific knowledge there are two components, the one given empirically with positivistic, denotative immediacy, the other given imaginatively and theoretically and of a character quite different from the empirically immediate. In the aforementioned paper Albert Einstein makes this point unequivocally clear. After telling us to watch what physicists do, he writes as follows: "Let us now cast an eye over the development of the theoretical system, paying special attention to the relations between the content of the theory and the totality of empirical fact. We are concerned with the eternal antithesis between the two inseparable components of our knowledge, the empirical and the rational. . . ." Upon this epistemological point Albert Einstein, notwithstanding all his other major departures from Kant, is a Kantian and a Greek empirical rationalist, rather than a Humean British positivistic empiricist. Albert Einstein, at a formative period in his intellectual life, did not study Immanual Kant's *Critique of Pure Reason* to no avail.

Furthermore, in the sentence immediately following the aforementioned quotation Einstein continues:

We reverence ancient Greece as the cradle of western science. Here for the first time the world witnessed the miracle of a logical system which proceeded from step to step with such precision that every one of its deduced propositions was absolutely indubitable—I refer to Euclid's geometry. This admirable triumph of reasoning gave the human intellect the necessary confidence in itself for its subsequent achievements. If Euclid failed to kindle your youthful enthusiasm, then you were not born to be a scientific thinker.[2]

There is, to be sure, the empirical, positivistically immediate, denotatively known component in scientific knowledge also. This Einstein immediately proceeds to designate:

But before mankind could be ripe for a science which takes in the whole of reality, a second fundamental truth was needed, which only became common property among philosophers with the advent of Kepler and Galileo. Pure logical thinking cannot yield us any knowledge of the empirical world; all knowledge of reality starts from experience and ends in it. Propositions arrived at by purely logical means are completely empty as regards reality. Because Galileo saw this, and particularly because he drummed it into the scientific world, he is the father of modern physics—indeed, of modern science altogether.

In short, there must be both the postulationally designated, deductively formulated theoretic component and the inductively given, denotative, empirical component in scientific knowledge. It might be thought from the last quotation, if nothing more by Einstein were read, that, because "knowledge of reality starts from experience and ends in it," what happens in between, as given theoretically and formulated deductively, reduces to the empirical component and hence adds to the conception of "reality" nothing of its own. The sentence, to the effect that "Propositions arrived at by purely logical means are completely empty as regards reality" might seem to suggest this. The point of the latter statement, however, is that logical implications are always carried through with expressions which contain variables; thus in themselves they designate nothing empirical. But logical deductions proceed from expressions containing variables which are postulates, or what Albert Einstein terms "axioms." And these axioms express a systematic relatedness. Consequently, when one finds empirically, by the method of Galileo, the inductive factors which function as material constants for the variables in the postulates of the deductive system, then to this inductively given material there is contributed a systematic relatedness which pure empiricism and induction alone do not exhibit. Thus the theoretically known systematic factor, between the experience with which scientific method begins and that with which it ends, contributes something of its own to what Einstein terms the scientific "knowledge of reality." Hence, Einstein concludes: "We have thus assigned to pure reason and experience their places in a theoretical system of physics. The structure of the system is the work of reason; the empirical contents and their mutual relations must find their representation in the conclusions of the theory."

Furthermore, Albert Einstein makes it clear that it is the rationalistic, deductively formulated, structural component which is the basic thing in mathematical physics and the empirical component which is derived. This was implicit in the last sentence just quoted, when it affirmed that "the empirical contents and their mutual relations must find their representation in the conclusions of the theory." They do not find their representation in the postulates or axiomatic basis of the deductively formulated theory.

Not only do the basic concepts and postulates of theoretical physics fail to reduce to purely nominalistic, denotatively given meanings, but they cannot be derived from the empirical, or what we have elsewhere[3] termed the aesthetic, component in scientific knowledge by any logical means whatever; neither the logical method of formal implication nor the more Aristotelian or Whiteheadian method of extensive abstraction. Upon these points Einstein is unequivocal.

He tells us that the deductively formulated theoretic component in scientific knowledge is a "free invention(s) of the human intellect. . . ." He adds,

Newton, the first creator of a comprehensive, workable system of theoretical physics, still believed that the basic concepts and laws of his system

[3] Chapters VIII and XII, *The Meeting of East and West* (Macmillan, New York, 1946).

could be derived from experience. This is no doubt the meaning of his saying, *hypotheses non fingo*. . . . the tremendous practical success of his doctrines may well have prevented him and the physicists of the eighteenth and nineteenth centuries from recognising the fictitious character of the foundations of his system. The natural philosophers of those days were, on the contrary, most of them possessed with the idea that the fundamental concepts and postulates of physics were not in the logical sense free inventions of the human mind but could be deduced from experience by 'abstraction'—that is to say by logical means. A clear recognition of the erroneousness of this notion really only came with the general theory of relativity, which showed that one could take account of a wider range of empirical facts, and that too in a more satisfactory and complete manner, on a foundation quite different from the Newtonian. But quite apart from the question of the superiority of one or the other, the fictitious character of fundamental principles is perfectly evident from the fact that we can point to two essentially different principles, both of which correspond with experience to a large extent; this proves at the same time that every attempt at a logical deduction of the basic concepts and postulates of mechanics from elementary experiences is doomed to failure.[4]

He adds that the "axiomatic basis of theoretical physics cannot be abstracted from experience but must be freely invented, . . . Experience may suggest the appropriate mathematical concepts, but they most certainly cannot be deduced from it."[5] In short, the method taking one from empirically given experience to the systematic factor in scientific knowledge designated by the postulates of deductively formulated scientific theory is not that of either extensive abstraction or formal implication.

But neither is it that of any explicitly formulatable scientific method grounded in probability rather than deductive certainty. It is precisely at this point, nothwithstanding his agreement with the positivists' emphasis upon empirical verification, that Albert Einstein, along with Max Planck, becomes so uneasy about positivism. The way from the empirical data to the postulates of deductively formulated physical science is a frightfully difficult one. Here, rather than anywhere else, the scientist's genius exhibits itself. The way is so difficult that no methods whatever must be barred; no sources of meaning whatever, imaginative, theoretical, of whatever kind, are to be excluded. It appears that nature covers up her basic secrets; she does not wear her heart upon her sleeve. Thus only by the freest play of the imagination, both the intuitive imagination and the non-intuitive, formal, theoretical imagination, can the basic concepts and postulates of natural science be discovered. In fact, Einstein writes, with respect to the discovery of "the principles which are to serve as the starting point . . ." of the theoretical physicist's deductive system, that "there is no method capable of being learnt and systematically applied so that it leads to the goal."[6]

In a paper on "The Problem of Space, Ether, and the Field of Physics," Albert Einstein adds that the "hypotheses with which it [theoretical physics] starts becomes steadily more abstract and remote from experience,"[7] the greater the number of empirical facts the logical deduction from the basic postulates includes. Consequently, the "theoretical scientist is compelled in an increasing degree to be guided by purely mathematical, formal considerations in his search for a theory, because the physical experience of the experimentor cannot lift him into the regions of highest abstraction. The predominantly inductive methods appropriate to the youth of science are giving place to tentative deduction."[8] Consequently, instead of hampering the theoretical physicist by epistemological prohibitions concerning the kind of meanings and their source permitted in his basic concepts, Albert Einstein writes that the "theorist who undertakes such a labour should not be carped at as 'fanciful'; on the contrary, he should be encouraged to give free reign to his fancy, for there is no other way to the goal." He adds: "This plea was needed . . .; it is the line of thought which has led from the special to the general theory of relativity and thence to its latest offshoot, the unitary field theory."[9]

But if Einstein's dictum that the "axiomatic basis of theoreti-

[6] *Ibid.*, 25.
[7] *Ibid.*, 91.
[8] *Ibid.*, 91-92.
[9] *Ibid.*, 92.

cal physics cannot be abstracted from experience but must be freely invented" entails the rejection on the one hand of the positivistic, purely empirical, Humean philosophy, which would reduce all scientific meanings to nominalistic particulars, and also, on the other hand, of the Aristotelian and Whiteheadian epistemology, which, while admitting universal or nontemporal invariant meanings, would nonetheless insist upon deriving them from empirical immediacy by the method of extensive abstraction, it equally rejects the Kantian epistemological thesis that the postulated, deductively formulated systematic relatedness of scientific knowledge is a categorical *a priori*. The more systematic relatedness of space and time in scientific knowledge is as tentative, even though not given purely empirically, as is the empirical content which may be observed and correlated with factors within the space-time relatedness. This is what Albert Einstein means when he speaks of the method of theoretical physics as the method of "tentative deduction."

There is, for Albert Einstein, as for Kant, spatio-temporal relatedness in scientific knowledge, which is not to be identified with sensed relatedness. But this systematic relatedness is not a universal and necessary presupposition of any possible empirical experience. It has to be discovered by a free play of the formal, mathematical, intellectual imagination, and it has to be tested by a long sequence of deductive implications, the resultant theorems of which are correlated with observable data. Thus, although the forms of space and time, or, to speak more accurately, the form of space-time, is *a priori* in the sense that it is not given empirically and must be brought to and combined with the local, diverse, contingent, inductive data located within it, nonetheless it is not *a priori* in the Kantian sense of being a universal and necessary form of any possible empirical experience whatever.

Nor is it *a priori* in the Kantian sense that it is brought to the Humean sensuous, contingent data of science by the epistemological knower. Thus Albert Einstein writes that it "cannot be justified . . . by the nature of the intellect. . . ."[20] Instead, it be-

---

[20] *Ibid.*, 33.

longs to and is the public physical relatedness of the public physical field of nature—in fact, it is that particular relatedness which exhibits itself as the gravitational field. Thus, in the epistemology of Albert Einstein, the structure of space-time is the structure of the scientific object of knowledge; it is not something which merely seems to belong to the object when its real basis supposedly is solely in the character of the scientist as knower.

This ultimate basis of space-time in the public, contingent, physical object of knowledge, rather than in the necessary constitution of the epistemological knower, follows from the tensor equation of gravitation in Einstein's general theory of relativity. Its ten potentials defining the gravitational field at the same time prescribe the metrical structure of space-time. Thus space-time has all the contingent character that the field strengths, determined by the contingent distribution of matter throughout nature, possess. Not even Kant would have referred these contingently distributed field strengths to the necessary constitution of the scientist as knower. The verification of the general theory of relativity indicates that there is no more justification for finding the basis of space-time in the knower.

Furthermore, this structure remains invariant for all possible physical objects which are chosen as the reference points for the empirical measurements of the astronomer or experimental physicist. Thus space-time escapes all relativity, not merely to frames of reference, but also to all the millions upon millions of human observers upon a single frame of reference such as the earth.

This means that, notwithstanding Albert Einstein's use of the word "fictitious" to designate the non-empirically given, theoretic component in scientific knowledge, this component is nonetheless not a Kantian or neo-Kantian or semantic logical positivist's subjective construct. The space-time of Einsteinian physics is the relatedness of the gravitational field of nature. It is fictitious in the sense that it is not a positivistically immediate, purely denotatively, inductively given datum; it is fictitious in the sense that it is discovered only by a free play of the scientist's imagination and not by the inductive method of extensive abstraction from empirical immediacy; it is fictitious also in the sense that it is only known positively by a leap of the imagination, a leap even of the formal, purely intellectual imagination; but it is *not* fictitious in the sense that the sole source of its being is in the knower or subject of knowledge. Instead, it constitutes and is literally the physical relatedness of the physical object of knowledge. It belongs to nature. It has its roots in nature; it is not restricted solely to the mind of man.

The foregoing consideration reminds us of the extent to which the Kantian epistemology is still working surreptitiously in the minds of even the contemporary logical positivists who suppose that they have repudiated Kant. The logical positivistic thesis that anything not given with Humean, inductive, purely empirical immediacy is a mere subjective logical construct is a hangover from the epistemology of Kant, a hangover, moreover, which the contemporary mathematical physics of Einstein has unequivocally repudiated.

This is why Albert Einstein is able to make another somewhat startling affirmation. It has been noted that he emphasizes the tentative character of the hypotheses embodied in the deductively formulated, indirectly verified theory of mathematical physics. So great, in fact, is the difference between nature as theoretically designated in its systematic relatedness by deductively formulated theory and nature as given with positivistic, empirical immediacy that Einstein affirms that neither the formal, logical relation of implication nor any probability or other formulation of induction can define the method by which the scientist goes from the empirical data to the basic postulates of scientific theory. The scientist has, by trial and error and the free play of his imagination, to hit upon the basic notions. Moreover, it has been noted that these basic notions receive their verification only through a long chain of deductive proofs of theorems which are correlated with the inductive data.

With time and new empirical information the traditional basic postulates have to be rejected and replaced by new ones.

Thus no theory in mathematical physics can be established as true for all time. Nor can the probability of the truth of any given theory be scientifically formulated. For there is neither an empirical frequency nor a theoretical *a priori* definition of all the possibles with respect to which any particular theory can function as a certain ratio in which the number of all the possibles is the denominator term. This was implicit in Albert Einstein's statement that there is no formulated method taking the scientist from the empirical data to the postulates of his deductively formulated theory.

Nonetheless, Einstein writes as follows: "If, then, it is true that this axiomatic basis of theoretical physics cannot be extracted from experience but must be freely invented, can we ever hope to find the right way? Nay more, has this right way any existence outside our illusions?"[11] There could hardly be a more unequivocal formulation of the query concerning whether the systematic spatio-temporal relatedness of nature, as specified in the postulates of the theory of mathematical physics, is a mere subjective construct.

Einstein's answer is unequivocal; he answers

without hesitation that there is, in my opinion, a right way, and that we are capable of finding it. Our experience hitherto justifies us in believing that nature is the realisation of the simplest conceivable mathematical ideas. I am convinced that we can discover by means of purely mathematical constructions the concepts and the laws connecting them with each other, which furnish the key to the understanding of natural phenomena. Experience may suggest the appropriate mathematical concepts, but they most certainly cannot be deduced from it. Experience remains, of course, the sole criterion of the physical utility of a mathematical construction. But the creative principle resides in mathematics. In a certain sense, therefore, I hold it true that pure thought can grasp reality, as the ancients dreamed.[12]

Nor is this mere faith or conjecture on Albert Einstein's part. For we have noted previously that it is an essential point in his general theory of relativity that the form of space-time is not something having its basis in a necessary form of the intellect

[11] *Ibid.*, 36.
[12] *Ibid.*, 36-37.

of the scientist as knower; instead, it is the relatedness of the gravitational potentials of the gravitational field. Thus it belongs to the object of scientific knowledge, as designated by the postulates of Einstein's general theory of relativity. When these postulates become verified through their deductive consequences, then nature as thus conceived—a gravitational field, with such and such potential distribution and such and such a space-time metric—is thereby confirmed as existing.

Albert Einstein supports this conclusion. For in the paragraph immediately succeeding the sentence last quoted he writes,

In order to justify this confidence ["that pure thought can grasp reality, as the ancients dreamed"], I am compelled to make use of a mathematical conception. The physical world is represented as a four-dimensional continuum. If I assume a Riemannian metric in it and ask what are the simplest laws which such a metric system can satisfy, I arrive at the relativist theory of gravitation in empty space. If in that space I assume a vector-field or an anti-symmetrical tensor-field which can be inferred from it, and ask what are the simplest laws which such a field can satisfy, I arrive at Clerk Maxwell's equations for empty space.[13]

These considerations indicate that if we are going to make scientific theory and scientific method our criterion of the epistemology of science, then the form of space-time belongs to physical nature, not to the knower. Thus Albert Einstein's contention that "pure thought can grasp reality, as the ancients dreamed" is justified.

Moreover, the scientific method by means of which this grasp is possible is evident. It is the method of postulation, with indirect verification by way of deduced consequences. There is nothing whatever in scientific method or in the relation of the scientist as knower to the subject matter he is trying to know which prevents the scientist from formulating postulationally the properties and systematic relatedness of the thing in itself, which is the subject matter. In fact, one of the outstanding accomplishments of the general theory of relativity is its scientific demonstration that, notwithstanding all the relativity of

[13] Ibid., 37.

reference frames and standpoints, inevitable in making specific measurements, science nonetheless arrives at a systematic conception of this subject matter which remains constant through all the relative standpoints.

Considerations such as these make it evident that science is much more than a weapon for utilitarian technology and prediction. It is also an instrument by means of which men are able to obtain systematic, deductively formulated, empirically verified conceptions of reality. Upon this point also Albert Einstein is explicit. He writes:

It is, of course, universally agreed that science has to establish connections between the facts of experience, of such a kind that we can predict further occurrences from those already experienced. Indeed, according to the opinion of many positivists the completest possible accomplishment of this task is the only end of science. I do not believe, however, that so elementary an ideal could do much to kindle the investigator's passion from which really great achievements have arisen. Behind the tireless efforts of the investigator there lurks a stronger, more mysterious drive: it is existence and reality that one wishes to comprehend. . . . When we strip [this] statement of its mystical elements we mean that we are seeking for the simplest possible system of thought which will bind together the observed facts. . . . The special aim which I have constantly kept before me is logical unification in the field of physics.[14]

In this connection it must be kept in mind, as has been previously noted, that this theoretically designated, logical unification is not a mere abstraction from purely empirical, positivistic immediacy, nor can it be logically deduced from this empirical immediacy. The postulated, deductively formulated, theoretically known component in scientific knowledge contributes something of its own. As Albert Einstein writes in his paper on "Clerk Maxwell's Influence on the Evolution of the Idea of Physical Reality," "the axiomatic sub-structure of physics" gives "our conception of the structure of reality. . . ."[15]

It may seem that Albert Einstein's conception of scientific procedure as "tentative deduction," which, because of the fallacy of affirming the consequent involved in its indirect method

[14] *Ibid.*, 137-138.
[15] *Ibid.*, 60.

of verification, prevents the achievement of scientific theories which are timelessly true, enforces the conception of such theory as a mere subjective construct and invalidates his conclusion that such theory designates the character and "the structure of reality." He is fully aware of the indirect method of verification, as a subsequent quotation from him will demonstrate. He knows that the scientifically verified conceptions of this structure change with the discovery of new empirical evidence and the investigations into the theoretical problems of physics by the theoretical physicists. But this means merely that our verified scientific theories give us more and more adequate conceptions of what the character and structure of reality are. It by no means follows from the tentative character of scientific theories that they are mere subjective constructs.

Furthermore, Albert Einstein points out that it is easy to exaggerate this tentativeness. Thus, in a paper entitled "Principles of Research" delivered before the Physical Society in Berlin, he writes:

The supreme task of the physicist is to arrive at those universal elementary laws from which the cosmos can be built up by pure deduction. There is no logical path to these laws; only intuition, resting on sympathetic understanding of experience, can reach them. In this methodological uncertainty, one might suppose that there were any number of possible systems of theoretical physics all with an equal amount to be said for them; and this opinion is no doubt correct, theoretically. But evolution has shown that at any given moment, out of all conceivable constructions, a single one has always proved itself absolutely superior to all the rest. Nobody who has really gone deeply into the matter will deny that in practice the world of phenomena uniquely determines the theoretical system, in spite of the fact that there is no logical bridge between phenomena and their theoretical principles; . . . Physicists often accuse epistemologists of not paying sufficient attention to this fact.[16]

The point here is that while Poincaré is undoubtedly right theoretically in his contention that no one knows all the possible theories of reality, and hence the uniqueness of any present theory can never be established, nevertheless, for all the possible theories which scientists are able to formulate in the light

---

[16] *Ibid.*, 22-23.

of mathematical and logical investigations into the possibles, it is actually the case that mathematical physicists, using the deductive method with its indirect mode of empirical verification, are able to show that, among the present possible theories, one is unique in its capacity to bring the widest possible range of empirical data under a single minimum set of assumptions. Moreover, it is not any subjective constructive power of the scientist which is the criterion of this uniqueness, but the correlation of the theory with the empirical data of nature. In short, the criterion of uniqueness is grounded in nature rather than in the subjective, constructive capacity of the knower of nature.

The manner in which the postulationally or axiomatically designated structure of nature is connected with the "wild buzzing confusion" of empirically given data, so that nature is found in itself to be a systematic unity, must now concern us. This connection becomes evident when one examines the method of mathematical physics as a whole. No one has stated the epistemological situation within which this method operates and to which it conforms more concisely than has Albert Einstein. In the first paragraph of his previously mentioned paper "On Clerk Maxwell's Influence" he writes:

The belief in an external world independent of the perceiving subject is the basis of all natural science. Since, however, sense perception only gives information of this external world or of 'physical reality' indirectly, we can only grasp the latter by speculative means. It follows from this that our notions of physical reality can never be final. We must always be ready to change these notions—that is to say, the axiomatic substructure of physics—in order to do justice to perceived facts in the most logically perfect way. Actually a glance at the development of physics shows that it has undergone far-reaching changes in the course of time.[17]

It will be worth our while to take up the sentences in the foregoing quotation one by one, bringing out the full content of their significance. The first sentence reads: "The belief in an external world independent of the perceiving subject is the basis of all natural science." The justification for this belief exhibits itself in Einstein's special theory of relativity.

[17] *Ibid.*, 60.

Albert Einstein has emphasized that the key idea in this theory is the thesis that the simultaneity of spatially separated events is not given empirically.[18] It is the case, however, as Alfred North Whitehead has emphasized, that we do immediately apprehend the simultaneity of spatially separated events. An explosion can be sensed beside one at the same time that one sees a distant flash in the sky. Clearly, these two events are separated spatially and they are sensed as occurring simultaneously. Why, then, does Einstein insist that the simultaneity of spatially separated events is not directly observed? The answer to this is that physicists want and require a simultaneity which is the same for all human beings at rest relative to each other on the same frame of reference.[19]

Immediately sensed simultaneity does not have this characteristic. If the observer is equidistant from two events he may sense them as simultaneous. Then any observer not equidistant from the two events will not sense them as simultaneous.

It is the required public simultaneity which is one of the elements going into the notion of the external world. In fact, the concept of the external world is the scientist's terminology for the distinction between publicly valid elements in scientific knowledge and purely private factors varying from one observer to another even on the same frame of reference. Thus Einstein's contention that belief in an external world is at the basis of science is not a dogmatic selection of one epistemological theory of physical science from many possible theories, but is something grounded in distinctions required by scientific evidence itself.

In this connection it may be noted also that Alfred North Whitehead's philosophy of physics, which affirms an immediately sensed meaning for the simultaneity of spatially separated events, is far nearer to positivism than is Albert Einstein's theory. Furthermore, Alfred North Whitehead's theory that all scientific concepts are derived from "the terminus of sense

[18] Albert Einstein, *The Theory of Relativity*, Fourth Edition (Methuen and Co., London, 1921), 21-24.
[19] See my "Whitehead's Philosophy of Science," in *The Philosophy of Alfred North Whitehead*, this *Library*, Vol. III, ch. 3.

awareness" by abstraction is much nearer to positivism than is the physics of Einstein, in which the theoretical concepts cannot be abstracted from or deduced from the empirical data.

Consider now Einstein's second sentence in the foregoing quotation: "Since, however, sense perception only gives information of this external world or of 'physical reality' indirectly, we can only grasp the latter by speculative means." The basis for this statement scientifically is in the method of hypothesis which deductively formulated scientific theory uses. But Albert Einstein realizes also that it follows epistemologically from Bishop Berkeley's analysis of the empirically given. Bishop Berkeley noted that all that is empirically given are sense qualities, that these are relative, private things, varying from person to person and hence relative to the mind that is apprehending them. Thus the physicist's concept of a physical object as something three-dimensional, possessing a back side which we do not sense, with right-angle corners constant through the varying sensed angles which we sense empirically is not guaranteed by positivistic, empirical observation. Even the notion of a common-sense object involves an imaginative leap by the method of hypothesis beyond pure fact. Not merely scientific objects such as electrons and electromagnetic fields, but also common-sense objects entail indirectly verified postulation.

Once this is noted, the shift of the logical positivists from the Berkeleyan sensationalism of Carnap's *Logischer Aufbau* to "physicalism" is seen to be a departure from positivism. The reason for this shift confirms the present analysis. The logical positivists wanted a scientific verification which gave objective, publicly valid meanings, not Berkeleyan solipsistic, private subjective meanings merely. But such objectivity is not given empirically; it is only given theoretically by postulation indirectly verified. This is what Einstein means when he says that "since sense perception only gives information of the external world or of 'physical reality' indirectly, we can only grasp the latter by speculative means."

His next sentence reads: "It follows from this that our notions of physical reality can never be final." The basis for this conclusion is that formal logic in scientific method runs not from the empirical data to the postulates of the deductively formulated theory but in the converse direction, from the postulates back through the theorems to the data. This means that, in scientific verification, the logic of verification is always committing the fallacy of affirming the consequent of the hypothetical syllogism. This does not entail that a theory thus verified is false. It means merely that it cannot be shown to be necessarily true. The fact that the theory is thus indirectly confirmed justifies its retention. The fact, however, that it is not related to empirical data necessarily forces one to hold it tentatively. But this is an asset rather than a liability; for otherwise we would be at a loss to explain how scientific, or even humanistic religious, theories can be empirically verified and yet shown later, with the advent of further empirical information and further theoretical investigation, to be inadequate and to require replacement by a different theory grounded in different postulates. Hence Albert Einstein's final two statements: "We must always be ready to change these notions—that is to say, the axiomatic sub-structure of physics—in order to do justice to perceived facts in the most logically perfect way. Actually a glance at the development of physics shows that it has undergone far-reaching changes in the course of time."

One additional element, often overlooked in scientific method, which Albert Einstein clearly recognizes, remains to be indicated in order to complete his conception of science. It has been noted that the basic concepts of deductively formulated scientific theory as conceived by him are neither abstracted from nor deduced from empirically given data. Consequently, they do not "reduce" to sentences about sense data, nor can they be derived from such sentences. In short, they are concepts of a kind fundamentally different from the nominalistic particulars which denote data given empirically.

This presents a problem so far as scientific verification is concerned. For, if the primitive concepts, in terms of which the deductively formulated scientific theory is constructed, gain their meanings by postulation, in terms of the formal properties of relations and other such logical constants, then the theorems deduced from the postulates of such theory must be concepts of the same character. An examination of scientific theory such as Maxwell's electromagnetic theory shows also that the concepts in the theorems refer no more to sense data than do the concepts in the postulates. They refer, instead, to numbers for wave lengths, etc. These are not sensuously qualitative things. But if this is the case, how, then, can concepts with such meanings, designating such empirically unobservable scientific structures and entities, be verified? For verification requires the relating of the theoretically designated to the positivistically and empirically immediate. This relation which must exist in scientific method remains, therefore, to be specified.

The foregoing considerations of this paper indicate that this relation, joining the theoretically designated factor in nature to the empirically given component, cannot be that of identity. What then, is the relation? In his paper "Considerations Concerning the Fundaments of Theoretical Physics" (*Science*, May 24, 1940), Albert Einstein answers this question as follows: "Science is the attempt to make the chaotic diversity of our sense experience correspond to a logically uniform system of thought. In this system single experiences must be correlated with the theoretic structure in such a way that the resulting co-ordination is unique and convincing." In other words, the relation between the theoretic component and the empirical component in scientific knowledge is the relation of correlation. Analysis of scientific method shows that this relation is a two-termed relation.[20]

The recognition of the presence of this relation in scientific method is the key to the understanding of Albert Einstein's conception of scientific method and scientific epistemology. Because the empirical component is joined to the theoretic component by correlation, one cannot get the latter from the former by either extensive abstraction or logical implication. For, in the two-termed relation of epistemic correlation, one term does not logically imply the other, nor is the theoretic term a mere ab-

---

[20] See the author's *The Meeting of East and West*, ch. XII, and *The Logic of the Sciences and the Humanities*, chs. VI-VIII (Macmillan, N.Y., 1947); also H. Margenau, in *The Monist*, XLII (1932), *Journal of the Philosophy of Science* (1934); and *Reviews of Modern Physics* (1941).

straction from the empirical term. And because the theoretic term cannot be derived from the empirical term, theoretic physics contributes something of its own to the scientific conception of nature and reality.

This means that the positivistic theory that all theoretical meanings derive from empirical meanings is invalid. Furthermore, the thesis that the theoretically designated knowledge gives us knowledge of the subject matter of science and of reality, rather than merely knowledge of a subjective construct projected by a neo-Kantian kind of knower, confirms the thesis that the thing in itself can be scientifically known and handled by scientific method. Thus ontology is again restored, as well as epistemology, to a genuine scientific and philosophical status.

Hence, although the positivists are wrong in their purely empirical theory of meaning in empirical science, they are right in their contention that philosophically valid propositions are scientifically verifiable propositions. The important thing is not where the meanings of scientific concepts come from, but that they be verified through their deductive consequences and attendant epistemic correlations with empirically given data, before anyone claims that they have philosophical validity as a correct designation of the nature of things.

The foregoing analysis of Einstein's conceptions of science shows that scientific concepts have two sources for their meanings: The one source is empirical. It gives concepts which are particulars, nominalistic in character. The other source is formal, mathematical and theoretical. It gives concepts which are universals, since they derive their meaning by postulation from postulates which are universal propositions.

It should be noted also that for Albert Einstein scientific method entails the validity of the principle of causality, not as conceived by Hume in terms of the hope that present sensed associations of sense data will repeat themselves, but in the sense of the mathematical physicist—the sense, namely, that with the empirical determination of the present state of a system, as defined by theoretical physics, the future state is logically implied. Albert Einstein tells us that he refused to accept certain ideas of his general theory of relativity for over a period of two years, because he thought they were incompatible with this theory of causality.[21] When this compatability did become evident to him, he went on with the investigation and publication of the general theory of relativity. Its type of causality is a theoretically given, indirectly verified causality, not a Humean empirical one. But this point is a special, more technical case of the general thesis that scientific knowledge involves a correlation of an empirically given component with a postulationally prescribed, systematic, theoretically designated component.

F. S. C. NORTHROP

DEPARTMENT OF PHILOSOPHY
YALE UNIVERSITY

[21] *Op. cit.*, 107.

15

E. A. Milne

GRAVITATION WITHOUT GENERAL RELATIVITY

GRAVITATION WITHOUT GENERAL RELATIVITY

G ENERAL relativity arose through the supposed impossibility of bringing gravitation within the scope of the Lorentz formulae of what has been called 'Special Relativity.' The Lorentz formulae are the expression of the equivalence of observers in uniform relative motion: an observer O, using Cartesian co-ordinates x, y, z and a time co-ordinate t, is enabled by the Lorentz formulae to infer the description of an event (x', y', z', t') (in his co-ordinates) which would be made by a second observer O' moving with some uniform velocity V relative to O. That is to say, O can calculate the values x', y', z', t' of the co-ordinates which would be attributed to the same event by O'. These formulae were originally obtained by Lorentz as the conditions that Maxwell's equations of the electro-magnetic field should take the same form for O' as for O. They were given a far more general derivation by Einstein, who showed that they could be deduced from the simple postulate that the speed of light was the same to O and O': that they were the linear transformation which made

$$c^2 t^2 - (x^2 + y^2 + z^2)$$

vanish when

$$c^2 t'^2 - (x'^2 + y'^2 + z'^2)$$

vanished. It is a consequence of these formulae that the so-called interval ds defined by

$$ds^2 = c^2 dt^2 - (dx^2 + dy^2 + dz^2)$$

is conserved by the transformation both in value and form, i.e.,

$$ds^2 = ds'^2,$$

where

$$ds'^2 = c^2 dt'^2 - (dx'^2 + dy'^2 + dz'_2).$$

The great success of these transformation-formulae as applied to the phenomena of electromagnetism made it all the more surprising that they appeared incapable of dealing similarly with gravitation. For example, a gravitational potential $\gamma m/r$ did not apparently transform into a gravitational potential $\gamma m/r'$ where r, r' were the distances of a material gravitating particle from O and O'. To remove this difficulty, Einstein abandoned the methods which had been so successful in the relativity of uniform motion. No longer insisting on the operational principle that only such symbols should be introduced into the theory as could be defined in terms of observations which could in principle be carried out, he introduced undefined co-ordinate systems, and required only that the value, but not necessarily the form, of the "interval" should be conserved. He allowed ds^2 to represent non-Euclidean spaces or space-times, and required that laws of nature should be describable in equivalent forms in *all* sets of co-ordinates; that is to say, he made *all* observers equivalent. Gravitation was then considered as the restriction defining the nature of space-time in the neighbourhood of gravitating matter.

But it is open to doubt whether the general principle of relativity, that all sets of co-ordinates will yield the same forms for laws of nature, i.e., that all observers are equivalent, should be expected to hold good in the universe at large. According to the views of Mach, gravitation, in particular, is a consequence of the general distribution of matter in the universe. If that be so, then only those observers who stand in the same relation to the whole distribution of matter in the universe would be expected to be equivalent, i.e., would find similar descriptions of the law of gravitation. Now the matter of the universe appears to be concentrated into galaxies, which are approximately homogeneously distributed and which are apparently receding from one another with velocities proportional to their distances from one another. Observers situated at the nuclei of the galaxies would be similarly related to the large-scale distribution of matter and motion in the universe, and might accordingly be expected to formulate similar accounts of the law of gravitation;

only such observers would be equivalent. If these observers are in fact equivalent observers, they can choose a scale of time so that they all appear to one another as in uniform relative motion. Since the Lorentz formulae are the expression of the equivalence of observers in uniform relative motion, they should, therefore, be applicable to descriptions of gravitation by observers at the nuclei of the external galaxies. The Law of Gravitation should, therefore, be capable of expression in Lorentz-invariant form by this restricted class of observers.

It should be noted that this mode of positing the equivalence of observers is more general, not less general, than the general principle of relativity. If the *general* principle of relativity holds good in the universe, in particular it will hold good for the transformation from the nucleus of one galaxy to the nucleus of any other; but our less restrictive principle could hold good without the general principle of relativity being necessarily true. In fact, the less restrictive principle here stated is scarcely an assumption at all; for in a rational universe, when the relation of one observer to the matter of the universe is identical with the relation of a second observer to the matter of the universe, there is no reason why their descriptions of laws of nature should not be identical.

The present article will describe some of the results of carrying out this programme, and some of the investigations suggested by it. But in executing a programme of this kind, it is desirable to begin as far back in physics as is reasonably possible. We do not, therefore, assume any of the results, or appeal to any of the results, of non-relativistic physics, but attempt to build up a physics from first principles. The intellectual climate of the present investigations is, therefore, different from that of contemporary physics. For example, we do not *assume* the Lorentz formulae, or derive them from a supposed physical principle of the constancy of the velocity of light to all observers in uniform relative motion. Instead, we show that they are essentially epistemological in content, expressing the necessary relations between the optical observations made by equivalent observers, without our assuming any properties of light. We attempt, in fact, to give to all the laws of nature covered by the investigation the character of *theorems*, deduced from the defining axioms.

In particular, we do not make the assumption that the "curvature of space" depends on the matter occupying it. We adopt the view that an observer can choose an arbitrary private space for the description of the phenomena presented to him in nature, together with an arbitrarily graduated clock. This position scarcely needs arguing. The observer merely makes a map of the events occurring in his world-wide *present*, and as he experiences the passage of time he makes a succession of such maps. We shall make little use of the notions of *space-time*, which is just as much an artificial construct as any chosen space, but which often obscures the physical content of the investigations in progress. Each map made by the observer is a mere correlation of the whole or part of the space he adopts, with the point events throughout the universe to which he assigns the same value of the time-co-ordinate *t*. For the purpose of this correlation, he can adopt Euclidean space if he chooses. The triple infinity of points in the whole or a portion of this Euclidean space can be brought into correlation with the events of any assigned *t*. Questions which then have to be answered arise as to the correlation between different observers' private spaces. But we attribute no physical properties to space itself.

Conditions of Equivalence of Observers

A primitive stage in the development of a physics is given when we endow every observer with a single measuring instrument, the clock. Since each observer is conscious of the passage of time at himself, he can correlate the occurrences of events at himself with the real numbers, and by a *clock*, in the first instance, we mean simply some such correlation. The clock is then arbitrarily graduated.

Consider two such observers *A* and *B*, each furnished with his own arbitrarily graduated clock, in any arbitrary type of a relative motion. Observer *A's* primitive type of observation consists in reading *B's* clock at the same instant as he reads his own. But to read a distant clock requires illumination. Let observer A provide his own illumination by striking a light. He can then note the reading of his clock when he first provides the illumination, say t_1, the reading of his clock (say t_3), when he first sees B's clock, and the reading of B's clock (say t_2') when first illuminated. It is *a priori* possible that t_3 might coincide with t_1, (it cannot precede it). We shall assume that this is not the case, and that t_3 is later than t_1. We can interpret this by saying that light takes a finite time to travel from A to B and back again. With a similar interpretation we can say that B has reflected the light at instant t_2' by B's clock, and that the reflected light has reached A at instant t_3 by A's clock.

Suppose this sequence of operations is repeated indefinitely often. Then A can construct the graph of t_2' as a function of t_1, and the graph of t_3 as a function of t_2'. Then it is possible for A to dictate to B a re-graduation of his (B's) clock so that after re-graduation, the new t_2' is the same function of t_1, as t_3 is of the new t_2'. If the relation of A to B is a symmetrical one, we can now say that A and B are provided with *congruent* clocks. In this way, for any B, it is possible to set up at B a clock congruent to A's arbitrarily graduated clock. All "transport" of clocks from A to a distant B is avoided, and we achieve in this way the setting up of a congruent clock at a distance. This procedure eventually obviates any need for the hypothetical transport of "rigid measuring rods," and so avoids all the difficulties of defining the latter expression. We now say that B is equivalent to A, and write $B \equiv A$.

The same observations, (but without need for B's clock-reading t_2'), permit the attribution by A of *co-ordinates* to B. Observer A assigns to the event of the reflection of light by B the co-ordinates (t, r), where

$$t = \tfrac{1}{2}\,(t_3 + t_1), \qquad\qquad r = \tfrac{1}{2}\,c\,(t_3 - t_1),$$

and c is an arbitrary number chosen by A. It is particularly to be noted that these assignments do not pre-suppose any equality of times of travel of light to and fro, though they lead to the inference of such equality. A can now attribute to B the instantaneous velocity $V = dr/dt$, and he finds also that c is the velocity he assigns to a light-signal—all by A's arbitrary clock.

Similarly B can complete his observations of A and assign co-ordinates to any event at A. More generally A and B can similarly assign co-ordinates to any event E in line with A and B.

If the observations of B by A are expressible by the formulae

$$t_2' = \theta_{12}(t_1), \qquad t_3 = \theta_{12}(t_2'), \tag{1}$$

then simple arguments show that, for any event E in line with A and B to which A, B respectively assign co-ordinates $(t\ r)$, $(t'\ r')$, we have

$$t' - r'/c = \theta_{12}(t - r/c) \qquad t' + r'/c = \theta_{12}^{-1}(t + r/c). \tag{2}$$

These are generalisations of the Lorentz-Einstein formulae, now made to refer to any relative motion of A and B, and to arbitrary but congruent clocks carried by A and B. They can be shown to reduce to the formulae of Lorentz-Einstein when we take the relative motion of B and A to be defined by

$$\theta_{12}(t) \equiv \alpha_{12}t,$$

in which case it can be shown that

$$\frac{V_{12}}{C} = \frac{\alpha_{12}^2 - 1}{\alpha_{12}^2 + 1}, \qquad \alpha_{12} = \left[\frac{1 + V_{12}/c}{1 - V_{12}/c}\right]^{1/2}, \tag{3}$$

where α_{12} is any constant and V_{12} is the constant relative velocity of B and A, as defined above.

The content of the Lorentz formulae is thus purely epistemological, and assumes no physics of a quantitative type. They express merely the self-consistency of the observations that A and B can make with arbitrarily-running but congruent clocks. These observations consist of the most elementary sense-data, namely those of visual perception. Moreover, any statement involving the co-ordinates (t, r) or $(t'\ r')$ can be immediately translated back into the observations from which the co-ordinates are assumed deduced. They do not involve the isolation of the concept of 'uniform time.'

To make further progress towards the isolation of the concept of 'uniform time' we consider a third observer C, in line with A and B, and suppose A has dictated to C regraduations of his (C's) clock which make C's clock congruent to A's. Then $B \equiv A$, $C \equiv A$. We require the condition that C's and B's clocks are now congruent, i.e., that $C \equiv B$. This condition is found to be of the nature of a restriction on C's motion relative to A, given B's motion relative to A. When this restriction is satisfied, we can consider a fourth collinear observer D, and find the condition that D is equivalent to A, B and C; and so on. A set of collinear observers who are all equivalent in pairs, i.e., who can be provided with congruent clocks, are said to form an *equivalence*. If, in the previous notation, $\theta_{pq}(t)$ is the *signal-function* connecting the equivalent observers A_p and A_q, so that, for a light-signal leaving A_p at time t by A_p's clock, reaching A_q at time t', by A_q's clock and returning to A_p at time t_3 by A_p's clock, we have

$$t_2' = \theta_{pq}(t_1), \; t_3 = \theta_{pq}(t_2')$$

then the condition that . . . A_p . . . A_q form an equivalence is that the signal functions are given by

$$\theta_{pq}(t) = \psi \alpha_{pq} \psi^{-1}(t), \tag{4}$$

where α_{pq} is a real number characteristic of the pair A_p, A_q and $\psi(t)$ is a monotonic increasing function characteristic of the whole equivalence and known as the generating function of the equivalence. Moreover

$$\alpha_{ps} = \alpha_{pq} \alpha_{qs}, \qquad \alpha_{qp} = \alpha_{pq}^{-1}. \tag{5}$$

These are the analytical conditions expressing the conditions that all the θ's commute in pairs,* $\theta_{pq} \theta_{rs}(t) = \theta_{rs} \theta_{pq}(t)$. The idea of an equivalence is readily extended to three dimensions; and once this has been done the appropriate generalisations of the transverse Lorentz formulae for any kind of relative motion can be obtained.

The main property of an equivalence is the re-graduation property: if all the clocks of an equivalence are regraduated from reading t to reading T, by a relation of the type $T = \chi(t)$ then the equivalence remains an equivalence. An equivalence is a definite kinematic entity, which has the property that all members of the equivalence can be given clocks which are congruent to one another, i.e., which in a well-defined sense "keep the same time." Essentially there is only one equivalence,

---

*We write $\theta_{pq}^{-1}(t) \equiv \theta_{qp}(t)$.

since any given equivalence may be transformed into any other given equivalence by a suitable regraduation of its clocks. In order, then, to set up a consistent system of time-keeping throughout the universe, we must find in the universe, or construct in the universe, an equivalence. The necessary circumstance that there is essentially only one equivalence corresponds in nature to the fact of the existence of only one universe. It is by no means necessary that there shall be a single "uniform" scale of time, and we shall see later that it is convenient to introduce *two* scales of time.

Another important property of an equivalence is that if ever two members of the equivalence coincide, then all the members of the equivalence coincide at the same instant. This instant I call the *natural origin of time*, for the equivalence. The most important example of an equivalence possessing an instant of coincidence for all its members, and thus a natural origin of time, is the *uniform relative motion* equivalence, in which the members all move with uniform but different relative velocities after parting company all at the same instant. This is given by the generating function $\psi(t) \equiv t$. The most important example of an equivalence not possessing an instant of coincidence is the *relatively stationary* equivalence, all of whose members are at relative rest. This is given by the generating function $\psi(t) \equiv t_o \log(t|t_o)$. These two equivalences are convertible, in accordance with the general theory: The regraduation which transforms the uniform motion equivalence into the relatively stationary equivalence is

$$\tau = t_0 \log(t/t_0) + t_0, \tag{6}$$

where t is the reading of any clock in the uniform motion equivalence, τ the reading of the same clock in the relatively stationary equivalence. It will be seen that $t = o$ corresponds to $\tau = -\infty$, so that the epoch corresponding to the event of coincidence in the t-equivalence is never reached however far we push the τ-equivalence backwards.

If consistent time-keeping is to be possible by observers situated at the nuclei of the external galaxies, then these galaxies must form an equivalence. We can then choose for the arbitrary graduations of their clocks that mode of graduation which makes each pair of galaxies in uniform relative motion. More generally, if the external galaxies themselves do not form an equivalence, we can construct a uniform motion equivalence and refer them to it. In either case the members of the equivalence will be referred to as the *fundamental particles* of the equivalence.

The question now arises, can we identify any one of the possible modes of graduation of the clocks of the equivalence with what is ordinarily understood as *physical time?* To solve this problem we need to leave the domain of mere kinematics, and to pass to that of dynamics. The essential step is, if possible, to deduce the equation of motion of an arbitrary free particle and compare it with the equation of motion of a free particle in Newtonian physics. Comparison should lead to the isolation of one mode of graduation of the clocks of an equivalence as that corresponding to Newtonian time.

The concept of a free particle is fundamental in Newtonian physics. By a *free* particle, in Newtonian physics, is meant a particle subject to no "external" force. To realise this freedom from external force, the particle must be thought of as removed to an indefinitely great distance from all gravitating matter. But in the universe as it actually is, it is impossible to consider a particle at an indefinitely great distance from all attracting matter, because we cannot even in imagination remove ourselves to an indefinitely great distance from all the extra-galactic nebulae: there are nebulae or galaxies everywhere, and however far we move from any one galaxy, we merely move into the neighbourhood of others. We must, therefore, modify the Newtonian concept of a free particle, replacing it by the concept of a particle at large in inter-galactic space. We require to calculate the acceleration of a particle moving through an arbitrary point at an arbitrary time with an arbitrary velocity, as reckoned by an observer and his clock situated at any fundamental particle of the system, i.e., situated at the centre of an arbitrary galaxy.

THE SUBSTRATUM

We have identified the motions of the galaxies with those of an equivalence, and we have arranged the graduations of the clocks of the fundamental observers so that these galaxies all appear in uniform relative motion, radially outwards from one another. That is, if O is an arbitrary fundamental observer, $\mathbf{P}$ the position-vector he assigns to an arbitrary galaxy at epoch t as reckoned by his ($O's$) clock, $\mathbf{V}$ its velocity by the same clock, then

$$\mathbf{P} = \mathbf{V}t \quad \text{or} \quad \mathbf{V} = \mathbf{P}/t, \tag{7}$$

t being reckoned from the natural zero of time for the system. But we have still to arrange the spatial distribution of the galaxies so that the relation of each pair is symmetrical, i.e., that each galaxy stands in the same relation to all the others. This arrangement is achieved by distributing the galaxies with density-distribution n per unit volume at time t, in the reckoning of the arbitrary fundamental observer O, where

$$n\,dx\,dy\,dz = \frac{Bt\,dx\,dy\,dz}{c^3(t^2 - \mathbf{P}^2/c^2)^2}. \tag{8}$$

Here B is an arbitrary multiplicative constant without real significance, and c, the arbitrary constant adopted by all observers in assigning distance co-ordinates, is identified with the velocity of light.

This density-distribution has many remarkable features. It is centrally symmetrical not only about the origin O, but also about any other member O' of itself when transformed by the Lorentz transformation from O to O'. Moreover it takes the same form about any member O' of itself taken as origin; that is to say, if (x',y',z') is the position at time t', in reckoning, of a typical galaxy, then the distribution appearing as (8) to O appears to O' as

$$n'\,dx'\,dy'\,dz' = \frac{Bt'\,dx'\,dy'\,dz'}{c^3(t'^2 - \mathbf{P}'^2/c^2)^2}. \tag{8'}$$

Thus although for any one origin the density increases outwards in all directions, the same holds good for any other particle, a member of the system, taken as origin. Each member, in its own view, is equally the centre of the rest. No member of the system is in a privileged position.

Locally the system is nearly homogeneous, but the density tends to infinity as $|\mathbf{P}| \to ct$. The system is wholly included within the sphere $r = ct$ centred at any arbitrary member of the system, in that member's private Euclidean space. The radius of this sphere is thus expanding with the speed of light. The sphere is itself a locus of singularities, each of which is the counterpart of the singularity of "creation," the initial singularity $t = o$, $r = o$. This sphere effectively prevents any intercourse between the interior of the sphere $r = ct$ and the exterior. No meaning attaches to any question about the space exterior to the sphere, since such space is completely screened from observation by the dense crowding of members of the system towards $r = ct$, in $O's$ description. Nevertheless, if an observer leaves the origin O and cruises in the interior with any speed not exceeding c, he always encounters regions of density smaller than that he left behind at O; he can never avoid the continuous process of density-dilution which accompanies the expansion. However fast he cruises, he is always in regions of local time later than the epoch at which he left O. Thus the singularities in density at the boundary are only apparent singularities.

The epochs of events witnessed by O as occurring on more and more distant nebulae are earlier and earlier in time, partly due to the time of transit of the light from the distant nebula, partly due to the Einstein slowing-down of the clock at the distant nebula occasioned by its rapid recession. Towards the apparent boundary $r = ct$, the local time t' of events now being witnessed by O tends to zero. An observer O' on such a fundamental particle, near $r = ct$ in $O's$ reckoning, would see himself just as much the centre of the whole system as O does. The actual locus $r = ct$ is for ever inaccessible.

It should be mentioned that the density-distribution (8) is preserved by the expansion-law (7) in the sense that the two together satisfy the equation of hydrodynamical continuity.

This model of the expanding universe of galaxies I shall call the *substratum*. It achieves in the private Euclidean space of each fundamental observer the objects for which Einstein developed his closed spherical space. Although it is finite in volume, in the measures of any chosen observer, it has all the properties of infinite space in that its boundary is forever inaccessible and its contents comprise an infinity of members. It is also homogeneous in the sense that each member stands in the same relation to the rest.

This description of the substratum holds good in the scale of time in which the galaxies or fundamental particles are receding from one another with uniform velocities. This choice of the scale of time, combined with the theory of equivalent time-keepers developed above, makes possible the application of the Lorentz formulae to the private Euclidean spaces of the various observers. It thus brings the theory of the expanding universe into line with other branches of physics, which use the Lorentz formulæ and adopt Euclidean private spaces. We see that there is no more need to require a curvature for space itself in the field of cosmology than in any other department of physics. The observer at the origin is fully entitled to select a private Euclidean space in which to describe phenomena, and when he concedes a similar right to every other equivalent observer and imposes the condition of the same world-view of each observer, he is inevitably led to the model of the substratum which we have discussed.

The present value of t, the present epoch reckoned from the natural origin of time, is obtained by applying the formulae $t = |\mathbf{P}|/|\mathbf{V}|$ to Hubble's data on the recession of the galaxies, as derived from the red-shifts in their spectra when interpreted as Doppler effects. The result is about $t = 2 \times 10^9$ years. This then is the age of the universe on the t-scale of time.

The Equation of Motion of a Free Particle

Having found, in the scale of time in which the fundamental particles are in uniform relative motion, a model for the substratum, we can take up again our enquiry as to the relation of this scale of time to that of Newtonian Physics. We require to deduce the equation of motion of a free particle in the presence of the substratum. A particle at position-vector $\mathbf{P}$, at epoch t, is projected with arbitrary velocity $\mathbf{V}$, (as reckoned by an arbitrary fundamental observer O) in the presence of the substratum. We wish to obtain the value of the acceleration vector $d\mathbf{V}/dt$ in terms of $\mathbf{P},\mathbf{V},t$.

Comparatively simple arguments based on the theory of the Lorentz transformation show that $d\mathbf{V}/dt$ must be of the form

$$\frac{d\mathbf{V}}{dt} = \frac{Y}{X}(\mathbf{P} - \mathbf{V}t)G(\xi), \qquad (9)$$

where $X = t^2 - \mathbf{P}^2/c^2$, $Y = 1 - \mathbf{V}^2/c^2$, $Z = t - \mathbf{P}.\mathbf{V}/c^2$, $\xi = Z^2/XY$, and $G(\xi)$ is some function of ξ still to be determined. The dimensionless number ξ is an invariant, taking the same value for all fundamental observers. The equation (9) preserves its form under a Lorentz transformation from O to any other fundamental observer.

Before we discuss the determination of $G(\xi)$, an inference of importance can be made from (9). We see that the acceleration of a free particle vanishes when $\mathbf{V} = \mathbf{P}/t$. Thus the fundamental particles, hitherto considered as moving *kinematically* according to this law, may be now considered as *free* particles. The substratum therefore constitutes a *dynamical* system. This could also have been seen from the circumstance that each fundamental particle is central in the field of the remainder, and if it is at local rest at any instant it will remain at local rest.

In order to determine the function $G(\xi)$ we have to introduce the negative consideration that the substratum is of hydrodynamical character, with a unique velocity at every point, and not a gas-like statistical system, with a velocity-distribution in the neighbourhood of every point. Rather complicated analysis, which cannot be reproduced here, results in the evaluation of $G(\xi)$ in the general case of a statistical system and then the interpretation of the expression for $G(\xi)$ as containing a term depending only on the substratum. The arguments consist essentially in determining the general distribution law of a statistical system and then ensuring that the accelerations to which it gives rise are compatible with the relation expressed by Boltzmann's equation. The function $G(\xi)$ for a pure substratum is then found to be

$$G(\xi) \equiv -1. \qquad (10)$$

The equation of motion of a free particle is thus found to be

$$\frac{d\mathbf{V}}{dt} = -\frac{Y}{X}(\mathbf{P} - \mathbf{V}t).\tag{11}$$

This can be shown to be equivalent to the pair of equations

$$\frac{1}{Y^{1/2}}\frac{d}{dt}\left(\frac{\mathbf{V}}{Y^{1/2}}\right) = -\frac{1}{X}\left(\mathbf{P} - \mathbf{V}\frac{Z}{Y}\right),\tag{12}$$

$$\frac{1}{Y^{1/2}}\frac{d}{dt}\left(\frac{c}{Y^{1/2}}\right) = -\frac{1}{X}\left(ct - c\frac{Z}{Y}\right),\tag{12'}$$

whose form, since $(\mathbf{P}, ct)$ and $(\mathbf{V}/Y^{1/2}, c/Y^{1/2})$ are 4-vectors and $Z/Y^{1/2}$ is an invariant, is obviously conserved under a Lorentz transformation from one fundamental observer to any other.

Equation (11) is not of Newtonian form. It will be found to have as an integral

$$\xi^{1/2} = \text{const.}\tag{13}$$

Further, if for a *non-free* particle we define an external force $(\mathbf{F}, F_t)$ by the equations

$$\frac{1}{Y^{1/2}}\frac{d}{dt}\left(m\xi^{1/2}\frac{\mathbf{V}}{Y^{1/2}}\right) = -\frac{m\xi^{1/2}}{X}\left(\mathbf{P} - \mathbf{V}\frac{Z}{Y}\right) + \mathbf{F}\tag{14}$$

$$\frac{1}{Y^{1/2}}\frac{d}{dt}\left(m\xi^{1/2}\frac{c}{Y^{1/2}}\right) = -\frac{m\xi^{1/2}}{X}\left(ct - c\frac{Z}{Y}\right) + F_t,\tag{14'}$$

and define the rate of performance of work by $(\mathbf{F}, F_t)$ in shifting the particle relative to its immediate cosmic environment by the relation

$$\mathbf{F}\cdot\left(\frac{\mathbf{V}}{Y^{1/2}} - \mathbf{P}\frac{Y^{1/2}}{Z}\right) - F_t\left(\frac{c}{Y^{1/2}} - ct\frac{Y^{1/2}}{Z}\right) = \frac{1}{Y^{1/2}}\frac{dW}{dt},\tag{15}$$

we are led to

$$\frac{dW}{dt} = \frac{d}{dt}(mc^2\xi^{1/2}).\tag{16}$$

These relations result in our identifying $m\xi^{1/2}$ as the *mass* M of a particle of rest mass m, and $mc^2\xi^{1/2}$ as its energy E, whence the relation

$$E = Mc^2, \tag{17}$$

originally due to Einstein. Since the invariant $\xi^{1/2}$ reduces to unity for a particle for which $\mathbf{V} = \mathbf{P}/t$ we see that all fundamental particles have the same mass. Moreover when we take as origin the fundamental observer O in the immediate neighbourhood of the particle in question, we calculate $\xi^{1/2}$ by putting $P = o$, when we get

$$E = |mc^2\xi^{1/2}|_{\mathbf{P}=0} = \frac{mc^2}{(1 - V^2/c^2)^{1/2}}, \tag{18}$$

also in agreement with Einstein. But now V is the velocity of the particle relative to the fundamental observer it is passing, i.e., its velocity relative to the local standard of rest in the substratum. Moreover the energy E of a moving particle is in this dynamics an invariant, the same for all fundamental observers, and not, as in Einstein's dynamics, the fourth component of a 4-vector. A consequence of this dynamics is that we must not attribute to the distant fast-receding galaxies vast stores of kinetic energy; all have precisely the same energy, m_0c^2 where m_0 is the rest-mass of a fundamental particle.

INTERPRETATION OF THE EQUATION OF MOTION OF A FREE PARTICLE

The equation of motion (11) gives an acceleration directed inwards to the apparent centre of the substratum $\mathbf{V}t$ in the frame in which the free particle is at rest. We can compare this acceleration with the acceleration calculated on Newtonian principles for a particle in the presence of the substratum. The acceleration near the observer, in the frame in which the particle is momentarily at rest, is by (11)

$$-\frac{r}{t^2} \tag{19}$$

where we have put r temporarily for $|\mathbf{P}|$. Now the particle-density of the substratum near the observer, as given by (8) is B/c^3t^3. Hence if m_0 is the mass of a fundamental particle, the mass enclosed in a sphere of radius r is $\frac{6}{4}\pi r^3 m_0 B/c^3t^3$, and the Newtonian gravitational acceleration due to this is

$$- \gamma \frac{\frac{4}{3}\pi r^3 m_0 B}{c^3 t^3} \cdot \frac{1}{r^2} \, . \tag{20}$$

Equating (19) and (20), we get

$$\gamma = \frac{c^3 t}{M_0}, \tag{21}$$

where

$$M_0 = \tfrac{4}{3}\pi m_0 B = \tfrac{4}{3}\pi (ct)^3 \frac{m_0 B}{c^3 t^3} \, . \tag{22}$$

Thus M_0 is the mass that would just fill the volume of the substratum $\frac{4}{3}\pi(ct)^3$ with matter of density equal to the density at the origin. In the t-scale, then, the Newtonian 'constant' of gravitation varies secularly with the epoch t. Its present value inserted in (21) gives

$$M_0 = \frac{(3 \times 10^{10})^3 \times 2 \times 10^9 \times 3.16 \times 10^8}{6.66 \times 10^{-8}} = 2.6 \times 10^{55} \text{ grams.}$$

We can use (21) also to calculate the mean space-density ϱ_0 near ourselves, for $\varrho_0 = m_0 B / c^3 t^3 = M_0 / \pi c^3 t^3$, giving on eliminating M_0,

$$\rho_0 = \frac{1}{\frac{4}{3}\pi\gamma t^2} = 0.9 \times 10^{-27} \text{ gram cm.}^{-3}$$

Quite a different interpretation of (10) is obtained by transforming the scale of time. For distances small compared with the radius ct of the substratum and for velocities small compared with c, the equation of motion (11) may be written

$$\frac{d\mathbf{V}}{dt} = - \frac{\mathbf{P} - \mathbf{V}t}{t^2},$$

or

$$\frac{d}{dt}\left(\mathbf{V} - \frac{\mathbf{P}}{t}\right) = 0. \tag{23}$$

But $\mathbf{V} - \mathbf{P}/t$ is the velocity of the free particle relative to the fundamental particle in its immediate neighbourhood, which has velocity $\mathbf{P}/t$ relative to O. The last equation accordingly states that the velocity of a free particle relative to its immediate cosmic environment remains constant. This resembles the Newtonian First Law of Motion, which states that the velocity of a particle in free space remains constant, and it suggests that the nuclei of the galaxies, here treated as in motion, are the fundamental inertial frames of Newtonian physics. Einstein and Infeld have pointed out the difficulty of defining an inertial frame, or Galilean frame of reference, in customary physics. Our analysis has at several points suggested that it is the nuclei of the galaxies which define local standards of rest and inertial frames.

We seek to transform (23) into the actual Newtonian equation of motion of a free particle, by re-graduating all the clocks of the equivalence so as to reduce the equivalence to relative rest. It was mentioned earlier that the required re-graduation is

$$\tau = t_0 \log (t/t_0) + t_0, \tag{24}$$

or

$$\frac{d\tau}{t_0} = \frac{dt}{t}. \tag{24'}$$

Co-ordinates r, t of a distant particle in t-measure will now be replaced by co-ordinates λ, τ as determined from the same observations made with clocks reading τ. Thus we have, using the earlier notation,

$$r = \tfrac{1}{2}c(t_3 - t_1), \qquad t = \tfrac{1}{2}(t_3 + t_1)$$
$$\lambda = \tfrac{1}{2}c(\tau_3 - \tau_1), \qquad \tau = \tfrac{1}{2}(\tau_3 + \tau_1)$$

where τ_3, τ_1, being actual clock-readings, are connected with t_3 and t_1 by

$$\tau_3 = t_0 \log (t_3/t_0) + t_0, \qquad \tau_1 = t_0 \log (t_1/t_0 + t_0.$$

Elimination of the signal times t_1, t_3, τ_1, τ_3, then gives

$$t = t_0 e^{(\tau - t_0)/t_0} \cosh (\lambda/ct_0). \tag{25}$$

The velocity-law for a fundamental particle, $dr/dt = r/t$, gives at once

$$r = ct_0 e^{(\tau - t_0)/t_0} \sinh (\lambda/ct_0). \tag{26}$$

so that the fundamental particles now appear at rest. For

near-by events, (25) and (26) yield approximately

$$\frac{d\lambda}{d\tau} = 0$$

so that

$$r = (t/t_0)\lambda,$$

This one can write as

$$V = \frac{dr}{dt} = \frac{\lambda}{t_0} + \frac{t}{t_0}\frac{d\lambda}{dt} = \frac{r}{t} + \frac{d\lambda}{d\tau} \cdot$$

$$\mathbf{v} = \frac{d\lambda}{d\tau} = \mathbf{V} - \frac{\mathbf{P}}{t},$$

and so, in terms of τ-measure, the equation of motion (23) reduces approximately to

$$\frac{d\mathbf{v}}{d\tau} = 0. \qquad (27)$$

This is the Newton-Galileo equation of motion of a free particle in empty space. The carrying through of the exact transformation (25), (26), applied to the exact equation of motion (11) shows that the τ-velocity in the now-stationary substratum remains constant.

The conclusion from this investigation is that, in Newtonian physics, the independent time-variable is τ, not t. The epoch co-ordinate τ of any event on the τ-scale can be shown to be independent of the observer measuring it, and so in the τ-scale there is a world-wide simultaneity. There is also a public space, in τ-measure, of hyperbolic character, extending to infinity, and in this space the non-stationary galaxies or fundamental particles are uniformly distributed. Instead of an expanding universe of galaxies, of finite age t and finite volume, distributed with apparently increasing density in all directions, we have a stationary universe, of history extending backwards to $\tau = -\infty$, of infinite volume and strictly homogeneous. There are merely two different descriptions of the same physical entity. The world-wide simultaneity of epochs τ is of course connected with the circumstance that in the τ-description all the fundamental particles are at relative rest.

Since the galaxies show an observed red-shift in their spectra, the frequency of a light-wave must be constant in t-measure. For in t-measure, the members of the substratum are receding, and the red-shift is then the usual Doppler effect. In τ-measure there is no Doppler effect, since the members of the substratum are relatively stationary, but the frequency of the comparison atoms increases secularly with the epoch, and hence the frequency of light emitted by distant nebulae, long ago, is by comparison slower.

The Gravitational Potential

It was stated earlier that in order to derive the equation of motion of a free particle in the presence of the substratum, we had to introduce the negative consideration that the substratum is not a statistical system but is of hydrodynamical character. A positive result of great value emerges however from the discussion of statistical systems: not only is the function $G(\xi)$ evaluated as identically -1 for a substratum, but also this function is evaluated for a system containing point-singularities, and the term corresponding to a point singularity suggests the Lorentz-invariant form for the elementary gravitational potential; the gravitational mass appears in the form of a constant of integration. The interpretation of the analysis, details of which are here omitted, is that the potential energy X of two point-masses m_1, m_2 located at points of position-vectors $\mathbf{P}_1$ and $\mathbf{P}_2$ with respect to an arbitrary fundamental observer O, a member of the substratum, is given by

$$\chi = - \frac{m_1 m_2 c^2}{M_0} \frac{X_{12}}{[X_{12}^2 - X_1 X_2]^{1/2}} \tag{28}$$

where $\qquad X_1 = t_1^2 - \mathbf{P}_1^2/c^2, \qquad X_2 = t_2^2 - \mathbf{P}_2^2/c^2,$
$$X_{12} = t_1 t_2 - \mathbf{P}_1.\mathbf{P}_2/c^2,$$

and t_1, t_2 refer to epochs at the respective particles. The values of X_1, X_2, X_{12} are invariant, the same for all observers O in the substratum, and the potential energy is therefore invariant for Lorentz transformations from any fundamental observer O to any other fundamental observer O'.

To see the physical meaning of (28), take the observer O to be at the fundamental particle which coincides with one of the particles, say m_2. Then in (28) we must take $\mathbf{P}_2 = o$, and accordingly $X_{12} = t_1 t_2$, $X_2 = t_2^2$, $X_{12}^2 - X_1 X_2 = t_2^2 \mathbf{P}_1^2 / c^2$. Then

$$\chi = - m_1 m_2 \frac{c^3 t_1}{M_0} \frac{1}{|\mathbf{P}_1|}. \tag{29}$$

But by (21), $c^3 t_1 / M_0$ is just γ_1, the value of the Newtonian 'constant' of gravitation at the epoch t_1 at the distant particle m_1. Thus (28) reduces to the elementary Newtonian potential energy of m_1, due to m_2 at the origin, namely $-\gamma_1 m_1 m_2 /|\mathbf{P}_1|$. It is particularly to be noted that it is independent explicitly of the epoch at m_2 when m_2 is taken as origin; and therefore without selecting a convention of simultaneity connecting t_2 and t_1 in (28), the formula for X is adequate to determine the orbit of a particle m_1 in the vicinity of a massive fundamental particle of mass m_2.

It has been shown by the present writer, in work in the course of publication,* that formula (29) introduced into the t-equations of motion of a particle m_1 moving in the vicinity of a massive fundamental particle yields orbits of spiral type, and leads eventually to a theory of the spiral nature of external galaxies. The spiral arms are such a well-marked characteristic of "late-type" galaxies that a gravitational explanation of them is urgently demanded. Though attempts have been made to explain the spiral character on Newtonian lines, it cannot be said that they have had a marked degree of success, and the way is therefore open for such a fundamental revision of the basis of gravitational theory as is implied by our conclusion that the so-called 'constant' of gravitation varies secularly with the epoch. It was to be expected that the present account of gravitation, which takes its origin in the grand phenomenon of the expanding universe of galaxies, should have something to contribute towards the explanation of the spiral character of the resolved galaxies. The

---

* Since the original writing of this essay published in *Monthly Notices* of the Royal Astronomical Society, 106, 180 (1946) and *ibid.*, 108, 309 (1948); also *Astrophysical Journal*, 106, 137 (1947).

general relativity theory of gravitation, making as it does only minute modifications in the Newtonian law, makes no contribution to this end.

Transformation of the scale of time from t to τ throws further light on the nature of the elementary gravitational potential given in Lorentz-invariant form by (28) or (29). Taking the origin again for simplicity at m_2, and substituting from (25) and (26) for the co-ordinates (t_1, P_1) of the event considered at the particle m_1, the potential energy (29) comes out to be

$$-\frac{m_1 m_2 c^2}{M_0} \frac{1}{\tanh(\lambda/ct_0)}, \tag{30}$$

which for distances λ not comparable with ct_0 reduces very closely to

$$-\frac{m_1 m_2 \gamma_0}{\lambda}. \tag{30'}$$

γ_0 being the value of the 'constant' of gravitation at the fixed epoch t_0. It will be seen that (30) contains no longer any reference to the epoch τ_1 at m_1; and it is readily shown that the more general formula (28), when transformed to τ-measure, contains no reference to either of the epochs τ_1 or τ_2.

To make the τ- and t-clocks agree at the present moment in rate, t_0 must be taken to be the present value of t, and γ_0 becomes the present value of the 'constant' of gravitation. But this must not be allowed to obscure the fact that the 'constant' of gravitation is secularly increasing, at the rate of one part in 2×10^9 per year, on the present theory of gravitation. Apart from this the τ-equations of motion reduce to the Newtonian equations to a first approximation.

It may be asked whether the present theory of gravitation accounts for those small effects like the motion of perihelion of a planet and the deflection of light by the sun whose experimental verification is claimed as triumphs for the general relativity theory of gravitation. The answer to this question is not yet known, for the sun is not at the nucleus of our galaxy, and the present theory as so far developed does not necessarily apply to the calculation of orbits about a centre of gravitational force which is not a fundamental particle. Tentative recent investigations by A. G. Walker in this direction show that the precise answers to the question of the so-called 'crucial phenomena' depend upon the exact way in which the gravitational potential (28) is introduced into the equation of motion. In Newtonian dynamics, the 'external force' acting on a particle is derived by taking the gradient of the potential; but in our t-dynamics, this gradient requires to be corrected by small terms depending on the variation of mass with velocity. The present writer's calculation of these small terms is not wholly accepted by A. G. Walker, who has proposed in unpublished work modifications which are capable of agreeing with the effects predicted by general relativity. But Walker has found as yet no unique way of fixing these small terms, and the whole question must be considered as *sub judice*.

Nevertheless, the present writer does not attach an importance to these small terms comparable with the importance of describing the main Newtonian phenomena within the scope of the Lorentz formulae and of transformations from one equivalent observer to another. Moreover, the present theory, with its dependence at each stage on the age of the universe reckoned from the natural zero of time can give an account of gravitation over periods of time comparable with the age of the universe which is beyond the scope of Newtonian gravitation.

Recapitulation

The present theory of gravitation without general relativity makes its first departure from Einstein's theory by not regarding all systems of co-ordinates, i.e., all observers, as equivalent. Since any observer is conscious of the passage of time at himself, a transformation of co-ordinates involving inter-connections between time and space co-ordinates means really a change of observer, and it is far from clear that all observers in the universe, whatever their motion, should be equivalent as regards the law of gravitation. Instead, the present theory imposes equivalence only on a limited class of observers, namely those associated with the nuclei of the galaxies, or fundamental observers, as they are here called. For only such observers can stand in the same general relation to the distribution of matter and motion in the universe at large, and so be equivalent.

Its second departure from Einstein's theory is that it regards the choice of a space as arbitrary for any observer. He is fully entitled to choose a private Euclidean space for the description and location of phenomena he observes. The object of relativity is then achieved by correlating the spaces and times used by different observers.

Its third departure from Einstein's theory is its denial of any natural measure of time which may be called 'proper time.' Instead, it regards the scale of time as at the observers' choice in the first instance. It then proceeds to find the conditions relating different observers' measures of time in order for them to be consistent with one another, i.e., in order that a meaning can be attached to saying that *congruent* clocks can be constructed at different observers. For simplicity, and because it envolves no *a priori* constants, the different *equivalent* observers then graduate their clocks so as to describe one another as in *uniform relative motion*, this corresponding to the generating function $\psi(t) \equiv t$ of the associated equivalence. This mode of time-keeping is called *kinematic* time t. The Lorentz formulae are then available for correlating the descriptions of events by the different equivalent observers.

These equivalent observers then set about describing one another, and the result is a model of the universe of receding galaxies constructed in the private Euclidean space and kinematic time used by any arbitrary member of the class. This model, though occupying a finite portion of Euclidean space bounded by an expanding sphere, describes an essentially homogeneous universe in expansion, with the same properties, at the same epoch, at every point. It involves a singularity, which one may call creation, at the natural origin of time; but like a Delphic oracle, it refuses to give answers as to the state of affairs at, or before, the epoch of creation. It contains an infinity of members, distributed with finite density at every accessible point, the singularity in density at creation re-appearing at the inaccessible frontier of the expanding sphere. It provides a natural class of frames of reference, or inertial frames, each at local rest, one being associated with each galactic nucleus or fundamental particle. In view of the equivalence of these frames of reference, laws of nature should be described in identical ways by the fundamental observers using them. This finite expanding sphere has many of the properties of infinite space, and it achieves the objects for which Einstein developed his spherical space as a model for the universe. The use of the Lorentz formulae in constructing this model involves no loss of generality. For it is always open to equivalent observers to regard themselves as in uniform relative motion, and for each of them to adopt a private Euclidean space.

In the presence of this model, or *substratum* as it may be called, two principal laws of nature are deduced: the law of motion of a free particle, arbitrarily projected, and the law of gravitational attraction between a pair of massive particles; and an associated dynamics has been constructed. This dynamics has the distinguishing feature that in it, *energy* is an invariant, therefore, the same for all fundamental observers, and not, as in Einstein's dynamics, the time-component of a 4-vector. A consequence is that the receding galaxies are not to be regarded as stores of kinetic energy.

The law of motion of a free particle can be compared with the Newtonian attraction on a free particle near the observer in a locally homogeneous universe; this results in the isolation of a formula for the Newtonian constant of gravitation which represents it as dependent on the velocity of light, the epoch, and a basic mass-constant, the mass of the apparent homogeneous universe. Or it may be compared with the Newtonian equation of a free particle in empty space; this shows that the non-Newtonian t-equation of motion transforms into the Newtonian law of zero acceleration when all clocks previously reading t are regraduated to read τ, which apart from a normalisation constant is substantially the logarithm of t. This transforms the t-dynamics into something akin to classical dynamics, and at the same time transforms the expanding substratum into a relatively stationary, infinitely extending, homogeneous universe devoid of singularity, for which the most convenient space to use is a public hyperbolic space. It must be remembered that the two modes of description, in t- and τ-time respectively, relate to the same entity, the substratum.

The law of gravitational attraction between two point masses is an expression in Lorentz-invariant form of the Newtonian elementary potential, with a Newtonian 'constant' of gravitation varying secularly with epoch. When converted to τ-measure, it yields an elementary potential which reduces to the Newtonian form at distances not comparable with the radius of the universe, and with a 'constant' of gravitation now *constant*, but involving the normalisation constant of the time-scale. This formulation of the law of gravitation is capable, in the writer's opinion, of accounting for the spiral character of resolved galaxies.

That the Newtonian 'constant' of gravitation varies secularly with the epoch is a property not confined to gravitation. Planck's 'constant' h can be shown, by later developments, to depend also secularly on the time.

In conclusion, the theory developed in the present article is believed to carry out the programme suggested by the success of Einstein's so-called 'special relativity' better than his later 'general relativity,' which, in the writer's opinion, is of a nature alien to the main tradition in mathematical physics. The present theory reposes none the less on the genius of Einstein.

E. A. MILNE

WADHAM COLLEGE
OXFORD UNIVERSITY

16

Georges Edward Lemaître

THE COSMOLOGICAL CONSTANT

THE COSMOLOGICAL CONSTANT

1. MATTER AS CURVATURE

ACCORDING to the general theory of relativity, matter can be described as a manifestation of the curvature of space-time. Let us recall how this inference is reached.

According to Riemann, curvature is a departure from flatness of a space, or space-time, which is, approximately, flat or Euclidean.

In Euclidean space, the square of the elementary distance of two points is a quadratic form of the differences of the co-ordinates of the points. When these co-ordinates are chosen conveniently, the quadratic form has constant coefficients.

In Riemannian space, it still is a quadratic form of the co-ordinates and these co-ordinates may be so chosen that their coefficients are constant approximately; thus geometry is Euclidean to the same approximation.

Nevertheless, the reduction to a form with constant coefficients cannot be achieved rigorously and, when regions are considered which are not too small, the effect of curvature, or lack of flatness, cannot be completely ignored.

Geodesics, i.e., the straightest lines in Riemannian space, are affected by curvature. In Euclidean analytic geometry, with co-ordinates such that the differential form has constant coefficients, geodesics are represented by linear equations. For space-time of three plus one dimensions, this is interpreted as rectilinear motion with constant velocity.

When curvature of space-time does not vanish, geodesics can no more be represented by linear equations and the corresponding motion is accelerated.

Planets are supposed to describe geodesics of space-time,

and their curvilinear motion is a manifestation of curvature.

Therefore curvature occurs in interplanetary space where there is no matter present. Matter is represented by curvature, but not every curvature does represent matter; there may be curvature "*in vacuo*." Mathematically, curvature is described by an array of quantities, collectively called a tensor: the Riemannian tensor which contains twenty independent components. If matter is described as curvature, it must be described, not by the whole Riemannian tensor, but by some combination of its components. Otherwise gravitation would not be effective outside matter and Newtonian attraction would not act at a distance. The combination of the whole Riemannian tensor which really describes matter must be carried out according to definite rules, the rules of tensor-calculus, which ensure the essential freedom of changing coordinates which characterises relativity. In short, matter will be described by some contracted tensor extracted from the complete Riemannian tensor.

This is not the whole story. If any values of the contracted Riemannian tensor could be a possible representation of matter, its actual distribution at some instant could be completely independent of its distribution in the past. Clearly matter does not behave in that way; matter varies, but not in a completely arbitrary way; matter is conserved; the possibilities of its evolution and therefore of the combination of the Riemannian tensor which is able to represent matter is essentially restricted by some tensorial relation, involving the variations in space and time of the components: some differential identity must be satisfied.

These requirements can be fulfilled, and when too complicated solutions, which would involve derivatives of a high order, are excluded, it is found that matter is represented by a two-indices-tensor $T_{\mu\nu}$ which can be written

$$T_{\mu\nu} = a(R_{\mu\nu} - \tfrac{1}{2}Rg_{\mu\nu}) + bg_{\mu\nu} \tag{1}$$

In this equation $g_{\mu\nu}$ are the coefficients of the differential form which describes the interval of space-time. They are ten independent quantities which are called, collectively, the metrical or fundamental tensor. $R_{\mu\nu}$ and R are called the contracted Riemannian tensor and the totally contracted Riemannian tensor, respectively. They are definite expressions of the $g_{\mu\nu}$ and their derivatives up to the second order. They must occur in the actual combination in order that $T_{\mu\nu}$ should be restricted by some differential identity.

a and *b* are two constants which are not determined by the foregoing discussion. Their values depend on the comparison of the theory with observation only.

This comparison may be simplified, by introducing some assumptions which are legitimate in astronomical applications and may be called the "Newtonian approximation."

First of all, in the actual world, departures from Euclidean geometry are not very conspicuous and, therefore, space can be described by Cartesian rectangular co-ordinates, in the usual way, with a rather high approximation. Similarly Newtonian time can be introduced and the simple Galilean expression can represent the interval of space-time as in special relativity. Of course, this expression is not taken as an exact one, and the acceleration of the geodesics is a manifestation of small departures from the Galilean values. For moderate velocities these accelerations are expressed by equations similar to those of classical mechanics such as

$$\frac{d^2x}{dt^2} = \frac{\partial U}{\partial x}$$

where the "Newtonian potential" U arises from the coefficient g_{44} of dt^2 in the quadratic form according to

$$g_{44} = c^2 - 2\,U,$$

c being the velocity of light, which is equal to unity when distances are measured by the light-time.

The leading component of the material tensor is T_{44}. It is the density ϱ of matter, or rather the corresponding density of energy ϱc^2. Other components are small, astronomical velocities being small compared with the velocity of light.

Within this Newtonian approximation, the equation of gravitation reduces to

$$- \tfrac{1}{2}\Delta g_{44} = - \frac{\mu}{2} T_{44} + \lambda g_{44}$$

where μ and λ are two constants which can replace a and b. ($\mu = - 1/a$, $\lambda = - b/a$). Δ is the Laplacian operator.

Writing

$$\lambda = \frac{\mu}{2} \rho_0 \qquad (2)$$

the equation becomes

$$\Delta U = - \frac{\mu}{2} c^2 (\rho - \rho_0) \qquad (3)$$

and is very similar to the Poisson equation

$$\Delta U = - 4\pi G \rho \qquad (4)$$

(G is the gravitational constant) which is equivalent to the Newtonian law of attraction.

The theory is therefore in agreement with observation if the constant μ (or a) is related to the gravitational constant in some obvious way and if ρ_0, which depends on the other constant b or λ, is small enough to produce only insensible perturbations in the motion of the planets. Within the limits imposed by the precision of planetary observations ρ_0 or λ is completely unknown.

When approximation higher than the Newtonian approximation is considered, the theory predicts small departures from the Newtonian law. They constitute the three astronomical tests of the theory: the gravitational red-shift, the deflection of light, double of the Newtonian expectation, and the advance of the perihelion of the planets. But even within the Newtonian approximation, theory provides for an unknown correction to gravitational attraction which can be represented by the so-called *cosmological constant* lambda or the corresponding *cosmical density* ρ_0.

The logical convenience of the second constant λ or ρ_0 was not realised at the early stages of the elaboration of the theory. It is rather by a happy accident that, in 1917, Einstein put the final touch to the equations of gravitation by introducing in it the cosmological constant lambda.

"Its original reason was not very convincing and for some years the cosmical term was looked on as a fancy addition rather than an integrated part of the theory."[1]

Even if the introduction of the cosmological constant "has lost its sole original justification, that of leading to a natural solution of the cosmological problem,"[2] it remains true that Einstein has shown that the structure of his equations quite naturally allows for the presence of a second constant besides the gravitational one. This raises a problem and opens possibilities which deserve careful discussion. The history of science provides many instances of discoveries which have been made for reasons which are no longer considered satisfactory. It may be that the discovery of the cosmological constant is such a case.

2. ENERGY AND GRAVITATIONAL MASS

Before investigating whether there are other empirical reasons to maintain lambda, besides Einstein's original one, I should like to insist on the logical convenience or even the theoretical necessity of its introduction.

Newtonian gravitation depends on the mass (through the density ϱ) and it produces on the planets a definite acceleration proportional to the attractive mass. Mass is but a form of energy and any form of energy has to be counted as mass. Energy essentially contains an arbitrary constant; it can be counted from a zero-level which can be chosen arbitrarily. Therefore, if gravitational mass, which has a definite effect, viz., the Newtonian attraction, must be identified with energy, which is defined but for an additive arbitrary constant, it is necessary that the theory should provide some possibility of adjustment when the zero-level from which energy is counted is changed arbitrarily.

Poisson's equation in its original form does not meet this requirement; but in the modified equation the density comes out as $\varrho - \varrho_0$ only. The arbitrary change of ϱ, arising from the change of zero-level, can then be compensated by an

---

[1] A. S. Eddington, *The Expanding Universe*, 24 (1932).
[2] A. Einstein, *The Meaning of Relativity*, 121 (1946).

equivalent change in the unknown constant ϱ_0 or in lambda. In this way no modification results in the gravitational attraction.

In other words, to suppose that lambda is exactly zero would mean that the conventional level, from which physicists are used to count energy, is more fundamental than any other they could have chosen just as well.

3. TIME-SCALE

In order to investigate the possibilities which are opened by the cosmological term, in questions connected with the evolution of the expanding universe, we must consider, in detail, the consequences of the introduction of this term into the gravitational equation.

The consequences of importance are connected with the equilibrium which might arise between the gravitational attraction and a new force which results from lambda, and also from the unstable character of this equilibrium.

Since this happens when the sign of λ or ϱ_0 is positive, we shall limit our discussion to that case.

Within the Newtonian approximation, and assuming spherical symmetry around some point, the equation of motion along the radius r is

$$\frac{d^2r}{dt^2} = -\frac{Gm}{r^2} + \frac{\lambda}{3} r.$$

This acceleration is the net result of two conflicting forces, the gravitational attraction and the cosmical repulsion arising from λ which is proportional to the distance r.

In this equation, m is the mass contained inside the sphere of radius r: $m = (4\pi/3) \varrho r^3$.

When $\varrho = \varrho_0$ the two forces balance one another, and, if the actual value of the velocities is zero, the system may remain in equilibrium.

If we do not make use of the Newtonian approximation, but assume, at least as an approximation, not only spherical symmetry but complete equivalence of each point and each direction, i.e., homogeniety and isotropy, so that spherical symmetry exists around any point, then the behaviour of the universe is completely described by the successive values taken by the variable radius of space R. The application of the gravitational equation gives in this case Friedmann's equation

$$\left(\frac{dR}{dt}\right)^2 = -1 + \frac{2M}{R} + \frac{\lambda}{3}R^2 \qquad (6)$$

with

$$M = \frac{4\pi}{3}\rho R^3.$$

When the values of M and λ are such that this equation can be written

$$\left(\frac{dR}{dt}\right)^2 = (R - R_E)^2 \frac{R + 2R_E}{R}, \qquad (7)$$

then $R = R_E$ is a possible solution. It is the case of equilibrium (static solution) originally found by Einstein.

This equilibrium is, on the grand scale, the same equilibrium we have just discussed within the Newtonian approximation.

The opposite case, where the density ϱ is very small in comparison with ϱ_o, has been considered by de Sitter.

In that case, radial motion occurs according to the equation

$$\frac{d^2r}{dt^2} = \frac{\lambda}{3}r$$

from which results

$$\left(\frac{dr}{dt}\right)^2 = \frac{\lambda}{3}r^2 + \text{constant}.$$

Comparison with Friedmann's equation shows that the constant is very small in the homogeneous case. Dropping the constant, we have

$$\frac{v}{r} = \frac{1}{T_H} = \sqrt{\frac{\lambda}{3}}. \qquad (8)$$

Velocities of recession are proportional to the distance and this constant ratio depends on the cosmological constant through the above equation.

The astronomic observations are given in kilometers per second per mega-parsecs, which is the inverse of the time T_H.

As an example of the conversion of one kind of units into the other, we may quote from Eddington: that a velocity ratio of 572 kilometer per mega-parsecs corresponds to a T_H of $1.72 \cdot 10^9$ years. The observed value given by Hubble in the *Realm of Nebulæ:* 530, is not very different.

T_H fixes the scale of time for the description of the expanding universe. Geometrically, it is the sub-tangent to the curve obtained by plotting r as ordinate against t as abcissa, or the radius R as a function of t. This meaning of Hubble's ratio is quite general and is independent of any hypothesis on the relative values of ϱ and ϱ_0. If ϱ_0 would vanish or be negative, then the acceleration should be negative and the curve would lie below its tangent; the time available for the evolution of the universe would be smaller than T_H.

If we are not ready to accept that the evolution of the universe did not last more than T_H, (which is the duration of the geological ages, known from the lead-content of radio-active minerals), then it is unavoidable to introduce the cosmological constant (with a positive sign).

Let us return to the hypothesis of de Sitter, $\varrho \ll \varrho_0$, in order to see if this hypothesis is consistent with observation.

The value of T_H quoted above corresponds to a definite value of the cosmical density ϱ_0. This value is $1.23 \cdot 10^{-27}$ gr. per cm^3. If de Sitter's hypothesis is tenable this must be much greater than the density of matter ϱ.

The value of this density is known with some precision. There are, in the mean, twelve nebulae per cubic- mega-parsecs.[3]

On the other hand, the masses of a few nebulae can be estimated from the observation of their spectroscopic rotation. The observations are difficult and in some instances corrections have been published even to the extent of reversing the

[3] This takes account of a statistical correction given by A. Fletcher, *Monthly Notices R.A.S.* 106 (1946), 123.

sign of the rotation. If the real masses were much greater, the observation would be comparatively easy.

The three available observations give a mean of $35 \cdot 10^9$ times the mass of the sun. They refer to exceptionally bright nebulae; the average nebula must be less massive. Assuming that the ratio of mass to luminosity is essentially the same for all nebulae, the mean mass is found as $2 \cdot 10^9$ times the mass of the sun.

This gives a density $\varrho = 1.6 \cdot 10^{-30}$, much smaller than ϱ_0.

From these figures, we may infer that actual distances are about ten times greater than at the time of equilibrium.

Therefore, astronomical observation definitely favours de Sitter's hypothesis that the actual value of the density is negligible; matter is, by no means, in equilibrium and the cosmical repulsion prevails on gravitation.

Of course conditions may have been very different in the past.

Equation (7) can be satisfied by other solutions than $R = R_E$. These solutions are expressed by elementary functions. R may start with initial values not much greater than R_E and slowly increase until finally it approaches the de Sitter case.

This special solution of Friedmann's equation, which had been emphasized by the author in 1927, has been described by Eddington as showing the instability of Einstein's equilibrium and giving instances of the rupture of this unstable equilibrium towards expansion.

If the relation between M and T, which reduces Friedmann's integral to elementary functions, is satisfied approximately only, i.e., if

$$(9) \qquad 3^{3/2} \, M/T = I + \eta$$

where η is small, then the process of evolution will not take an infinite time.

If η is negative, the actual expansion would have been preceded by a similar contraction, the minimum radius being a little greater than the equilibrium value.

In the more interesting case, where η is positive, the value of the radius has been initially smaller than the equilibrium value, and, theoretically at least, started from zero. In the early stages of the evolution the cosmological constant was therefore quite negligible. When the value of the radius reached the equilibrium value, the velocity of expansion, though small, did not vanish, and the radius was able to go beyond the equilibrium value; then cosmical repulsion began to dominate and expansion started again with resumed vigour until the de Sitter condition, $\varrho \ll \varrho_o$ should be realised.

This ever-expanding type of expansion was called by Friedmann the monotonic universe.

It is possible to compute the time elapsed from the instant where the radius started from zero to the one where its value amounts to about ten times the equilibrium value. This depends on the small value of η and, if we write this quantity:

$$(10) \qquad \eta = 10^{-n},$$

the duration of evolution just defined is given by the approximate expression

$$1.3\,(n+2)\,T_H.$$

How far exceedingly small values of η may retain physical significance is a matter of judgment. One more zero before the significant figures increases the available time by $2.7\ 10^9$ years only. We may conclude that evolution during 15 to 20 10^9 years is within the realm of possibility. The other type of motion would lead to essentially the same figures.

This definitely steers clear of the dangerous limit fixed by the known duration of the geological ages; but the margin so gained is not very large. Here again, the way out of the difficulty comes out of the instability of the equilibrium.

4. INSTABILITY

In order to discuss the effect of instability on matter going through equilibrium, we must make some assumption about the state of matter at that time. It would be meaningless to suppose that matter was already arranged into stars and extragalactic nebulae, since we, precisely, intend to explain the formation of stars and nebulae; but we must consider some simpler state of matter from which, as an effect of instability, stars and nebulae would result.

We shall suppose that, at that time, matter was arranged into gaseous clouds, similar to the actual diffuse nebulae, and that these clouds had large relative velocities. The question of the origin of these clouds must, of course, be postponed; presently we shall investigate if they could account, in the moderate time available, for the actual universe, formed of galaxies of stars and diffuse nebulae.

The state of matter we postulate may be compared to a gas; it is a kind of super-gas, the molecules of which are the individual clouds. Nevertheless this comparison cannot be stressed too far. Although collisions between "molecules" would occur sometimes, they would, unlike collisions in a gas, not be elastic, and they would not bring about any statistical equilibrium or anything like Maxwell's law of distribution of velocities.

We may even suppose that collisions are rare. Then each cloud behaves independently of the others under the effect of the common gravitational field, or rather under the effect of the fluctuations of this gravitational field, because the main effect is neutralised by the cosmic repulsion.

Under these circumstances, we could understand that some cloud, or some accidental arrangement of clouds, moving with nearly equal velocities, may act as an attractive center, which would retain under its dominating influence other clouds which approach this attractive center with moderate relative velocities.

A larger condensation will result which will move along with the velocity of the initial attractive center and which will not disperse when the universe resumes expansion.

The net result is that, after passage through the unstable equilibrium, the universe will be formed of local condensations which remain condensed, while their mutual distances increase.

This would look like the actual universe formed of condensed structures, the extragalactic nebulae, arranged in an expanding assembly. It would help us to understand how these nebulae have a rather large dispersion of their proper velocities (i.e., departure from the mean velocity which constitutes the expansion). This velocity is given as 200 KM/sec. for field nebulae and is much greater in the big clusters of nebulae.

As long as collisions are neglected, the agglomeration of

clouds would arrange themselves with some concentration at the center and correspondingly with greater velocities. In the central region, the higher density and the greater velocity will give more chance to collision. These collisions would occur with velocities of the order of 300 kilometer sec. and such collisions would not be elastic collisions. The colliding clouds would merge one into the other and the kinetic energy would be dissipated into radiation. Further central condensation with an increase of density and of speed will result and therefore more collisions. The colliding clouds would finally turn into stars and the system of stars and remaining clouds (the diffuse nebulae) would gain a strong degree of central condensation. It is clear, that, at least in a preliminary qualitative way, we reach here the essential features of our actual universe. It would not be wise to go into more minute details at this point, but it is clear that this whole process could be accomplished in time of a few T_H. Thus the difficulty arising from the shortness of the time-scale can be avoided.

Let us summarize our argument in favour of the cosmological constant; we have shown that the introduction of this term into the equations of gravitation was necessary to make acceptable the short scale of time which is imposed by the value of the red-shift of the nebulae. This is achieved in two ways: first, by providing a positive acceleration, it enlarges the scale and makes it definitely greater than the duration of geologic ages; possibility ten times greater; secondly, by the mechanism of the instability of the equilibrium between Newtonian attraction and cosmical repulsion it produces, within the short time available, great differentiations in the distribution of matter as an effect of small accidental fluctuations in the original distribution, and thus might account for the formation of stars and nebulae.

5. Beginnings

We have postponed the question of the origin of the clouds from which stars and nebulae have been formed. Our discussion would not be complete unless we inquire if it is possible to derive these clouds, by a natural process of evolution, from some simpler original state of matter.

The gaseous clouds are not the only thing which we have to explain; we must realise that it is also necessary to include the cosmic rays in the discussion.

It is not likely that these rays are actually formed in the galaxy. All presumptions point to a far more remote origin; therefore we can assume that they uniformly fill up the whole space between the galaxies.

Their energy can be estimated from the number of ions they are able to produce, not only in their passage through the atmosphere, but down to the bottom of the lakes or even at extreme depths in coal mines where their presence can still be detected. The whole energy thus found is given as $3 \cdot 10^{-3}$ erg per cm². These figures can be turned into a density of energy by being divided by their velocity, which is nearly the velocity of light c. Finally, for the purpose of comparison with the density of matter: $1.6 \cdot 10^{-30}$ gr. per cm³, resulting from the estimation of the masses of the nebulae and of their mean distances, they have to be turned into density of mass by being divided again by c^2. In that way, the energy of the cosmic rays is found to be $1.1 \cdot 10^{-34}$ gr. per cm³. This energy amounts to one ten thousandth of the energy of matter.

Cosmic rays must, therefore, be looked upon as essential constituents of matter and their existence must be explained, as well as that of the gaseous clouds, by great velocities which are needed at the time of equilibrium.

At that time the energy of the cosmic rays was even greater than now, because this energy has been reduced as an effect of the expansion.

In the same way, the dispersion of the velocities of the nebulae, or rather of the centers of condensations which have caused their formations, was ten times greater than now. Judging from the actual dispersions of velocities of the field-nebulae, 200 km per sec., it was 2000 km per sec. at the time of equilibrium.

The cosmic rays amounted to one thousandth of the total (nuclear) energy of matter. Of course, if they did originate when the radius of space was much smaller, or if they have been appreciably absorbed, their original energy was even nearer the amount of energy of matter.

It is not easy to conceive any simple arrangement of matter which could give rise to cosmic rays and to the gaseous clouds with great relative velocities. One might think of adapting the hypothesis of a primaeval nebula to the expansion of space. When the radius was small, the whole of matter existed as a unique mass of gas with exceedingly high temperature and pressure. Under such conditions radiation similar to cosmic rays could have been produced inside this mass.

It is difficult to explain how this continuous mass could have split into separated clouds, and how the original cosmic rays, formed within the mass, have managed to go through the distended gases without being transformed or absorbed in a way similar to what happens when they enter the earth's atmosphere.

Furthermore, even if the clouds could separate, how did they acquire these great relative velocities? Some separation could, of course, be achieved by going through an unstable equilibrium; but that process can not have happened twice, and we need it for the formation of stars and nebulae.

The requirements of the cosmical problem can be met by the primaeval atom hypothesis.

The idea of this hypothesis arose when it was noticed that natural radioactivity is a physical process which disappears gradually and which can, therefore, be expected to have been more important in earlier times. If it were not for a few elements of average lifetimes comparable to T_H, natural radioactivity would be completely extinct now. It might be thought, therefore, that radioactive elements did exist which are actually completely transformed into stable elements.

Furthermore, artificial disintegration shows that, besides the stable elements, there are a great number of radioactive elements of short mean life so that any stable element may be the product of disintegration of some radioactive one. We know these new radioactive elements in the vicinity of Mendelyeev's line of stable elements only; but there is no indication that they are limited to this vicinity, and when more powerful means shall be available, it may be expected that they will be found farther away from the Mendelyeev line as well.

The hypothesis that all the actually existing elements have resulted from the disintegration of heavier elements now extinct finds some support, therefore, in nuclear physics. This support was not available, however, when the hypothesis was first proposed.[4]

Elements are described by two numbers: their atomic number and their atomic weight. We do not suggest that elements existed with much greater atomic numbers, but that elements, which were isotopes of the actual stable elements or of the neutron, existed temporarily with much higher atomic weight.

In its extreme form the hypothesis suggests, as the simplest conceivable origin of the universe, a unique atom, isotope of the neutron which had an atomic weight equal to the total mass of the universe. From the successive disintegrations of this atom and of the smaller atoms resulting of its fragmentation, all actual stable atoms have been formed.

Let us discuss this hypothesis in its broad outlines and see if it meets the requirements of the cosmical problem.

It is not very profitable to insist on [the precise nature of] the extreme physical conditions which arose at the very beginning. Strictly speaking, if matter existed as a single atomic nucleus, it makes no sense to speak of space and time in connection with this atom. Space and time are statistical notions which apply to an assembly of a great number of individual elements; they were meaningless notions, therefore, at the instant of the first disintegration of the primaeval atom.

When the individual fragments became numerous enough space and time progressively acquired definite meaning. Then it is possible to think of space as spherical space with a small radius, the value of which was increasing very rapidly.

If some rays, which were emitted in the splitting process, have been able to reach us, they have been reduced enormously, in the ratio of the increase of the radius; they cannot form any significant part of the cosmic rays.

Nature, May 9, 1931.

Radioactive process must have continued when the radius was getting larger, say one hundredth of the actual value. If the greater part of the observed rays come out of this epoch, their original energy was about one per cent of the nuclear energy.

Further progress in nuclear physics must be awaited before some definite analysis of the production of the rays in that way can be attempted. Nuclear fragments with extremely high kinetic energy may have existed, and collisions between these fragments may have produced many kinds of rays.

We must content ourselves to notice that this process would make understandable not only the extremely high individual energy of the rays, but also their total intensity, which is a notable part of the remaining energy of matter.

It is easy to understand how some important part of the rays, produced in this way, have escaped, being absorbed by gaseous matter. Actually they separated when gaseous matter was not yet formed.

The formation of gaseoeus matter is somewhat difficult to understand. Originally the atomic fragments must have had enormous kinetic energy (recoil energy), and then elastic collision could not have happened. But these relative velocities are attenuated by the expansion process. After a while collisions with moderate relative velocities might have arisen. If these collisions were mild enough to be elastic collisions, then the process of uniformization of the velocities which leads to Maxwell's distribution and to the statistical equilibrium, which characterises a gas, could have worked progressively.

It is clear that such a progress depends on chance encounters and that the enormous original velocities must result in large velocities of the individual clouds which have been formed in that way.

6. Velocities

The reduction of the proper velocities as a consequence of the expansion has played an essential part in the theory, not only in order to explain the formation of the clouds, but also in the red-shift of light and the attenuation of the energy of the cosmic rays. I should like to make some remarks which might help to shed some light upon the theory of this essential phenomenon, and also to discuss its importance in relation to the clustering of the nebulae.

There are two ways of discussing this phenomenon, each of which emphasizes some different aspect of the question.

The most rigorous way is to consider the trajectories of individual particles as geodesics of the universe of variable radius, defined by the quadratic form:

$$ds^2 = - R^2 d\sigma + dt^2$$

Strictly speaking, σ is three-dimensional, it is the angular distance in an elliptic space of radius one; but this circumstance can be ignored in the actual question.

If it were not for the minus sign, which emphasises the essential difference between space and time, this quadratic form would be the line element on a surface of revolution (the t axis being the axis of symmetry).

A well known theorem of Clairaut states that, for geodesics on a surface of revolution, the sine of the angle made by the geodesics with the meridian plane varies as the inverse of the distance from the axis.

Computation of the geodesics, essentially as in the demonstration of Clairaut's theorem, shows that for the geodesic the relation ($R \, d\sigma/dt = C\tau/R$) is satisfied.

The velocity, or more strictly the momentum (because the denominator is ds and not dt, so that the variation of mass with velocity is taken into account) is reduced in proportion to the ratio of the expansion.

This extends the theory of the red-shift, so that it can be applied to material particles of any velocity.

There is another way of presenting the theory in a more elementary manner. Instead of using angular space with co-ordinates which follow the mean motion of matter, we may resort to Galilean local co-ordinates, around some point taken as a center of the description.

Then, the mean motion is a radial motion away from the center, with velocities proportional to distance. This defines the mean velocity or, let us say, the normal velocity.

The proper velocity of a material particle shows as a difference between the motion of this particle and the normal velocity at the place where the particle happens to be.

Now, it is easy to see, that a particle with abnormal velocity has a tendency to reach places where its velocity is not so abnormal.

Consider, for definiteness, an abnormal positive velocity along the radius drawn from the center of the representation. The particle travels quicker than the normal particles (which have the normal velocity), and therefore it outruns normal particles which have greater and greater velocities. The difference between its own velocity (assumed to be constant) and the normal velocity at the place it has reached has therefore diminished. That is its proper velocity, and we see that it is reduced as an effect of the expansion. The magnitude of this effect can be computed as a courier problem and gives the same result as the more rigorous proof given above.

A further application of this effect is shown in the correlation which is found between the fluctuations in the distribution of the densities and the fluctuations in the distribution of the velocities. In the great clusters of the nebulae, which have failed to expand as the field nebulae and have retained a density not very different from the cosmical density ϱ_o, the proper velocities are much greater than for the field nebulae.

Actually the velocities in the clusters are only three times greater than for field nebulae, whereas a velocity ten times greater might have been expected from the value of the density. It is difficult to decide if the discrepancy is to be ascribed to uncertainty of the observational data or to some aspect not yet understood in the theory of the clusters of nebulae.

G. Lemaître

Bruxelles, Belgium

17

Karl Menger

THE THEORY OF RELATIVITY AND GEOMETRY

THE THEORY OF RELATIVITY AND GEOMETRY

I. A Brief History of Geometry

A FUTURE historian of geometry, if pressed for space, might devote to the period between Euclid and Einstein a passage somewhat like the following four paragraphs:

(1) The Greeks began the systematic study of objects such as points, lines, planes, polygons, conic sections, and spheres. They discovered how to draw, from a very few assumptions about these objects, an astonishing number of conclusions. Euclid's assumptions (some of which he never stated explicitly) about points, lines, and planes involved a two-fold idealization of the relations between small dots, rigid rods, and flat boards. First, he neglected the extension of the dots as well as the thickness of the rods and boards. Secondly, he assumed the length of the rods to exceed any finite bound. The Greeks also included in their studies a few curves and surfaces more complicated than the conic sections and the sphere. These turned up in the course of their pursuit of certain geometric hobbies, such as the trisection of angles. Archimedes discovered methods for computing the areas bounded by some curves as well as the slopes of their tangents. But it was not until the eighties of the nineteenth century that the foundation of this postulational or "synthetic" geometry was completed. Pasch was the first to formulate explicitly all the assumptions on which a particular branch of geometry is based, and in addition to list all the concepts involved. On these as a foundation he built up the whole theory by purely logical reasoning. Since then, it has become common knowledge that a deductive theory (such as synthetic geometry) is necessarily based on concepts which, within the theory, remain undefined, and on propositions which, within the theory, remain unproved.

(2) In the seventeenth century, after navigators had char-

acterized the points on the surface of the earth by latitude and longitude, Descartes and Fermat introduced analogous methods into theoretical geometry. To do this, they chose as a frame of reference three mutually perpendicular planes. Each point in space they characterized by three numbers, called the co-ordinates of the point in question. These numbers are the perpendicular distances from the three planes of reference to the point. According to this scheme, each of the simple geometrical objects studied by the Greeks is characterized by a simple numerical relation between the co-ordinates (x, y, z) of its constituent points. For example, the sphere of radius 1 with its center at $(0, 0, 0)$ is characterized by the relation $x^2 + y^2 + z^2 = 1$. Conversely, every simple relation between three numbers x, y, and z characterizes an object treated in the Greek geometry. For example, the relation $y = 3x$ characterizes the points of a particular plane. To every assumption and every theorem of the Greek geometry, there corresponds an algebraic theorem about triples of numbers. There was no reason to confine this new .method to simple numerical relations; consequently Descartes included within the realm of geometry objects corresponding to numerical relations more complicated than those which characterized the objects of Greek geometry. An example is the equality $y = x^3$. In fact, Descartes began the systematic study of all curves and surfaces defined by numerical relations. In the course of this study, it appeared that the few rather complicated objects known to the Greeks were merely very special individuals in the now immensely increased geometric population. The application of differential and integral calculus to co-ordinate (also called "analytic") geometry resulted in the systematic description of the local properties of curves, such as their slopes, radii of curvature, etc. This so-called "differential" geometry, a broad generalization of Archimedes' results, was later extended by Euler, Monge, and Gauss to surfaces. But differential geometry, by its very nature, is restricted to objects accessible by the methods of calculus—that is, to smooth objects which at all points have tangent lines or planes, curvatures, etc. (A triangle at its vertices has neither curvature nor tangent.) About 1900, Study gave a sound foundation to analytic geometry by developing it as a theory in which (in contrast to synthetic geometry) the objects are explicitly defined: points by pairs or triples of numbers; lines by linear equations, etc. These arithmetically defined objects are then treated by the methods of algebra and calculus.

(3) During the nineteenth century, the very concept of space was profoundly generalized. It was found that assumptions incompatible with those of Euclid can be used as the foundations for consistent deductive geometries. These systems (particularly the first one, developed by Bolyai and Lobachewsky) were called non-Euclidean geometries. In analytic geometry, pairs and triples of complex numbers (of the form $a + b \sqrt{-1}$) were admitted as points, and were treated just as the pairs and triples of real numbers had previously been treated in the analytic geometry of the Euclidean plane and space. Quadruples and quintuples, etc., of numbers were called points in four and five etc. dimensional spaces. Gauss studied surfaces intrinsically— that is, without reference to the space in which they are embedded. He regarded them as generalizations of the plane. Riemann developed n-dimensional spaces which had the same generality and variety as the smooth objects embedded in them. An Italian school studied the effects which a transformation of the frame of reference has on the description of an object— effects similar to those produced by a transformation of the object without change in the frame of reference. An earlier French school had created projective geometry, that is, the geometry dealing with those properties which an object retains when it is projected on another object. For instance, the straightness of a line is left unchanged by a projective transformation, its length, in general, is not. Lie developed a profound theory dealing with groups of transformations. Klein's classification of geometrical properties according to the groups of transformations under which they are invariant, was in fashion for some decades about 1900.

Among the most fundamental characteristics of an object are its so-called topological properties. These properties are the ones which an object retains when it undergoes such an irregular transformation as a diagram undergoes if it be drawn on a rubber sheet, and the sheet then stretched, compressed or distorted in any way which does not result in tearing the fabric apart or cementing it together. Such a transformation may not only alter the length of a curve but may change a straight line into a curved one. Any object which can be obtained from a straight segment (between the points p and q) by a topological transformation is called an "arc." By an "interior" point of an arc is meant any point which is the transform of any point other than p or q of the straight segment. (Interior points can also be defined intrinsically, that is, without reference to the original straight segment and the transformation.) Every arc has the characteristic property that, by the omission of any one of its interior points, it is decomposed into exactly two connected parts. Y-shaped objects and circles (into which a straight segment cannot topologically be transformed) cannot be thus decomposed. If a plane contains two triples of points, and if each point of one triple is connected by an arc with each point of the other triple, then at least two of the nine arcs have at least one interior point in common. This fact is a topological property of the plane, since it remains true no matter how the plane is topologically transformed. On the surface of an anchor ring (a surface into which a plane cannot be topologically transformed) two triples of points can be connected by nine arcs, no two of which have an interior point in common.

(4) During the nineteenth century, the concept of a numerical relation as a basis for the definition of geometric objects was slowly but steadily generalized. The curve represented by $y = x^3$ had already been admitted to the realm of plane curves at a time when some Renaissance geometers denied that $y = 3^x$ represented a legitimate geometric object. Even after such smooth "transcendental" curves had been admitted, conservatives still made smoothness a *sine qua non*. But Cauchy pointed out that a V-shaped curve (which has no tangent at its lowest point) corresponds to the equation $y = + \sqrt{x^2}$, and Weierstrass showed that even curves which have no tangent at any point correspond to generally recognized numerical expressions. The same is true of some objects which defy all graphic representation. Take for example the set consisting of all those points on the line $y = 0$ which have an irrational abscissa together with

all those points on the line $y = 1$ which have a rational abscissa. Dirichlet noticed that this set could be defined by the equation

$$y = \lim_{n \to \infty} \lim_{m \to \infty} \cos^{2m}(n!\pi x)$$

an expression essentially of the same nature as the equations customarily used in the Fourier analysis of periodic phenomena.

It was Cantor who, about 1880, took the final step in this program of liberalization by opening the domain of geometry to all sets of points, not only those defined by numerical relations, but those defined in any other way—say, by the joining or intersecting of simpler sets; by omitting parts; by selecting one point from each of a family of sets and uniting the selected points into one set; etc. The new objects introduced into geometry by this point set theory were so vast in number that they dwarfed the additions introduced by analytic geometry during the Renaissance. Some of these new objects exhibited such unexpected properties and deviated so radically from traditional patterns that they were said to defy intuition. But the tremendous new world disclosed by set theory was soon found to be governed by general laws: partly extensions and generalizations of classic results obtained by analytic geometry; partly new laws of the most unexpected kind dealing with radically new patterns, where smoothness, instead of being the general rule, turned out to be a rare and not very important exception.

As a parallel to the extension just described, the very notion of space was broadened until it attained the same generality and variety as the spatial objects contemplated by set-theoretical geometry. According to Fréchet, a general metric space is any set which fulfills the following requirements. With every pair of elements there is associated a number, called the distance between them. This number is positive whenever the elements are distinct, and zero when they are identical. Of the three distances defined by three distinct points, no one is greater than the sum of the other two. (This last stipulation generalizes the theorem that in a Euclidean triangle the length of any one side cannot exceed the sum of the lengths of the other two sides.) There have been formulated conditions under which the elements of such a general metric space can be described by coordinates, and still stronger conditions under which these elements behave in every respect like the points of Euclidean space.

II. The Theory of Relativity and Classical Geometry

One of Einstein's most fundamental contributions to scientific thought was his introduction of non-Euclidean geometry into the foundations of physics. Poincaré had discussed the possibility of describing Nature by some non-Euclidean system; but he offered this suggestion only to dismiss it, for he believed that Euclidean geometry had an inherent simplicity which no other geometry possessed. In direct contradiction to this idea, Einstein greatly simplified the description of Nature by assuming a non-Euclidean space.[1] But, as he and others have emphasized, this assumption is not of a geometric nature. For geometry, in its synthetic aspect, deals with undefined objects (called points, lines, planes, etc., cf. I, 1) and, in its analytic aspect, with arithmetically defined objects (triples of numbers, linear equations, etc., cf. I, 2). Einstein's assumption, on the other hand, deals with physical objects such as cross-hairs in telescopes and the light rays observed by astronomers, etc. It amounts, in fact, to the hypothesis that certain physical objects behave like points and lines of a non-Euclidean rather than a Euclidean space. However, in formulating his hypothesis about the physical world, Einstein employed a geometric terminology. Indeed, his fundamental idea may be split into two parts: (1) That a light ray always follows the shortest path; and (2) that these shortest paths have the properties of lines in a non-Euclidean space. In this sense he geometrized certain basic parts of physics, particularly the theory of gravitation.

[1] The recent development of hyperbolic geometry indicates that Euclidean geometry lacks even the distinction of logical simplicity. For in Euclidean geometry "congruent" and "perpendicular" cannot be defined in terms of intersectional constructions, and hence these (or similarly complicated) relations must be incorporated in the list of undefined concepts on which Euclidean geometry is based. Even "between," while capable of an intersectional definition, cannot be proved to enjoy the properties of linear order except on the basis of complicated assumptions. The only geometry which indeed is simple in the indicated sense is (as has been shown in the Reports of a Mathematical Colloquium, 2nd series) the hyperbolic geometry initiated by Bolyai and Lobachewsky. Hyperbolic geometry is the only one which can be developed from a few simple assumptions concerning "joining," "intersecting," and "continuity" alone.

Einstein, in carrying out his program, went so far as—and essentially no farther than—to assume that the space-time of the physical world is a four-dimensional Riemann space (cf. I, 3). For the quantitative (metric) description of the objects in this space, each observer of the physical world carries with him his own particular frame of reference. Furthermore, Einstein made extensive use of the Italian theorems concerning the transformations of frames of reference (cf. I, 3).

A simple, non-relativistic example may illustrate how physical facts may suggest assumptions even about the qualitative topological properties of a space. Imagine a world the structure of which resembles that of a very thin but infinitely extended sheet of paper. And imagine this world to be inhabited by intelligent beings who are not aware that their world has any thickness at all. They use plane geometry, although their geometers have defined the concept, to them unpicturable, of a three-dimensional space. They have developed chemistry to the structural stage. Their chemists have devised plane diagrams for many simple molecules without finding any two valence bonds with an interior point in common. At last they run across a compound P_3N_3 in which each of three atoms of nitrogen is joined by one valence bond to each of three atoms of phosphorus. For the molecules of this substance the chemists cannot draw a diagram of the usual sort because, in a plane, it is impossible to join each of three points to each of three other points by nine arcs no two of which have an interior point in common (cf. I, 3). But a two-dimensional Einstein living in this paper plane might explain everything by suggesting that the world in question was one of the three-dimensional continua developed by his mathematical colleagues, and that the nitrogen and phosphorus atoms composing any molecule of P_3N_3 were arranged on the surface of a little anchor ring in this continuum. So long as terrestrial chemists confine themselves to one-dimensional valence bonds (valence arcs) they are not forced to assume that their space is a thin slice of a four-dimensional continuum, because, according to a basic theorem of dimension theory, every object composed of arcs can be depicted in three-dimensional space—that is to say, it can be topologically transformed into an object contained in three-dimensional space. The situation might be different if chemists were to find it necessary to use surfaces as bonds. Suppose, for instance, there were two kinds of ozone of different stability, and suppose it were decided to represent one of these by three oxygen atoms joined by the three sides of a triangle, and the other by three oxygen atoms situated at the corners of a triangular surface. The extension of such a system might cause difficulties, because not every object composed of triangular surfaces can be depicted in three-dimensional space. In fact, Flores discovered some which cannot be transformed topologically into any object of a space of less than five dimensions.

III. Some Trends in Modern Geometry

The close relation between modern differential geometry (the work of Levi-Cività, Cartan, Weyl, Schouten) and the theory of relativity is generally known and will undoubtedly be treated elsewhere in this volume. Here I shall discuss certain trends of modern geometry which are less commonly known.

(A). Undoubtedly the most striking feature in the development of geometry during the last 2000 years is the continued expansion of the concept "geometric object." This concept began by comprising only the few curves and surfaces of Greek synthetic geometry; it was stretched, during the Renaissance, to cover the wide domain of those objects defined by analytic geometry; more recently, it has been extended to cover the boundless universe treated by point-set theory. The tree planted by Descartes still continues to bloom, and its admirers have indeed repeatedly tried to exterminate the somewhat bizarre shoots which have sprung from the seed sown by Cantor—growths which, in the natural course of events, seem destined to surround and cover the venerable tree. But although the trend, particularly in the last decade, has been against point-set theory,[2] I do not believe that its antagonists will, in the long run, stunt its growth, any more than their intellectual ancestors, at the time of the Renaissance, harmed analytic geometry by denying

[2] It is a curious fact that some opponents of set theory introduce set theory into the foundation of other branches of mathematics, such as projective geometry, and into parts of analysis which can be developed in a purely algebraic way.

that the equation $y = 3^x$ represents a legitimate geometric object (cf. I, 4). The exponential and logarithmic curves, once denounced as ungeometric, have emerged unscathed from the struggle. Those who claim that Euclid and Descartes would not recognize most point-sets as legitimate objects for geometric treatment are undoubtedly right. But it is equally likely that neither Pythagoras nor Palestrina would recognize a modern symphonic tone poem as music.

(B). Another important modern trend is the transition from the quantitative to the qualitative point of view. Projective geometry began by ignoring length; then came the general theory of order which neglects distances and concentrates attention on mere arrangement. These movements, however, are but steps along the road to topology. In this connection, it is worth noting that even modern algebra, by devoting itself principally to the study of groups, rings and fields, has largely abandoned the quantitative point of view.

(C). A third modern tendency is the one away from co-ordinates. It was by way of co-ordinates that quantity, in the seventeenth century, invaded geometry. But objections to co-ordinates may be raised even by a geometer interested in quantitative results, for every set of co-ordinates refers to just one frame of reference, and it is fair to ask "Why this particular frame?" Indeed, in tensor calculus the co-ordinates of an object are computed with respect to every frame, if the co-ordinates of that object with respect to any one frame are known; and in the theory of invariants, geometers and algebraists have systematically studied properties and relations which are valid no matter what frame is chosen. Why then introduce any frame at all? Unfortunately, in analytic geometry, many relations which are independent of any frame must be expressed with reference to some particular frame. It is therefore preferable to devise new methods—methods which lead directly to intrinsic properties without any mention of co-ordinates. The development of topology of general spaces and of the objects which occur in them, as well as the development of the geometry of general metric spaces (cf. I, 4) are steps in this direction.

(D). The last modern trend which we shall mention is the

one away from assumptions of differentiability. There is no valid reason to restrict numerical relations by such assumptions, even if attention is confined to points defined by co-ordinates, and to objects introduced by equations. In other words, there is no valid reason why only smooth objects should be studied. The motives which prompt so many mathematicians and physicists to limit themselves to the consideration of such objects are, in origin, historical and psychological. The concepts of calculus first opened the field of local geometric properties (e.g., tangents, curvatures, cusps, points of inflection, etc.) to investigation; and the methods of calculus have suggested to geometers problems which have kept them busy for 250 years. The training of mathematicians, and particularly of physicists, begins with calculus, and the spirit of the calculus permeates their later studies. Whatever is customary appears natural and simple. Students, when their mathematical training is finished, handle higher partial derivatives as easily as they handle common fractions; and they are thereby misled into the belief that such derivatives represent natural and simple concepts. In my opinion, the concepts so represented are neither geometrically as natural nor logically as simple as many of the concepts of general topology or general metric geometry, which appear complicated to some mathematicians and abstruse to most physicists. Assumptions of smoothness should be eliminated except where they are really indispensable. For instance, the length of a curve and many related quantities (which in calculus are expressed as integrals involving derivatives) have actually nothing to do with the smoothness of the curve in question. In fact, the concept of length, applied to a polygon, is clearer than the same concept applied to a circle, although the polygon is not smooth and the circle is. Moreover, many general theorems do not hold within the restricted field of smooth curves. Goldschmidt showed that some curves which minimize certain simple and important expressions, have corners, and Hahn discovered that some of these minimizing (!) curves are even of infinite length. Consequently, an *a priori* limitation to smooth curves of finite length often eliminates the very solutions of the minimum problems under consideration. It is only by reason of historical inertia that, even where smoothness has no bearing on either the problem or its solution, differentiability is postulated in order that the traditional methods of the calculus may be applied.

IV. Modern Trends in Geometry and the Theory of Einstein

A geometer who attempts to connect the trends just mentioned with the work of Einstein finds himself in an unenviable position. On the one hand, he realizes that the theory of relativity, one of the greatest achievements of the human intellect, is based entirely on a form of geometry which today deserves to be called classic. On the other hand, he is forced to admit that, no matter how much significance he may attach to the recent progress just indicated, he has only a few suggestions and no substantial results to offer to the physicist. Even so, if he is convinced of the importance of the recent developments in his own field, he cannot help feeling that some day the new geometry must be of use to physicists, particularly in the field of relativity. And since it was Einstein who introduced into physics geometric ideas which, before his day, had been regarded as mere mathematical speculations, an essay on relativity and geometry seems to be the appropriate place for a geometer to air his opinions and his hopes.

Historically, the first attempt to apply modern geometry to physics was not auspicious. The speculations about Nature in which the founder of set theory briefly indulged were not on a par with his profound mathematical ideas. He attempted to connect heat and electricity with denumerability and indenumerability, two quantitative properties of infinite sets. Today, despite the greatly increased knowledge about the regularities and irregularities of point-sets (cf. III, A), it is difficult to imagine how general sets could be applied to physics. Take, for example, only one of the most astonishing conclusions which Banach and Tarski deduced from a discovery made by Hausdorff. It is possible to divide a large sphere (say, of the size of the sun) into a finite number of mutually disjoint parts which together exhaust the volume of the large sphere, and to move each one of these parts (without changing its size or shape) into a small sphere (say, of the size of a pea) in such a way that the moved parts remain mutually disjoint and together exhaust the volume of the small sphere. This statement means that, if a man could only break up the large sphere in the proper clever way, he could put the whole of it into his pocket. Admirable as this result is mathematically, to attempt to apply its method to physics would be hopeless. For, although the theory clearly defines the parts into which the large sphere is to be broken, and precisely describes the motion of each one of these parts into the small sphere, such a construction, since it involves an infinite number of operations, cannot be applied to any physical object. Indeed the same difficulty crops up, though in a milder form, whenever the attempt is made to apply to the physical world the concept of an irrational number. The only conclusion which might be drawn from theorems such as the one just mentioned is an argument in favor of the atomistic structure of matter—or at least in favor of the theory that matter is composed of lumps, each of which is again composed of lumps and so on perhaps *ad infinitum*, but that at every stage of this structure there is empty space between the lumps. A philosopher of nature, trained in logic, might find it worth his while to formulate assumptions on the basis of which this argument and others like it (some of which were anticipated by the scholastic philosophers) might be transformed into rigorous proofs. At present, however, it seems unlikely that the theory of complicated sets can contribute much to the theory of relativity or to physics in general.

Between the sets of set-theoretical geometry and the smooth world lines of the Riemann space with which the theory of relativity deals, there are, however, many intermediate stages. But before these are discussed, a word should be devoted to the qualitative and quantitative concepts (cf. III, B) in mechanics. The antithesis between these concepts is roughly parallel to the antithesis between the synthetic and the analytic points of view in this branch of physics.

Philosophers of science may be interested to know that, considered as synthetic theories, some branches of biology and economics have attained a degree of perfection higher than that hitherto attained by mechanics—the science which, in its analytic phase, is the most highly perfected form of applied mathematics. Indeed, some of the so-called axiomatizations of mechanics are reminiscent of Spinoza's *Ethics* rather than the geometric work of Pasch, Pieri, Hilbert, or Veblen. They have the form of a postulational theory without exhibiting the spirit of rigorous reasoning which is so splendidly displayed in analytic mechanics. Postulational geometry begins with qualitative assumptions about undefined objects. Von Staudt and Hilbert developed this theory to the stage where systems of numbers may be associated (in many different ways) with the undefined objects considered. These systems of numbers are the co-ordinates relative to various frames of reference. There is no reason why a similar postulational mechanics (in the sense of either Newton or Einstein) should be impossible. Such a theory would begin with qualitative assumptions about undefined concepts and would culminate by associating systems of numbers (in many different ways) with the undefined objects. These systems of numbers would be the quantitative co-ordinates of analytical mechanics.

Einstein's theory of relativity looks for smooth lines of minimal length in Riemann spaces which are far more general than the Euclidean space. But in spaces which are still more general, lines of minimal length need not be smooth (cf. III, D). Indeed, Riemann spaces and their immediate generalizations are by no means the last word in generality, even if attention is confined to homogeneous spaces devoid of set-theoretical singularities (cf. I, 4). The day may well come when physicists will take advantage of the wide generality and enormous variety provided by the concepts of modern geometry. The points of general metric spaces are not indeed defined by co-ordinates, but the disadvantages inherent in the use of co-ordinates have already been mentioned (cf. III, C). The relativity theory of the future may seek to formulate intrinsic relations between the lines of general metric spaces, without reference to any arbitrarily chosen frame.

In connection with this prophecy, I venture to elaborate Minkowski's dictum that the laws of nature may find their most perfect expression in the statement of relations between world-lines. It might be suggested to the physicists that they try to express qualitative physical laws by statements about intrinsic topological relations between world-lines in some fairly general continuum. These statements should not mention co-ordinates but should be capable of being expressed with quantitative precision in regard to any particular frame of reference.

V. Future Tasks for Geometers

The further geometrization of physics is bound to raise new problems for geometers—problems other than that of preparing the ground for some generalization of the theory of relativity such as the one outlined in the preceding section.

Postulational non-Euclidean geometries and the analytic geometries of smooth Riemann spaces modify Euclid's idealization of the properties of a rod as its length increases beyond any finite bound (cf. I, 1). This statement is not contradicted by the fact that the geometry used in the present theory of relativity is a differential geometry of the type which, in the eighteenth century, used to be called "the geometry of the infinitely small;" for, paradoxically, this differential geometry has been applied to the macrocosmos, in fact, to astronomical distances. Euclid's other idealization, his neglect of the thickness of rods and planes (cf. I, 1), has not yet been profoundly changed. In fact, a specific geometry of the microcosmos has not yet been well developed. I venture the conjecture that, for the geometrization of physics, especially the physics of the microcosm, idealizations very different from those of Euclid might prove more adequate than his.

One such alternative is a geometry where points are not primary entities. What is here contemplated is a geometry of lumps—that is, a theory in which lumps are undefined concepts, whereas points appear as the results of limiting or intersectional processes applied to these lumps. The reader interested in the details of this idea is referred to the exposition of it which appeared in the Rice Institute Pamphlets of 1940. As a conclusion for the present paper, another possibility is here indicated,—namely, the introduction of probability into the foundations of geometry.

Poincaré, in several of his famous essays on the philosophy of science, characterized the difference between mathematics and physics as follows: In mathematics, if the quantity A is equal to the quantity B, and B is equal to C, then A is equal to C; that is, in modern terminology: mathematical equality is a transitive relation. But in the observable physical continuum "equal" means indistinguishable; and in this continuum, if A is equal to B, and B is equal to C, it by no means follows that A is equal to C. In the terminology of the psychologists Weber and Fechner, A may lie within the threshold of B, and B within the threshold of C, even though A does not lie within the threshold of C. "The raw result of experience," says Poincaré, "may be expressed by the relation

$$A = B, B = C, A < C,$$

which may be regarded as the formula for the physical continuum." That is to say, physical equality is not a transitive relation.

Is this reasoning cogent? It is indeed easy to devise experiments which prove that the question whether two physical quantities are distinguishable cannot always be answered by a simple Yes or No. The same observer may regard the same two objects sometimes as identical and sometimes as distinguishable. A blindfolded man may consider the simultaneous irritation of the same two spots on his skin sometimes as one, and sometimes as two tactile sensations. Of two constant lights, he may regard the first sometimes as weaker than, sometimes as equal to, and sometimes as stronger than the second. All that can be done in this situation is to count the percentage number of instances in which he makes any one of these two or three observations. In the observation of physical continua, situations like the one just described seem to be the rule rather than the exception.

Instead of distinguishing between a transitive mathematical and an intransitive physical relation of equality, it thus seems much more hopeful to retain the transitive relation in mathematics and to introduce for the distinction of physical and physiological quantities a probability, that is, a number lying between 0 and 1.

Elaboration of this idea leads to the concept of a space in

which a distribution function rather than a definite number is associated with every pair of elements. The number associated with two points of a metric space is called the distance between the two points. The distribution function associated with two elements of a statistical metric space might be said to give, for every x, the probability that the distance between the two points in question does not exceed x. Such a statistical generalization of metric spaces appears to be well adapted for the investigation of physical quantities and physiological thresholds. The idealization of the local behavior of rods and boards, implied by this statistical approach, differs radically from that of Euclid. In spite of this fact, or perhaps just because of it, the statistical approach may provide a useful means for geometrizing the physics of the microcosm.

Perhaps the most promising way to attack local geometric problems would be with a combination of the two ideas outlined in this section, the statistical approach and a geometry of lumps.

KARL MENGER

ILLINOIS INSTITUTE OF TECHNOLOGY
CHICAGO

18

Leopold Infeld

ON THE STRUCTURE OF OUR UNIVERSE

ON THE STRUCTURE OF OUR UNIVERSE

I

SPECULATIONS about the Universe in which men live are as old as human thought and as art; as old as the view of shining stars on a clear night. Yet it was the general relativity theory which, only thirty years ago, shifted cosmological problems from poetry or speculative philosophy into physics. We can even fix the year in which modern cosmology was born. It was in 1917 when Einstein's paper appeared in the Prussian Academy of Science under the title "Cosmological Considerations in General Relativity Theory."[1]

Although it is difficult to exaggerate the importance of this paper, and although it created a flood of other papers and speculations, Einstein's original ideas, as viewed from the perspective of our present day, are antiquated if not even wrong. I believe Einstein would be the first to admit this.

Yet the appearance of this paper is of great importance in the history of theoretical physics. Indeed, it is one more instance showing how a wrong solution of a fundamental problem may be incomparably more important than a correct solution of a trivial, uninteresting problem.

Why is Einstein's paper so important? Because it formulates an entirely new problem, that of the structure of our universe; because it shows that the general theory of relativity can throw new light upon this problem.

The classical physicists thought about our physical space as a three-dimensional Euclidean continuum, our physical time as a one-dimensional continuum common to all observers, whether in

[1] A. Einstein, "Kosmologische Betrachtungen zur allgemeinen Relativitäts-theorie," *S. B. Preuss. Akad. Wiss.* (1917), 142-152.

relative motion or not. These concepts were changed completely when Einstein, in 1905, formulated the special theory of relativity. The physicist learned that, in ordering physical events, it is much more convenient and simple to consider a four-dimensional pseudo-Euclidean time-space continuum as the background for these events. Then, in 1914, he had to learn again that, in order to understand the phenomena of gravitation, he must generalize his concepts once more. In the general theory of relativity, the universe is represented by a four-dimensional manifold, its metric shaped by masses, their motion and radiation; far from masses and sources of energy, this Riemannian space-time continuum more and more closely approaches the pseudo-Euclidean space-time continuum of the special theory of relativity.

In theoretical physics new ideas are born by the genius and imagination of men who can look upon an old problem from an entirely new and unexpected point of view. This is how the special and the general theories of relativity were born; this is how quantum theory entered into physics. In Einstein's paper on cosmology we see the same ability to look upon old problems in a new way. Yet, as we know today, there is an essential difference. Whereas the special and general theories of relativity stand in our present day almost as fresh and complete as in the days when they were formulated, whereas in the last thirty years nothing of fundamental importance has been added to Einstein's structure, the problem of cosmology looks very different today from the way it did in the days when Einstein wrote his celebrated paper.

To consider our universe as a whole means to do something similar to what a child does when he looks at the globe of our earth. He becomes familiar with the general shape of our earth, by ignoring the mountains and valleys, houses and towns, by considering the earth as a smooth surface, by forming a highly idealized picture, useless if he wants to find his way through his back-yard, but useful if he wishes to understand the path of an aeroplane journey around the world. Similarly, in cosmological problems, when we consider our universe as a whole, we must form a highly idealized picture, ignoring small disturbances and local concentrations of masses, smoothing out irregularities and considering the geometry of our universe taken as a whole. Thus, according to Einstein, in such a simplified picture of our universe, matter should be at rest in a suitably chosen co-ordinate system and the proper distances of nebulae from the observer should not change with time.

Experiments later on showed that such a postulate contradicts the law of red-shift, which was discovered some years after Einstein's paper appeared. It is ironical that Einstein wished to form a general picture of our universe in which matter does not run away; yet the famous experiments on the red-shift of nebulae convince us that matter behaves as though it were running away! Thus the fundamental Einstein assumption seems to be too narrow to fit the facts as they were observed later.

The next assumptions which Einstein made were those of *isotropy* and *homogeneity*. Unlike the first assumption, these two (formulated rather implicitly) have survived up to now, although it is not at all sure whether future observations made with new, more powerful, telescopes, will not force us to change them. Yet, mostly because of their simplicity, these two assumptions form the basis of all modern cosmologies.

What is the meaning of these assumptions?

Isotropy means simply that in a proper co-ordinate system an observer looking in different directions will never notice that any of them are preferred. In a suitably chosen co-ordinate system the smoothed out, idealized universe appears the same in all directions, or, as we say, it is *isotropic*.

The assumption of *homogeneity* means that observers placed at different points of the universe, describing its history in different, but properly chosen co-ordinate systems will find these histories identical in their contents; that it is impossible in this way to distinguish one place in the universe from another. Similarly, the two-dimensional inhabitants of a perfect sphere or plane could not distinguish one point of their surface from another.

Thus the two postulates, that of isotropy and homogeneity are implicitly contained in Einstein's work.

These two assumptions survived beyond Einstein's first attempt to formulate a cosmological theory. They are present (explicitly or implicitly) in all modern cosmologies.

We could ask: Is our universe really isotropic? Is our universe really homogeneous? These questions mean: can we formulate a theory consistent with the observed facts by assuming homogeneity and isotropy? At the present time our observations can penetrate only a small corner of our universe. It is possible that future observation may force us to retreat from these simple assumptions. Yet these assumptions are the most obvious ones and we shall change them only under the impact of new discoveries.

Besides isotropy and homogeneity Einstein assumed, as we said before, that in a proper co-ordinate system, the masses at large, which form the universe, are at rest and that the average density of matter ϱ_0 is constant.

Are these assumptions consistent? Let us recall that in the general theory of relativity, Einstein formulated new gravitational equations which must be satisfied by every gravitational field. Is it possible, we ask, to satisfy the postulates of isotropy, homogeneity, and that of constant density of resting masses? A straightforward investigation provides the answer: No! These three postulates together contradict Einstein's original gravitational equations. Thus something must be changed to make the general theory of relativity consistent with Einstein's cosmological considerations. In his paper, Einstein proposed to make the scheme consistent by changing the gravitational equations of the general relativity theory. The change is small, characterized by the appearance of an additional small cosmological term. Whenever in the past the general theory of relativity was confirmed by experiment, it will be confirmed again, if we add this small cosmological term. Its appearance matters little, if we consider the phenomena in our solar system or even in our galaxy. But this cosmological term becomes important, if we consider our universe as a whole. It is this term which makes it possible to satisfy Einstein's cosmological postulates in the now generalized frame of relativity theory.

One could argue that the additional introduction of a new term, which we shall call the *cosmological term*, is artificial;

that a satisfactory theory must not introduce new constants, leaving their numerical determination to experiment. There is no doubt that such objections are valid; that the introduction of a cosmological constant—without theoretical specification of its numerical value—does have the character of an *"ad hoc"* hypothesis. Yet, in spite of all that, Einstein's paper, because of the originality of its ideas, because of its imaginative formulation of a new problem, from a new point of view, played a fundamental rôle in the development of our knowledge about the structure of the universe.

Let us add to our discussion a sketch of its mathematical formulation. The so-called Einstein universe is characterized by the following metrical form:

$$ds^2 = R^2 \left[d\tau^2 - d\varrho^2 \, sin^2\varrho (d\theta^2 + sin^2\theta \, d\varphi^2) \right] \qquad (I, 1)$$

Here τ is the time co-ordinate, ϱ, φ, θ are the space co-ordinates, and c, the velocity of light, is taken to be one. R is a constant called "the Radius of the Einstein universe." If ϱ is very small we can by introducing

$$\varrho = r/R$$
$$\tau = ct/R; \; (c = \text{velocity of light})$$

write the above equation in the following form:

$$ds^2 = c^2 \, dt^2 - dr^2 - r^2 (d\theta^2 + sin^2\theta \, d\varphi^2) \qquad (I, 2)$$

This is the ordinary form of the Minkowski or pseudo-Euclidean space-time continuum where the space part is written in a polar co-ordinate system.

The space part in (I, 1) represents an isotropic and homogeneous three-dimensional manifold, the geometry of which is a generalization of the geometry of a two-dimensional sphere. Much can be deduced from the quadratic form (I, 1) without going into the dynamical equations of the general theory of relativity. Let us discuss now the possible *topologies* of a manifold represented by (I, 1), a point to which little attention was paid when Einstein formulated his cosmological theory, and a point, which, I believe, is of great importance for the understanding of cosmological problems.

The angles φ and θ which have the same meaning as in a polar co-ordinate-system also have the same range:

$$0 \leq \varphi < 2\pi$$
$$0 \leq \theta \leq \pi$$

What about the angle ϱ? Take any point characterized by $\varrho = 0$, φ, θ, then, any point characterized by $\varrho = \pi$, φ, θ. The line element ds^2 will have the same form and the same value at these two points for neighbouring events with the same $d\tau$, $d\varrho$, $d\varphi$, $d\theta$. How will the observer distinguish between the two pairs of neighbouring events? The metrical form is the same. If we solve a physical problem on such a geometrical background (e.g., the behaviour of the electromagnetic field) we usually see that the physical events are also identical in two such points. Thus we are faced with two possibilities:

1. The universe is a *mirror* universe. To every event O there corresponds an identical event O′ at its antipodal point. In such a universe ϱ ranges from 0 to π, but events at $\varrho = \pi$ mirror those at $\varrho = 0$. It is easy to make jokes about such a universe in which someone like you is reading a treatise on cosmology at this moment. But in our cosmological, idealized and smoothed-out universe, the individuals and even the stars are of little importance.

Such a *mirror* universe is called a *spherical* universe.

2. Another, less paradoxical interpretation assumes: O and O′ are *identical* points and the events in them are *identical* events. The points with the co-ordinates $\varrho = 0$ and $\varrho = \pi$ are *the same* points. Such a universe is called an *elliptical* universe.

Both universes, the spherical and elliptical, have the same metric but a different topology, or connectivity. Cut out a piece of paper and form a cylinder from it and you will get a surface with the same metric as on the plane but with a different topology. The edges of the paper regarded as different points are now identified in the case of a cylinder.

It is almost obvious that, faced with a choice between these two interpretations, we should rather choose the second one than populate our universe with ghost-events.

Let us return to our quadratic form (I, 1) and draw from it some simple conclusions:

1. At any point in space, in a co-ordinate system characterized by (I, 1), we can imagine a particle at rest, not changing its position with time. Rest of a free particle *is* consistent with the Einstein universe and with the relativistic law of motion, according to which every free particle moves along a geodetic line.

2. A light ray sent out from a point returns to it after a time interval either 2π or π, depending on whether we consider the Einstein universe as a spherical or elliptical one. The small and simple number 2π or π is not astonishing. It is due to our choice of the time unit as given by (I, 1). Indeed we could say that our unit of time as used in (I, 1) is tremendously great. In ordinary units the period after which light returns would be

$$T = 2\pi R/c \text{ in a spherical universe}$$
$$T = \pi R/c \text{ in an elliptic universe.}$$

As R is of the order 10^{28} cm (for reasons to be explained later), we see that the period which light takes to travel around our universe is of the order of 10^{18} second or 10^{11} years!

Other conclusions can be drawn if we assume, besides the metrical form (I, 1), Einstein's dynamical equations generalized by the appearance of the cosmological constant. These equations are:

$$G_{kl} + \Lambda\, g_{kl} = -k\, T_{kl} \qquad\qquad (I, 3)$$

Let us discuss these equations briefly without going into the details of their mathematical structure.

These are 10 equations, or one tensorial equation. The indices k, l take any of the values 0, 1, 2, 3, and all tensorial expressions with indices are symmetric, that is $g_{kl} = g_{lk}$; $G_{kl} = G_{lk}$; $T_{kl} = T_{lk}$. The symmetric tensor g_{kl} is the metric tensor. It is completely known in our case, because the metrical form (I, 1) is given. The symmetric Einstein tensor G_{kl}, depending on g_{kl} and its derivatives can be calculated explicitly if the g_{kl} are known, that is when the metrical form (I, 1) is given. Now the expression $\Lambda\, g_{kl}$ is *the* additional cosmological expression which appeared for the first time in Einstein's paper in 1917. Put $\Lambda = 0$ and you will have the old gravitational equations.

The constant k appearing on the right-hand side of (I, 3) is known, and depends in a simple manner on the gravitational constant of Newton's theory and the velocity of light. Thus our equation determines T_{kl}, if the metric form is given and if Λ is known. T_{kl} are the components of the so-called energy-momentum tensor characterizing masses, their motion and radiation energy. If the geometry of our universe is known (that is the g_{kl} tensor), if Λ is known, then the physics of our universe (that is the energy-momentum tensor) is known too.

In Einstein's universe, as we saw before, masses at large are at rest. This, translated into the language of tensors, means that the only surviving component of the T_{kl} tensor will be the T_{oo} component. It is this component which represents the density ϱ_o of matter. Only if we introduce a proper cosmological constant can we achieve the vanishing of all components of T_{kl} with the exception of T_{oo}. The T_{oo} component will then be constant and represent the density of matter in the world.

From Einstein's dynamical equations we can draw two new conclusions:

1. The radius R is known if ϱ_o is known. The oo equation (I, 3) gives us a simple connection between ϱ_o and R. From Hubble's nebuli counts we can at least estimate roughly the mean density of matter. Its order of magnitude seems to be 10^{-30} gram per cubic centimeter. From that we can deduce the order of magnitude of R. This is how the value $R \sim 10^{28}$ cm, quoted before, was obtained. Also, the cosmological constant can be calculated if we know R. We have $\Lambda = 1/R^2 \sim 10^{-57}$ cm^{-2}. Indeed, the additional cosmological term is very small!

2. The total mass of the universe is finite. This is so, because the density of the mass is finite and the volume of the universe is finite. Knowing (or rather assuming we know) the mean density of matter in our universe, and having deduced from it the radius of the universe, we can now calculate its total mass. But again we have to distinguish between a spherical and elliptic space. The total mass in a spherical universe is twice as great as that in an elliptic one.

Thus Einstein's work presents us for the first time with a mathematical model of our universe. The three dimensional parts of our metrical form (I, 1) (if we put $d\tau = 0$) is a generalization to three dimensions of the ordinary two-dimensional sphere or the one-dimensional circle. The universe (I, 1) is sometimes called the "Einstein cylindrical universe." The circle of the ordinary two-dimensional cylinder may be said to correspond in this picture to our three-dimensional sphere; the height to the time dimension. In such a universe free particles may retain their proper distances in space, and light circumvents such a universe in finite time.

We shall have to abandon this picture because it is inconsistent with observation. Yet it was this picture which formed a basis for all further work on cosmology.

II

We shall now sketch briefly the story of fifteen years of development, covering the period 1917-1931, which ends with the appearance of Einstein's two papers on cosmology.

Since Einstein wrote his paper in 1917 great observational progress has been achieved. The human eye has penetrated far beyond the Milky Way, far beyond our galaxy.

As far as we can reach with our most powerful telescopes, we find matter agglomerated into a large number of separate aggregates, the *nebulae*.

Observation on these nebulae has revealed to us the following characteristic features of our universe:

On a tremendous scale, large compared with the distances between nebulae, the distribution of nebulae is *isotropic* and *homogeneous*. This important result is deduced from two facts. First: A comparison of nebular counts to great depths in different portions of the sky shows that the nebulae have an isotropic distribution. Secondly: The number N of nebulae to within a certain distance d (in cm.), is, for sufficiently large d, given by

$$N = 4 \times 10^{-71} d^3.$$

Since the nebular masses are of the same order of magnitude (10^{41} grams per nebula) a mean density of luminous matter can be calculated:

$$\varrho_0 = 10^{-30} \ gr \ cm^{-3}.$$

Hubble estimates that the mean density of matter may actually be one thousand times greater because of dust, gas, or unobservable moving particles in intergalactic space.

A further very important result of observational cosmology was the discovery of the *red-shift*. The spectra of nebulae, when compared with the corresponding terrestrial spectra, are shifted towards the red in an overwhelming majority of cases. For any individual nebula the displacement $\Delta\lambda$ of the wave-length λ of any line of the nebulae spectrum is proportional to λ. Thus we may measure the red-shift of the nebulae by $(\Delta\lambda)/\lambda$. The obvious interpretation is to imagine that these nebulae run away from us and the red-shift is due to the Doppler effect. However, the velocities calculated in this way are so tremendous that we may fear that such an obvious interpretation is too obvious to be the correct one. And, besides, what is the reason for such a rapid motion?

This red-shift, as given by observation, appears to depend on the remoteness of the distance of the nebulae. The farther away the nebulae are, the greater the red-shift, the greater seems their velocity. As far as our telescopes penetrate, the relationship between red-shift and distance is approximately linear. We have

$$(\Delta\lambda)/\lambda = kd + \text{departure of higher order and}$$
$$k = 5.68 \times 10^{-28} \ cm^{-1}.$$

Thus, if we look back upon the Einstein universe, we see that the idea of isotropy and homogeneity seems to be confirmed by observation. But there is no place for the red-shift in the Einstein universe! Einstein's model seems to prevent the nebulae from running away. Ironically enough it was invented to do just that. But the nebulae do seem to run away! Thus Einstein's model will not do, and has to be replaced by another. Once, however, the problem was raised by Einstein, it was comparatively easy to look for different models to retain some of Einstein's ideas and to reject others. It was again Einstein's genius which opened a new path into the unknown.

Before we discuss further generalizations, let us return once more to the principles of isotropy and homogeneity. Obviously, in our search for a generalization of our cosmological model, we would like to stick to these assumptions. If for no other reasons than because these assumptions *are* the simplest possible and they are not contradicted by experiment. But does not the phenomenon of the red-shift contradict these assumptions? How is it possible that in a homogeneous universe the nebulae seem to run away from *our* galaxy? The answer to this question is obvious. If we wish to save the principle of homogeneity we must not assume that *our* galaxy is distinguished in any way; that nebulae show their aversion by running away from our galaxy; that this aversion increases with the distance of the nebulae. On the contrary! We must form a model in which the red-shift can be observed from *any* nebula. The history of our universe and its description must be such that it won't matter from what point in space we describe our universe. Putting it more mathematically; the laws of our universe viewed at large must be invariant in form and content with respect to a proper transformation connecting the arbitrary points in space.

Let us now form a very simplified and highly idealized picture of our universe. In it, all local irregularities due to the agglomeration of matter into nebulae or even nebular clusters are neglected; so are all random motions. In such a smoothed-out, idealized model we assume a very dense and uniform distribution of particles. One such particle in our model corresponds to a nebula. We can imagine its presence whenever we wish and we shall call this dense collection of particles—*fundamental particles*. With each such particle we imagine an observer and we shall call him the *fundamental observer*. The law of red-shift seems to indicate that nebulae move with great velocities. Thus in our model we shall assume a vector field, the vector at each point of space indicating the velocity of the fundamental particle and, therefore, representing the motion of a nebula.

Thus we have a picture similar to that we use in hydromechanics: a fluid composed of fundamental particles, their motion prescribed by the vector field.

The law of red-shift broadened our vision of the universe. It cannot be the static Einstein universe.

Can we reconcile the postulates of homogeneity and isotropy

with the observed red-shift and still remain on the ground of the general relativity theory?

Shortly after Einstein's paper appeared, de Sitter[2] proposed a new model of our universe, which reconciles the principles of isotropy and homogeneity on the one hand with the observed facts of red-shift on the other. As a matter of fact, de Sitter formulated his paper before the law of red-shift was discovered. It forms a very beautiful instance of theory predicting experimental results.

The de Sitter universe is mathematically more attractive than Einstein's universe. Whereas the Einstein universe is—vaguely speaking—like a three-dimensional sphere the de Sitter universe is—equally vaguely speaking—like a four-dimensional sphere immersed in a five-dimensional space. Yet, just because it can be represented as a sphere, the demands of isotropy and homogeneity are automatically fulfilled.

We have already mentioned the importance of fundamental particles and their motion. We could ask now: what is the motion of such fundamental particles in the de Sitter universe? Unfortunaely, it is not easy to answer this question for two reasons. First: the description will depend on the choice of our co-ordinate system. Second: there are not one, but three possible de Sitter universes with different kinds of motions. What we shall do now is to pick out *one* of these universes, ignoring the other two. We shall discuss it in a co-ordinate system which unfortunately does not reveal the four-dimensional symmetry of this universe but has other redeeming features which will make our discussion simple.

A universe with the quadratic form

$$ds^2 = \frac{\tau_0{}^2}{\tau^2} (d\tau^2 - dx^2 - dy^2 - dz^2) \qquad \text{(II, 1)}$$

is the de Sitter universe. Here τ_0 is a constant, τ is time and x, y, z the space co-ordinates.

We see that in our co-ordinate system, in which the de Sitter

[2] W. de Sitter, "On the Relativity of Inertia." Remarks concerning Einstein's latest Hypothesis. *Proc. Arad. Wetensch*, Amsterdam (Vol. 19, 1917), 1217-1225. "On Einstein's Theory of Gravitation, and Its Astronomical Consequences: III." *Monthly Not. Roy. Astron. Soc.* (Vol. 78, 1917), 3-28.

universe is represented by (II, 1), the laws of light-geometry will be the same as in a Minkowski (or pseudo-Euclidean), universe. Indeed, the only difference between the de Sitter universe, as represented by (II, 1), and the Minkowski universe, is the presence of the factor $\tau_0{}^2/\tau^2$ in (II, 1). But the presence of this factor means nothing for light-rays, which are zero-geodetic lines. For them we always have $ds^2 = 0$.

The next remark concerns the fundamental particles. For the kind of de Sitter universe *we* have chosen, for the kind of co-ordinate system we have chosen, the fundamental particles are at rest. (There are two other de Sitter universes possible, with the same quadratic form and with the fundamental particles moving in a well defined way, prescribed by the conditions of isotropy and homogeneity.)

We could ask: how is a red-shift possible if the particles are at rest? The red-shift is due partially to the motion of fundamental particles, but partially to the gravitational field. How we divide the total effect into these two components (gravitational and Doppler-effect) will depend upon the co-ordinate system. The total effect will, of course, be independent of the choice of the co-ordinate system. In the de Sitter universe, which we consider, the total effect is due only to the gravitational field.

Let us now derive the important law of red-shift from our quadratic form and from our knowledge of relativity theory.

Imagine that a nebula at a distance r sends to us radiation received *here* ($r = 0$) and *now* ($\tau = \tau_0$). The radiation was sent at the time $\tau_0 - r$, (where $r^2 = x^2 + y^2 + z^2$), because the laws of light propagation are the same as in Minkowski's space and because the velocity of light was assumed to equal "one." Now, according to relativity theory, an atom keeps its rhythm in the *proper* time. Thus if $_{(s)}\nu$ is the proper frequency and δs is the period of one oscillation, if $_{(\tau)}\nu$ is the period in τ time, and $\delta\tau$ the frequency in τ time, we have because of the form (II, 1):

$$\delta s = \frac{1}{_{(s)}\nu} = \frac{\tau_0 \delta\tau}{\tau_0 - r} = \frac{\tau_0}{(\tau_0 - r)\,_{(\tau)}\nu}. \qquad \text{(II, 2)}$$

Through its journey in space the radiation preserves its rhythm in τ time because the laws of radiation have nothing to do with the factor $(\tau_0/\tau)^2$ in (II, 1) and are the same in the Minkowski world as in the de Sitter world. Thus, on our earth we can compare the unchanging rhythm of our atomic clock *here*, that is its $_{(s)}\nu$ with the frequency $_{(\tau)}\nu$ sent to us from a distant nebula. We find, from (II, 2):

$$\frac{_{(\tau)}\nu}{_{(s)}\nu} = \frac{\tau_0}{(\tau_0 - r)} = \frac{1}{1 - \dfrac{r}{\tau_0}}.$$

Here and *now* on our earth where $r = 0$, the τ and *s* frequency coincide. Introducing two wave lengths $_{(s)}\lambda = 1/_{(s)}\nu$ and $_{(\tau)}\lambda = 1/_{(\tau)}\nu$ we have:

$$\frac{_{(s)}\lambda}{_{(\tau)}\lambda} = 1 - \frac{r}{\tau_0}$$

and therefore

$$\frac{_{(\tau)}\lambda - _{(s)}\lambda}{_{(\tau)}\lambda} = \frac{\Delta\lambda}{\lambda} = \frac{r}{\tau_0},$$

which gives the famous law of the red-shift. Thus the red-shift is proportional to the "distance" of the source of light. (The quotation marks around the word "distance" indicate that it is an open question whether *r* as defined above deserves to be called "distance.") We see that the de Sitter universe as considered here gives us the law of red-shift and from its experimental determination we can find the present cosmological τ_0. We see also that a similar consideration repeated for the static Einstein universe would not give us the law of red-shift.

Yet in spite of the mathematical beauty of the de Sitter universe, in spite of the fact that it gives us the law of red-shift, two grave objections can be raised against this mathematical model.

The first objection is common to both the de Sitter and Einstein universes. They both require the change in dynamical equations of relativity theory, they both satisfy the gravitational equations for the gravitational field only if we introduce into them the cosmological constant Λ. But we are also faced with another difficulty peculiar to the de Sitter universe.

If we introduce the metrical form (II, 1), into the gravitational equations (I, 3), then we can calculate the average density of matter. True, the fundamental particles are at rest, but we would expect them to have some density as they had in the case of the Einstein universe. But here the density turns out to be zero! The de Sitter universe is empty! Thus the presence of elementary particles with which we must populate our universe in order to represent the nebulae and their motion, contradicts the dynamical equations of the general theory of relativity. Of course, it is an open question whether we should stick to the equations of dynamics in our cosmological approach. We have violated them, in any case, by adding the cosmological expression. We could violate them further by changing the dynamical equations, so that the density of matter defined in a new way would turn out to be different from zero. But such a procedure would be ugly, and it is doubtful whether a logically consistent theory could be built in this way. Einstein's work is characterized by a rare search for logical simplicity, beauty and clarity. Within the framework of the relativity theory there is no place for *ad hoc* assumptions and artificial hypotheses. They would spoil not only the beauty but also the self-consistency of the general theory of relativity.

The first theoretical recognition that the law of red-shift does follow from de Sitter's model of our universe is due to Weyl. We have here one of the instances where theory predicted events later confirmed by experiment. Indeed, Weyl's theoretical paper appeared in 1923,[3] whereas experimental evidence of red-shift became known only in 1929,[4] when Hubble published his results on red-shift measurement of 46 nebulae, and established experimentally the linear relation between $(\Delta\lambda)/\lambda$ and distance.

The further development of theoretical cosmology is mostly connected with three names: Friedmann (1922),[5] Lemaître

[3] Hermann Weyl, "Zur allgemeinen Relativitätstheorie," *Phys. Zeitschr.* (Vol. 24, 1923), 230-232.

[4] E. P. Hubble, "A Relation between Distance and Radial Velocity among Extra-Galactic Nebulae," *Proc. Nat. Acad. Sci.* (Vol. 15, 1929), 168-173.

[5] A. Friedmann, "Über die Krümmung des Raumes," *Zeitschr. f. Physik* (Vol. 10, 1922), 377-386.

(1927),[6] and Robertson (1929).[7] Each of them dealt with the same problem: to find a more general model of our universe, to go beyond that of Einstein and de Sitter. Indeed, it turned out that both the Einstein and de Sitter universes form, so to speak, two limiting cases of a universe either full of matter or of a universe empty of matter. Between these two limiting cases there is an infinite variety of possible universes.

From the philosophical point of view the most satisfactory discussion of the cosmological problem was given by Robertson. It is general, based on very few assumptions, and kinematical in its character, that is, it ignores the dynamical equations of the general theory of relativity altogether.

In its essence Robertson's problem can be stated as follows: Our universe, taken as a whole, is characterized by a metrical four-dimensional form. What, we ask, is the most general quadratic form that would describe an isotropic and homogeneous universe in a co-ordinate system in which the fundamental particles are at rest. Here is Robertson's answer to this question: Imagine a three-dimensional space with constant curvature. Without loss of generality we may assume that the Riemannian curvature k has the values

$$+1, \ 0, \ -1.$$

(Indeed the curvature can be positive, zero, or negative; therefore it can be made $1, 0, -1$, by a proper change of units). Such a three-dimensional space with constant curvature is both isotropic and homogeneous. Mathematically, the three metrical forms can be written in the following ways:

(A) $d\sigma^2 = d\varrho^2 + sin^2 \ \varrho \ (d\theta^2 + sin^2 \ \theta \ d\varphi^2)$ for $k = +1$.

(B) $d\sigma^2 = d\varrho^2 + \varrho^2 \ (d\theta^2 + sin^2 \ \theta \ d\varphi^2)$ for $k = 0$.   (II, 3)

(C) $d\sigma^2 = d\varrho^2 + sinh^2 \ \varrho \ (d\theta^2 + sin^2 \ \theta \ d\varphi^2)$ for $k = -1$.

In relativity theory our universe is represented as a four-dimensional space-time manifold. The demand for isotropy and

[6] G. Lemaître, "Un Univers Homogène de Masse Constante et de Rayon Croissant, Rendant Compte de la Vitesse Radiale de Nébuleuses Extra-galactiques," *Ann. Soc. Sci.* (Bruxelles, Vol. 47A, 1927), 49-59.
[7] H. P. Robertson, "On the Foundations of Relativistic Cosmology," *Proc. Nat. Acad. Sci.*, (Vol. 15, 1929), 822-829.

homogeneity will be preserved, that is, all fundamental observers will describe our universe in the same way, if its metrical form is:

$$ds^2 = R^2(\tau)(d\tau^2 - d\sigma^2),$$

where $d\sigma^2$, is one of the three forms written out before in (II, 3). Thus we have now the most general form for all universes satisfying the conditions of isotropy and homogeneity.

Indeed, take $R = R_0 =$ constant and $d\sigma^2$ of the form (A) and you will have the Einstein universe. Take $R(\tau) = \tau_0/\tau$ and $d\sigma^2$ of the form (B) and you will have the de Sitter universe.

Thus we see that we are faced with a tremendous number of possible cosmological models. True, there are only *three* possibilities for $d\sigma^2$, but an infinite number of possibilities for $R^2(\tau)$, and therefore for ds^2. Many of these models will give us the red-shift. Some of them may give us a violet shift and will, therefore, have to be rejected. Some of them may give us a negative mass or density, or violate some other reasonable dynamic requirements. Yet many possibilities remain. Such a situation is not encouraging. We expect a good theory to lead us to definite conclusions, to a model that can be accepted or rejected by experiment. This is not true in this case. There are too many possibilities!

III

In 1931 Einstein[8] indicated a way of restricting the many cosmological possibilities. He suggested the dropping of the cosmological constant which he had introduced in 1917. We remember how the introduction of Λ generalized Einstein's dynamic equations, so that they could be satisfied by the metric of the Einstein universe. Yet we have learned since then that Einstein's universe is only *one* of the many possible; that, besides, it is inconsistent with the law of red-shift. Thus it would

[8] A. Einstein, "Zum kosmologischen Problem der allgemeinen Relativitätstheorie," S. B. Preuss. Akad. Wiss. (1931), 235-237.

A. Einstein and W. de Sitter, "On the Relation between the Expansion and the Mean Density of the Universe," Proc. Nat. Acad. Sci. (Vol. 18, 1932), 213 f.

seem proper to retreat to the old position held by relativity theory before 1917 and abandon the cosmological constant Λ. In this way the possibilities will become more restricted. The two universes which we considered here in greater detail, the Einstein and de Sitter universes, will not be among those admitted, because they both satisfy only the *generalized* dynamic equations.

In his first paper on this subject, Einstein investigated a cosmological model with $k = 1$ and $R(\tau)$ so chosen that the metric form was consistent with the original dynamic equations, that is those with $\Lambda = 0$. Thus the model which Einstein suggested was a generalization of the previous Einstein universe. But, the fact that $R(\tau)$ was no longer constant made red-shift possible.

In the following year Einstein and de Sitter jointly investigated an especially simple universe. Indeed, in some respects it is the simplest universe yet investigated (of course, with the exception of Minkowski's universe).

The metrical form of this *Einstein-de Sitter* universe, as we shall call it, is:

$$ds^2 = \left(\frac{\tau}{\tau_0}\right)^4 (d\tau^2 - d\sigma^2) \qquad \text{(III, 1)}$$

where $d\sigma^2$ is of the form (B), that is the Euclidean three-dimensional space. A straightforward calculation shows that the metrical form of such a universe is consistent with the original dynamic equations of relativity theory. There is one important conclusion which follows for the absence of the constant Λ and which we shall try to explain now.

Before, we could have argued roughly in the following way: The metrical form introduced a constant, like the constant R_0 in the Einstein universe, or the constant τ_0 in the de Sitter universe. The dynamic equations introduce another constant Λ. Now, generally, such constants as τ_0 can be determined from the observational data on the red-shift. Such constants as Λ can be determined from Hubble's data on nebulae count, that is, from the average density of matter. This is certainly not a satisfactory situation: two constants both determined by measurements.

From the philosophical point of view the Einstein-de Sitter universe appears more satisfactory. Here we have only *one* arbitrary constant, that is τ_0. Its value can be determined from the observation of the red-shift. But if τ_0 is determined, then the value of the density of matter can be *calculated* from it. Thus the theory passes its first test if it gives us reasonable data for the density. In the case of the Einstein-de Sitter universe these data are fairly reasonable.

The density is $6 \times 10^{-28}\ cm^{-3}$, consistent with the upper limit of Hubble's estimation.

Is our universe of such a simple type?

Again we can raise objections both of a practical and of a philosophical nature.

In the first approximation the red-shift is linearly dependent upon the distance. Such a dependence can be explained by many models through a proper choice of a constant (like τ_0) in the metric form. But a more thorough experimental examination shows that the red-shift depends on expressions of *higher* order too. As experimental evidence accumulates, as we are able to reach further and further into our universe, the demands on a theory of our universe will become more and more stringent. A good theory will have to explain the *total* red-shift and not only the approximate red-shift as represented by the linear term. But even now, with our imperfect knowledge of the red-shift effects of the higher order, we know that the Einstein-de Sitter universe is not in close agreement with the experimental results.

The next difficulty is shared both by the Einstein-de Sitter universe and many other models too. We have seen that the red-shift effect allows us to find τ_0, the *"now"* of our universe. Thus we can easily calculate how long—in proper time—the universe has existed until the present moment. The result is 10^9 years, a period which seems too small to squeeze the complicated history of our universe into it. It seems almost too short for even only the geological history of one insignificant member of our universe, the earth.

There is one more argument against the Einstein-de Sitter universe though much more difficult to explain, because it is of a rather philosophical and mathematical character.

Our universe can be either *open* or *closed*. We call our universe closed, if a light-ray sent from a point o ultimately returns to it; the universe is open, if a light-ray does not return to its point of departure. If a co-ordinate system is such that all fundamental particles are at rest in it, then, in an isotropic homogeneous universe, the quadratic form must be of the form (II, 3). The universe is open, if the quadratic form in such a co-ordinate-system is (B) or (C). The universe is closed if it is of the form (A).

Thus among the universes that we have considered until now, the Einstein universe is closed, but the de Sitter universe and the Einstein-de Sitter universes are open. (We may remark in passing that one of the three possible de Sitter universes—not considered here—*is* closed.)

Before we decide the question: what is the particular quadratic form of our universe, we would like to decide a more fundamental question: is our universe *open* or *closed?* This question is more general and more important than the specialized question regarding the metric of our universe, that is, the choice of the function $R(\tau)$. We do not know the answer to this question. Yet every mathematician—if given the choice—would rather see our universe closed than open. There is mathematical beauty in such a universe which reveals itself when we consider any mathematical problem on such a cosmological background. In such a closed universe we have simple boundary conditions and do not need to worry about infinities in time and space. Compared with the closed universe the open one of Einstein-de Sitter appears to be dull and uninspired.

The Einstein universe can be regarded as a prototype of a closed universe. Yet, we remember, there are two possible Einstein universes. An Einstein universe can be either *spherical* or *elliptical*. In the quadratic form (I, 1) we identify the points $\varrho = 0$ and $\varrho = \pi$, if the universe is elliptic. We have mirror events in a spherical universe. They become identical events in an elliptic universe.

This difference between a spherical and elliptic universe appears in every *closed* universe. There is no such distinction in the case of an open universe. Thus if our universe is closed we would have to answer an additional question. Is it spherical with mirror events, or is it elliptic? Scant attention was paid to this question, because it is of little importance if we explore only the neighbourhood of our galaxy. But the description of some phenomena may be very different on two such backgrounds. Indeed, the solution of Dirac's quantum mechanical equation, for example, depends very essentially on the spherical or elliptical character of our universe.[9]

IV

In the last thirty years the centre of investigation has shifted from relativity theory to quantum theory. Yet this statement may be misleading, because it is too much simplified. It ignores the tremendously important rôle played by relativity theory in the development of quantum mechanics. I would like to indicate only one instance: the great progress achieved by Dirac's equations is due to his success in reconciling relativity theory and quantum mechanics. But even the problem of cosmology became connected with the problem of the atom. We ask: are the laws governing our universe independent of the quantum mechanical laws governing the atom? Different theoretical physicists answer this question differently. Some of them believe that there is a connection between the structure of the universe and the structure of the atom. The most outstanding representative of this school of thought is Sir Arthur Eddington, who devoted many years to the difficult task of constructing a conceptual bridge between quantum theory and relativity theory. His work, undoubtedly very audacious and imaginative, is admired by some physicists, but regarded as too speculative and formal by others. Some physicists (Dirac, Schroedinger) believed that Eddington was at least on the right track. Others reject the idea that there is any connection between the fine structure constant, the ratio of proton to electron mass on the one hand and constants characterizing our universe on the other.

[9] L. Infeld and A. Schild, "A New Approach to Kinematic Cosmology," *Phys. Rev.* (Vol. 68, 1945), 250-272, and (Vol. 70, 1946), 410-425.

It is not up to me to say what Einstein's views on this question are. His recent paper[10] would indicate that at present he
does not believe in the connection between the structure of the
universe and the atom. In it he has shown that local problems
like that of a particle or that of our solar system are not affected
by the structure of our universe considered as a whole.

Yet I believe that there may be some connection between the
description of local phenomena and the structure of our universe, though it may be less spectacular than that searched for
by Eddington, and lie in an entirely different direction. Let
us take as an example Maxwell's equations and try to find
their solution on a cosmological background. If we assume our
universe to be an *open* one, then there is no difference between
a solution in such a universe and that in a Minkowski world.
In other words, the structure of our universe does not reveal
itself in Maxwell's equations if the universe is open. But the
situation changes radically if we solve the same Maxwell equations in a *closed* universe. It does not change because of the
metric, but because of the identification of points $\varrho = 0$ and
$\varrho = \pi$. Such an identification changes our problem into a boundary value problem, and we obtain characteristic values for frequencies. In a closed universe the frequency of radiation has its
lowest value, the spectrum, on its red side, can not reach the frequency zero. It does not matter whether the problem is solved
in an Einstein space or in any other closed space; the solution is
always the same. Thus, not the *metric* but the *topology* of the
universe influences the character of Maxwell's solutions.

A similar situation prevails if we consider Dirac's equations
upon a cosmological background. Again the solutions in an open
universe are those of the Minkowski space, whereas the solutions in a closed universe are different, not because of the metric,
but because of the topology of our universe.

We have tried to sketch briefly the scientists' efforts to grasp
the architecture of our universe. These efforts, though linked
with observation, are essentially of a speculative character. In

[10] A. Einstein and E. G. Straus, "Influence on the Expansion of Space on the
Gravitation Fields Surrounding the Individual Stars," *Rev. of Mod. Physics* (Vol.
17, 1945), 120-125.

the last thirty years we have succeeded in formulating a new problem and in viewing some of the possible solutions; but our answers are neither decisive nor final. Indeed, *there are no final and decisive answers in science.* Yet all our cosmological speculations, though they have gone far from Einstein's original paper, grew from the ideas of the theory of relativity. In the history of human thought they represent one of the many paths emanating from a common source: relativity theory, the creation of one man of genius.[11]

LEOPOLD INFELD

UNIVERSITY OF TORONTO
TORONTO, CANADA

[11] For a fuller quotation of literature and for a more technical exposition of the cosmological problem, the reader is referred to the following sources: H. P. Robertson, "Relativistic Cosmology," in *Review of Modern Physics* (1935), 62-90. R. C. Tolman, *Relativity, Thermodynamics and Cosmology* (Oxford, At the Clarendon Press, 1934). A. Schild, "A New Approach to Kinematic Cosmology" (University of Toronto thesis, 1946).

19

Max von Laue

INERTIA AND ENERGY

19
INERTIA AND ENERGY

I. Introduction

IN MODERN physics the laws of conservation are of fundamental importance. Essentially, there are three of them: The principle of inertia, which states the conservation of linear momentum; the energy principle, which asserts the conservation of energy; and the law of the conservation of the quantity of electricity. There are two more conservation laws, dealing with the conservation of the angular momentum and of the inert mass. The first of these two, however, is a necessary consequence of the law of conservation of linear momentum, and the latter, as far as we still acknowledge it to be correct, has become identical with the law of the conservation of energy. Finally the laws of conservation of linear momentum and of energy fuse into one for modern relativistic considerations. The discussion that follows is concerned with these unifications of originally distinct laws.

Let us first consider the conservation of the quantity of electricity. The history of this law is soon told, though it extends over a century or more. Under the tremendous impact of Newton's law of gravitational attraction, this law was hypothetically postulated for the electrical attraction and repulsion in the early 18th century. The conservation of mass in which one believed with good reason, was transferred to the electric "Fluida," with the only modification that positive and negative charges cancel each other. Several investigators deduced the inverse proportionality to the square of the distance a long time before Coulomb from the screening effect of electrically conducting enclosures. Coulomb himself cites this effect in a paper on his famous experiment with the torsion balance as a second proof of this law. Only a few persons, however, understood this argu-

ment at the time; thus it was forgotten. The proportionality
between forces and charges was accepted implicitly by all scientists of that time. They could not have proved it, if for no other
reason than that they did not posses a well-defined quantitative
measure of the charge. The idea of defining the quantity of
electricity from Coulomb's law itself was originated by Carl
Friedrich Gauss (about 1840). And the experimental proof of
charge conservation was first given by the ice-bucket experiment
of Michael Faraday in 1843.

The apparatus consisted of a metal vessel with a relatively
small opening, the ice-bucket. This vessel was connected to an
electrometer, but was otherwise insulated. Faraday lowered an
electrically charged body into it, suspended by an insulating
string; immediately the electrometer showed a deflection proportional to the charge. And this deflection remained unchanged, no matter what was done with the charge inside the
ice-bucket, e.g., whether it was transferred to the wall, or
whether it was added to other charges present before the start
of the experiment, which might perhaps compensate for the
new charge. Perhaps this proof is not too accurate. As an in-
tegrating component of Maxwell's theory of electricity, however, the law of conservation of charge is supported by the
numerous and exact experimental confirmations of this theory.
Nowadays nobody doubts it.

This fundamental result has never caused even approximately the same sensation as the law of the conservation of
energy, which was proved at nearly the same time. History
makes us understand this difference. Generations of scientists
have striven for it, but the conservation of the quantity of charge
corresponded to the "*communis opinio*" already a hundred years
before Faraday.

In what follows we shall relate the much more eventful
story of the two other conservation laws and their interrelation-
ship.

II. The Law of Momentum in Newton's Mechanics

The laws of conservation of momentum and energy are results of modern times. The law of momentum is probably the

earlier of the two, because it was clearly formulated, and its significance recognized, sooner than the law of energy, even when we think only of the law of energy in mechanics. It is true, antiquity has left us permanently valuable knowledge for statics, the science of mechanical equilibrium. But influenced by the doctrines of Aristotle, it had advocated a proposition diametrically opposed to the principle of inertia, namely, that a permanent action from without is necessary for maintaining any motion. It was not until the time of Galileo Galilei (1564-1642), that this brilliant originator of the theory of motion, dynamics, in his long life of research, realized that the motion of a body free of outside interaction does not stop, but continues for all time with constant velocity. It is significant that the consideration which led him to this result is based on energy considerations in the modern sense.

It runs as follows: a body on the surface of the earth which falls from a certain altitude, be it directly, on an inclined plane, on the circular path of a pendulum, or otherwise, must obtain precisely that velocity which it requires to return to its former level. For any deviation from this law would furnish a method for making the body ascend by means of its own gravity, perhaps through the inversion of the process of motion which is always possible; and Galileo thinks that this is impossible. Moreover, he confirms his conviction by means of certain experiments. Now let a body ascend again on an inclined plane after it has fallen downwards a certain distance. The lower the inclination toward the horizontal, the longer the path which it requires to obtain its former level on the inclined plane. And if the plane is horizontal, then the body will keep on flying (on it) to infinity with undiminished velocity.

This transition to the limit is not stated explicitly in Galileo's papers, because this rigorous empiricist knew that a plane is not a level surface, because of the spherical shape of the earth, and he avoided intentionally any hypothesis concerning conditions as they might be encountered somewhere away from the earth. But the reader of his *Discorsi* on the mechanics (1638) could not help drawing this conclusion himself. Thus the simplest form of the law of inertia, that the velocity of each force-free body is maintained with respect to direction and magnitude, has become the common property of all scientists since Galileo.

It was soon observed, however, that a more general law was hidden in the law of inertia, when the interaction of two bodies was considered. Collisions were then considered to be the simplest kind of interaction; thus even before Newton a whole series of collision theories had arisen. Few of them were based on exact experiments, but all of them were in agreement that the masses of the colliding bodies were important, their masses simply being identified with the weights. As weighing never showed changes in the weight of a body, the mass, too, was considered to be constant. This important step was taken apparently without misgiving, as a matter of course. Incidentally, these earliest collision theories considered only the central impact of two balls, where all motions take place on a straight line (the connecting line of the mid-points).

From the mass m and the velocity q René Descartes (1596-1650) already formed the *quantity of motion* mq and asserted the conservation of the sum of the quantities of motion of all bodies, and in particular of two colliding bodies, on the basis of philosophic-theological speculations which to us appear strange. But he understood the velocity merely as a number, as a scalar quantity in oûr terminology, without considering its direction, i.e., its vector properties. Thus his considerations naturally did not lead to successful results.

In 1668 the Royal Society in London made the theory of collisions the topic for a contest. Three papers were submitted. The first candidate, John Wallis (1616-1703), well-known in mathematics by the "Wallis formula," observed, indeed, that opposite velocities had to be provided with opposite signs when the above-mentioned quantity of motion is formed. Otherwise he retained the Cartesian idea of the constancy of the quantity of motion; but of course he could not determine the two momenta after an impact (considered by him as in-elastic) from the initial velocities with the help of this single requirement only; he, therefore, introduces additional assumptions which, being incorrect, vitiate his result.

Christian Huygens (1629-1695) first submitted to the Royal

Society his results only, but he gave the proofs later in a paper (*De motu corporum ex percussione*) published in his *Opuscula posthuma* in 1703. He realized correctly that not only the sum (formed with the correct signs) of the quantities of motion $m \cdot q$ has the same value before and after a perfectly elastic collision, but also the sum of the products of the respective masses m by the squares of the associated velocities, $m \cdot q^2$. These two statements are in fact sufficient to solve the problem. Here we encounter the first application of the principle of mechanical energy, though without any realization of its comprehensive significance. By the way, Christopher Wren (1632-1723), the third candidate, used the principle in the same manner. It is very interesting, however, that Huygens used in his paper the principle of relativity, of course only the one which corresponds to the mechanics of his time and which we call today the Galilean principle of relativity to distinguish it from that of Einstein. In order to generalize the law that two equal elastic balls with equal velocities and opposite signs simply exchange their velocities on impact, Huygens assumes that the impact occurs on a moving ship, and he observes it from shore. Thus he transforms, as we should call it today, from one system of reference to another.

But all these investigations became dated when Isaac Newton (1642-1727) published his *"Principia"* (*Philosophiæ Naturalis Principia Mathematica*) in 1687. In this treatise we find the two pronouncements that the rate of change of (linear) momentum of a mass point per unit time equals the force acting on it, and that the forces between two mass points are equal and opposite (equality of action and reaction). It follows immediately that the interaction of an arbitrary number of mass points never changes their total momentum, but that this total momentum is constant for any system not subject to external forces. Newton calculates the total momentum as a vector quantity, by adding vectorially the individual momenta. His formulation of the first law above appears almost prophetic: He equates the force not to the product of mass and acceleration, but to the rate of change of momentum, even though both formulations are equivalent if the momentum is assumed to be the product *m q*. Newton's formulation, however, is co sistent with present-day relativity, whereas the other formulation has been disproved by the experiments on the deflection of fast electrons.

Newton's mechanics obtained its principal empirical confirmation from astronomical experience, because he could derive mathematically the planetary motions from its laws and from his law of gravitational attraction. But all the other great ideas of his work, the theory of tides, the calculation of the flattening of the earth and other planets, the derivation of the velocity of sound, etc., lent credence to the law of momentum, once they were verified by experience, because they are all based on it. In the following centuries, the thousandfold empirical verifications of Newton's mechanics produced an almost unlimited confidence in the law of momentum. In the minds of many scientists this law assumed the quality of a mathematical truth—which it is not.

The conservation of the angular momentum is one of the most important mathematical consequences of the law of linear momentum; the angular momentum is a directed quantity (a vector), which is determined by the momentum of a mass point and the radius vector assumed to be drawn to it from a fixed point in space. The angular momentum is perpendicular to these two vectors; its amount is obtained by multiplying the momentum component normal to the radius vector by the length of the latter. The earliest examples for the conservation of angular momentum are the two laws of Kepler, which state that the path of a planet is plane and that the radius vector drawn from the sun to the planet covers equal areas in equal times. Later on, the angular momentum law achieved prominence when, in 1765, Leonhard Euler (1707-1783), with analytical methods, developed the theory of the rotation of a rigid body about a fixed point; then, somewhat later (1834), Louis Poinsot (1777-1859) solved the same problem with the help of synthetic-geometrical methods. All that is needed in this case is the application and mathematical interpretation of the law of angular momentum. The top provides the most obvious example of the types of motion that can be treated with its help. When no point of the rigid body is held fixed, then the translatory motion of its center of mass is controlled by the law of linear momentum alone, and the rotation about this point by the law of angular momentum alone.

As a *physical* problem mechanics was completely solved by Newton. The mathematicians, however, worked on it for another century and a half. They erected a structure with an architectural beauty which Newton, himself, had never divined. The fact, however, that the architects were mathematicians and that they required no new experiment or new observations proves that the foundation laid by Newton was fully sufficient to support this structure. And, since the scientists of that time proposed to reduce all of physics to mechanics, they thought that it would also suffice to support the far greater building of physics. This belief inspired physical research till the end of the nineteenth century. Only then new ideas gained hold in mechanics as well as throughout the other branches of physics.

Newton's mechanics assumed action at a distance between the different bodies. His law of gravitational attraction shows this very distinctly. It is beside the point whether Newton himself had considered this law to be more than an approximation, to be replaced eventually by a law incorporating a finite velocity of propagation. The notion of the rigid body, where each force attacking one part affects the entire body instantaneously, also is based on the idea of action at a distance. More fundamentally, the axiom of the equality of action and reaction shows the importance of action at a distance in Newton's theory: in case body *A* is the source of an action which changes its momentum and which *only later* reaches a body *B*, where it produces an equal and opposite change of momentum, the sum of the momenta of both bodies is evidently not the same during the interval of transfer as before and after. In a later section we are going to show how physics has been able to maintain the law of conservation of momentum by expanding the momentum concept.

We shall conclude this section with a remark concerning the invariability of mass. As mentioned above, this invariability **was taken for granted** because repeated weighings had never indicated any change in the weight of a body. After the revolutionary chemical discoveries of the eighteenth and nineteenth centuries, the question arose whether the chemical reactions left the total weight of the matter unchanged. Hans Landolt (1831-1914) achieved the highest accuracy for the necessary weight determinations for fifteen different reactions in a long series of tests which lasted from 1893 to 1909. He was able to exclude relative variations in weight greater than 10^{-6}. In a few cases he obtained even higher accuracy.

III. The Law of Energy

In mechanics, the beginnings of the knowledge of the law of energy coincide with those of the law of momentum, as shown by the aforementioned energy considerations of Galileo and Huygens. Newton's theory of planetary motion naturally includes the fact that the planet always possesses the same velocity when it returns to the same distance from the sun. For Newton, however, this was only one of the many conclusions from the law of momentum. Gottfried Wilhelm Leibniz (1646-1716) was the first to devote his attention to the product of mass and squared velocity, $m\,q^2$. In 1695 he called this expression *"Vis viva,"* and this term was used until the middle of the nineteenth century. Following Gustave Gaspard Coriolis (1792-1843), it was applied to one-half of $m\,q^2$, the value of $(m/2)\,q^2$. Johannes Bernoulli (1667-1748) gave us the expression *"energy,"* but this name did not gain the upper hand until later. We use "energy" today in a broader sense and denote the *"vis viva"* as *kinetic energy.* The kinetic energy first came to public attention through the well-known, endless quarrel between the Cartesians on the one hand and Leibniz and his disciples on the other, whether $m \cdot q$ or $m \cdot q^2$ represents the correct measure of force. Actually both quantities play important but different rôles in mechanics; the whole dispute concerned a fictitious problem, caused by the then ambiguous meaning of the word "force" (*vis*). In the eighteenth century, however, the force concept was still so overgrown with mysticism that profound thinkers were seriously concerned with the dispute.

A further step in the interpretation of the law of energy was taken by the above-mentioned Swiss mathematicians Johannes Bernoulli and Leonhard Euler. They emphasized that the change in kinetic energy in a closed mechanical system did not at all result in a reduction in its "capacity of action" (*Facultas agendi*), but only in its transition to other forms. In 1826 Jean Victor Poncelet (1788-1867) first introduced the term "work" for that product of a force by the path of its point of application, measured in the direction of the force, which in mechanics equals the change in energy. The kinetic energy is again of great importance in the papers on collision by Thomas Young (1773-1829), which were published in 1807. As one of the results of mechanics it was established by the end of the eighteenth century that it was impossible to construct with mechanical components a *perpetuum mobile*, a machine that would permanently create mechanical work from nothing. That this result had a more general significance was probably suspected even then; at least the Academy of Paris decided in 1775 not to accept any further supposed solutions of the problem of the *perpetuum mobile*, on the grounds that it had already wasted too much of its time examining these schemes. That these negative results could lead to important positive conclusions remained unrecognized at that time.

The stimulus for a generalization of the mechanical to a universal conservation law was furnished by the experience of long standing that kinetic energy or mechanical work could be lost while the temperature of the bodies involved was increased, as through friction, and also by the much more recently observed fact, on the steam engine, that one might gain work from thermic processes. It was with the steam engine that Sadi Carnot (1796-1832) concerned himself in 1824 in a very remarkable paper, which led to the basic result that the production of work was contingent on the transition of heat from the high temperature of the boiler to the lower temperature of the surroundings. His work was marred, however, by the erroneous belief, then current, that heat is an indestructible substance. His successor, Bénoit Clapeyron (1799-1864), still retained the same error in a paper in 1843. But even before, in the first decades of the nineteenth century, there had been voices which asserted the existence of a uniform "force," which was to account equally for the phenomena of heat, light, electricity, magnetism, chemical affinity, etc. Added to these were discussions of the metabolism of food in the body as the source of animal heat as well as their capacity to do work. A discovery was in the air, and several scientists independently made important contributions in its direction.

The first was Julius Robert Mayer (1814-1878), a physician, who (according to M. Planck's 1885 paper on the conservation of energy) "preferred, in his whole mental attitude, to generalize in the manner of a philosopher rather than build piecemeal and by experimental methods." In his brief paper of May, 1842, he operated with the principles *"Ex nihilo nihil fit"* (from nothing grows nothing) and *"Nil fit ad nihilum"* (nothing leads to nothing), applying them to the "power to fall," to motion, and to heat; what is of permanent value in his paper is that he gives a reasonably correct value for the mechanical equivalent of heat. How he obtained his value, he does not tell until 1845; his computation is one still familiar, from the difference in the two specific heat capacities of perfect gases, where he assumes by implication, but correctly, that their internal energy is independent of the volume. Ludwig August Colding (1815-1888) obtained almost precisely the same value in 1843 from experiments involving friction; however, his justification for the general conservation law appears to us even more fantastic than the one given by Mayer. The latter considers electric and biological processes already in his second publication, while in his third, in 1848, he raises the question of the origin of solar heat, explains the incandescence of meteors from their loss of kinetic energy in the atmosphere, and applies the law of conservation to the theory of tides. Quite obviously, Mayer fully realized the significance of his discovery. Nevertheless, at first he remained quite unkown and received the recognition due him only much later. Men like Joule and Helmholtz cannot be blamed for not having known at first of Mayer's sparsely distributed works and therefore for not having quoted him.

Whatever we may think of Mayer's arguments, this much we

must admit: Since it is the task of physics to discover the general laws of nature, and since one of the simplest forms of a general law is to assert the conservation of some particular quantity, the search for constant quantities is not only a legitimate line of inquiry, but is exceedingly important. This approach was always present in physics. We owe to this approach the early conviction concerning the constancy of electric charge. The actual decision, whether a quantity believed to be subject to a conservation law does really possess that property can, of course, be reached only by experimentation. The energy principle is an experimental law just as much as the law of conservation of electricity. But Mayer really took the road of the experiment in determining the mechanical equivalent of heat. For other fields of physics, the principle remained for him a program, to be carried through by others.

As the second contributor we must mention James Prescott Joule (1818-1889), who early in 1843 wrote a paper on the thermic and chemical effects of the electric current (this paper was not printed until 1846). He established by measurements that the heat developed in the electric wire of a galvanic cell (which later, appropriately, was called *Joule's heat*) equals the chemical heat of reaction if the reaction takes place in an open-circuited cell, and provided, as we must add today, that the current is produced by the cell without the development of heat. Shortly after and again in 1845, Joule reports determinations of the mechanical heat equivalent, in which he converts mechanical work into heat either directly, electrically, or through the compression of gases.

However, the man whose universally educated mind enabled him to develop the energy principle with all its implications was Hermann Ludwig Ferdinand von Helmholtz (1821-1894). Like Mayer, whose works he did not know and whose results he had to obtain independently, he approached the principle starting from medical investigations. In 1845 he had corrected, in a short paper, an error of Justus von Liebig's (1803-1873), by pointing out that one could not simply equate the heat of the combustion of food stuffs in the animal body to the heat of combustion of the constituent chemical elements; at the same time, he had made a brief survey of the implications of the energy principle for the different fields of physics.

His lecture before the Physical Society of Berlin, on July 27, 1847, goes farther into the ramifications of this idea. In contrast to Mayer, Helmholtz adopted the point of view of the mechanical nature of all processes of nature, to be comprehended by the assumption of attractive and repulsive central forces, as did most of his contemporaries. In this point of view he saw a sufficient and (erroneously) necessary condition for the impossibility of the *perpetuum mobile*. But in his deductions he did not use the mechanistic hypothesis at all, but derived the various expressions for the energy directly from the impossibility of the *perpetuum mobile*—if for no other reason than that the reduction of all processes to central forces had by no means been carried through. Thus, his results did not depend on the mechanistic hypothesis and therefore were able to survive it. His original contributions included the concept of potential energy (*"Spannkraft"*—stress) for mechanics, the expressions for the energy of gravitation, for the energy of static electric and magnetic fields, and his energy considerations applied to the production of electric current in galvanic cells and thermocouples as well as to electrodynamics, including electromagnetic induction. When, today, we compute the energy of a gravitational field as the product of masses and potentials, that of an electrostatic field as the product of charges and potentials, we are employing Helmholtz's methods directly.

It would lead us too far to go into the details. The further development of the principle cannot be treated here either. The final formulation only, due to William Thomson (later Lord Kelvin of Largs, 1824-1907) may be mentioned: "We denote as energy of a material system in a certain state the contributions of all effects (measured in mechanical units of work) produced outside the system when it passes in an arbitrary manner from its state to a reference state which has been defined *ad hoc*." The words "in an arbitrary manner" contain the physical law of the conservation of energy.

Helmholtz's considerations were not at all generally accepted; the older of his contemporaries were afraid of a revival of the phantasies of Hegel's natural philosophy, against which they had had to fight for such a long time. Only the mathematician Gustav Jakob Jacobi (1804-1851), who has made his own important contributions to mechanics, saw in them the logical continuation of the ideas of those mathematicians of the eighteenth century who had built up the science of mechanics. When, however, by about 1860 the law of energy had finally received general recognition, it became very soon a cornerstone of all natural science. Now every new theory, particularly in physics, was evaluated first by examining whether it was consistent with the law of energy. About 1890 many scientists, such as the well-known physical chemist Wilhelm Ostwald (1859-1932), were so enthralled by it that they not only undertook to deduce all other natural laws from it, but they actually made it the central thesis of a new *Weltanschauung*, energetics. Such exaggerations, however, were soon brought to an end by less excitable contemporaries.

The notion of energy also penetrated into engineering. Every machine was judged according to its balance of energy, i.e., the extent to which its energy input is transformed into the desired form of energy. Nowadays the energy concept is part of the working knowledge of every educated person. Only in regard to atomic physics, about 1924, was the principle of energy seriously doubted. For a time Niels Bohr, H. A. Kramers, and J. C. Slater thought that energy was not conserved in the individual scattering process involving x-rays or γ-rays, but only as the average for many such processes. But in 1925 the famous coincidence experiments by Hans Geiger (1882-1945) and Walter Bothe established that their views were in error.

The problem of basing mechanics solely on the energy principle arose also in the epoch of energetics. We shall state the answer here, because it holds in modern relativistic mechanics even though originally it was obtained on the basis of Newton's mechanics. The law of momentum cannot be deduced from the principle of energy alone; it contains more than it. But if we add the principle of relativity—at that time of course only that of Galileo—to the law of energy, according to which there is not only one correct system of reference for the fundamental equations of mechanics but an infinite number of them, all of which move with respect to one another with constant velocity, in other words if we require that the sum of potential and kinetic energy is conserved in *each* system of reference of this kind, it necessarily follows that the total momentum of the closed system considered remains constant.[1] The connection between the two laws of conservation which is hereby revealed, is related to the inertia of energy, toward which our presentation is aimed.

But when the principle of energy was found to hold beyond mechanics, it first seemed to lose this connection entirely. It had to be accepted as being much more comprehensive than the purely mechanical law of momentum. How the law of momentum, too, gradually grew beyond the sphere of mechanics we are going to show in the following sections.

IV. The Theory of the Flow of Energy

Time changed, the knowledge of physics became more profound. No sharp dividing line, however, separates the epoch which concluded with the triumph of the principle of energy from the following period which is characterized by the displacement of the theories of action at a distance by the theories of local action, which better correspond to the principle of causality. The dates in our presentation clearly show that the transition was gradual and that the two epochs partly overlap.

[1] Let us consider an isolated system of any number of mass-points m_i with the velocities q_i relative to a first system of reference, the potential energy of which is a function of the relative co-ordinates of the m_i, such as Φ. From the law of energy we have:

$$\tfrac{1}{2} \sum m_i q_i^2 + \Phi = C,$$

where C is a quantity independent of time.

In a second system of reference which moves with the constant velocity $\mathbf{v}$ relative to the first system, the mass-point m_i has the velocity $q_i - \mathbf{v}$. Relative to this system the law of energy becomes:

$$\tfrac{1}{2} \sum m_i (q_i - \mathbf{v})^2 + \Phi = C'$$

Again C' is independent of time; Φ has the same value in both cases. Subtracting the first equation from the second we therefore obtain:

$$\tfrac{1}{2}\mathbf{v}^2 \sum m_i - (\mathbf{v} \cdot \sum m_i\, q_i) = C' - C.$$

According to this equation the scalar product $(\mathbf{v} \cdot \sum m_i\, q_i)$ is independent of time, no matter what direction and amount $\mathbf{v}$ may have. And this is possible only if $\sum m_i\, \mathbf{q}_i$, the total momentum of all mass-points, is constant with time.

The principle of local action and that of finite velocity of propagation, even in a vacuum, which is connected with it, first triumphed in electrodynamics; we are convinced of it, since Heinrich Hertz (1855-1894) discovered the electromagnetic waves in 1888. Nowadays we are also convinced that gravitation progresses with the speed of light. This conviction, however, does not stem from a new experiment or a new observation, it is a result solely of the theory of relativity. But that belongs to a later period.

Of course, the idea of local action for all domains filled with matter was known to former physicists. The oldest theory involving local action is contained in the theory of elastically deformable bodies, including fluid dynamics. The origins of that theory date back to the life-time of Newton. Not only was the *total* potential energy of a stressed body calculated without difficulty, but the potential energy could be localized, i.e., its share could be attributed to each part of the body. It was also generally accepted that a fluid moving under pressure not only conveys energy by transport, but also conducts an additional amount of energy, which is proportional to its velocity and pressure. In 1898 this theory was completed by Gustav Mie, when he taught us how to calculate the flow of energy for any motion of elastically stressed bodies. The assumption that energy flows like a substance can be carried through quite generally. In the driving belt, which connects the motor with a machine consuming energy, the energy flows against the motion of the stretched half of the belt. In the rotating and twisted shaft, which connects the engine of the ship with the propeller, it flows parallel to the shaft axis, i.e., at right angles to the velocity of the material parts.

For electromagnetic processes Helmholtz's method at first furnished merely a formula for the total energy; as long as one believed in action at a distance without a transmitting medium, the question of localization lacked meaning. But Michael Faraday (1791-1867), in the course of his long career of scientific investigation, developed the concept of the *field* as the medium transmitting such action; the field was considered as a change in the physical state of a system which was essentially located in the dielectric, or even in the empty space between the carriers of electric charge and electric current and between the magnets. With this approach, the problem of localization became significant; Maxwell's theory of electricity and magnetism, proposed in 1862, does, in fact, contain the expressions for calculating the energy density which is composed additively of an electric and a magnetic term. This development is a necessary supplement of the field concept.

J. H. Poynting (1852-1914) led the theory a step farther, by adding to it, in 1884, the notion of a *flux* of electromagnetic energy, long before Mie carried through this idea for the theory of elasticity. He took this step on the basis of a mathematical conclusion from Maxwell's equations, but accomplished much more, the creation of an entirely new physical concept. According to him, there is a flux of electromagnetic energy wherever an electric and a magnetic field are present at the same time. Now it was possible to determine the route by which the chemical energy, which in the galvanic cell is transformed into electromagnetic energy, gets to the wire that completes the circuit, where that energy is converted into Joule's heat; likewise we can trace the energy on its way into the electric motor which transforms it into mechanical work. For us, this approach has become almost a matter of course; during Poynting's time, it was the cause of considerable conceptual difficulties and took a long time to gain acceptance.

For a special case the concept of a spatially distributed energy and its flow through empty space had already been developed, and this circumstance greatly facilitated the assimilation of Poynting's innovation. A body which radiates light or heat loses energy; this energy will not appear as the energy of a particular body until the radiation strikes another body. Therefore, if the sum total of all energies of the system is to remain constant, the radiated energy must in the meantime exist as *radiation energy*. And now Maxwell's theory, confirmed so brilliantly by Hertz's experiments, reveals light and heat radiation to be electromagnetic vibrations; its formulas for the density and for the flux of electromagnetic energy turned out to correspond precisely to the customary ideas concerning radiation. Thus, physicists of the last decade of the nineteenth century gradually learned to appreciate the new concepts also for other electromagnetic fields.

But the concept of linear momentum required a similar generalization. Clerk Maxwell (1831-1879), in his comprehensive work, *Treatise of Electricity and Magnetism,* 1873, had shown that a body which absorbs a light ray experiences a force in the direction of the ray; its magnitude per unit cross section of the ray equals the energy flux S, divided by the velocity of light c. This assertion was confirmed experimentally much later, by P. Lebedew (1901), E. F. Nichols and G. F. Hull (1903), and, with an accuracy of about two parts in a hundred, by W. Gerlach and A. Golsen (1923). But even earlier there arose the question of the validity of the law of momentum.

Now it is true that the body which emits a ray experiences the opposite force of the one which absorbs it; and, since emission and absorption take equally long times, the two changes in linear momentum eventually compensate for each other exactly. However, while the ray passes from one body to the other, the total mechanical momentum is certainly different from that measured, either before the process of emission or after absorption. If we wish to maintain the law of conservation of momentum, we cannot but ascribe to the ray an *electromagnetic momentum* and to assert the law of conservation for the sum of mechanical and electromagnetic momenta. And then one cannot but extend this new concept to all electromagnetic fields, instead of restricting it to rapidly vibrating fields like heat and light radiations. It turns out that the field must contain momentum of the magnitude of S/c^2 per unit volume, where the symbol S denotes the magnitude of electromagnetic energy flux; both of these vectors possess the same direction.

$$g = S/c^2$$

is the momentum density of the field. Science owes this fundamental step to Henri Poincaré (1854-1912); his publication is contained in the Lorentz Anniversary Volume of 1900.

According to this theory, static fields, too, may give rise to energy flux, if only electric and magnetic fields overlap. The paths of this flow, though, are always closed, the energy current leads back into itself without being converted anywhere into other forms of energy. This conclusion has occasionally been used as a counter-argument in discussions of Poynting's law. As a matter of fact, in energy considerations it is perfectly permissible to disregard this closed energy current entirely.

But according to Poincaré, in such static fields we shall also encounter linear momentum. For the field as a whole, the total momentum is always zero; but the local momenta will in general give rise to an angular momentum whose sum total is different from zero. A system consisting of electric charges and of magnets at rest represents an electromagnetic top whose angular momentum corresponds to that of a mechanical top. As long as the state of the system remains unchanged, the angular momentum of either top remains unobservable. However, any change of the electromagnetic field, affecting either the magnitude or the direction of the angular momentum, must produce a torque on the material carriers of the electric charge and on the magnets, because the change in angular momentum of the field must be compensated for by a corresponding change of the mechanical angular momentum. This conclusion, which at first may appear surprising, actually results merely in the well-known forces experienced by moving charges in a magnetic field and by moving magnets in an electric field, once the calculations are carried out. But it is clear now that the electromagnetic momentum is observable not only in heat and light radiation.[2]

Of greater importance is another conclusion from the equation $g = S/c^2$. If we displace a carrier of electric charge, then the motion of the corresponding electric field gives rise to a magnetic field, and their coexistence leads both to a current

[2] If we permit ourselves in passing to operate with a (fictitious) single magnetic pole of magnitude m and if we form a system containing in addition a single electric charge of magnitude e, then the angular momentum of the field has the direction from e toward m, if both are positive or both negative (otherwise the direction is reversed), and its magnitude is independent of the distance and equals em/c. Starting with this law, and by applying vector addition, we can get the angular momentum for a charge in the field of a magnetic dipole and also for more complicated cases.

of energy and to a momentum; if the system satisfies certain symmetry conditions, e.g., if the body is a sphere, these two vectors are parallel to the velocity of the body. Here, for the first time we encounter the *inertia* of electromagnetic energy; for this additional momentum represents an additional inertial mass. True, for a macroscopic body this additional mass is negligible for all charges that are experimentally feasible. But for the electron, considered a rigid sphere with a radius of about 10^{-13} cm, it was not difficult to find out that this additional inertial mass is of the same order of magnitude as the observed mass; in fact, it was suspected that the whole mass of the electron might be of electromagnetic origin. Many physicists tended toward this view soon after 1900. This hypothesis was examined most carefully by Max Abraham (1875-1922) in a famous investigation in 1903; the most striking result was that the electromagnetic momentum is proportional to the material velocity only for very small velocities, but otherwise increases more rapidly, in fact it increases without limit as the velocity of the electron approaches the velocity of light, c. The differentiation between two masses, both of which depend on the velocity, the *longitudinal mass* and the *transversal mass*, originated with this investigation; but it also showed that this result modifies the basic structure of mechanics only slightly. These investigations stimulated the performance of many experiments in which the deflection of fast electrons by electric and magnetic fields was measured with ever increasing accuracy. The results showed uniformly that the momentum increases more rapidly than the velocity, but even more rapidly than is predicted by Abraham's mechanics. These results led subsequently to a decision between his mechanics and relativistic mechanics.

For small velocities, both of the masses postulated by Abraham go over into the rest mass m, which is related to the electrostatic energy of the electron, E_0, by the equation

$$m = \frac{4}{3} \frac{E_0}{c^2}.$$

Theoretical investigations of the dynamics of cavity radiation inside a uniformly moving envelope are part of the same general approach. Since Planck's radiation law of 1900, the problem of cavity radiation at rest was completely settled. In 1904, F. Hasenöhrl (1874-1915) began to generalize the theory for cavities in motion, and K. v. Mosengeil and M. Planck completed the investigation with an improved theoretical approach. At rest all rays, no matter what their direction of propagation, have the same intensity, whereas in motion those are more intensive which form an acute angle to the direction of motion. As a consequence, we have a resultant momentum in the direction of motion. This momentum increases with the velocity, but more rapidly than the latter, and it would increase beyond all limits, if the velocity should approach that of light, c, but even more rapidly than in the case of Abraham's model of the electron. What is common to both cases is the relationship between the rest mass m and the rest energy E_0. We have here a special case of relativistic dynamics, but treated without explicit reference to the principle of relativity; the derivation from Maxwell's theory by itself assures consistency with that principle.

In the case of the sphere as well as in the case of cavity radiation, the total linear momentum is parallel to the velocity. In most other cases, however, the total momentum possesses a component at right angles to the velocity. Even when the motion is purely translatory, the angular momentum will change, and, to compensate for this change, the material carriers of the charge must experience a torque which will produce this compensatory change in the mechanical angular momentum. Thus it appeared reasonable that an electrically charged condenser, if suspended so that it could turn freely, would assume a particular orientation relative to the velocity of the Earth, the one in which that angular momentum vanishes. This conclusion is inescapable in Newtonian mechanics. However, in 1903 Fr. T. Noble and H. R. Trouton searched for this effect in vain, and even the much more accurate repetition of their experiment by R. Tomaschek (1925-26) showed no trace of the effect. Their result is just as convincing a proof of the principle of relativity as Michelson's interference experiment. Both of these experiments proved the necessity for a new mechanics; Michelson's experiment because it showed the contraction of moving bodies in the direction of motion, and the experiment by Trouton and Noble because it showed that an angular momentum does not necessarily lead to a rotation of the body involved.

Thus, a new epoch in physics created a new mechanics. This epoch, too, partly overlaps with the preceding one; it began, we might say, with the question as to what effect the motion of the Earth has on physical processes which take place on the Earth. Hendrik Anton Lorentz (1853-1928) had centered the general interest on this question through a famous essay in 1895. But in this case we can assign to the dividing line between epochs a precise date: It was on September 26, 1905, that Albert Einstein's investigation entitled "On the Electrodynamics of Bodies in Motion" appeared in the *Annalen der Physik*. Our presentation here need not report on the theory of relativity as a whole; we shall restrict ourselves to the question, how this theory led to the recognition that *all* forms of energy possess inertia.

And here we must first of all take exception to a prime example of national-socialist forgery of history, this time in the field of physics. Because of the work of Fritz Hasenöhrl which was mentioned above, Philipp Lenard and his cronies tried, during the period of the "Third Reich," to give credit for the law of inertia, which had received the limelight of attention because of its applications in nuclear physics, to this worthy physicist, who had long since died. But an examination of the literature shows conclusively that Hasenöhrl in 1904 applied the then current notion of the inertia of electromagnetic energy with partial success to the problem of cavity radiation. The idea of the inertia of other forms of energy occurred to him no more than to other physicists prior to Einstein.

Incidentally, we must emphasize that our division into epochs applies only to macrophysics. Simultaneously, the development of molecular physics proceeded at a different pace; initially it received more stimulus from macrophysics than it was able to return. Since Planck's law of radiation, which is based on molecular-statistical considerations, this relationship has undergone a gradual change, so that for later times we can no longer speak of two separate approaches in physics; but for our present purposes, this is rather unimportant.

V. The Inertia of Energy

The recognition of the inertia of energy as such was published by Einstein in 1905 (*Ann. d. Physik, 18,* 639), in the same year as his basic paper on the theory of relativity. Einstein derived this law relativistically. And, in fact, a rigorous derivation must start from there. But a year later Einstein gave another presentation which is merely approximate, but which possesses the great advantage of being more intuitive and of avoiding the relativistic foundation. For our purposes, it will be sufficient to trace the second argument.

Let a large cylindrical cavity which has been evacuated float in empty space; let its length be L and its mass M. Placed on its end faces there are two bodies, A and B, respectively, whose masses are sufficiently small compared to M that they can be disregarded in all sums involving M (Fig. 1). Let A transmit

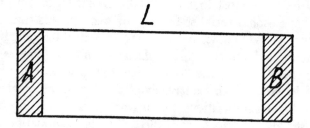

Fig. 1

to B an amount of energy ΔE in the form of Hertz vibrations or as light, and let B absorb that energy completely. The time required for emission and the equal time required for absorption shall be small compared to the time $T = L/c$, which is the time of travel through the interior of the cavity. During emission the body A receives a total impulse $G = \Delta E/c$, because of the radiation pressure, and through A, the cylinder as a whole receives the same impulse; the center of mass of the cylinder will therefore assume a velocity $q = G/M$ and, since it will retain this velocity during the time T, it will undergo a displacement

$$qT = \frac{L\Delta E}{Mc^2}$$

in the direction $B \to A$.

After the body B has stored the energy received in some arbitrary form, we displace it by means of forces which originate inside the cylinder until it touches A. If we denote the mass of B at this stage by m_1, then the center of mass of the cylinder will be displaced by an amount Lm_1/M in the direction $A \to B$. Now let B transfer the energy ΔE back to A and subsequently return B to its original position, again by means of internal forces. If the mass of B is m_2 after it has lost the energy ΔE, then the displacement of the center of mass will amount to Lm_2/M in the direction $B \to A$. In the final state the distribution of energy is the same as it was initially: But there remains a resultant displacement of the center of mass of magnitude

$$\frac{L}{M}\left(\frac{\Delta E}{c^2} + m_2 - m_1\right)$$

in the direction $B \to A$.

Shall we believe that the cylinder can shift its center of mass (and, therefore, in effect, itself) without any action from without and without any change in its interior? Such a possibility is not only inconsistent with mechanics but with our whole physical intuition, which, after all, contains a good deal of ancient valuable experience, even if that experience is often unconscious or uncomprehended. But the displacement will be zero only if the mass m_1 of the body possessing greater energy exceeds m_2, in fact if

$$m_1 - m_2 = \frac{\Delta E}{c^2}.$$

This is the amount by which the mass of a body must increase when it receives the energy ΔE, no matter in what form.

If q_1 was the velocity of B while it was moving toward A, then its momentum was

$$m_1 q_1 = \left(m_2 + \frac{\Delta E}{c^2} \right) \cdot q_1.$$

Let us divide this expression through by the volume V of the body B in order to obtain the momentum density (momentum per unit volume) and the energy density

$$\epsilon = \frac{\Delta E}{V},$$

to the extent that these quantities depend on the energy ΔE.

$$g = \frac{\epsilon}{c^2} q_1$$

is then the contribution of ΔE to the momentum density. On the other hand ϵq_1 is the flux S of the energy carried along convectively. As a result, we find the relationship

$$g = \frac{S}{c^2}$$

for the momentum density due to energy carried convectively.

Now we can modify the conceptual experiment which we have described by returning the energy ΔE to A not convectively, but for instance by means of a shaft which extends between A and B and which is rotated and twisted. We saw in Section IV that in such a shaft mechanical energy passes along the axis. Or, alternatively, we could return the energy by means of heat conduction. With every such type of energy flow there must be present an impulse in the same direction, if the center of mass of the cylinder is to return at the end to its original location. We require no lengthy calculations to show that momentum density and energy flux must always obey the same relationship indicated above.[3] Following Max Planck, who was

---

[3] If S is the density of the energy current in the shaft or in the heat conductor that returns the energy ΔE to A, if Q is the cross section of the carrier of this energy current and T' the time that it takes the current to return the energy ΔE, then we find

$$SQT' = \Delta E.$$

On the other hand, if G is the momentum possessed by the shaft or heat conductor

the first to point out this relationship in 1908, we consider it the most general expression for the inertia of energy. The formula

$$m_1 - m_2 = \frac{E}{c^2}$$

makes use of the concept of mass, which loses its significance when momentum and velocity are no longer parallel to each other. And this is usually not the case, as was pointed out repeatedly; the rotating shaft is merely one striking instance.

Now if for a material body there is a difference in direction between its momentum and its velocity, then a purely translatory motion will change its angular momentum according to our previous remarks. Because of the law of conservation of angular momentum, it will require an angular momentum to *prevent* angular acceleration. This is the explanation for the experiment by Trouton and Noble. The condenser is stressed elastically by the forces of its own electric field. Its mechanical momentum therefore is inclined toward its velocity. The torque which, according to Section IV, the field exerts on the condenser is just sufficient to make possible its translatory motion.

---

because of the energy current in the direction $B \to A$ and g the momentum density, then

$$G = gQL,$$

and

$$G/M = gQL/M$$

is the velocity which the center of mass of the cylinder receives because it must acquire the compensatory momentum $-G$; the direction of the velocity is from A toward B. During the time T', the center of mass will travel a distance

$$G'T'/M = GQLT'/M.$$

Now this displacement must equal the preceding displacement in the direction $B \to A$.

$$L \cdot \Delta E/Mc^2 = SQLT'/Mc^2,$$

and we conclude again that

$$g = S/c^2.$$

In this connection, one should not object that in the event of heat conduction or other irreversible processes the entropy will increase and that at least in this respect the initial condition of the system cannot be recovered. Increase in entropy by itself cannot cause a displacement of the center of mass, if for no other reason than that the direction of the displacement would remain completely undetermined.

But if an angular momentum is associated with translatory motion, is not the original law of inertia cancelled or at least its validity severely restricted? This law stated that a body *free of external forces* conserves its state of motion. Not at all! In the case of a force-free body (an isolated static system, in technical language), the momentum is always in the direction of the velocity. Only for parts of the system can the momentum deviate from that direction. The material parts of the condenser are not free of force, they are subject to the action of the field. However, the physical system which consists of the condenser plates and the field is an isolated static system. Thus we must conclude that the condenser will not begin to rotate just because it participates in the translatory motion of the Earth.

Energy possesses inertial mass. Can, then, *all* of the inertial mass of a body be ascribed to its energy content? Do we have the farther reaching relationship $m = E/c^2$? The theory of relativity has given a positive answer to this question from the beginning. That is why it was able to combine the energy density, energy flux, and momentum density into a single mathematical quantity, the energy-momentum tensor. This development is due to Hermann Minkowski (1864-1909) who, in an exceedingly beautiful mathematical representation, introduced this quantity and rewrote the two conservation laws in the form of a single brief formula. Much more clearly than in Newtonian mechanics, we recognize here the fusion of the two laws with the help of a relativity principle. Experience has subsequently confirmed the validity of this daring step in a surprising manner. The last Section (VI) will deal with these developments.

First, however, we must explain why Abraham's model of the electron as well as cavity radiation yield the different relationship $m = (4/3) (E_0/c^2)$. The reason is the same in both cases. The electromagnetic field is not capable of existing by itself alone, it requires certain supports of a different nature ("material supports"). Cavity radiation can exist only within an envelope, and the charged sphere would fly apart if it were not for certain cohesive forces. In both cases, motion will give rise to an energy current within the material supports which is directed opposite to the motion. It contributes to the total momentum a negative amount and reduces the factor 4/3 to 1. (We are disregarding here the energy inherent in the supports themselves.) For the sphere, we have to consider in addition that, in contradiction to Abraham's assumptions, a moving sphere, because of its contraction in the direction of motion, turns into a rotational ellipsoid. That is why the dependence of the momentum on the velocity obeys relativistic dynamics rather than Abraham's.

The generalized law of the inertia of energy then provides that every inertial mass is due to energy, every momentum due to energy flux. The concept of mass, formerly a basic concept of physics and a measure for the quantity of matter as such, is demoted to a secondary rôle. The law of conservation of mass is eliminated; for the energy of a body can be changed by the transfer of heat or work. What is left of that law is absorbed by the energy law. On the other hand, the energy concept is expanded tremendously. We have reason to doubt that we know all forms of energy at the present time. But quite independently of that question, we can determine the total amount of energy in a body from its mass. We thereby get rid of the arbitrariness of the zero point of energy which the former definition of energy (cf. Section III) was forced to introduce. There are not merely energy *differences*, as before; the energy possesses a physically meaningful absolute value.

One type of energy, however, the new physics must eliminate from its list, and that is kinetic energy. For the energy E of a body possessing the velocity q, relativistic dynamics furnishes the equation

$$E = \frac{E_0}{\sqrt{1 - \left(\frac{q}{c}\right)^2}},$$

in which E_0 is the energy in the state of rest. Each type of energy therefore increases in the same manner as a result of motion. And in fact, if we consider all of the inertia as an attribute of energy, then we cannot base a particular type of energy in turn on the inertia. That is how fundamental the changes are which the law of the inertia of energy causes in our whole picture of the physical universe.

How do these conclusions agree with the conservation of mass as established by experiment, in particular with the accurate confirmations that Landolt achieved by his investigations of chemical reactions (cf. Section II)? After all, the reagents occasionally lose considerable amounts of heat in the course of the reaction.

Let us consider, as an instance, the combination of one mol of oxygen with two mols of hydrogen to form two mols of liquid water. If we compute from the well-known heat of reaction of this chemical reaction the corresponding loss of mass, we find that it amounts to less than the 10^{-10}th part of the total mass involved. Landolt's limit of accuracy was of the order of 10^{-6}. Thus he could not possibly have ascertained the relativistic loss of mass. For all changes of phase, such as the condensation from the gaseous state to a liquid or solid, or the solidification of a liquid, the mass losses are even much smaller.

However, already in his first paper, Einstein pointed out one possibility for determining the loss of mass connected with the transfer of energy: In radioactive nuclear transformations the amounts of energy liberated are much larger relative to the masses involved than even in the most powerful chemical reactions. The same is true of artificial nuclear transformations, about which we have learned so much since Lord Rutherford's great discovery in 1919. This aspect will be the topic of our last Section.

VI. The Inertia of Energy in Nuclear Physics

The chemist Jean Charles Galissard de Marignac of Geneva (1817-1894) in 1865 wrote in a paper concerned with completed and planned determinations of atomic weights in *Liebigs Annalen* as follows:

If in these future determinations we should find to the same extent elements whose atomic weights approach integral values so remarkably close, then it appears inevitable to me that Prout's law be placed beside those of Gay-Lussac and Mariotte and that we recognize the presence of an essential cause according to which all atomic weights should exhibit simple numerical ratios, with secondary causes accounting for slight deviations from these ratios.

In all probability, Marignac merely expressed an opinion which was widespread at the time. Prout's hypothesis of the composition of all atoms from one or a few common original building stones has always been fascinating. Of course, science had to travel a long way before this opinion could assume definite shape. One of the preliminary conditions was, for instance, the discovery of isotopes by Frederic Soddy in 1910. Nowadays we know several atoms of different atomic weight at nearly each point of the periodic table; if we define the "unit of mass," by setting the atomic weight of the most frequent oxygen-isotope equal to 16.000 units, the atomic weight of each kind of atoms is really very close to an integer, the "mass number." This assertion, however, does not hold for the chemical elements composed of several isotopes. Another preliminary condition was the discovery of the neutron by J. Chadwick in 1930. Soon thereafter Jg.Tamm and Ivanienko, a little later W. Heisenberg, found that the composition of all atomic nuclei of protons and neutrons (which have nearly the same weight) is the essential cause for the integral numbers of the atomic weights, and that the energy loss accompanying the combination of these elementary particles and the loss of mass due to the inertia of energy is the secondary cause for the deviations from this law.

Two examples may show this: the atomic weights of the neutron and of the proton are 1.00895 and 1.00813 respectively; their sum is 2.01708. The deuteron, however, which consists of a neutron and a proton, has only the atomic weight of 2.01472. The difference, amounting to 0.00235 units of mass, is the mass defect of the deuteron, the result of an energy loss of 3.51×10^{-6} erg due to the fusion of a neutron and a proton. The nucleus of a lithium atom consists of 3 neutrons and 3 protons; but this atom does not have the weight 3 times $2.01708 = 6.051124$, but only 6.01692; the mass defect, therefore, is 0.03432, corresponding to a loss of energy of 5.11×10^{-5} erg when this atomic nucleus is formed from its components. The mass defect increases with the atomic number up to 0.238 for uranium. The example of lithium shows that it can be as much as half a percent of the mass; this is quite a different order of magnitude from the above defect of 10^{-10} when water is formed.

The accuracy of the law of inertia, $E = m\,c^2$, was proved by W. Braunbeck (*Zs. f. Physik* 107, p. 1 (1937)), by calculating the velocity of light c according to that equation for a series of nuclear reactions for which the loss of energy and the masses of the reacting atoms before and after the reaction are measured independently of each other. For instance, he finds a mass defect of 0.02462 units of mass for the transmutation of the above-mentioned isotope of lithium with the mass number 6 plus a deuteron into two atoms of helium; this mass defect corresponds to $4.087 \times 10^{-26}g$; the loss of energy is 3.534×10^{-5}. This results in the velocity of light of 2.94×10^{10} cm/sec. Forming the mean value over many different transmutations of nuclei, Braunbeck obtains the value 2.98×10^{10}, which is only 0.4 per cent below the value of 2.998×10^{10} cm/sec, measured electrically or optically.

All these tests, however, concern only the *variations* of energy and mass, not the entire mass of body. All the more important was a quite unexpected observation made in the Wilson chamber in connection with C. D. Anderson's discovery of the positron, the electron with a positive charge. In the proximity of an atomic nucleus, which serves only as a catalyst, γ-radiation can be transformed into a pair of electrons, a negative and a positive one. Not each γ-radiation can do this; its frequency ν has to be so high, its quantum of radiation $h\nu$ so great, that it is above 1.64×10^{-6} erg. As the rest mass of an electron—be it negative or positive—amounts to $9.1 \times 10^{-28}g$, it has a rest energy of 8.2×10^{-7} erg. This means: the γ-quantum has to be large enough to supply two electrons with their rest energy; what remains is used to give the electrons a certain velocity. The law of conservation of the electric charge is not disturbed here. The electron pair has the total charge zero.

Also, the reverse process of pair formation is possible. It is true, we have never observed in the Wilson chamber how a negative and a positive electron annihilate each other while emitting γ-radiation. But otherwise this annihilation radiation is well known experimentally; for example, Jesse DuMond measured its wave length in 1949 with a crystal spectrometer at 2.4×10^{-10} cm. According to all these observations, the law of inertia may be considered to be one of the results of physics which is best confirmed.

Thus we have followed the history of the laws of conservation of momentum and energy up to their amalgamation in the recent state of physics. Every thinking person cannot but be strongly impressed by the last consequence, which is extreme, but confirmed by experience, that at least for electrons the mass is nothing but a form of energy which can occasionally be changed into another form. Up to now our entire conception of the nature of matter depended on mass. Whatever has mass, —so we thought—, has individuality; hypothetically at least we can follow its fate throughout time. And this is certainly not true for electrons. Does it hold for other elementary particles, e.g., protons and neutrons? If not, what remains of the substantial nature of these elements of all atomic nuclei, i.e., of all matter? These are grave problems for the future of physics.

But there are more problems. Can the notions of momentum and energy be transferred into every physics of the future? The uncertainty-relation of W. Heisenberg according to which we cannot precisely determine location and momentum of a particle at the same time—a law of nature precludes this—, can, for every physicist who believes in the relation of cause and effect, only have the meaning that at least one of the two notions, location and momentum, is deficient for a description of the facts. Modern physics, however, does not yet know any substitute for them. Here we feel with particular intensity that physics is never completed, but that it approaches truth step by step, changing forever.

MAX VON LAUE

MAX PLANCK INSTITUTE OF PHYSICS
GÖTTINGEN, GERMANY

20

Herbert Dingle

SCIENTIFIC AND PHILOSOPHICAL IMPLICATIONS OF THE SPECIAL THEORY OF RELATIVITY

SCIENTIFIC AND PHILOSOPHICAL IMPLICATIONS OF THE SPECIAL THEORY OF RELATIVITY

EINSTEIN'S theory of relativity is unique among the great epoch-marking ideas of the world in that it caused a revolution by keeping to tradition; its heterodoxy lay in the strictness of its orthodoxy. The outstanding characteristic of the movement which in the seventeenth century inaugurated the modern scientific age was the requirement that every conception used in the description of phenomena should be directly referable to experience. Ideas not so referable were "hypotheses" or "occult qualities" according to Newton, and "mere names" according to Galileo; such ideas "put a stop to philosophy," and their avoidance was a prime necessity of right scientific thinking.

It is easy to accept a general principle while violating it in particular applications. The physicists of the nineteenth century were not conscious of having been caught in the trap against which Newton had warned them, when they spoke of the length of a moving body without having convinced themselves in detail whether such a quantity could be unambiguously determined. They had forgotten that Galileo had written: "I will endeavour to show that all experiments that can be made upon the Earth are insufficient means to conclude its mobility, but are indifferently applicable to the Earth moveable or immoveable;" and, if this passage had been brought to their attention, they would doubtless have replied that Galileo's outlook was too limited, without considering the possibility that it might have been their own which was too confused. By the beginning of the twentieth century the simple, essential principles of Galileo and Newton had become so entangled in the

network of incompatible physical theory that a genius as great
as theirs was needed to bring those principles again to light.
It is the glory of Einstein and the good fortune of the present
age that he possessed that genius.

Now that the ground has been cleared it is comparatively
easy to survey the fallen structure of post-Newtonian physics
and see wherein it was essentially faulty. It is not so easy to
build a more lasting structure; but here also Einstein has
shown the way—or at least *a* way—in which it can be begun.
The special theory of relativity reiterated the essential relativity
of uniform motion; the general theory extended that relativity
to all motion of the kind called "gravitational," and so rendered
still less valid the Aristotelian distinction between natural and
violent motions. The next extension—to motions in the electromagnetic field—though not yet so definitely established, bids
fair finally to abolish the Aristotelian distinction altogether, so
far as non-living matter is concerned, and to comprehend the
whole science of motion in one supreme generalisation. It is
indeed amazing that out of a simple recall to the Galilean
principle of relating conceptions to experience, so mighty an
issue should have come.

From another point of view it is perhaps equally surprising
that, the potentiality of that principle having been established,
it should not have been immediately applied to other physical
phenomena; for in at least one other field of study (namely,
that of temperature, or "black body," radiation) the same over-
sight has occurred. We observed motion of one body with
respect to another, and quite illegitimately we ascribed to each
an absolute motion, which we had no means of detecting.
Similarly, we observe radiation from one body to another, and
ascribe an absolute radiation to each, which we have no means
of detecting. If two bodies were relatively at rest we said their
absolute motions were equal, and so postulated two superfluous
unobservable processes which neutralised one another. Similarly,
if two bodies are at the same temperature we say that their
exchanges of absolute radiation are equal, and so postulate two
superfluous unobservable processes that neutralise one another.
The medium—an aether—which we invoke to serve as the

vehicle of these absolute radiations is the same as that which we invoked, and have now discarded, to serve as the frame of reference for the absolute motions. In order to construct laws of motion on the basis of the assumed absolute motions we found it necessary to assume two properties of bodies—inertial mass and gravitational mass—which were mysteriously equal. Similarly, in order to construct laws of radiation on the basis of the assumed absolute radiations we find it necessary to assume two properties of bodies—radiative power and absorptive power—which are mysteriously equal.

Now it seems clear that the principle which demanded a revision of classical mechanics, because of its detachment from possible experience, demands equally a revision of classical radiation theory for the same reason. Prévost's theory of exchanges is equivalent in one domain to motion with respect to the aether in the other. Moreover, the correspondence just indicated suggests that the actual technique employed in re-expressing the laws of motion might be effective also in re-expressing the laws of radiation. The parallelism is, of course, not exact; there is above all the great difference between the phenomena of motion and radiation which is usually expressed by saying that the laws of motion are reversible and those of radiation are not, so that the matter of the universe can exhibit eternal movement but not eternal radiation. But such differences are, from the technical point of view, matters of detail; they will lead us to expect equations of different form, but not needing a different mode of derivation. Again, there is no reason to suppose that the Stefan-Boltzmann law of radiation is inaccurate, as was the classical law of composition of velocities. We have found it applicable sufficiently close to the limiting temperature—the "absolute zero"—to make unlikely a modification similar to that which mechanical relativity demanded in the neighbourhood of the limiting velocity, viz., the velocity of light. We may suppose rather that the present laws of radiation correspond to the classical laws of motion with the Lorentz transformation formulae substituted for the Newtonian. Many of the phenomena observed will then be consistent with them, but they will lack the power of generalisation to cover more complex situations than those corresponding to radiation at uniform temperature, and so act as a barrier to progress without showing marked disagreement with observation in a limited field.

From the purely *scientific* point of view, therefore, it seems most desirable to explore the possibility of applying to the phenomenon of radiation the treatment which has been so successful with motion; from the general *philosophical* point of view the argument is compelling. We cannot urge the necessity of building only on experience in one part of physics and evade that necessity in another. Let us see, then, how the reform can be achieved.

The first thing to do in attempting to generalise a theory is to express that theory in the most suitable form for the purpose. An outstanding example of this is, of course, afforded by the theory of relativity itself. It is well known that, in its original form, all efforts at extending the application of the theory from uniform to accelerated motions were unsuccessful. Only when Minkowski gave it a geometrical expression was Einstein able to show how the generalisation could be made. Minkowski made no essential change in the theory: he simply expressed it in a different way. Our first task, therefore, is to see how the theory of mechanical relativity can be expressed so as to make clear the way in which its principle can be applied to the phenomenon of radiation.

To do this let us suppose we are about to start the study of motion, having no preconceptions in the matter at all. We must first devise some method of *measuring* motion; i.e., of representing each movement we observe by a number obtained by a strictly specified process. There are various processes which we could choose. We could construct some form of speedometer, or make use of the displacement of spectrum lines known as the Doppler effect, or construct a scale of movements such as that suggested by P. W. Bridgman,[1] or doubtless, if we are ingenious, invent other ways of achieving our purpose. Actually, however, physicists have chosen none of these devices, but, following Galileo, they have measured motion by the space covered by the moving

---

[1] P. W. Bridgman, *The Logic of Modern Physics*, 99.

body in a given time. This choice is so fundamental in physics that it is often assumed to be not a choice at all but a necessity. That is not so, however; and it is important to realise this at the outset, because when we come to compare motion with radiation we shall see that a similar choice is open there; radiation may be measured by candle-power, by the stellar magnitude scale, by a number of other observable quantities, or by the energy or entropy emitted by the radiating body in a given time. Naturally we shall choose the method indicated by the previous choice for motion.

Having decided, then, to measure motion by the space covered in a given time, we must now decide how to measure space and time. Here again considerable freedom of choice is open, but (taking space first) we select the familiar process based on the adoption of a rigid rod as a standard of length. This choice has been criticised by E. A. Milne[2] on the ground that a rigid rod is indefinable. He has usually been answered by the contention that definition is unnecessary, provided that physicists are consistent in their practice. I would agree with Milne that a definition is desirable, but I would not agree that it is impossible. The definition, which in fact is implied in modern physical theory, is that a rigid rod is a rod such that, if a source of monochromatic light and a spectroscope be placed at one end and a mirror at the other, the spectra seen by direct and reflected light always coincide. Whether the standard metre at Paris fulfills this condition we do not know, for the observation is too difficult to carry out with sufficient exactitude, but that this definition actually is implied by modern physics is clear from the following consideration. In the periodical comparisons of standards of length made at the National Physical Laboratory in England it is found that systematic changes occur. In the year 1936, for instance, the standard bar known as P.C.VI was found to be shrinking with respect to the Imperial Standard Yard at the rate of 1.92×10^{-7} cm. a year.[3]

[2] Cf. e.g. *Astrophysical Journal*, *91*, 138 (1940).

[3] Report by the Board of Trade on the Comparisons of the Parliamentary Copies of the Imperial Standards with the Imperial Standard Yard, etc. (H. M. Stationery Office, 1936).

This, though certainly an actual change and not an error of observation, was regarded as practically negligible. For most purposes, of course, it is; but, taking the rate of recession of the nebulae as 528 km. a second per megaparsec (i.e., 5.4×10^{-8} cm. a year per metre), it is evident that one standard is expanding with respect to the other at nearly four times the rate of the expansion of the universe. Consequently, the universe may be expanding with respect to one and contracting with respect to the other. We are therefore not justified in saying, as Eddington does, for example,[*] that the universe is expanding with respect to "the standards of length ordinarily accepted—the metre bar, for example." The nebular spectrum shift, however, is unambiguously towards the red, and therefore the only standard with respect to which we can say definitely that the universe is expanding—or, more generally, that a Doppler red-shift indicates recession—is one whose rigidity is guaranteed by the Doppler effect itself. We do not know which, if any, of our standards that is.

Let us take it, however, that we know how to measure space: the next thing is to decide how to measure time. Broadly speaking, we can choose between two types of process. We can choose a series of recurring events—pulse beats, maxima of a variable star, passages of a particular star across the meridian, etc.,—and call the time intervals between successive events equal; or we can choose a process in which a measurable quantity changes continuously, and define equal times as those in which it changes by equal amounts. Examples of such continuous changes are afforded by a moving body (continuous change of position in space), a radio-active body (continuous change of mass), a radiating body (continuous change of energy), etc. The current practice in physics on this point is exceedingly ill-defined. Officially we choose an example of the first type; the standard in the C.G.S. system of units is the mean solar second, which is a certain fraction of the interval between successive passages of a star across the meridian, i.e., a certain fraction of the sidereal rotation period of the Earth. But it is now generally

[*] *The Expansion of the Universe*, Chapter III.

agreed that the Earth's rotation is gradually slowing down, and for this to be conceivable an unnamed ulterior standard of time measurement must be implied. Examination of the evidence for the slowing down of the Earth shows that this ulterior standard is that defined by Newton's first law of motion—equal times are those in which a moving body free from forces covers equal spaces. That law therefore ceases to be an assumption to be tested and becomes a definition of the time-scale used.

Einstein introduced a formal change in this definition: for a moving body free from forces he substituted a beam of light *in vacuo*. It is, of course, possible to maintain a time-scale defined by Newton's first law and regard the relativity postulate of the constancy and invariance of the velocity of light as an assumption vulnerable to experiment. This, however, would be a very unsatisfactory procedure, for it would mean that the whole structure of physics would rest on an assumption which it was impossible to test in actual practice. By taking the constancy of the velocity of light as a definition of the time-scale used we avoid all assumptions and introduce into physics for the first time a practicable time-scale which leads to simple expressions of natural laws. The ideal clock then becomes a beam of light travelling along a rigid space-measuring scale, and the time at any instant is the reading of the scale at the position of the wave-front.

The point of fundamental importance in this is that, having decided to represent motion as change of position in space with time, we choose to measure time in terms of space. We thus get a measure of time peculiarly fitted to express laws of *motion* (but not necessarily laws of radiation or anything else), for whatever effect motion has on space-measurement is necessarily carried over into time-measurement also. Thus, if we find that a space-measuring scale is contracted with motion, we must also find that the time-scale is contracted, for the space-scale is an essential part of our ideal clock. It is therefore because of our voluntary choice of measuring processes that we can speak of the "union" of space and time into "space-time." This has nothing to do with any philosophical notions of space and time in themselves; it is a consequence of the wisdom of making sure that, after expressing motion in terms of space and time, the measurement of time shall depend on the measurement of space. Only on this account is it possible, as Minkowski did, to represent the time-co-ordinate as a fourth space-co-ordinate and describe motion geometrically as a track in a four-dimensional continuum.

The next step is to obtain the equations of transformation connecting measurements made with one set of instruments (measuring-rod and clock) with those made with another set moving with uniform velocity with respect to the first. In each set, of course, the measuring-rod and clock are relatively stationary: i.e., the rod used for the measurement of space is stationary with respect to the similar rod which forms part of the ideal clock. It is a basic principle of the theory of relativity that no state of motion is fundamentally different from any other, so that, if we have a large number of pairs of instruments, all moving at different uniform speeds, the same laws of motion must be equally applicable to them all. Experiments such as that of Michelson and Morley indicate what the transformation laws must be in order that this shall be so: we obtain the well-known Lorentz equations, from which the measurements appropriate to any of our pairs of instruments can be calculated, when those made with a set moving with a known uniform velocity with respect to it are known. This completes the essential structure of the special theory of relativity; all that remains follows by calculation.

This description of the fundamentals of Einstein's achievement has been framed, as was indicated earlier, with the view of affording the easiest possible passage from the relativity of motion to the relativity of radiation. The procedure to be adopted is clearly first to represent radiation as a change of some measurable quantity (η, let us call it) with time; and secondly to measure time in terms of η. We may then construct an η-time which in the theory of radiation will play the rôle of space-time in the theory of motion. The whole apparatus of the tensor calculus and the geometry of the particular manifold arrived at will then be applicable to derive laws of radiation along the lines which Einstein has established for the laws of mechanical motion.

The measurable quantity which seems best fitted to serve as η is obtained as follows.[5] Suppose the radiating body under consideration has a Kelvin temperature θ. Let its radiation be received isothermally by one gram-molecule of a perfect gas at a temperature θ_0, and suppose that in consequence the pressure of the gas changes during a certain interval from p_1 to p_2. We choose for η the quantity $\beta \log_e (p_2/p_1)$, where β is a constant to be chosen to give the unit a convenient value. It is easy to see that this is closely related to the entropy received by the gas (or by the η-measuring instrument, as we will call it), for the energy received is, by the well-known formula, $-R\,\theta_0\,\log_e (p_2/p_1)$ (where R is the universal gas constant) and θ_0 is the temperature. Radiation is thus measured by the η recorded by the instrument in unit time.

We must now define the time-scale, in which η will play the part played by space in the time-scale for the study of motion. Just as the ideal mechanical clock was a beam of light travelling along a space-measuring scale, so the ideal radiation clock will be a body at constant temperature radiating to an η-measuring instrument. Choose for this body one gram-molecule of a perfect gas having the same volume as the initial volume of the gas in an η-measuring instrument, but a slightly higher pressure ($p_1 + dp_1$ instead of p_1, say), and let its volume and pressure be maintained constant. We know that it will then have a slightly higher temperature ($\theta_0 + d\theta_0$) than the temperature of the η-measuring instrument and so will continuously radiate to the latter. Time is then measured by the reading of the instrument, unit time being that in which it records unit (or any other convenient) quantity of η.

These instruments—the η-measuring instrument and the radiation clock—provide measurements by which the process of radiation can be described in terms analogous to Einstein's description of the process of motion. We have now, following our pattern, to derive transformation equations for pairs of instruments in different states of uniform radiation—or, in more

[5] For a fuller treatment see *Phil. Mag.* 35, 499 (1944).

ordinary language, at different temperatures. For this purpose we have the experimental result embodied in the Stefan-Boltzmann law, namely that the gross rate of energy radiation is proportional to the fourth power of the Kelvin temperature of the body, the net rate, of course, being obtained by subtracting from this the radiation received from the surroundings. This is the "Michelson-Morley experiment of radiation," and it is easy to show that it is sufficient to solve our problem.

Let $d\eta$ represent the change of reading of the η-measuring instrument at Kelvin temperature θ_0 when a given body at constant temperature θ radiates to it for a time dt as measured by the radiation clock. We write

$$\tau \equiv \frac{d\eta}{dt} \tag{1}$$

and clearly τ will be a measure of the temperature of the body, whose Kelvin temperature is θ, referred to an arbitrary zero of temperature represented on the Kelvin scale by θ_0. τ, of course, will measure temperature on a different scale from the ordinary ones, but that is because we do not ordinarily measure temperature in terms of a temporal process: we deliberately choose to do so here in order to be able to follow the procedure of mechanical relativity. τ is now analogous to velocity, defined as $V \equiv ds/dt$, whereas the Kelvin temperature scale is more analogous to a measure of velocity in terms of the Doppler effect, e.g., $V \equiv c \, d\lambda/\lambda$, in that time is not explicitly involved. For the measuring instruments themselves, as indicated, $\tau = 0$, for if a body at the same temperature as the instruments is presented to them, the η-measuring instrument will clearly record nothing.

Now let the same body, at Kelvin temperature θ and temperature τ on the τ-scale when measured by instruments at Kelvin temperature θ_0 and τ-scale temperature zero, be presented to instruments at Kelvin and τ-scale temperatures θ_1 and τ_1, respectively. The problem is, what will be the values of $d\eta'$, dt' and τ', corresponding to $d\eta$, dt and τ with the former instruments, when these new instruments define the arbitrary zero of temperature? (In the case of motion the corresponding problem is this: let a body moving with velocity V and travelling a distance ds in time dt, when measured by a measuring-rod and clock at rest, be examined by a measuring rod and clock moving with velocity V_1; what will be the values of ds', dt' and V'' with these instruments?) The algebra is given elsewhere;[6] here we need only the result—"the thermal Lorentz equations"—namely,

$$
\left.
\begin{aligned}
d\eta' &= \frac{d\eta - \tau_1 dt}{(1 + \tau_1/\zeta)^{1/4}} \\
dt' &= (1 + \tau_1/\zeta)^{3/4} dt \\
\tau' &= \frac{\tau - \tau_1}{1 + \tau_1/\zeta}
\end{aligned}
\right\}
\tag{2}
$$

Here ζ is a constant whose numerical value depends on the arbitrary choice of the increment of pressure, dp_1, in the clock (i.e., in effect on the unit of time chosen) and which corresponds to the temperature on the τ-scale of the Kelvin absolute zero. It is easily seen that it is a limiting temperature, having the same value for all "co-ordinate systems," and that it plays the same part in these equations as the velocity of light, c, in the Lorentz equations.

One difference is at once noticeable between these equations and the corresponding kinematical ones, namely, that these are unsymmetrical; it is not possible to interchange primed and unprimed quantities in them. That is because the limiting velocity is the same in opposite directions, but the limiting temperature is $+\infty$ in one direction and $-\zeta$ in the other. The difference, however, is not intrinsic in the nature of the phenomena; it is introduced by differences in the kinds of measurement chosen.

The process can be carried further. Just as the interval ds^2 in the relativity theory of motion, defined by

$$
ds^2 \equiv c^2 dt^2 - dx^2 - dy^2 - dz^2
\tag{3}
$$

is invariant to a Lorentz transformation, so the "thermal interval," $d\sigma^4$, defined by

$$
d\sigma^4 \equiv dt(dt + d\eta/\zeta)^3
\tag{4}
$$

is invariant to the transformation (2). It is easily seen that whereas $d\eta$ corresponds to the net loss of entropy suffered by

[6] *Loc. cit.* in fn. 5 above.

the radiating body after the radiation by the η-measuring instrument back to the body has been taken into account, $d\sigma$ corresponds to the *gross* loss of entropy. It is the invariance of $d\sigma$ in this view of the process that corresponds to the "absoluteness" of the Kelvin temperature according to the ordinary view.

Just as equation (3) permits a geometrical interpretation of motion, so equation (4) permits a geometrical interpretation of radiation. The manifold indicated, however, ("η-time," it may be called), differs from the Euclidean—or, in its general form, Riemannian—manifold ("space-time") used in the description of motion in that it is two-dimensional instead of four-dimensional and, on the other hand, has a metric of the fourth degree instead of the second. The suggestion is inevitable that a generalisation along the lines of Einstein's general theory should be attempted. The most general laws of radiation would be expected to be given by the vanishing of a tensor derived from the metric

$$d\sigma^4 = g_{\alpha\beta\gamma\delta}dx^\alpha dx^\beta dx^\gamma dx^\delta \qquad (\alpha, \beta, \gamma, \delta = 1, 2). \qquad (5)$$

The mathematical difficulties, however, appear very formidable. "Spaces" of this character have been studied by Cartan[7] and Berwald,[8] among others, and their work seems to indicate that, even if the right tensor were identified, the mere labour of the application to a particular case would be excessive. That, however, is not of prime importance for our present purpose. It is sufficiently evident that the great clarification of the foundations of physics which Einstein achieved, and the mathematical technique which he employed, not only provide a solution of problems in the particular field of study with which he was concerned, immensely important though that was, but open the possibility of a much farther-reaching generalisation. Let us consider briefly the possible implications of this extension.

We may conveniently divide them into scientific and philosophical implications, though there is no clear dividing line between these classes. On the scientific side it is first to be noted that equations (2) and (4) are simply a re-expression, without

[7] "Les Espaces de Finsler" (*Act. Sci. et Indus.*, No. 79, 1934).
[8] *Math. Zeits*, 25, 40 (1926).

modification, of existing radiation theory. A generalisation of the metric might lead to new knowledge, but the "special" theory of thermal relativity, in its actual existing state, is precisely equivalent to what is already known and accepted; it is in its potentiality that its advantage lies. In this, as has already been pointed out, it differs from the special theory of mechanical relativity, which introduced new equations of transformation entailing consequences (e.g., the dependence of mass on velocity) not previously known.

The greater potentiality of the new expression lies first in its suggestion that phenomena in which radiation plays an essential part should be invariant to the transformation (2); i.e., that the laws of such phenomena should not depend on the temperature of the instruments used for investigating them. By an application of this requirement, for instance, it has been possible to show[9] that the electrical resistance of a pure metallic conductor should be proportional to its Kelvin temperature, a result which agrees with observation as closely as could be expected from the inexactness with which the ideal conditions are realisable in practice. Of greater interest is the application to the spectrum of black body radiation.[10] If it be accepted that radiation is associated with a continuous range of frequencies, then the law of distribution of the radiation among the frequencies, when these are reckoned on the thermal time-scale, should be invariant to the transformation (2). This condition, though necessary, is unfortunately not sufficient to determine the law, but it is possible to show that the Planck distribution law satisfies it, whereas the Rayleigh-Jeans law does not. In general, indeed, it may be said that the new expression places at the disposal of the theory of radiation the powerful apparatus of the tensor calculus, and so creates the possibility of a wide range of consequences which cannot be immediately foreseen.

As an example of the kind of simplification which the relativity expression might make possible, consider the following problem: given a sphere of known material, placed at a known initial temperature in an enclosure maintained at a constant and

[9] *Phil. Mag.*, 37, 58 (1946).
[10] *Phil. Mag.* 37, 47 (1946).

uniform lower temperature, to determine the surface temperature of the sphere at any instant during its cooling. It is difficult
to imagine an intrinsically simpler radiation problem than this;
yet in terms of present conceptions it cannot be solved. We need
to know the laws of variation of specific heat and thermal conductivity with temperature, and we know them only approximately and semi-empirically. This would appear to be clear
enough evidence that such concepts as specific heat and thermal
conductivity, however necessary for engineering purposes, are
unsuitable for the expression of theoretically simple laws. In
the thermal relativity theory they would be expected to be as
irrelevant as mass and force in mechanical relativity, and the
theoretically important and tractable quantities would be the
components of a tensor from which the specific heat and thermal
conductivity, if needed, could be calculated.

Of more general interest is the prospect of a new system of
thermodynamics. The existing science of thermodynamics,
whether considered in the macroscopic or the microscopic form,
is an interpretation of thermal phenomena in terms of classical
Newtonian mechanics. Tolman[11] has indeed considered how
the thermal quantities must be transformed when the kinematical co-ordinate system is changed; but this is more of the nature
of a correction to a fundamentally Newtonian thermodynamics
than the creation of a thermodynamics essentially relativistic.
The problem which now suggests itself is that of amalgamating
the Riemannian manifold of mechanics with the more general
manifold corresponding to (5), so that both thermal and mechanical measurements can be expressed in terms of characteristics of the same "space." Such a union of the two sciences
might be expected, among other things, to throw light on problems of the remote history of the physical universe.

Turning to the philosophical aspects of the theory, the first
point to be noticed is the light which it throws on *the meaning
of time* in physics. This has been perhaps the most widely misunderstood part of Einstein's theory. It has been supposed that
the relativity theory gives us some insight into what is called
the "nature" of time, and has shown that it is at bottom identi-

[11] *Relativity, Thermodynamics and Cosmology*, Sections V and IX.

cal with the nature of space, so that these two things are simply arbitrarily separated parts of an objectively existing entity called space-time. It must be confessed that Minkowski's famous remark, "From henceforth space in itself and time in itself sink to mere shadows, and only a kind of union of the two preserves an independent existence," lends itself naturally enough to this interpretation; although Einstein himself has always insisted that the theory has no metaphysical implications. The fact is that time has become associated with space in physics simply because we have chosen to measure time in terms of space measurements. The choice is voluntary, and, although this is completely revealed by Einstein's original theory when that is carefully considered, it becomes immediately obvious when we find that by measuring time in terms of other measurements, such as η, an "η-time" appears which is analogous in all essential respects to space-time. If, instead of η (or entropy), it had been found convenient to measure radiation in terms of the *energy* radiated per unit time, there would have been an "energy-time," no more and no less philosophically important than space-time or η-time. What relativity theory illuminates is not the metaphysical nature of time, but the function which time measurement can perform in physics. It appears to be a most powerful means of studying any phenomenon which can be represented as a temporal process, i.e., as the variation of some measurable quantity with time. You then choose to measure time in terms of that quantity and so create a manifold of measurements amenable to treatment by generalised geometrical methods. Such an enlargement of the scope of scientific method is altogether more significant than any of the speculations concerning the mystic nature of time which seem, unfortunately, to have been inspired by this development.

It should be pointed out, however, that the various systems of time measurement thus envisaged do not necessarily give different time *scales* in the sense of giving discordant measurements of the same duration. It is indeed a fundamental principle of relativity, considering even the relativity of motion alone, that a wide variety of such discordant scales are legitimate; although in practice one is so much more convenient than the others that it is the obvious choice to make. It happens that this same scale is the obvious one for radiation also; that is to say, the time-scale, according to which the velocity of light is constant, is also the time-scale according to which a body at constant temperature radiates uniformly. It is thus not necessary for physicists to keep a variety of clocks; for at a given temperature and in a given state of motion our ordinary familiar clocks can be used for either phenomenon. This identity of time-scales clearly suggests itself as a starting-point for constructing the relativistic thermodynamics already mentioned. The importance of adapting the system of time-measurement to the phenomenon studied lies not in the values of the clock-readings yielded but in the nature of the transformation to be used when we change the state of motion, the temperature, etc. of the instruments used; for the laws of the phenomenon in question are determined by the fact that they must be invariant under such transformations.

Another important philosophical implication of this extension of the relativity principle lies in its bearing on the question whether the physical world is fundamentally continuous or discontinuous in character. Hitherto a large and important part of physics (including universal gravitation) has been explicable only in terms of conceptions of continuity—field theory, as it is called—whereas another large and important part (atomic physics) has been explicable only in terms of conceptions of discontinuity. True, a part of the latter, which involves the discontinuity of matter only, has been amenable to treatment also in continuous terms (thus we have classical thermodynamics and statistical mechanics as alternative descriptions of the same set of phenomena), but the more fundamental part, which involves the discontinuity of energy, in which Planck's constant, h, appears, has so far resisted any interpretation which does not imply such discontinuity. Poincaré, in fact, went so far as to say that no interpretation of the spectrum of black-body radiation was possible without the basic conceptions of the quantum theory.[12]

The relativistic treatment of radiation, however, suggests that this statement might need revision. It has been stated above that

[12] *Journ. de Phys.*, January 1912.

Planck's formula satisfies the condition of invariance to the transformation (2), but is not the only formula to do so. It is, of course, a characteristic of the relativity technique that it imposes necessary, but not always sufficient, conditions on possible laws of nature; but in this case the number of mathematical alternatives is unfortunately large. It is not impossible, however, that they are reducible by macroscopic considerations alone, and, to make the most modest claim, we may say that Poincaré's dictum can no longer be accepted as final. The most general form of Planck's equation which satisfies the condition of invariance involves only one constant, B, to be determined by observation, and this is proportional to θ_0^2 (ah/kR), where θ_0 is the Kelvin temperature of the instruments used (B, though constant in any one thermal "co-ordinate system," is not invariant to change of system), a is Stefan's constant, h, Planck's constant, k, Boltzmann's constant, and R the universal gas constant. Hence we have a relation between an experimental constant, whose significance is purely macroscopic (continuous) and a combination of constants whose significance is purely microscopic (discontinuous).

The implication of this is that the alternatives of continuity and discontinuity have nothing to do with nature but are applicable to our conceptions alone; and, further, that a possibly complete parallelism might exist between the descriptions of the world in terms of the respective conceptions. Even if only one phenomenon in which hitherto the atomicity of energy has seemed inevitable should be found to be describable in terms of continuity (or even if, by an appropriate choice of β, determining the unit of η, in terms of Boltzmann's constant, k, the resulting value of ζ could be related to h, so that the atomicity of energy could be shown to depend on that of matter), the present complete antagonism of microscopic and macroscopic physics would have been broken down, and the view now so widely held, that the microscopic scheme of things, with its attendant conceptions of probability, uncertainty and the like, is the essential framework of nature itself, would no longer be tenable. Such a scheme, though legitimate as a means of expression of natural laws, would be seen as an alternative to a possibly equally comprehensive expression in purely macroscopic terms. Its elements would be no longer inherent in the physical world, but characteristics of a possible way of describing the physical world. Admittedly this is not yet established; but its likelihood must be taken into account by the scientific philosopher.

From our present point of view, however, the main purport of this article is to indicate what a profound and far-reaching achievement Einstein accomplished when he first recalled to physicists the forgotten principles of their own philosophy and next introduced to them the technique by which those principles could be applied to derive the ultimate laws of nature. In a survey of the phenomena with which the physicist is concerned, two stand out above all others as universally and eternally significant—motion and radiation. Unless we are altogether deceived, two pieces of matter placed anywhere at all in an otherwise empty universe will necessarily influence one another in two ways, and, so far as we know, in two ways only: they will affect one another's motion, and they will affect one another's temperature. The genius of Einstein explicitly derived the law of operation of the first phenomenon; it now appears that at the same time it implicitly derived the law of operation of the second.

HERBERT DINGLE

UNIVERSITY OF LONDON
LONDON, ENGLAND

21

Kurt Gödel

A REMARK ABOUT THE RELATIONSHIP BETWEEN RELATIVITY THEORY AND IDEALISTIC PHILOSOPHY

A REMARK ABOUT THE RELATIONSHIP
BETWEEN RELATIVITY THEORY
AND IDEALISTIC PHILOSOPHY

ONE of the most interesting aspects of relativity theory for the philosophical-minded consists in the fact that it gave new and surprising insights into the nature of time, of that mysterious and seemingly self-contradictory[1] being which, on the other hand, seems to form the basis of the world's and our own existence. The very starting point of special relativity theory consists in the discovery of a new and very astonishing property of time, namely the relativity of simultaneity, which to a large extent implies[2] that of succession. The assertion that the events A and B are simultaneous (and, for a large class of pairs of events, also the assertion that A happened before B) loses its objective meaning, in so far as another observer, with the same claim to correctness, can assert that A and B are not simultaneous (or that B happened before A).

Following up the consequences of this strange state of affairs one is led to conclusions about the nature of time which are very far reaching indeed. In short, it seems that one obtains an unequivocal proof for the view of those philosophers who, like Parmenides, Kant, and the modern idealists, deny the objectivity of change and consider change as an illusion or an appearance due to our special mode of perception.[3] The argu-

[1] Cf., e.g., J.M.E. McTaggart, "The Unreality of Time." *Mind*, 17, 1908.

[2] At least if it is required that any two point events are either simultaneous or one succeeds the other, i.e., that temporal succession defines a complete linear ordering of all point events. There exists an absolute partial ordering.

[3] Kant (in the *Critique of Pure Reason*, 2. ed., 1787, p. 54) expresses this view in the following words: "those affections which we represent to ourselves as changes, in beings with other forms of cognition, would give rise to a perception in which the idea of time, and therefore also of change, would not occur

ment runs as follows: Change becomes possible only through the lapse of time. The existence of an objective lapse of time,[4] however, means (or, at least, is equivalent to the fact) that reality consists of an infinity of layers of "now" which come into existence successively. But, if simultaneity is something relative in the sense just explained, reality cannot be split up into such layers in an objectively determined way. Each observer has his own set of "nows," and none of these various systems of layers can claim the prerogative of representing the objective lapse of time.[5]

This inference has been pointed out by some, although by surprisingly few, philosophical writers, but it has not remained

---

at all." This formulation agrees so well with the situation subsisting in relativity theory, that one is almost tempted to add: such as, e.g., a perception of the inclination relative to each other of the world lines of matter in Minkowski space.

[4] One may take the standpoint that the idea of an objective lapse of time (whose essence is that only the present really exists) is meaningless. But this is no way out of the dilemma; for by this very opinion one would take the idealistic viewpoint as to the idea of change, exactly as those philosophers who consider it as self-contradictory. For in both views one denies that an objective lapse of time is a possible state of affairs, a fortiori that it exists in reality, and it makes very little difference in this context, whether our idea of it is regarded as meaningless or as self-contradictory. Of course for those who take either one of these two viewpoints the argument from relativity theory given below is unnecessary, but even for them it should be of interest that perhaps there exists a second proof for the unreality of change based on entirely different grounds, especially in view of the fact that the assertion to be proved runs so completely counter to common sense. A particularly clear discussion of the subject independent of relativity theory is to be found in: Paul Mongré, Das Chaos in kosmischer Auslese, 1898.

[5] It may be objected that this argument only shows that the lapse of time is something relative, which does not exclude that it is something objective; whereas idealists maintain that it is something merely imagined. A relative lapse of time, however, if any meaning at all can be given to this phrase, would certainly be something entirely different from the lapse of time in the ordinary sense, which means a change in the existing. The concept of existence, however, cannot be relativized without destroying its meaning completely. It may furthermore be objected that the argument under consideration only shows that time lapses in different ways for different observers, whereas the lapse of time itself may nevertheless be an intrinsic (absolute) property of time or of reality. A lapse of time, however, which is not a lapse in some definite way seems to me as absurd as a coloured object which has no definite colours. But even if such a thing were conceivable, it would again be something totally different from the intuitive idea of the lapse of time, to which the idealistic assertion refers.

unchallenged. And actually to the argument in the form just presented it can be objected that the complete equivalence of all observers moving with different (but uniform) velocities, which is the essential point in it, subsists only in the abstract space-time scheme of special relativity theory and in certain empty worlds of general relativity theory. The existence of matter, however, as well as the particular kind of curvature of space-time produced by it, largely destroy the equivalence of different observers[6] and distinguish some of them conspicuously from the rest, namely those which follow in their notion the mean motion of matter.[7] Now in all cosmological solutions of the gravitational equations (i.e., in all possible universes) known at present the local times of all *these* observers fit together into one world time, so that apparently it becomes possible to consider this time as the "true" one, which lapses objectively, whereas the discrepancies of the measuring results of other observers from this time may be conceived as due to the influence which a motion relative to the mean state of motion of matter has on the measuring processes and physical processes in general.

From this state of affairs, in view of the fact that some of the known cosmological solutions seem to represent our world correctly, James Jeans has concluded[8] that there is no reason to abandon the intuitive idea of an absolute time lapsing objectively. I do not think that the situation justifies this conclu-

[6] Of course, according to relativity theory all observers are equivalent in so far as the laws of motion and interaction for matter and field are the same for all of them. But this does not exclude that the structure of the world (i.e., the actual arrangement of matter, motion, and field) may offer quite different aspects to different observers, and that it may offer a more "natural" aspect to some of them and a distorted one to others. The observer, incidentally, plays no essential rôle in these considerations. The main point, of course, is that the world itself has certain distinguished directions, which directly define certain distinguished local times.

[7] The value of the mean motion of matter may depend essentially on the size of the regions over which the mean is taken. What may be called the "true mean motion" is obtained by taking regions so large, that a further increase in their size does not any longer change essentially the value obtained. In our world this is the case for regions including many galactic systems. Of course a true mean motion in this sense need not necessarily exist.

[8] Cf. *Man and the Universe*, Sir Halley Stewart Lecture (1935), 22-23.

sion and am basing my opinion chiefly[9] on the following facts and considerations:

There exist cosmological solutions of another kind[10] than those known at present, to which the aforementioned procedure of defining an absolute time is not applicable, because the local times of the special observers used above cannot be fitted together into one world time. Nor can any other procedure which would accomplish this purpose exist for them; i.e., these worlds possess such properties of symmetry, that for each possible concept of simultaneity and succession there exist others which cannot be distinguished from it by any intrinsic properties, but only by reference to individual objects, such as, e.g., a particular galactic system.

Consequently, the inference drawn above as to the non-objectivity of change doubtless applies at least in these worlds. Moreover it turns out that temporal conditions in these universes (at least in those referred to in the end of footnote 10) show other surprising features, strengthening further the idealistic viewpoint. Namely, by making a round trip on a rocket ship in a sufficiently wide curve, it is possible in these worlds to travel into any region of the past, present, and future, and back again, exactly as it is possible in other worlds to travel to distant parts of space.

This state of affairs seems to imply an absurdity. For it enables one e.g., to travel into the near past of those places where

[9] Another circumstance invalidating Jeans' argument is that the procedure described above gives only an approximate definition of an absolute time. No doubt it is possible to refine the procedure so as to obtain a precise definition, but perhaps only by introducing more or less arbitrary elements (such as, e.g., the size of the regions or the weight function to be used in the computation of the mean motion of matter). It is doubtful whether there exists a precise definition which has so great merits, that there would be sufficient reason to consider exactly the time thus obtained as the true one.

[10] The most conspicuous physical property distinguishing these solutions from those known at present is that the compass of inertia in them everywhere rotates relative to matter, which in our world would mean that it rotates relative to the totality of galactic systems. These worlds, therefore, can fittingly be called "rotating universes." In the subsequent considerations I have in mind a particular kind of rotating universes which have the additional properties of being static and spatially homogeneous, and a cosmological constant < 0. For the mathematical representation of these solutions, cf. my paper forthcoming in *Rev. Mod. Phys.*

he has himself lived. There he would find a person who would be himself at some earlier period of his life. Now he could do something to this person which, by his memory, he knows has not happened to him. This and similar contradictions, however, in order to prove the impossibility of the worlds under consideration, presuppose the actual feasibility of the journey into one's own past. But the velocities which would be necessary in order to complete the voyage in a reasonable length of time[11] are far beyond everything that can be expected ever to become a practical possibility. Therefore it cannot be excluded *a priori*, on the ground of the argument given, that the space-time structure of the real world is of the type described.

As to the conclusions which could be drawn from the state of affairs explained for the question being considered in this paper, the decisive point is this: that for *every* possible definition of a world time one could travel into regions of the universe which are passed according to that definition.[12] This again shows that to assume an objective lapse of time would lose every justification in these worlds. For, in whatever way one may assume time to be lapsing, there will always exist possible observers to whose experienced lapse of time no objective lapse corresponds (in particular also possible observers whose whole existence objectively would be simultaneous). But, if the experience of the lapse of time can exist without an objective lapse of time, no reason can be given why an objective lapse of time should be assumed at all.

It might, however, be asked: Of what use is it if such conditions prevail in certain *possible* worlds? Does that mean anything for the question interesting us whether in *our* world there

---

[11] Basing the calculation on a mean density of matter equal to that observed in our world, and assuming one were able to transform matter completely into energy the weight of the "fuel" of the rocket ship, in order to complete the voyage in *t* years (as measured by the traveller), would have to be of the order of magnitude of $\dfrac{10^{22}}{t^2}$ times the weight of the ship (if stopping, too, is effected by recoil). This estimate applies to t $\ll 10''$. Irrespective of the value of t, the velocity of the ship must be at least $1/\sqrt{2}$ of the velocity of light.

[12] For this purpose incomparably smaller velocities would be sufficient. Under the assumptions made in footnote 11 the weight of the fuel would have to be at most of the same order of magnitude as the weight of the ship.

exists an objective lapse of time? I think it does. For, (1) **Our** world, it is true, can hardly be represented by the particular kind of rotating solutions referred to above (because these solutions are static and, therefore, yield no red-shift for distant objects); there exist however also *expanding* rotating solutions. In such universes an absolute time also might fail to exist,[13] and it is not impossible that our world is a universe of this kind. (2) The mere compatibility with the laws of nature[14] of worlds in which there is no distinguished absolute time, and, therefore, no objective lapse of time can exist, throws some light on the meaning of time also in those worlds in which an absolute time *can* be defined. For, if someone asserts that this absolute time is lapsing, he accepts as a consequence that, whether or not an objective lapse of time exists (i.e., whether or not a time in the ordinary sense of the word exists), depends on the particular way in which matter and its motion are arranged in the world. This is not a straightforward contradiction; nevertheless, a philosophical view leading to such consequences can hardly be considered as satisfactory.

KURT GÖDEL

INSTITUTE FOR ADVANCED STUDY
PRINCETON, NEW JERSEY

[13] At least if it required that successive experiences of one observer should never be simultaneous in the absolute time, or (which is equivalent) that the absolute time should agree in direction with the times of all possible observers. Without this requirement an absolute time always exists in an expanding (and homogeneous) world. Whenever I speak of an "absolute" time, this of course is to be understood with the restriction explained in footnote 9, which also applies to other possible definitions of an absolute time.

[14] The solution considered above only proves the compatibility with the general form of the field equations in which the value of the cosmological constant is left open; this value, however, which at present is not known with certainty, evidently forms part of the laws of nature. But other rotating solutions might make the result independent of the value of the cosmological constant (or rather of its vanishing or non-vanishing and of its sign, since its numerical value is of no consequence for this problem). At any rate these questions would first have to be answered in an unfavourable sense, before one could think of drawing a conclusion like that of Jeans mentioned above. *Note added Sept. 2, 1949:* I have found in the meantime that for *every* value of the cosmological constant there do exist solutions, in which there is no world-time satisfying the requirement of footnote 13. K.G.

22

Gaston Bachelard

THE PHILOSOPHIC DIALECTIC OF THE CONCEPTS OF RELATIVITY

THE PHILOSOPHIC DIALECTIC OF THE CONCEPTS OF RELATIVITY*

I

PHILOSOPHERS have removed the great cosmic drama of Copernican thought from the dominion of reality to the dominion of metaphor. Kant described his Critical philosophy as a Copernican revolution in metaphysics. Following the Kantian thesis, the two fundamental philosophies, rationalism and empiricism, changed places, and the world revolved about the mind. As a result of this radical modification, the knowing mind and the known world acquired the appearance of being relative to each other. But this kind of relativity remained merely symbolic. Nothing had changed in the detail or the principles of coherence of knowledge. Empiricism and rationalism remained face-to-face and incapable of achieving either true philosophical co-operation or mutual enrichment.

The philosophic virtues of the Einsteinian revolution could be quite differently effective, as compared to the philosophic metaphors of the Copernican revolution, if only the philosopher were willing to seek all the instruction contained in relativity science. A systematic revolution of basic concepts begins with Einsteinian science. In the very detail of its concepts a relativism of the rational and the empirical is established. Science then undergoes what Nietzsche called "an upheaval of concepts," as if the earth, the universe, things, possessed a different structure from the fact that their explanation rests upon new foundations. All rational organization is "shaken" when the fundamental concepts undergo dialectical transformation.

Moreover, this dialectic is not argued by an automatic logic, as is the dialectic of the philosopher too often. In relativity,

---

* Translated from the French manuscript by Forrest W. Williams.

the terms of the dialectic are rendered solid and cohesive to the point of presenting a philosophical synthesis of mathematical rationalism and "technological" empiricism. This, at least, is what we would like to show in the present article. First, we will present our view in respect to the "shaking" of some isolated concepts; then, we shall endeavor to show the value of the philosophical synthesis which is suggested by Einsteinian science.

II

As we know, as has been repeated a thousand times, relativity was born of an epistemological shock; it was born of the "failure" of the Michelson experiment. That experiment should contradict theoretical prediction is in itself not a singular occurrence. But it is necessary to realize how and why a negative result was, this time, the occasion for an immense positive construction. Those who live in the realm of scientific thinking doubtless do not need these remarks. They are nonetheless polemically indispensable for assessing the philosophical utility of relativity.

For this notion of the negative quality of experiment must not be allowed to subsist. In a well-performed experiment, everything is positive. And Albert Einstein understood this fact when he pondered over the Michelson experiment. This pseudo-negative experiment did not open upon the mystery of things, the unfathomable mystery of things. Its "failure" was not even a proof of the ineptitude of rationalism. The Michelson experiment proceeded from an *intelligent* question, a question which had to be asked. Contemporary science would be hanging "in mid-air," if the Michelson experiment had not been conceived, then actualized, then meticulously actualized in the full consciousness of the sensibility of the technique; then varied, then repeated on the floors of valleys and the peaks of mountains, and always verified. What capacity for self-doubt, for meticulous and profound doubt, for *intelligent* doubt, was contained in this will to test and measure again and again! Are we sure that Michelson died with the conviction that the experiment had been well performed, perfectly performed, with the conviction that the *negative* bases of the experiment had been reached? Thus, instead of an universal doubt, an intuitive doubt, a Cartesian doubt, technological science yields a precise doubt, a discursive doubt, an implemented doubt. It was as a consequence of this explicit doubt that the mechanistic dogmatism was shattered by relativity. To paraphrase Kant, we might say that the Michelson experiment roused classical mechanics from its dogmatic slumber.

For the negative aspect of the Michelson experiment did not deter Einstein. For him, the experimental failure of a technique thus scientifically pursued suggested the need for new theoretical information. It became indispensable to hope for a minute "Copernican revolution" in which all philosophy of reality and of reason must begin a new dialectic. In order that this dialectic may possess its full instructive value for the philosopher, it is necessary to beware of sweeping philosophical designations. It is not highly instructive to say, with Meyerson, that Einstein is a *realist*. Without a doubt, Einstein submits to experience, submits to "reality." But must we not inquire: to what experience, to what reality? That of the infinitesimal decimal upon which the Michelson experiment turned, or that solid reality of the whole number, of solid, ordinary, common, gross verification? It would seem that the philosopher who acknowledges the lessons of relativity must at the very least, envisage a *new reality*. And this *new reality* enjoins him to *consider* reality *differently*.

Where, then, must the philosophy of science find its initial convictions? Must it give precedence to the lessons to be found in the beginning of experience, or in the end of experience? By building upon the first structures or upon the final structures? We shall see that the latter is correct, that it is *l'esprit de finesse* which reveals the foundations of *l'esprit géometrique*.

III

Which, then, are the concepts that are "shaken"? Which concepts undergo at the rational level, in the superb light of rational philosophy, a Nietzschean transmutation of rational values?

They are the concepts of:

> absolute space,
> absolute time,
> absolute velocity.

Is so little required to "shake" the universe of spatiality? Can a single experiment of the twentieth century annihilate—a Sartrian would say "*néantiser*"—two or three centuries of rational thought? Yes, a single decimal sufficed, as our poet Henri de Regnier would say, to "make all nature sing."

Upon what, in fact, did the notion of absolute space rest? Did it rest upon an absolute reality or upon an absolute intuition of the Kantian variety? Is it not philosophically strange that absoluteness could be attributed as well to a *reality* as to an *a priori intuition*? This double success of a raw realism and an over-simple intuitionism seems spurious. This twofold success makes a double failure. Therefore, it is necessary to investigate this double possibility of philosophical interpretation from the standpoint of the precision of modern scientific experiment. Uncriticized experience is no longer admissible. The *double philosophy* of the experience of space—realistic philosophy and Kantian philosophy—must be replaced by a *dialectical philosophy* of space, by a philosophy which is at once experimental and rational. In short, the philosophy of ultra-refined experience and the philosophy of physical theory are firmly *coupled* in relativity. The new philosophy of science will prove to be a critical philosophy more subtle and more synthetic than was Kantian philosophy in respect to Newtonian science. Relativistic criticism does not limit itself to a revoluton of means of explanation. It is more profoundly revolutionary. It is more *génial*.

Thus, we come face-to-face with the fundamental assertion of Einstein: the *position* of an absolute space as the affirmation of a kind of materialization of immobility and as the residence of an unconditioned subject in the center of all the conditioned relations, is a *position* without proof. Therefore, one must— Copernican revolution at the level of an unique concept— formulate the essential relativity of the intuition of localization and the experience of localization, which simultaneously destroys two absolutes: first, the intuition of an observer has no absolute character; and secondly, the extension of an objective world has no absolute character. The essentially discursive method of reference will, therefore, always have to be explicitly considered in relation to the real phenomena studied in the extremity of scientific precision. Extreme experimental dexterity will underlie any knowledge of space. The Michelson experiment, at first sight so particular in character, will form the basis of the most far-reaching generalization.

It is, moreover, quite striking that the Michelson laboratory was, properly speaking, *cosmic*. There, the most artificial physics imaginable was referred to the space of the world. The decimal which they wished to reveal by means of the interferometer, the decimal which is of the order of three-fourths of the wavelength of a vibration of light, was related to the orbital speed of the earth, a speed of the order of eighteen miles per second. The precision of such a question posed by this technique in respect to the space of the world, this attempt to experience the immobility of space in its cosmic significance, ought to set the metaphysicians thinking who study the place of man in the world; if only these metaphysicians would give their attention to the lengthy discursive processes which lead science to build new intuitions.

IV

The new intuitions of time likewise demand lengthy preparation. They must struggle against the blinding clarity of common intuitions, and against the equally over-hasty formulation of Kantian criticism.

Here, the concept which experiences the "Nietzschean upheaval" is that of *simultaneity*. In regard to this concept, so evident, so familiar, the Einsteinian claim is pregnant. This claim collides with common sense; it is contrary to common experience; it puts in question again the very basis of classical mechanics. It demands therefore, a decisive intellectual mutation which must reverberate among the most fundamental philosophical values. More precisely, if the notion of simultaneity, which was not *criticized* by Kant, must receive a *neo-critical* examination, empiricism and rationalism must, at the same time, be *rectified* and related to each other in a new way.

To formulate a doubt concerning the notion of simultaneity is, in our opinion, to transcend the hyperbolic doubt of Cartesian philosophy. A doubt attaching to so simple, so positive, so direct a notion no longer bears the marks of a formal doubt, an universal doubt. As long as one remains within the horizons of Cartesian doubt, one is in the contingency of doubt. The Einsteinian revolution demands a necessary doubt regarding a notion which has always passed for fundamental. Concomitantly, the putting in doubt of a rational and realistic notion cannot remain provisional. Such a doubt will always carry with it a decisive pedagogical effect. It will remain an imprescriptible cultural fact. Whoever, for the rest of time, would teach relativity would have to put in doubt the absolute character of the notion of simultaneity. This necessity constitutes, in some sense, an *electro-shock* for rationalistic philosophies and hardened realistic philosophies.

Granting a renunciation of the right to posit an absolute space, what is the Einsteinian claim in regard to the simultaneity of events which occur at two different points in space? Einstein demands that one define a *positive* experiment, a *precise* experiment expressible in well-defined scientific terms. There is no longer any question of retreating into the intuition of internal sensibility, whether this intuition be Kantian or Bergsonian, formalistic or realistic. One must be able to describe and institute objective experiments which enable one to *verify* this simultaneity. Immediately, a metaphysical nuance appears which the philosopher too often neglects. Here we have a *verified* reality in place of a given reality. Hereafter, if an idealist must make an initial declaration, he will be forced to do so from a point one step closer to a rationalism which is linked with reality. He cannot be satisfied with repeating after Schopenhauer: "The world is my representation;" he must say, if he is to assume the full extent of scientific thought: "The world is my verification."

More precisely, the objective world is the aggregate of facts verified by modern science, the world rendered by the conceptions verified by the science of our time. Further, *experimental verification* implies the *coherence* of the experimental method. Since a science is founded upon the Michelson experiment, this Michelson experiment must be comprehended in the very definition of simultaneity. To be sure, we are concerned with the Michelson experiment as it is, not as it was for a long time thought to be. The Michelson experiment, as it is, then, must assign reality at the outset to the convention of signaling.

Without a doubt, any number of conventions of signalling could have been adopted. One could create a meta-acoustics based upon a simultaneity verified by the transmission of sounds. But physics would gain nothing from such specialization. Hereafter, physics is cosmic. The most rapid and reliable signals which are both human and universal are light signals. The Michelson experiment discloses a privileged character which accrues to these signals. They require no support; they are not conditioned by a medium, by a transmitting ether. They are independent of the *relative* movements of the observers who utilize them. They are truly the most "reasonable" ("*rational-isables*") of all signals. Thus, one would define the simultaneity of two events which occur in two different places in terms of an exchange of light signals and of the result, henceforth regarded as positive, of the Michelson experiment which justifies the following postulate: the velocity of light is the same in all directions irrespective of the observers who measure it, regardless of the relative motion of these observers.

This *operational* definition of simultaneity dissolves the notion of *absolute* time. Since simultaneity is linked to physical experiments which occur in space, the temporal contexture (*contexture*) is one with spatial contexture. Since there is no absolute space, there is no absolute time. And it is due to the solidarity of space-experiments and simultaneity-experiments that a reconstitution of space and time must accompany any thorough examination of space and time. Therefore, from the standpoint of philosophy, it is evident that scientific thought requires a rebuilding of the notions of space and time in terms of their solidarity. As a consequence of this necessity to provide a new basis for space and time, relativity will emerge philosophically as a *rationalism of second order* (*rationalisme de deuxième position*), as an enlightened rationalism which necessitates a new departure.

But before building, one must destroy. One must convince oneself that any analysis which from the outset separates spatial characters and temporal characters is a crude analysis. Doubtless, such an analysis is valid for common knowledge, and no less valid for an enormous quantity of scientific thought. But for its denunciation one need only note that it masks certain well-defined problems. Looking to the new synthetic notion of space-time, henceforth indispensable for a grasp of electromagnetic phenomena, one can perceive the philosophical weakness of any attempt at vulgarization. It is not a matter of basing a synthesis upon an analysis. One must conceive the *a priori synthesis* which underlies the notion of space-time. All the tales of passing trains which signal an observer standing in a station, of aviators who smoke cigars in lengthened or contracted periods of time—to what purpose are they?—or, more precisely, for whom are they designed? Surely not for those who have not understood the *mathematical organization* of relativity. And those who have understood the *mathematical organization* of relativity require no *examples*. They install themselves in the clear and certain *algebraism* of the doctrine. It is on the basis of the synthesis of algebraism and scientific experiment that one may correctly designate the rationalistic revival implied in the doctrines of Einstein. Let us demonstrate this neo-Kantian aspect. It did not escape Léon Brunschvicg, who wrote: "The advancement on Kant (effected by these new doctrines) consisted in transporting the *a priori* synthesis from the region of intuition to the region of intellect, and this is decisive for the passage to physics."

And, in fact, any Kantian philosophy holds that space is not a concept drawn from experience of the external world, since the intuition of space is a *sine qua non* condition of experience of the external world. A similarly inverted formulation is enunciated in respect to time, which is given as the *a priori* form of internal sensibility. The *sine qua non* is the pivot of the Copernican revolution of intuitions of space and time.

And, in the same manner, in the same philosophical fashion, if one would determine the epistemological function of the space-time notion in relativistic science, one must say that the *space-time algebraic complex* is a *sine qua non* condition of the general validity of our knowledge of electromagnetism. Knowledge of electromagnetic phenomena during the nineteenth century was co-ordinated by the laws of Maxwell. Reflection upon these laws led to the conviction that they must remain *invariant* for any change of reference system. This invariance defined the transformation [formulas] of Lorentz. It established a Lorentz group which possesses the same philosophical significance for relativity geometry which the group of displacements and similitudes possesses for Euclidean geometry. Thus, it is the Lorentz transformation which underlies the notion of space-time, and the Lorentz group which forbids the separation of spatial co-ordinates and temporal co-ordinates. The notion of space-time takes shape in a perspective of *necessity*. To see in it a mere linguistic structure, a mere condensation of means of expression, would be to underestimate its philosophical significance. It is a conception, a necessary conception. If the rôle of the philosopher is, as we believe, to think thought, then he must think space-time in the totality of its functions, in its algebraic nature, and in its informing value for scientific phenomena.

If one adds now, that due to the operational definition of simultaneity the velocity of light enters into geometrical-mechanical references, and if one recalls that light is an electromagnetic phenomenon, one reaches the conclusion that the notion of space-time is hereafter a basic notion for an ultra-precise understanding of phenomena.

Thus, the concept of space-time, as suggested by Lorentz, as achieved by Einstein, appears as an *a priori* form, functionally *a priori*, permitting the comprehension of precise electromagnetic phenomena. It is of little importance, philosophically, that this form occurs tardily in the history of science. It is installed as functionally *primary* by the *enlightened rationalism* which constitutes one of the most clear-cut aspects of the theory of relativity. Once having aligned oneself with this enlightened rationalism, one sees that there is a *naïve rationalism* in the same sense that there is a *naïve realism*. And if one would reap all the philosophical benefits of scientific culture, one must realize psychologically the soundness of the *new foundations;* one must abandon the old points of departure, and *begin again.* At the close of the eighteenth century, in his history of astronomy, Bailly maintained that calculated astronomy procured a *peace of mind* in contrast to any theory of imaginative astronomy. Newtonian thinkers, he said, "chose to adopt the notion of attraction to fasten their imagination, to rest their thoughts."

The function of Einsteinian rationalism is likewise salutary The algebraic notion of space-time rids us of vulgarizing images. It frees us from a falsely profound reverie upon space and time. In particular, it precludes the irrationalism associated with an unfathomable duration. The mind *rests* in the truth of its constructions.

Once the *algebraic* nature of the Einsteinian formulation is realized, one is prepared for a philosophic inversion of the abstract and concrete characters of scientific culture; or, to speak more precisely, one accedes to the *abstract-concrete* character of scientific thought. One may well say that the concept of *space-time* is more concrete, despite its intellectual character, than the two separate notions of space and time, since it consolidates two perspectives of experience. Naturally, the notion of space-time will, whenever necessary, be divided and analyzed so as to reinstate those separate functions of time and space, in view of the *simplifications* which are useful in classical mechanics. But relativity will be on guard against all *simplifications.* It *rests* upon the summit of its synthesis. From this vantage point, it judges confidently all analytical perspectives.

How shall philosophers be led to this summit? But philosophers no longer care, it seems, for synthetic thoughts. They do not wish to found knowledge upon its highest achievement. They claim to cut Gordian knots at a time when science is striving to *knit together* the most unforeseen relations, at a time when physico-mathematical science resolutely declares itself abstract-concrete.

Rather than to return ceaselessly to the base of common knowledge, as if what suffices for life could suffice for knowledge, we have the means, by pursuing Einsteinian science, to develop a terminal rationalism, a differentiating rationalism, a dialectical rationalism. This differentiaton, this dialectic appears in knowledge at a second stage of approximation. In short, there occurs an inversion in [the order of] epistemological importance. The first approximation is only the opening move. Common knowledge regards it as basic, though it is only provisional. The structure of scientific understanding emerges only from refinement, through an analysis as thorough as possible of every functionality.

One may, in application, limit these functionalities, cognizant that a potentiality remains unrealized, that a sensibility is smothered. One would recognize that in quantum mechanics in numerous cases there occurs *degeneration* (*"dégénérescence"*), that is to say, extinction of a structural possibility. But the new theories yield the whole hierarchy of rationalistic and empiricist values. Classical science and common knowledge have their [respective] places in the system of epistemological values. The dialectic of relativistic mechanics and classical mechanics is an enveloping dialectic. It seems that relativity risked everythng which lent certainty to the classical conception of reality, but, having risked all, lost nothing. It has retained all that was scientifically known during the last century. A shift of the finer structures reveals the ancient bonds. Thus, relativity permits a retrospective re-enactment of the entire history of mechanistic rationalism.

V

This possibility of recurring to simplified philosophies will be better understood if we can now show the notably firm nature of the coupling of rationalism and realism effected by relativity. To this end, it will suffice to consider the algebraic form, *space-time*, in its ordering functions in mechanics and electromagnetism.

Space-time is not merely a simple epistemological necessity evoked by reflection upon the conditions of invariance stipulated by the Maxwell equations. This initial synthesis propagates its ordering power. The notion of space-time conditions quadrivectors which accentuate the synthetic character of the relativistic [mode of] organization.

For example, by extending the classical conception of mechanical impulsion, which is a vector of three-dimensional space, relativity attains the conception of the impulsion of the universe as a quadrivector of four-dimensional space. This impulsion has the three components of classical momentum as its spatial component, and energy divided by the velocity of light as its temporal component. But the quadrivector of the impulsion does not consist of a simple juxtaposition of the momentum- and energy-aspects. So powerful a conceptual fusion is achieved that the principle of the conservation of momentum and the principle of the conservation of energy are summated. In an isolated material system, the geometric sum of the quadrivectors of the impulsion remains constant when applied to different bodies in the system. Recalling that Descartes formulated his mechanics in terms of the notion of momentum whereas Leibniz advanced the notion of mechanical energy, one would perceive, from the summit of this synthesis, the historical recurrence as a profound synthesis of Descartes and Leibniz achieved by Einstein.

This same inspiration led to Einstein's discovery of the algebraic homogeneity of energy and mass. This discovery of mathematical, *rationalistic* origin had considerable *realistic* import. The mass-energy amalgam, first established for kinetic energy, clearly extends to all forms of energy. Doutbless the philosopher who thinks in words, who believes that scientific concepts have an absolute root in common notions, is shocked by the phrase *"inertia of energy."* And yet it is this concept of the inertia of energy which marks Einsteinian science as a new science, as a conceptually synthetic science.

In effect, the realistic aspect of this mass-energy amalgam consists in none other than the union of the so different classical principles of the conservation of mass and the conservation of energy. Considered in their historical evolution, the concepts of mass and energy appear bereft of an *absolute.* Now it is necessary to establish between them a profound *relation,* an ontological relation.

In other words, in order to realize this relativization of so realistic a principle as that of the conservation of mass, one must accept once more the Copernican revolution of relativity, one must install mathematics at the *center* of experience, one must take mathematics as the inspiration of scientific experiment. For, after all, experiments as precise as those of chemistry cast no doubt upon the principle of Lavoisier. Chemistry was, in this respect, the recital of an immense success. Chemistry codified the *absolute* character of a materialism of balances. *Scientific* realism was, on this point, on a par in conviction with *naïve realism.* Let us firmly underscore that efficacious thought proceeds in the direction of rationalism → realism. Primacy belongs, not to the principle of conservation (in realistic fashion), but to a principle of invariance (in rationalistic fashion). It is the conditions of invariance in the mathematical expression of the laws which permit a definition of the meaning and validity of the true *principles of conversation.* Insofar as it was thought possible to characterize the philosophy of relativity by the too-simple label of "realism" from the sole fact that relativity substantiates principles of conservation, this epistemological evolution must be the more definitively formulated. For our part, we are of the opinion that the manner of conserving is more important than what is conserved. To conserve mass and energy in a single formula is not really to ground one's faith in the reality conserved but, rather, to become conscious of the rationalistic power of the invariance of the laws.

Doubtless, experiment in its most refined, meticulous forms sanctioned the ingenious views of Albert Einstein; consequently, [the concept of the] inertia of energy possesses hereafter an undeniably realistic character. But these very *conceptions* were *original* and *inspired;* they were not psychologically *natural* and they led to scientific experiments which were quasi-*supernatural.* For example, the entirety of nuclear physics falls within the jurisdiction of the principle of *inertia of energy.* And the power of nuclear physics has been sufficiently emphasized, perhaps to the neglect of its ultra-phenomenal character. The scientist has already smashed more uranium nuclei in the space of five years than Nature in a millennium. The laboratory technician has succeeded in *implementing* by means of the atomic pile the Einsteinian principle of inertia of energy. The reality which slumbered in his materials was *provoked* by mathematically-founded experiments. Seen from the nuclear level, one might well say that matter evokes a neo-materialism in which substance and energy are interchangeable entities. Reality is no longer nature pure and simple. It must be wrought to become the object of scientific experiment. Thus, the philosophy of contemporary science as it issued from the revolutions of the beginning of the century appears as a dialectic of enlightened rationalism and elaborated realism. In order to lose none of the philosophical implications of science the two concepts of invariance and conservation must be synthesized in an *abstract-concrete* philosophy by introducing an additional unifying trait in the form of an *invariance-conservation*. Here is a philosophical *doublet* which would be mutilated by an unilateral philosophical interpretation, whether rationalistic or realistic. Science requires hereafter a bi-certitude. It must satisfy the requirements of mathematical coherence and minute experimental verification.

VI

We have followed rapidly a development of relativistic thought to a synthetic center of the science of mechanics. The synthesis on the side of electromagnetism was not less important. The components of the two tri-dimensional vectors by which classical physics defined separately the electric field and the magnetic field are recognized by relativity as the components of a single tensor. This fact endows the Maxwell-Lorentz equations with an extreme generality which goes hand in hand with an extreme algebraic condensation.

It is not the least paradoxical character of general relativity to find in the development of its doctrine this dialectic of rational condensation and extension of empirical significations. When enlightened rationalism takes hold of reality by such condensed symbols, one experiences, there too, a great peace of mind. Tensor calculus, Paul Langevin liked to say, knows relativity better than the relativist himself. Tensor calculus becomes, in some manner, charged for us with subaltern thought; it is our guarantee of forgetting nothing; it arranges for particular analyses. These symbols are in no way mystical. They are translucent to the mathematician and they render the physicist perspicacious. The unifying formulas of general relativity are philosophical syntheses which reunite rationalism and realism.

VII

If we were to consider dialectically the *principle of equivalence* of inert mass and heavy mass, the principle which founded general relativity, we would be led to the same philosophical conclusions.

In effect, to reunite *inert mass* and *heavy mass* in a single concept amounts to amalgamating inertia, a quality inhering in a given body, and weight, a quality whose seat is, in some manner, external to the body in question. Thus, we have a prime example of the correlation of a force and a structure of space-time. This correlation inscribed in the Einsteinian principle of equivalence is greatly extended in the development of the doctrine.

Here, again, the philosopher may find instruction; for the principle of equivalence constitutes a denial of the [supposed] logical priority habitually assigned to force over against its manifestations. In fact, force is contemporaneous with phenomena. There is no circuit of being which assigns being to matter, then to its forces, then to the deformations of matter. As Eddington said, "Matter is not a cause, it is an index."[1] All exists together as the structure of space-time.

Relativity, therefore, seems to us to modify philosophically the principles of *"causalism"* in quite as thoroughgoing fashion as those of *realism*. *Abstract-concrete* philosophy will have to be formulated in terms of a new trait of metaphysical union and will have to think of scientific phenomena as *cause-functions*. There occurs an endosmosis of mathematical consequences and physical causes.

---

[1] A. S. Eddington, *Space, Time and Gravitation* (Cambridge, 1921), 191.

Thus, relativity ceaselessly calls scientific thought to a philosophical activity which is both *central* and *dialectic*. The traditional problem of the dualism of mind and body is posed in a precise central locus, with the benefit of an extreme sensibility. Here the most rigorous mathematician and the most meticulous physicist agree. They understand each other. They instruct each other. Thought would become empty, experience would become obscure, if one were not to accept, in the regions in which relativity functions, the synthesis of enlightened rationalism and elaborated realism.

GASTON BACHELARD

THE SORBONNE
PARIS, FRANCE

23

Aloys Wenzl

EINSTEIN'S THEORY OF RELATIVITY, VIEWED
FROM THE STANDPOINT OF CRITICAL
REALISM, AND ITS SIGNIFICANCE
FOR PHILOSOPHY

EINSTEIN'S THEORY OF RELATIVITY, VIEWED FROM THE STANDPOINT OF CRITICAL REALISM, AND ITS SIGNIFICANCE FOR PHILOSOPHY*

THE battle in epistemology is, in the final analysis, conditioned by the various degrees of confidence in our capacity to know. It could be said that the issue is that of finding the right Aristotelian mean between the extremes of naïveté and scepticism. Naïve realism as well as so-called subjective idealism drop out from the beginning if what we are concerned with is real and significant knowledge; for if science and philosophy are to be pursued seriously, they certainly cannot be satisfied with an uncritical acceptance of our impressions of the outside world as faithful reproductions of the same, nor carry doubt so far that our determinations are seen as nothing more than our ideas, our perceptions as nothing more than our imaginings. This would also lead to a splitting of theory and practice. The (only) applicable epistemological points of view, therefore, are the critical idealism of Kant, positivism, and critical realism. Kant emphasizes that he can and wants to make assertions only concerning appearances, although he acknowledges a reality independent of consciousness as the cause of those appearances. Positivism in its various forms wants to limit itself to mastering of experience under the viewpoint of usefulness, simplicity, and uniformity; it merely wishes to bring the facts of experience into an ordered system. Critical realism is concerned with combining criticism and the positive knowledge of reality. It appears inconsistent [to the critical realist] to destroy the bridge between appearance and reality, and unsatisfactory to the human striving for knowledge to be satisfied with merely useful or

* Translated from the German manuscript by Paul Arthur Schilpp.

even with the most useful ordering of the variety of experiences; this would not be knowledge and [certainly] no justification of the motive of all scientific endeavor to arrive at the most responsible world-picture. In Germany we do not understand under critical realism quite the same thing as what is thus named in America; but we do assert our faith in the programmatic theses, formulated by the *Critical Realism* of 1920, that, although the things-in-themselves do not enter our consciousness, appearances are by no means merely subjective, but that there is such a thing as objective truth and that logic is valid. In Germany critical realism is connected with the names of Eduard von Hartmann, Hermann Lotze, Hans Driesch, Oswald Külpe, Erich Becher, Bernhard Bavink, *et al.:* to the perceptual appearances, relations, and qualities correspond the relations and qualities of objective reality; neither the sense-qualities of color, of sound, etc., nor the spatial and temporal distances are objective or absolute, but they do correspond to qualities and relations which are independent of consciousness; out of the agreement between deduced suppositions and their conclusions with experience, moreover, we may conclude concerning the truth content of the proffered hypotheses.

It is thus that critical realism becomes the basis for an inductive metaphysics, i.e., it is possible to posit, even if only hypothetically, a unitary picture of the world which does most justice to experience and is scientifically [respectable] responsible. A theory is, therefore, neither a [mere] ideational work of art nor a mere convention, but a pointer with external and inner probability on the basis of validation and consistency; and its scientific character remains preserved even in its hypothetical nature by virtue of the fact that the presuppositions of the accepted assumptions are stated. It is only on such a point of view that from the standpoint of critical realism, a theory actually contributes to what we call knowledge. What, now, are the philosophically most important results of Einstein's theory of relativity. We consider them to be the following:

1. The equal validity of all straight-line equally moving systems not only as regards the laws of mechanics, but also as concerns those of electro-magnetism, of optics, and

the constancy of the *velocity of light*, the two axioms, that is to say, from which the relativizing of spatial and temporal measurements follow and which demand the co-ordination into a four-dimensional continuum.

2. The equivalence of mass and energy, which is expressed in the already classical equation $E = mc^2$ and which connects the concepts of *mass and energy*, which had played the rôle of substance in classical physics and in natural philosophy.

3. The formation (curvature) of the space-time continuum by mass and energy in such fashion that the *metric* becomes the expression for the reality of what appears to us as material-energic. True, this conception of matter and its fields as a realization of the metrical characteristics of the space-time continuum has thus far been carried through in Einstein's general theory of relativity only for the field of gravitation; but one is confident that the charges and the electromagnetic fields will also be capable of being interpreted metrically.

4. The *cosmological* development: the world is a spatially limited, finite non-Euclidean continuum, its radius increases and the universe expands.

5. The *cosmogonic* development: our universe originated in an "explosion" or "expansion" of a "cylindrical world" or else by means of the increasing formation of material particles (P. Jordan).

The philosophical problematics includes, therefore:

1. The problem of space-time, especially as concerns the reality of time and of motion—the problem which already had its inception with the opposition between the philosophy of the Eleatics and that of Heraclitus.

2. The problem of substance and of the original stuff, which began with the antique problem of the ether—viz., of the still indeterminate *apeiron* of Anaximander—continues in Aristotle's and scholasticism's concept of the *materia prima*, and which was contained also in the modern problem of the physical ether. Since Democritus the doctrine of continuity, which dominates these theories, has been

opposed by a theory of discontinuity; the opposition and the question of a [possible] synthesis of continuity and discontinuity reaches right down to the present and constitutes the basic problem as regards the union of the theory of relativity and quantum theory.

3. The Pythagorean-Platonic Ideal: Reality is the realization of mathematical ideas, "God is always doing mathematics."

4. The cosmological-cosmogonic theories, which reached their first height in Kant's "theory of the heavens," but which has by no means proved itself unobjectionable.

5. There must be added the problem of determinism, related on the one hand to the problem of time, and, on the other hand, to the opposition between the theory of relativity and quantum theory; an old philosophical problem also, which was central [in importance] from Augustine to Spinoza, for Leibniz and Kant, as well as for Schopenhauer and Fechner.

We now shall take a stand on these problems from the point of view of critical realism.

1. The Constancy of the Velocity of Light

Philosophically the most exciting assertion and therefore the one which has aroused most philosophic opposition is the second axiom of the special theory of relativity, viz., the constancy of the velocity of light, from which follows the relativity of spatial and temporal measurements. One could say, that the observers of various moving systems are like Leibniz's monads and that Leibniz's idea of a pre-established harmony finds an analogy in the theory of relativity: Just as the world is mirrored differently in each monad and yet the sights of all monads are related to each other and translatable into each other, so also does the "absolute" four-dimensional world-continuum appear in different values of spatial and temporal measurements to every observer imprisoned [as he is] in his own system, yet all sights are transformable into each other. But if, on the one hand, Hans Driesch calls Leibniz's system of the pre-established harmony bizarre, many critics of the theory of relativity have even declared its principle to be a logical contradiction:[1] if light spreads out—independently of the motion of its source—equally in all directions, if it is a reality—whether wave or corpuscle is at this point of no concern—which moves, then it can not proceed with objectively equal velocity with reference to an observer A, on the one hand, and with reference to an independently moving observer B. As a way out [of this difficulty] the explanation is offered that the axiom of the constancy of the velocity of light in all qualified co-ordinate systems is simply an arbitrary determination, which we posit. In this case it remains ununderstandable, however, that this arbitrary determination validated itself in experience and that it makes possible the astounding consistency of the mathematical forms of the theory of relativity. Objective matters of fact seem, therefore, to provide the foundation for this [arbitrary] determination, after all.

A second possibility of interpretation offers itself in the following. Spatial and temporal qualities are objectively not at all divisible, in fact, spatiality and temporality are nothing objective at all; motion is merely appearance which arises by splitting the world-continuum into space and time; it is merely our consciousness which goes along with the world-line of our body; and the objectively real is precisely the four-dimensional continuum. In this way we get to Minkowski's world, a world of absolute existence, the Eleatic world. From the standpoint of the physicist this is a thoroughly consistent solution. But the physicist will [doubtless] understand the objection, raised by philosophy, that time is by no means merely a physical matter. Time is, as Kant put it, the form not merely of our outer but

---

[1] So, among others, O. Kraus, who writes: "The proposition that velocity of light is identical in all 'Galilean' systems, uninfluenced by the motion of the source of light, does not offend habits of thought but *a priori* self-evident judgments; the relativizing of simultaneity is very much like the explanation of the principle of contradiction as a habit of thought." And P. F. Linke writes: "A proposition is absurd not only if it contradicts formal logic, but also when it asserts a proposition which contradicts the essence of the object to which it refers. That is to say, a proposition is just as absurd if its assertion does not lie within the meaning of such a propositional object, which latter can itself be given at any time in immediate confrontation, as if it were in a formal sense illogical." *Annalen der Philosophie*, Vol. II, No. 3, 1921.

also of our inner sense. Could everything which we call development [evolution] be really an untemporal order? Should our experiences of successiveness and of memory be mere illusion, our whole existence, with all its bodily conditioned and bodily expressed strivings and actions be, so to speak, already pre-existent and also still post-existent—in so far as one could speak in such an absolutely existing world of pre and post at all; should we, in the final analysis be trans-temporal beings? And with this does not the question of *freedom* receive an answer from physics alone and a negative answer at that, without regard for those experiences which have always spoken for freedom of the will, such as responsibility, shame, and regret, and without regard for the freedom which is today particularly emphasized by the philosophy of existentialism, that freedom in which every later act is, after all, dependent upon former decisions? One understands in any case that the relativizing of time, of simultaneity, of temporal dilatation, in brief, the subjectivizing of temporality as such is felt as a much greater demand than the relativizing of spatial magnitudes, as, e.g., by means of the Lorentz-contraction. And what matters is not the measurement of time, but the saving of temporality as a principle of our world as such. However, is it possible to maintain temporality in its specific quality—even in the theory of relativity time is by no means entirely homogeneous with the spatial co-ordinates, but is multiplied by the imaginary unity, and a space-like and a time-like area are differentiated—and nevertheless avoid the contradiction that a physical reality, which moves, can not move with objectively identical velocity with reference to different observers? This can, indeed, be done, but one must draw the conclusion that [in that case] light may neither be treated nor be viewed as a material body, nor as a wave which moves on in a three-dimensional space.

Already in the special theory of relativity we meet, for the first time, the inadequacy of the two sides of that "double nature," whether of the corpuscle or of the wave in any perceptual sense. Obviously we dare not regard light either as moving particles nor as real waves of a system-bound medium. On the other hand, there is no reason why light should not be regarded as a signal which actually behaves towards all systems disinterestedly and impartially, which is neither imprisoned in nor bound to a material system, but is supersystemic [or: above all systems]. Only in that case we may not regard it [i.e., light] as something already material, but must consider it as something still "immaterial," "pre-material," "potential." But what does this mean? For the concept of the potential is by no means at home merely in ancient ontology, but also in physics; considerable clarification might therefore be expected from a uniting of the often underestimated ingenuity to be found in the thought-structures erected by Aristotle and scholasticism as if out of thin air, with the concept of potentiality which is already familiar in physics from the doctrines of force and energy, and which has entered, in even an expanded degree, into modern physics. What then does it mean [to say] that light is still "above the systems"?

Let us think of two systems moving towards each other, in which A and B, on the one hand, and A' and B', on the other, stand to each other in a relatively identical relation of order, in the same relation, in the same "distance" from and for each other; and let us imagine that, at the very moment when A and A' coincide (with each other), there proceeds a signal, a disturbance, from A, resp. from A', then one can certainly see no reason why B should not be reached in the identical temporal duration as B'. "Light" is the signal of the change in existential relations, no longer and not yet materialized and therefore not yet system-bound, but rather, as the dissolution of a former material order, the mere announcement and communication of a new possibility. It is an as yet potential situation,[2] which does not refer to a *single* system, but which restores the disturbed order precisely because of its reference to all. If one wishes to retain the old concept of the ether, one simply dare not regard the ether itself again as a material reality which itself constructs or distinguishes or belongs to *one* system, but inversely, only as a field of possibility to which all systems be-

[2] The introduction of a concept of potentiality, in the sense of a real possibility, of a multi-potential being, is met with in modern biology in the notion of a germinal substance, and in psychology in that of the unconscious.

long even as do planes to space; the mathematical models, which already exist, would merely have to be interpreted in this sense. If we attribute a sphere of existence to every system, we would have to say, in traditional fashion, that their [resp.] "ethers" penetrate each other reciprocally without disturbance; which would simply mean that they are no longer to be treated materially. It would be closer to our way of thinking today to take the systems together in an over-all concept of a "space-like" area, which would require four dimensions and to permit the signal, the pre-proclamation for possible corpusculations, to move ahead in this ["space-like" area]. What moves ahead is, therefore, a potential; that is to say, in every system the changed existential situation can "announce itself" successively according to the distance relation between the origin of the disturbance and the recipient. The "geometrical location" of the appearance of a disturbance and dissolution, the possibility of the occurrence of new localized elements, photons, transmits itself uniformly in reference to all systems, and only by this process is the foundation created for the spatial and temporal measurements of the individual systems. If we are still to use a neutral designation, we would have to say that potential energy propagates itself in order to actualize itself again when it hits a "wall." Only this sounds unaccustomed; until now physics has been using the concept of potential energy in the first place for the working capacity which inheres in a body or field, but which is still restrained, not yet released; here, however, we have to form the concept of an expanding potential energy, of an expanding capacity for individuation as photons, of a disinterestedly, impartially, and super-systemically expanding possibility in such way that every system can have a basis for its measurements in its inter-systematic relations of spatial and temporal distance. If, therefore, one speaks of the undulatory and corpuscular nature of light, the contradiction, which has created so many difficulties, is solved [by pointing out] that the continuous wave-nature corresponds to energy in its potential state, to the expansion of a super-systemic field of possibilities, whereas the particle nature is to be associated with the actualization in a system. By doing this temporality is in principle preserved, without having had to demand an absolute *measurement* of time, which could have been claimed by one system. Perhaps the gap between the double nature of light and matter could also be bridged by this same procedure.

2. The Problem of Substance

For classical physics mass with its attributes of inertia and gravity was *the* substance, which remains preserved through all changes. Electromagnetism added charges and the attribute of polarity, and with that the problem of the reducibility of mechanics to electromagnetism emerged. But energy also claimed the character of substance and it seemed to play the unity-producing rôle. True, even though the equivalence-statements are valid for the comparison of mechanical and electromagnetic energy, the question is still open whether it is possible thereby to arrive at a real monism; for the conversion of Joule into *mkg* does not prove that the two forms of energy are in essence the same, just as one can not say of an electron that it *is* mass merely because one can say of it that it *has* mass. Also connected with this is the question, whether it is more suitable to retain for the absolute system of measurement the three old magnitudes of "mass, length, and time," or to introduce a fourth magnitude for the "charge." In microphysics one believed to have at last found the very original building-stones. And now the theory of relativity brought to synthetic view, by way of the famous equation $E = mc^2$, viz., mass represents localized energy, it is an agglomeration, a centre, a concentration of energy, an energy-knot, and inversely an area of space filled with energy has inertia and gravity. Both, of course— mass and energy—proved themselves as dependent upon the state of motion of the observer. The general theory of relativity made possible the compression of the conservation principles of energy and impulse; and the sum of the energy of matter and of the gravitational field proved to be invariant. In the general theory of relativity the "world-plane" with its invariants is itself the ultimate reality, the "substance." The laws of the conservation of energy and impulse follow from the equations for the field of gravitation and for the physical fields. That is to say, valid for every system is [the proposition] that in a restricted spatial area the balance between the total energy present in it and the addition or subtraction of energy by way of the surface of the area must remain preserved. But what precisely is energy? Physics defines it [viz., energy] as working capacity, that is to say as something potential; moreover, it is not merely the potential energy but the kinetic energy also which is, strictly speaking, potential: it *can* actualize itself. It is a special instance, a sub-concept of what Aristotle called *energeia*. Force, itself again a potential concept, enters constitutively into the field of energy; and mass into the kinetic energy; mass too is a potential concept, it implies space-control-potency and the tendency to lay claim to space; the mass-bodies and mass-particles are themselves bearers of the energy-content $E = mc^2$. Substance, therefore, whether mass or energy, is from the beginning a capacity to make itself effective according to mathematical order; spatially-temporally, therefore, material reality appears to us where and only where potentiality actualizes itself and where, by so doing, it becomes comprehensible for us.

3. The Metric of the World-Continuum

To the question, what both: matter and energy, are, the general theory of relativity gives us the [following] answer: they are that which creates the metric. The metric of the space-time-continuum is the expression of the intensity of the stresses of their essence, which is unknown to us, of their "inner," to use the expression employed by Hermann Weyl and Richard Woltereck. The measurement-worthiness, the metric, the space-curvature, space-determination, space-signing, or however we care to put it, is the expression of the potency of this "inner." The Riemann continuum really refers to the fields, the masses are really asymptotic-symmetrical positions; Hermann Weyl speaks of "channels" along the world-line; the energetic events, the actualizations of the potency represent singularities.

The most noteworthy fact, object of marvelling which can not be great enough, is this: that it is possible to comprehend and represent the physical magnitudes (mass, impulse, force, energy) as producers of geometrical characteristics as they occur in the theory of planes, and to be able to treat the field-forces also [in terms of] differential geometry. For this is by no means self-evident nor simply the invention of a great mathematico-artistic ingenuity; yet *in this possibility lies the decisive objec-tive epistemological value of the general theory of relativity.* The name [of this theory] already shows that it arose out of the (now called "special") theory of relativity by looking for and finding an invariant form of natural laws not merely for Galilean systems of inertia but for any [number and types of] accelerated systems. That was still a matter of mathematics, a mathematical problem. The enlightening main thought, by which this general theory of relativity became the theory of gravitation was the equivalence of inert and heavy mass and, along with that, of accelerated systems and gravitational fields. The classical example for this, which has become famous, is the thought experiment of the indistinguishable nature of a free fall in an elevator which is at rest in a gravitational field, and a body at rest in an elevator which is accelerated upwards in gravitation-empty space. It is also possible, therefore, to regard the co-efficients of the line-elements in an accelerated system without gravitational field as the co-efficients in a gravitational field at rest. In proceeding this way, however, it must not be overlooked that it is true that every accelerated system can be thought of as substituted by one at rest in a gravitational field with appropriate distribution of masses, but that it is not possi-ble to substitute an accelerated system for every gravitational field. In spite of this, with the g_{ik} and with the differential-geometrical tensors, vectors, and scalars, which can be formed out of the g_{ik}, one possesses the tool with which the gravita-tional fields can be treated as metrical fields. And this means that matter and energy impress a geometrical structure upon the world, fields of force are producers of metric and inversely the metric expresses itself dynamically.

What has occurred is a return to Descartes on a higher plane of mathematical and philosophical development: in Descartes extension was the attribute of matter. Leibniz raised the objection to this that extension is no real attribute at all, that it is force which is real (in one of his discussions with Descartes he actually found the law of the conservation of "living force"). Now the characteristics of space—although not those of extension but of metrical structure—viz., its characteristics of curvature, have become *the* attribute of matter after all; which latter [namely, matter] actually creates the physically real space by means of those characteristics. Geometry itself has become real. Instead of saying, matter produces a field of force under whose influence the motions result, one can now say, reality means the formation of the world-continuum, the creation of a metric field, in which the movements follow on the principles of variation. What we call material and physical is an "inner," which expresses itself mathematically and which, therefore, is capable of being mathematically expressed. Material reality is actualized mathematics. True, in the general theory of relativity this is valid only for the gravitational fields; the metrical representation of electromagnetic fields is still an unsolved problem.

4. The Problem of Cosmology and Cosmogony

If we turn our attention to the external world as a whole, the first question which arises is whether space, filled with matter and energy, is finite or infinite. For the naïve unprejudiced person it is difficult to assume infinity, but he is more or less forced to it by the idea of an unbounded Euclidean space; and it is, moreover, the commitment to the principle of sufficient reason which thus forces him. Why should the space filled with material and energic reality come to an end at some boundary and beyond that be nothing but infinite unfilled space? This thought, of course, is by no means logically conclusive; in fact, it would lie close to our ideational requirement to think of an asymptotic fulfillment which approximates to the limiting value of zero. However, from the standpoint of natural science the objection raised against this [view] is that it is pure speculation, and, from that of philosophy, that empty space is here spoken of as if such were a reality. However, through the development of the general theory of relativity the question has taken on a completely new look: The universe is finite, but not a universe which is subsumed in Euclidean space, lives in such space or is embedded in it; but the universe is finite just as a non-Euclidean space of finite radius is finite (just as the surface of a three-dimensional "ball" in a four-dimensional continuum). This closed non-Euclidean space is not something which exists prior to or alongside of material reality, but is produced by it and at the same time together with it; the question concerning "something beyond" makes no sense, since one dare not make the mistake, almost always made by the mathematical layman, to think of a non-Euclidean continuum in a Euclidean one of equally as many dimensions. By the way, mathematicians and philosophers often talk past each other at this point; the former insists that through the physical theory of the closed space it is now decided that "space" is not Euclidean; and the latter declare that, on the basis of our powers of perception, it is impossible that "space" could be anything but Euclidean. Actually the matter stands as follows: Even though the physically filled space with its relationships corresponds to a closed non-Euclidean system of relations, it nevertheless remains true that the Euclidean space plays not merely a mathematical but also a psychologically excellent rôle, insofar as Euclidean geometry is in fact the only one which corresponds to our powers of perception. Inversely: Although I must proceed from this form of perception in all empirical investigations, it nevertheless remains true that the cohesion of all observations may demand a system of relations which is not Euclidean. The closedness and finitude of the universe relates, therefore, to matter-filled space as a whole and declares that a body or a ray, which moves in one direction without deviating towards any of the three perceptual dimensions, nevertheless returns upon itself, just as the idea of red, moving towards orange and yellow, returns upon itself. It is true that, if we want a perceptual model for this imperceivable fact, we shall have to have recourse to an analogy: Just as we must imagine the band of colors in the last named example, we would have to imagine the progression of the ray or of the moving body in a continuum of four dimensions. The fourth dimension would be that one in which the body on a sphere returns to its point of departure; since, however, our power of imagination does not suffice for four dimensions, we must suppress one dimension and imagine, for example, the progression of a beam of light on a plane, one of the dimensions of which is the not perceivable, not appearing "fourth dimension." To the mathematician all of this is so familiar that it becomes actually difficult for him to note and recognize the epistemological difficulty.

But, back to the issue: Physical space is a non-Euclidean continuum of finite radius. Matter and space are indissoluble from each other. Matter manifests itself as actualization of a many-dimensioned continuum which appears to us in space and time. And now came the next step. The radius itself grows, the universe expands.

And with that a double problem is raised. Temporality enters again into the physical consideration and the cosmological problem becomes at the same time a cosmogonic one. What is the situation at the beginning?

The idea which has dominated all cosmogony-schemes of a physico-astronomic kind until now has been essentially the Kant-Laplace theory: The becoming of our world of experience arose out of a chaotic primeval fog. Against the carrying through of this idea there arose, however, quite aside from all references to a teleological element in the world order, physical objections also, which C. F. von Weizsäcker has recently attempted to remove by [means of] supplementary hypotheses. Within the framework of the theory of relativity itself Einstein's cylindrical world could be regarded as an ideal state of equilibrium, from which the expansion took place. What, however, was the cause of this, and how would this cylindrical world have come to be? Most recently P. Jordan attempted a radical solution, which unites microphysical and macrophysical problems, the becoming of the material world from a minimum number of particles, say two neutrons, which move away [from each other] and in so doing make "space" for the appearance of new particles.

Jordan rejects the question concerning any "before" as meaningless; for time arises precisely as does space with matter.

What, however, can not be rejected is the question concerning the "before" in the causal sense: What causes the first particles to form themselves? No man can disregard the "*ex nihilo fit nihil.*" Even for religious faith the world is a creation out of nothing only insofar as matter itself had a beginning; but not insofar as its appearance came out of nothing; rather in the sense of the story of creation it is the will and idea of God— to whom himself is ascribed timeless eternity—which constitute the ground for the genesis of space, time, and matter. Consequently one would still have to imagine pre-posited a potential state without any materialization of corpuscles before the cosmogony of Jordan; a potential state whose transition to the empirical form of being introduced at the same time a temporal becoming. Once again, therefore, potentiality would precede actuality. But, in the final analysis, this means: Every physical cosmogony comes necessarily to the boundary of transcendence and must end with an unsolved problem. And every attempt at a solution [of this problem] on the part of philosophy will only be able to be a speculation. If the philosopher risks such [a speculation]—and he may do this, if only to assert that it is only a speculation, an idea, which he creates for himself—he will have to organize it into a transcendent *Weltanschauung*, which would have to be called "Real-Idealism" (*Real-Idealismus*).

In any case we desire to express the basic thought of such an interpretation: What appears to us as external reality is the putting itself forward of a will; matter is the expression of a mathematically expressible form of its inner essence. Its will finds its expression in the actualization of mathematical structures. Were we to resolve the differential equations, which constitute the basic laws of the universe, and give to arbitrary functions and constants, which occur in the resolution, a definite value, we should have created the world, which appears in a way which is binding for all beings. In an epistemological sense such a world structure would be realism, because it recognizes a reality independent of consciousness. Metaphysically speaking it would be idealism, because the essence of what appears would be the "will to appear," and because the mathematical structures, in which it appears, or which are at least ideationally implied, are the expression of a non-material "inner" (understanding this word approximately in the sense of Hermann Weyl and Richard Woltereck). But, as already stated, this reaches way beyond experience and is merely interpretation.

5. BOUNDARY PROBLEMS OF THE THEORY OF RELATIVITY

However imposing and impressive the intellectual work of art of the general theory of relativity, nonetheless great is the suspense with which both theoretical physics and the philosophy of nature await the solution of the riddles which are propounded by it. These are:

1. The description of the electromagnetic fields in analogy to the fields of gravitation by means of metric characteristics of the space-time world. This demands a mathematically-formal differentiation of the metric of the general theory of relativity, a refinement of its geometry, and a refinement of the existential concepts of such nature that the polarity of the charges and their relation to the mass is included, i.e., that the dualism of mechanics and electromagnetism is resolved by placing both on a common foundation.

2. A synthesis of the continuum and discontinuity views and, with that, of the two lines of development of modern physics: the theory of relativity and the quantum theory, macrophysics and microphysics, in the sense of the old philosophical problematic: the doctrine of original substance and of the hypothesis of original building-blocks. All of these problems of a refined structure of the theory of relativity on the one hand, and of a synthesis on the other, are obviously very closely connected with each other.

Philosophy will enter this problematic mainly from the standpoint of the problem of determinism. The general theory of relativity rates as an avowedly deterministic doctrine. Quantum mechanics has led to the indeterminacy relation of Heisenberg, which at least leaves open the possibility of some play for freedom in the area of elementary events, or, more carefully, let's say a threshold of indeterminacy. This possibility will at least have to be taken into consideration. For the attempt to save determinism at all events by interpreting the indeter-

minateness of the two complementary factors as mere inde-
termin*able*ness (because of the impossibility of knowing exactly
the respective present, and because of the disturbing interference in the case of an experiment), this attempt only pushes
the problem back [a step] and does not explain that the product
of the imprecisions of impulse and location, or of energy and
time, is precisely equivalent to such an important universal constant, and that the final equations, at which we arrive, are equations of probability; that possibility and probability, therefore,
are not anything secondary, but something primary. But, entirely aside from this, philosophy cannot make its attitude to
the problem of determinism become dependent merely upon the
formation of physical theories. We already have weighty reasons to assume that life-events are taking place not *merely*
according to mathematically formulable laws, such as Hamilton's principles, for example; and that [life] does precisely
not run its course according to laws of probability; that, shall we
say, the arbitrary functions which enter into the solution of
differential equations leave great latitude for meaningful and
complete (*ganzheitliche*) events. Perhaps the formative forces
of life make use of a wide range of indetermination in the
microphysical realm. However, even independently of these
theories we need to cling to what is given us in life's experience "existentially," to use the word which is so common today.
And here it must be stated that we cannot get by [without
recognizing] the experience of a double freedom: If there is
not to loom up an unbridgeable gulf between theory and practice, and if we are not to discount our confidence in our immediate and most important experience as just nothing, then we
must acknowledge that as original phenomenon we are confronted by:

1. The experience of arbitrary decisions, which, although
they may not at all be of any particular consequence, are not
unequivocally determined by the situation; the hypothesis that
we are deceived by unconscious motives must not be generalized
to such an extent that nothing but illusions remain; otherwise
one would unnecessarily have to invent nothing but hypothetical causes.

2. Above all, however, the experience of moral responsibility; without the acknowledgment of moral freedom the concepts of guilt and expiation become just as empty fictions as the emotions of indignations, of shame and of remorse. From the "inner point of view," to use a word of Planck's we are free. The "external point of view," the view which considers every event as unequivocally causally determined, is not applicable there. We make the [causal] presupposition in order to carry on science and to make predictions; but we may, of course, reach limits; and the presupposition is [only] an hypothesis, whereas the consciousness of freedom is obvious in experience. If, however, existence at the human level demands freedom, or at least possibly demands it, does not then an aspect of freedom enter into all strata of existence, even into those of the vital and material? Any reality which would be nothing but driven, pushed, pulled, and kicked would be a purely passive being, and such a world would be a world of marionettes which is [merely] being played. Determinateness does not in any case belong as ideational necessity to the concept of being. To the contrary, real active being includes within itself a degree of determination of the indeterminate.

However, we neither shall nor can unroll here the question of the pro and con, but only raise it conditionally: *If* an aspect of freedom runs through reality at all levels of its being, is it, and how is it, compatible with the theory of relativity, what does it mean in its framework and what does the theory of relativity mean within the framework of such a view of being? Well then, the world continuum of the theory of relativity is simply the framework of possibility and of probability within which the actual happening takes place. Just as macrophysics grows out of the microphysical possibilities and actualizations, just as the macrophysical laws grow out of the microphysical laws of probability for a large number of particles and their fields, just so is the metric of the world continuum so to speak the epitome, the integral of all fields of probability. Or if, instead of proceeding from the discrete particles and moving on to the continuum as totality, we, inversely, proceed from the continuum as totality: Just as the fields of probability are not mere mathematical-ideal structures, but rather the lead fields of a super-individual potentiality for the occurrence of actual elements, just so is the metric not merely a mathematical-ideal structure, but the world continuum is the all comprehensive field into which all microfields are bedded. The indeterminateness of the elementary events would, therefore, mean a refined structure of the world-plane just as [is the case with] a vitally or psychically conditioned event; but it would have as little meaning for the macro-structure as the falling of a bit of dust for the path of the earth. Indeterminism in microphysical events would therefore be just as compatible with the theory of relativity as are the autonomy of life and the psychic conditioning of the behavior of living things.

How, then, is it with the double nature of light and matter? Already when discussing the constancy of the velocity of light in the special theory of relativity we hit upon the necessity of depriving the expanding radiation of the characteristics both of particles as well as of those of a system-bound wave. We said: an immaterial signal expands in the entire space-like area (really on the boundary of the temporal); the geometrical location for the possibility of the occurrence of photons expands itself super-systemically and thereby creates the foundation for the systematic space- and time-measurements. In this process the contradiction disappears that a physical reality could not propagate itself objectively equally rapidly with reference to systems and observers moving at different rates of speed. Therewith the other contradiction disappears also which seemed to exist between the undulatory and the corpuscular nature in microphysics. As one and the same reality the same something can indeed not at one and the same time be corpuscle, viz., be localized, and be wave, viz., be not localized. But nothing stands in the way of referring the localization only to the actual occurrence in energy and in situations of energic character, or of referring the nature of waves only to the progress of possibilities and of geometrical locations to the occurrence of corpuscles. As a matter of fact—and this is particularly important from the positivistic standpoint—we must clearly recognize that what we at any particular time observe experimentally are always particles and that what makes us conclude that there are waves, [namely] the interferences, refers only to expansion. We reach, therefore, so to speak, the following proportion: Wave nature is to the nature of particles what super-individual potentiality is to individual actuality. For, for the so-called waves of matter—because of their excess over the speed of light—immateriality, i.e., pure potentiality, is valid from the very beginning.

SUMMARY

SIGNIFICANCE FOR OUR PICTURE OF THE WORLD

In a prize essay of 1923 on "The Relation of Einstein's Theory of Relativity to Contemporary Philosophy" (which was composed in response to a prize offered by the *Annalen der Philosophie*, and to which the prize was awarded by a committee of judges consisting of Max von Laue, Ernst von Aster, and Moritz Schlick, and which was also favorably adjudged by Albert Einstein) the author had already pointed out the compatibility of the theory of relativity with critical realism and had contended for its significance for our scientific worldpicture. Favoring the objective epistemological worth of the theory of relativity in the sense of critical realism is, on the one hand, the possibility of its consistent execution, which is by no means self-evident, and, on the other hand, its validation within experience. Today I would summarize this significance in the following manner:

1. The order of things and events which appears to us as space, and that which appears to us as time with regard to the external world, are, of course, not interchangeable, but neither are they separated by a sharp boundary. There is, therefore, a space-like and a time-like "sphere." A "distance" in the sense of merely being apart from each other may, according to differing conditions, appear as a more spatial or as a more temporal [kind of a] distance.[*] This is connected with the fact

[*] The order becomes unequivocally temporal only if a cause and effect relation is involved. Without such [a relation] it makes no sense to speak of any objective simultaneity or after-each-other; for finite system-bound beings could not establish such; and for an infinite being, capable of surveying everything, there could be no temporality at all.

that reality, which is the foundation of all appearances, is obviously a many-dimensional arrangement of order, which demands more dimensions than are at the disposal of our perceptual capacity. And this in turn is connected with the fact that before that which becomes real there lies a greater richness of possibilities. What appears to us as matter in an unformed Euclidean space and in an homogeneous time is something which creates a four-dimensional Riemannian continuum which, for a "graphic" description of its intensity, would require a ten-dimensional Euclidean space.[4] If we were to conceive of the four-dimensional continuum as a whole (under neglect of two dimensions) as a plane in a three-dimensional (actually: five-dimensional) space, and do this with regard to the expansion of the universe as a plane whose cross-sections have an increasing radius, then a thus described world would have at its disposal a fifth dimension for a stratum of possibilities.[5]

2. The invariants occur in the four-dimensional synopsis. This does not mean the elimination of time as such, but points to the fact that spatial and temporal extensions and distances, which are bound to each other, belong to real being and happening. The fact should be pondered that even in microphysics, in Planck's equation $E \cdot \tau = h$ and in Heisenberg's uncertainty-relation we are confronted by this solidarity of spatial and temporal extensions.

3. The reality of the external world is not so material as was held by materialism, which got its bearings from the ideas of classical physics of impenetrable, fixed, extended and well-defined bodies. What is it possible to say concerning it today at all? Nothing, except that it is a [type of] reality which effectively confronts us and which is so well mathematically describable that it can be regarded as the realization of mathematical structures and forms, as something which realizes mathematically expressible relations of order (space-time struc-

---

[4] It is possible to say that a Riemannian space of four dimensions lies in a Euclidean space of ten dimensions. In this case tensors can be interpreted geometrically by extensions which bring about a deformation of space. (Cf. Herbert Lang, *Zur Tensor-Geometrie in der Relativitätstheorie:* Dissertation, 1919).

[5] Compare the author's *Wissenschaft und Weltanschauung* (Leipzig, 1st ed., 1935, p. 280; 2nd ed., 1949), 308f.

tures). Being effectual for each other and towards us, being the expression and the expressibleness of the orderly relations in mathematically couchable forms: these are today the attributes of "material reality." Is this peculiar? Mathematical expressibility, we already said, is marvellous. But what lies at the base of material appearance is a being-related-to and a becoming-effectual: this simply lies in the concept of being. For being means nothing else than "being for itself" or "being for someone," expressing itself with regard to other being, making an appearance and becoming effective.

If we raise the question at all concerning the essence, concerning the "inner nature" of matter, concerning the bearer of the orderly relations, we must recognize the fact that we shall either have to waive any claim to any answer—which would still be no reason for saying that the question has become meaningless; for questions are meaningless only if they already contain within themselves a contradiction or a lack of relation between subject and predicate[6]—or else we shall have to weigh the possibility of placing the "inner nature," the "essence" of the being of matter in analogy with the only being with which we cannot connect any meaning at all, namely with the becoming effective, which is grounded upon a "will." This appears to be pure speculation. In fact, however, not one of the however greatly differing *Weltanschauungen* has been able to get around the necessity—nor will any such ever be able to get around it—of taking into account a volitional element which expresses itself in actuality. The religious *Weltanschauungen* speak of the will of the creator; the pantheists have a dim notion of the will of the soul of nature; Schopenhauer made the will itself the principle of the world; Nietzsche misinterpreted it as the mere will to power, and by doing so made it empty of meaning; in Eduard von Hartmann it received its content from an unconscious; in Bergson it appeared in the form of an *élan vital*; but in a dynamic conception of nature

---

[6] Questions today are all too readily cut off by the dictum that they are meaningless. The question is meaningless as to whether a primary number is red, or which integral co-efficients must have an equation of the n'th degree, amongst whose roots the circular number and the basis of natural logarithms occurs. But a question is not meaningless because it is empirically unanswerable.

also is the idea of the will—not, of course, in an anthropo-morphizing sense—basic. Whether we regard matter as the appearance of a divine or of a natural will, of a meaningful or of a blind will or as the expression of an inner dynamic—and we offer no opinion on the subject—, the content of this "will" is, in any case, of such a nature that it seems at one and the same time to arise out of a both irrational and rational principle. In the realization of the principles of mathematical order there expresses itself the content of a will which we would have to call Logos; in the distribution [on the other hand there seems to be] a contingency, chance, arbitrariness: for the empirical world does not appear to be what one would call a harmonious whole. Here we confront a bifurcation of the roads which try to interpret the world meaningfully: Is there a divided principle at the foundation of the world? Or is the arbitrary element, the aspect of chance included in the self-willedness of finite beings who nevertheless are under meaningful direction?

The theory of relativity has simultaneously made us freer and richer by showing in the realm of physics, not merely by way of abstract advice but in concrete performance, that our intellectual capacity of knowledge reaches farther than our sensory capacity of perception. It is the same step in the realm of ideas as that in geometry from Euclidean to non-Euclidean geometry. Our perceptual capacity is limited to three dimensions of a homogeneous continuum of the curvature zero. Our thought-capacity reaches farther. We do not feel ourselves imprisoned in the world of appearances and of the workaday world. But neither do we need to resign ourselves so much, as did Kant, who could say nothing aside from his forms of perception and the forms of thought. We do not assert that with the theory of relativity we have reached reality as such; concerning its inner essence we shall never be able to speak otherwise than by analogy and suppositions. But we have obviously come closer to objective reality than by way of our perceptual capacity. Philosophically this means at the same time that we have moved farther away from materialism even through the development of physics. For we now assert of matter only that it is something which is expressed and can be expressed differential-geometrically, by means of differential equations for a many-dimensioned continuum. Our cautiousness must go so far that we are willing to leave undecided whether there is such a thing as a continuous existence of world-bodies and particles, or whether only discrete actual events take place in the interplay of energy, so that only super-individual potential being can still be thought of as continuous. In the continuous world of potentiality, within the "frame" of being, temporality has become a mere dimension which enters into the world continuum just as do the dimensions of space. Only in actual individuation does a real temporalisation and localisation occur again.

Alongside of the tasks of theoretical physics named above there will be the task of creating a clear system of concepts in a new physical ontology, concepts which are demanded by the evolution of physics and which can now only be intimated.

ALOYS WENZL

PHILOSOPHISCHE FAKULTÄT
UNIVERSITÄT MÜNCHEN
GERMANY

24

Andrew Paul Ushenko

EINSTEIN'S INFLUENCE ON CONTEMPORARY PHILOSOPHY

EINSTEIN'S INFLUENCE ON CONTEMPORARY PHILOSOPHY

1. A General Survey

EINSTEIN'S influence on philosophy has taken many forms. This means that no complete account can be expected within the space of the present essay. At the same time, the writer, if he is not to appear arbitrary, must explain his choice of contents. Such influence as is mainly negative in character or effect will be disregarded. Accordingly, the story of the setback, after a period of unprecedented success, of Bergson's philosophy of absolute time—unquestionably under the impact of relativity—is not to be told here. Again, there will be no adequate discussion of Einstein's influence on thinkers who would not go beyond the boundaries of tradition in philosophy. Many able men have tried to assimilate the new physics within the context of a congenial type of classical philosophy without realizing the necessity of reciprocal adjustments: their efforts have not led to a new metaphysics. For example, physicists, as a rule, have interpreted relativity within the frame of some classical version of idealism. Eddington advocates some sort of Kantian apriorism; Jeans goes for neo-Platonism enriched with a mathematician God; Weyl concocts a mixture of ideas derived from Leibniz and Husserl; Dingle is a phenomenalist; and Einstein himself occupies an intermediate position between Cassirer's neo-Kantianism and Mach's positivism. Interesting as such attempts to interpret relativity in terms of traditional philosophy may be in some instances, I shall disregard them all in favor of philosophers who were inspired by Einstein in starting an entirely new departure of metaphysics, including both epistemology and ontology. Philosophers to be examined have managed to render the traditional issue between idealism and materialism obsolete by showing that the distinction between "mental" and "physical" is epistemological and not ontological. Preoccupation with the novel departure in philosophy, in the spectacular form of its presentation by Whitehead and Russell, enables me to interpret the title of this paper in the following narrow but literal sense. I shall be dealing with Einstein's conceptions in philosophy which are characteristic of contemporary mentality, as contrasted with tradition. Accordingly, my chief concern is to connect certain tenets of relativity physics with the philosophical principle which, either in the negative form of exposing "the fallacy of bifurcation," or, in a positive formulation, as "neutral monism," has been embedded in a metaphysics of events to be opposed to the traditional metaphysics of material or mental things. Concentration upon the philosophies of events has a further advantage of forming a link between the Einstein volume and its predecessors in *The Library of Living Philosophers*. Thus I have an opportunity of straightening the matter whenever misunderstanding of the relation between Einstein and the philosophies of Whitehead and Russell has led some contributors to the third and fifth volumes of the *Library* towards unfair criticism; and correction of misinterpretation is particularly important in the case of Whitehead who was unable to write a reply to his critics. This accounts for the critical discussion, in the second and third sections (of this paper), of articles by F. C. S. Northrop, and E. Nagel. The outcome of the examination of the above philosophers is the conclusion, in fulfilment of the intention to trace a connection between this and the third and fifth volumes, that Whitehead and Russell present a "united front" with regard to the concept of nature, and that they differ from Einstein in ways which are more subtle, and at the same time less profound, than their explicit pronouncements may lead one to expect. (*The Library of Living Philosophers* will be referred to by initials, as "LLP.")

On certain points Einstein's influence on Whitehead and Russell may have been indirect. For example, Russell tells me in a letter of December 12, 1946, that it was Whitehead who led him, around 1914, "to abandon Newtonian absolute time and space and also particles of matter, substituting systems of events." Russell's conviction that the philosophy of events "fitted in well with Einstein," as he puts it, "confirmed me [i.e., Russell] in the views I got from Whitehead, but Einstein was not their source for me, and I think not for Whitehead." If Russell is right concerning Whitehead, the latter may have developed his philosophy of nature under Einstein's indirect but formative influence, for example, through contact with T. P. Nunn or S. Alexander. However this may be, there are other important points, such as the principle that contemporary events are physically independent of one another, where the influence could have hardly been anything but direct.

Reduction of the scope of discussion to a concern with two philosophers, together with some doubt about the measure of Einstein's positive influence, makes us wonder why the number of metaphysicians who have studied relativity physics to their profit is unquestionably smaller than it should be. I believe the explanation is that metaphysicians generally do not consider themselves sufficiently competent to deal with technical physics, while feeling that popular expositions are unreliable. And, if the explanation is satisfactory, the only remedy short of turning metaphysicians into professional physicists, the only way which would enable philosophers to assimilate the ideas of relativity, is to raise the level of popular presentation. Although abundance of allegories and metaphors, in such popularisers as Eddington and Jeans, is stimulating to imagination, it leaves a philosopher at a loss in his effort to understand the logic of modern physics. Even Einstein himself, as explained in the second section, has misled philosophers on the crucial point of the relativity of simultaneity, although the book in which he gives the misleading illustration[1] can be recommended as a model of popular account. These remarks give additional support to a rejection of an alternative explanation, according to which metaphysicians are not interested in contemporary

[1] *Relativity: the Special and General Theory.* (Henry Holt & Co., 1921.)

physics simply because physics and metaphysics have nothing in common.

I am not raising here the issue of the possibility or meaning of metaphysical statements. I fully agree with Einstein when he tells us that the fear of metaphysics is a "malady of contemporary empiricistic philosophizing"[2] and I expect that the days of anti-metaphysicians are numbered. I am concerned with the current opinion, shared by men who show a respect for metaphysics, that physics is neutral with regard to philosophy. To illustrate the opinion in question let me quote from an able physicist-philosopher. In his presidential address, prepared for the Pacific Division of the American Philosophical Association, V. F. Lenzen says: "It is a thesis of the present discussion that it is desirable, and indeed possible, to expound the concepts of science in a manner that is neutral with respect to theory of knowledge."[3]

Neutrality, of course, may mean several things. And I should agree with Lenzen, if he merely meant to point out that science does not logically entail, in the sense of formal logic, any particular type of theory of knowledge or ontology, say realism, to the exclusion of other types. Accordingly, I grant that there is no contradiction in a belief which combines science with any self-consistent metaphysics whatsoever. The point is, however, that entailment is not the only kind of conformity or requiredness. Science may require a particular metaphysics because of a peculiar relation of fitness or harmony between the two. This is to call the reader's attention to the kind of exclusive relevance which the scientist himself recognizes at least in practice. In plotting the graph of a completed continuous process, of which only a finite number of disconnected observations is available, the scientist joins the points that represent the data of observation by a "smooth" curve which he chooses, on the grounds of simplicity, to the exclusion of any of the infinite number of odd or "irrelevant" curves, although the latter are logically equally consistent with the same data. Simplicity is not

[2] *LLP*, v. 5, 289.
[3] *The Philosophical Review* (July, 1945), 341.

required by formal logic; whether a requirement of aesthetics or economy, the principle of simplicity stands for an extra-scientific consideration. And the fact that science must rely on such extra-scientific considerations proves that science is biased in favor of, and not neutral, with regard to, the latter. If I am asked to mention some particular metaphysics which clearly does not fit in with the theory of relativity, I should name solipsism. This I am prepared to do in spite of H. Dingle's disapproval in a review of my *Philosophy of Relativity*.[4] For an essential part of the meaning of the term "relative property," as is brought forth by such pronouncements as "The shape A is a square in relation to a particular observer O_1 but is elongated in relation to another observer O_2, provided these observers are in relative motion," implies the existence of at least two observers. A solipsist, even with a split personality, could not actually move in relation to his alter ego. This, as well as other considerations, may or may not mean that relativity and solipsism are logically incompatible; but, at any rate, they enable me to hold, contrary to Dingle, that solipsism does not fit in with, or is not naturally conformable to, relativity or, for that matter, any physics. As Russell has pointed out, "relativity physics, like all physics, assumes the realistic hypothesis, that there are occurrences which different people can observe."[5] In order to avoid the ambiguity of the noun "physics" we must not overlook, in this connection, the physicist's intention to describe the nature of the external world, i.e., of facts which are there independently of his own existence. Subsequently to divorce the description from the original intention, to argue that there is nothing to describe but a private field of dreams, or to contend that the description describes nothing at all and should be treated as an instrument for successful prediction of private observations, is a travesty of truth or language. And if positive grounds enable us to eliminate solipsism, and thereby show that relativity is not neutral in regard of metaphysics, we may also expect evidence for the existence of a particular type of phi-

[4] *Philosophy* (1937).
[5] *The Analysis of Matter* (Harcourt, Brace & Co., 1927), 48.

losophy which is, as it were, sponsored by Einstein's physics. The philosophies of events are, as I shall attempt to demonstrate, in such a privileged position.

2. The Relativity of Simultaneity: Einstein's Illustration of the Train

In order to decide whether world-elements are things or events a philosopher must understand the bearing of the relativity of simultaneity on his problem. For in one way, which a relativist can disregard because the size of physical bodies is negligible in comparison with the astronomical scale of phenomena that he is dealing with, the bearing would seem to be noteworthy. A material thing of classical physics occupies a definite volume of space—to be recognized by all observers regardless of their state of motion—which it carries with it, from moment to moment throughout the period of its existence, and thereby provides an absolute differentiation between space, the invariant volume of the body, and time, the succession of moments. And since, theoretically, we can imagine a body of an immense size, this conception of a material thing naturally fits in with the idea of absolute simultaneity which allows for an instantaneous volume of space—the same for all observers—regardless how large the latter is required to be. On the other hand, if simultaneity of spatially separated parts of a body is relative, and observers in relative motion must associate with the body different physical configurations, the conception of a definite material thing is no longer theoretically clear. If this is understood, the paramount question in the philosopher's mind is: how compelling is the evidence for the relativity of simultaneity, and, in particular, to what extent do observable data enter into the situation? Einstein's example of the train, illustrated by Fig. 1, has the merit of providing evi-

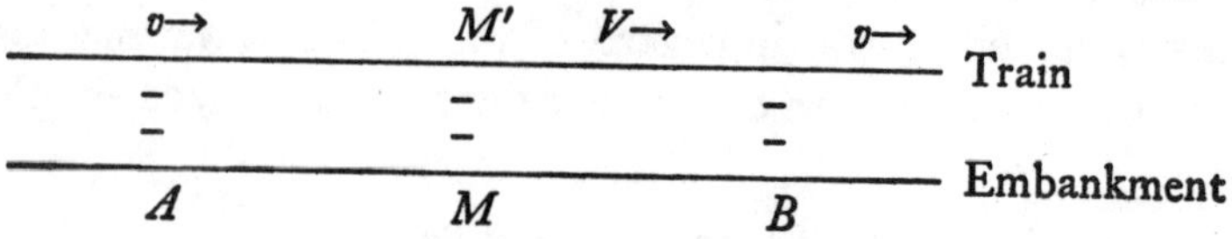

$$v\rightarrow \qquad M' \quad V\rightarrow \qquad v\rightarrow$$
—————————————————————— Train
$$A \qquad\qquad M \qquad\qquad B$$
—————————————————————— Embankment

FIG. 1

dence which is, in principle, observable. A passenger seated at M' in a train observes two events A and B, two strokes of lightning, in close succession, while a man on the embankment at M observes the same events simultaneously. But such conflicting observations, assuming that they would be obtained in the case of an extremely long train moving at a superlative speed, form evidence for the relativity of simultaneity only within the context of certain plausible assumptions. Some of these assumptions Einstein has stated explicitly and clearly, but his exposition is confusing, if not confused, on the following two crucial points.

First, observation of simultaneity of spatially separated events does not imply the identification between seen simultaneity and physical simultaneity, except in the case where the observer happens to be situated midway between the physical sources of the simultaneously seen events. Accordingly, the relativist would agree with the astronomer who tells us that the explosion of a distant star happened long before the nearby flash of lightning even though both are recorded at the present moment. Second, in order to infer physical simultaneity from seen simultaneity, the observer's state of motion must be discounted as immaterial. This is to say that, in agreement with physical experiment, observers in relative motion, for example, the man on the embankment and the passenger in the train, establish the same constant velocity c with which light travels *in vacuo*. With these two points in mind, let us turn to Einstein's own presentation of the matter.

We suppose a very long train travelling along the rails with the constant velocity v and in the direction indicated in Fig. 1. People travelling in this train will with advantage use the train as a rigid reference-body (co-ordinate system); they regard all events in reference to the train. Also the definition of simultaneity can be given relative to the train in exactly the same way as with respect to the embankment. . . . When we say that the lightning strokes A and B are simultaneous with respect to the embankment, we mean: the rays of light emitted at the places A and B, where the lightning occurs, meet each other at the midpoint M of the length A—B, of the embankment. But the events A and B also correspond to positions A and B on the train. Let M' be the mid-point of the distance A—B on the travelling train. Just when the flashes (as judged from the embankment) of lightning occur, this point M' naturally coincides with the point M, but it moves towards the right in the diagram with the velocity v of the train. If an observer sitting in the position M' in the train did not possess this velocity, then he would remain permanently at M, and the light rays emitted by the flashes of lightning A and B would reach him simultaneously, i.e., they would meet just where he is situated. *Now in reality* (considered with reference to the railway embankment) he is hastening towards the beam of light coming from B, whilst he is riding ahead of the beam of light coming from A. Hence the observer will see the beam of light emitted from B earlier than he will see that emitted from A. Observers who take the railway train as their reference-body *must* therefore come to the conclusion that the lightning from B took place earlier than the lightning from A. We thus arrive at the important result: Events which are simultaneous with reference to the embankment are not simultaneous with respect to the train, and vice versa.[6]

I have italicized in this passage three words which are particularly misleading. The words "in reality" suggest that the real reason why the passenger must see two flashes in succession is his rushing towards one and away from the other, and that therefore the relative speed of the two beams of light depends on his state of motion and is not the same. The explanatory clause in brackets, inserted immediately after the words "in reality," does not help much because it can be misinterpreted in the sense that the embankment is a privileged frame of reference and that only description with respect to the embankments represents the real situation. And this misinterpretation is likely to be strengthened by Einstein's subsequent explanation which appears to require correction for the motion of the train in order to account for the disagreement between the passenger and the observer on the embankment. In other words, the explanation is given in terms which would be entirely acceptable to a classical physicist and therefore fail to make clear the new position. Under these circumstances, the italicized "must" leads to an additional misunderstanding: the reader may think that correction for the motion of the train is re-

* Einstein, *Relativity: the Special and General Theory*, 30ff.

jected because seen succession is identifiable with physical succession.

A physicist, who knows better, because of his familiarity with technical expositions, is apt to minimize the danger of misinterpretation. I can assure him that the danger is quite real. For a number of men, prominent in philosophy, have been actually misled by Einstein, exactly along the above mentioned lines, and thereby arrived at the conclusion that philosophy had better disregard the alleged relativity of simultaneity. Consider, for example, A. O. Lovejoy's article "The Dialectical Argument against Absolute Simultaneity."[7] Commenting on Einstein's example of the train, Lovejoy, first, points out that the relativity of simultaneity can follow only if the passenger, unlike the man on the embankment, "has not remained permanent at M," and then contends, in disregard of the principle that the train and the embankment are on a par as alternative frames of reference, that the fact that the passenger continues to be seated midway between two points, which Lovejoy calls A' and B', where the lightning strokes A and B hit the train, is immaterial to the argument because "it is not necessary to suppose that the observer on the train is unaware that he is moving relatively to the embankment in the direction A—B."[8] Thus, according to Lovejoy, the passenger can always correct the results of his observation for the motion of the train and establish that in reality the lightning bolts struck at the same time. However, Lovejoy believes that even if the passenger were unaware of his motion he could establish simultaneity, because

if it is still maintained that each observer can have empirical information only about events on his own system, what follows is that the signals will arrive simultaneously both at M and M' . . . since, upon the principles of relativity physics and the apparent evidence of Michelson-Morley experiment, the velocity of light is constant over equal distances on any given system irrespective of its relative motion.[9]

Let me admit that at this point Lovejoy's premises are correct,

[7] *The Journal of Philosophy* (1930), 650.

[8] *Ibid.*, 650.

[9] *Ibid.*, 650.

so that momentarily the fault is with his own reasoning for which we cannot blame Einstein. Lovejoy's error is that momentarily he overlooks (a) that the succession of flashes is assumed to be observed at M' (an assumption which he recognizes elsewhere through the requirement that observable succession must be corrected for the motion of the train), and (b) that, on the premises of the theory of relativity, observed succession of flashes at the mid-point M' can only mean that, in relation to the train, the lightning strokes A and B are *not* physically simultaneous. Lovejoy may have sensed that something is wrong with his remark because he hastens to add:

But in this case [i.e., on the premises of relativity physics] the two observers would not in fact be judging about the same pair of events; the one would be judging about events occurring at A and B, the other about events occurring at A' and B'. Hence, if their conclusions did disagree in the case supposed (though they would not), the fact would have no significance, since the two observers would be talking about different things.[10]

The additional point does not help Lovejoy, because A' occurs in the immediate neighborhood of, and therefore is virtually identical with, A, and the same is true about B' and B. And perhaps he is not easy about this point either because he relinquishes the momentary advantage of proceeding from correct premises and reverts to the original misunderstanding by concluding that Einstein himself assumes "that the observer on the train as well as the one on the embankment is judging about events occurring at A and B, i.e., at points on the embankment." The quoted conclusion is intended to reinstate what Lovejoy takes Einstein's example to imply, the privileged position of the embankment as a frame of reference.[11]

[10] *Ibid.*, 650.

[11] Lovejoy is by no means alone in his misunderstanding. F. S. C. Northrop and DeWitt H. Parker, to mention two men of reputation among philosophers, have also been misled by Einstein. In his *Science and First Principles* (The Macmillan Co., N.Y., 1932, 73), Northrop gives a lucid and correct account of the example of the train, but concludes with the following statement: "Obviously, then, if the light rays arrive simultaneously for the man on the ground, they will not

A slight modification of Einstein's example would remove the cause of misunderstanding by philosophers. For instance, two trains on parallel tracks might serve better the purpose of illustrating the parity of alternative reference systems because of a common experience, in looking out of the window of a train at another, of the inability to tell which of the trains is actually moving. Accordingly, let two passengers, P in the train T and P' in the train T', take each his own train as the frame of reference. We may imagine that a lightning stroke L_1 hit both trains and left a burned spot A on T and A' on T', while another lightning stroke L_2, at the opposite end of the trains, left its mark B on T and B' on T'. We further assume P to be seated midway between the marks A and B, and P' between the marks A' and B'. Under these circumstances, and because the beams of light from both L_1 and L_2 move with the same critical velocity in both trains, the fact that one of the passengers observes the flash coming from the engine before the flash from the rear, while the other passenger observes both flashes at the same time, can be explained only by the proposition that L_1 and L_2 are in succession in relation to one train, but simultaneous in relation to the other.

3. Whitehead's Conception of Simultaneity

In a penetrating essay on "The Philosophy of Whitehead," John Dewey observes that experience of causal compulsion—"the direct evidence as to the connectedness of one's immediate present occasion of experience with one's immediately past occasions"[12]—serves as the pattern of connectedness in

---

do so for the man of the train, since the latter is moving towards the ray coming from the front of the train and away from the one coming from the rear." If this statement were the explanation of the difference in observation, correction for the motion of the train would establish, in contradiction to Northrop's preceding account, the non-relative physical simultaneity of the lightning strokes. Parker, likewise, gives an excellent exposition of Einstein's illustration only to wind it up with the unaccountable contention that Einstein is not concerned with physical simultaneity but with the time when light messages reach the observers concerned: "And relativity theory gives an absolutely correct picture *with regard to the messages. . . .*" *Experience and Substance*, (The University of Michigan Press, 1941, 168).

[12] *LLP*, v. 3, 647.

nature in the metaphysics of events and thereby supports Whitehead's opposition to the traditional separation between mind and matter. On a further page of the same essay Dewey adds:

The new philosophical departure [i.e., Whitehead's rejection of the bifurcation between mind and matter] initiated by deep reflection upon the general significance of the new physics in its contrast with Newtonian cosmology was . . . carried through by taking human experience to be a specialization of the traits of nature thus disclosed.[13]

Dewey's remarks leave no doubt as to where to look to among the doctrines of the new physics in order to establish the crucial point of Einstein's influence upon the metaphysics of events. This crucial point is the conception of the causal structure of physical space-time, the principle, that is, that because of the finite but unsurpassable velocity of light, the occurence of any event is the apex of a double light-cone which leaves the events along the alternative cross-sections of simultaneity, i.e., within the regions of space-time in-between the two cones, causally disconnected and therefore physically independent of one another. This principle, except for the identification of the critical velocity with the velocity of light *in vacuo*, Whitehead accepts *in toto* as a basis of metaphysics. "Contemporary events happen in causal independence of each other," writes Whitehead, and a footnote adds: "This principle lies on the surface of the fundamental Einsteinian formula for the physical continuum."[14]

In order to understand the importance which the principle of physical independence of contemporaries has for Whitehead, let us consider the principle in the context of the metaphysics of events, and, in particular, of Whitehead's theory of perception. As is well known, his ultimate elementary events are organized acts, or, rather, agent-acts combined, of perception—I shall call them *percipients*—where perception ranges, with respect to complexity of organization, from human experience down to blind electronic response, or sensitiveness, to the surrounding physical field. Because percipients are events im-

---

[13] *Ibid.*, 656.
[14] *Process and Reality* (Cambridge University Press, 1929), 84.

mutably fixed each at a definite region of space-time, mutual perception is their only way of transaction. And since perception of another event requires propagation of causal influence from the latter to the percipient, experience of causal compulsion—in Whitehead's terminology perception in the "mode of causal efficacy"—is the major ontological pattern of correlation. Conformably to this pattern, and in agreement with the conception of the causal structure of space-time, Whitehead accounts for creativity, which is his ultimate and most universal feature of process, in terms of the unique and original perception of the world which each percipient brings forth with its occurrence. This is to say that the actual world of each percipient is different from the actual world of any of its contemporaries: in each case the actual world can be represented by the unique light-cone of the past with the corresponding percipient at the apex. In this connection Whitehead explicitly refers to the theory of relativity:

Curiously enough, even at this early stage of metaphysical discussion, the influence of the 'relativity theory' of modern physics is important. According to the classical 'uniquely serial' view of time, two contemporary actual entities define the same actual world. According to the modern view no two actual entities define the same actual world. Actual entities are called 'contemporary' when neither belongs to the 'given' actual world defined by the other.[18]

Recognition that contemporary percipients are physically independent of one another, in conjunction with the principle of "one world," or what Whitehead calls "the solidarity of one common world," lead to a complication in the theory of perception. Important as the mode of causal efficacy is, this mode is insufficient because it leaves out contemporaries, contrary to the requirement of solidarity, completely disconnected. Hence Whitehead supplements his basic perception of causal compulsion by a second mode of perception, which he calls the "mode of presentational immediacy," which is designed to provide non-causal correlation among contemporaries. In the mode of presentational immediacy a percipient is directly cognizant of the *extension* of the contemporary external world but not of the nature or character of events that happen jointly to fill up

[18] *Ibid.,* 90f.

this extension. This is to say that the percipient has no access to such colors, shapes, or other perceptual and physical manifestations that actually belong to the external world at the moment of perception but only to the regions of the surrounding medium where the inaccessible properties reside, in Whitehead's words, only to the "presented locus" of contemporary events. Of course, under normal conditions of the so-called veridical perception and at close range, perceived qualities are likely to be similar, or at any rate relevant, to actual manifestations; and under no circumstances is there perception of pure and bare extension. But error, not with regard to the presented locus but to perceptual presentations within the locus, is always possible, because manifestations which illustrate to a percipient his contemporary external‸world are in fact derived, through the mode of causal efficacy, from the past (and therefore represent the world as it was and not as it is) to be unconsciously "projected" upon the extended surroundings of the present. An important difference in the function of the two modes of perception is this: in the causal mode the world reaches the percipient where and when the latter happens to be, i.e., at the latter's spatio-temporal standpoint, whereas in the non-causal mode the percipient manages to reach, beyond the volume of its own body and by means of a felt geometrical prolongation of bodily strains, for places where contemporaries abide.[16] We may express this difference, in terms of the well

[16] An obvious objection against the theory of two perceptual modes, that we find no evidence for the existence of distinct kinds of perception, is met by Whitehead when he points out that *ordinary human perception* is the outcome of a pre-conscious interplay between the two modes; he calls this interplay "symbolic reference." However, Whitehead has also mentioned unusual instances when each mode operates singly. For examples of experience in the mode of causal efficacy alone see *Process and Reality*, 247f. The mode of presentational immediacy can be illustrated with the aid of the difference between our perception of a chair and as we turn around, of the mirror-image of the chair. The mirror-image *presents a region behind the mirror*, but the chair-like shape and color, which are projected upon that region, are derived from the actual chair in front of the mirror and give no idea as to the actual contents of the space thus illustrated. Another example is an astronomer's perception of the explosion of a star at a distant region in the sky: the astronomer knows that the star actually exploded long ago and therefore only an image of the past event illustrates the contemporary distant region.

known issue between direct and representative realism, by saying that the regions of a contemporary world can be presented *directly*, but the nature of events there (directly given there in the aspect of extension) is represented, and sometimes misrepresented, by characteristics that are causally derived from their antecedents. Whitehead himself sums up the matter as follows:

> Thus the presented locus must be a locus with a systematic geometrical relation to the body. According to all the evidence, it is completely independent of the contemporary actualities which in fact make up the nexus of actualities in the locus. For example, we see a picture on the wall with direct vision. But if we turn our back to the wall, and gaze into a good mirror, we see the same sight as an image behind the mirror. Thus, given the proper physiological state of the body, *the locus presented in sense-perception is independent of the details of the actual happenings which it includes.* This is not to say, that sense-perception is irrelevant to the real world. It demonstrates to us the real extensive continuum in terms of which these contemporary happenings have their own experience qualified. Its additional information in terms of the qualitative sensa has relevance in proportion to the relevance of the immediate bodily state to the immediate happenings throughout the locus. Both are derived from a past which is practically common to them all. Thus there is always some relevance; *the correct interpretation of this relevance is the art of utilizing the perceptive mode of presentational immediacy as a means for understanding the world as a medium.*[17]

I have italicized some of Whitehead's statements in order to forestall F. C. S. Northrop's contention, to be examined presently, that Whitehead and Einstein have essentially different conceptions of simultaneity because the former fails to differentiate between perceptual or phenomenal events, on the one hand, and physical events on the other. I think that the required differentiation follows from the statement that the presented locus is independent of the actual happenings which it includes, since the presented locus appears in the guise of immediately sensed events, whereas actual happenings are physical events. Furthermore, Whitehead explicitly recognizes that, in order to establish which physical events reside within the pre-

[17] *Loc. cit.,* 178.

sented locus, we must resort to interpretation, or correlation, of the data in the mode of presentational immediacy.

An examination of Northrop's contention is in order not only because in the context of his interesting article on "Whitehead's Philosophy of Science" the misinterpretation enjoys an appearance of plausibility, but also because Northrop may have succeeded in misleading Einstein. In an attempt to explain to Einstein Whitehead's position Northrop made the following statement:[18]

When Whitehead affirms an intuitively given meaning of simultaneity of spatially separated events he means immediately sensed phenomenological events, not postulated public physically defined events. . . . We certainly do see a flash in the distant visual space of the sky now, while [and subsequently?] we hear an explosion beside us. His reason for maintaining that this is the only kind of simultaneity which is given arises from his desire, in order to meet epistemological philosophical difficulties, to have only one continuum of intuitively given events, and to avoid the bifurcation between these phenomenal events and the postulated physically defined public events.

Northrop tells us that Einstein's comment on Whitehead's theory thus presented was: "on that theory there would be no meaning to two observers speaking about the same event." This comment is a *reductio ad absurdum* not of Whitehead's view but of Northrop's account of the latter.

I do not deny that Whitehead passed some adverse criticism upon Einstein's definition of simultaneity, and if E. McGilvary is right (*LLP*, v. 3, 215ff.), the criticism is questionable. But if Whitehead misunderstood Einstein, this merely shows that the philosopher assumed the existence of disagreement where there was none. In order not to exaggerate their difference, let me point out, first, that in all his publications which are subsequent to *The Principles of Natural Knowledge,* and therefore may be taken as a more considerate treatment of the matter, Whitehead has omitted his original criticism of Einstein's definition, and, second, that the point of the original criticism is not that Einstein's procedure—whereby simultaneity of spatially separated events can be ascertained by the use of light signals—is in-

[18] *LLP*, v. 3, 204.

adequate, but that, whatever the procedure, the meaning of simultaneity is the same regardless of whether simultaneous events are far apart or in immediate proximity. Apparently Northrop has missed Whitehead's point, the differentiation between the *meaning* of simultaneity and the *procedure* whereby simultaneity can be established, because he argues, as if Whitehead should reject the scientist's ways of knowing simultaneity, that simultaneity of spatially separated events is scientifically "known by postulated theory, which is confirmed indirectly through its deductive consequences and not by immediate apprehension."[19]

In support of his interpretation Northrop quotes Whitehead's statement that "Nature is nothing else than the deliverance of sense-awareness." But Whitehead's statement, an expression of his opposition to the "fallacy of bifurcation," must not be taken to mean that immediate sense-awareness discloses *everything* there is in nature. Whitehead does not even claim that perception accounts for every item of human knowledge. His position is simply that there are no *kinds* of things in nature except the kinds which, in principle, can be known directly through perception. This position leaves ample room for knowledge by inference, and application of Whitehead's own "method of extensive abstraction" provides many illustrations of such knowledge.[20] Hence there is no reason whatsoever to expect that Whitehead is unable, on the basis of his allowance for inference, to deal with the following situations:

Consider two immediately sensed explosions: one in West Haven and the other in East Haven, which are so loud that they can be heard at every point between the two places. . . . We all know it to be a

---

[19] *LLP*, v. 3, 194.

[20] For example, Whitehead uses the method of extensive abstraction in order to account for such scientific objects as atoms or electrons. On p. 158 of *The Concept of Nature* he describes an electron as "a systematic correlation of the characters" of events, and contrasts a scientific object, such as an electron, with both observable physical objects, such as chairs, and sense-objects, such as colors or noises. Thus Northrop is completely mistaken when he asserts that, to Whitehead, "both atoms and sense data are immediately sensed adjectives of immediately sensed events, and that an electron is 'a sensed adjective qualifying all the event particles' in a 'historical route,' i.e., a Minkowskean world-line" (*LLP*, v. 3, 190).

phenomenological fact, and hence one which Whitehead cannot escape, that if a person midway between these two explosions immediately senses them as simultaneous, then all other observers who are nearer the one explosion than the other will not. This example shows both, that we do have an immediately sensed simultaneity for spatially separated events for the individual sense awareness of the individual observer, and that this intuitively given simultaneity does not provide [rather need not provide if the observer is not midway between the two explosions or if some such interference as the wind causes the speed of sound coming from one explosion to be greater than the speed from the other] a publicly valid simultaneity the same for all observers at rest relative to each other on the same frame of reference—in this instance on the earth's surface.[21]

It is amazing that Northrop can imagine that his example should embarrass Whitehead, or that an epistemology which would be embarrassed by such examples is worth refutation. Actually Whitehead requires no more than the possibility of knowing simultaneity of spatially separated events through the deliverance of sense-awareness, for example, in the case of the observer midway between the two explosions. Whitehead recognizes the existence of a public temporal relation between two events, the same for all observers using the same frame of reference, to be established by correction for differences in distance, and the like. Thus, on p. 53 of *The Principles of Natural Knowledge*, he says: "The same definition of simultaneity holds throughout the whole space of a consentient set in the Newtonian group."[22] And, in accordance with his theory

---

[21] *LLP*, v. 3, 200.

[22] The phrase "consentient set" designates a frame of reference of the special theory of relativity. And while, as the context of the phrase shows, "the same definition of simultaneity" is to be distinguished from Einstein's procedure of establishing public simultaneity within a particular frame of reference (because actually light signals do not travel *in vacuo* and therefore represent only an approximation to the constant velocity *c*, however close this approximation may be), Whitehead's recognition of the existence of alternative consentient sets, even when observers in relative motion pass by each other at virtually the same place and therefore momentarily have the same field of vision, proves that he does not identify public simultaneity with sensed simultaneity of spatially separated events. The distinction between a consentient set and the associated perceptual space reappears, with a greater measure of elaboration, in *Process and Reality* in the form of the differentiation between a "locus in unison of becoming" (with the

of perception, he would say, concerning Northrop's example, that there is no public physical sound at the sources of the explosions by the time a distant observer hears the noise. The inevitable conclusion is that there is no essential disagreement between Whitehead and Einstein of the special theory of relativity, at any rate not on the distinction between seen and physical simultaneity.

The truth is that Einstein's influence on Whitehead is, if anything, excessive. For the principle of independence of contemporaries is strictly valid only if events are understood in Einstein's sense of world-points. According to Whitehead, on the other hand, an event or a percipient is not without extension but a quantum of duration, a protensive entity. And when the duration of an event, as exemplified by the specious present in human experience, takes an appreciable fraction of a second,

---

given percipient) and the associated "presented locus." The additional elaboration brings Whitehead even closer to Einstein: "Thus the *loci* of 'unison of becoming' are only determinable in terms of actual happenings of the world." (*Process and Reality*, 180.)

There is, of course, much difference between the physical theories of Whitehead and Einstein, but I am not concerned with this aspect of the matter. And, in so far as a physical theory is conditioned by a philosophy of nature, I think Whitehead exaggerates his departure from Einstein, when he opposes his conception of "contingent" physical laws superimposed upon the uniform structure of space-time to the conception of the general theory of relativity, according to which spatio-temporal curvature expresses the presence of matter. As Whitehead himself has pointed out in the "Preface" to *The Principle of Relativity*, his requirement of uniformity would be satisfied by an elliptic or hyperbolic as well as by a flat space-time. Furthermore, Whitehead's prolongation of the presented *locus* beyond the set of strains of the percipient's body cannot be expected to disclose the exact structure of space-time on an astronomical scale; and on the scale of terrestrial transaction the validity of Euclidean geometry can be ascertained within the errors of observation. On the other hand, the general theory of relativity is concerned with astronomical distances, and proceeds upon the premise of a large scale uniformity of space-time: the relativist either assumes a uniform and static distribution of the nebulae or, if he argues for an expanding universe, systematic motions in the matter accountable for the cosmic curvature. The idea of the expanding universe practically obliterates the philosophical difference (under consideration) between Whitehead and Einstein, for, to quote from H. P. Robertson's article "The Expanding Universe," (*Science in Progress*, 2nd Series, 166), this idea leads to "a more or less unique stratification of space-time into space and time (which in a sense reintroduces a universal time), in which the geometry of space is one of the congruence geometries."

two such contemporary events can be physically interconnected, provided they are not too far from each other. Consider, for example, two men at the opposite ends of an open field. If both must strain their eyes in order to watch each other, the facial expression of strain can be perceived by each, because of the negligible amount of time required to carry a light-message from one of them to the other, before his percipient act is over. And, although Whitehead allows for a kind of "passage" from earlier to later phases within the duration of a single percept, he would not let us say that the beam of light that leaves one observer at an early phase of his percept reaches only a later phase within the percept of the other man. For this manner of speaking implies a division into earlier and later phases that occupy earlier and later intervals of physical time, a breakdown of the temporal quantum. "This genetic passage from phase to phase is not in physical time."[23] Hence contemporary percipients, on Whitehead's premise of protensive events, need not be physically independent of one another.

4. THINGS AND CORRELATIONS OF EVENTS

Since Einstein, and still more since Heisenberg and Schrödinger, the physical world is no longer regarded as consisting of persistent pieces of matter moving in a three-dimensional space, but as a four-dimensional manifold of events in space-time. The old view resulted from an attempt to make the common-sense concept of "things" available for science; the new view means that "things" are no longer part of the fundamental apparatus of physics. . . . The essential business of physics is the discovery of "causal laws," by which I mean any principles which, if true, enable us to infer something about a certain region of space-time from something about some other region or regions.[24]

Thus, succinctly, Russell has stated the basis of the philosophies of events. On this basis his road to "neutral monism," the contention that the distinction between mind and matter is functional or epistemological but not an ontological disparity, is clear. If there is no need for material things, the ground is removed from under their alleged mental counterparts, per-

---

[23] *Process and Reality*, 401.
[24] *LLP*, v. 5, 701.

cipient things. And if causal laws do not unexpectedly break down when a physical stimulus causes the occurrence of a percept, we must not expect the percept to be fundamentally, or ontologically, different from a physical effect which the same stimulus would have caused at the same spot if the percipient had not been present there.

The theory that perceiving depends upon a chain of physical causation is apt to be supplemented by a belief that to every state of the brain a certain state of the mind 'corresponds,' and vice versa, so that, given either the state of the brain or the state of the mind, the other could be inferred by a person who sufficiently understood the correspondence. If it is held that there is no causal interaction between mind and brain, this is merely a new form of the pre-established harmony. But if causation is regarded—as it usually is by empiricists—as nothing but invariable sequence or concomitance, then the supposed correspondence of brain and mind involves causal interaction.[25]

As this passage shows, Russell's causal theory of perception leads to neutral monism because the alternatives, the doctrine of pre-established harmony and the notion of double effect (i.e., the notion that the same physical cause which is regularly followed by a definite physical effect is occasionally followed by an additional mental effect), are "fantastic." Although the question whether Einstein accepts the causal theory of perception, and, if he does, how far he would go with Russell towards neutral monism is very interesting, I do not have sufficient evidence for an answer. In fact, and this is the question I am concerned with, I am not sure whether Einstein would accept without qualification the basis of the philosophies of events as stated by Russell in the beginning of this section. Unquestionably there is much agreement between them:

In the pre-relativity physics space and time were separate entities. . . . It was not observed that the true element of the space-time specification was the event specified by the four numbers x_1, x_2, x_3, t. . . . Upon giving up the hypothesis of the absolute character of time, particularly that of simultaneity, the four-dimensionality of the time-space concept was immediately recognized. It is neither the point in space, nor the

[25] B. Russell, *Physics and Experience* (Henry Sidgwick Lecture, Cambridge University Press, 1945), 6.

instant in time, at which something happens that has physical reality, but only the event itself. There is no absolute (independent of the space of reference) relation in space, and no absolute relation in time between two events, but there is an absolute (independent of the space of reference) relation in space and time. . . . The circumstance that there is no objective rational division of the four-dimensional continuum into a three-dimensional space and a one-dimensional time continuum indicates that the laws of nature will assume a form which is logically most satisfactory when expressed as laws in the four-dimensional space-time continuum.[26]

Nevertheless, when it comes to dispensing with material things in favor of events, Einstein demurs. And, of course, there is no single decisive reason why we should not use both the concept of event and the concept of thing in an account of the physical world. But taken in conjunction such reasons as I have mentioned in the beginning of the preceding section are impressive. The main consideration, however, is that we can dispense with the concept "thing" because in relativity physics events are sufficient. This is to say that, although the language of things cannot do away with the events that happen to a thing, the language of events enables us to translate a statement about a thing into an equivalent statement about a sequence, or string, of events. In particular, a material particle becomes, in the language of relativity, a series of world-points along a definite world-line. "It is hardly correct to say that a particle *moves* in a geodesic; it is more correct to say that a particle *is* a geodesic (though not all geodesics are particles)."[27] In the face of this consideration Einstein's reluctance to eliminate the concept of material things requires explanation. As far as I can see, he has two reasons, the operational basis of physics and the technical meaning of the term "event," each of which I shall proceed to examine separately at some length.

Physics, including relativity, involves the use of instruments, such as clocks and practically rigid measuring rods, which must be identifiable at different dates and through displacement.

[26] A. Einstein, *The Meaning of Relativity* (Princeton University Press, 1945), 30f.

[27] B. Russell, *The Analysis of Matter* (Harcourt, Brace, & Co., 1927), 313.

And, as Einstein has pointed out, "we are still far from possessing such certain knowledge of theoretical principles as to be able to give exact theoretical construction of solid bodies and clocks."[28] Einstein's remark may mean that translation of statements about things into statements about more ultimate elements, such as events, although desirable, is premature at the present stage of science. If this were all he meant, there would be no essential disagreement between him and Russell. In this case both might agree to draw a line of demarcation between the theory of relativity, with events as basic elements, and the metatheory of physics (through the medium of which relativity is to be presented), with provisional employment of the concept, "thing." But Einstein's recent criticism of Russell shows that his present position is much more uncompromising: "Over against that [i.e., against Russell's view] I see no 'metaphysical' danger in taking the thing (the object in the sense of physics) as an independent concept into the system together with the proper spatio-temporal structure."[29] These words may show no more than disagreement with Russell's latest attempt to dispense with substances (including particular events) altogether by reducing things into bundles of qualities. But Einstein's reason for disagreement suggests opposition to reduction of any kind. His reason, as the following quotation shows, is that Russell is unable to account for the distinction between two bundles of qualities which are exactly alike except by including the differentiating spatial relations among sense data: "Now the fact that two things are said to be one and the same thing, if they coincide in all qualities, forces one to consider the geometrical relations between things as belonging to their qualities. (Otherwise one is forced to look upon the Eiffel Tower in Paris and that in New York as 'the same thing'.)"[30] Einstein's implicit criticism, I take it, is twofold: (1) A thing cannot be constructed out of, or reduced to, a set of sensory qualities, and (2) Geometrical, and presumably spatio-temporal, entities are not sense data. And this leads us to an

---

[28] A. Einstein, *Sidelights of Relativity* (Methuen and Co., 1922), 36.

[29] A. Einstein in *LLP*, v. 5, 291.

[30] A. Einstein in *LLP*, v. 5, 290.

examination of events in the technical sense of spatio-temporal elements or world-points.

Events in the sense of world-points are without extension. And, unless these extensionless elements of space-time can be constructed out of, or logically derived from, ordinary and extended happenings or events, there would be no advantage in sacrificing things for the sake of the latter. Of course, Russell explicitly recognizes the distinction between a world-point and an ordinary event: "The points of space-time have, of course, no duration as well as no spatial extension."[31] But a question is raised on which Einstein and Russell are apart: Is there a way to abstract, or logically derive, world-points from events that are given in sense experience? The fact that both world-points and ordinary events are identifiable by specifying a position and a date prompts us to answer "Yes." Einstein, however, says "No." For world-points are theoretical concepts, and Einstein rejects the "idea that the fundamental concepts and postulates of physics were not in the logical sense free inventions of the human mind but could be deduced from experience by 'abstraction'—that is by logical means."[32] This is not to say that Einstein denies that world-points, or any other scientific concepts, serve to correlate events of observation or sense experience; but his idea of correlation or what he calls "representation," is not correlation in Russell's sense of logical construction. As far as "representation" in terms of world-points is concerned, it consists of *assignment* of distinct world-points to distinct observations. The assignment is controlled by the condition of numerical agreement between the spatio-temporal relations among the assigned world-points, on the one hand, and the relationships, established by clock readings and displacements of measuring rods, that bind the represented phenomena, on the other. According to Einstein, "representation" of data by means of world-points is an obvious extension from three to four dimensions of the usual correlation between Euclidean geometry and actual, or possible, configurations exhibit-

[31] B. Russell, *The Analysis of Matter*, 57.
[32] A. Einstein, *The World as I See It* (Covici & Friede, N.Y., 1934), 35.

ed by solid bodies on the earth in relation to one another: "Solid bodies are related, with respect to their possible dispositions, as are bodies in Euclidean geometry of three dimensions. Then the propositions of Euclid contain affirmations as to the relations of practically-rigid bodies."[33] Hence the difference between Einstein and the philosophers of events concerning the part played by ordinary events in the constitution of nature depends on the opposition of the procedure of "representation" to that of logical construction. The question is: Which of the two conceptions of correlation is more adequate?

I believe Einstein is wrong when he asserts that such scientific concepts as points, or world-points, cannot be "deduced from experience by 'abstraction'—that is to say by logical means." The method of extensive abstraction (in the development and use of which Russell has followed Whitehead) can do just that. For example, in Chapter 28 of *The Analysis of Matter*, Russell applies the method of extensive abstraction in a successful construction of a world-point out of sets of overlapping ordinary events. Such constructions are supposed to be given exclusively on the basis of observable data, such as the sequence of overlapping notes struck one after another on the keyboard of the piano, and by means of formal logic and mathematics alone, i.e., with the aid of such terms as "the logical sum of classes," "infinite number," and the like. Furthermore, these constructions satisfy the following two conditions: (1) The constructed elements must be related to one another in agreement with the theorems of the corresponding geometry; and (2) The statement that "A region of space-time can be exhaustively analyzed into sets of points," and other statements of the same kind, must have a definite empirical meaning in terms of the constructed elements. Accordingly, construction of points, or world-points, by means of the method of extensive abstraction is a question of semantics or meaning; there is no intention to provide instruction for the purpose of locating, or exhibiting, a particular point, or world-point, in the actual set-up of practice and experiment. Hence, granted that the method is technically correct,

---

[33] A. Einstein, in *Sidelights of Relativity*, 32.

the observation that the procedure of a practicing physicist is something entirely different is no objection against the method as such.[34] Yet some critics have made this observation as if it were an objection. For example, E. Nagel writes as follows:

[34] As far as I know no one has attempted to show that the method of extensive abstraction involves some logical or technical error. The usual criticism is that a geometrical "element," constructed by means of the method, is not observable because it contains an infinite number of regions. This criticism is invalid. For the infinite number (of regions) is allowed not because it is observable but because it is a legitimate concept of formal mathematics. Accordingly, the method does not require an actual exhibition of *all* regions that constitute a point; the requirement is that *any* constituent region should be, in principle, observable. In fact a weaker condition is sufficient in order to provide the construction of a point with an empirical basis. This is to say that identification of a particular region or member of a co-punctual group, i.e., within a group that forms a point by definition, is not required. All that we really need is an illustration of the *kind* of thing that the definition is about. For example, Whitehead gives the following illustration of an abstractive set. "Such a set . . . has the properties of the Chinese toy which is a nest of boxes, one within the other, with the difference that the toy has a smallest box, while the abstractive class has neither a smallest event nor does it converge to a limiting event which is not a member of the set" (*The Concept of Nature*, 79f.). The difference between the illustration and the abstractive set cannot, and need not, be illustrated because of being fully accounted for in terms of pure logic and mathematics. These considerations, I think, take care of E. Nagel's objection which runs as follows: "Assuming that events have been isolated, co-punctual groups of events must next be found. However, since a co-punctual group may have an indefinite number of event-numbers, the assertion that a given group is co-punctual will in general be a *hypothesis*. The situation does not become easier when the physicist next tries to identify those co-punctual groups which are points: the assertion that a class of events is a point will be a conjecture for which only the most incomplete sort of evidence can be available." (*LLP*, v. 5, 344.) Nagel overlooks the fact that if a co-punctual group could be perceptually given *in toto*, recognition, or identification of a point would follow by definition. On the other hand, the fact that a total co-punctual group cannot be perceptually given is immaterial in a concern with meaning, i.e., in so far as the proposed definition of a point is meaningful. I believe now that my own objection against Whitehead's definition of a point, the observation that we cannot exhibit even a part of the required abstractive set, because this presupposes an antecedent acquaintance with points and other exact geometrical figures such as sets of concentric circles (cf. *Power and Events*, Princeton University Press, 1926, 251f.), is a mistake, or, at any rate, needs qualification. For even if precision of enclosure cannot be exemplified except through some such configuration as a set of concentric circles, the definition to be understood and empirically justified, may need illustration but does not require exemplification. In other words, Whitehead's definition is a conceptual or logical construction. Furthermore, if we insist upon dealing with events of any odd shape, we can follow Russell's alternative definition without giving up the use of the method of extensive abstraction altogether.

Russell's definition exhibits no concern whatever for the way in which physicists *actually use* expressions like "point." In the first place, it is certainly not evident that physicists do in fact apply the term to structures of events. On the contrary, there is some evidence to show that they employ it in a somewhat different fashion, using it in connection with bodies identifiable in gross experience and whose magnitudes vary from case to case according to the needs of specific problems. To be sure, the application of the term is frequently sloppy and vague, and its rules cannot in general be made precise. But the vagueness and sloppiness are facts which a philosophy of science must face squarely, and they cannot be circumvented by an ingenious but essentially irrelevant proposal as to how the term *might* be used.[35]

How widely Nagel's shot misses the target becomes evident when we ascertain that Russell's philosophy of science faces squarely the facts with which Nagel is concerned. Thus, we read:

Sometimes it would seem as if the whole earth counted as a point: certainly one physical laboratory does so in the practice of writers on relativity. . . . The fact that such a view is appropriate in discussions of relativity makes it unnecessary to be precise as to what is meant by saying that two events occupy the same point, or that two world-lines intersect.[36]

But Nagel's admission that "the application of the term is frequently sloppy and vague" does not mean that there is no need for a precise meaning of the term "point." And Nagel overlooks the theoretical need for a precise meaning when the physicist is concerned with the correlation of statements which belong to different branches of physics. To illustrate: It is no longer unnecessary to be precise when a relativist contends that his own statement that "Two world-lines intersect at a world-point" and the quantum principle that "A simultaneous specification of a world-point of a particle and of its momentum and energy is impossible" are not entirely disconnected propositions.[37] The relativist may then consider that in his own practice

[35] E. Nagel in *LLP*, v. 5, 344f.

[36] B. Russell, *The Analysis of Matter*, 57.

[37] I cannot resist the temptation, which this illustration offers to a philosopher, of a footnote query to the professional physicist: Is the quantum principle, quoted in the illustration, in conflict with the equation of the general theory of relativity, according to which the "curvature" tensor is *equated* to the "matter" tensor?

he is dealing with an approximation, corresponding to the nature of the particular problem, to the precise meaning which is empirically justified by the method of extensive abstraction. In fact, Nagel's characterization of the practice as "sloppy and vague" would be meaningless, if he were altogether unaware of successive approximations to precision. And if the application of the term "point" were arbitrary and uncontrolled by any consideration of the precise meaning, even to the extent to which the measure of precision in the act of application may turn out to depend upon the specific nature of the problem, the successful outcome in practice, as far as correlation and prediction of observations is concerned, would be an utter mystery. Einstein himself is ready to accept the success with which scientific terms are applied to experience as a mystery that "we shall never understand."[38] But to a philosopher an epitemological mystery spells failure in analysis. Thus, whereas Einstein, on p. 23 of *The World as I See It*, says, concerning the relation between theoretical principles and phenomena: "This is what Leibniz describes so happily as a 'pre-established harmony,'" to Russell the notion of a pre-established harmony appears "fantastic."[39] And, in the case of the relation between the theoretical term "point" and observable phenomena, the philosopher has actually dispelled the mystery with the aid of the method of extensive abstraction.

The issue between Einstein and the philosophy of events has not been settled yet, however. For we must not overlook the fact that world-points are elements within the continuum of space-time; and if the latter is a conceptual scheme or order that cannot be derived from the world of experience, and therefore, in Einstein's own words, "in guiding us in the creation of such an order of sense experiences, success in the result is alone the determining factor,"[40] abstraction of an isolated world-point from a set of ordinary events is of no consequence. This consideration raises the problem of the ontological status of space-time.

[38] "Physics and Reality," *Franklin Institute Journal* (1936), 351.
[39] B. Russell, *Physics and Experience*, 6.
[40] "Physics and Reality" 351.

5. THE PROBLEM OF SPACE-TIME

"Space-time, as it appears in mathematical physics, is obviously an artifact, i.e., a structure in which materials found in the world are compounded in such a manner as to be convenient for the mathematician."[41] On the face of it Russell's statement leads beyond Einstein's semi-Kantian conceptualism toward positivism or conventionalism. For, in order to appreciate Einstein's comparatively conservative stand, we must not be misled by such phrases as "the purely fictitious character of the fundamentals of scientific theory,"[42] which serve to emphasize the part played by the scientist's creative intelligence in the advance of knowledge, but take them in conjunction with Einstein's explanation that the scientist's "liberty of choice . . . is not in any way similar to the liberty of a writer of fiction . . . , but to that of a man engaged in solving a well designed word puzzle . . . ; there is only one word which really solves the puzzle in all its forms."[43] The concept of space-time affords an excellent illustration of Einstein's epistemological position. The scientist's freedom of choice is fully exercised in the construction of a curved four-dimensional continuum, since no experience could dictate to him the idea. Yet his invention also happens to be an intuition or discovery of an objective physical reality. For spatio-temporal invariance provides the word that solves the puzzle of alternative differentiation between space and time within frames of reference which are set in relative motion. The illustration brings out invariance as the ultimate criterion of physical reality. In accordance with this criterion variable or alternative perspectives of differentiated space and time are relegated to the status of shadowy being: hence Einstein's endorsement of Minkowski's dictum that "henceforth space in itself and time in itself dissolve into shadows and only a kind of union of the two retains an individuality." Of course, to such an empiricist as Russell this sort of about face, which starts with building physics on the evidence of observations within the terrestrial frame of differentiated space and time

[41] B. Russell, *The Analysis of Matter*, 376.
[42] A. Einstein, in *The World as I See It*, 34.
[43] "Physics and Reality," 353.

only to end with casting metaphysical doubts upon the reality of the latter, is unacceptable. And to counteract the physicist's influence Russell has pointed out that space-time, as it appears in mathematical physics, is an artifact. But Russell's observation does not mean that he rejects the existence of space-time altogether. On the contrary, his statement suggests a differentiation between the artificial mathematical, and possibly metrical, structure of space-time in relativity physics, on the one hand, and space-time as the physical medium in which ordinary events are embedded and without which there could be no continuous, and therefore unobservable, causal chains from external sources to actual percepts, on the other. As a medium of events and percepts space-time is no less real than these events and percepts themselves, although their modes of reality may be different. In its capacity of a medium space-time provides distinct happenings in the world with distinct, and mutually external, regions; and this fact of externality, which is represented in experience by the opposition between the "now" or "here" and whatever takes place "elsewhere," is, however unique its mode of being may be, more than a mental act of correlating observations. This conception of space-time Russell makes explicit, and accepts as his own, in another statement: "I think it may also be assumed that one event may extend over a finite extent of space-time, but on this point the theory is silent, so far as I know."[44] As these words show, the identification of space-time with a medium of extended events appears to Russell so natural that he is prepared to take it as part of the theory of relativity although he leaves the question open. Actually, of course, there is no such question: if it is permissible to identify the theory of relativity with Einstein's position, and if my account of Einstein is substantially correct, the theory is not silent but rejects Russell's assumption. The real question is: What can be said for and against the conception of space-time as a medium?

A relativist may object to Russell's differentiation between the ontological basis of a space-time medium and the mathematical superstructure, an artifact, as follows. Either the hypothetical medium of events has a definite intrinsic structure or

[44] B. Russell, *The Analysis of Matter*, 57.

not. On Russell's realist premises, the second alternative, of an indeterminate space-time, would seem to be excluded. But if space-time has structure, then mathematical, and metrical, specifications in relativity physics, unless they are no more than a fairy tale, must have a certain measure of conformity to that structure. And therefore, to the extent to which there is conformity, space-time of mathematical physics is not an artifact. The argument is telling and leaves only two ways of escape.

There is Einstein's way which is closed to Russell, because of the rejection of the medium of extended events as an independent physical reality, independent, that is, of the scientist's mathematical construction. Einstein can make allowance for the conventional, or fictitious, features of mathematical space-time without raising the question of conformity to a would-be ontological counterpart. However, he has to pay a high price for his advantage. There remains the mystery—which Einstein himself is forced to recognize as such—of successful prediction. And, except for this mystery, the imposition of the conceptual order of space-time upon facts can only mean that, if physical occurrences were left to themselves, free from theoretical intervention by the scientist, they would be mutually disconnected.[45]

The second alternative, which might be acceptable to Russell, if it were not for his prejudice against the idea of potentiality, takes the medium of events, in opposition to the determinate or specific structure of mathematical space-time, to be plastic or determinable rather than fixed and fully specified. This alternative denies that the medium of space-time is a ready made, antecedently established actuality of which mathematical space-time is a conceptual copy or replica. The contention is that the

[45] Let me enlarge, in this connection, upon an earlier remark about Einstein's epistemology. If we differentiate between *a priori* meaning and truth, we may say that Einstein, following Kant, accepts the *a priori* meaning of scientific concepts and theories whereas, in agreement with the positivists, he contends that truth in science is established *a posteriori* by the success of prediction. Thus Einstein is not a positivist: the latter questions the very meaning of an empirical statement that, admittedly, cannot be derived from experience by abstraction, induction, or some other logical means. Furthermore, it would seem that Einstein relies, in addition to the pragmatic criterion of successful prediction, on the *a priori* intuition that the acceptable theory is the closest available approximation to the limit of an absolute truth.

medium exists in a state of disposition, or potentiality, to be variously specified in conception or description; and mathematical space-time of relativity is one such specification. This contention enables us to treat the peculiarities of mathematical specification, to the extent to which they go beyond the specifiable, as a matter of convention and, at the same time, to recognize a measure of conformity between theory and physical reality, in case the disposition to be theoretically specified has not been positively distorted by the subsequent theory. On the other hand, lack of specificity or actuality does not prevent the medium of events from connecting them with one another independently of, and antecedently to, the supervening correlation, by means of a mathematical construct, in the mind of a mathematician. Let me illustrate the point, first, with a three-dimensional analogue to a situation in space-time. Suppose a cone to be at rest in the frame of reference containing two observers. One of them perceives the cone from aside, in the shape of a triangle; the other from below, in the shape of a circle. The total, three-dimensional shape of the cone is not represented by either of the two actual percepts. Moreover, the total shape cannot be actual, or subject to perception, because any actual percept would exclude, or be incompatible with, the shape of a circle or a triangle. We seem to have no other choice but to admit that the cone, as contrasted with its alternative actual aspects such as a circle or a triangle, exists in the state of disposition or potentiality. This is to say that the cone is the disposition, or power, to show an actual aspect of a triangle within one perspective and some alternative aspect, for example, a circle, within another. The alternative aspects exclude each other as actual observations—no observer can have two of them at the same time—but as observable, i.e., in the capacity to appear in different perspectives, they are connected and co-exist. Of course, we also have the mathematical formula for the cone to correlate its various perspectival aspects in our minds. But the formula cannot literally *do* anything to either the cone itself or to its aspects, and the point of mental correlation is conformity to antecedent correlation in fact, even though the latter means no more than disposition or power to be actualized in alternative aspects.

We now turn to the analogue in space-time. Alternative frames of reference, moving in relation to one another, provide alternative actual aspects upon the same region of space-time. These alternative aspects are co-exclusive, because each represents a different way of separating space from time. Again there are mathematical formulas, the transformation equations of relativity, that enable us to correlate the diverse systems of space and time. But again we may assume the ontological counterpart of the mathematical correlation to be antecedent to the latter. The question is: What are the minimum requirements which the ontological counterpart must satisfy? One thing is clear. Whatever else the disposition to yield a variety of systems of space and time may be, it is, at least, just this, a disposition or power. And there is another consideration. To be susceptible to alternative separations between space and time the disposition in question must provide neutral, or impartial, grounds for all of them—as the term medium appropriately connotes—and that can only mean that the medium of potentiality exists as a fusion of space with time. The logic that leads to the invariant space-time as a medium for a variable differentiation between space and time, let us note, does not depend, except for the conception of alternative systems of space and time, on the theory of relativity. At any rate the logic does not commit us to the mathematical peculiarity of space-time in physics. Accordingly, we are in a position to accept what I take to be Russell's distinction between the ontological basis and the conventional superstructure, the artifact, of space-time.

The contention that space-time is a field of potentiality or power may be altogether unacceptable to Russell.[46] Nor is the

[46] Yet one line of his argument leads Russell to what he calls "ideal" elements of reality that would not seem to be essentially different from elements of potentiality. I have in mind his theory of unobserved aspects within a causal chain that terminates in a percept of a material thing. To describe an unobserved aspect Russell uses the term "ideal" with the proviso, which is directed against phenomenalism, that "the only thing rejected is the view that 'ideal' elements are unreal." (*The Analysis of Matter*, 215) The employment of the term "ideal" to connote reality would be awkward if Russell were not concerned with the kind of reality that, like potentiality or power, is to be contrasted with actual observation. On the other hand, in his later book, *An Inquiry into Meaning and Truth*, Russell has proposed a theory of particulars which would do away with any substantial medium, whether actual or potential.

present contention derived from Whitehead. Whitehead characterizes the "extensive continuum" of physical space-time as "the most general scheme of real potentiality."[47] Yet this characterization does not enable me to claim agreement with Whitehead because he does not make his meaning, even within the context of further elaboration, sufficiently clear. For, according to Whitehead, clarity requires that "every entity should be a specific instance of one category of existence";[48] but he fails to classify either the extensive continuum or potentiality under any of his eight categories of existence. The extensive continuum, Whitehead's own term, "scheme," and E. McGilvary's interpretation[49] notwithstanding, cannot be meant to be an eternal object, a Platonic form, since, as Whitehead has pointed out,[50] eternal objects are no more than pure or general potentialities whereas space-time is said to be "the first determination of order—that is, of real potentiality—arising out of the general character of the world." If we try the remaining categories of existence one by one, we may conclude that only the category "proposition," in Whitehead's peculiar sense of "matter of fact in potential determination," appears to be adjustable to fit in with his description of the extensive continuum. And if the conclusion is correct, Whitehead's extensive continuum is an aspect—to be derived by abstraction either conceptually or through perception of the "presented locus"—of actuality. An aspect of actuality is, of course, something different from a medium of potentiality. On the other hand, his refusal to follow Einstein beyond the special theory of relativity indicates that Whitehead would be in favor of our distinction between space-time and the mathematical specification of the latter.

The proposed distinction enables us to justify directly, on the grounds of observability, the conception of the medium of events, and, indirectly, the mathematical space-time of relativity. We recognize that space-time as a whole, mathematical or

[47] A. N. Whitehead, *Process and Reality,* 93.
[48] *Ibid.,* 27.
[49] *LLP*, v. 3, 239.
[50] Whitehead, *op. cit.,* 90f.

otherwise, is beyond experience. And we know that the "curved" continuum of general relativity cannot be perceived even in parts. I may also admit that the percipient's field of experience coincides with a particular frame of reference in which space and time are set apart. Yet a glimpse into the world of dynamics, a four-dimensional fragment, is not irregular or uncommon in perception. For even within a frame of separation between space and time their union is in a measure restored in a percept of some dynamic shape the presentation of which cannot be given by an arrested figure, like a snapshot, because it requires the completion of a process or movement. The shape of a waving flag, for example, is perceivable, but only through the period of an enduring experience. And similarly with the shape of a dance. Occasionally we may even perceive the four-dimensional intersection of two distinct frames of reference, when we happen to participate in both. Whitehead gives an illustration of this possibility:

> When the bulk of the events perceived are cogredient in a duration other than that of the percipient event, the percipience may include a double consciousness of cogredience, namely the consciousness of the whole within which the observer in the train is 'here,' and the consciousness of the whole within which the trees and bridges and telegraph posts are definitely 'there.'[51]

Such fragments of four-dimensional experience, let me repeat, form direct evidence in favor of a determinable or specifiable medium of space-time. But whereas we can correlate two things, both of which lack specificity, we may wonder whether sound logic would ever establish a correlation between the indefinite and fragmentary dynamic manifestations, on the one hand, and the precise specification of space-time, on the other. Under the circumstances, neither Einstein's procedure of "representation" nor Whitehead's method of extensive abstraction appear to be serviceable. The question is whether there exists a different method of correlation.

The required principle of correlation is to bridge the gap between factual indeterminacy and theoretical precision. Hence

[51] A. N. Whitehead, *The Concept of Nature*, 111.

we can expect a form of idealization; only not the usual practice of idealization which has been discredited by entanglement in arbitrariness, dogmatism, and wishful thinking. With the need for drastic restriction in mind, let us try the following tentative statement of the principle of legitimate idealization. A theoretical conception is empirically justified if, and only if, determinable experience, a sense datum or percept, is not sufficiently specific or explicit to enable the observer positively to establish its failure as an exemplification. To illustrate the function of the principle let us consider Euclid's conception of an extensionless point. In answer to Whitehead's criticism of the conception, to the effect that there is nothing in nature that would not show under close inspection some amount of extension, we can point out that perception is part of nature and that a percept of a dot may not be determinate enough to be positively distinguishable from what would be an extensionless point. If we look from some distance at a corner of this page, we are unable to discern within the visual datum a length or width or depth: the corner of the page, as we see it, does not positively fail to exemplify Euclid's ideal. Or, to take another illustration, observe a road-map in relation to the percept of the countryside. As we drive along the highway, we understand the map to be an idealization because we do not find representation of minor curves on the road or other perceptible detail. But we accept the idealization as legitimate because we know that under different perceptual conditions, for example, while looking down from an airplane, the percept of the road would no longer be sufficiently definite and detailed to be contrasted with the outline on the map. Similarly, with the mathematical conception of space-time. If no other method except "representation" or "extensive abstraction" were available, such peculiarities of the mathematical conception as "curvature" would be entirely artificial; the principle of legitimate idealization, however, enables us to reconsider the matter. Space-time "curvature" is an empirically justifiable notion so long as the scale of human perception, together with the inevitable inexactitude of measurement, leave within the field of experience a margin of indeterminacy that does not let us positively decide in

favor either of flatness or of small curvature. Here as elsewhere, the principle of legitimate idealization can yield only
an ambiguous result. The same empirical evidence justifies
both the conception of "curvature" and of flatness. The justification is a question of meaning and not of truth. If the scientist
prefers a curved space-time, his reasons are beyond the scope of
a philosopher. A philosopher is only concerned with the ontological status of space-time. And if his philosophy prompts him
to accept the independent physical existence of space-time (independent of the mind, that is), he need not go beyond the
idea of specifiable medium of events, in a state of potentiality
or power, into considerations of actual specification.[52]

ANDREW PAUL USHENKO

DEPARTMENT OF PHILOSOPHY
PRINCETON UNIVERSITY

[52] On the other hand, the physicist is not concerned with the distinction between
power and actuality, and the contention that space-time is a medium of potentiality is likely to leave him cold. Yet, let us remind him, except for experiments and
pointer-readings, which are actual events, physics, as the terminology of physical
science clearly demonstrates, is entirely preoccupied with potentialities. For an
analysis of the physicist's terminology shows, in addition to such terms as potential
energy, an abundance of dispositional adjectives, such as elastic, combustible, com-
pressible, and the like, and of differential equations which, as Russell has observed,
must be interpreted in terms of tendencies. And when a physical law is translated
from the language of symbols into the language of words, contrary-to-fact con-
ditionals, which are meant to convey that there is something independent of
actuality, provide the appropriate linguistic form of translation.

25

Virgil G. Hinshaw, Jr.

EINSTEIN'S SOCIAL PHILOSOPHY

EINSTEIN'S SOCIAL PHILOSOPHY

THE PRESENT sketch is intended as a brief investigation of certain aspects of Albert Einstein's social philosophy. One of the difficulties of such a study is that it is hard to discover, in Einstein's speeches and writings, any systematic position in social ethics. Thus, in most cases, I prefer to speak of his convictions, rather than position, in social philosophy.

SCIENCE AND VALUES

"Concern for man himself and his fate must always form the chief interest of all technical endeavors. . . . Never forget this in the midst of your diagrams and equations."—*Albert Einstein*

Ever since finding this quotation, about ten years ago, in Robert Lynd's *Knowledge for What?*,[1] I have felt that it epitomized Einstein's convictions concerning the place of values in a world of science. I am here using "value" in that familiar sense wherein a value may be defined as "any object of any interest."[2] In this sense I shall distinguish between values as *interests*, in what has (sometimes) been called axiology, and ethical imperatives, in what has sometimes been called deontology.[3] In what follows, I shall be keeping in mind a certain preconception:

Einstein seems to be thinking of values more nearly as interests than as ontologically grounded norms. His ethic is, it seems to me, closer to an empirical, than to an ontological ethic. His

---

[1] Robert S. Lynd, *Knowledge for What?*, (Princeton, 1939), 114. In most cases, my documentation is supplemented by a conversation I was privileged to have with Professor Einstein at Princeton in May, 1949.

[2] In particular, R. B. Perry's interest theory of value as developed in his *General Theory of Value*, (New York, 1926).

[3] Compare W. Frankena, "Ethics" article (D. Runes (ed.)) *Dictionary of Philosophy*, (New York, 1942), 98-100.

cosmos is more nearly "one-layered," like the monist's, than "two-layered," like the Platonist's.

In the article from which the above quotation was taken, Einstein suggests that we must have this concern for man in order that "the creations of our mind shall be a blessing and not a curse to mankind." Such a statement could be given several interpretations; however, Einstein's meaning is this. For us human beings, our mutual behavior and our conscious striving for our goals is much more important than any factual knowledge. Moreover, Einstein is actually evincing a broader conviction, somewhat like St. Paul's, that charity is of greater value than faith and hope, than the gift of prophecy and the possession of all knowledge. Compare also his statement, in another place, that "only a life lived for others is the life worthwhile."[4]

In recent years, of course, the issues regarding science and values have been sharpened by the atomic bomb, the possibility of atomic energy, and the problem of their control. It is at such a time as this that Einstein, important contributor to the development of the atomic bomb and atomic energy, has reasserted his conviction with increased vigor.

On the one hand, he is a man who has maintained a type of balance, perhaps only possible for one with his scientific background and ethical maturity. "I do not believe," says Einstein, "that civilization will be wiped out in a war fought with the atomic bomb. Perhaps two-thirds of the people of the earth might be killed; but enough men, capable of thinking, and enough books would be left to start again, and civilization could be restored."[5] Likewise, he has tried to outline wisely the rôle of both the scientist and the man of letters in these times of crisis. "The intellectual workers," he says, ". . . cannot successfully intervene directly in the political struggle. They can achieve, however, the spreading of clear ideas about the situation and the possibility of successful action. They can contribute through enlightenment to prevent able statesmen from being hampered in their work by antiquated opinions and prejudices."[6]

[4] *New York Times* (hereafter NYT), 20 June 1932, p. 17, col. 3.
[5] *Ibid.*, 24 February 1946, sect. 6, p. 42, col. 3.
[6] *Ibid.*, 18 November 1946, p. 25, col. 1.

On the other hand, Einstein has shown considerable leadership in showing the way, as he sees it, to the resolution of the "major moral problem of our age." His position concerning the control of atomic energy is too well known to require detailed documentation. Nevertheless, as Chairman of the Emergency Committee of Atomic Scientists, Einstein has said many things worth repeating. For example, his telegram soliciting funds for the Committee: "Our world faces a crisis as yet unperceived by those possessing power to make great decisions for good or evil. The unleashed power of the atom has changed everything save our modes of thinking and we thus drift toward unparalleled catastrophe." In short, "a new type of thinking is essential if mankind is to survive and move toward higher levels."[7]

Mention must here be made, as it will again presently, of Einstein's insistence upon social action on the part of the intellectual of our times. Take his interview entitled "The Real Problem is in the Hearts of Men," which we shall have occasion to cite shortly. Again, remember the fact that Einstein was one of the first members of the Commission for Intellectual Co-operation with the League of Nations. Still again, compare his being asked about the advisability of establishing a "Court of Wisdom,"[8] as was originally suggested at the Harvard Tercentenary Conference. Such a Court, similar to the medieval University of Paris, would be able, it was thought, to bring forth powerful moral judgments. If established, Einstein answered, such a body could represent a "conscience of mankind;" and it could, in the course of time, exert a "highly beneficial and . . . even a standard-setting influence on the development of the social and economic affairs of the world." Affirming that such a Court would necessarily call for concentrated efforts of the best minds, Einstein actually outlines how members of the Court ought to be elected and how vacancies ought to be filled. In short, in this letter of 1939 (as elsewhere, later), Einstein indicates that he is devoting much thought to the question concerning the means of organizing the intellectual and spiritual

---

[7] *Ibid.*, 25 May 1946, p. 13, col. 5.
[8] The quotations concerning the "Court" are found in NYT, 14 March 1939, p. 1, col. 3.

forces of the world into a unified moral force, which would serve as "a sort of conscience of mankind."

Moreover, the conviction concerning the rôle of the intellectual in social action is, once again, embodied explicitly in his urging the intellectual workers, of the United States and other free countries, to organize and fight for the establishment of a supra-national political force as protection against aggression. Specifically, the aim of such a union of intellectual workers would be to supply, for the majority of people, the clear thinking necessary if international co-operation is to become a fact. "In the organization and promotion of enlightenment on this subject, I see the most important service . . . intellectual workers can perform in this historical moment."[9]

To Einstein's concern with social action I shall revert throughout the remainder of this sketch.

Finally, a word about the "neutrality" of the scientist in the process of valuation. This is the hackneyed, though substantial, problem: How can the scientist (who, insofar as possible, maintains complete objectivity in the laboratory) even be interested in, let alone concerned with, value-judgments—which are, by their very nature, either largely subjective if concerned with *interests* or, if concerned with *ethical norms* or *imperatives*, investigable only by philosophic methods? Though he fails to face squarely in his writings some of the issues involved, Einstein surely envisages the major problem. Moreover, in a letter of February 6, 1939, Einstein, in effect, resolves the problem by distinguishing (essentially) two rôles of the intellectual worker: his rôle as scientist or man of letters, *and* his rôle as citizen.

In this letter (a reply to Lincoln's Birthday Committee), he urged united collective action by scientists in their rôles *as citizens* to protect the freedom of teaching and publication. This, in a word, is his answer to the problem.

But his thinking (in this particular letter, along the lines of academic freedom) does not stop there. He agreed that scientists must stand guard against *any* infringement of the freedom of scientific research and teaching. Moreover, Einstein called on the government to protect teachers against influences brought on by economic pressure.

THE STATE AND THE INDIVIDUAL

"Never do anything against conscience, even if the state demands it."
—*Albert Einstein*

"But Peter and the apostles answered and said, we must obey God rather than men."—*The Acts*, V, 29

In broad strokes, Einstein's convictions concerning the ethical duty of the individual in relation to the state are these. A moral man cannot identify himself with the state. If the state decides upon a certain course of moral action, the individual must always evaluate this decision for himself. Einstein suggests as a maxim: "Never do anything against conscience, even if the state demands it."[10] And the spirit of this maxim is reflected in the answer of Peter and the apostles, "we must obey God rather than men."

In explaining this maxim, Einstein suggests that we consider the recent Nürnberg Trials. He believes the Trials indicate that we do, as a matter of fact, think in terms of the guilt of nations. And, if the term "guilt" is to have genuine meaning here, moral judgment beyond nationalism is implied. In short, Einstein insists that these trials were supra-national. The fact of the trials, therefore, Einstein believes, gives evidence that we all do (more or less) accept the maxim.

Succinctly, Einstein suggests that each man should distinguish law of duty from law of the state. A man's duty often clashes with the will of the state. When this occurs, the moral man will side with the deliverances of his own conscience. Here, as elsewhere, the final arbiter of all ethical decisions is conscience. (To some of these points we must again return shortly.)

But surely a misgiving concerning his interpretation of the Trials arises at this point. For my part, I would want to make the following qualification. I would qualify Einstein's belief that we do think in terms of the guilt of nations, with the clause, "If the Trials have any genuine moral and ethical

---

[a] From notes of private conversation.

significance whatsoever." It is certainly not obvious that the Trials are necessarily significant either for valuation or for obligation—either for axiology or for deontology. The sense in which the Trials may have been farcical has been too often noted to require repetition or comment. And, of course, if they were a mockery of justice, the Trials are more important for the sociology of morals than for social philosophy proper.

Moreover, if the thesis of Reinhold Niebuhr's *Moral Man and Immoral Society* is accurate at all, a further qualification of Einstein's belief is in order. In short, if a "sharp distinction must be drawn between the moral and social behavior of individuals and of social groups ... ," then "this distinction justifies and necessitates political policies which a purely individualistic ethic must always find embarrassing."[11] The concept of the guilt of nations surely requires careful scrutiny in the light of Niebuhr's remarks.

PACIFISM, THE BOMB, AND THE OUTLAWRY OF WAR

That Albert Einstein has been pacifist during most of his lifetime, is a well known fact which requires little more than acknowledgment in this sketch. The truth of the matter is that Einstein has always been anti-militaristic. As to pacifism, his conviction is this: the only exception to adherence, in our times, to pacifism is the case of militant fascism, specifically, German Nazism. With Gandhi,[12] he would recommend passive resistance. But, unlike Gandhi, he believes in passive resistance only up to a certain point. He believes that one should resort to violence whenever militant fascism arises; that is, whenever militant fascism, as did Nazism, seeks to wipe out humanity's best. If militant fascism tries to destroy the intellectual class of any given society, then violence is not only fully justified, but actually necessary. The only course of action open to moral man in such times is his resorting to violence. No moral man could do otherwise, while relying wholly upon the dictates of his conscience.

[11] Reinhold Niebuhr, *Moral Man and Immoral Society*, (New York, 1932), xi.
[12] He did contribute (p. 79-80) on "Gandhi's Statesmanship" to a memorial volume: *Mahatma Gandhi*—Essays and reflections on his life and work presented to him on his seventieth birthday, edited by S. Radhakrishnan, (London, 1944).

Here one can see close resemblance of position to the Quakers' convictions. Reliance upon the "inner light" both first and last is germane to both positions. Regarding war and peace, the deliverances of conscience are for Einstein and the Quaker quite similar. As a matter of fact, Einstein feels that, in this respect, the Quakers are the only true Christians.

In the article "The Real Problem is in the Hearts of Men,"[13] Einstein clearly states his position regarding the atomic bomb and its immediate implications for our social conduct. In the light of new knowledge, that is, of atomic science, a world authority and an eventual world state are not only desirable but necessary for survival. "Today we must abandon competition and secure co-operation. . . ." "Past thinking and methods did not prevent world wars (but) future thinking *must* prevent wars." America's present superiority in the way of armaments gives her the responsibility of leading mankind's effort to surmount this crisis.

There is no foreseeable (military or scientific) defense against the bomb. "Our defense," says Einstein, "is not in armaments, nor in science, nor in going underground. Our defense is in law and order." Henceforth foreign policy must be judged by this consideration: Does it lead to law and order or to anarchy and death? Einstein does not believe that we can prepare for war and, at the same time, for world community. Likewise, he does not believe the "bomb secret" should be turned loose but asks, "Are we ardently seeking a world in which there will be no need for bombs or secrets, a world in which science and men will be free?" The whole problem, as Bernard Baruch has said, is not one of physics, but of ethics. There has been, it seems to Einstein, too much emphasis on legalisms and procedure. "It is easier," he says, "to denature plutonium than it is to denature the evil spirit of man."

Once again, Einstein insists on the need for supra-nationalism and the conception of world government which it implies; and, from his many statements, one infers that he has seriously considered the possibility of a world government. His optimism,

[13] NYT, 23 June 1946, sect. 6, p. 7, col. 42-43. All quotations up to footnote 14 are taken from this particular article.

therefore, should be judged accordingly. In working toward supra-nationalism as against nationalism, he avers, it is obvious that national spirit will survive longer in armies than anywhere else. Further, Einstein discusses problems involved in world organization. In mentioning Fremont Rider's book,[14] wherein the representation dilemma of the United Nations might be solved by granting it on the basis of education and literacy, Einstein agrees that backward nations, therefore, ought to be told: " 'to get more votes you must *earn* them.' "

Einstein flatly challenges the wisdom of having used the bomb over Japan. The old type of thinking, he asserts, can, of course, raise thousands of objections about the lack of "realism" in this simplicity of belief—in particular, concerning the proposal that the bomb should not have been used, but should have been demonstrated in some isolated area, where (say) the Japanese could have observed its effects. But the thinking evoked in such objections ignores psychological realities. All men fear atomic war. "Between the realities of man's true desires and the realities of man's danger, what are the obsolete 'realities' of protocol and military protection?" Mere reading about the bomb, claims Einstein, promotes knowledge in mind, but "only talk between men promotes feeling in the heart."

The bomb is a real threat, not only to politicians and generals, but to all mankind. Once more, Einstein says too much faith is placed in legalisms, treaties and mechanisms. In the final analysis, the decisions of the United Nations rest on those made in village squares. It is to village squares that facts of atomic energy must be carried. Public understanding of the dilemma facing mankind today is of the essence. Only then will decisions be the "embodiment of a message to humanity from a nation of human beings." The real problem is in the minds and hearts of men. Such is Albert Einstein's conviction.

Finally, I turn, for a moment, to Einstein's convictions as regards the relations between the USA and the USSR. There has been frequent criticism of the man on this score; but, it seems to me, it is not only more charitable to him, but far wiser

[14] *The Great Dilemma of World Organizations.*

for us, to know exactly what his position is before criticism comes.

First, Einstein believes that the Russia of today differs considerably from Nazi Germany, particularly as to basic aims and goals. Whereas Nazi Germany sought to "liquidate" the intellectual and his product, in Russia Einstein sees no similar trend. It is true, however, that the recent surge of nationalism in genetics—of "Russian genetics," if you like—perturbs him. But, it seems to me, he fails sufficiently to integrate this worry with other convictions like freedom for the intellectual worker, toleration of the truth no matter what its consequences, and reliance upon the dictates of conscience.

As far as nationalism is concerned, Einstein deplores it in any form. However, he fears the growth of nationalism in the United States more than in the Soviet Union; and this, because he observes among us a kind of mob hysteria, unbecoming to otherwise so great a nation.

In the same manner, Einstein faces the charge of "fellow traveling with Communist Front organizations." Of course, Einstein's insistence upon freedom of conscience, in and of itself necessarily differentiates his position from that of the Communist. In any case, he feels more nearly like Harold C. Urey, Nobel savant, than like the kindly, yet naïve, old man so many take Einstein to be in this matter. Compare Urey's recent statement: "I can't help it if the Communists fellow travel with me on the Spanish line. I do not fellow travel with them."[15] At times, nevertheless, Einstein seems to justify his membership in so many so-called "Communist Front" organizations simply as a reaction to the hysteria among people in this country. Still, one must not forget that Einstein is fully in sympathy with many minority groups and unpopular causes. Compare, for example, his espousal of liberal doctrines by approval of their liberal authors. Such men as Roosevelt, Willkie and Wallace, he thinks,[16] are in a category of men above the petty bickering of the day and without any selfish interest. One must agree, he

---

[15] *Chicago Daily Tribune*, 20 May 1949, p. 1, col. 6.
[16] NYT, 30 March 1948, p. 25, col. 4.

continues, with the fundamental premises of Henry Wallace's *Toward World Peace*, if one reads without prejudice. "This book is as clear, honest and unassuming as its author."

Finally, Einstein feels that his reaction to our hysteria is more than justified by the fact of our technological superiority over the Russians. Rightly or not, he believes that we are a nation superior to Russia in sheer productive and military strength. Hence, he argues, the guilt of the United States in the present world situation is greater than that of Russia. Being more powerful, we are actually in control of the situation; and, when crises arise, we are (therefore) more culpable than the Soviet Union.

Moreover, Einstein thinks that with our greater strength, we also have greater responsibility than Russia. The duty of a great nation is to accept its responsibility as a great nation. Likewise, the duty of the greatest nation is to acknowledge its place among nations; and Einstein is suggesting that, with our greatness of power, we should also accept our moral responsibility. If we are the most powerful nation, let us try to be the most moral by accepting, with humility and wisdom, this greatness so recently thrust upon us. And, of course, the only genuine resolution, for Einstein, of the USA-USSR problem is premised upon supra-national grounds. Before cavalierly criticizing Einstein as social thinker, one should remember his statement that there is "no other salvation for civilization and even for the human race than the creation of a world government with security on the basis of law."[17]

JUDAISM AND ZIONISM

It seems to me that Einstein's own religious conviction is not at all unrelated to his social philosophy. Moreover, his belief in Zionism is far from irrelevant to his ethical outlook. In reading certain passages from his essays and speeches, I cannot help but think that one does substantial injustice to Einstein's social philosophy if he neglects Einstein's religious beliefs. To a brief sketch of such of his beliefs I now turn.

[17] *Ibid.*, 15 September 1945, p. 11, col. 6.

"In the philosophical sense," says Einstein, "there is, in my opinion, no specifically Jewish point of view. Judaism seems to me to be concerned almost exclusively with the moral attitude in life and to life."[18] "Judaism is not a creed: the Jewish God is simply a negation of superstition, an imaginary result of its elimination. It is also an attempt to base the moral law on fear, a regrettable and discreditable attempt."[19]

"Judaism is thus," Einstein believes, "no transcendental religion; it is concerned with life as we live it and as we can, to a certain extent, grasp it, and nothing else." ". . . no faith but the sanctification of life in a supra-personal sense is demanded of the Jew."[20] The "sanctity of life" and the "sanctification of life" are, claims Einstein, the fundamental principles of Judaism. " 'When a Jew . . . says that he's going hunting to amuse himself, he lies.'—Walter Rathenau. The Jewish sense of the sanctity of life could not be more simply expressed."[21] In defense of Judaism, Einstein has this to say: ". . . it is time to remind the western world that it owes to the Jewish people (a) its religion and therewith its most valuable moral ideals, and (b) to a large extent, the resurrection of the world of Greek thought."[22]

In another place, Einstein holds that "the insistence on the solidarity of all human beings finds still stronger expression [in Judaism], and it is no mere chance that the demands of Socialism were for the most part first raised by Jews."[23]

Einstein's conception of God has been the subject of considerable conjecture. On more than one occasion, he has made himself quite clear as to his conviction in the matter. "I believe in Spinoza's God who reveals Himself in the orderly harmony of what exists, not in a God who concerns himself with

[18] Albert Einstein, *The World as I See It* (hereafter *World*), (New York, 1934), by Covici Friede, Inc., 143. Originally published as *Mein Weltbild*, 1933, by Querido Verlag, Amsterdam. Translated from the German by Alan Harris; Compare items 361-363 in Bibliography of this Volume.

[19] *Ibid.*, 144.

[20] *Ibid.*, 144-145.

[21] *Ibid.*, 146.

[22] *Ibid.*, xv.

[23] *Ibid.*, 146.

fates and actions of Human beings."[24] Of this cablegram, Rabbi Herbert S. Goldstein drew the following interpretation. He made use of it to substantiate his own belief that Einstein was neither atheist nor agnostic. Says Rabbi Goldstein: "Einstein points to a unity." If carried out to its logical conclusion, his theory "would bring to mankind a scientific formula for monotheism."[25]

In one place, Einstein has explicitly stated his conception of religion in general. There he speaks of three conceptions, each one differing in essential respects. First, he distinguishes the most primitive conception of religion, with its anthropocentric God. Second, ". . . on the higher levels of social life, the religion of morality predominates."[26] Third, there is what Einstein thinks of as "cosmic religious feeling."[27] It is this last conception of religion in which Einstein believes; or, rather, it is this sort of religion which he lives.

For a moment, I turn to Einstein's convictions about Zionism. "The object which the leaders of Zionism have before their eyes," he says, "is not a political but a social and cultural one."[28] "Palestine is not primarily a place of refuge for the Jews of Eastern Europe but the embodiment of the reawakening corporate spirit of the whole Jewish nation."[29] "The first step in that direction [i.e., toward 'mutual toleration and respect'] is that we Jews should once more become conscious of our existence as a nationality and regain the self-respect that is necessary to a healthy existence."[30]

"It is not enough," he continues, "for us to play a part as individuals in the cultural development of the human race, we must also tackle tasks which only nations as a whole can perform. Only so can the Jews regain social health." And, with these words, Einstein concludes: "It is from this point of view that I would have you look at the Zionist movement. Today

[24] NYT, 25 April 1929, p. 60, col. 4.
[25] Ibid.
[26] World, 263.
[27] Ibid., 264-265.
[28] Ibid., 152.
[29] Ibid., 154.
[30] Ibid., 156.

history has assigned to us the task of taking an active part in the economic and cultural reconstruction of our native land."[31]

Such are some of the ethical and religious convictions of Albert Einstein. In this sketch, I have made no attempt to indicate in what specific ways these beliefs comprise a consistent and adequate social ethic. I have, rather, only outlined the main trends of Einstein's thought regarding social issues and social action. Such a catalogue of his convictions serves to document the breadth of thought characteristic of the man. What is so commendable in Einstein is that, as intellectual worker in his rôle as citizen, he has seriously faced so many of the vital social questions of his day. The fact that, in so doing, he follows his own precepts demonstrates, as nothing else could, the sincerity of his concern with issues in social ethics.

VIRGIL G. HINSHAW, JR.

DEPARTMENT OF PHILOSOPHY
THE OHIO STATE UNIVERSITY

[31] *Ibid.*, 157. These remarks were made sometime during or before 1933, the publication date of *Mein Weltbild*. Compare footnote 18, above.

Albert Einstein

REPLY TO CRITICISMS

REMARKS CONCERNING THE ESSAYS BROUGHT TOGETHER IN THIS CO-OPERATIVE VOLUME*

BY WAY of introduction I must remark that it was not easy for me to do justice to the task of expressing myself concerning the essays contained in this volume. The reason lies in the fact that the essays refer to entirely too many subjects, which, at the present state of our knowledge, are only loosely connected with each other. I first attempted to discuss the essays individually. However, I abandoned this procedure because nothing even approximately homogeneous resulted, so that the reading of it could hardly have been either useful or enjoyable. I finally decided, therefore, to order these remarks, as far as possible, according to topical considerations.

Furthermore, after some vain efforts, I discovered that the mentality which underlies a few of the essays differs so radically from my own, that I am incapable of saying anything useful about them. This is not to be interpreted that I regard those essays—insofar as their content is at all meaningful to me—less highly than I do those which lie closer to my own ways of thinking, to which [latter] I dedicate the following remarks.

To begin with I refer to the essays of Wolfgang Pauli and Max Born. They describe the content of my work concerning quanta and statistics in general in their inner consistency and in their participation in the evolution of physics during the last half century. It is meritorious that they have done this: For only those who have successfully wrestled with the problematic situations of their own age can have a deep insight into those situations; unlike the later historian, who finds it difficult to make abstractions from those concepts and views which appear to his generation as established, or even as self-evident. Both authors

* Translated (from the German typescript) by Paul Arthur Schilpp.

deprecate the fact that I reject the basic idea of contemporary statistical quantum theory, insofar as I do not believe that this fundamental concept will provide a useful basis for the whole of physics. More of this later.

I now come to what is probably the most interesting subject which absolutely must be discussed in connection with the detailed arguments of my highly esteemed colleagues Born, Pauli, Heitler, Bohr, and Margenau. They are all firmly convinced that the riddle of the double nature of all corpuscles (corpuscular and undulatory character) has in essence found its final solution in the statistical quantum theory. On the strength of the successes of this theory they consider it proved that a theoretically complete description of a system can, in essence, involve only statistical assertions concerning the measurable quantities of this system. They are apparently all of the opinion that Heisenberg's indeterminacy-relation (the correctness of which is, from my own point of view, rightfully regarded as finally demonstrated) is essentially prejudicial in favor of the character of all thinkable reasonable physical theories in the mentioned sense. In what follows I wish to adduce reasons which keep me from falling in line with the opinion of almost all contemporary theoretical physicists. I am, in fact, firmly convinced that the essentially statistical character of contemporary quantum theory is solely to be ascribed to the fact that this [theory] operates with an incomplete description of physical systems.

Above all, however, the reader should be convinced that I fully recognize the very important progress which the statistical quantum theory has brought to theoretical physics. In the field of *mechanical* problems—i.e., wherever it is possible to consider the interaction of structures and of their parts with sufficient accuracy by postulating a potential energy between material points—[this theory] even now presents a system which, in its closed character, correctly describes the empirical relations between statable phenomena as they were theoretically to be expected. This theory is until now the only one which unites the corpuscular and undulatory dual character of matter in a logically satisfactory fashion; and the (testable) relations, which are contained in it, are, within the natural limits fixed by the indeterminacy-relation, *complete*. The formal relations which are given in this theory—i.e., its entire mathematical formalism—will probably have to be contained, in the form of logical inferences, in every useful future theory.

What does not satisfy me in that theory, from the standpoint of principle, is its attitude towards that which appears to me to be the programmatic aim of all physics: the complete description of any (individual) real situation (as it supposedly exists irrespective of any act of observation or substantiation). Whenever the positivistically inclined modern physicist hears such a formulation his reaction is that of a pitying smile. He says to himself: "there we have the naked formulation of a metaphysical prejudice, empty of content, a prejudice, moreover, the conquest of which constitutes the major epistemological achievement of physicists within the last quarter-century. Has any man ever perceived a 'real physical situation'? How is it possible that a reasonable person could today still believe that he can refute our essential knowledge and understanding by drawing up such a bloodless ghost?" Patience! The above laconic characterization was not meant to convince anyone; it was merely to indicate the point of view around which the following elementary considerations freely group themselves. In doing this I shall proceed as follows: I shall first of all show in simple special cases what seems essential to me, and then I shall make a few remarks about some more general ideas which are involved.

We consider as a physical system, in the first instance, a radioactive atom of definite average decay time, which is practically exactly localized at a point of the co-ordinate system. The radioactive process consists in the emission of a (comparatively light) particle. For the sake of simplicity we neglect the motion of the residual atom after the disintegration-process. Then it is possible for us, following Gamow, to replace the rest of the atom by a space of atomic order of magnitude, surrounded by a closed potential energy barrier which, at a time $t = 0$, encloses the particle to be emitted. The radioactive process thus schematized is then, as is well known, to be described—in the sense of elementary quantum mechanics—by a ψ-function in three dimensions, which at the time $t = 0$ is different from zero only inside of the barrier, but which, for positive times, expands into the outer space. This ψ-function yields the probability that the particle, at some chosen instant, is actually in a chosen part of space (i.e., is actually found there by a measurement of position). On the other hand, the ψ-function does not imply any assertion *concerning the time instant of the disintegration* of the radioactive atom.

Now we raise the question: Can this theoretical description be taken as the *complete* description of the disintegration of a single individual atom? The immediately plausible answer is: No. For one is, first of all, inclined to assume that the individual atom decays at a definite time; however, such a definite time-value is not implied in the description by the ψ-function. If, therefore, the individual atom has a definite disintegration-time, then as regards the individual atom its description by means of the ψ-function must be interpreted as an incomplete description. In this case the ψ-function is to be taken as the description, not of a singular system, but of an ideal ensemble of systems. In this case one is driven to the conviction that a complete description of a single system should, after all, be possible; but for such complete description there is no room in the conceptual world of statistical quantum theory.

To this the quantum theorist will reply: This consideration stands and falls with the assertion that there actually is such a thing as a definite time of disintegration of the individual atom (an instant of time existing independently of any observation). But this assertion is, from my point of view, not merely arbitrary but actually meaningless. The assertion of the existence of a definite time-instant for the disintegration makes sense only if I can in principle determine this time-instant empirically. Such an assertion, however, (which, finally, leads to the attempt to prove the existence of the particle outside of the force barrier), involves a definite disturbance of the system in which we are interested; so that the result of the determination does not permit a conclusion concerning the status of the undisturbed system. The supposition, therefore, that a radioactive atom has a definite disintegration-time is not justified by anything whatsoever; it is, therefore, not demonstrated either that the ψ-function can not be conceived as a complete description of the individual system. The entire alleged difficulty proceeds from the fact that one postulates something not observable as "real." (This the answer of the quantum theorist.)

What I dislike in this kind of argumentation is the basic positivistic attitude, which from my point of view is untenable, and which seems to me to come to the same thing as Berkeley's principle, *esse est percipi*. "Being" is always something which is mentally constructed by us, that is, something which we freely posit (in the logical sense). The justification of such constructs does not lie in their derivation from what is given by the senses. Such a type of derivation (in the sense of logical deducibility) is nowhere to be had, not even in the domain of pre-scientific thinking. The justification of the constructs, which represent "reality" for us, lies alone in their quality of making intelligible what is sensorily given (the vague character of this expression is here forced upon me by my striving for brevity). Applied to the specifically chosen example this consideration tells us the following:

One may not merely ask: "Does a definite time instant for the transformation of a single atom exist?" but rather: "Is it, within the framework of our theoretical total construction, reasonable to posit the existence of a definite point of time for the transformation of a single atom?" One may not even ask what this assertion *means*. One can only ask whether such a proposition, within the framework of the chosen conceptual system— with a view to its ability to grasp theoretically what is empirically given—is reasonable or not.

Insofar, then, as a quantum-theoretician takes the position that the description by means of a ψ-function refers only to an ideal systematic totality but in no wise to the individual system, he may calmly assume a definite point of time for the transformation. But, if he represents the assumption that his description by way of the ψ-function is to be taken as the *complete* description of the individual system, then he must reject the postulation of a specific decay-time. He can justifiably point to the fact that a determination of the instant of disintegration is not possible on an isolated system, but would require disturbances of such a character that they must not be neglected in the critical examination of the situation. It would, for example, not be possible to conclude from the empirical statement that the transformation has already taken place, that this would have been the case if the disturbances of the system had not taken place.

As far as I know, it was E. Schrödinger who first called attention to a modification of this consideration, which shows an interpretation of this type to be impracticable. Rather than considering a system which comprises only a radioactive atom (and its process of transformation), one considers a system which includes also the means for ascertaining the radioactive transformation—for example, a Geiger-counter with automatic registration-mechanism. Let this latter include a registration-strip, moved by a clockwork, upon which a mark is made by tripping the counter. True, from the point of view of quantum mechanics this total system is very complex and its configuration space is of very high dimension. But there is in principle no objection to treating this entire system from the standpoint of quantum mechanics. Here too the theory determines the probability of each configuration of all its co-ordinates for every time instant. If one considers all configurations of the co-ordinates, for a time large compared with the average decay-time of the radioactive atom, there will be (at most) *one* such registration-mark on the paper strip. To each co-ordinate-configuration corresponds a definite position of the mark on the paper strip. But, inasmuch as the theory yields only the relative probability of the thinkable co-ordinate-configurations, it also offers only relative probabilities for the positions of the mark on the paperstrip, but no definite location for this mark.

In this consideration the location of the mark on the strip plays the rôle played in the original consideration by the time of the disintegration. The reason for the introduction of the system supplemented by the registration-mechanism lies in the following. The location of the mark on the registration-strip is a fact which belongs entirely within the sphere of macroscopic concepts, in contradistinction to the instant of disintegration of a single atom. If we attempt [to work with] the interpretation that the quantum-theoretical description is to be understood as a complete description of the individual system, we are forced to the interpretation that the location of the mark on the strip is nothing which belongs to the system *per se*, but that the existence of that location is essentially dependent upon the carrying out of an observation made on the registration-strip. Such an interpretation is certainly by no means absurd from a purely logical standpoint; yet there is hardly likely to be anyone who would be inclined to consider it seriously. For, in the macroscopic sphere it simply is considered certain that one must adhere to the program of a realistic description in space and time; whereas in the sphere of microscopic situations one is more readily inclined to give up, or at least to modify, this program.

This discussion was only to bring out the following. One arrives at very implausible theoretical conceptions, if one attempts to maintain the thesis that the statistical quantum theory is in principle capable of producing a complete description of an individual physical system. On the other hand, those difficulties of theoretical interpretation disappear, if one views the quantum-mechanical description as the description of ensembles of systems.

I reached this conclusion as the result of quite different types of considerations. I am convinced that everyone who will take the trouble to carry through such reflections conscientiously will find himself finally driven to this interpretation of quantum-theoretical description (the ψ-function is to be understood as the description not of a single system but of an ensemble of systems).

Roughly stated the conclusion is this: Within the framework of statistical quantum theory there is no such thing as a complete description of the individual system. More cautiously it might be put as follows: The attempt to conceive the quantum-theoretical description as the complete description of the individual systems leads to unnatural theoretical interpretations, which become immediately unnecessary if one accepts the interpretation that the description refers to ensembles of systems and not to individual systems. In that case the whole "egg-walking" performed in order to avoid the "physically real" becomes superfluous. There exists, however, a simple psychological reason for the fact that this most nearly obvious interpretation is being shunned. For if the statistical quantum theory does not pretend to describe the individual system (and its development in time) completely, it appears unavoidable to look elsewhere for a complete description of the individual system; in doing so it would be clear from the very beginning that the elements of such a description are not contained within the conceptual scheme of the statistical quantum theory. With this one would admit that, in principle, this scheme could not serve as the basis of theoretical physics. Assuming the success of efforts to accomplish a complete physical description, the statistical quantum theory would, within the framework of future physics, take an approximately analogous position to the statistical mechanics within the framework of classical mechanics. I am rather firmly convinced that the development of theoretical physics will be of this type; but the path will be lengthy and difficult.

I now imagine a quantum theoretician who may even admit that the quantum-theoretical description refers to ensembles of systems and not to individual systems, but who, nevertheless, clings to the idea that the type of description of the statistical quantum theory will, in its essential features, be retained in the future. He may argue as follows: True, I admit that the quantum-theoretical description is an incomplete description of the individual system. I even admit that a complete theoretical description is, in principle, thinkable. But I consider it proven that the search for such a complete description would be aimless. For the lawfulness of nature is thus constituted that the laws can be completely and suitably formulated within the framework of our incomplete description.

To this I can only reply as follows: Your point of view—taken as theoretical possibility—is incontestable. For me, however, the expectation that the adequate formulation of the universal laws involves the use of *all* conceptual elements which are necessary for a complete description, is more natural. It is furthermore not at all surprising that, by using an incomplete description, (in the main) only statistical statements can be obtained out of such description. If it should be possible to move forward to a complete description, it is likely that the laws would represent relations among all the conceptual elements of this description which, *per se*, have nothing to do with statistics.

A few more remarks of a general nature concerning concepts and [also] concerning the insinuation that a concept—for example that of the real—is something metaphysical (and therefore to be rejected). A basic conceptual distinction, which is a necessary prerequisite of scientific and pre-scientific thinking, is the distinction between "sense-impressions" (and the recollection of such) on the one hand and mere ideas on the other. There is no such thing as a conceptual definition of this distinction (aside from circular definitions, i.e., of such as make a hidden use of the object to be defined). Nor can it be maintained that at the base of this distinction there is a type of evidence, such as underlies, for example, the distinction between red and blue. Yet, one needs this distinction in order to be able to overcome solipsism. Solution: we shall make use of this distinction unconcerned with the reproach that, in doing so, we are guilty of the metaphysical "original sin." We regard the distinction as a category which we use in order that we might the better find our way in the world of immediate sensations. The "sense" and the justification of this distinction lies simply in this achievement. But this is only a first step. We represent the sense-impressions as conditioned by an "objective" and by a "subjective" factor. For this conceptual distinction there also is no logical-philosophical justification. But if we reject it, we cannot escape solipsism. It is also the presupposition of every kind of physical thinking. Here too, the only justification lies in its usefulness. We are here concerned with "categories" or schemes of thought, the selection of which is, in principle, entirely open to us and whose qualification can only be judged by the degree to which its use contributes to making the totality of the contents of consciousness "intelligible." The above mentioned "objective factor" is the totality of such concepts and conceptual relations as are thought of as independent of experience, viz., of perceptions. So long as we move within the thus programmatically fixed sphere of thought we are thinking physically. Insofar as physical thinking justifies itself, in the more than once indicated sense, by its ability to grasp experiences intellectually, we regard it as "knowledge of the real."

After what has been said, the "real" in physics is to be taken as a type of program, to which we are, however, not forced to cling *a priori*. No one is likely to be inclined to attempt to give up this program within the realm of the "macroscopic" (location of the mark on the paperstrip "real"). But the "macroscopic" and the "microscopic" are so inter-related that it appears impracticable to give up this program in the "microscopic" alone. Nor can I see any occasion anywhere within the observable facts of the quantum-field for doing so, unless, indeed, one clings *a priori* to the thesis that the description of nature by the statistical scheme of quantum-mechanics is final.

The theoretical attitude here advocated is distinct from that of Kant only by the fact that we do not conceive of the "categories" as unalterable (conditioned by the nature of the understanding) but as (in the logical sense) free conventions. They appear to be *a priori* only insofar as thinking without the positing of categories and of concepts in general would be as impossible as is breathing in a vacuum.

From these meager remarks one will see that to me it must seem a mistake to permit theoretical description to be directly dependent upon acts of empirical assertions, as it seems to me to be intended [for example] in Bohr's principle of complementarity, the sharp formulation of which, moreover, I have been unable to achieve despite much effort which I have expended on it. From my point of view [such] statements or measurements can occur only as special instances, viz., parts, of physical description, to which I cannot ascribe any exceptional position above the rest.

The above mentioned essays by Bohr and Pauli contain a historical appreciation of my efforts in the area of physical statistics and quanta and, in addition, an accusation which is brought forward in the friendliest of fashion. In briefest formulation this latter runs as follows: "Rigid adherence to classical theory." This accusation demands either a defense or the confession of guilt. The one or the other is, however, being rendered much more difficult because it is by no means immediately clear what is meant by "classical theory." Newton's theory deserves the name of a classical theory. It has nevertheless been abandoned since Maxwell and Hertz have shown that the idea of forces at a distance has to be relinquished and that one cannot manage without the idea of continuous "fields." The opinion that continuous fields are to be viewed as the only acceptable basic concepts, which must also [be assumed to] underlie the theory of the material particles, soon won out. Now this conception became, so to speak, "classical;" but a proper, and in principle complete, *theory* has not grown out of it. Maxwell's theory of the electric field remained a torso, because it was unable to set up laws for the behavior of electric density, without which there can, of course, be no such thing as an electro-magnetic field. Analogously the general theory of relativity furnished then a field theory of gravitation, but no theory of the field-creating masses. (These remarks presuppose it as self-evident that a field-theory may not contain any singularities, i.e., any positions or parts in space in which the field-laws are not valid.)

Consequently there is, strictly speaking, today no such thing as a classical field-theory; one can, therefore, also not rigidly adhere to it. Nevertheless, field-theory does exist as a program: "Continuous functions in the four-dimensional [continuum] as basic concepts of the theory." Rigid adherence to this program can rightfully be asserted of me. The deeper ground for this lies in the following: The theory of gravitation showed me that the non-linearity of these equations results in the fact that this theory yields interactions among structures (localized things) at all. But the theoretical search for non-linear equations is hopeless (because of too great variety of possibilities), if one does not use the general principle of relativity (invariance under general continuous co-ordinate-transformations). In the meantime, however, it does not seem possible to formulate this principle, if one seeks to deviate from the above program. Herein lies a coercion which I cannot evade. This for my justification.

Nevertheless I am forced to weaken this justification by a confession. If one disregards quantum structure, one can justify the introduction of the g_{ik} "operationally" by pointing to the fact that one can hardly doubt the physical reality of the elementary light cone which belongs to a point. In doing so one implicitly makes use of the existence of an arbitrarily sharp optical signal. Such a signal, however, as regards the quantum facts, involves infinitely high frequencies and energies, and therefore a complete destruction of the field to be determined. That kind of a physical justification for the introduction of the g_{ik} falls by the wayside, unless one limits himself to the "macroscopic." The application of the formal basis of the general theory of relativity to the "microscopic" can, therefore, be based only upon the fact that that tensor is the formally simplest covariant structure which can come under consideration. Such argumentation, however, carries no weight with anyone who doubts that we have to adhere to the continuum at all. All honor to his doubt—but where else is there a passable road?

Now I come to the theme of the relation of the theory of relativity to philosophy. Here it is Reichenbach's piece of work which, by the precision of deductions and by the sharpness of his assertions, irresistibly invites a brief commentary. Robertson's lucid discussion also is interesting mainly from the standpoint of general epistemology, although it limits itself to the narrower theme of "the theory of relativity and geometry." To the question: Do you consider true what Reichenbach has here asserted, I can answer only with Pilate's famous question: "What is truth?"

Let us first take a good look at the question: Is a geometry —looked at from the physical point of view—verifiable (viz., falsifiable) or not? Reichenbach, together with Helmholtz, says: Yes, provided that the empirically given solid body realizes the concept of "distance." Poincaré says no and consequently is condemned by Reichenbach. Now the following short conversation takes place:

Poincaré: The empirically given bodies are not rigid, and consequently can not be used for the embodiment of geometric intervals. Therefore, the theorems of geometry are not verifiable.

Reichenbach: I admit that there are no bodies which can be *immediately* adduced for the "real definition" of the interval. Nevertheless, this real definition can be achieved by taking the thermal volume-dependence, elasticity, electro- and magneto-striction, etc., into consideration. That this is really [and] without contradiction possible, classical physics has surely demonstrated.

Poincaré: In gaining the real definition improved by yourself you have made use of physical laws, the formulation of which presupposes (in this case) Euclidean geometry. The verification, of which you have spoken, refers, therefore, not merely to geometry but to the entire system of physical laws which constitute its foundation. An examination of geometry by itself is consequently not thinkable.—Why should it consequently not be entirely up to me to choose geometry according to my own convenience (i.e., Euclidean) and to fit the remaining (in the usual sense "physical") laws to this choice in such manner that there can arise no contradiction of the whole with experience?

(The conversation cannot be continued in this fashion because the respect of the [present] writer for Poincaré's superiority as thinker and author does not permit it; in what follows therefore, an anonymous non-positivist is substituted for Poincaré.—)

Reichenbach: There is something quite attractive in this conception. But, on the other hand, it is noteworthy that the adherence to the objective meaning of length and to the interpretation of the differences of co-ordinates as distances (in prerelativistic physics) has not led to complications. Should we not, on the basis of this astounding fact, be justified in operating further at least tentatively with the concept of the measurable length, as if there were such things as rigid measuring-rods? In any case it would have been impossible for Einstein *de facto* (even if not theoretically) to set up the theory of general relativity, if he had not adhered to the objective meaning of length.

Against Poincaré's suggestion it is to be pointed out that what really matters is not merely the greatest possible simplicity of the geometry alone, but rather the greatest possible simplicity of all of physics (inclusive of geometry). This is what is, in the first instance, involved in the fact that today we must decline as unsuitable the suggestion to adhere to Euclidean geometry.

Non-Positivist: If, under the stated circumstances, you hold distance to be a legitimate concept, how then is it with your basic principle (meaning = verifiability)? Do you not have to reach the point where you must deny the meaning of geometrical concepts and theorems and to acknowledge meaning only within the completely developed theory of relativity (which, however, does not yet exist at all as a finished product)? Do you not have to admit that, in your sense of the word, no "meaning" can be attributed to the individual concepts and assertions of a physical theory at all, and to the entire system only insofar as it makes what is given in experience "intelligible?" Why do the individual concepts which occur in a theory require any specific justification anyway, if they are only indispensable within the framework of the logical structure of the theory, and the theory only in its entirety validates itself?

It seems to me, moreover, that you have not at all done justice to the really significant philosophical achievement of Kant. From Hume Kant had learned that there are concepts (as, for example, that of causal connection), which play a dominating rôle in our thinking, and which, nevertheless, can not be deduced by means of a logical process from the empirically given (a fact which several empiricists recognize, it is true, but seem always again to forget). What justifies the use of such concepts? Suppose he had replied in this sense: Thinking is necessary in order to understand the empirically given, *and concepts and "categories" are necessary as indispensable elements of thinking.* If he had remained satisfied with this type of an answer, he would have avoided scepticism and you would not have been able to find fault with him. He, however, was misled by the erroneous opinion—difficult to avoid in his time —that Euclidean geometry is necessary to thinking and offers *assured* (i.e., not dependent upon sensory experience) knowledge concerning the objects of "external" perception. From this easily understandable error he concluded the existence of synthetic judgments *a priori*, which are produced by the reason alone, and which, consequently, can lay claim to absolute validity. I think your censure is directed less against Kant himself than against those who today still adhere to the errors of "synthetic judgments *a priori*." —

I can hardly think of anything more stimulating as the basis for discussion in an epistemological seminar than this brief essay by Reichenbach (best taken together with Robertson's essay).

What has been discussed thus far is closely related to Bridgman's essay, so that it will be possible for me to express myself quite briefly without having to harbor too much fear that I shall be misunderstood. In order to be able to consider a logical system as physical theory it is not necessary to demand that all of its assertions can be independently interpreted and "tested" "operationally;" *de facto* this has never yet been achieved by any theory and can not at all be achieved. In order to be able to consider a theory as a *physical* theory it is only necessary that it implies empirically testable assertions in general.

This formulation is insofar entirely unprecise as "testability" is a quality which refers not merely to the assertion itself but also to the co-ordination of concepts, contained in it, with experience. But it is probably hardly necessary for me to enter upon a discussion of this ticklish problem, inasmuch as it is not likely that there exist any essential differences of opinion at this point. —

Margenau. This essay contains several original specific remarks, which I must consider separately:

To his Sec. 1: "Einstein's position . . . contains features of rationalism and extreme empiricism. . . ." This remark is entirely correct. From whence comes this fluctuation? A logical conceptual system is physics insofar as its concepts and assertions are necessarily brought into relationship with the world of experiences. Whoever desires to set up such a system will find a dangerous obstacle in arbitrary choice (*embarras de richesse*). This is why he seeks to connect his concepts as directly and necessarily as possible with the world of experience. In this case his attitude is empirical. This path is often fruitful, but it is always open to doubt, because the specific concept and the individual assertion can, after all, assert something confronted by the empirically given only in connection with the entire system. He then recognizes that there exists no logical path from the empirically given to that conceptual world. His attitude becomes then more nearly rationalistic, because he recognizes the logical independence of the system. The danger in this attitude lies in the fact that in the search for the system one can lose every contact with the world of experience. A wavering between these extremes appears to me unavoidable.

To his Sec. 2: I did not grow up in the Kantian tradition, but came to understand the truly valuable which is to be found in his doctrine, alongside of errors which today are quite obvious, only quite late. It is contained in the sentence: "The real is not given to us, but put to us (*aufgegeben*) (by way of a riddle)." This obviously means: There is such a thing as a conceptual construction for the grasping of the inter-personal, the authority of which lies purely in its validation. This conceptual construction refers precisely to the "real" (by definition), and every further question concerning the "nature of the real" appears empty.

To his Sec. 4: This discussion has not convinced me at all. For it is clear *per se* that every magnitude and every assertion of a theory lays claim to "objective meaning" (within the framework of the theory). A problem arises only when we ascribe group-characteristics to a theory, i.e., if we assume or postulate that the same physical situation admits of several ways of description, each of which is to be viewed as equally justified. For in this case we obviously cannot ascribe complete objective meaning (for example the x-component of the velocity of a particle or its *x*-co-ordinates) to the individual (not eliminable) magnitudes. In this case, which has always existed in physics, we have to limt ourselves to ascribing objective meaning to the general laws of the theory, i.e., we have to demand that these laws are valid for every description of the system which is recognized as justified by the group. It is, therefore, not true that "objectivity" presupposes a group-characteristic, but that the group-characteristic forces a refinement of the concept of objectivity. The positing of group characteristics is heuristically so important for theory, because this characteristic always considerably limits the variety of the mathematically meaningful laws.

Now there follows a claim that the group-characteristics determine that the laws must have the form of differential equations; I can not at all see this. Then Margenau insists that the laws expressed by way of the differential equations (especially the partial ones) are "least specific." Upon what does he base this contention? If they could be proved to be correct, it is true that the attempt to ground physics upon differential equations would then turn out to be hopeless. We are, however, far from being able to judge whether differential laws of the type to be considered have any solutions at all which are everywhere singularity-free; and, if so, whether there are too many such solutions.

And now just a remark concerning the discussions about the Einstein-Podolski-Rosen Paradox. I do not think that Margenau's defense of the "orthodox" ("orthodox" refers to the thesis that the ψ-function characterizes the individual system *exhaustively*) quantum position hits the essential [aspects]. Of the "orthodox" quantum theoreticians whose position I know, Niels Bohr's seems to me to come nearest to doing justice to the problem. Translated into my own way of putting it, he argues as follows:

If the partial systems *A* and *B* form a total system which is described by its ψ-function $\psi/(AB)$, there is no reason why any mutually independent existence (state of reality) should be ascribed to the partial systems *A* and *B* viewed separately, *not even if the partial systems are spatially separated from each other at the particular time under consideration.* The assertion that, in this latter case, the real situation of B could not be (directly) influenced by any measurement taken on A is, therefore, within the framework of quantum theory, unfounded and (as the paradox shows) unacceptable.

By this way of looking at the matter it becomes evident that the paradox forces us to relinquish one of the following two assertions:

(1) the description by means of the ψ-function is *complete*
(2) the real states of spatially separated objects are independent of each other.

On the other hand, it is possible to adhere to (2), if one regards the ψ-function as the description of a (statistical) ensemble of systems (and therefore relinquishes (1)). However, this view blasts the framework of the "orthodox quantum theory."

One more remark to Margenau's Sec. 7. In the characterization of quantum mechanics the brief little sentence will be found: "on the classical level it corresponds to ordinary dynamics." This is entirely correct—*cum grano salis;* and it is precisely this *granum salis* which is significant for the question of interpretation.

If our concern is with macroscopic masses (billiard balls or stars), we are operating with very short de Broglie-waves, which are determinative for the behavior of the center of gravity of such masses. This is the reason why it is possible to arrange the quantum-theoretical description for a reasonable time in such a manner that for the macroscopic way of viewing things, it becomes sufficiently precise in position as well as in momentum. It is true also that this sharpness remains for a long time and that the quasi-points thus represented behave just like the mass-points of classical mechanics. However, the theory shows also that, after a sufficiently long time, the point-like character of the ψ-function is completely lost to the center of gravity-co-ordinates, so that one can no longer speak of any quasi-localisation of the centers of gravity. The picture then becomes, for example in the case of a single macro-mass-point, quite similar to that involved in a single free electron.

If now, in accordance with the orthodox position, I view the ψ-function as the complete description of a real matter of fact for the individual case, I cannot but consider the essentially unlimited lack of sharpness of the position of the (macroscopic) body as *real*. On the other hand, however, we know that, by illuminating the body by means of a lantern at rest against the system of co-ordinates, we get a (macroscopically judged) sharp determination of position. In order to comprehend this I must assume that that sharply defined position is determined not merely by the real situation of the observed body, but also by the act of illumination. This is again a paradox (similar to the mark on the paperstrip in the above mentioned example). The spook disappears only if one relinquishes the orthodox standpoint, according to which the ψ-function is accepted as a complete description of the single system.

It may appear as if all such considerations were just superfluous learned hairsplitting, which have nothing to do with physics proper. However, it depends precisely upon such considerations in which direction one believes one must look for the future conceptual basis of physics.

I close these expositions, which have grown rather lengthy, concerning the interpretation of quantum theory with the reproduction of a brief conversation which I had with an important theoretical physicist. He: "I am inclined to believe in telepathy." I: "This has probably more to do with physics than with psychology." He: "Yes." —

The essays by Lenzen and Northrop both aim to treat my occasional utterances of epistemological content systematically. From those utterances Lenzen constructs a synoptic total picture, in which what is missing in the utterances is carefully and with delicacy of feeling supplied. Everything said therein appears to me convincing and correct. Northrop uses these utterances as point of departure for a comparative critique of the major epistemological systems. I see in this critique a masterpiece of unbiased thinking and concise discussion, which nowhere permits itself to be diverted from the essential.

The reciprocal relationship of epistemology and science is of noteworthy kind. They are dependent upon each other. Epistemology without contact with science becomes an empty scheme. Science without epistemology is—insofar as it is thinkable at all—primitive and muddled. However, no sooner has the epistemologist, who is seeking a clear system, fought his way through to such a system, than he is inclined to interpret the thought-content of science in the sense of his system and to reject whatever does not fit into his system. The scientist, however, cannot afford to carry his striving for epistemological systematic that far. He accepts gratefully the epistemological conceptual analysis; but the external conditions, which are set for him by the facts of experience, do not permit him to let himself be too much restricted in the construction of his conceptual world by the adherence to an epistemological system. He therefore must appear to the systematic epistemologist as a type of unscrupulous opportunist: he appears as *realist* insofar as he seeks to describe a world independent of the acts of perception; as *idealist* insofar as he looks upon the concepts and theories as the free inventions of the human spirit (not logically derivable from what is empirically given); as *positivist* insofar as he considers his concepts and theories justified *only* to the extent to which they furnish a logical representation of relations among sensory experiences. He may even appear as *Platonist* or *Pythagorean* insofar as he considers the viewpoint of logical simplicity as an indispensable and effective tool of his research.

All of this is splendidly elucidated in Lenzen's and Northrop's essays. —— ——

And now a few remarks concerning the essays by E. A. Milne, G. Lemaître, and L. Infeld as concerns the cosmological problem:

Concerning Milne's ingenious reflections I can only say that I find their theoretical basis too narrow. From my point of view one cannot arrive, by way of theory, at any at least somewhat reliable results in the field of cosmology, if one makes no use of the principle of general relativity.

As concerns Lemaître's arguments in favor of the so-called "cosmological constant" in the equations of gravitation, I must admit that these arguments do not appear to me as sufficiently convincing in view of the present state of our knowledge.

The introduction of such a constant implies a considerable

renunciation of the logical simplicity of theory, a renunciation which appeared to me unavoidable only so long as one had no reason to doubt the essentially static nature of space. After Hubble's discovery of the "expansion" of the stellar system, and since Friedmann's discovery that the unsupplemented equations involve the possibility of the existence of an average (positive) density of matter in an expanding universe, the introduction of such a constant appears to me, from the theoretical standpoint, at present unjustified.

The situation becomes complicated by the fact that the entire duration of the expansion of space to the present, based on the equations in their simplest form, turns out smaller than appears credible in view of the reliably known age of terrestrial minerals. But the introduction of the "cosmological constant" offers absolutely no natural escape from the difficulty. This latter difficulty is given by way of the numerical value of Hubble's expansion-constant and the age-measurement of minerals, completely independent of any cosmological theory, provided that one interprets the Hubble-effect as Doppler-effect.

Everything finally depends upon the question: Can a spectral line be considered as a measure of a "proper time" (*Eigen-Zeit*)*ds* $(ds^2 = g_{ik}dx_i dx_k)$, (if one takes into consideration regions of cosmic dimensions)? Is there such a thing as a natural object which incorporates the "natural-measuring-stick" independently of its position in four-dimensional space? The affirmation of this question made the invention of the general theory of relativity *psychologically* possible; however this supposition is logically not necessary. For the construction of the present theory of relativity the following is essential:

(1) Physical things are described by continuous functions, field-variables of four co-ordinates. As long as the topological connection is preserved, these latter can be freely chosen.

(2) The field-variables are tensor-components; among the tensors is a symmetrical tensor g_{ik} for the description of the gravitational field.

(3) There are physical objects, which (in the macroscopic field) measure the invariant *ds*.

If (1) and (2) are accepted, (3) is plausible, but not necessary. The construction of mathematical theory rests exclusively upon (1) and (2).

A *complete* theory of physics as a totality, in accordance with (1) and (2) does not yet exist. If it did exist, there would be no room for the supposition (3). For the objects used as tools for measurement do not lead an independent existence alongside of the objects implicated by the field-equations. — — It is not necessary that one should permit one's cosmological considerations to be restrained by such a sceptical attitude; but neither should one close one's mind towards them from the very beginning. — — —

These reflections bring me to Karl Menger's essay. For the quantum-facts suggest the suspicion that doubt may also be raised concerning the ultimate usefulness of the program characterized in (1) and (2). There exists the possibility of doubting only (2) and, in doing so, to question the possibility of being able adequately to formulate the laws by means of differential equations, without dropping (1). The more radical effort of surrendering (1) with (2) appears to me—and I believe to Dr. Menger also—to lie more closely at hand. So long as no one has new concepts, which appear to have sufficient constructive power, mere doubt remains; this is, unfortunately, my own situation. Adhering to the continuum originates with me not in a prejudice, but arises out of the fact that I have been unable to think up anything organic to take its place. How is one to conserve four-dimensionality in essence (or in near approximation) and [at the same time] surrender the continuum? —

L. Infeld's essay is an independently understandable, excellent introduction into the so-called "cosmological problem" of the theory of relativity, which critically examines all essential points. — — —

Max von Laue: An historical investigation of the development of the conservation postulates, which, in my opinion, is of lasting value. I think it would be worth while to make this essay easily accessible to students by way of independent publication. — — —

In spite of serious efforts I have not succeeded in quite under-standing H. Dingle's essay, not even as concerns its aim. Is the idea of the special theory of relativity to be expanded in the sense that new group-characteristics, which are not implied by the Lorentz-invariance, are to be postulated? Are these postu-lates empirically founded or only by way of a trial "posited"? Upon what does the confidence in the existence of such group-characteristics rest? — — —

Kurt Gödel's essay constitutes, in my opinion, an important contribution to the general theory of relativity, especially to the analysis of the concept of time. The problem here involved disturbed me already at the time of the building up of the gen-eral theory of relativity, without my having succeeded in clarifying it. Entirely aside from the relation of the theory of relativity to idealistic philosophy or to any philosophical formulation of questions, the problem presents itself as follows:

If P is a world-point, a "light-cone" ($ds^2 = o$) belongs to it. We draw a "time-like" world-line through P and on this line observe the close world-points B and A, separated by P. Does it make any sense to provide the world-line with an arrow, and to assert that B is *before P, A after P?* Is what remains of temporal connection between world-points in the theory of relativity an asymmetrical relation, or would one be just as much justified, from the physical point of view, to indicate the arrow in the opposite direction and to assert that A is *before P, B after P?*

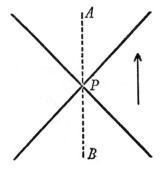

In the first instance the alternative is decided in the negative, if we are justified in saying: If it is possible to send (to tele-graph) a signal (also passing by in the close proximity of P) from B to A, but not from A to B, then the one-sided (asym-metrical) character of time is secured, i.e., there exists no free choice for the direction of the arrow. What is essential in this is the fact that the sending of a signal is, in the sense of thermo-dynamics, an irreversible process, a process which is connected with the growth of entropy (whereas, *according to our present knowledge,* all elementary processes are reversible).

If, therefore, B and A are two, sufficiently neighboring, world-points, which can be connected by a time-like line, then the assertion: "B is before A," makes physical sense. But does this assertion still make sense, if the points, which are connectable by the time-like line, are arbitrarily far separated from each other? Certainly not, if there exist point-series connectable by time-like lines in such a way that each point precedes temporally the preceding one, *and if the series is closed in itself.* In that case the distinction "earlier – later" is abandoned for world-points which lie far apart in a cosmological sense, and those paradoxes, regarding the *direction* of the causal connection, arise, of which Mr. Gödel has spoken.

Such cosmological solutions of the gravitation-equations (with not vanishing Λ-constant) have been found by Mr. Gödel. It will be interesting to weigh whether these are not to be excluded on physical grounds.

* * * * * *

I have the distressing feeling that I have expressed myself, in this reply, not merely somewhat longwindedly but also rather sharply. This observation may serve as my excuse: one can really quarrel only with his brothers or close friends; others are too alien [for that]. —

P.S. The preceding remarks refer to essays which were in my hands at the end of January 1949. Inasmuch as the volume was to have appeared in March, it was high time to write down these reflections.

After they had been concluded I learned that the publication of the volume would experience a further delay and that some additional important essays had come in. I decided, nevertheless, not to expand my remarks further, which had already become too long, and to desist from taking any position with reference to those essays which came into my hands after the conclusion of my remarks.

INSTITUTE OF ADVANCED STUDY
PRINCETON, NEW JERSEY
FEBRUARY 1, 1949

A. Einstein.

BIBLIOGRAPHY OF THE WRITINGS OF ALBERT EINSTEIN

TO MAY 1951

Compiled by

MARGARET C. SHIELDS

PREFACE TO THE BIBLIOGRAPHY

OVER the fireplace in the professors' lounge of Fine Hall, the home of the Princeton University department of mathematics, are these words of Einstein, *"Raffiniert ist der Herr Gott, aber boshaft ist er nicht,"* ("God is subtle, but he is not malicious") which are said not to have been taken from any writing, but to have been treasured from a conversation. This instance may perhaps be taken as representative of the way in which the thoughts of the man have been sown broadcast over the earth so that any attempt to collect even his printed words with any degree of completeness is beyond attainable possibility.

A fairly complete list of his scientific work may be presumed contained in the following pages, but the published material representing his other interests is much more difficult to garner, and the present record of it is clearly inadequate. Of these widely scattered items, multitudinous and significant even when brief, relatively few could be traced through periodical indexes. Many have been published in minor German weeklies, etc., which are not covered by the *Bibliographie der Deutschen Zeitschriften* and its *Beilage,* and most of these publications, at least for the period 1920-1930, are not available in this country for direct searching. Four items from this *Bibliographie* have been included though the Library of Congress reports they are not in any American library. The several Einstein anthologies, with one exception, fail to indicate the original places of publication of the items in their contents, and the circumstances of the years since the anthologies were issued have made it impossible to obtain this information from either editor or publisher. The editor of this volume will be most grateful to readers who will report to him citations for missing items to be inserted in a second edition; there are at least a score of items of this period of which the compiler knows the existence but which she has failed to locate.

Even for the last few years with free access to the original manuscripts the task is quite as clearly impossible. One finds among these manuscripts a letter to the Jews of Montevideo which was reprinted there in facsimile as a broadside on June 5, 1948, captioned *Fuer unsere Haganah*. One finds a message to the Japanese people on peace and security which was printed in the New Year 1948 issue of a Japanese language paper, *Ahasi*. Neither of these could be included in the bibliography, though both may have been several times reprinted in the far corners of the earth. There are messages to gatherings like the World Federalists Conference at Montreux, August 17, 1947, radio broadcasts, endorsements of worthy persons and worthy causes, which once made public may be printed in an endless variety of places, but which are not to be located by any reasonable process of search, or which, such as letters quoted on book jackets, are not suitable for inclusion.

Some points may be mentioned as to details of the bibliography, particularly certain modifications of the style prevailing in earlier volume of this series which have kindly received the sanction of the editor. The remaining departures from normal library procedure it is hoped will be as kindly overlooked. Mistakes on the part of the compiler there may be which require, not forgiveness, but correction.

The material has been divided into three categories; such division is clearly suggested by the material itself and will increase, it is hoped, the convenience of the bibliography for its users. The first major division is the scientific writings; the second, publications other than those in Part III bearing on his wide humanitarian interests; third, the text of speeches, letters, etc., published in the *New York Times*.

Reprinted items are recorded only under the date of first publication, with a note indicating subsequent reprintings. In case of items not reprintings, textually similar but bibliographically distinct, they have been so listed under the appropriate year.

The dates used in case of periodical articles are the dates appearing on the title pages of completed volumes; when the periodical year does not coincide with the calendar year, this date may follow by one year the actual date of issue of the paper, but for the purpose of seeking out the article in a library the title page date is the more convenient.

Many of the monographs, particularly those in the *Sitzungsberichte* of the Prussian Academy, are listed in dealers' catalogs as separates with the high prices of collectors' items. These are entered here, however, only as are other periodical articles.

Within each year the order is first books, then periodical articles arranged alphabetically by the periodical title, for convenience in locating a particular item when one has only that much information to begin on.

To all the large number of libraries and individuals who have been approached with questions, whether they were able to supply information or not, the compiler again extends her warm thanks, and to those who will turn to the bibliography for service her regret that it is not more perfect.

MARGARET C. SHIELDS

FINE HALL LIBRARY
PRINCETON UNIVERSITY
JUNE 1, 1948

BIBLIOGRAPHY

I

SCIENTIFIC WRITINGS

1901

1. Folgerungen aus den Kapillaritätserscheinungen.
Annalen der Physik, ser. 4, vol. 4, pp. 513-523.

1902

2. Thermodynamische Theorie der Potentialdifferenz zwischen Metallen und vollständig dissoziierten Lösungen ihrer Salze, und eine elektrische Methode zur Erforschung der Molekularkräfte.
Annalen der Physik, ser. 4, vol. 8, pp. 798-814.

3. Kinetische Theorie des Wärmegleichgewichtes und des zweiten Hauptsatzes der Thermodynamik.
Annalen der Physik, ser. 4, vol. 9, pp. 417-433.

1903

4. Theorie der Grundlagen der Thermodynamik.
Annalen der Physik, ser. 4, vol. 11, pp. 170-187.

1904

5. Allgemeine molekulare Theorie der Wärme.
Annalen der Physik, ser. 4, vol. 14, pp. 354-362.

1905

6. EINE NEUE BESTIMMUNG DER MOLEKÜLDIMENSIONEN. Bern, Wyss. 21 pp.

> Inaugural-dissertation, Zürich Universität. Published also in *Annalen der Physik*, (item 11).

7. Über einen die Erzeugung und Verwandlung des Lichtes betreffenden heuristischen Gesichtspunkt.
Annalen der Physik, ser. 4, vol. 17, pp. 132-148.

> This paper and item 13 present the fundamental photoelectric equation in explicit form though not in current notation. It was nominally for this work that the Nobel prize was awarded Einstein. (See also item 45).

694

8. Die von der molekularkinetischen Theorie der Wärme geforderte Bewegung von in ruhenden Flüssigkeiten suspendierten Teilchen.
Annalen der Physik, ser. 4, vol. 17, pp. 549-560.

Included in item 157 and item 198.

9. Elektrodynamik bewegter Körper.
Annalen der Physik, ser. 4, vol. 17, pp. 891-921.

This is the initial paper on special relativity.

At a war bond rally in Kansas City a manuscript copy was sold for six million dollars and deposited with the Library of Congress. (see *New York Times*, Feb. 5, 1944, p. 5, and Aug. 4, p. 15)

The paper was reprinted in H. A. LORENTZ: *Das Relativitätsprinzip, eine Sammlung von Abhandlungen*, Leipzig, Teubner, 1913, and also in its subsequent editions. This book is also available in an English translation by W. Perrett and G. B. Jeffery, H. A. LORENTZ: *The principle of relativity, a collection of original memoirs* . . . London, Methuen, 1923.

See also item 128 for another English translation, item 189 for a French translation.

Excerpts are included in BUILDERS OF THE UNIVERSE, Los Angeles, 1932 (See item 345).

10. Ist die Trägheit eines Körpers von seinem Energieinhalt abhängig?
Annalen der Physik, ser. 4, vol. 18, pp. 639-641.

In subject matter this is closely associated with item 9; it is included in the LORENTZ there mentioned, and in its translation. For French translation see item 189.

1906

11. Eine neue Bestimmung der Moleküldimensionen.
Annalen der Physik, ser. 4, vol. 19, pp. 289-306.

This is his inaugural-dissertation, item 6, with a brief "Nachtrag." It is also included in his *Untersuchungen über die Theorie der Brownschen Bewegungen*, item 157, and its translation, item 198.

12. Zur Theorie der Brownschen Bewegung.
Annalen der Physik, ser. 4, vol. 19, pp. 371-381.

Included in items 157 and 198.

13. Theorie der Lichterzeugung und Lichtabsorption.
Annalen der Physik, ser. 4, vol. 20, pp. 199-206.

See note under item 7.

14. Prinzip von der Erhaltung der Schwerpunktsbewegung und die Trägheit der Energie.
    Annalen der Physik, ser. 4, vol. 20, pp. 627-633.

15. Eine Methode zur Bestimmung des Verhältnisses der transversalen und longitudinalen Masse des Elektrons.
    Annalen der Physik, ser. 4, vol. 21, pp. 583-586.
    French translation in *L'Éclairage électrique*, vol. 49, pp. 493-494.

1907

16. Plancksche Theorie der Strahlung und die Theorie der spezifischen Wärme.
    Annalen der Physik, ser. 4, vol. 22, pp. 180-190, and p. 800 (Berichtigung).

17. Gültigkeitsgrenze des Satzes vom thermodynamischen Gleichgewicht und die Möglichkeit einer neuen Bestimmung der Elementarquanta.
    Annalen der Physik, ser. 4, vol. 22, pp. 569-572.

18. Möglichkeit einer neuen Prüfung des Relativitätsprinzips.
    Annalen der Physik, ser. 4, vol. 23, pp. 197-198.
    An analysis of the Doppler effect.

19. Bemerkung zur Notiz des Herrn P. Ehrenfest: Translation deformierbarer Elektronen und der Flächensatz.
    Annalen der Physik, ser. 4, vol. 23, pp. 206-208.

20. Die vom Relativitätsprinzip geforderte Trägheit der Energie.
    Annalen der Physik, ser. 4, vol. 23, pp. 371-384.

21. Relativitätsprinzip und die aus demselben gezogenen Folgerungen.
    Jahrbuch der Radioaktivität, vol. 4, pp. 411-462, and vol. 5, pp. 98-99 (Berichtigungen)
    On page 443 appear probably for the first time explicit statements both of the equivalence of inertial and gravitational mass, and of the equation for mass in terms of energy which has been blazoned since August 1945 on so many graphic presentations of the release of atomic energy.

22. Theoretische Bemerkungen über die Brownsche Bewegung.
    Zeitschrift für Elektrochemie, vol. 13, pp. 41-42.
    Included in items 157 and 198.

1908

23. Electromagnetische Grundgleichungen für bewegte Körper, with J. Laub.
Annalen der Physik, ser. 4, vol. 26, pp. 532-540, and vol. 27, p. 232 (Berichtigungen).
See also Item 27.

24. Die im elektromagnetischen Felde auf ruhende Körper ausgeübten ponderomotorischen Kräfte, with J. Laub.
Annalen der Physik, ser. 4, vol. 26, pp. 541-550.

25. Neue elektrostatische Methode zur Messung kleiner Elektrizitätsmengen.
Physikalische Zeitschrift, vol. 9, pp. 216-217.

26. Elementare Theorie der Brownschen Bewegung.
Zeitschrift für Elektrochemie, vol. 14, pp. 235-239.
Included in items 157 and 198.

1909

27. Bemerkungen zu unserer Arbeit: Elektromagnetische Grundgleichungen für bewegte Körper, with J. Laub.
Annalen der Physik, ser. 4, vol. 28, pp. 445-447.

28. Bemerkung zur Arbeit von Mirimanoff: Die Grundgleichungen.
Annalen der Physik, ser. 4, vol. 28, pp. 885-888.
Points out correspondence of this work with that of Minkowski.

29. Zum gegenwärtigen Stande des Strahlungsproblems.
Physikalische Zeitschrift, vol. 10, pp. 185-193.
Ibid., pp. 323-324, under the same title there appears a clarification of his point of view in this paper vs. that of W. Ritz.

30. Entwicklung unserer Anschauungen über das Wesen und die Konstitution der Strahlung.
Physikalische Zeitschrift, vol. 10, pp. 817-825.
Address before the 81st assembly of the Gesellschaft Deutscher Naturforscher, Salzburg, 1909. It is also published in *Deutsche physikalische Gesellschaft, Verhandlungen*, Jahrg. 11, pp. 482-500.

1910

31. Über einen Satz der Wahrscheinlichkeitsrechnung und seine Anwendung in der Strahlungstheorie, with L. Hopf.
Annalen der Physik, ser. 4, vol. 33, pp. 1096-1104.
See item 79 for further discussion of the topic.

32. Statistische Untersuchung der Bewegung eines Resonators in einem Strahlungsfeld, with L. Hopf.
   Annalen der Physik, ser. 4, vol. 33, pp. 1105-1115.

33. Theorie der Opaleszenz von homogenen Flüssigkeiten und Flüssigkeitsgemischen in der Nähe des kritischen Zustandes.
   Annalen der Physik, ser. 4, vol. 33, pp. 1275-1298.

34. Principe de relativité et ses conséquences dans la physique moderne.
   Archives des sciences physiques et naturelles, ser. 4, vol. 29, pp. 5-28, and 125-244.

   The translation is by E. Guillaume, but it is not of item 21.

35. Théorie des quantités lumineuses et la question de la localisation de l'énergie électromagnétique.
   Archives des sciences physiques et naturelles, ser. 4, vol. 29, pp. 525-528.

36. Forces pondéromotrices qui agissent sur les conducteurs ferromagnétiques disposés dans un champ magnétique et parcourus par un courant.
   Archives des sciences physiques et naturelles, ser. 4, vol. 30, pp. 323-324.

1911

37. Bemerkung zu dem Gesetz von Eötvös.
   Annalen der Physik, ser. 4, vol. 34, pp. 165-169.

38. Beziehung zwischen dem elastischen Verhalten und der spezifischen Wärme bei festen Körpern mit einatomigem Molekül.
   Annalen der Physik, ser. 4, vol. 34, pp. 170-174, and p. 590.

39. Bemerkungen zu den P. Hertzschen Arbeiten: Mechanische Grundlagen der Thermodynamik.
   Annalen der Physik, ser. 4, vol. 34, pp. 175-176.

40. Berichtigung zu meiner Arbeit: Eine neue Bestimmung der Moleküldimensionen.
   Annalen der Physik, ser. 4, vol. 34, pp. 591-592.

   See items 6 and 11.

41. Elementare Betrachtungen über die thermische Molekularbewegung in festen Körpern.
   Annalen der Physik, ser. 4, vol. 35, pp. 679-694.

42. Einfluss der Schwerkraft auf die Ausbreitung des Lichtes.
  Annalen der Physik, ser. 4, vol. 35, pp. 898-908.

  This paper returns to the ideas of item 21, and deduces from those ideas for the first time the consequence that star beams must be bent in passing the edge of the sun's disc.

  It appears in the third and later editions of H. A. LORENTZ: *Relativitätsprinzip* and in its English translation (see item 9).

43. Relativitätstheorie.
  Naturforschende Gesellschaft, Zürich, Vierteljahresschrift, vol. 56, pp. 1-14.

  Vortrag gehalten in der Sitzung der Gesellschaft.

44. Zum Ehrenfestschen Paradoxon.
  Physikalische Zeitschrift, vol. 12, pp. 509-510.

  Corrects a misapprehension of the Lorentz contraction.

1912

45. Thermodynamische Begründung des photochemischen Äquivalentgesetzes.
  Annalen der Physik, ser. 4, vol. 37, pp. 832-838, and vol. 38, pp. 881-884.

46. Lichtgeschwindigkeit und Statik des Gravitationsfeldes.
  Annalen der Physik, ser. 4, vol. 38, pp. 355-369.

47. Theorie des statischen Gravitationsfeldes.
  Annalen der Physik, ser. 4, vol. 38, pp. 443-458.

48. Antwort auf eine Bemerkung von J. Stark: Anwendung des Planckschen Elementargesetzes.
  Annalen der Physik, ser. 4, vol. 38, p. 888.

49. Relativität und Gravitation: Erwiderung auf eine Bemerkung von M. Abraham.
  Annalen der Physik, ser. 4, vol. 38, pp. 1059-1064.

50. Bemerkung zu Abraham's Auseinandersetzung: Nochmals Relativität und Gravitation.
  Annalen der Physik, ser. 4, vol. 39, p. 704.

51. État actuel du problème des chaleurs spécifiques.
  pp. 407-435 of INSTITUTS SOLVAY. CONSEIL DE PHYSIQUE, 1er, 1911. *Rapports*. Paris, Gauthier.

  For German text see item 63.

52. Gibt es eine Gravitationswirkung die der elektrodynamischen Induktionswirkung analog ist?

Vierteljahrsschrift für gerichtliche Medizin, ser. 3, vol. 44, pp. 37-40.

1913

53. ENTWURF EINER VERALLGEMEINERTEN RELATIVITÄTSTHEORIE UND EINE THEORIE DER GRAVITATION. I. Physikalischer Teil von A. Einstein. II. Mathematischer Teil von M. Grossmann. Leipzig, Teubner. 38 pp.

Sonderdruck aus *Zeitschrift für Mathematik und Physik*, vol. 62, pp. 225-261 (Physikalischer Teil, pp. 225-244).

This paper may be called a review of the ideas developing in items 21, 42, 46 and 47. For critical comment see item 68.

54. Einige Argumente für die Annahme einer molekular Agitation beim absoluten Nullpunkt, with O. Stern.

Annalen der Physik, ser. 4, vol. 40, pp. 551-560.

55. Déduction thermodynamique de la loi de l'équivalence photochimique.

Journal de physique, ser. 5, vol. 3, pp. 277-282.

Not a translation of item 45, but an address March 27, 1913, before the Société Française de Physique.

56. Physikalische Grundlagen einer Gravitationstheorie.

Naturforschende Gesellschaft, Zürich, Vierteljahrsschrift, vol. 58, pp. 284-290.

Address before this Swiss society, Sept. 9, 1913. A résumé is printed in *Schweizerische naturforschende Gesellschaft, Verhandlungen*, 1913, Part 2, pp. 137-138.

57. Max Planck als Forscher.

Naturwissenschaften, vol. 1, pp. 1077-1079.

58. Zum gegenwärtigen Stande des Gravitationsproblems.

Physikalische Zeitschrift, vol. 14, pp. 1249-1266.

Address at 85th Versammlung Deutscher Naturforscher, Wien, Sept. 21, 1913. The citation above includes the open discussion of the paper.

Also published in *Gesellschaft deutscher Naturforscher und Ärzte, Verhandlungen*, 1914, pp. 3-24. A "referat" was published in *Himmel und Erde*, vol. 26, pp. 90-93.

1914

59. Nordströmsche Gravitationstheorie vom Standpunkt des absoluten Differentialkalküls, with A. D. Fokker.

Annalen der Physik, ser. 4, vol. 44, pp. 321-328.

60. Bases physiques d'une théorie de la gravitation. [Translated by E. Guillaume]

Archives des sciences physiques et naturelles, ser. 4, vol. 37, pp. 5-12.

For German original see item 56.

61. Bemerkung zu P. Harzers Abhandlung: Die Mitführung des Lichtes in Glas und die Aberration.

Astronomische Nachrichten, vol. 199, pp. 8-10.

62. Antwort auf eine Replik P. Harzers.

Astronomische Nachrichten, vol. 199, pp. 47-48.

63. Zum gegenwärtigen Stande des Problems der spezifischen Wärme.

Deutsche Bunsengesellschaft, Abhandlungen, nr. 7, pp. 330-364.

This volume is the German edition of the proceedings of the first Solvay congress (see item 51). Pages 353-364 of the citation are the questions and answers of the general discussion.

64. Beiträge zur Quantentheorie.

Deutsche physikalische Gesellschaft, Berichte, 1914 (or its *Verhandlungen*, vol. 16), pp. 820-828.

65. Zur Theorie der Gravitation.

Naturforschende Gesellschaft, Zürich, Vierteljahrsschrift, vol. 59, pp. 4-6.

66. [Review of] H. A. LORENTZ: Das Relativitätsprinzip.

Naturwissenschaften, vol. 2, p. 1018.

67. Nachträgliche Antwort auf eine Frage von Reissner.

Physikalische Zeitschrift, vol. 15, pp. 108-110.

On the question of the mass of a gravitational field.

68. Principielles zur verallgemeinerten Relativitätstheorie und Gravitationstheorie.

Physikalische Zeitschrift, vol. 15, pp. 176-180.

Reply to comment by G. Mie on the relation of Einstein's work as represented in item 53 to Minkowski's.

69. Antrittsrede.

Preussische Akademie der Wissenschaften, Sitzungsberichte,
1914, pt. 2, pp. 739-742.

On the relative rôles of theoretical and experimental physics. Included
in *Mein Weltbild* and in its translation (cf. 361 and 362).

70. Formale Grundlage der allgemeinen Relativitätstheorie.

Preussische Akademie der Wissenschaften, Sitzungsberichte,
1914, pt. 2, pp. 1030-1085.

71. Zum Relativitätsproblem.

Scientia (Bologna), vol. 15, pp. 337-348.

An exposition in reply to two papers of the opposition previously
issued in this journal.

72. Physikalische Grundlagen und leitende Gedanken für eine Gravitationstheorie.

Schweizerische naturforschende Gesellschaft, Verhandlungen,
Vol. 96, pt. 2, p. 146.

Listed by title only. Lecture delivered at the 96th session of the
Swiss society Sept., 19 1913; item 56 is the same lecture.

73. Gravitationstheorie.

Schweizerische naturforschende Gesellschaft, Verhandlungen,
vol. 96, pt. 2, pp. 137-138.

For full text see item 56.

74. Relativitätsprinzip.

Vossische Zeitung, 26 April 1914, pp. 33-34.

A rather full and serious popular presentation, not identifiable with
any other.

75. Kovarianzeigenschaften der Feldgleichungen der auf die verall-
gemeinerte Relativitätstheorie gegründeten Gravitationstheorie,
with M. Grossmann.

Zeitschrift für Mathematik und Physik, vol. 63, pp. 215-225.

1915

76. Theoretische Atomistik.

pp. 251-263 of DIE PHYSIK unter Redaktion von E. Lecher.
Leipzig, Teubner. (Kultur der Gegenwart, teil 3, abt. 3,
bd. 1.).

For a revised edition see item 191.

77. Relativitätstheorie.
   pp. 703-713 of DIE PHYSIK.

   See item 76 for bibliographic detail.
   For a revised edition see item 192.

78. Proefondervindelijk bewijs voor het bestaan der moleculaire stroomen van Ampère, with W. J. de Haas.
   Akademie van wetenschappen, Amsterdam, Verslag., ser. 4, vol. 23, pp. 1449-1464.

   A translation into Dutch of item 80.

79. Antwort auf eine Abhandlung M. von Laues: Ein Satz der Wahrscheinlichkeitsrechnung und seine Anwendung auf die Strahlungstheorie.
   Annalen der Physik, ser. 4, vol. 47, pp. 879-885.

   Discussion bearing upon item 31.

80. Experimenteller Nachweis der Ampèreschen Molekularströme, with W. J. de Haas.
   Deutsche physikalische Gesellschaft, Verhandlungen, vol. 17, pp. 152-170, and p. 203 (Berichtigung).

   Notiz zu unserer Arbeit, *ibid.*, p. 420.
   For an English translation see item 88.

81. Experimenteller Nachweis der Ampereschen Molekularströme, with W. J. de Haas.
   Naturwissenschaften, vol. 3, pp. 237-238.

   A preliminary note covering item 80.

82. Grundgedanken der allgemeinen Relativitätstheorie und Anwendung dieser Theorie in der Astronomie.
   Preussische Akademie der Wissenschaften, Sitzungsberichte, 1915, pt. 1, p. 315.

   This is an abstract; published in full as items 83 and 84.

83. Zur allgemeinen Relativitätstheorie.
   Preussische Akademie der Wissenschaften, Sitzungsberichte, 1915, pt. 2, pp. 778-786, 799-801.

84. Erklärung der Perihelbewegung des Merkur aus der allgemeinen Relativitätstheorie.
   Preussische Akademie der Wissenschaften, Sitzungsberichte, 1915, pt. 2, pp. 831-839.

85. Feldgleichungen der Gravitation.
Preussische Akademie der Wissenschaften, Sitzungsberichte, 1915, pt. 2, pp. 844-847.

1916

86. GRUNDLAGE DER ALLGEMEINEN RELATIVITÄTSTHEORIE. Leipzig, Barth. 64 pp.

> "Sonderdruck aus *Annalen der Physik,*" (item 89), with "Inhalt" and "Einleitung" added. It has gone through several printings, at least up to the "5. unveränderter Abdruck," Barth, 1929.
>
> For English and French translations see items 128 and 266, respectively.

87. Vorwort.
ERWIN F. FREUNDLICH: *Grundlagen der Einsteinschen Gravitationstheorie.* Berlin, Springer.

> This preface is likewise in all later German editions of the Freundlich and in its two English translations, Cambridge university press, 1920, and Methuen, 1924; also in the Polish translation, Warsaw, about 1923.

88. Experimental proof of the existence of Ampère's molecular currents, with W. J. de Haas.
Akademie van wetenschappen, Amsterdam, Proceedings, vol. 18, pp. 696-711.

> An English translation of item 80.

89. Grundlage der allgemeinen Relativitätstheorie.
Annalen der Physik, ser. 4, vol. 49, pp. 769-822.

> This—the first complete exposition of a penetrating generalization of the original theory—was added in the third edition of H. A. LORENTZ: *Relativitätsprinzip* Teubner, 1920, and is in its English translation. There is another English translation in item 128, and a French translation in item 266. It has also been issued as a separate (see item 86.)

90. Über Fr. Kottlers Abhandlung: Einsteins Äquivalenzhypothese und die Gravitation.
Annalen der Physik, ser. 4, vol. 51, pp. 639-642.

91. Einfaches Experiment zum Nachweis der Ampèreschen Molekularströme.
Deutsche physikalische Gesellschaft, Verhandlungen, vol. 18, pp. 173-177.

"Vorlesungsexperiment . . . eine Variante der . . . mit de Haas ausgeführten Versuche," (item 88).

92. Strahlungs-emission und -absorption nach der Quantentheorie.
Deutsche physikalische Gesellschaft, Verhandlungen, vol. 18, pp. 318-323.

93. Quantentheorie der Strahlung.
Physikalische Gesellschaft, Zürich, Mitteilungen, vol. 16, pp. 47-62.

94. [Review of] H. A. LORENTZ: Théories statistiques en thermodynamique.
Naturwissenschaften, vol. 4, pp. 480-481.

95. Elementare Theorie der Wasserwellen und des Fluges.
Naturwissenschaften, vol. 4, pp. 509-510.

96. Ernst Mach.
Physikalische Zeitschrift, vol. 17, pp. 101-104.

97. Neue formale Deutung der Maxwellschen Feldgleichungen der Elektrodynamik.
Preussische Akademie der Wissenschaften, Sitzungsberichte, 1916, pt. 1, pp. 184-187.

98. Einige anschauliche Überlegungen aus dem Gebiete der Relativitätstheorie.
Preussische Akademie der Wissenschaften, Sitzungsberichte, 1916, pt. 1, p. 423.

This is an abstract showing that the paper dealt with the behavior of clocks and the Foucault pendulum; never published in full.

99. Näherungsweise Integration der Feldgleichungen der Gravitation.
Preussische Akademie der Wissenschaften, Sitzungsberichte, 1916, pt. 1, pp. 688-696.

100. Gedächtnisrede auf Karl Schwarzschild.
Preussische Akademie der Wissenschaften, Sitzungsberichte, 1916, pt. 1, pp. 768-770.

101. Hamiltonsches Prinzip und allgemeine Relativitätstheorie.
Preussische Akademie der Wissenschaften, Sitzungsberichte, 1916, pt. 2, pp. 1111-1116.
This is included in the third and later editions of H. A. LORENTZ:

Relativitätsprinzip, and is in the English translation, Methuen, 1923.
(See note under item 9 for further bibliographic detail.)

1917

102. ÜBER DIE SPEZIELLE UND DIE ALLGEMEINE RELATIVITÄTS-THEORIE, GEMEINVERSTÄNDLICH. Braunschweig, Vieweg. 70 pp. (Sammlung Vieweg, Heft 38).

> The only comprehensive survey by Einstein of his theory, and his most widely known work.
>
> See items 110, 129, 130, 137-141, 154, 169 and 215 for other editions and translations.

103. Zum Quantensatz von Sommerfeld und Epstein.
Deutsche Physikalische Gesellschaft, Verhandlungen, vol. 19, pp. 82-92.

104. [Review of] H. v. HELMHOLTZ: Zwei Vorträge über Goethe.
Naturwissenschaften, vol. 5, p. 675.

105. Marian von Smoluchowski.
Naturwissenschaften, vol. 5, pp. 737-738.

106. Quantentheorie der Strahlung.
Physikalische Zeitschrift, vol. 18, pp. 121-128.

107. Kosmologische Betrachtungen zur allgemeinen Relativitätstheorie.
Preussische Akademie der Wissenschaften, Sitzungsberichte, 1917, pt. 1, pp. 142-152.

> This is included in the third and later editions of H. A. LORENTZ: *Relativitätsprinzip*, and is in the English translation, Methuen, 1923.

108. Eine Ableitung des Theorems von Jacobi.
Preussische Akademie der Wissenschaften, Sitzungsberichte, 1917, pt. 2, pp. 606-608.

109. Friedrich Adler als Physiker.
Vossische Zeitung, Morgen Ausgabe (no. 259) May 23, p. 2.

1918

110. ÜBER DIE SPEZIELLE UND DIE ALLGEMEINE RELATIVITÄTS-THEORIE, GEMEINVERSTÄNDLICH. 3. aufl. Braunschweig, Vieweg. 83 pp.

> For first edition see item 102. The third to ninth editions (1918-1920) have an appendix: "Einfache Ableitung der Lorentz-transformation. Minkowskis vierdimensionale Welt."

111. Motiv des Forschens.
   pp. 29-32 of ZU MAX PLANCKS 60. GEBURTSTAG: AN-
   SPRACHEN IN DER DEUTSCHEN PHYSIKALISCHEN GESELL-
   SCHAFT. Karlsruhe, Müller.
   This was reprinted in *Mein Weldbild*, and is in its translation.

112. Prinzipielles zur allgemeinen Relativitätstheorie.
   Annalen der Physik, ser. 4, vol. 55, pp. 241-244.

   Impelled by various comments, Einstein here sets himself the goal
   "lediglich die Grundgedanken herauszuheben wobei ich die Theorie
   als bekannt voraussetze."

113. Lassen sich Brechungsexponenten der Körper für Röntgenstrahlen
   experimentell ermitteln?
   Deutsche Physikalische Gesellschaft, Verhandlungen, vol. 20,
   pp. 86-87.

114. Bemerkung zu Gehrckes Notiz: Über den Äther.
   Deutsche physikalische Gesellschaft, Verhandlungen, vol. 20,
   p. 261.

115. [Review of] H. WEYL: Raum, Zeit, Materie.
   Naturwissenschaften, Vol. 6, p. 373.

116. Dialog über Einwände gegen die Relativitätstheorie.
   Naturwissenschaften, vol. 6, pp. 697-702.

117. Notiz zu Schrödingers Arbeit: Energiekomponenten des Gravitationsfeldes.
   Physikalische Zeitschrift, vol. 19, pp. 115-116.

118. Bemerkung zu Schrödingers Notiz: Lösungssystem der allgemein
   kovarianten Gravitationsgleichungen.
   Physikalische Zeitschrift, vol. 19, pp. 165-166.

119. Gravitationswellen.
   Preussische Akademie der Wissenschaften, Sitzungsberichte,
   1918, pt. 1, pp. 154-167.

120. Kritisches zu einer von Hrn. de Sitter gegebenen Lösung der
   Gravitationsgleichungen.
   Preussische Akademie der Wissenschaften, Sitzungsberichte,
   1918, pt. 1, pp. 270-272.

121. Der Energiesatz in der allgemeinen Relativitätstheorie.
   Preussische Akademie der Wissenschaften, Sitzungsberichte,
   1918, pt. 1, pp. 448-459.

1919

122. Prüfung der allgemeinen Relativitätstheorie.
Naturwissenschaften, vol. 7, p. 776.

> A few lines based on a telegraphic report of the May 29, 1919, eclipse.

123. Spielen Gravitationsfelder im Aufbau der materiellen Elementarteilchen eine wesentliche Rolle?
Preussische Akademie der Wissenschaften, Sitzungsberichte, 1919, pt. 1, pp. 349-356.

> This appears in the third and later editions of H. A. LORENTZ: *Relativitätsprinzip,* and in the English translation, Methuen, 1923. (see item 9 for bibliographic detail).

124. Bemerkungen über periodische Schwankungen der Mondlänge, welche bisher nach der Newtonschen Mechanik nicht erklärbar schienen.
Preussische Akademie der Wissenschaften, Sitzungsberichte, 1919, pt. 1, pp. 433-436.

> Einstein's reply to comment on this paper is found, *ibid.,* pt. 2, p. 711.

125. Feldgleichungen der allgemeinen Relativitätstheorie vom Standpunkte des kosmologischen Problems und des Problems der Konstitution der Materie.
Preussische Akademie der Wissenschaften, Sitzungsberichte, 1919, pt. 1, p. 463.

> Title only. "Im wesentlichen ein Referat über "Spielen Gravitationsfelder. . . ?" (See item 123).

126. My theory.
Times, London, November 28, 1919, p. 13.

> Copied under title "Time, space and gravitation" in *Optician, The British optical journal,* vol. 58, pp. 187-188. Noted, with quotations in *Nature,* vol. 104, p. 360. Reprinted in *Living age,* vol. 304, pp. 41-43. German text is in *Mein Weltbild,* pp. 220-228, under the title "Was ist Relativitätstheorie?" (cf. item 361.)

127. Leo Arons als Physiker.
Sozialistische Monatshefte, vol. 52, (Jahrgang 25, pt. 2) pp. 1055-1056.

1920

128. THE PRINCIPLE OF RELATIVITY: ORIGINAL PAPERS by A. Einstein and H. Minkowski, translated by M. N. Saha and

S. N. Bose, with an historical introduction by P. C. Mahalanobis. Calcutta, University of Calcutta. xxiii, 186 pp.

Contains translations of items 9 and 89.

129. ÜBER DIE SPEZIELLE UND DIE ALLGEMEINE RELATIVITÄTS-THEORIE, GEMEINVERSTÄNDLICH. 10 aufl. Braunschweig, Vieweg. 91 pp.

For first edition see item 102. Editions up to the fourteenth, 1922, are recorded; this last including the sixty-fifth thousand. Editions 10 to 14 contain a third section in the appendix: "Rotverschiebung der Spektrallinien."

130. RELATIVITY, THE SPECIAL AND THE GENERAL THEORY: A POPULAR EXPOSITION. London, Methuen. xiii, 138 pp., port.

Authorized translation by Robert W. Lawson from the fifth German edition, item 110. It contains a brief biographical sketch by Dr. Lawson, a brief bibliography of other books in English on relativity, and an appendix specially written for this edition: "Experimental confirmation of the general theory of relativity." So-called second and third editions were also issued by Methuen in 1920, up to the tenth in 1931. *Autobiography of science*, ed. by F. R. MOULTON, New York, Doubleday, 1945, quotes portions of this text on pp. 524-536. A "condensation" is included in J. W. Knedler: *Masterworks of science*, Doubleday, 1947, pp. 599-637.

131. ÄTHER UND RELATIVITÄTSTHEORIE: REDE GEHALTEN AM 5. MAI 1920 AN DER REICHS-UNIVERSITÄT ZU LEIDEN. Berlin, Springer. 15 pp. Lecture given in Leiden, October 27, 1920.

For an English translation see item 152; for French and Italian translations, items 145 and 153 respectively. A Polish translation by L. Freudenheim, *Eter a teorja wzglednosci*, was published in Lwow without date.

132. Bemerkung zur Abhandlung von W. R. Hess: Theorie der Viscosität heterogener Systeme. *Kolloidzeitschrift*, vol. 27, p. 137.

133. Inwiefern lässt sich die moderne Gravitationstheorie ohne die Relativität begründen? *Naturwissenschaften*, vol. 8, pp. 1010-1011.

134. Trägheitsmoment des Wasserstoffmoleküls. *Preussische Akademie der Wissenschaften, Sitzungberichte*, 1920, p. 65.

Abstract of a paper never published.

135. Schallausbreitung in teilweise dissoziierten Gasen. *Preussische Akademie der Wissenschaften, Sitzungsberichte,* 1920, pp. 380-385.

136. Meine Antwort über die antirelativitätstheoretische G.m.b.H. [Gesellschaft mit beschränkter Haftung]. *Berliner Tageblatt und Handelszeitung,* 27 August 1920, (no. 402), pp. 1-2.

1921

137. RELATIVITY, THE SPECIAL AND THE GENERAL THEORY: A POPULAR EXPOSITION. New York, Holt. xiii, 168 pp.

> This differs from the English edition (item 130) only in page arrangement. The same book appears with the imprint, New York, Smith [1931], and again with the imprint, New York, Hartsdale House, Inc., 1947.

138. TEORIA DE LA RELATIVIDAD ESPECIAL Y GENERAL, Trad. de la 12ª ed. alemana por F. Lorente de Nó. Toledo, Peláez, 1921. 79 pp.

> Translation of item 129. There are two later Spanish editions, called 2ª and 3ª, of 127 pp., with imprints respectively Cuenca, Ruiz de Lara, 1923, and Toledo, Medina, 1925.

139. SULLA TEORIA SPECIALE E GENERALE DELLA RELATIVITÀ: VOLGARIZZAZIONE. Trad. di G. L. Calisse. Bologna, Zanichelli. xii, 125 pp.

> Italian translation of item 129.

140. TEORIIA OTNOSITEL'NOSTI: OBSHCHEDOSTYPNOE IZLOZHENIE. [Berlin] Slowo. 150 pp., portrait.

> Russian translation by G. B. Itel'son of item 129. Also the same with imprint date 1922.

141. LA THÉORIE DE LA RELATIVITÉ RESTREINTE ET GÉNERALISÉE, traduit d'après la 10ᵉ éd. allemande par Mlle. J. Rouviere. Paris, Gauthier. xii, 120 pp.

> Translation of item 129.

142. THE MEANING OF RELATIVITY: FOUR LECTURES DELIVERED AT PRINCETON UNIVERSITY, May, 1921. Transl. by Edwin P. Adams. Princeton University Press. 123 pp.

> Contents:—Space and time in pre-relativity physics.—Theory of

special relativity.—General theory of relativity.—General relativity (continued).

> Reprinted with dates 1922 and 1923. The same title also with the imprint London, Methuen [1922], and [1924]. See items 166, 167, 179 for other translations; 156 for German text; 297 for a second edition.

143. GEOMETRIE UND ERFAHRUNG, ERWEITERTE FASSUNG DES FESTVORTRAGES GEHALTEN AN DER PREUSSISCHEN AKADEMIE. Berlin, Springer, 20 pp.

> The original paper, "zur Feier des Jahrestages König Friedrichs II" is in the academy *Sitzungsberichte*, 1921, pp. 123-130, (item 148). A Polish translation of this was issued in Lwow without date under title, *Geometrja a doswiadczenie*. See items 144, 152, 153 for other translations.

144. LA GÉOMÉTRIE ET L'EXPÉRIENCE, traduit par Maurice Solovine. Paris, Gauthier, 20 pp.

> Translation of item 143. A second edition also issued by Gauthier in 1934, 24 pp.

145. L'ÉTHER ET LA THÉORIE DE LA RELATIVITÉ, traduit par Maurice Solovine. Paris, Gauthier, 15 pp.

> A translation of item 131. Another printing carries the date 1925.

146. Einfache Anwendung des Newtonschen Gravitationsgesetzes auf die kugelförmigen Sternhaufen.

> pp. 50-52 of KAISER WILHELM GESELLSCHAFT ZUR FÖRDERUNG DER WISSENSCHAFT, Festschrift . . . zu ihrem zehnjährigen Jubiläum . . . Berlin, Springer.

147. A brief outline of the development of the theory of relativity, [translated by R. W. Lawson].
Nature, vol. 106, pp. 782-784.

> Written for a special issue of *Nature* devoted to relativity.

148. Geometrie und Erfahrung.
Preussische Akademie der Wissenschaften, Sitzungsberichte, 1921, pt. 1, pp. 123- 130.

> See item 143.

149. Eine naheliegende Ergänzung des Fundamentes der allgemeinen Relativitätstheorie.
Preussische Akademie der Wissenschaften, Sitzungsberichte, 1921, pt. 1, pp. 261-264.

150. Ein den Elementarprozess der Lichtemission betreffendes Experiment.

Preussische Akademie der Wissenschaften, Sitzungsberichte, 1921, pt. 2, pp. 882-883.

On the bearing of quantum theory upon the Doppler phenomenon. The proposed experiment was apparently never carried through. But see the related paper, item 202.

151. [Report of lecture at King's College on the development and present position of relativity, with quotations].

Nation and Athenaeum, vol. 29, pp. 431-432.

The German text is included in *Mein Weltbild,* (item 361) pp. 215-220, and a full translation in *The world as I see it.* It is reported without direct quotation in the *Times, London,* June 14, p. 8, also in *Nature,* vol. 107, p. 504.

1922

152. SIDELIGHTS ON RELATIVITY: I. ETHER AND RELATIVITY. II. GEOMETRY AND EXPERIENCE, transl. by G. B. Jeffery and W. Perrett. London, Methuen. 56 pp.

Translations of items 131 and 143. The same was published with the imprint New York, Dutton, 1923. *Geometry and experience* is reproduced complete as chapter 8 of CHICAGO UNIVERSITY: *Methods of the sciences,* 2nd ed., 1947.

153. PROSPETTIVE RELATIVISTICHE DELL'ETERE E DELLA GEOMETRIA, trad. di R. Cantù e T. Bembo. Milan, Andare. 54 pp.

Translations of items 131 and 143.

154. A KÜLÖNLEGES ÉS AZ ÁLTALÁNOS RELATIVITÁS, ELMÉLETE. Budapest, Patheon irodalmi. 94 pp.

Hungarian translation of item 129.

155. O FIZICHESKOI PRIRODIE PROSTRANSTVA, transl. by G. B. Itel'son. Berlin, Slowo. 52 pp.

The translated Russian title is "Physical nature of space." It comprises translations of items 131 and 143.

156. VIER VORLESUNGEN ÜBER RELATIVITÄTSTHEORIE, GEHALTEN IM MAI, 1921, AN DER UNIVERSITÄT PRINCETON. Braunschweig, Vieweg. 70 pp.

The German text of item 142. There is also a second printing by Vieweg of date 1923.

157. Untersuchungen über die Theorie der Brownschen Bewegungen, hrsg. von R. Fürth. Leipzig, Akademische Verlagsgesellschaft. 72 pp. (Ostwalds Klassiker der exakten Wissenschaften, Nr. 199).

> A reissue of items 8, 11, 12, 22, 26, with notes by the editor on the history of specific points, derivation of formulæ, etc. For an English translation see item 198.

158. Theoretische Bemerkungen zur Supraleitung der Metalle.

> pp. 429-435 of Leyden. Rijksuniversiteit. . . . Natuurkundig Laboratorium, Gedenkboek aangeboden aan H. Kamerlingh Onnes . . . Leiden, Ijdo.

159. Bemerkung zur Seletyschen Arbeit: Beiträge zum kosmologischen Problem.

> *Annalen der Physik,* ser. 4, vol. 69, pp. 436-438.

160. [Review of] W. Pauli: Relativitätstheorie.

> *Naturwissenschaften,* vol. 10, pp. 184-185.

161. Emil Warburg als Forscher.

> *Naturwissenschaften,* vol. 10, pp. 823-828.

162. Theorie der Lichtfortpflanzung in dispergierenden Medien.

> *Preussische Akademie der Wissenschaften, Phys.-math. Klasse, Sitzungsberichte,* 1922, pp. 18-22.

163. Bemerkung zu der Abhandlung von E. Trefftz: Statische Gravitationsfeld zweier Massenpunkte. . . .

> *Preussische Akademie der Wissenschaften, Phys.-math. Klasse, Sitzungsberichte,* 1922, pp. 448-449.

164. Quantentheoretische Bemerkungen zum Experiment von Stern und Gerlach, with P. Ehrenfest.

> *Zeitschrift für Physik,* vol. 11, pp. 31-34.

165. Bemerkung zu der Arbeit von A. Friedmann: Über die Krümmung des Raumes.

> *Zeitschrift für Physik,* vol. 11, p. 326.

> The criticism was withdrawn in a later note, *ibid.* vol. 16, p. 228.

1923

166. Cztery Odczyty o Teorji Wzglednosci Wygloszone w 1921 na Uniwersytecie w Princeton. Wien, and Stanislawow, Renaissance-Verlag.

Polish translation by A. Gottfryda of item 156 (142).

167. Matematicheskija Osnovy Teorii Otnositel'nosti. Berlin, Slowo, 106 pp.

Russian translation by G. B. Itel'son of item 156 (142).

168. Grundgedanken und Probleme der Relativitätstheorie. Stockholm, Imprimerie royale. 10 pp.

Address in acknowledgement of the Nobel prize, delivered before the Nordische Naturforscherversammlung, Göteborg. Also contained in *Nobelstiftelsen, Les prix Nobel en 1921-22.*

169. [Yiddish translation, printed in Hebrew characters, of item 129] Warsaw, Gitlina. 109 pp.

E. P. Goldsmith and Co., Ltd., Old Bond St., London, list this in an old catalog. No copy has been located in the United States.

170. Bemerkung zu der Notiz von W. Anderson: Neue Erklärung des kontinuierlichen Koronaspektrums.
Astronomische Nachrichten, vol. 219, p. 19.

171. Experimentelle Bestimmung der Kanalweite von Filtern, with H. Mühsam.
Deutsche medizinische Wochenschrift, vol. 49, pp. 1012-1013.

172. Beweis der Nichtexistenz eines überall regulären zentrisch symmetrischen Feldes nach der Feldtheorie von Kaluza, with J. Grommer.
Jerusalem University, Scripta, vol. 1, no. 7, 5 pp.

Hebrew text also.

173. Theory of the affine field.
Nature, vol. 112, pp. 448-449.

This is a relatively non-mathematical statement on electromagnetic and gravitational fields as generalized Riemannian geometry. Translated by R. W. Lawson, but not from item 175.

174. Zur allgemeinen Relativitätstheorie.
Preussische Akademie der Wissenschaften, Phys.-math. Klasse, Sitzungsberichte, 1923, pp. 32-38, 76-77.

175. Zur affinen Feldtheorie.
Preussische Akademie der Wissenschaften, Phys.-math. Klasse, Sitzungsberichte, 1923, pp. 137-140.

176. Bietet die Feldtheorie Möglichkeiten für die Lösung des quanten-problems?
Preussische Akademie der Wissenschaften, Phys.-math. Klasse, Sitzungsberichte, 1923, pp. 359-364.

177. Théorie de relativité.
Société française de philosophie, Bulletin, vol. 22, pp. 97, 98, 101, 107, 111-112.

> A discussion to which Einstein contributes two statements as to the relation of his theory to Kant's and to Mach's. These are quoted in full in *Nature,* vol. 112, p. 253.

178. Quantentheorie des Strahlungsgleichgewichts, with P. Ehrenfest.
Zeitschrift für Physik, vol. 19, pp. 301-306.

1924

179. QUATRE CONFERENCES SUR LA THÉORIE DE LA RELATIVITÉ, FAITES À LA UNIVERSITÉ DE PRINCETON, traduit par Maurice Solovine. Paris, Gauthier, 104 pp.

> French translation of item 156 (142).
> A second printing, Gauthier, 1925. 96 pp.

180. Geleitwort.
> vol. 2, p. vi, a-b, of *Lucretius, De rerum natura,* lateinisch und deutsch, von H. DIELS, Berlin, Weidmann.

181. Antwort auf eine Bemerkung von W. Anderson.
Astronomische Nachrichten, vol. 221, pp. 329-330.

182. Komptonsche Experiment.
Berliner Tageblatt, April 20, 1924, 1. Beiblatt.

183. Ideas fundamentales y problemas de la teoria de la relatividad.
Fénix (or *Phoenix*), Buenos Aires. vol. 4, pp. 103-111.

> Translation of address in acknowledgement of Nobel prize. (See item 168.)

184. Zum hundertjährigen Gedenktag von Lord Kelvins Geburt.
Naturwissenschaften, vol. 12, pp. 601-602.

185. Quantentheorie des einatomigen idealen Gases.
Preussische Akademie der Wissenschaften, Phys.-math. Klasse, Sitzungsberichte, 1924, p. 261-267.

> Continued in item 194.

186. Über den Äther.
   Schweizerische naturforschende Gesellschaft, Verhandlungen,
   vol. 105, pt. 2, pp. 85-93.

   An historical survey.

187. Theorie der Radiometerkräfte.
   Zeitschrift für Physik, vol. 27, pp. 1-6.

188. [Note appended to paper by Bose: Wärmegleichgewicht im Strahlungsfeld bei Anwesenheit von Materie].
   Zeitschrift für Physik, vol. 27, pp. 392-393.

1925

189. SUR L'ÉLECTRODYNAMIQUE DES CORPS EN MOUVEMENT, traduit par Maurice Solovine. Paris, Gauthier. 56 pp., port. (Maîtres de la pensée scientifique).

   A translation of items 9 and 10.

190. Anhang: Eddingtons Theorie und Hamiltonsches Prinzip.
   p. 366-371, of A. S. EDDINGTON. *Relativitätstheorie in mathematischer Behandlung.* Berlin, Springer.

   Written especially for this German edition of Eddington.

191. Theoretische Atomistik.
   pp. 281-294 of DIE PHYSIK, 2. Aufl. Leipzig, Teubner.

   A revision of item 76.

192. Relativitätstheorie.
   pp. 783-797 of DIE PHYSIK, 2. Aufl. Leipzig, Teubner.

   A revision of item 77.

193. Elektron und allgemeine Relativitätstheorie.
   Physica, vol. 5, pp. 330-334.

194. Quantentheorie des einatomigen idealen Gases. 2. Abhandlung.
   Preussische Akademie der Wissenschaften, Phys.-math. Klasse, Sitzungsberichte, 1925, pp. 3-14.

   A continuation of item 185.

195. Quantentheorie des idealen Gases.
   Preussische Akademie der Wissenschaften, Phys.-math. Klasse, Sitzungsberichte, 1925, pp. 18-25.

   A general condition is deduced which must be satisfied by every theory of a perfect gas.

196. Einheitliche Feldtheorie von Gravitation und Elektrizität.
Preussische Akademie der Wissenschaften, Phys.-math. Klasse, Sitzungsberichte, 1925, pp. 414-419.

197. Bemerkung zu P. Jordans Abhandlung: Theorie der Quantenstrahlung.
Zeitschrift für Physik, vol. 31, pp. 784-785.

1926

198. INVESTIGATIONS ON THE THEORY OF THE BROWNIAN MOVEMENT, edited with notes by R. Fürth, transl. by A. D. Cowper. London, Methuen. 124 pp.

> Translation of item 157. The same was issued with the imprint New York, Dutton.

199. W. H. Julius, 1860-1925
Astrophysical Journal, vol. 63, pp. 196-198.

200. Ursache der Mäanderbildung der Flussläufe und des sogenannten Baerschen Gesetzes.
Naturwissenchaften, vol. 14, pp. 223-224.

> Read before the Prussian Academy, January 7, 1926. Included in *Mein Weltbild* and in its translation (items 361 and 362).

201. Vorschlag zu einem die Natur des elementaren Strahlungs-emissions-prozesses betreffenden Experiment.
Naturwissenschaften, vol. 14, pp. 300-301.

> A preliminary note covering item 202.

202. Interferenzeigenschaften des durch Kanalstrahlen emittierten Lichtes.
Preussische Akademie der Wissenschaften, Phys.-math. Klasse, Sitzungsberichte, 1926, pp. 334-340.

> The prediction here made that canal rays radiate as do classical Hertz oscillators was experimentally verified by Rupp (*Ibid.,* pp. 341-351).

203. Geometría no euclídea y física.
Revista matemática hispano-americana, ser. 2, vol. 1, pp. 72-76.

1927

204. [Introduction]
to T. SHALIT: *Di spetsyele relativitets-teorye.* Berlin, [privately printed] 240 pp.

> Both Yiddish and German texts are given.

205. Einfluss der Erdbewegung auf die Lichtgeschwindigkeit relativ zur Erde.

Forschungen und Fortschritte, vol. 3, pp. 36-37.

206. Formale Beziehung des Riemannschen Krümmungstensors zu den Feldgleichungen der Gravitation.

Mathematische Annalen, vol. 97, pp. 99-103.

> Read before Prussian Academy, 1926, under title: Anwendungen einer von Rainich gefundenen Spaltung des Riemannschen Krümmungstensors.

207. Isaac Newton.

Manchester Guardian weekly, vol. 16, pp. 234-235.

> Also in the *Manchester Guardian* of March 19, 1927; reprinted in *Observatory*, vol. 50, pp. 146-153, and in *Smithsonian Institution, Report* for 1927, pp. 201-207.

208. Newtons Mechanik und ihr Einfluss auf die Gestaltung der theoretischen Physik.

Naturwissenschaften, vol. 15, pp. 273-276.

> Included in *Mein Weltbild*, and in its translation (items 361 and 362).

209. Zu Newtons 200. Todestage.

Nord und Süd, Jahrg. 50, pp. 36-40.

210. [Letter to Royal Society on the occasion of the Newton bicentenary]

Nature, vol. 119, p. 467; *Science*, new ser., vol. 65, pp. 347-348.

211. Establishment of an international bureau of meteorology.

Science, new ser., vol. 65, pp. 415-417.

> Report of a subcommitttee of the International Committee on Intellectual Cooperation, signed also by M. Curie and H. A. Lorentz.

212. Kaluzas Theorie des Zusammenhanges von Gravitation und Elektrizität.

Preussische Akademie der Wissenschaften, Phys.-math. Klasse, Sitzungsberichte, 1927, pp. 23-30.

213. Allgemeine Relativitätstheorie und Bewegungsgesetz. (First part with J. Grommer.)

Preussische Akademie der Wissenschaften, Phys.-math. Klasse, Sitzungsberichte, 1927, pp. 2-13, 235-245.

214. Theoretisches und Experimentelles zur Frage der Lichtentstehung.

Zeitschrift für angewandte Chemie, vol. 40, p. 546.

Editorial report of a lecture before the Mathematische-physikalische Arbeitsgemeinschaft, Universität Berlin, 23 Feb.

1928

215. Al Torath ha-Yahasiuth ha-Peratith weha-Kelalith (Harzaah Popularith). Tel-Aviv, Dvir. 102 pp.

Hebrew translation by Jacob Greenberg of item 129.

216. H. A. Lorentz.

Mathematisch-naturwissenschaftliche Blätter, vol. 22, pp. 24-25.

Extract from an address at the Leyden University memorial service. In *Mein Weltbild*, p. 25 (item 361).

217. Riemanngeometrie mit Aufrechterhaltung des Begriffes des Fern-Parallelismus.

Preussische Akademie der Wissenschaften, Phys.-math. Klasse, Sitzungsberichte, 1928, pp. 217-221.

218. Neue Möglichkeit für eine einheitliche Feldtheorie von Gravitation und Elektrizität.

Preussische Akademie der Wissenschaften, Phys.-math. Klasse, Sitzungsberichte, 1928, pp. 224-227.

219. À propos de "La déduction relativiste" de M. E. Meyerson.

Revue philosophique de la France, vol. 105, pp. 161-166.

1929

220. Space-time.

Encyclopedia Britannica, 14th ed., vol. 21, pp. 105-108.

This is reprinted without revision in the 1942 edition.

221. Über den gegenwärtigen Stand der Feldtheorie.

pp. 126-132 of Festschrift Prof. Dr. A. Stodola Überreicht. Zürich, Füssli.

A survey much less technical than that in item 235, with emphasis on the antecedents of the theory.

222. Ansprache an Prof. Planck [bei Entgegennahme der Planckmedaille].

Forschungen und Fortschritte, vol. 5, pp. 248-249.

223. [Quotation from interview with (London) *Daily Chronicle* of Jan. 26, on the unitary field theory, in advance of publication of his paper on the subject, item 226].
Nature, vol. 123, p. 175.

224. [Note appended to a reprinting of Arago's Memorial address on Thomas Young before the French Academy.]
Naturwissenschaften, vol. 17, p. 363.

225. The new field theory.
Times, London, of 4 Feb., 1929.
Translated by L. L. Whyte. Quoted in full in *Observatory*, vol. 52, pp. 82-87 and 114-118, 1930.

226. Einheitliche Feldtheorie.
Preussische Akademie der Wissenschaften, Phys.-math. Klasse, Sitzungsberichte, 1929, pp. 2-7.
This paper represents a new development which was immediate news. (See *New York Times* item for Feb. 3rd.) A trustee of Wesleyan University purchased the manuscript directly, for desposit in the Olin Library at Wesleyan. (See *New York Times*, April 8, p. 4, col. 3.) *Scientific monthly*, vol. 28, p. 480, published a facsimile of one page. The critical note by Eddington in *Nature* of Feb. 23 (vol. 123, pp. 280-281) is also of interest in connection with the paper.

227. Einheitliche Feldtheorie und Hamiltonsches Prinzip.
Preussische Akademie der Wissenschaften, Phys.-math. Klasse, Sitzungsberichte, 1929, pp. 156-159.

228. Sur la théorie synthéthique des champs, with Th. de Donder.
Revue générale de l'électricité, vol. 25, pp. 35-39.

229. Appreciation of Simon Newcomb.
Science, new ser., vol. 69, p. 249.
Translation of a letter to Newcomb's daughter dated July 15, 1926.

230. Sesión especial de la Academia, 16 abril 1925.
Sociedad científica Argentina, Anales, vol. 107, pp. 337-347.
Debate with R. G. Loyarte on the equivalence of mass and energy, and discussion with H. Damianovich on the bearing of relativity on a possible "chemical field."

1930

231. Begleitwort.
D. REICHINSTEIN: *Grenzflächenvorgänge in der unbelebten und belebten Natur*. Leipzig, Barth.

232. Über Kepler.
Frankfurter Zeitung, 9 Nov. 1930, p. 16, col. 3-4.

German text is reprinted in *Mein Weltbild,* and a translation in *The World as I see it* (items 361 and 362).

233. Raum-, Feld- und Äther-problem in der Physik.
World power conference, 2nd, Berlin, 1930. Transactions, vol. 19, pp. 1-5.

An invitation address, widely reported; a rather full account, for example, in *Dinglers polytechnisches journal,* vol. 345, p. 122.

234. Raum, Äther und Feld in der Physik.
Forum Philosophicum, vol. 1, pp. 173-180.

This is followed by an English translation by E. S. Brightman, pp. 180-184. The subject matter of this exposition is similar to that of item 233, but the phraseology distinctly different. Both items, in turn, are different from "Das Raum-, Äther-, und Feld-problem der Physik" contained in *Mein Weltbild,* p. 229-248. See item 415.

235. Théorie unitaire du champ physique.
Institut H. Poincaré, Annales, vol. I, pp. 1-24.

A comprehensive survey of the problem.

236. Auf die Riemann-Metrik und den Fern-Parallelismus gegründete einheitliche Feldtheorie.
Mathematische Annalen, vol. 102, pp. 685-697.

237. Das Raum-Zeit Problem.
Koralle, vol. 5, pp. 486-488.

A much simplified and abbreviated form of the material of item 220.

238. [Review of] S. WEINBERG: *Erkenntnistheorie.*
Naturwissenschaften, vol. 18, pp. 536.

239. Kompatibilität der Feldgleichungen in der einheitlichen Feldtheorie.
Preussische Akademie der Wissenschaften, Phys.-math. Klasse, Sitzungsberichte, 1930, pp. 18-23.

240. Zwei strenge statische Lösungen der Feldgleichungen der einheitlichen Feldtheorie, with W. Mayer.
Preussische Akademie der Wissenschaften, Phys.-math. Klasse, Sitzungsberichte, 1930, pp. 110-120.

241. Theorie der Räume mit Riemannmetrik und Fernparallelismus.
Preussische Akademie der Wissenschaften, Phys.-math. Klasse,
Sitzungsberichte, 1930, pp. 401-402.

242. Address at University of Nottingham, [transl. by Dr. I. H.
Brose].
Science, new ser., vol. 71, pp. 608-610.

> A brief survey of special and general relativity and field theory. A
> summary is published in Nature, vol. 125, pp. 897-898, under the
> title "Concept of space."

243. Über den gegenwärtigen stand der allgemeinen Relativitätstheorie.
Yale University. Library. Gazette. vol. 6, pp. 3-6.

> Followed on pp. 7-10 by a translation by Prof. Leigh Page. Yale
> University possesses the autographed manuscript. As Prof. Page re-
> calls, " a Yale graduate persuaded Dr. Einstein to write this state-
> ment in his own hand;" it was not a lecture.

1931

244. Foreword.
p.v of R. De Villamil: Newton, the man. London, Knox.

245. Maxwell's influence on the development of the conception of
physical reality.
pp. 66-73 of James Clerk Maxwell: A Commemoration
Volume. Cambridge, University press.

> German original is in Mein Weltbild, and a different English version
> in its translation (items 361 and 362).

246. Foreword.
p. vii-viii of Sir Isaac Newton: Optiks . . . reprinted from
the 4th ed., [London, 1730] New York, McGraw.

> Written expressly for this volume.

247. Theory of Relativity: Its Formal Content and Its Present Problems.

> Rhodes lectures at Oxford University, May, 1931. These dealt in
> Prof. Einstein's opinion with questions "in too fluid a state" for
> publication, and they have consequently never been published. Their
> content is briefly described in Nature, vol. 127, pp. 765, 790, 826-
> 827.

248. Knowledge of past and future in quantum mechanics, with R. C.
Tolman and B. Podolsky.
Physical Review, ser. 2, vol. 37, pp. 780-781.

249. Zum kosmologischen Problem der allgemeinen Relativitätstheorie.
  Preussische Akademie der Wissenschaften, Phys.-math. Klasse,
  Sitzungsberichte, 1931, pp. 235-237.

250. Systematische Untersuchung über kompatible Feldgleichungen
  welche in einem Riemannschen Raume mit Fern-Parallelismus
  gesetzt werden können, with W. Mayer.
  Preussische Akademie der Wissenschaften, Phys.-math. Klasse,
  Sitzungsberichte, 1931, pp. 257-265.

251. Einheitliche Theorie von Gravitation und Elektrizität, with W.
  Mayer.
  Preussische Akademie der Wissenschaften, Phys.-math. Klasse,
  Sitzungsberichte, 1931, pp. 541-557.

  A French translation is contained in item 266. Continued in item 261.

252. Thomas Alva Edison, 1847-1931.
  Science, new ser., vol. 74, pp. 404-405.

253. Gravitational and electrical fields. [Translation of preliminary
  report for the Josiah Macy, Jr. foundation.]
  Science, new ser., vol. 74, pp. 438-439.

254. [Reply to congratulatory addresses at a dinner given by the California Institute of Technology, January 15, 1931.]
  Science, new ser., vol. 73, p. 379.

  Stresses the support given his work by experimental physicists. The
  text of the other addresses is given in the same article.

255. Gedenkworte auf Albert A. Michelson.
  Zeitschrift für angewandte Chemie, vol. 44, p. 658.

1932

256. Prologue,
  pp. 7-12 of M. PLANCK: *Where is science going?* New York,
  Norton.

  A characterization of the work of Planck and of theoretical physicists generally.

257. Epilogue: a socratic dialogue, interlocutors, Einstein and Murphy.
  pp. 201-213 of MAX PLANCK: *Where is science going?* New
  York, Norton.

  "An abridgment of stenographic reports made . . . during various
  conversations." Essentially on the scientific basis for a philosophy of
  determinism.

258. On the relation between the expansion and the mean density of the universe, with W. de Sitter.

> *National academy of sciences, Proceedings,* vol. 18, pp. 213-214.

259. Zu Dr. Berliners siebzigstem Geburtstag.

> *Naturwissenschaften,* vol. 20, p. 913.

>> Reprinted in *Mein Weltbild,* pp. 29-32 (item 361).

260. Gegenwärtiger Stand der Relativitätstheorie.

> *Paedagogischer Führer* (then called *Die Quelle*), vol. 82, pp. 440-442.

261. Einheitliche Theorie von Gravitation und Elektrizität, 2. Abhandlung, with W. Mayer.

> *Preussische Akademie der Wissenschaften. Phys.-math. Klasse, Sitzungsberichte,* 1932, pp. 130-137.

>> A continuation of item 251.

262. Semi-Vektoren und Spinoren, with W. Mayer.

> *Preussiche Akademie der Wissenschaften, Phys.-math. Klasse. Sitzungsberichte,* 1932, pp. 522-550.

263. Unbestimmtheitsrelation.

> *Zeitschrift für angewandte Chemie,* vol. 45, p. 23.

>> Abstract of a Colloquium, University of Berlin, Nov. 4, 1931.

1933

264. ON THE METHOD OF THEORETICAL PHYSICS. The Herbert Spencer lecture delivered at Oxford, June 10, 1933. Oxford, Clarendon press. 15 pp.

> The same text was published with the imprint New York, Oxford university press, 1933. 20 pp. It was also reprinted in *Philosophy of science,* vol. 1, pp. 162-169 in 1934. The German text is published in *Mein Weltbild,* pp. 176-187, and a more colloquial translation in *The world as I see it* (items 361 and 362). Selections from it are included (pp. 391-397) in *New worlds in science,* ed. by H. WARD, New York, McBride, 1941.

265. ORIGINS OF THE GENERAL THEORY OF RELATIVITY. Lecture on the George A. Gibson foundation in the University of Glasgow, June *20th*, 1933. Glasgow, Jackson. 11 pp. (Glasgow university publications, no. 30.)

> German text is contained in *Mein Weltbild* pp. 248-256. A different

English version is published in *The world as I see it* (item 362). An abstract, with quotations, is in *Nature*, vol. 132, p. 21.

266. Les Fondements de la Théorie de la Relativité Générale. . . . traduit par Maurice Solovine. Paris, Hermann. 109 pp.

> Three essays: translations of items 89 and 251, and "Sur la structure cosmologique de l'espace" (pp. 99-109) which was specially written for this volume. This last is an amplified treatment of the expanding universe (compare items 249 and 258), including the historical setting of the topic. The volume is reputed rare.

267. Dirac Gleichungen für Semi-Vektoren, with W. Mayer.
Akademie van wetenschappen, Amsterdam, Proceedings, vol. 36, pt. 2, pp. 615-619. 1934

268. Spaltung der natürlichsten Feldgleichungen für Semi-Vektoren in Spinor-Gleichungen vom Diracschen Typus, with W. Mayer.
Akademie van wetenschappen, Amsterdam, Proceedings, vol. 36, pt. 2, pp. 615-619.

1934

269. Introduction.
pp. 5-6, of L. Infeld: The World in Modern Science. London, Gollancz.

> Written especially for this English translation. German original on p. 275.

270. Darstellung der Semi-Vektoren als gewöhnliche Vektoren von besonderem Differentiations Charakter, with W. Mayer.
Annals of mathematics, ser. 2, vol. 35, pp. 104-110.

271. [Review of] R. Tolman: Relativity, thermodynamics and cosmology.
Science, new ser., vol. 80, p. 358.

1935

272. Elementary derivation of the equivalence of mass and energy.
American mathematical society, Bulletin, vol. 41, pp. 223-230.

> Josiah Willard Gibbs lecture, before the American Association for the Advancement of Science, Dec. 28, 1934.

273. Can quantum-mechanical description of physical reality be considered complete? with B. Podolsky and N. Rosen.
Physical Review, ser. 2, vol. 47, pp. 777-780.

> An abstract of this paper by H. T. Flint appears in *Nature*, vol. 135,

pp. 1025-1026. For a news story on the paper see *New York Times*, May 4, 1935, p. 11, col. 4, and May 7, p. 21, col. 5.

274. The particle problem in the general theory of relativity, with N. Rosen.

Physical Review, ser. 2, vol. 48, pp. 73-77.

1936

275. Physik und Realität.

Franklin Institute, Journal, vol. 221, pp. 313-347.

A translation by J. Piccard follows, pp. 349-382. The German text is reprinted in *Zeitschrift für freie deutsche Forschung*, Paris, vol. 1, no. 1, pp. 5-19; no. 2, pp. 1-14, (1938).

276. Two-body problem in general relativity theory, with N. Rosen.

Physical Review, ser. 2, vol. 49, pp. 404-405.

277. Lens-like action of a star by deviation of light in the gravitational field.

Science, vol. 84, pp. 506-507.

1937

278. On gravitational waves, with N. Rosen.

Franklin Institute, Journal, vol. 223, pp. 43-54.

1938

279. THE EVOLUTION OF PHYSICS: THE GROWTH OF IDEAS FROM EARLY CONCEPTS TO RELATIVITY AND QUANTA, with L. Infeld. New York, Simon and Schuster. x, 319 pp.

As explained in the preface, this is "not a systematic course in elementary facts and theories," but is aimed "to give some idea of the eternal struggle of the inventive human mind for a fuller understanding of the laws governing physical phenomena." Contents cover the rise and decline of the mechanical view; field and relativity; quanta.

280. DIE PHYSIK ALS ABENTEUER DER ERKENNTNIS. Leiden, Sijthoff. viii, 222 pp.

German edition of item 279.

281. DREI EEUWEN PHYSICA VAN GALILEI TOT RELATIVITEITS-THEORIE EN QUANTUMTHEORIE. Amsterdam, Centen. viii, 319 pp.

A translation into Dutch by M. C. Geerling of item 279.

282. L'ÉVOLUTION DES IDÉES EN PHYSIQUE DES PREMIERS CONCEPTS AUX THÉORIES DE LA RELATIVITÉ ET DES QUANTA. Traduit par Maurice Solovine. Paris, Flammarion. vii, 298 pp.

French translation of item 279.

283. Gravitational equations and the problems of motion, with L. Infeld and B. Hoffmann.
Annals of mathematics, ser. 2. vol. 39, pp. 65-100.

For continuation see item 286.

284. Generalization of Kaluza's theory of electricity, with P. Bergmann.
Annals of mathematics, ser. 2, vol. 39, pp. 683-701.

1939

285. Stationary system with spherical symmetry consisting of many gravitating masses.
Annals of mathematics, ser. 2, vol. 40, pp. 922-936.

1940

286. Gravitational equations and the problems of motion. II, with L. Infeld.
Annals of mathematics, ser. 2, vol. 41, pp. 455-464.

Continuation of item 283.

287. Considerations concerning the fundamentals of theoretical physics.
Science, new ser., vol. 91, pp. 487-492.

Address at the 8th *American scientific congress*, Washington, May, 1940. Published also in the *Proceedings* of the Congress, vol. 7, pp. 19-27 (1942), and in slightly abridged form in *Nature*, vol. 145, pp. 920-924 (1940).

1941

288. Five-dimensional representation of gravitation and electricity, with V. Bargmann and P. G. Bergmann.
pp. 212-225 of THEODORE VON KARMAN ANNIVERSARY VOLUME. Pasadena, California Institute of Technology.

289. Science and religion.
pp. 209-214 of CONFERENCE ON SCIENCE, PHILOSOPHY, AND RELIGION, 1st, New York, 1940.

Reported in *New York Times* Sept. 11, 1940, p. 30, col. 2, and also in *Nature*, vol. 146, pp. 605-607.

290. Demonstration of the non-existence of gravitational fields with a non-vanishing total mass free of singularities.

> *Tucumán universidad nac., Revista,* ser. A, vol. 2, pp. 11-16.

>> Same in Spanish, *ibid.* pp. 5-10. This represents an address before a joint meeting of the American Physical Society and the American Association of Physics Teachers in Princeton, Dec. 29, 1941, under the title "Solutions of finite mass of the gravitational equations."

1942

291. Foreword.

> p. v of PETER G. BERGMANN: *Introduction to the theory of relativity.* New York, Prentice-Hall.

292. The work and personality of Walter Nernst.

> *Scientific monthly,* vol. 54, pp. 195-196.

1943

293. Non-existence of regular stationary solutions of relativistic field equations, with W. Pauli.

> *Annals of mathematics,* ser. 2, vol. 44, pp. 131-137.

1944

294. Remarks on Bertrand Russell's theory of knowledge.

> pp. 277-291 of *The philosophy of Bertrand Russell,* edited by PAUL A. SCHILPP. Evanston, Northwestern University. (Library of living philosophers, vol. 5)

295. Bivector fields, I, with V. Bargmann.

> *Annals of mathematics,* ser. 2, vol. 45, pp. 1-14.

296. Bivector fields, II.

> *Annals of mathematics,* ser. 2, vol. 45, pp. 15-23.

>> Just before its publication the manuscript of this paper was sold at a Kansas City bond auction for $5,500,000 (*New York Times,* 5 February 1944, p. 5, col. 3). It was presented to the Library of Congress (*New York Times,* 4 August 1944, p. 15, col. 5).

1945

297. THE MEANING OF RELATIVITY. Princeton, Princeton University press, 135 pp.

>> This is a second edition of item 142. An appendix has been added covering The cosmological problem, Four-dimensional space which is isotropic with respect to three dimensions, Field equations, Spatial

curvature, Generalization with respect to ponderable matter. This
appendix was translated by Ernst G. Straus. A so-called third edition with the imprint London, Methuen, 1946, is the same as the
American edition except for a change of pagination to 130 pp.

298. On the cosmological problem.
American scholar, vol. 14, pp. 137-156; correction, p. 269.

This is a preprinting of part of the appendix to item 297.

299. Generalization of the relativistic theory of gravitation.
Annals of mathematics, ser. 2, vol. 46, pp. 578-584.

300. Influence of the expansion of space on the gravitation fields surrounding the individual stars, with E. G. Straus.
Reviews of modern physics, vol. 17, pp. 120-124; corrections
and addition, *ibid.,* vol. 18, pp. 148-149.

1946

301. Generalization of the relativistic theory of gravitation, II, with E.
G. Straus.
Annals of mathematics, ser. 2, vol. 47, pp. 731-741.

302. Elementary derivation of the equivalence of mass and energy.
Technion journal, (Yearbook of American Society for Advancement of the Hebrew Institute of Technology in Haifa.)
vol. 5, pp. 16-17.

A derivation not published before, which uses the principle of special
relativity but not its formal machinery.
Published also in Hebrew in vol. 2 (1947) of Hebrew Technical
College (Institute of Technology), Haifa, *Scientific publications.*

1947

303. The problem of space, ether and the field in physics.
pp. 471-482 of SAXE COMMINS, and R. N. LINSCOTT, ed.,
Man and the universe. Random House.

Reprinted from *The world as I see it,* pp. 82-100 (item 362). The
original has not been identified (see note attached to item 234).

1948

304. EL SIGNIFICADO DE LA RELATIVIDAD, trad. por Dr. Carlos E.
Prélat. Buenos Aires, Espasa-Calpe. 165 pp.

Spanish translation of item 297.

305. Einstein's theory of relativity.
vol. 9, p. 19 of GROLIER ENCYCLOPEDIA, New York, Grolier

society, 1947. (Actual date of issue is 1948.)

> Einstein wrote only this portion of the article *Relativity: time, space and matter.*

306. Relativity: essence of the theory of relativity.
Vol. 16, col. 604-608, of AMERICAN PEOPLES ENCYCLOPEDIA.
Chicago, Spencer press [1948]

307. Quantenmechanik und Wirklichkeit.
Dialectica, vol. 2, pp. 320-324.

308. Generalized theory of gravitation.
Reviews of modern physics, vol. 20, pp. 35-39.

> "A new presentation . . . which constitutes a certain progress in clarity as compared with previous presentations," prepared for the Robert A. Millikan commemorative issue.

1949

309. Motion of particles in general relativity theory, with Leopold Infeld.
Canadian journal of mathematics, vol. 3, pp. 209-241.

II
NON-SCIENTIFIC WRITINGS
Starred titles are not available in the United States.

1920

311. Interview on interplanetary communication.
Daily Mail, London, Jan. 31, 1920.

> Indirect quotation in *New York Times*, Feb. 2, p. 24, col. 2.

1921

312. [Interview for Nieuwe Rotterdamsche Courant on impressions of the United States.]
Berliner Tageblatt, 7 July 1921, p. 2.

> Partly quoted in *Mein Weltbild* (item 361), pp. 54-60, and partly presented in the *New York Times*, 31 July 1921, sect. 2, p. 4, col. 3.

313. Einstein on education.
Nation and Athenaeum, vol. 30, pp. 378-379.

> Contains Quotations, but fails to indicate their source.

1922

314. In Memoriam Walther Rathenau.
Neue Rundschau, vol. 33, pt. 2, pp. 815-816.

315. Conditions in Germany.
New Republic, vol. 32, p. 197.

> Letter to H. N. Brailsford.

1923

316. My impressions of Palestine.
New Palestine, vol. 4, p. 341.

> Included in item 328, pp. 57-60.

1924

317. Une interview [on the League of Nations].
Journal des debats politiques et littéraires, édition hebdomadaire.
vol. 31, pt. 2, p. 184.

318. An die polnische Judenheit.
* *Leipziger jüdische Zeitung,* vol. 3, nr. 46.

1925

319. Botschaft.
Jüdische Rundschau, vol. 30, p. 129 (no. 14, Feb. 17).

> Copied from *La Revue juive.*
> On nationalism as an enemy of peace and as opposed by Zionism.

320. Ein Wort auf den Weg.
Juedische Rundschau, vol. 30, p. 245. (No. 27/28, Mar. 4).

> On the opening of the Hebrew University in Jerusalem.

321. Pan-Europa.
Das junge Japan, vol. I, pp. 369-372.

322. Mission of our university.
New Palestine, vol. 8, p. 294.

> Included in item 328, pp. 63-66.

1926

323. Interview urging extension of the Jewish telegraphic agency and
support of Dr. Weizmann in his leadership of United Palestine
appeal.
New Palestine, vol. 11, p. 334.

1927

324. Soll Deutschland Kolonial-politik treiben? Eine Umfrage. [Einstein's reply].
Europäische Gespräche, vol. 5, p. 626.

1929

**325. GELEGENTLICHES . . . ZUM FÜNFZIGSTEN GEBURTSTAG . . .
DARGEBRACHT VON DER SONCINO-GESELLSCHAFT DER FREUNDE
DES JÜDISCHEN BUCHES ZU BERLIN. 32 pp.**

> Published in a limited edition.
>
> Consists of small fragments: Über Wissenschaft und Politik, (including "Motive des Forschens" and Internationalität der Wissenschaft"),
> Judenfrage (various fragments), Vorrede zur hebräischen Übersetzung
> der Relativitätstheorie, a poem to Alexander Moszkowski, etc. The
> choicest portions are perhaps "Neun Fragen über das eigene Schaffen"
> —concise questions and answers, and "Antwort auf neun Fragen über
> das Erfinderwesen"—more expansive statements. These have not been
> found elsewhere.

326. Palestine troubles.

> *Manchester Guardian weekly*, vol. 21, p. 314.
>
> A letter first published in the *Manchester Guardian* of Oct. 12. Reprinted in item 328, pp. 71-85.

327. G. Stresemanns Mission.

> *Nord und Süd*, Jahrgang 52, pp. 953-954.
>
> Included as a "Foreword," pp. v-vii, to A. VALLENTIN, *Stresemann*. New York, Smith; London, Constable, 1931, but not to the
> German edition.

1930

**328. ABOUT ZIONISM: SPEECHES AND LETTERS, transl. and edited
by Sir Leon Simon. London, Soncino press. 68 pp.**

> Published also with the imprint New York, Macmillan, 1931. 94 pp.
> Passages from *Manchester Guardian*, *Jüdische Rundschau* (Berlin),
> *New Palestine* (New York), *Jewish Chronicle* (London), *Jüdischer
> Almanach* (Prague), etc., which are dated but not identified as to
> precise location of original. Selections are arranged under the captions "Assimilation and nationalism," "Jews in Palestine," "Jew and
> Arab."

329. Wissenschaft und Diktatur.

> p. 108 of O. FORST-BATTAGLIA, *Prozess der Diktatur*. Zürich,
> Amathea-verlag.
>
> A three-line statement, the source of which is not indicated.
>
> An English translation occurs on p. 107 of both English and American
> editions of the book, 1930 and 1931 respectively, which are entitled
> *Dictatorship on trial*.

330. Science and God: a dialog.
Forum and Century, vol. 83, pp. 373-379.

> With J. Murphy and J. W. N. Sullivan.
>
> The conversation touches also the relation of science to other aspects of life, the question of Jewish racial characteristics, etc. It is entirely distinct from item 257.

331. What I believe.
Forum and Century, vol. 84, pp. 193-194.

> The thirteenth of the Forum series "Living philosophies," republished as pp. 3-7 of LIVING PHILOSOPHIES, New York, Simon and Schuster, 1931. It was reprinted in the *Forum* vol. 95, pp. 174-176, 1936. It also appears under the title "Meeting-place of science and religion" on pp. 91-102 of *Has science discovered God?*, edited by E. H. COTTON, New York, Crowell, 1931. The original text is in *Mein Weltbild*, pp. 11-17 (item 361).

332. Judentum im Kampfe für den Frieden, with O. Wassermann.
*Leipziger jüdische Zeitung (or *Allgemeines jüdisches Familien-Blatt*), vol. 11, nr. 3, p. 3.

333. Religion and science.
New York Times, 9 November 1930, sect. 5, pp. 1-4.

> Written expressly for the *New York Times Magazine*.
>
> Reprinted as the title essay in *Cosmic religion* (item 335).
>
> German text was published in *Berliner Tageblatt*, 11 November 1930, 1. Beiblatt, p. 1, and reproduced in *Mein Weltbild*, pp. 36-45 (item 361).

334. [Welcome to World power conference]
Vossische Zeitung, 8 June 1930, p. 4.

> A short paragraph included with greetings from other Berlin scientists.

1931

335 COSMIC RELIGION, WITH OTHER OPINIONS AND APHORISMS. New York, Covici-Friede, 109 pp.

> Contains a biographical note "prepared by the publishers," and an appreciation by George Bernard Shaw. The title essay is item 333; the section captioned "Pacifism" contains item 343 and other fragments; two other sections are headed "The Jews," and "Opinions and Aphorisms." "The Jewish homeland," pp. 71-83, is a composite of quotations also found in item 328.

336. Tagore talks with Einstein.
   Asia, vol. 31, pp. 138-142, with special portrait.

> Republished in abbreviated form, *ibid*, vol. 37, pp. 151-152, 1937. This conversation is on Eastern music, in a lighter vein than item 340, and reported by Tagore himself.

337. A day with Albert Einstein: interview by Prof. Chaim Tscherno-witz.
   Jewish sentinel, vol. 1, no. 1 (September), pp. 19, 44, 50.

> Conversation on Jewish philosophy, leading up to Zionism.

338. Mitarbeit am Palästina-Werk.
   * *Leipziger jüdische Zeitung*, vol. 12, no. 13, p. 3.

339. Abrüstungskonferenz, 1932.
   Luxemburg Zeitung, 9 November 1931.

> This is a letter dated Berlin, Sept. 4, 1931.

340. The nature of reality.
   Modern review, Calcutta, vol. 49, pp. 42-43. Also *Living age*, vol. 340, pp. 262-265.

> Authorized version of a conversation with Tagore, largely on the nature of truth and beauty.

341. The 1932 Disarmament conference.
   Nation, vol. 133, p. 300.

> Original German text is included in *Mein Weltbild*, p. 89-92 (cf. 361).

342. Wehrpflicht und Abrüstung.
   Neue freie Presse, Wien. 22 Nov. 1931, pp. 1-2.

> This is reprinted in *Mein Weltbild*. pp. 83-89 (item 361).

343. Militant pacifism.
   World tomorrow, vol. 14, p. 9.

> Address before the New History Society, New York City, 14 December 1930, translated by Mme. Rosika Schwimmer. Quoted in part in *New York Times*, 21 December 1930, sect. 9, p. 4, col. 1. Reprinted in items 335 and 353. It was also issued by the NEW HISTORY FOUNDATION in a pamphlet entitled *Torchbearers* (pp. 26-28), which contains as well the other addresses on the same occasion.

1932

344. Message of felicitation to Justice Brandeis.

p. 3, AVUKAH ANNUAL of 1932. New York, American student Zionist federation.

345. Introduction
pp. 9-10 of BUILDERS OF THE UNIVERSE. Los Angeles, U. S. library association.

346. Address to students of the University of California at Los Angeles, February, 1932.
pp. 91-96 of BUILDERS OF THE UNIVERSE, U. S. library association.

> Text in both German and English; on science as coordination of observed facts, exemplified in the progression from special relativity to unified field theory.

347. To American Negroes.
Crisis, vol. 39, p. 45.

348. Is there a Jewish view of life?
Opinion, vol. 2, issue of 26 September 1932, p. 7.

1933

349. WARUM KRIEG? EIN BRIEFWECHSEL, Albert Einstein und Sigmund Freud. Paris, Internationales Institut für geistige Zusammenarbeit, Völkerbund. 62 pp. (Nummerierte Aufl. von nur 2000 Exemplaren).

> Einstein's letter is pp. 11-21.

350. WHY WAR? Paris, International institute of intellectual cooperation, League of nations, 56 pp. (Open letters, no. 2.)

> Einstein's letter is pp. 11-20.
> English translation by Stuart Gilbert of item 349.
> Reprinted in London, 1934, as New Commonwealth [pamphlet], series A, no. 6. Also reprinted in *Free World*, vol. 11, March issue, pp. 23-25, 1946; and in LEAGUE OF NATIONS, INTELLECTUAL COOPERATION ORGANISATION, *Bulletin*, vol. 1, pp. 239-245.

351. POURQUOI LA GUERRE? Paris, Institut international de coopération intellectuelle, Société des nations. 62 pp. (Limited ed. of 3,000 copies).

> Translation into French by B. Briod of item 349.

352. WAAROM OORLOG Amsterdam, Seyffardt. 61 pp.

> Translation into Dutch by E. Straat of item 349.

353. THE FIGHT AGAINST WAR, ed. by Alfred Lief. New York, John Day. 64 pp. (John Day pamphlets, no. 20).

Selections from Einstein's writings and speeches covering the period 1914-1932. The historical setting is given for each, and where possible a specific reference. Among the items not readily available elsewhere is the "Counter-manifesto" drawn up by Einstein, Georg F. Nicolai and Wilhelm Foerster in October, 1914, as a protest against the manifesto signed by ninety-three German intellectuals. This is otherwise published only in Nicolai's *Biologie des Krieges*. Zürich, Fussli, 1919, and its translation, New York, Century, 1918. Another is a speech before an Opponents of War International Conference at Lyons, August 1, 1931, under the caption "Now is the time," which was quoted in part in *New York Times*, 2 August 1931, sect. 1, p. 3, col. 5.

354. A declaration.

p. 5 of LES JUIFS. Paris, Société anonyme 'Les Illustrés Français.'

355. On peace, a letter to the editor [Dr. Frederick Kettner].
Biosophical review, vol. 3, p. 27.

356. Zur Deutsch-Amerikanischen Verständigung.
pp. 4-8 of *California Institute of Technology, Bulletin*, vol. 42, no. 138.

An English translation follows, pp. 9-12.

This was part of a symposium on America and the world situation broadcast January 23, 1933. (See *New York Times*, 24 Jan. 1933, p. 2, col. 2.)

357. Address [at a dinner under the auspices of American friends of the Hebrew University in Palestine in New York, March 15]
Science, new ser., vol. 77, pp. 274-275.

358. [Open letter to the Prussian Academy on the matter of his resignation from that body]
Science, new ser., vol. 77, p. 444.

All the correspondence on this occasion is included in *Mein Weltbild*, pp. 120-128, and in *The world as I see it*, pp. 174-182 (items 361 and 362).

359. Victim of misunderstanding.
Times, London. 25 September 1933, p. 12, col. d.

Letter on his position as to Communism.

360. Albert Hall speech: Civilization and science.
Times, London. 4 October 1933, p. 14, col. e.

This was also published as "Europe's danger, Europe's hope," see item 365.

A French translation appeared in 1934 in *Revue bleu* (Item 368).

1934

361. MEIN WELTBILD. Amsterdam, Querido. 269 pp.

> Permission was given "to one of his intimates, J. H." to make "a selection to give a picture of the man"—his writings in the fields of science, Judaism, politics, and pacifism. Some of the contents are noted under the separate items of this bibliography. The book itself gives no clue as to where items were originally published; some may never have appeared in print previously.
>
> There is also a "2. Aufl." with the same imprint.

362. THE WORLD AS I SEE IT. New York, Covici-Friede. 290 pp.

> A translation by Alan Harris of item 361, though the order of arrangement is different. The same text is also published with the imprint London, Lane, 1935. 214 pp. These editions carry a "Foreword" by Einstein which is not in the German edition. The Philosophical Library, New York, has announced an abridged edition for publication in the fall of 1949.

363. COMMENT JE VOIS LE MONDE. Paris, Flammarion. 258 pp.

> A translation by Col. Cros of item 361.

364. Sauvons la liberté.
Annales politiques et littéraires, vol. 102, pp. 377-378.

365. Europe's danger; Europe's hope.
Friends of Europe. Publications. no. 4, 6 pp.

> Address at a meeting in Royal Albert Hall, Oct. 4, 1933, organized by Refugee Assistance Fund. Reprinted under the caption "Personal liberty" by the *New York Herald-Tribune,* 4 February 1934. On the inter-relation of personal freedom and collective security, ending with the words "Only through peril and upheaval can nations be brought to further development."

366. An opinion of H. W. Krutch's article: Was Europe a success?
Nation, vol. 139, p. 373.

367. Education and world peace.
Progressive education, vol. 11, p. 440.

> A message read at a New York regional conference of the Progressive Education Association. Quoted in full in the *New York Times,* 24 November 1934, p. 17, col. 4.

368. La science et la civilization, trad. par L. Baillon de Wailly.
Revue bleu, littéraire et politique, vol. 72, pp. 641-642.

> Albert Hall speech of October 4, 1933. See items 360 and 365.

1935

369. D'MUTH OLAMI. Tel-Aviv, Stybel publ. co. 224 pp.

> Hebrew translation by S. Ettinger of *Mein Weltbild*, item 361.

370. LAMAH MILHAMAH? Tel-Aviv, 1935? 16 pp.

> Hebrew translation of item 349.

371. Appeal for Jewish unity: address before Women's division of the American Jewish Congress.

> *New Palestine*, vol. 25, issue of 1 March (no. 9), p. 1.

372. Statement on Prof. Hugo Bergmann, newly appointed Rector of the Hebrew University in Jerusalem.

> *New Palestine*, vol. 25, issue of 22 November (no. 36), p. 2.

373. Peace must be waged, an interview by R. M. Bartlett.

> *Survey graphic*, vol. 24, p. 384, with portrait.

1936

374. Some thoughts concerning education.

> *School and society*, vol. 44, pp. 589-592.

>> Address for a convocation of the University of the State of New York, Albany. Translated by Lina Arronet.

375. Freedom of learning.

> *Science*, new ser., vol. 83, pp. 372-373.

>> Reprint of a letter to the *Times, London*, signed also by E. Schroedinger and V. Tchernavin. (Mar. 25, p. 17, col. e.)

1938

376. Why do they hate the Jews?

> *Collier's weekly*, vol. 102, Nov. 26, pp. 9-10, '38, with portrait.

> Translated by Ruth Norden.

1939

377. Humanity on trial.

> A radio address in support of the United Jewish Appeal, printed as a four-page leaflet by this organization for wider circulation. The text is quoted in the *New York Times*, 22 March 1939, p. 10, col. 2. Also published under the title "Europe will become a barren waste," in *New Palestine*, vol. 29, issue of March 24, pp. 1-2.

378. The Goal.

> Lecture at a summer conference at Princeton Theological Seminary. Circulated in mimeographed form only.

379. Spirit of faith: comment on a British White Book on Palestine.
Aufbau, vol. 5, issue of 1 June (no. 10), p. 7.

380. Message to United Palestine Appeal convened in Washington.
New Palestine, vol. 29, issue of Jan. 20, box on p. 3.

381. On Zionism.
New Palestine vol. 29, issue of March 17, p. 3.

> A special issue in honor of Einstein's sixtieth birthday presents a page of quotations from his writings (cf. item 328).

382. Statement issued on sixtieth birthday, on the American scientific spirit.
Science, new ser., vol. 89, p. 242.

1940

383. Freedom and science.

> pp. 381-383 of *Freedom: its meaning*, edited by Ruth N. Anshen, New York, Harcourt, Brace, and Co.

> Translated by Prof. James Gutmann from a manuscript prepared for this volume. There is also an edition of this book with the imprint London, Allen, 1942.

384. Neuer Bund der Nationen.
Aufbau, vol. 6, issue of June 28 (no. 26), pp. 1-2.

> Based on interview at the time he received American citizenship.

385. Meine Stellung zur jüdischen Frage.
Aufbau, vol. 6, issue of December 27 (no. 52), box on p. 9.

386. The hour of decision.
Saturday review of literature, vol. 22, issue of October 19, p. 7.

1941

387. Credo as a Jew.

> Vol. 4, pp. 32-33 of UNIVERSAL JEWISH ENCYCLOPEDIA, edited by I. Landman.

> Quoted in translation, with facsimile of German manuscript; no other source credited.

388. [Statement on significance of American citizenship]
pp. 43-47 of I AM AN AMERICAN, edited by R. S. Benjamin.
New York, Alliance Book Corp.

> This volume had its origin in a series of broadcasts under the auspices of the U.S. Immigration and Naturalization Service. (Also in *New York Times*, 23 June 1940, p. 6, col. 2.)

1942

389. The common language of science.
Advancement of science, vol. 2, (no. 5), p. 109.

> An address radioed to the meeting of the British Association for the Advancement of Science, Sept., 1941.

1943

390. [Address before student body, California Institute of Technology, 16 February 1931, on the misuse of scientific discovery].
pp. 43-44 of *Treasury of science*, ed. by H. SHAPLEY, et al. New York, Harper.

> The date given in the anthology is incorrect; the text is to be found in the *New York Times*, 17 February 1931, p. 6, col. 3.

1944

391. LETTERA A B. CROCE E RISPOSTA DEL CROCE. Bari, Laterza. 7 pp.

> Einstein's letter is pp. 1-2; there is no clue as to publication elsewhere.

392. Gandhi's statesmanship.

> pp. 79-80 of MAHATMA GHANDHI: ESSAYS AND REFLECTIONS ON HIS LIFE AND WORK, presented to him on his seventieth birthday, 1939, edited by S. Radhakrishnan. London, Allen and Unwin, [1944].

393. TEST CASE FOR HUMANITY. London, Jewish agency for Palestine. 7 pp.

> This is a pamphlet reprint of item 399, accompanied by quotations from *About Zionism*, item 328.

394. THE ARABS AND PALESTINE, with E. Kahler. New York, Christian Council on Palestine and American Palestine Committee. 16 pp.

> Two articles originally published in the *Princeton Herald* of 14 April and 28 April 1944 (items 399 and 400).

395. The problem of today and tomorrow.
    Aufbau, vol. 10, no. 11 (March 17), box on p. 1.

    A brief birthday message from London.

396. Grüsse zum "I am an American" Day.
    Aufbau, vol. 10, no. 20 (May 19), p. 1.

397. Our goal unity, but the Germans are unfit: an interview.
    Free world, vol. 8, pp. 370-371.

398. The ethical imperative.
    Opinion, vol. 14, March issue, p. 10.

    In tribute to Rabbi Stephen S. Wise.

399. Palestine setting of sacred history of Jewish race, with Eric
    Kahler.
    Princeton Herald, April 14, 1944, pp. 1, 6.

    This and the following item constitute a reply to a letter by Prof.
    Hitti on the Palestinian question in *Princeton Herald* April 7, p. 1.

    Reprinted as part of item 394.

400. Arabs fare better in Palestine than in Arab countries, with Eric
    Kahler.
    Princeton Herald, April 28, 1944, pp. 1, 6.

    Reprinted as part of item 394.

1945

401. A testimonial from Prof. Einstein.
    pp. 142-143 of JACQUES S. HADAMARD, *An essay on the psy-
    chology of invention in the mathematical field*. Princeton Uni-
    versity Press.

    This same testimonial is included in the second printing of the book,
    1949.

402. Einstein on the atomic bomb, edited by Raymond Gram Swing.
    Atlantic monthly, vol. 176, November issue, pp. 43-45.

    Quoted in *New York Times*, Oct. 27, p. 17, col. 6. He clarified his
    meaning in a statement issued in *New York Times*, October 29, p. 4,
    col. 3.

    A reprint was distributed November 1947 with an appeal for
    financial support by the Emergency Committee of Atomic Scientists,
    and again January 1948 with a letter signed only by Einstein.

403. Gedenkworte für F.D.R.
  Aufbau, vol. 11, no. 17 (April 27), p. 7.

404. Message für Town Hall.
  Aufbau, vol. 11, no. 46 (November 16), p. 17.

405. Einstein verdammt Lessing Rosenwald.
  Aufbau, vol. 11, no. 50 (Dec. 14), p. 11.

406. Interview with Einstein, by Alfred Stern.
  Contemporary Jewish record, vol. 8, pp. 245-249.

  On American science and general scientific questions.

1946

407. ONLY THEN SHALL WE FIND COURAGE.

  An eight-page pamphlet, consisting of reprints of the interview with
  M. Amrine in the *New York Times Magazine* (June 23, sect. 6, p. 7)
  and a supporting article by Dean Christian Gauss entitled "Is Einstein right?" from *The American Scholar* (vol. 15, pp. 469-476),
  which was published by the Emergency Committee of Atomic
  Scientists for wide circulation in its campaign for funds. As evidence
  of its extensive dissemination one may cite an editorial in *Étude* for
  May, 1947, vol. 65, p. 243, which is based upon it.

408. Social obligation of the scientist.
  pp. 318-319 of *Treasury for the free world*, edited by R.
  RAEBURN. New York, Arco Publ. Co.

  In the form of questions and answers; not found elsewhere, though
  most other items in the anthology are from the *Free world*.

409. The way out.
  pp. 76-77 of *One world or none*, ed. by D. MASTERS and
  K. WAY. New York, McGraw.

410. Introduction.
  pp. ix-xi of RUDOLF KAYSER, *Spinoza: portrait of a spiritual
  hero*. New York, Philosophical Library.

  Not in the German edition.

411. [Quotations from letters on uranium fission research of Aug. 2,
  1939, Mar. 7 and Apr. 25, 1940, as read by Dr. Alexander
  Sachs.]

  pp. 10, 16-17, 19-20 of U.S. SENATE. SUBCOMMITTEE ON
  ATOMIC ENERGY. *Hearings pursuant to Senate Resolution 179.*

Quoted in *New York Times*, Nov. 28, 1945, p. 2, col. 2. See also item 412.

412. [Letter to President Roosevelt, Aug. 2, 1939]

This is published in full in "A statement of purpose" by the Emergency Committee of Atomic Scientists, an eight-page pamphlet distributed in December 1946 as part of its campaign for funds.

413. An die jüdischen Studenten.
Aufbau, vol. 12, no. 1 (Jan. 4), p. 16.

A telegram to the world conference meeting in Paris.

414. Die Welt muss neu denken lernen.
Aufbau, vol. 12, no. 38, pp. 1-2 and no. 39, p. 5, (Sept. 20 and 27).

This is the German text of the interview by M. Amrine published in the *New York Times* of June 23, 1946 (q.v., and also item 407).

415. Why war?
Free world, vol. 11, March issue, pp. 23-25.

A reprint of item 350.

416. Year one—Atomic age. A message.
Survey graphic, vol. 34, issue for January, box on p. 23.

Included with speeches at a New York meeting of Americans United for World Organization.

417. $E = mc^2$: the most urgent problem of our time.
Science illustrated, vol. 1, no. 1, April issue, pp. 16-17.

An explanation of the formula for the general reader by analogy.

1947

418. The military mentality.
American scholar, vol. 16, pp. 353-354

Reprinted in *Bulletin of the atomic scientists*, vol. 3, pp. 223-224.

419. Atomic war or peace, as told to Raymond Swing.
Atlantic monthly, vol. 180, pp. 29-33 of November issue.

Distributed as a separate by the Emergency Committee of Atomic Scientists with a plea for financial support. The German text, "Atomkrieg oder Frieden?", was published in *Aufbau*, vol. 13, no. 50 (December 12), pp. 1-2, 27.

420. Dear friends in the Mid-West: a Christmas greeting.
Chicago daily tribune, 24 December, p. 9.

Presented by Marshall Field Co.

421. World unity demanded.
    Cleveland news, 11 November (vol. 106, no. 266). Home final ed., p. 1, col. 7 and p. 4, col. 5.

> Address radioed from Princeton to convocations of World Security Workers at Western Reserve University, Case Institute of Technology, Fenn College, John Carroll University and Cleveland School of Art.

422. Musical visit with Einstein: interview by Lili Foldes.
    Etude, vol. 65, issue of January, p. 5.

423. Paul Langevin.
    La Pensée: revue du rationalisme moderne, new ser., no. 12 (mai-juin), pp. 13-14.

424. Telegraphic response to the editor on Walter White's article: Why I remain a negro.
    Saturday review of literature, vol. 30, issue of November 1, p. 21.

425. An open letter to the General Assembly of the United Nations, on "the way to break the vicious circle."
    United Nations world, vol. 1, issue of October, pp. 13-14.

> Quotations from it and comment in *New York Times*, Sept. 23, p. 16, col. 2.

426. Science "gag" can even crimp military use.
    Washington post, August 3, p. 1 of special Atomic energy supplement.

1948

427. Introduction
    p. 1 of DANIEL Q. POSIN: *I have been to the village*. Ann Arbor, Edwards.

428. Foreword.
    pp. 1-2 of LINCOLN BARNETT: *The universe and Dr. Einstein*. New York, Sloane.

> This volume is an expansion of articles appearing under this title in Harper's during April, May and June 1948, very carefully prepared.

429. [Letter on universal military training addressed to the Chairman of the Senate Committee]

p. 267 of U.S. CONGRESS. SENATE. COMMITTEE ON ARMED SERVICES. *Universal military training.* Hearings. . . .

> Read at hearing of March 24.

430. A plea for international understanding.
Bulletin of the atomic scientists, vol. 4, p. 1.

> Addressed to the Foreign Press Association of the United Nations, Nov. 11, 1947, in accepting the Association's award. First published in *New York Times*, 12 November 1947, p. 1, col. 7.

431. Reply to Soviet scientists.
Bulletin of the atomic scientists, vol. 4, pp. 33-34.

> A statement prepared for the *Bulletin* in reply to a letter published in the *New Times* of Moscow, Nov. 26, 1947, "About certain fallacies of Albert Einstein." This is largely quoted in *New York Times*, 30 January 1948, p. 1, col. 2-3 and p. 12, col. 6.

432. Message to the World Congress of Intellectuals, Warsaw.
Bulletin of the atomic scientists, vol. 4, pp. 295, 299.

> Dissimilar version released in Poland appears on p. 320. Both documents appeared first in the *New York Times*, 29 August 1948, sect. 1, p. 1 and 18.

433. Letter [on new financial arrangements for this Bulletin].
Bulletin of the atomic scientists, vol. 4, p. 354.

> Later distributed as a circular letter.

434. Religion and science: irreconcilable?
Christian register, vol. 127, June issue, p. 19.

> Message addressed to a national Unitarian conference.

435. Atomic science reading list.
Magazine of the year, January 1948 issue, pp. 60-61.

> Einstein's choice of six titles with his annotations.

436. Looking ahead.
Rotarian, issue for June, p. 8-10.

> This includes a reprinting of items 430 and 431, his message to a citizens' meeting for world government in Portland, Maine, December 11, 1946, and a report of an interview with the editor of the *Rotarian* on the feasibility of world government now.

437. [Letter urging support of a supra-national organization, addressed to the General Conference of the Methodist Church].
Zion's herald, vol. 126, p. 453.

438. Epoche des Friedens?
UNESCO, *Monatsschrift für Erziehung, Wissenschaft und Kultur der Österreichischen Liga für die Vereinigten Nationen,* Jahrg. 1, pp. 435-436 (Heft 10).

> An interview with Dr. Helmut Leitner, Consul General of Austria in New York.

1949

439. [Letter to Prof. Archibald Henderson on the occasion of the publication of his *Bernard Shaw: playboy and prophet.* Appleton, 1932. 872 pp.]
p. 92 of ARCHIBALD HENDERSON: THE NEW CRICHTON, ed. by Samuel S. Hood. New York, Beechhurst press.

440 [Article by A. Werner in token of Einstein's seventieth birthday, containing questions and answers of an interview.]
Liberal Judaism, vol. 16, issue for April-May, pp. 4-12.

> Also quotes his Credo (item 387).

441. Why socialism.
Monthly review: an independent socialist magazine. vol. 1, issue for May (no. 1), pp. 9-15.

442. A true prophet: greeting to Rabbi Stephen Wise on his seventy-fifth birthday.
Opinion, vol. 19, issue for March (no. 5), p. 12.

443. Facsimile of greeting to ORT convention.
ORT *Bulletin,* vol. 2, issue for May (no. 9), p. 7.

444. Most fateful decision in recorded history.
Southern Patriot, May.

> Reprinted in *Motive,* November (Vol. X, No. 2, p. 36).

445. Notes for an autobiography.
Saturday Review of Literature, Nov. 26 (Vol. XXXII, No. 46), 9ff.

> Excerpts from "Autobiographical Notes," pp. 1-95 of *Albert Einstein: Philosopher-Scientist,* edited by Paul A. Schilpp, Evanston (Library of living philosophers, vol. 7).

III

INTERVIEWS, LETTERS AND SPEECHES
QUOTED IN *NEW YORK TIMES**

(Omitting items more completely published elsewhere)

Letter to Dr. Haenisch on his affection for Berlin. 21 Nov. 1920, sect. 2, p. 10, col. 5.

Reply to tribute paid him at meeting of National Academy of Sciences. placing joy of discovery above personal renown. 27 April 1921, p. 21, col. 2.

Statement on the Edison test for college men. 18 May 1921, p. 18, col. 2.

Speech in Berlin on anti-German attitude in America. 2 July 1921, p. 3, col. 5.

Statement on scientific life in the United States. 31 July 1921, sect. 2, p. 4, col. 3.

Interview in Berlin by Cecil Brown on the theory connecting gravitation and electricity. 27 March 1923, p. 18, col. 8.

Letter resigning from the League of Nations Committee on Intellectual Cooperation, in protest at inadequacy of the League. 28 June 1923, p. 15, col. 4.

Quotation in a special article by H. Bernstein on Europe's craving for peace. 17 May 1925, sect. 9, p. 4, col. 5.

On greatness, from an interview. 18 April 1926, sect. 9, p. 12, col. 4.

Interview on the 200-inch telescope, etc., while an important new discovery is pending. 4 November 1928, p. 1, col. 3, and p. 15, col. 5.

Field theories, old and new, written expressly for the *New York Times.* 3 February 1929, sect. 9, p. 1, col. 1-8.
    A simplified presentation of item 225.

Letter to a thirteen-year Los Angeles boy who had written on relativity for a Los Angeles paper. 10 February 1929, p. 26, col. 3.

* These titles have been in almost every case supplied by the editor of this bibliography, since the newspaper captions were either entirely lacking or not specific enough.

Poem acknowledging a birthday greeting. 21 April 1929, sect. 10, p. 7, col. 4-5.

Belief in the God of Spinoza. 25 April 1929, p. 60, col. 4.

Interview, with portrait, by S. J. Woolf; several direct quotations on the philosophy of life, etc. 18 August 1929, sect. 5, p. 1-2.

Text of a broadcast in connection with Edison semicentennial of incandescent lighting. 23 October 1929, p. 3, col. 2.

Cable to *New York Times* on the possibility of disarmament by a single nation. 21 January 1930, p. 5, col. 3.

Lecture at Kroll Opera House, Berlin, on development of physical theories. 17 June 1930, p. 3, col. 1-3.

Address on the marvel and the social significance of radio at opening of radio exhibit, Berlin. 23 August 1930, p. 1, col. 6.
> German original in *Berliner Tageblatt*, Abend Ausgabe, August 22, 1. Beiblatt.

Interview on philosophy of science and art, by Emil Lengyel. 14 September 1930, sect. 5, p. 9, col. 1-4.

Quotations from paper read before International Congress of Palestine Workers in Berlin, Sept. 27. 28 September 1930, sect. 2, p. 5, col. 1.

Reply to George Bernard Shaw at Ort and Oze Society dinner, London, on his attitude toward Jews. 29 October 1930, p. 12, col. 2, and 2 November 1930, sect. 9, p. 2, col. 1.

Religion and science, written expressly for the *New York Times*. 9 November 1930, sect. 5, p. 1, col. 1-4. (see also item 333)

Statement given to Zionist Organization of America criticizing British Zionist policy. 3 December 1930, p. 15, col. 1.

New Year's greeting to America, on its joy in work, and other points. 1 January 1931, p. 13, col. 1.

Letter to A. Geller on his determinist views. 28 January 1931, p. 2, col. 2.

An interview on several subjects, quoted from the *Yale News*. 3 February 1931, p. 8, col. 1.

Science and Happiness. 22 February 1931, sect. 9, p. 2, col. 1. This is his speech at California Institute of Technology reprinted from the issue of 17 February 1931, p. 6, col. 3.

Appreciation of his American reception. Radio address and cable. 15 March 1931, p. 1, col. 2.

Letter read at meeting of International Philosophical Society at Barbizon Plaza, New York, answering questions on theories of art, etc. 17 April 1931, p. 25, col. 7.

Statement to International Conference of Opponents of War, Lyons, August 1, 1931. 2 August 1931, sect. 1, p. 3, col. 5. Quoted in item 353.

Lecture at Berlin planetarium on aim of physicists. 5 October 1931, p. 11, col. 4.

Address on current economic questions at California Institute of Technology dinner. 26 January 1932, p. 13, col. 2.

Talk to university representatives in Pasadena advocating economic boycott in war. 28 February 1932, sect. 2, p. 4, col. 4.

A one-sentence rule for success, quoted from *Youth* published by Young Israel of Williamsburg. 20 June 1932, p. 17, col. 3.

Letter read at Spinoza tercentenary, City College, New York. 24 November 1932, p. 27, col. 8.

Speech at dinner of American Friends of the Hebrew University in Palestine on the significance of the university. 16 March 1933, p. 10, col. 2. Also in *Science* vol. 77, pp. 274-275. (Item 357)

Letter to Prussian Academy to deny his spreading of propaganda on anti-semitic atrocities. 12 April 1933, p. 16, col. 5.

Letter to A. Nahon on application of pacifist principles to the problems of Belgium. 10 September 1933, p. 14, col. 4. Previously published in *La Patrie Humaine.*

Address at Albert Hall, London: a plea for the freedom and integrity of scholarship. 4 October 1933, p. 17, col. 3-4. See item 360.

Address at Nobel centenary, Hotel Roosevelt, New York. 19 December 1933, p. 18, col. 2.

Excerpt from essay on U.S. high school system and importance of education, written for celebration at Weequahic High School, Newark, N.J. 18 March 1934, sect. 4, p. 4, col. 7.

Message on Brotherhood Day stating need of churches to mobilize good will. 30 April 1934, p. 17, col. 6.

Praises P. H. Phenix, Princeton 1934, for senior thesis, "The absolute significance of rotation." 26 July 1934, p. 21, col. 7.

Speech at American Jewish physicians' meeting praising Hebrew University. 28 October 1934, p. 31, col. 2.

Tribute to Dr. W. de Sitter as an astronomer. 22 November 1934, p. 21, col. 1.

Tribute to Madame Curie. 24 January 1935, p. 21, col. 5.

Article quoted from *Daily Princetonian* approving student anti-war movement. 13 April 1935, p. 1, col. 5.

Interview with Henry Rosso, Princeton High School senior, originally printed in special issue of High School paper, *Tower*. 14 April 1935, sect. 2, p. 1, col. 6.

Speech on Maimonides at celebration of the 800*th* anniversary of his birth, Hotel Pennsylvania. 15 April 1935, p. 15, col. 5.

Speech on Palestine urging Jewish-Arab amity, at Passover celebration at the Manhattan Opera House. 21 April 1935, sec. 2, p. 4, col. 7.

The late Emmy Noether: Letter in appreciation. 4 May 1935, p. 12, col. 5-6.

Speech on perils which Judaism faces, to United Jewish Appeal meeting. 27 June 1935, p. 13, col. 5.

Speech at luncheon honoring Max Reinhardt. 29 June 1935, p. 16, col 1.

Message sent for unveiling of a cairn in honor of Simon Newcomb's centenary. 31 August 1935, p. 28, col. 6.

Address at meeting sponsored by American Christian Committee for German Refugees and the Emergency Committee in Aid of Polish Refugees from Nazism. 23 Ocober 1935, p. 22, col. 5.

Comments on extension of relativity theory by Prof. Page, and Dr. L. Silberstein's criticism of theory. 8 February 1936, p. 13, col. 8.

Address at dedication of Museum of Science and Industry. 12 February 1936, p. 1, col. 4.

Comment on ignoring of the ether in relativity theory. 1 March 1936, sect. 10, p. 6, col. 2.

Speech at Jewish Forum dinner, on Jews in Germany. 9 March 1936, p. 21, col. 2.

Letter refuting L. Silberstein's attack on relativity in the *Physical Review* (vol. 49, pp. 268-270). 7 March 1936, p. 10, col. 1.

On games, particularly chess. 28 March 1936, p. 17, col. 2.

Message read at dinner of National Labor Committee, opposing a legislative council for Palestine. 12 April 1936, p. 34, col. 2.

Letter on Hightstown, New Jersey, model farm community. 18 May 1936, p. 6, col. 2.

Message at the 18*th* anniversary of the Jewish Seminary, warning against the menace of materialism. 8 June 1936, p. 22, col. 2.

Address at the convocation of the University of the State of New York on economic struggle for survival. 16 October 1936, p. 11, col. 1.

Appreciative letter to Independent Order of B'rith Abraham for naming lodge after him. Urges cooperation in Jewish cause. 23 January 1937, p. 12, col. 3.

Message to National Labor Committe for Jewish Workers in Palestine. 29 March 1937, p. 6, col. 3.

Telegram to New York City mass meeting on Spanish Civil War, warning of the danger in Spanish loss of political freedom. 19 April 1937, p. 4, col. 5.

Message to Y.M.C.A. on world conditions, urges war on tyranny and preservation of truth. 11 October 1937, p. 19, col. 3.

Message to National Council for Jewish Women, urging Jewish unity. 28 January 1938, p. 22, col. 5.

Tribute at a special stage performance of Jewish stars. Praises work of United Palestine Appeal. 7 April 1938, p. 19, col. 4.

Speech on anti-semitism at a New York dinner of the National Labor Commission for Palestine. 18 April 1938, p. 15, col. 3.

> Published in *New Palestine*, vol. 28, issue of April 29, under the title "Our debt to Zionism."

Interview praising Dr. H. E. Ives' new proof of relativity theory. 27 April 1938, p. 25, col. 2.

Address at Swarthmore College commencement, criticizes barbarity abroad and aloofness here. 7 June 1938, p. 16, col. 1.

Letter put in New York World's Fair time capsule, describes fear and terror in the life of today, with hope for a better world. 16 September 1938, p. 22, col. 1.

Address at American Jewish Congress dedication of refugee home, urging aid for refugees. 30 October 1938, p. 19, col. 2.

Message to New York City Zionist meeting begs England to support Balfour declaration in Palestine. 3 November 1938, p. 16, col. 2.

Speech on presentation of A. Einstein medal to Dr. Thomas Mann. 29 January 1939, p. 23, col. 1.

Letter replying to Lincoln's Birthday Committee for democracy and intellectual freedom. 6 February 1939, p. 19, col. 4.

Letter replying to questionnaire on law linking all physical phenomena and on world science association. 14 March 1939, p. 1, col. 3.

Explanation of radio altimeter at visit to Newark airport. 23 March 1939, p. 25, col. 6.

Speech on cosmic rays on the occasion of the first illumination of the World's Fair when cosmic rays were demonstrated to 200,000 persons. 1 May 1939, p. 6, col. 5.

Speech by radio to Town Hall assembly of Jewish National Workers Alliance on importance of British friendship in Palestine. 28 May 1939, p. 13, col. 1.

Address at dedication of Palestine Pavilion at World's Fair. 29 May 1939, p. 7, col. 1.

In symposium of five Nobel Prize winners, "World Leaders on Peace and Democracy," at World's Fair, Einstein urges an international superior court. 2 July 1939, p. 13, col. 1.

Warning to World Student Association convention on spread of fascism. 17 August 1939, p. 15, col. 8.

Address to New Jersey Education Association on education in democracy. 11 November 1939, p. 34, col. 2.

Defense of Bertrand Russell's appointment as Professor of Philosophy at City College of New York. 19 March 1940, p. 22, col. 4.

At Testimonial dinner asks fund for Hebrew Institute of Technology in Haifa. 9 May 1940, p. 15, col. 2.

Telegram urging Roosevelt to aid allies, heads list of 17 members of Princeton University to sign it. 21 May 1940, p. 12, col. 5.

International broadcast, predicts armed League of Nations needed to preserve peace. 23 June 1940, p. 6, col. 2.

Message sent to United Palestine Appeal rally for war fund. 25 February 1941, p. 46, col. 2.

Speech at Hechalitz Organization dedication of Hightstown, New Jersey, farm. 16 June 1941, p. 9, col. 1.

Interview on change in his pacifist attiude. 30 December 1941, p. 9, col. 4.

Adddress at Russian war relief Jewish council dinner on USSR rôle in the peace. 26 October 1942, p. 17, col. 2.

"Einstein's theory of living", interview by D. Schwarz. 12 March 1944, sect. 6, p. 16, col. 38-39.

Tribute to war-time heroism of British public. 14 March 1944, p. 20, col. 3.

Statement sent to National Wartime Conference urging a union of thinkers. 29 May 1944, p. 17, col. 8.

Message sent to a meeting of American Fund for Palestinian Industry. 6 June 1944, p. 18, col. 2.

Statement repudiating biography of himself by Dr. Marianoff, former son-in-law, and P. Wayne as unreliable and un-authorized. 5 August 1944, p. 13, col. 6. German text in *Aufbau*, 1944, no. 32, p. 14.

Statement urging Roosevelt reelection, as important to securing lasting peace. 10 October 1944, p. 15, col. 3.

Statement on acceptance of honorary chairmanship of New York City Fund drive for Institute of Religion. 22 July 1945, p. 39, col. 1.

Explanation of solar and nuclear energy in interview. 12 August 1945, p. 29, col. 3.

On harnessing solar energy. (Quoted from a 1920 interview in the *Manchester Guardian.*) 14 August 1945, p. 18, col. 3.

Interview, asserts world government is prerequisite to lasting peace. 15 September 1945, p. 11, col. 6.

Letter thanking *New York Times* for articles of October 27, and recommending Emery Reves' book, *The anatomy of peace.* 1 November 1945, p. 22, col. 7.
   See item 402.

Address at the American Nobel Anniversary Commission dinner. Message on peace, transcribed. 11 December 1945, p. 15, col. 1.

Testifies against British policy in Palestine before Anglo-American Committee of Inquiry on Palestine. 12 January 1946, p. 7, col. 1.

Letter sent to meeting of Progressive Palestine Association, Washington, D.C., urging that UNO run Palestine. 15 February 1946, p. 2, col. 2.

Statement on civilization's capacity to survive atomic warfare. 24 February 1946, sect. 6, p. 42, col. 3.

Letter sent to Jewish Council for Russian Relief urging American Jews to continue relief shipments to USSR. 17 April 1946, p. 27, col. 4.

Address at Lincoln University upon receipt of doctorate. Sees future for Negro. 4 May 1946, p. 7, col. 4.

Message sent to National Council of Organization for Yeshiva University stating its importance to Jewish tradition. 6 May 1946, p. 6, col. 3.

Telegram asking prominent persons for funds for Atomic Scientists' Emergency Committee. 25 May 1946, p. 13, col. 5.

Radio speech to Students for Federal World Government at Chicago rally; on international peace and the need for United States-Soviet accord. 30 May 1946, p. 18, col. 5. (National radio broadcast on ABC.)

"The real problem is in the hearts of men," interview with M. Amrine. 23 June 1946, sec. 6, p. 7, col. 42-43. (See items 407 and 414.)

Statement on atomic bomb for *France-Soir*. 22 June 1946, p. 6, col. 8.

Statement on atomic bomb for *Sunday Express*, London. 19 August 1946, p. 1, col. 7.

Letter to Pres. Truman on lynching. [partially quoted] 23 September 1946, p. 16, col. 4.

Letter to Urban League for Service among Negroes. [partially quoted] 25 September 1946, p. 38, col. 2.

Nation-wide radio address opening the campaign for a million dollar educational fund for the Emergency Committee of Atomic Scientists. 18 November 1946, p. 25, col. 1

Einstein backs Lilienthal for Atomic Energy Commission [partially quoted] 22 February 1947, p. 4, col. 3-4.

Plea made in concert with the Federation of American Scientists for United Nations control of atomic energy. 16 July 1947, p. 2, col. 4. and 20 July 1947, sect. IV, p. 8, col. 4.

Conference with H. C. Usborne on world government. 29 September 1947, p. 7, col. 1.

Message on the occasion of the dedication of Riverside Drive Memorial to six million martyred Jews of Europe. 16 October 1947, p. 30, col. 4.

Message to United World Federalists, testifying to their support by the Emergency Committee of Atomic Scientists. 2 November 1947, p. 50, col. 3.

Message read at dinner of the American committee for the Weizmann Institute. 26 November 1947, p. 6, col. 4.

Commendation of Henry Wallace's *Toward World Peace*. 30 March 1948, p. 25, col. 4.
   This letter was also quoted on the dust jacket of the book.

Letter to the Editor. Palestine cooperation: appeal made to Jews to work for the goal of the common welfare. 18 April 1948, sect. IV, p. 8. col. 6.
   Letter is signed jointly with Leo Baeck.

Speech read in Carnegie Hall at presentation of "One World Award," decrying U.S. rearmament. 28 April 1948, p. 2, col. 2.

Assails education today. 13 March 1949, sect. 1, p. 34, col. 1.
Forms part of an article assembled by William Laurence in honor of Einstein's seventieth birthday. Einstein's part is a quotation from the autobiographical chapter of the book *Albert Einstein: Philosopher-Scientist, ed.* by PAUL ARTHUR SCHILPP, Library of living philosophers, volume VII, Evanston, Ill.

Proposes international society of social studies to break the spell of nationalism. 11 August 1949, p. 8, col. 6.
Full text is included in a report to be submitted by Secretary-General Trygve Lie to the UN Committee for the establishment of a research laboratory.

ADDENDA TO THE WRITINGS OF ALBERT EINSTEIN

WRITINGS

1950

446. Out of My Later Years, New York, Philosophical Library.
A collection of articles and essays written since 1934.

447. Introduction to *Relativity - a Richer Truth,* by Philipp Frank, Beacon Press, Boston.

448. Generalized Theory of Gravitation.
Published as appendix II to *The Meaning of Relativity*, Princeton University Press, Princeton 1950.

449. Preface to *Explaining the Atom,* by Selig Hecht, Lindsay Drummond Ltd., London 1950.

Interviews, Letters, Speeches

Statement on occasion of receiving Honorary Degree from Hebrew University, 16 March, 1949, p. 29, col. 4.

Message of congratulations to Hebrew University on 25th Anniversary, 23 October, 1949.

Statement for Symposium, Morris R. Cohen Memorial Fund, City College of New York, 17 November, 1949.

Broadcast for United Jewish Appeal Conference in Atlantic City, 29 November, 1949.

Message for Manilal Gandhi, editor of *Indian Opinion,* Phoenix, Natal, So. Africa, on the occasion of Indian Independence, December, 1949.

Sixteen, including A. Einstein and T. Mann sign statement protesting censure of attorneys who defend minority and labor groups, 1 February, 1950, p. 19, col. 5.

Broadcast on Mrs. Eleanor Roosevelt's television program concerning the dangers of atomic warfare, etc., 13 February, 1950, p. 3, col. 2.

Message to the Southern Conference for the Fight Against Racial Discrimination, Atlanta University, 8 April, 1950.

Message for the 25th Anniversary of the Hebrew University of Jerusalem, May, 1950.

Einstein urges Jewry support cultural institutions to provide openings for youth, 11 May, 1950, p. 27, col. 4.

Statement in interview for documentary program on atomic energy, "Year of Decision" in UN radio series entitled "The Pursuit of Peace," June, 1950.

Einstein urges international control of A-bomb stock piles, 19 June, 1950, p. 10, col. 3.

Message to 42nd meeting of Societa Italiana par il Progresse de la Scienze in Lucca, Italy, published in issue 3-4, Vol. I, 1950 of *Impact,* periodical of UNESCO, Paris.

Letter to Viscount Samuel, published in the latter's *Essay in Physics,* Basil Blackwell, Oxford, November, 1950.

Address (tape recording) to the convention of the International College of Surgeons on the occasion of being named an Honorary Fellow, Cleveland, Ohio, 3 November, 1950.

Article by Gertrude Samuels "Where Einstein Surveys the Cosmos," November, 1950, Sec. VI, p. 14.

Message for U.I.T. (University of Jerusalem, Weizmann-Institute Rechovoth and Technion, Haifa) Dinner, Waldorf-Astoria, New York, 30 November, 1950, p. 15, col. 2.

Statement to the Society for Social Responsibility in Science, 22 December, 1950, in *Science*, Vol. CXII, p. 160.

Dr. Einstein's secretary, Miss Helen Dukas, quotes briefly Einstein's comment on Gertrude Samuels' article, 24 December, 1950, Sec. VI, p. 2, col. 3.

Dr. Einstein holds UN can become world government only if Assembly representatives are elected directly by the people, 27 December, 1950, p. 2, col. 6.

Statment to Fyke Farmer on the necessity of world government, for the Geneva Convention, December, 1950.

Message for the 75th Anniversary of the Ethical Cultural Society, New York, 6 January, 1951, p. 16, col. 6.

Message of congratulations for the Israel Symphony Orchestra, January, 1951.

Message for 400th Anniversary of University of San Marcos on receiving honorary doctor's degree, Lima, Peru, May 1951.

Letter of recommendation for Meyer Levin's book, *In Search*, Horizon Publishers, New York, 1950.

SUPPLEMENT TO ADDENDA TO EINSTEIN'S WRITINGS

Editor's Note

The editor would like to thank Miss Helen Dukas, compiler of the *Biographical Checklist and Index to the Collected Writings of Albert Einstein* (New York: Readex Microprint Corporation, 1960), for bringing to our attention the following omissions and errata in our own Einstein Bibliography.

1920—#131, the date given is: 5 Mai 1920; it should read 27 October 1920.

1922—"Über die gegenwärtige Krise in der Theoretischen Physik," *Kaizo* (Tokyo), 4, No. 12 (December, 1922).

1923—*Collected Works*, translated into Japanese by Professor Ishiwara, with a Foreword by Professor Einstein, Tokyo, dated December 27, 1922.

1924—Review of "Relativitäts-Theorie u. Erkenntnislehre" by J. Winternitz (Berlin: Verlag B. G. Teubner, 1923; Sammlg. Wissenschaft u. Hypothese), *Deutsche Literaturzeitung*, Heft 1, pp. 20-22.

1924—Review of Max Planck's "Wärmestrahlung. Vorlesungen über die Theorie der Wärmestrahlung," 5. Aufl. J. A. Barth, Leipzig, 1923. In *Deutsche Literaturzeitung*, 13, pp. 1153-54.

1925—German original article "Nichteuklidische Geometrie in der Physik," in *Neue Rundschau* (Berlin: Fischer-Verlag, 1925), pp. 16-20. Listed in Spanish translation (*Revista matematica hispano-americana*, 1926) by Shields, #203.

1928—"Fundamental Concepts of Physics and Their Most Recent Changes," *St. Louis Post-Dispatch*, Supplement, December 9, 1928, 7:1-4. This is the text (translation) of an address by

Albert Einstein at the Davoser Hochschulkurse, March 18, 1928, at Davos, Switzerland. The German text was not published, only the introductory part (spoken from notes, not in manuscript) was printed in *Mein Weltbild* and its translations. Carl Seelig, editor of the Europa-Verlag, Zürich, edition of *Mein Weltbild* gives particulars in his editorial comments, pp. 235-36. See also *Ideas and Opinions* (New York: Crown Publishers, 1954), p. 54.

1932—"Bemerkungen über den Wandel der Problemstellung in der Theoretischen Physik," a contribution to *Emanuel Libman Anniversary Volume* (New York: The International Press, 1932), pp. 363-64.

1933—#357, listed erroneously under 1933; the address was actually given in 1932, and reprinted in *Science* a year later.

1950—"On the Generalized Theory of Gravitation," a report concerning the published expansion of the General Theory of Relativity within the framework of its historical and philosophical background, *Scientific American* 182, No. 4 (April, 1950), pp. 13-17. Reprinted in *Ideas and Opinions*, pp. 341-56.

1953—"Einleitende Bemerkungen über Grundbegriffe," an essay contributed to the volume entitled *Louis de Broglie, Physicien et Penseur* (Paris: Editions Albin Michel, 1953). This essay appeared together with its French translation: "Remarques preliminaries sur les concepts fondamenteaux."

1905—Über einen die Erzeugung und Verwandlung des Lichtes betreffenden heuristischen Gesichtspunkt. [7]

1905—Die von der molekularkinetischen Theorie der Wärme geforderte Bewegung von in ruhenden Flüssigkeiten suspendierten Teilchen. [8]

1905—Elektrodynamik bewegter Körper. [9]

1905—Ist die Trägheit eines Körpers von seinem Energieinhalt abhängig? [10]

1906—Zur Theorie der Brownschen Bewegung. [12]

1906—Theorie der Lichterzeugung und Lichtabsorption. [13]

1907—Plancksche Theorie der Strahlung und die Theorie der spezifischen Wärme. [16]

1907—Relativitätsprinzip und die aus demselben gezogenen Folgerungen. [21]

1910—Theorie der Opaleszenz von homogenen Flüssigkeiten und Flüssigkeitsgemischen in der Nähe des kritischen Zustandes. [33]

1911—Beziehung zwischen dem elastischen Verhalten und der spezifischen Wärme bei festen Körpern mit einatomigem Molekül. [38]

1911—Einfluss der Schwerkraft auf die Ausbreitung des Lichtes. [42]

1913—Entwurf einer verallgemeinerten Relativitätstheorie und eine Theorie der Gravitation. [53]

1915—Experimenteller Nachweis der Ampèreschen Molekularströme. [80]

1915—Erklärung der Perihelbewegung des Merkur aus der allgemeinen Relativitätstheorie. [84]

1916—Experimental proof of the existence of Ampère's molecular currents. [88]

1916—Grundlage der allgemeinen Relativitätstheorie. [89]

1916—Strahlungs-Emission und -Absorption nach der Quantentheorie. [92]

INDEX

Arranged by

SURINDAR SURI AND KENNETH G. HALVORSEN

THE LIBRARY OF LIVING PHILOSOPHERS

PAUL ARTHUR SCHILPP, FOUNDER AND EDITOR 1939–1981
LEWIS EDWIN HAHN, EDITOR 1981–

Paul Arthur Schilpp, Editor
THE PHILOSOPHY OF JOHN DEWEY (1939, 1971, 1989)
THE PHILOSOPHY OF GEORGE SANTAYANA (1940, 1951)
THE PHILOSOPHY OF ALFRED NORTH WHITEHEAD (1941, 1951)
THE PHILOSOPHY OF G. E. MOORE (1942, 1971)
THE PHILOSOPHY OF BERTRAND RUSSELL (1944, 1971)
THE PHILOSOPHY OF ERNST CASSIRER (1949)
ALBERT EINSTEIN: PHILOSOPHER-SCIENTIST (1949, 1970)
THE PHILOSOPHY OF SARVEPALLI RADHAKRISHNAN (1952)
THE PHILOSOPHY OF KARL JASPERS (1957; AUG. ED., 1981)
THE PHILOSOPHY OF C. D. BROAD (1959)
THE PHILOSOPHY OF RUDOLF CARNAP (1963)
THE PHILOSOPHY OF C. I. LEWIS (1968)
THE PHILOSOPHY OF KARL POPPER (1974)
THE PHILOSOPHY OF BRAND BLANSHARD (1980)
THE PHILOSOPHY OF JEAN-PAUL SARTRE (1981)

Paul Arthur Schilpp and Maurice Friedman, Editors
THE PHILOSOPHY OF MARTIN BUBER (1967)

Paul Arthur Schilpp and Lewis Edwin Hahn, Editors
THE PHILOSOPHY OF GABRIEL MARCEL (1984)
THE PHILOSOPHY OF W. V. QUINE (1986, AUG. ED., 1998)
THE PHILOSOPHY OF GEORG HENRIK VON WRIGHT (1989)

Lewis Edwin Hahn, Editor
THE PHILOSOPHY OF CHARLES HARTSHORNE (1991)
THE PHILOSOPHY OF A. J. AYER (1992)
THE PHILOSOPHY PAUL RICOEUR (1995)
THE PHILOSOPHY OF PAUL WEISS (1995)
THE PHILOSOPHY OF HANS-GEORG GADAMER (1997)
THE PHILOSOPHY OF RODERICK M. CHISHOLM (1997)
THE PHILOSOPHY OF P. F. STRAWSON (1998)
THE PHILOSOPHY OF DONALD DAVIDSON (1999)

In Preparation:
Lewis Edwin Hahn, Editor
THE PHILOSOPHY OF SEYYED HOSSEIN NASR
THE PHILOSOPHY OF MARJORIE GRENE
THE PHILOSOPHY OF ARTHUR C. DANTO
THE PHILOSOPHY OF MICHAEL DUMMETT
THE PHILOSOPHY OF JAAKKO HINTIKKA
THE PHILOSOPHY OF HILARY PUTNAM
THE PHILOSOPHY OF RICHARD M. RORTY